Scotland's Tourist Areas

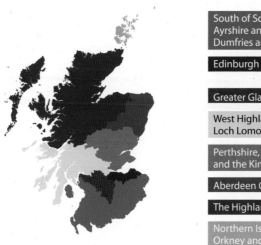

TOURING GUIDE 2010

Invercoe Caravan and Camping Park near Glencoe Village, Highlands

Published by VisitScotland, 2010

Photography Paul Tomkins / VisitScotland / Scottish Viewpoint / Alistair Firth / Kelburn Castle / Richard Campbell

visitscotland.com

Eilean Donan Castle, Highlands

WELCOME TO SCOTLAND

Scotland is a wonderful place for holidaymakers and once you've been, expect to return time and again. From the briefest of breaks to annual vacations, Scotland has so much to offer that you'll never run out of options.

Flick through the pages of this guide and you'll immediately get a flavour of Scotland's diversity. You'll discover an array of fascinating places, each with its own unique attractions and regional favours, and you are sure to find your ideal home from home in the pages ahead.

Though it's a relatively small country, Scotland is remarkably varied. You can climb mountains in the morning and still be on the beach in the afternoon. You can canoe across a remote loch and never see another soul all day long or you can join the party at one of Scotland's world-famous festivals. Relax in a tearoom after exploring a beautiful garden in full bloom on a summer's day or join in with some traditional music round a welcoming log fire in a cosy pub on a cold winter's night. Whether you are an adventure-seeker or art-lover, Scotland is a world-class holiday destination all year round.

A touring holiday can benefit greatly from local knowledge. From the friendly B&B owner who points you in the direction of an off-the-beaten-track attraction to the patrons of a welcoming restaurant or pub who are more than happy to suggest a local hidden gem, Scotland has a proud reputation of friendly, hospitable people who just love to welcome visitors into their own home.

And touring offers flexibility; from big cities to remote getaways, there are all sorts of places with comfortable rooms and tasty home-made food which can be explored at your own pace. It's an economical way to travel and the list of accommodation on offer is endless.

Discover a charming former fishermen's cottage by the sea, a lighthouse perched on a clifftop or lovely little house in a tranquil Highland glen. For those looking for something a little more grand, why not set up camp in a historic hunting lodge or even a castle?

When you're camping or caravanning, you can get close to nature and explore a wilder side of Scotland. Though many of Scotland's caravan sites are now very sophisticated with a wide range of home comforts, this really is the best way to escape the trappings of modern life and experience the great outdoors. Discover an excellent range of holiday parks and, with sites all over the country, each time you move on you can step out in the morning to savour another stunning view.

When you've found the ideal place, you can look forward to a rousing welcome in a country that is renowned for its hospitality. Nobody loves a good time like the Scots. Whether it's bringing in the New Year with a wee dram, swirling your partner at a ceilidh or sampling the finest local produce at a farmers' market or food festival, unforgettable experiences are never far away.

There's always the chance too that you'll meet some great folk – locals and visitors alike – some of whom could well become friends for life. That's all just part of a visit to Scotland.

As they say in the Gaelic tongue, ceud mille failte – 'a hundred thousand welcomes'. Come and enjoy our beautiful country

Kelvingrove Art Gallery and Museum, Glasgow

Top left: Walkers on the Tweedside Walk near Peebles, Scottish Borders   Top right: Red deer stag in Glen Coe, Highlands
Above: A couple stroll along the sandy beach at Traigh An Iar on the Isle of Harris, Outer Hebrides

DON'T MISS

Walking

From the rolling hills in the south to the mountainous north, Scotland is perfect for walkers - whether it's a gentle stroll with the kids or a serious trek through the wilderness.

Beaches

Scotland's beaches are something special whether it's for a romantic stroll, or to try some surfing. Explore Fife's Blue Flag beaches or the breathtaking stretches of sand in the Outer Hebrides.

Wildlife

From dolphins in the Moray Firth to red deer in the Highlands and seals and puffins on the coastline, you never know what you might spot.

Culture & Heritage

From the mysterious standing stones in Orkney and the Outer Hebrides to Burns Cottage and Rosslyn Chapel, Scotland's fascinating history can be found everywhere.

Rosslyn Chapel, Roslin, Midlothian

To find out more go to visitscotland.com

Adventure

From rock climbing to sea kayaking, you can do it all. Try Perthshire for unusual adventure activities or the south of Scotland for the 7stanes centre bike trails.

Two cyclists on a country road near Newton Stewart

Shopping

From Glasgow's stylish city centre to Edinburgh's eclectic Old Town and friendly farmers' markets, Scotland is a shopper's paradise with lots of hidden gems to uncover.

The terrace above Victoria Street, Edinburgh

Golf

The country that gave the world the game of golf is still the best place to play it. With more than 500 courses in Scotland, take advantage of one of the regional golf passes on offer.

A golfer at Turnberry Golf Club, Ayrshire

Castles

Wherever you are in Scotland you are never far from a great Scottish icon, whether it's an impressive ruin or an imposing fortress, a fairytale castle or country estate.

Glamis Castle near Forfar, Angus

Highland Games

From the famous Braemar Gathering in Aberdeenshire to the spectacular Cowal Highland Gathering in Argyll, hot foot it to some Highland Games action for pipe bands, dancers, and tossing the caber.

Highland dancing competition at the Ballater Highland Games

Events & Festivals

In Scotland there's so much going on with fabulous events and festivals throughout the year, from the biggest names to the quirky and traditional.

The Scottish Traditional Boat Festival at Portsoy

If you love food, get a taste of Scotland. Scotland's natural larder offers some of the best produce in the world. Scotland's coastal waters are home to an abundance of lobster, prawns, oysters and more, whilst the land produces world famous beef, lamb and game.

There's high quality food and drink on menus all over the country often cooked up by award-winning chefs in restaurants where the view is second to none. You'll find home cooking, fine dining, takeaways and tearooms. Whether you're looking for a family-friendly pub or a romantic Highland restaurant there's the perfect place to dine. And there's no better time to indulge than when you're on holiday!

Traditional fare

Haggis and whisky might be recognised as traditional Scottish fare but why not add cullen skink, clapshot, cranachan, and clootie dumpling to the list…discover the tastes that match such ancient names. Sample some local hospitality along with regional specialities such as the Selkirk Bannock or Arbroath Smokies. Or experience the freedom of eating fish and chips straight from the wrapper while breathing in the clear evening air. Visit **eatscotland.com** and see our 'Food & Drink' section to find out more.

Farmers' markets

Scotland is a land renowned for producing ingredients of the highest quality. You can handpick fresh local produce at farmers' markets in towns and cities across the country. Create your own culinary delights or learn from the masters at the world famous Nick Nairn Cook School in Stirling. Savour the aroma, excite your taste buds and experience the buzz of a farmers' market. To find out more visit the Farmers Market information on the **eatscotland.com** website that can be found in the 'Food & Drink' section.

EATING AND DRINKING

Events

Scotland serves up a full calendar of food and drink festivals. Events like Taste of Edinburgh and Highland Feast are a must for foodies. Whisky fans can share their passion at the Islay Malt Whisky Festival, the Highland Whisky Festival, or the Spirit of Speyside Whisky Festival. Visit **eatscotland.com** to find out more about the events and festivals that are on in the 'What's on' section.

Tours and trails

If you're a lover of seafood spend some time exploring the rugged, unspoilt coastline of mid-Argyll following The Seafood Trail. Or if you fancy a wee dram visit the eight distilleries and cooperage on the world's only Malt Whisky Trail in Speyside.

EatScotland Quality Assurance Scheme

EatScotland is a nationwide Quality Assurance Scheme from VisitScotland. The scheme includes all sectors of the catering industry from chip shops, pubs and takeaways to restaurants.

A trained team of assessors carry out an incognito visit to assess quality, standards and ambience. Only those operators who meet the EatScotland quality standards are accredited to the scheme so look out for the logo to ensure you visit Scotland's best quality establishments.

The newly launched EatScotland Silver and Gold Award Scheme recognises outstanding standards, reflecting that an establishment offers an excellent eating out experience in Scotland.

To find great EatScotland places to dine throughout the country visit **eatscotland.com**

Beach at Elie in Fife

GREEN TOURISM

Scotland is a stunning destination and we want to make sure it stays that way. That's why we encourage all tourism operators including accommodation providers to take part in our Green Tourism Business Scheme. It means you're assured of a great quality stay at an establishment that's trying to minimise its impact on the environment.

VisitScotland rigorously assesses accommodation providers against measures as diverse as energy use, using local produce on menus, or promoting local wildlife walks or cycle hire. Environmentally responsible businesses can achieve Bronze, Silver or Gold awards, to acknowledge how much they are doing to help conserve the quality of Scotland's beautiful environment.

Look out for the Bronze, Silver and Gold Green Tourism logos throughout this guide to help you decide where to stay and do your bit to help protect our environment.

For a quick reference see our directory at the back of the book which highlights all quality assured accommodation that has been awarded with the Gold, Silver or Bronze award.

green-business.co.uk

Bronze Green Tourism Award

Silver Green Tourism Award

Gold Green Tourism Award

Find all you want to do in Scotland, in one place.

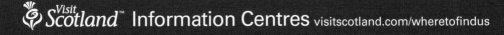

VisitScotland, under the Scottish Tourist Board brand, administers the 5-star grading schemes which assess the quality and standards of all types of visitor accommodation and attractions from castles and historic houses to garden centres and arts venues. We quality assure over 70 per cent of the accommodation in Scotland and 90 per cent of the visitor attractions – so wherever you want to stay or visit, we've got it covered. The schemes are monitored all year round each establishment is reviewed once a year. We do the hard work so you can relax and enjoy your holiday.

The promise of the stars:

★ It is clean, tidy and an acceptable, if basic, standard

★★ It is a good, all round standard

★★★ It is a very good standard, with attention to detail in every area

★★★★ It is excellent – using high quality materials, good food (except self-catering) and friendly, professional service

★★★★★ An exceptional standard where presentation, ambience, food (except self-catering) and service are hard to fault.

 This means that a bothy or bod has been inspected

 The Thistle symbol recognises a high standard of caravan holiday home

 This means individual caravan holiday homes have been inspected

IT'S WRITTEN IN THE STARS...

How does the system work?

Our advisors visit and assess establishments on up to 50 areas from quality, comfort and cleanliness to welcome, ambience and service. The same star scheme now runs in England and Wales, so you can follow the stars wherever you go.

Graded visitor attractions

Visitor attractions from castles and museums to leisure centres and tours are graded with 1-5 stars depending on their level of customer care. The focus is on the standard of hospitality and service as well as presentation, quality of shop or café (if there is one) and toilet facilities.

We want you to feel welcome

Walkers Welcome and Cyclists Welcome. Establishments that carry the symbols below pay particular attention to the specific needs of walkers and cyclists.

 Cyclists Welcome

 Walkers Welcome

There are similar schemes for Anglers, Bikers, Classic Cars, Golfers, Children and Ancestral Tourism. Check with establishment when booking.

Further information:
Quality Assurance (at VisitScotland)
Tel: 01463 244111
Fax: 01463 244181
Email: qainfo@visitscotland.com

Access all areas

The following symbols will help visitors with physical disabilities to decide whether accommodation is suitable. The directory at the back of this book will highlight all quality assured establishments that have suitable accommodation.

 Unassisted wheelchair access

 Assisted wheelchair access

 Access for visitors with mobility difficulties

We welcome your comments on star-awarded properties
Tel: 01463 244122
Fax: 01463 244181
Email: qa@visitscotland.com

The Glenfinnan Viaduct, near Fort William, Highlands

TRAVEL TO SCOTLAND

It's really easy to get to Scotland whether you choose to travel by car, train, plane, coach or ferry. And once you get here travel is easy as Scotland is a compact country.

By Air

Flying to Scotland couldn't be simpler with flight times from London, Dublin and Belfast only around one hour. There are airports at Edinburgh, Glasgow, Glasgow Prestwick, Aberdeen, Dundee and Inverness. The following airlines operate flights to Scotland (although not all airports) from within the UK and Ireland:

bmi
Tel: 0870 60 70 555
From Ireland: 1332 64 8181
flybmi.com

bmi baby
Tel: 09058 28 28 28
From Ireland: 1 890 340 122
bmibaby.com

British Airways
Tel: 0844 493 0787
From Ireland: 1890 626 747
ba.com

Eastern Airways
Tel: 08703 669 100
easternairways.com

easyJet
Tel: 0905 821 0905
From Ireland: 1890 923 922
easyjet.com

Flybe
Tel: 0871 700 2000
From Ireland: 1392 268513
flybe.com

Ryanair
0871 246 0000
From Ireland: 0818 30 30 30
ryanair.com

Air France
Tel: 0871 66 33 777
airfrance.co.uk

Aer Arann
Tel: 0870 876 76 76
From Ireland: 0818 210 210
aerarann.com

Jet2
Tel: 0871 226 1737
From Ireland: 0818 200017
jet2.com

Air Berlin
Tel: 0871 5000 737
airberlin.com

Aer Lingus
Tel: 0871 718 5000
From Ireland: 0818 365 000
aerlingus.com

To find out more go to visitscotland.com

By Rail

Scotland has major rail stations in Aberdeen, Edinburgh Waverley and Edinburgh Haymarket, Glasgow Queen Street and Glasgow Central, Perth, Stirling, Dundee and Inverness. There are regular cross border railway services from England and Wales, and good city links. You could even travel on the First ScotRail Caledonian Sleeper overnight train service from London and wake up to the sights and sounds of Scotland.

First ScotRail
Tel: 08457 55 00 33
scotrail.co.uk

Virgin Trains
Tel: 08457 222 333
virgintrains.co.uk

East Coast
Tel: 08457 225 225
eastcoast.com

National Rail
Tel: 08457 484950
nationalrail.co.uk

By Road

Scotland has an excellent road network from motorways and dual carriageway linking cities and major towns, to remote single-track roads with passing places to let others by. Whether you are coming in your own car from home or hiring a car once you get here, getting away from traffic jams and out onto Scotland's quiet roads can really put the fun back into driving. Branches of the following companies can be found throughout Scotland:

Arnold Clark
Tel: 0845 607 4500
arnoldclarkrental.com

Enterprise Rent-A-Car
Tel: 0870 350 3000
enterprise.co.uk

National Car Rental
Tel: 0870 400 4560
nationalcar.com

Avis Rent A Car
Tel: 08445 818 181
avis.co.uk

Europcar
Tel: 0870 607 5000
europcarscotland.co.uk

Sixt rent a car
Tel: 0844 499 3399
sixt.co.uk

Budget
Tel: 0844 544 3439
budget.co.uk

Hertz
Tel: 08708 44 88 44
hertz.co.uk

Alamo Rent A Car
Tel: 0870 191 6937
alamo.co.uk

easyCar
Tel: 08710 500444
easycar.com

By Ferry

Scotland has over 130 inhabited islands so ferries are important. And whether you are coming from Ireland or trying to get to the outer islands, you might be in need of a ferry crossing. Ferries to and around the islands are regular and reliable and most carry vehicles. These companies all operate ferry services around Scotland:

Stena Line
Tel: 08705 204 204
stenaline.co.uk

Western Ferries
Tel: 01369 704 452
western-ferries.co.uk

John o'Groats Ferries
Tel: 08456 000 449
northlinkferries.co.uk

P&O Irish Sea
Tel: 0871 66 44 777
poirishsea.com

Northlink Ferries
Tel: 08456 000 449
northlinkferries.co.uk

Pentland Ferries
Tel: 01856 831246
pentlandferries.co.uk

Caledonian MacBrayne
Tel: 08000 665000
calmac.co.uk

By Coach

Coach connections include express services to Scotland from all over the UK, and there is a good network of coach services once you get here too. You could even travel on the Postbus - a special feature of the Scottish mail service which carries fare-paying passengers along with the mail in rural areas where there is no other form of transport, bringing a new dimension to travel.

National Express
Tel: 08717 818 177
nationalexpress.com

City Link
Tel: 08705 50 50 50
citylink.co.uk

Postbus
Tel: 08457 740 740
royalmail.com/postbus

DRIVING DISTANCES

	ABERDEEN	BIRMINGHAM	CARDIFF	DOVER	DUMFRIES	DUNDEE	EDINBURGH	FORT WILLIAM	GLASGOW	HARWICH	HAWICK	HULL	INVERNESS	KYLE OF LOCHALSH	LONDON	MANCHESTER	NEWCASTLE	OBAN	PERTH	PRESTWICK	ROSYTH	STIRLING	STRANRAER	THURSO	TROON	ULLAPOOL
BIRMINGHAM	421 687																									
CARDIFF	529 851	113 182																								
DOVER	617 993	200 322	224 361																							
DUMFRIES	214 344	234 376	335 539	436 700																						
DUNDEE	71 114	357 575	465 749	553 890	149 240																					
EDINBURGH	131 210	290 467	398 641	486 782	80 128	62 99																				
FORT WILLIAM	161 258	396 637	504 811	592 952	179 288	123 197	138 221																			
GLASGOW	152 243	286 461	394 634	482 776	76 122	84 134	45 72	108 173																		
HARWICH	604 972	187 300	242 390	130 210	370 595	540 869	473 761	578 931	469 754																	
HAWICK	178 287	243 391	344 554	417 671	53 86	113 182	50 81	185 298	85 137	370 596																
HULL	387 619	137 221	251 405	255 411	205 330	318 509	255 408	384 614	275 440	214 346	206 331															
INVERNESS	118 189	446 717	553 890	641 1032	239 385	134 214	162 259	69 110	178 285	628 1011	209 337	444 710														
KYLE OF LOCHALSH	200 320	469 755	577 929	665 1070	253 407	179 286	207 331	76 122	184 294	652 1049	254 408	459 734	82 131													
LONDON	549 878	118 190	150 242	75 122	349 561	481 770	412 659	514 822	406 650	78 126	358 576	216 346	573 917	590 944												
MANCHESTER	345 556	93 150	201 324	281 453	157 252	281 453	214 345	320 515	210 338	268 431	166 267	95 154	370 595	393 633	201 322											
NEWCASTLE	244 390	208 336	323 519	350 563	91 147	175 280	112 179	267 427	159 254	309 498	64 102	148 237	274 438	343 549	288 461	147 237										
OBAN	190 304	385 620	493 794	581 935	168 270	121 194	125 200	50 80	96 154	568 914	175 281	371 594	112 180	125 200	502 803	309 498	310 496									
PERTH	86 139	348 560	449 723	550 884	128 205	21 34	43 69	104 166	64 104	484 778	96 155	319 513	114 183	158 254	463 744	271 436	152 245	94 151								
PRESTWICK	177 285	304 489	411 662	500 804	61 98	113 182	79 127	131 210	32 52	486 783	105 168	279 449	201 324	204 329	418 673	228 366	168 271	120 193	96 155							
ROSYTH	115 185	324 522	425 684	477 768	104 170	48 77	14 23	124 200	47 76	430 692	67 108	265 426	145 233	189 304	437 703	247 398	123 198	114 183	31 49	79 127						
STIRLING	120 193	313 503	414 666	514 823	92 149	55 89	38 61	97 157	29 47	448 722	87 141	284 456	145 234	172 277	427 688	236 379	143 231	87 140	37 60	61 99	26 42					
STRANRAER	241 386	297 478	404 651	489 787	71 115	172 275	133 213	196 314	89 142	475 765	125 202	284 454	265 424	272 435	415 664	224 358	161 259	172 277	149 240	54 87	131 211	114 611				
THURSO	234 374	555 893	663 1066	750 1208	348 560	250 400	278 445	183 293	293 469	737 1186	319 513	559 894	112 180	177 283	690 1104	499 798	391 626	233 373	221 311	355 500	254 409	252 406	382 183			
TROON	183 295	314 505	415 668	516 830	64 104	119 191	82 132	126 203	35 56	450 724	106 171	285 459	209 336	200 322	429 690	237 381	171 276	116 186	101 162	5 8	80 129	63 101	60 96	316 508		
ULLAPOOL	179 286	499 803	607 976	695 1118	293 472	194 310	222 355	119 190	238 381	681 1097	263 424	504 806	63 101	91 146	635 1016	444 710	335 536	169 270	168 270	255 411	199 320	199 320	128 205	327 523	263 423	
YORK	343 552	132 212	246 396	273 439	151 243	279 449	191 308	318 511	208 335	233 374	152 245	41 65	367 591	391 630	208 335	70 113	90 146	307 495	237 382	226 363	212 341	230 370	477 767	218 352	231 372	421 678

M KM

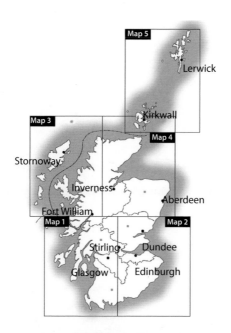

MAPS

MAP 1

Locations shown indicate establishments that are advertised in this Touring Scotland publication and our Indulge in Scotland publication. Please use a current road atlas for route planning and touring.

MAP 2

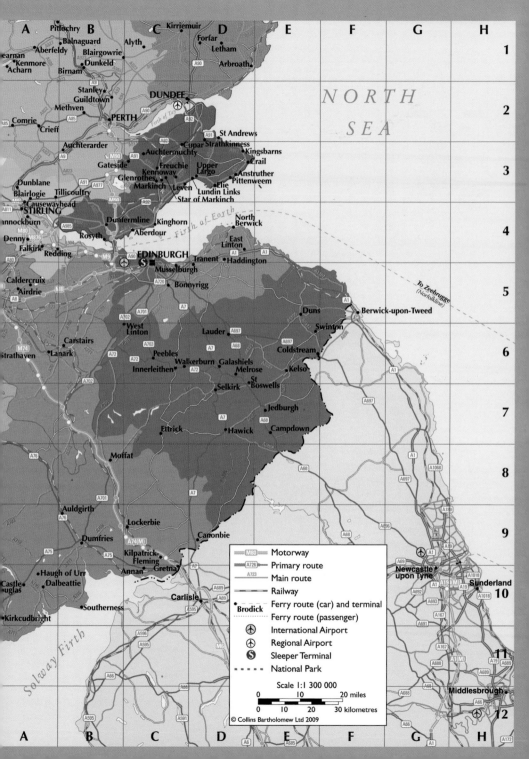

MAP 3

Locations shown indicate establishments that are advertised in this Touring Scotland publication and our Indulge in Scotland publication. Please use a current road atlas for route planning and touring.

MAP 3   MAP 4

OUTER HEBRIDES

LEWIS

Uig
Stornoway
Back
Aignish

Scourie
Kylesku
Clachtoll
Lochinver
ASSYNT

Tarbert
HARRIS
Seilebost
Leverburgh
Rodel

Laide
Dundonnell
Ullapool
Braemore
A835

Gairloch

The Minch

Staffin

Lochmaddy
Locheport
NORTH
UIST

Uig
A87
Glenhinnisdal
Snizort
Waternish
Dunvegan
Carbost
Portree

Torridon
Lonbain
Applecross
Achnasheen

BENBECULA

Lochcarnan
SOUTH
UIST

SKYE
Struan
Sconser
A87

RAASAY

Plockton
Kyle of
Lochalsh
Balmacara
Broadford
Kylerhea
Glenelg
Achmore
Dornie
Letterfearn
Cannic

Glen Shiel
Glen
Morist

Lochboisdale

CANNA

Isle Ornsay
Teangue
Ardvasar
Armadale

A87
Invergarry

BARRA
Castlebay

RUM

EIGG

Mallaig
Arisaig
A830
Loch Morar

Glenfinnan
A830

Spean
Bridge
Inverroy
Torlundy
Banavie
Corpach
Fort
William
A82

Loch
Lochy
A82

MUCK

Acharacle
Salen
Kinlochleven
A82
S

A   B   C   D   E   F   G   H

MAP 4

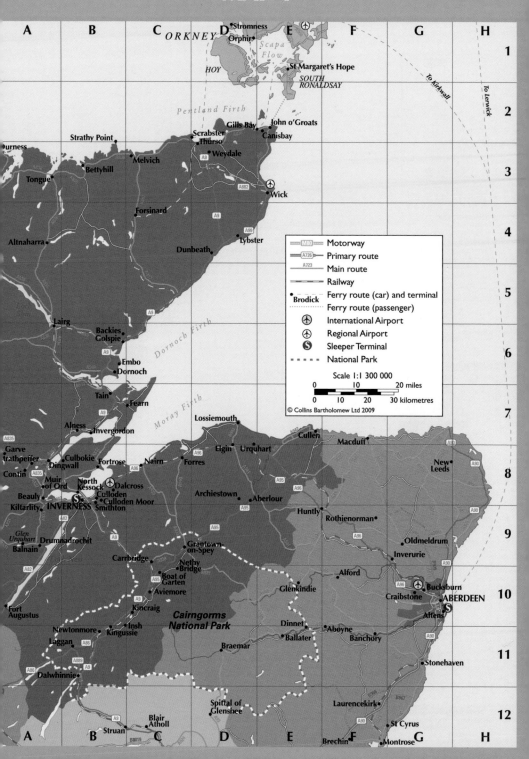

Legend:

- Motorway — M80
- Primary route — A726
- Main route — A723
- Railway
- Ferry route (car) and terminal — Brodick
- Ferry route (passenger)
- International Airport
- Regional Airport
- Sleeper Terminal — S
- National Park

Scale 1:1 300 000

0   10   20 miles
0   10   20   30 kilometres

© Collins Bartholomew Ltd 2009

ORKNEY

Stromness
Orphir
HOY
Scapa Flow
St Margaret's Hope
SOUTH RONALDSAY

Pentland Firth

To Kirkwall
To Lerwick

Strathy Point
Gills Bay
John o'Groats
Scrabster
Thurso
Canisbay
Weydale

Strathy Point
Melvich
Bettyhill
Tongue
urness

Forsinard

Wick

Altnaharra

Dunbeath
Lybster

Lairg
Backies
Golspie
Embo
Dornoch

Dornoch Firth

Tain
Fearn
Alness
Invergordon

Moray Firth

Lossiemouth
Cullen
Macduff

Garve
trathpeffer
Contin
Culbokie
Dingwall
Fortrose
Nairn
Forres
Elgin
Urquhart

New Leeds

Beauly
Muir of Ord
North Kessock
Dalcross
Culloden
Culloden Moor
Smithton
INVERNESS
Kiltarlity

Archiestown
Aberlour
Huntly
Rothienorman

Glen Urquhart
Drumnadrochit
Balnain

Grantown-on-Spey
Nethy Bridge
Boat of Garten
Carrbridge
Aviemore

Oldmeldrum
Inverurie

Alford

Bucksburn
Craibstone
ABERDEEN
Altens
S

Fort Augustus
Kincraig

Cairngorms National Park

Glenkindie
Dinnet
Aboyne
Banchory

Newtonmore
Insh
Kingussie
Laggan

Braemar
Ballater

Stonehaven

Dalwhinnie

Spittal of Glenshee

Laurencekirk

Struan
Blair Atholl

St Cyrus
Brechin
Montrose

MAP 5

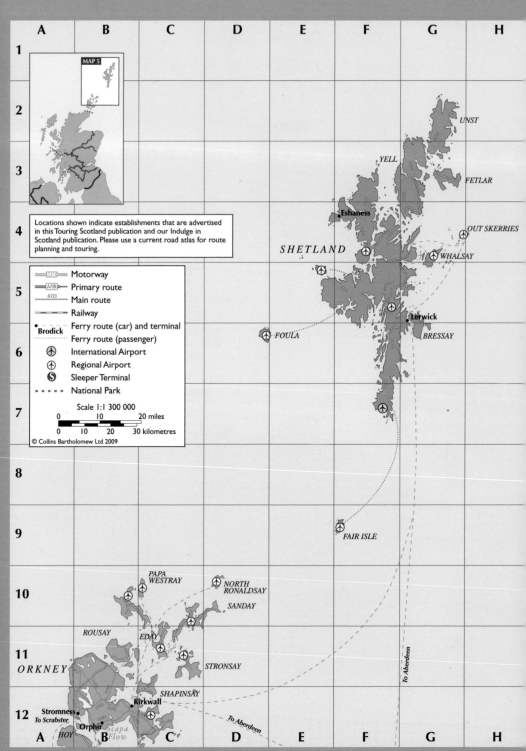

	A	B	C	D	E	F	G	H

1

MAP 5

2

UNST

3

YELL

FETLAR

4

Eshaness

OUT SKERRIES

SHETLAND

WHALSAY

Locations shown indicate establishments that are advertised in this Touring Scotland publication and our Indulge in Scotland publication. Please use a current road atlas for route planning and touring.

5

FOULA

Lerwick

BRESSAY

M80 — Motorway
A726 — Primary route
A723 — Main route
━━ Railway
• Brodick Ferry route (car) and terminal
···· Ferry route (passenger)
⊕ International Airport
⊕ Regional Airport
Ⓢ Sleeper Terminal
- - - National Park

6

Scale 1:1 300 000

0   10   20 miles
0   10   20   30 kilometres

© Collins Bartholomew Ltd 2009

7

8

9

FAIR ISLE

10

PAPA WESTRAY

NORTH RONALDSAY

SANDAY

ROUSAY

EDAY

11

STRONSAY

To Aberdeen

ORKNEY

SHAPINSAY

12

Stromness
To Scrabster

Kirkwall

Orphir

HOY

Scapa Flow

To Aberdeen

| A | B | C | D | E | F | G | H |

Great Scotland Breaks...

Whether it's a 900 year old castle or a Highland retreat we have the perfect locations for a weekend break.

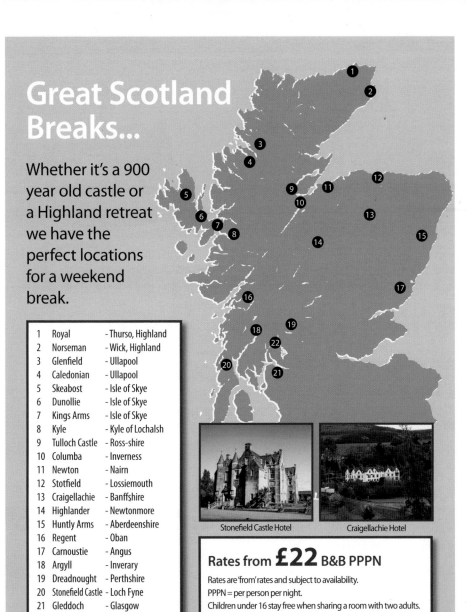

1	Royal	- Thurso, Highland
2	Norseman	- Wick, Highland
3	Glenfield	- Ullapool
4	Caledonian	- Ullapool
5	Skeabost	- Isle of Skye
6	Dunollie	- Isle of Skye
7	Kings Arms	- Isle of Skye
8	Kyle	- Kyle of Lochalsh
9	Tulloch Castle	- Ross-shire
10	Columba	- Inverness
11	Newton	- Nairn
12	Stotfield	- Lossiemouth
13	Craigellachie	- Banffshire
14	Highlander	- Newtonmore
15	Huntly Arms	- Aberdeenshire
16	Regent	- Oban
17	Carnoustie	- Angus
18	Argyll	- Inverary
19	Dreadnought	- Perthshire
20	Stonefield Castle	- Loch Fyne
21	Gleddoch	- Glasgow
22	Arrochar	- Argyll & Bute

Stonefield Castle Hotel

Craigellachie Hotel

Rates from £22 B&B PPPN

Rates are 'from' rates and subject to availability.
PPPN = per person per night.
Children under 16 stay free when sharing a room with two adults.
Terms & conditions apply, please confirm at time of booking.

0871 376 9900
reservations@ohiml.com
www.oxfordhotelsandinns.com

OXFORD
HOTELS & INNS

75417

19

4 & 5 star **holiday parks** in The Highlands, Perthshire & South West Scotland

Choose from our wide range of cosy holiday homes at one of our holiday parks by some of Scotland's most stunning beaches, beautiful rolling countryside or peaceful woodlands.

- Top quality caravan & lodge holiday homes
- Central heating & double glazing available
- FREE heated indoor pools
- FREE kids' clubs from tots to teens
- FREE live family entertainment
- Sports courts & adventure play areas
- Cafés, bars & restaurants
- We've **excellent touring & camping** facilities & welcome caravans, tents & motorhomes.

Grannie's Heilan' Hame, Highlands
Nairn Lochloy, Highlands
INVERNESS
ABERDEEN
Wemyss Bay, Clyde Coast
Tummel Valley, Perthshire
PERTH
Sundrum Castle, Ayrshire
GLASGOW   EDINBURGH
AYR
Southerness, Dumfries
NEWCASTLE
CARLISLE

Parkdean

Six award winning parks in Scotland

Extra savings online!

To book or to order a FREE brochure

parkdean.com
0844 335 3728

All our parks have received national **4 & 5** star gradings

49204

Thistle Holiday Home Parks
Top-Class Self-Catering

Thistle Holiday Home Parks are the best caravan parks for self-catering holiday homes in Scotland. All the parks have been awarded four or five stars by VisitScotland and you can enjoy a relaxing holiday in their top-class Thistle holiday home caravans.

Thistle caravans are awarded a 'Thistle' because they are all of a very high standard, are less than six years old, and are very well maintained. They have a lounge, a kitchen and dining area, and either two or three bedrooms, plus a shower room and a toilet. All are double-glazed and with heating throughout and they have mains water, electricity and drainage.

The caravan parks may be quite small and ideal for a quiet break, or much bigger, with a shop, restaurant, bar, games room and play areas on site, so great for a family holiday. Whether you want to visit castles and gardens, historic houses and distilleries or prefer to picnic on the beach, follow the waymarked trails or enjoy exploring the local area – choose a 'Thistle' for your holiday.

There are over sixty Thistle Holiday Home Parks in Scotland, so you can take your pick and enjoy a relaxing self-catering holiday with plenty to do every day.

Thistle **Top-Class Self-Catering**

For a free brochure call VisitScotland on 0845 22 55 121 or e.mail info@visitscotland.com or go to www.thistleparks.co.uk

Walking by the White Water in Glen Doll at the head of Glen Clova, Angus

To find out more go to visitscotland.com

A hotel overlooking Loch Fyne, Argyll

ACCOMMODATION LISTINGS

- Establishments are listed by type **Hotels, Guest Houses/B&B, Self Catering and Camping & Caravan Parks** then by **location** in alphabetical order.

- At the back of this book there is a directory showing all VisitScotland quality assured **Accommodation**. This directory shows **Accessible Accommodation** for visitors with mobility difficulties and also lets you know what **Green Award** has been obtained.

- You will also find an **Index by location** which will tell you where to look if you already know where you want to go.

- Inside the back cover flap you will find a **key to the symbols**.

Looking over to the hills of Arran from the beach at Troon

SOUTH OF SCOTLAND

Ayrshire & Arran,
Dumfries & Galloway,
Scottish Borders

The South of Scotland has everything to offer for the perfect break, from its fascinating history and traditions to the many outdoor activities to pursue.

The scenery is spectacularly varied, from the lush countryside to a stunning coastline, with its picturesque harbour towns, beaches and rocky cliffs. And to experience all this magnificent terrain in one day, visit the beautiful Isle of Arran, which really does have it all, from history and culture to fine food and relaxation.

This region is steeped in history. Discover a wealth of ancient abbeys, medieval castles, stately homes, stone circles and chambered cairns; all nestled amongst beautiful rolling hills, at the centre of vast estates or perched grandly on cliff-top locations.

Visit the South of Scotland and discover a proud history. Follow in the footsteps of the Border Reivers, where hundreds of years raiding over the border are marked by the Common Ridings. Join thousands of spectators who attend these spectacular horseback parades across the many town boundaries each summer. Explore Robert Burns country and visit the places where Scotland's national bard lived and worked. From the poet's Ayrshire birthplace, a simple Auld Clay Biggin in Alloway, to Dumfries, where Burns worked as an excise man and lived with his wife, Jean Armour.

Walkers love this part of the country. walkers love this part of the country' with: 'The South of Scotland is a walker's paradise'- the 212-mile Southern Upland Way - there's also the likes of the Ayrshire Coastal Path, Isle of Arran Coastal Way or Borders Abbeys Way, offering scenic landscapes and charming historical attractions along the way. Don't miss the pretty harbour towns of Dumfries & Galloway, which have served to inspire artists for hundreds of years keen to capture the light and landscapes of the region. The picturesque Kirkcudbright is a must for art lovers, with its many galleries and studios to explore.

And for cyclists, there are endless open spaces and quiet country roads on offer, with routes to suit all abilities and the opportunity to spot an abundance of wildlife along the way.

Play golf in splendid surroundings; Ayrshire is famed as the birthplace of the Open Championship, home to Turnberry and Royal Troon, the Isle of Arran can offer a remarkable seven courses, while the Roxburghe and the Cardrona golf club can be found in the Scottish Borders. As well as a host of quality courses, the South of Scotland also offers quality for money when it comes to hitting the greens with some great value golf passes.

Make the most of the delicious local produce which flourishes in this region; sample delicious seafood landed fresh along the coast and flavoursome game from the hills. Whether it's wandering around a local farmers' market to pick up supplies, or relaxing in one of the revered eateries each region has to offer, there is something to satisfy any gourmet's appetite.

The South of Scotland has it all. Exciting places, beautiful scenery and the perfect place to unwind with a holiday experience you will never forget.

Mountain bikers on McMoab, at Kirroughtree (forest), near Newton Stewart

What's On?

Scottish Grand National
16 - 17 April 2010
Witness some of the most exciting races in the country at Ayr Racecourse.
ayr-racecourse.co.uk

Arran Wildlife Festival
12 - 19 May 2010
Discover Arran's diverse wildlife in a selection of tours, talks and walks.
arranwildlife.co.uk

The Festival of the Horse
19 - 31 May 2010
visitscottishborders.com/
EventsCalendar

Scottish Borders Common Ridings
Various around the region from May to August.
visitscottishborders.com/
EventsCalendar

Spring Fling
29-31 May 2010
Open Studios event – an opportunity to see the artists and craft-makers at work in their own studios.
spring-fling.co.uk

burns an' a' that! Festival
27-31 May 2010
Celebrate the rich legacy of Scotland's national bard.
visitscotland.com/burns

The Wickerman Festival
23-24 July 2010
Watch the 30ft Wickerman go up in flames and enjoy a diverse selection of music.
thewickermanfestival.co.uk

Largs Viking Festival
28 August - 5 September 2010
Viking extravaganza complete with a spectacular burning of the longship, Viking battle re-enactment and fireworks display.

Scottish Borders Festival of Walking
September 2010
visitscottishborders.com/
EventsCalendar

Wigtown Book Festival
Meet famous writers and broadcasters in the idyllic Galloway countryside.
wigtownbookfestival.com

All dates correct at time of publication. Please check before booking. VisitScotland cannot be held responsible for any inaccuracies

25

Map labels:

dinburgh

VisitScotland Information Centres

To help you plan and book your trip to Scotland email our travel experts at info@visitscotland.com. When you arrive call into one of our Information Centres where our friendly experts can offer advice on all things local as well as sharing their wider knowledge of Scotland. We don't just advise either. We can sort out your accommodation and all your travel needs, as well as tickets for events across Scotland. So if you're looking to get the most from your visit, there really is only one place to go.

Ayrshire & Arran

Ayr	22 Sandgate, Ayr, KA7 1BW
Brodick	The Pier, Brodick Isle of Arran, KA27 8AU

Dumfries & Galloway

Dumfries	64 Whitesands Dumfries DG1 2RS
Gretna	Unit 38, Gretna Gateway Outlet Village, Glasgow Road Gretna, DG16 5GG
Kirkcudbright	Harbour Square Kirkcudbright DG6 4HY
Southwaite	M6 Service Area Southwaite CA4 0NS
Stranraer	Burns House, 28 Harbour Street Stranraer, Dumfries DG9 7RA

Scottish Borders

Hawick	Tower Mill, Heart of Hawick Campus, Kirkstile Hawick, TD9 0AE
Jedburgh	Murray's Green Jedburgh, TD8 6BE
Melrose	Abbey House Abbey Street, TD6 9LGR
Peebles	23 High Street Peebles, EH45 8AG

Map labels:

Eyemouth
Berwick-upon-Tweed
Duns
Swinton
Lauder
Coldstream
Galashiels
Melrose Kelso
eithen
lkerburn
To Newcastle
St Boswells
Selkirk
Hawick
Jedburgh
Campdown
ck
To Hexham
A7
Canonbie
k-
ng
Gretna
M6
To Carlisle
Southwaite Services

 Open All Year

 Seasonal

 Live it. Visit *Scotland.*
visitscotland.com/wheretofindus

- LOCAL KNOWLEDGE
- WHERE TO STAY
- ACCOMMODATION BOOKING
- PLACES TO VISIT
- THINGS TO DO
- MAPS AND GUIDES
- TRAVEL ADVICE
- ROUTE PLANNING
- WHERE TO SHOP AND EAT
- LOCAL CRAFTS AND PRODUCE
- EVENT INFORMATION
- TICKETS

Glen Rosa, Isle of Arran

Ayrshire & Arran

Ayrshire & Arran is a beautiful corner of Scotland, where you are always guaranteed a warm welcome from the locals.

The birthplace of Robert Burns, Scotland's national poet, Ayrshire combines bustling market towns with picturesque villages and rolling countryside. This is also golf country, with over 50 courses to choose from, including championship greats Turnberry and Royal Troon.

Across the water beckons the Isle of Arran, known as 'Scotland in miniature' because it offers everything that's good about Scotland in a compact but addictive package. From walking to wildlife, adventure to relaxation, mountains to sea, this is Scotland at its best.

With miles of unspoilt coastline and rolling green hills, both Ayrshire & Arran offer an enormous diversity of fresh and natural quality produce. From ales and whiskies to lamb, beef and ice cream - all are readily available. There is also an abundance of seafood, creamy cheese and organic vegetables and herbs.

A stunning coastline coupled with hidden treasures make this part of Scotland a treat to discover and explore. The relaxing character and breathtaking beauty of Ayrshire & Arran is easily accessible with fantastic sea, road, rail and bus networks, as well as flights into Prestwick or Glasgow airports. It is the ideal choice for a short break.

DON'T MISS

1   Often described as the jewel in the crown for the National Trust of Scotland, **Culzean Castle & Country Park** has a romantic cliff-top setting and overlooks Ailsa Craig and the Firth of Clyde. Designed by Robert Adam in 1777 it has period furnishing, beautiful gardens, and adventure playground and a deer park. A delight to explore.

2   Wander around the rustic courtyard of **Balmichael Visitor Centre** and discover the very best of shopping on the Isle of Arran - crafts, jewellery, designer gifts, antiques, island wares and more. For fun try the quad bikes, archery, spin art and pottery painting. Top it off with a treat from the coffee shop.

3   If you want to escape the fast pace of modern life, indulge in some magical **'island time'**. Take a relaxing 55-minute ferry ride from Ardrossan and discover the Isle of Arran. Offering history, mystery, adventure and relaxation, it's the ideal location to try a number of outdoor pursuits. The island of Great Cumbrae, only a 10-minute hop on the ferry from Largs, has an undeniable charm and a fabulous setting on the Clyde with views towards Arran. The capital, Millport, is a model Victorian resort.

4   **Brodick Castle & Country Park** is a stunning castle, with an amazing history, set in beautiful gardens. The country park has waterfalls, gorges and an adventure playground.

5   If you enjoy a good day out, **Ayr Racecourse** is the perfect venue for thrills and excitement. Home to the Scottish Grand National and Ayr Gold Cup Festival, a number of races and events take place during the year.

6   See what happens when you bring four of the world's best graffiti artists to Scotland and provide them with a castle as a canvas. This is exactly what the owners of Kelburn Castle did. Kelburn is the ancient home of the Earls of Glasgow and dates back to the 13th century. The **graffiti project** on the castle is a spectacular piece of artwork, surrounded by a beautiful country estate and wooden glen. There is plenty to interest all the family.

WALKING/OUTDOORS

7   The River Ayr Way (66km) is the first source to sea path network, which follows the river from its source at Glenbuck to the sea at Ayr. With beautiful scenery and abundant wildlife it is enjoyable to walk all or part of this route.

8   The Ayrshire Coastal Path from Glenapp to Skelmorlie runs 100 miles along one of the finest panoramic coastlines in the British Isles. Crowned with a superb backdrop across the Firth of Clyde of the ever-changing profile of the mountains of Arran, this coastline is steeped in history and teeming with wildlife.

9   At 874 metres, Goatfell is Arran's highest point. It draws thousands of hill walkers to the island every year and the spectacular views from the top are ample reward for the climb.

10   The Isle of Arran Coastal Way allows you to walk around the island. It is 100 km long, but can be broken down into seven more manageable sections. This route offers spectacular scenery and enjoyable challenges. Guide books are available at the VisitScotland Information Centre in Brodick.

FOOD & DRINK

11   The newly opened Braehead Cook School has already gained five-star status and offers a huge range of cookery courses to tempt all tastes and capabilities. Run by Steven Doherty, the first ever British head chef of a three-star Michelin restaurant, the school has a number of guest chefs.

12   The west coast is renowned for its delicious seafood and an array of fresh produce is hauled ashore daily and served up in a variety of delicious ways. Visit an up-market fish and chip shop and enjoy a simple yet delicious al fresco meal along the waterfront. Or sample the dish-of-the-day at one of the many excellent seafood restaurants.

13   With an abundance of natural and local ingredients to inspire, it is no wonder that Ayrshire & Arran has such fabulous restaurants and eateries. From Michelin star and AA rosette-winning restaurants to innovative gastro pubs, Ayrshire & Arran will satisfy any gourmet's appetite.

14   Opened in 1995, the Isle of Arran Distillery at Lochranza enjoys a spectacular location and is among the most recent to begin production in Scotland. The distillery has a visitor centre that offers fully guided tours, and the opportunity to pour your own bottle. Peat and artificial colourings aren't used in Arran whisky, which the distillers proudly claim offers 'the true spirit of nature'.

GOLF

15 Ayrshire & Arran has some of the finest and most famous links golf courses in the world; Western Gailes, Glasgow Gailes, West Kilbride, Royal Troon, Prestwick, Prestwick St Nicholas, Turnberry Ailsa and Shiskine on the Isle of Arran are all part of the Great Scottish Links collection.

16 Ayrshire & Arran offer three different golf passes which are great value for money. By spending less on the course, you will have more to spend in the legendary 19th hole!

17 As birthplace of the Open Championship, Ayrshire has a proud golfing history. The Open was hosted at Turnberry in 2009, while the Ailsa course is celebrated as the location of Jack Nicklaus and Tom Watson's 'Duel in the Sun' in 1977. This remains a fantastically challenging course which presents the best of links golf. Royal Troon is the other championship venue still on the circuit, which boasts the 'Postage Stamp' as its signature hole. These courses are accessible to visitors, but book well ahead to avoid disappointment.

18 Amazingly for its size, the Isle of Arran has seven golf courses. Shiskine boasts a challenging 12-hole layout which can test the skills of most golfers. The Arran Golf Pass offers fantastic value and allows you to play each of the courses.

HISTORY

19 On 25 January 1759, Scotland's National Bard was born in the picturesque village of Alloway, a must-visit for admirers of the man and his work. Here, you can visit Burns National Heritage Park, which includes Burns Cottage, Monument and Museum, containing prized artefacts such as an original manuscript of Auld Lang Syne. Surrounding sites, including the Brig O' Doon and Kirk Alloway, are familiar from Burns' epic poem Tam O'Shanter, which even has an entire visitor attraction dedicated to it.

20 The Isle of Arran Heritage Museum can be found on the main road at Rosaburn, just north of Brodick. The present group of buildings were once a working croft and smiddy, and include a farmhouse, cottage, bothy, milk house, laundry, stable, coach house and harness room. The fascinating exhibits reflect the social history, archaeology and geology of the island.

21 Situated in Kilmarnock, Dean Castle & Country Park covers over 200 acres and boasts beautiful woodland walks, adventure playground, pets corner, visitor centre, tearoom, shop and a fantastic 14th century castle housing world class collections including historic weapons, armour and musical instruments. A fascinating place to visit, for all ages.

22 Take a tour of Dumfries House, the Georgian masterpiece designed by the renowned Scottish architect, Robert Adam. The house, which sits in 2,000 acres of East Ayrshire countryside, is the former home of the Marquises of Bute and has remained virtually unchanged for the last 250 years.

Ayrshire & Arran

Hotels

Largs
Willowbank Hotel

Open: All year   **Map Ref: 1F5**

★★★
HOTEL

96 Greenock Road, Largs, North Ayrshire, KA30 8PG
T: 01475 672311/675435 E: iaincsmith@btconnect.com W: thewillowbankhotel.com

Indicated Prices:

Single	from £75.00 per room	Twin	from £100.00 per room
Double	from £100.00 per room	Family	from £130.00 per room

64306

Guest Houses and B&Bs

Isle of Arran, Brodick
Dunvegan House

Open: All year excl Xmas & New Year   **Map Ref: 1F6**

★★★★
GUEST HOUSE

58 Shore Road, Brodick, Isle of Arran, KA27 8AJ
T: 01770 302811 E: dunveganhouse1@hotmail.com W: dunveganhouse.co.uk

Indicated Prices:

Single	from £45.00 per room	Twin	from £40.00 per person
Double	from £40.00 per person		

23879

Isle of Arran, Whiting Bay
Mingulay Bed and Breakfast

Open: All year

Map Ref: 1F7

★★★
BED AND BREAKFAST

Middle Road, Whiting Bay, Isle of Arran, KA27 8QH
T: 01770 700346 E: belle@ithomson.fsnet.co.uk W: arranwelcome.co.uk/mingulay

Indicated Prices:

Single	from £30.00 per room	Twin	from £23.00 per person
Double	from £23.00 per person	Family	from £23.00 per person

38522

Ayr
Sunnyside Bed and Breakfast

Open: All year

Map Ref: 1G7

★★★★
BED AND BREAKFAST

26 Dunure Road, Alloway, Ayr, Ayrshire KA7 4HR
T: 01292 441234 E: ayrbandb@hotmail.com W: ayrbandb.co.uk

Indicated Prices:

Single	from £39.50 per room	Twin	from £59.00 per room
Double	from £59.00 per room	Family	from £70.00 per room

57253

Ayr
Leslie Anne Guest House

Open: All year excl Xmas

Map Ref: 1G7

A warm welcome and comfortable accommodation awaits you at our family run Victorian guest house. Close to Ayr railway station and town centre. Prestwick Airport is five miles. Ideally situated for golf courses, Ayr Race Course, Burns Country, Culzean Castle and the Ayrshire coast. Private parking. Two ground floor rooms.

★★★
BED AND BREAKFAST

13 Castlehill Road, Ayr, KA7 2HX
T: 01292 265646 E: leslieanne2@btinternet.com W: leslieanne.org.uk

Indicated Prices:

Single	from £30.00 per room	Twin	from £50.00 per room
Double	from £50.00 per room		

35320

For a full listing of Quality Assured accommodation, please see directory at back of this guide.

33

Ayrshire & Arran

Largs
Whin Park

Open: All year excl Feb

Map Ref: 1F5

★★★★
GUEST HOUSE

16 Douglas Street, Largs, KA30 8PS
T: 01475 673437 E: enquiries@whinpark.co.uk W: whinpark.co.uk

Indicated Prices:

Single	from £38.00	Twin	from £35.00
Double	from £35.00		

63959

Self Catering and Camping & Caravan Parks

Isle of Arran, Lamlash
Sunnybank

Open: All year

Map Ref: 1F7

★★★
SELF CATERING

The Brae, Lamlash, Isle of Arran, KA27 8NA
T: 01142 680019 E: info@sunnybank-arran.co.uk W: sunnybank-arran.co.uk

1 Bungalow	2 Bedrooms	Sleeps 2-4

Prices – Bungalow:
£250.00-£390.00 Per Week

Short breaks available

68472

by Ayr, Coylton
Sundrum Castle Holiday Park

Open: Mar-Nov

Map Ref: 1G7

★★★★★
HOLIDAY PARK

Coylton, by Ayr, Ayrshire, KA6 5JH
T: 0844 335 3728 E: via website W: parkdean.com

Take the A70 to Cumnock then follow main road for three miles and you'll find us before the village of Coylton.

Park accommodates 30 pitches. Total touring pitches: 30.
Prices per pitch:
(30) £13.00-£32.00

Holiday Caravans for Hire:
(67) £179.00-£639.00 per week.

Thistle

57225

Isle of Cumbrae, Millport
1 Guildford Street

Open: All year

Map Ref: 1F6

★★ UP TO ★★★★
SELF CATERING

Mrs B McLuckie, Muirhall Farm, Larbert, Stirlingshire, FK5 4EW
T: 01324 551570 E: b@1-guildford-street.co.uk W: 1-guildford-street.co.uk

| 1 House | 3 Bedrooms | Sleeps up to 8 |
| 5 Flats | 1-2 Bedrooms | Sleeps 2-10 |

| Prices – House: | | Flats: | |
| £374.00-£678.00 | Per Week | £156.00-£650.00 | Per Week |

Short breaks available only out of high season

42593

Wemyss Bay
Wemyss Bay Holiday Park

Open: Mar-Nov

Map Ref: 1F5

★★★★
HOLIDAY PARK

Wemyss Bay, Renfrewshire, PA18 6BA
T: 0844 335 3728 E: via website W: parkdean.com
Take the A78 to Wemyss Bay. The park is located opposite the railway station.

Lodges:
(3) £369.00-£839.00 per week.

Holiday Caravans for Hire:
(100) £179.00-£619.00 per week.

63559

A standing stone on Machrie Moor, the Isle of Arran

For a full listing of Quality Assured accommodation, please see directory at back of this guide.

35

Looking across a sandy beach at Killantringan Bay north west of Portpatrick

Dumfries & Galloway

Dumfries & Galloway is a naturally inspiring place, where 200 miles of coastline meet the tide and impressive hills rise up to greet the vast clear sky. Add to that rolling countryside, beautiful light and wide open spaces, and you could only be in the stunning south west of Scotland.

From the Galloway Forest Park to the Solway Coast, there are so many picturesque places to explore and an abundance of wildlife habitats. Look out for red deer, rare red kites, wild goats and even ospreys at Wigtown, Scotland's Book Town.

And there is plenty to see and do. Remember to visit Kirkcudbright Artists' Town with its thriving artistic community, studios and galleries. Poets and artists have made Dumfries & Galloway their base for generations, inspired to capture the look and feel of this beautiful region. For those looking for adventure, world class mountain biking, challenging golf courses and many activity centres are waiting to offer an adrenaline rush.

Whatever you choose to do, you'll find Dumfries & Galloway the perfect setting for a great holiday adventure.

The harbour at Kirkcudbright, a small town on the River Dee

DON'T MISS

1   Discover some of Scotland's most relaxing environments and natural **beauty spots**. At every turn, there is something new to inspire - stroll along quiet sandy beaches, explore glorious gardens that bask in the balmy air of the Gulf Stream, spot wildlife in the nature reserves and conquer cliff-tops for the stunning views. When it comes to inspiring scenery, Dumfries & Galloway never fails to impress.

2   Lovers of the great outdoors are at home in the south west of Scotland. There are endless opportunities to get **active** in the countryside, from walking parts of the famous Southern Upland Way to mountain biking at the 7stanes centres, from world class fishing in the lochs, rivers and sea to teeing off from one of the many fantastic golf courses. Take an activity break to this beautiful and varied countryside and discover nature's playground.

3   This region is home to an abundance of **wildlife**, including the graceful red kite which has been successfully reintroduced to Galloway. The Galloway Red Kite Trail takes a circular route around Loch Ken, designed to take you closer to this elusive raptor with observation points and interpretation boards. Ospreys are also back in Galloway after a break of more than 100 years. Visit the County Buildings in Wigtown where you can watch live CCTV coverage of the ospreys.

4   As you travel through Dumfries & Galloway taking in the breathtaking scenery, you will come face to face with some amazing environmental **artworks** set in the landscape: head carvings in a sheep pen in the Galloway Forest Park, sculpture within Creetown town square, Andy Goldsworthy's Striding Arches near Moniaive. You never know what intriguing works you'll discover around the next corner!

5   Dumfries & Galloway has a packed calendar of **events and festivals** throughout the year, so there's bound to be something exciting happening whenever you choose to visit. Discover the Dumfries Film Festival in May, the ever-popular Wickerman Festival at the end of July and a number of agricultural shows across the region from late summer into autumn.

6   **Logan Botanic Garden**, under the care of the Royal Botanic Garden, Edinburgh is Scotland's most exotic garden where a fabulous array of bizarre and exotic plants and trees flourish outdoors. Warmed by the Gulf Stream, the climate provides ideal growing conditions for many plants from the southern hemisphere including a number of palm trees, which means you may forget where you are!

GOLF

7   The **Gateway to Golf Pass** is a scheme unique to Dumfries & Galloway, making it really easy to enjoy a great golf break at excellent value. The pass is available for three or six rounds and can be used at 26 courses across the region. Every course is within easy reach of the next one with some great places to visit and superb views in between. There are three fantastic golf trails offering something for every level of skill and handicap.

8   The **Tiger Trail** is the most challenging, boasting the six top courses in the area, leading from one side of the region to the other. Remember your handicap certificate as you could be asked for it on these courses. Start at Powfoot Golf Club on the Solway Firth. This beautiful James Braid designed course is a challenging mixture of links and parkland with breathtaking views of the North Lakes mountains.

9   The majority of golfers find the **Challenge Trail** offers the perfect combination of excellent courses amidst a variety of beautiful landscapes. This trail includes Thornhill Golf Club, a mixture of parkland and heathland with spectacular views of the Southern Uplands and Wigtownshire Country Golf Club, a links course on the shores of the scenic Luce Bay.

10   For bags of entertainment at superb rates, play some 9-hole golf on the **Little Gems Trail**. There are 10 courses on this trail and, although you are playing a shorter game, there are some real tests. Tee off in the morning and you'll have the rest of the day free to explore.

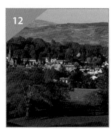

WALKING

11   The region is synonymous with great walking. Acres of sky, miles of rugged coastline, sandy beaches, mysterious forests, rolling hills and tranquil lochs offer endless opportunities. Request a copy of Dumfries & Galloway's **Twelve Walks** - a selection of handpicked routes - and you'll be met by an amazing array of cultural and historic attractions along the way.

12   There are many great walks around **Moffat**, Scotland's first 'Walkers are Welcome' town, where a warm welcome is guaranteed. The Grey Mare's Tail, in the care of the National Trust for Scotland, just a short drive from Moffat along the Selkirk Road, provides a glorious walk up the side of this impressive 61m waterfall. Join an experienced walk leader to discover more great walks during the Moffat Walking Festival, held in October each year.

13   The **Solway Coast Heritage Trail** is a waymarked driving route between the vast tidal flats of the Solway Firth at Annan and the towering sea cliffs of the Rhins. There are wonderful walks from various points along the trail. Wildlife lovers can take in Luce Bay and Sands, the Solway Firth and the Mull of Galloway, which are Special Areas of Conservation (SACs).

14   The **Southern Upland Way** is one of Scotland's national trails and the only coast-to-coast long distance footpath. With 212 miles (340kms) of glorious, unspoilt and varied terrain, many sections offer wonderful short walks. The coastal section from Portpatrick to Killantringan Lighthouse is a great place to start or why not try the 7½ mile section between Wanlockhead and Sanquhar for a completely different experience of the Way.

ARTS AND CULTURE

15 Dumfries & Galloway is a naturally inspiring place, something which is reflected by the wealth of **arts and crafts** produced across the region. More than 400 contemporary artists and craftsmen currently make the region their home, with many incorporating the natural world around them into their works. Pick up some unique gifts as you wander around the various charming shops.

16 The pretty harbour town of Kirkcudbright has earned a reputation as a hotbed of **creativity**, as artists from far and wide find the scenery and light a constant source of inspiration. Spend a day weaving in and out of the many little galleries, workshops and studios and find out more about the historical significance of this picture perfect town to the world of art.

17 Take the opportunity to discover the wealth of artistic talent in this region on a tour of selected studios at the annual **Spring Fling**, held over the May bank holiday weekend. This unique event sees more than 60 studios open their doors to the public. Follow one of the artistic trails or make up your own itinerary.

EATING OUT

18 Discover wonderful restaurants making the most of the delicious local produce and indulge in a spot of **fine dining**. Sample the culinary delights at the award-winning Blackaddie Country House Hotel, which is nestled amidst two acres of secluded gardens on the outskirts of the village of Sanquhar.

19 Explore Dumfries & Galloway using our extensive network of quiet B Roads. Have a deliciously fun day at **Cream o' Galloway**, a family run farm nestled in the beautiful countryside. Join the behind the scenes tour of the organic farm, which is timed to coincide with the dairy herd coming in for their afternoon milking. The tour ends with a free scoop of ice cream, frozen smoothie or frozen yoghurt - all Cream o' Galloway specialties.

20 **Local produce** is a way of life in Dumfries & Galloway. It does boast the 'food town' of Castle Douglas, after all. Sample freshly baked Wigwam bread from Creetown, jams, pickles and mustards from Galloway Lodge Preserves, or even try out the local beer from Sulwath Brewery. With so much temptation on offer, you won't leave empty handed.

21 All kinds of fresh **seafood** are brought ashore and served up in restaurants daily, much of it caught off the coast of Galloway. Smokehouses are a common feature in this region, expertly flavouring a range of delicious delicacies over smouldering whisky cask chippings. Visit the award-winning Galloway Smokehouse on the banks of Wigtown Bay and the Marrbury Smokehouse of Bargrennan, at Carsluith Castle, for luxury gifts.

Hotels

Dumfries
Aston Hotel Dumfries

Open: All year

Map Ref: 2B9

Located on the wonderful Crichton Estate extending to over 100 acres. Aston offers king size bedrooms with power showers and complimentary wi-fi. It blends state of the art facilities with traditional Scottish hospitality, with interiors creating an atmosphere of luxurious simplicity. Brasserie and Bar 59 offers a varied selection of menus.

★★★
HOTEL

The Crichton, Bankend Road, Dumfries, DG1 4ZZ
T: 01387 272410 E: enquiries@astonhoteldumfries.co.uk W: astonhoteldumfries.co.uk

Indicated Prices:

Single	from £69.00	Twin	from £79.00 per room
Double	from £79.00 per room	Family	from £79.00 per room

58714

Gretna
Garden House Hotel

Open: All year

Map Ref: 2C10

★★★
HOTEL

Sarkfoot Road, Gretna, DG16 5EP
T: 01461 337621 E: june@gardenhouse.co.uk W: gardenhouse.co.uk

Indicated Prices:

Single	from £65.00 per room	Twin	from £90.00 per room
Double	from £90.00 per room		

27233

Important: Prices stated are estimates and may be subject to amendments. Prices are per person per night unless otherwise stated.

Lockerbie
Ravenshill House Hotel   Open: All year excl Boxing Day & 1st-4th Jan   Map Ref: 2B9

★★
SMALL HOTEL

12 Dumfries Road, Lockerbie, DG11 2EF
T: 01576 202882 E: reception@ravenshillhotellockerbie.co.uk W: ravenshillhotellockerbie.co.uk

Indicated Prices:

Single	from £50.00 per room	Twin	from £75.00 per room
Double	from £75.00 per room	Suite	from £120.00 per room
		Family	from £85.00 per room

51167

Moffat
Buccleuch Arms Hotel   Open: All year   Map Ref: 2B8

One of the most service-driven hotels you are likely to come across. Nestled in the Moffat Hills and centre of the Southern Upland Way, they have earned many awards for their food, wine and service. Passionate about quality of food and local produce. Seriously motorcycle, walker, cyclist and dog friendly.

★★★
SMALL HOTEL

High Street, Moffat, Dumfriesshire, DG10 9ET
T: 01683 220003 E: enquiries@buccleucharmshotel.com W: buccleucharmshotel.com

Indicated Prices:

Single	from £50.00 per room	Twin	from £80.00 per room
Double	from £80.00 per room	Family	from £90.00 per room

16754

For a full listing of Quality Assured accommodation, please see directory at back of this guide.

Guest Houses and B&Bs

Annan
The Old Rectory   **Open: All year**   **Map Ref: 2C10**

Elegant Victorian villa close to town centre and rail station. Charming, comfortable en-suite bedrooms. Breakfast features quality local ingredients, vegetarian and gluten free choices available. Bike and fishing storage. Motorbikes welcome. Private parking. In-house massage and reflexology treatments available. Treatment breaks and special offers, see website for details. Free wi-fi.

★★★
GUEST HOUSE

12 St John's Road, Annan, Dumfries & Galloway, DG12 6AW
T: 01461 202029   E: info@theoldrectoryscotland.com   W: theoldrectoryscotland.com

Indicated Prices:

Single	from £27.00 per room	Twin	from £60.00 per room
Double	from £60.00 per room	Family	from £65.00 per room

73973

Auldgirth, Dumfries
Low Kirkbride Farmhouse B&B   **Open: All year**   **Map Ref: 2A9**

★★★
FARM HOUSE

Low Kirkbride, Auldgirth, Dumfries, DG2 0SP
T: 01387 820258   E: lowkirkbride@btinternet.com   W: lowkirkbridefarm.com

Indicated Prices:

Single	from £30.00	Twin	from £25.00 per person
Double	from £25.00 per person		

36483

Dumfries & Galloway

Canonbie
Four Oaks

Open: All year excl Xmas & New Year

Map Ref: 2D9

★★★
BED AND BREAKFAST

Canonbie, Dumfriesshire, DG14 0TF
T: 01387 371329 E: gwen@mmatthews.fsbusiness.co.uk W: 4-oaks.co.uk

Indicated Prices:
Single   from £26.00 per person   Twin   from £26.00 per person
Double   from £26.00 per person

26661

Dumfries
Inverallochy Bed & Breakfast

Open: All year

Map Ref: 2B9

★★★
BED AND BREAKFAST

15 Lockerbie Road, Dumfries, DG1 3AP
T: 01387 267298 E: shona@inverallochy.com W: inverallochy.com

Indicated Prices:
Single   from £27.00 per room   Twin   from £54.00 per room
Double   from £54.00 per room

31906

Kirkcudbright
Number One Bed & Breakfast

Open: All year excl Xmas & New Year

Map Ref: 2A10

★★★★ GOLD
BED AND BREAKFAST

1 Castle Gardens, Kirkcudbright, DG6 4JE
T: 01557 330540 E: annenisbet1@btinternet.com W: number1bedandbreakfast.co.uk

Indicated Prices:
Double   from £70.00 per room

70404

Moffat
Hartfell House

Open: All year excl Xmas

Map Ref: 2B8

★★★★
GUEST HOUSE

Hartfell Crescent, Moffat, DG10 9AL
T: 01683 220153 E: enquiries@hartfellhouse.co.uk W: hartfellhouse.co.uk

Indicated Prices:
Single   from £40.00 per room   Twin   from £70.00 per room
Double   from £70.00 per room   Family   from £80.00 per room

29655

For a full listing of Quality Assured accommodation, please see directory at back of this guide.

Moffat
Woodhead Farm

Open: All year

Map Ref: 2B8

★★★★
BED AND BREAKFAST

Woodhead, Old Carlisle Road, Moffat, DG10 9LU
T: 01683 220225　E: sylvia@woodhead4.freeserve.co.uk

Indicated Prices:
Single	from £40.00 per room	Twin	from £75.00 per room
Double	from £70.00 per room		

64514

Portpatrick
Braefield Guest House

Open: All year

Map Ref: 1F10

★★★
GUEST HOUSE

Braefield Road, Portpatrick, DG9 8TA
T: 01776 810255　E: mjohn@btconnect.com　W: portpatrick-braefield.co.uk

Indicated Prices:
Single	from £30.00 per person	Twin	from £30.00 per person
Double	from £30.00 per person		

15984

Stranraer
East Challoch Farm

Open: All year excl Xmas & New Year

Map Ref: 1F10

★★★
FARM HOUSE

Dunragit, Stranraer, DG9 8PY
T: 01581 400391　W: eastchalloch.co.uk

Homely, spacious, friendly quality accommodation with spectacular views over Luce Bay. All rooms ensuite and tastefully decorated. Delicious home cooked breakfasts. Ideally situated for local gardens and touring the unspoilt Galloway coast. Great for birdwatching, walking or cycling and golf courses nearby. **Self catering also available.**

Indicated Prices:
Single	from £29.00 per room	Twin	from £48.00 per room
Double	from £48.00 per room		

24096

Stranraer
The Ivy House & Ferry Link

Open: All year

Map Ref: 1F10

★★★
GUEST HOUSE

3 Ivy Place, London Road, Stranraer, DG9 8ER
T: 01776 704176 E: ivyplace3@hotmail.com W: ivyplace.worldonline.co.uk

Indicated Prices:

Single	from £25.00-£35.00 per person	Twin	from £25.00-£28.00 per person
Double	from £25.00-£28.00 per person	Room only from £18.00-£20.00 per person	

32384

Self Catering and Camping & Caravan Parks

by Castle Douglas, Haugh of Urr
Croys Lodge

Open: All year

Map Ref: 2A10

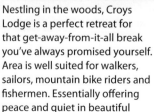

Nestling in the woods, Croys Lodge is a perfect retreat for that get-away-from-it-all break you've always promised yourself. Area is well suited for walkers, sailors, mountain bike riders and fishermen. Essentially offering peace and quiet in beautiful surroundings.

★★★
SELF CATERING

Croys, Haugh of Urr, DG7 3EX
T: 01556 650237 E: alanwithall@aol.com W: croys-lodge.co.uk

1 Lodge	3 Bedrooms	Sleeps 6

Prices – Lodge:
£450.00-£900.00   Per Week

Short breaks available

39397

For a full listing of Quality Assured accommodation, please see directory at back of this guide.

45

Gatehouse-of-Fleet
Mr Martin Howe
Open: All year   **Map Ref: 1H10**

★★★
SELF CATERING

41 Hotspur Street, Tynemouth, Tyne & Wear, NE40 4EN
T: 07968 873485 E: martin@martinhouse.com

1 Cottage   3 Bedrooms   Sleeps 2-6

Prices – Cottage:
£400.00-£475.00   Per Week

Short breaks available

74504

---

by Gretna Green
Cove House
Open: All year   **Map Ref: 2C9**

★★★★
SELF CATERING

Cove Estate, Kirkpatrick Fleming, by Gretna Green, Dumfriesshire, DG11 3AT
T: 01461 800285/07779 138694 E: info@coveestate.co.uk W: coveestate.co.uk

2 Apartments   2 Bedrooms   Sleeps 4-6
Prices – Apartments:
£70.00-£90.00   Per Night
£450.00-£600.00   Per Week
Short breaks available

83629

Newton Stewart
Barholm Croft
Open: All year   **Map Ref: 1H10**

★★
SELF CATERING

Barholm Croft, Creetown, Newton Stewart, DG8 7EN
T: 01671 820440 E: petra.winters@virgin.net

1 Cottage   1 Bedroom   Sleeps 3

Prices – Cottage:
£150.00-£225.00   Per Week

Short breaks available

14288

Southerness, Dumfries
Southerness Holiday Park
Open: Mar-Oct   **Map Ref: 2B10**

★★★★
HOLIDAY PARK

Southerness, Dumfries, DG2 8AZ
T: 0844 335 3728 E: via website W: parkdean.com
Approximately 14 miles from Dumfries following the A710 and a mile past the village of Kirkbean.

Park accommodates 100 pitches. Total touring pitches: 100.   Holiday Caravans for Hire:
Prices per pitch: (77) £175.00-£665.00 per week.
(100) £12.00-£30.00

Thistle

49157

Important: Prices stated are estimates and may be subject to amendments. Prices are per person per night unless otherwise stated.

Whithorn
Mrs Morag Forsyth

Open: Easter-end October

Map Ref: 1H11

★★★
SELF CATERING

Mid Bishopton Bungalow, Whithorn, DG8 8DE
T: 01988 500754 E: morag@whithorn.net W: bishopton-farm-holidays.co.uk

1 Bungalow | 2 Bedrooms | Sleeps 4

Prices – Bungalow:
£120.00-£275.00   Per Week

Short breaks available

48237

Whithorn
Seagulls

Open: All year

Map Ref: 1H11

★★
SELF CATERING

42 Laigh Isle, Isle of Whithorn, DG8 8LS
T: 023 9259 3468 E: thehammonds58@gmail.com W: laighisle.co.uk

1 Chalet | 2 Bedrooms | Sleeps 5+cot

Prices – Chalet:
£210.00-£260.00   Per Week

Short breaks available

10261

Looking across the River Nith to the Devorgilla Bridge in the town of Dumfries

For a full listing of Quality Assured accommodation, please see directory at back of this guide.

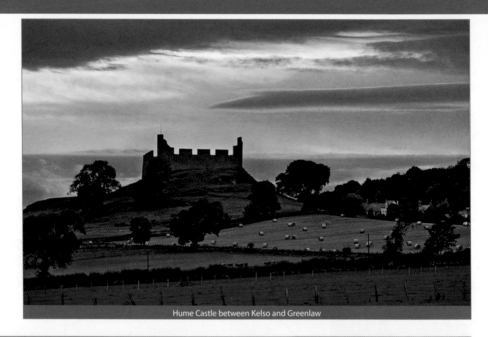
Hume Castle between Kelso and Greenlaw

Scottish Borders

The Scottish Borders stretches from the rolling hills and moorland in the west, through gentler valleys to the rich agricultural plains of the east, and on to the rocky Berwickshire coastline with its secluded coves and picturesque fishing villages.

It should also come as no surprise that an area so rich in hills and moorland, valleys and rivers should have mastered so many ways of enjoying the great outdoors. The area is a paradise for hillwalkers and cyclists of all types, while in the River Tweed and its many tributaries you'll find some of the best fishing in Scotland.

Discover an array of castles, abbeys, stately homes and museums that illustrate the fascinating history of the area. The very history which is commemorated by the Common Ridings and other local festivals, creating colourful pageants much enjoyed by visitors and locals alike. As the Scottish Borders is a region famed for its textiles, a major attraction for many is to browse and buy beautiful tweeds, tartans, cashmere and the highest quality knitwear direct from the local mills and shops.

Whenever you choose to visit, there is sure to be a packed calendar of exciting events and festivals. And you are always guaranteed a warm welcome in the Scottish Borders, a destination for all seasons.

Mountain Bikers, Glentress, near Peebles

DON'T MISS

1   The beautiful and varied landscapes of the Scottish Borders create ideal conditions for **golf**. Indeed The Roxburghe, near Kelso, is one of the most highly rated courses in Scotland. This 7,100 yard 72-par course follows natural contours, mature beech woods, dramatic water hazards, and uses clever bunkering to spectacular effect. Look out for signature hole 'The Viaduct', the views of the River Teviot and viaduct from the elevated tee of the 14th hole are simply stunning.

2   The Scottish Borders has it all for those keen to do a spot of **fishing**. From the internationally famous salmon fishing on the River Tweed to the excellent sea trout fishing on its tributaries, from the rainbow trout in the local lochs to wild brown trout in the rivers, and from the course fishing of the lower Tweed to sea fishing off the Berwickshire coast. There is something for everyone – and all of it surrounded by magnificent scenery.

3   With miles of wide open spaces and relatively quiet roads, **cyclists** can explore this unspoilt countryside at a relaxed pace. Whether it's a five mile route that takes in one of the best places to see otters, an eight mile tour of the stunning Berwickshire coast, or a more challenging 53 mile route covering three of the region's most beautiful stretches of water, the Scottish Borders has trails to suit all levels of cyclist.

4   There's some great **walking** in the Scottish Borders with over 1,500 miles of designated walking routes. The St Cuthbert's Way stretches 62 miles from Melrose to Lindisfarne, the Southern Upland Way is a 212 mile coast to coast trek taking in forest, farmland and hills, while the Borders Abbeys Way is a very pleasant 65 mile circular route visiting all four historic abbeys in Kelso, Melrose, Jedburgh and Dryburgh.

5   Discover a strong sense of **history** and tradition in this region, with imposing castles, abbeys, ancient fortifications, battlefields and dramatic ruins at every turn. This rich legacy is celebrated with a year-round calendar of events and festivals, including the annual Common Ridings, when the towns commemorate the age-old tradition of riding the boundaries to ward off invaders.

6   Thanks to the rolling hills and moorland in the west, which gradually turn to gentler valleys and high agricultural plains in the east, the Scottish Borders boasts some of the most varied **local produce** in Scotland. You can be sure the chefs in this region know just how to make the most of the game, fish, cheese, beef, lamb, fruit and vegetables that flourish on their doorstep.

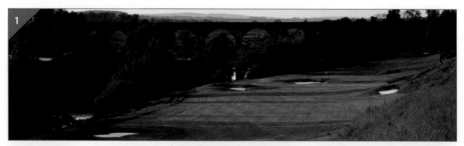

GOLF

7. With 21 courses to choose from, including two championship standard courses - The Roxburghe, near Kelso and Cardrona golf and country club, near Peebles - the Scottish Borders has some great golf on offer. **Freedom of the Fairways** adult and senior golf passports are available for 3 and 5 days and offer unbelievable value.

8. With 21 highly rated courses on offer in the Scottish Borders, often the hardest part for golfers is deciding where to begin. But while you can be sure of a quality round, you can be equally certain of a **warm welcome** at the clubhouses. The 18-hole Hirsel and Minto courses and 9-hole St Boswells and Selkirk courses were recently recognised as the friendliest in the region.

9. The beauty of playing **18-hole golf** in this region is the sheer variety of courses on offer. Eyemouth in Berwickshire is the only coastal course in the Scottish Borders and the 6th hole has been named the 'most extraordinary golf hole in Britain', a breathtaking par 3 where the tee shot is played over a vast gully with thunderous crashing waves below. Travel inland to gentler inclines at The Woll in Selkirk, one of the newest 18-hole courses in the Scottish Borders, which boasts scenic views and has excellent facilities.

10. For those keen to enjoy a spot of golf, but also find the time to explore some of other attractions on offer, there are some challenging **9-hole courses** to whet your appetite. St Boswells, which is nestled beautifully alongside the River Tweed, is an enjoyable test for all levels of ability. Travel further north and find Lauder - a classic course laid out by Willie Park Jnr, which has some lovely features offers fantastic value for money.

FISHING

11. The **River Tweed** may be most famous for its salmon fishing, but it also has an excellent run of sea trout both in the summer and the autumn, good quality wild trout fishing and some first rate winter grayling fishing. Ghillies are provided by most beats to look after anglers, and they give invaluable help to the many beginners who try their hand each year.

12. Often called the queen of **salmon rivers**, the River Tweed boasts famous salmon pools such as Weetles, Galoshan and Carry Wiel, which attract anglers from all over the world to test their skills with rod and line.

13. The Tweed, with its tributaries the Teviot, Ettrick, Leader, Whiteadder and many other small streams, provides fishing for **brown trout**, many of them wild.

14. Eyemouth is just one of a string of attractive fishing ports on the Berwickshire coastline. All offer excellent and varied **sea fishing**, from both boat and shore, with stunning coastal scenery to match.

CYCLING

15 The Scottish Borders is highly rated by cyclists thanks to 1,800 square miles of open spaces, which range from miles of meandering country lanes to river valleys, gently sloping moorland and coastal tracks. Discover the region's **waymarked cycling routes** and be sure to stop for refreshments in some of the charming towns and villages along the way.

16 The **Tweed Cycleway** starts 650 feet above sea level near Biggar and runs close by to the River Tweed through the Scottish Borders to the finish at Berwick upon Tweed. This 89 mile way-marked route can be broken down into sections and it takes in lovely towns en-route, including Peebles, Melrose, Kelso and Coldstream.

17 The **Borderloop** is a magnificent 250 mile way-marked circular route linking Peebles in the west with the Berwickshire coast at Eyemouth. The route celebrates a wonderful literary legacy, taking in romantic castles, historic abbeys and grand country houses along the way.

18 The 200-mile **Coast and Castles** route links the Forth and Tyne estuaries, taking in some of Britain's best built and natural heritage. This is a truly memorable journey between Newcastle and Edinburgh, passes Hadrian's Wall World Heritage site, unspoilt coastline and the beautiful Tweed valley and Scottish Borders coastal towns.

WALKING

19 The **Borders Abbeys Way** is a circular route linking the four great ruined Border Abbeys in Kelso, Jedburgh, Dryburgh and Melrose. The full route is 105km/65 miles in length and can easily be broken down into stages and completed at your own pace.

20 The life and progress of St Cuthbert provided the inspiration for the **St Cuthbert's Way** walking route. Starting in Melrose and ending on Holy Island (Lindisfarne) it passes through rolling farmland, river valleys, sheltered woods, hills and moorland culminating in The Holy Island Causeway, passable only at low tide. The full route is 100km/60 miles in length but this can be broken down into shorter stages.

21 The **Southern Upland Way** is Britain's first official coast to coast long distance footpath. It runs 212 miles (340km) from Portpatrick in the west to Cockburnspath on the Berwickshire coast. This route takes in some of the finest scenery in Southern Scotland and, of the total route, 130km/82 miles is in the Scottish Borders. The Southern Upland Way goes through many remote uplands areas, providing a real challenge for the experienced walker, while some parts lie within easy reach of towns and villages and are more suitable for families and the less ambitious.

Scottish Borders

Hotels

Lauder
The Lodge, Carfraemill   **Open: All year excl New Year's Day**   **Map Ref: 2D5**

Enjoy our award winning hotel perfectly situated on the junction of the A68/A697 at the gateway to the Scottish Borders and only half an hour from Edinburgh. We offer very comfortable accommodation in individually designed bedrooms and really good home-cooked food using the best of local produce.

★★★★
RESTAURANT WITH ROOMS

Carfraemill, Lauder, Berwickshire, TD2 6RA
T: 01578 750750 E: enquiries@carfraemill.co.uk W: carfraemill.co.uk

Indicated Prices:

Single	from £60.00 per room	Twin	from £90.00 per room
Double	from £90.00 per room	Family	from £100.00 per room

59541

Melrose
The Townhouse Hotel   **Open: All year excl Boxing Day and 4-12 Jan**   **Map Ref: 2D6**

★★★
TOWN HOUSE HOTEL

Market Square, Melrose
T: 01896 822645 E: enquiries@thetownhousemelrose.co.uk W: thetownhousemelrose.co.uk

Indicated Prices:

Single	from £90.00 per room	Twin	from £116.00 per room
Double	from £116.00 per room	Suite	from £128.00 per room
		Family	from £130.00 per room

58138

Important: Prices stated are estimates and may be subject to amendments. Prices are per person per night unless otherwise stated.

Swinton
The Wheatsheaf

Open: All year excl 24, 25, 26 Dec 2009; 3-14 Jan 2010

Map Ref: 2E6

★★★★
RESTAURANT WITH ROOMS

Main Street, Swinton, Berwickshire, TD11 3JJ
T: 01890 860257 E: reception@wheatsheaf-swinton.co.uk W: www.wheatsheaf-swinton.co.uk

Indicated Prices:

Single	from £75.00 per room	Superior Twin	from £148.00 per room
Double	from £112.00 per room		

63940

Walkerburn
Windlestraw Lodge

Open: All year excl Xmas & New Year

Map Ref: 2C6

A stunning house in the country with spectacular views of the Tweed Valley. This luxurious hideaway owned by chef Alan Reid and his wife Julie offers the warmest of welcomes, sublime food and ultimate relaxation. The perfect location for exploring the Borders, Edinburgh and Northumberland.

★★★★
COUNTRY HOUSE HOTEL

Galashiels Road, Walkerburn
T: 01896 870636 E: reception@windlestraw.co.uk W: windlestraw.co.uk

Indicated Prices:

Single	from £85.00 per room	Twin	from £150.00 per room
Double	from £130.00 per room	Family	on request

62318

For a full listing of Quality Assured accommodation, please see directory at back of this guide.

53

Guest Houses and B&Bs

Galashiels
Ettrickvale
Open: All year excl Xmas & New Year

Map Ref: 2D6

★★★
BED AND BREAKFAST

33 Abbotsford Road, Galashiels, TD1 3HW
T: 01896 755224 E: ettrickvale@btinternet.com W: ettrickvale.co.uk

Indicated Prices:
Double   from £22.50 per person   Twin   from £25.00 per person

45019

---

by Hawick
Whitchester Christian Guest House
Open: All year excl Xmas

Map Ref: 2D7

★★★
GUEST HOUSE

Borthaugh, Hawick, Scottish Borders, TD9 7LN
T: 01450 377477 E: enquiries@whitchester.org.uk W: www.whitchester.org.uk

Indicated Prices:
Single   from £38.00 per person   Twin   from £38.00 per person
Double   from £38.00 per person   Suite   from £48.00 per person
                                        Family   from £45.00 per person

63994

---

by Kelso, Hume
Sarah Freer
Open: Apr-Oct

Map Ref: 2E6

★★★
BED AND BREAKFAST

The Bield, Hume, Kelso, TD5 7TS
T: 01573 470349 E: thebieldhume@tiscali.co.uk W: thebieldhume.co.uk

Indicated Prices:
Single   from £30.00 per room   Twin   from £56.00 per room
Double   from £56.00 per room

58215

Important: Prices stated are estimates and may be subject to amendments. Prices are per person per night unless otherwise stated.

Peebles
Lyne Farmhouse B&B

Open: All year excl Xmas

Map Ref: 2C6

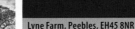
★★★
FARM HOUSE

Lyne Farm, Peebles, EH45 8NR
T: 01721 740255 E: lynefarmhouse@btinternet.com W: lynefarm.co.uk

Indicated Prices:

Single	from £30.00	Twin	from £25.00 per person
Double	from £25.00 per person		

36638

St Boswells
Mainhill

Open: All year

Map Ref: 2D7

★★★
BED AND BREAKFAST

Mainhill, St Boswells, Roxburghshire, TD6 0HG
T: 01835 823788 E: annmainhill@hotmail.co.uk

Indicated Prices:

Single	from £40.00 per room	Twin	from £65.00 per room

42404

Selkirk
Sunnybrae House

Open: All year excl Xmas & New Year

Map Ref: 2D7

★★★
BED AND BREAKFAST

75 Tower Street, Selkirk, TD7 4LS
T: 01750 21156 E: bookings@sunnybraehouse.fsnet.co.uk

Indicated Prices:

Single	from £40.00	Twin	from £28.00 per person
Double	from £28.00 per person	Family	from £28.00 per person

12349

West Linton
Jerviswood B&B

Open: All year excl Xmas & New Year

Map Ref: 2C6

★★
BED AND BREAKFAST

Linton Bank Drive, West Linton, Peeblesshire, EH46 7DT
T: 01968 660429

Indicated Prices:

Single	from £25.00 per person	Twin	from £20.00 per person
Double	from £20.00 per person		

43942

For a full listing of Quality Assured accommodation, please see directory at back of this guide.

55

Self Catering and Camping & Caravan Parks

Coldstream
Mrs Sheila Letham Open: All year Map Ref: 2E6

★★★
SELF CATERING

Fireburn Mill, Coldstream, TD12 4LN
T: 01890 882124 E: andrewletham@tiscali.co.uk

2 Cottages Bedrooms 3 Sleeps 2-6

Prices – Cottages:
from £200.00 Per Week

Short breaks available

37989

by Jedburgh
Overwells Country Cottages Open: All year Map Ref: 2E7

Converted millhouse on a farm three miles from Jedburgh. Maintained to highest standards overlooking the water garden of a nearby farmhouse and beyond to the Cheviot Hills. Sleeps four. An ideal base for touring beautiful scenic countryside, all sporting activities or just to chill out in peaceful surroundings.

★★★★
SELF CATERING

Millhouse, Overwells, Jedburgh, TD8 6LT
T: 01835 863020 E: abfraser@btinternet.com W: overwells.co.uk

1 Cottage 2 Bedrooms Sleeps 1-4

Prices – Cottage:
£250.00-£400.00 Per Week

Short breaks available

48862

Important: Prices stated are estimates and may be subject to amendments. Prices are per person per night unless otherwise stated.

Peebles
Rosetta Road

Open: All year

Map Ref: 2C6

★★★

SELF CATERING

Contact: Christine Napier, 6 Ash Grove, Norwich, NR3 4BE
T: 01603 301702 E: jandcnapier40@btinternet.com W: peeblesholidayflat.webeden.co.uk

1 Flat	1 Bedroom	Sleeps 2

Prices – Flat:
£280.00   Per Week
Short breaks available

42735

near Selkirk
Mrs L Bernard

Open: Apr-Sept

Map Ref: 2C7

MINIMUM STANDARD HOLIDAY CARAVAN

West Deloraine, Ettrick, Selkirk, TD7 5HR
T: 01750 62207 E: thefarm@westdeloraine.co.uk W: westdeloraine.co.uk
On B7009 12½ miles from Selkirk.

Holiday Caravans for Hire:
(2) £200.00 per week. Sleeps 6 max.

68955

Melrose Abbey, in the centre of Melrose, Scottish Borders

or a full listing of Quality Assured accommodation, please see directory at back of this guide.

57

Food & Drink

Lauder
The Lodge, Carfraemill

Open: All year

Map Ref: 2D5

★★★★
RESTAURANT WITH ROOMS

Culinary Type:
SCOTTISH

Lauder, Berwickshire
T: 01578 750750
E: enquiries@carfraemill.co.uk
W: carfraemill.co.uk

Best For:
   • Kids and Families • Special Occasions
   • Budget Meals • Breakfast • Group Dining

Prices:
Starter from:	£3.50
Main Course from:	£8.50
Dessert from:	£5.00

Opening Times:
   Lunch from 1200, all day
   Dinner from 1700, last orders 2100.
   Good food available all day!

59541

Award-winning restaurant with rooms, situated on the junction of
the A68/A697 just half an hour south of Edinburgh. Enjoy delicious
home-cooked locally produced food in a choice of eating areas; the
wood-panelled dining room, bistro bar or unique Jo's Kitchen with its
own ruby red Aga.

EatScotland.com

Discover Scotland's superb produce and great places to dine.

Floors Castle, near Kelso, Scottish Borders

For a full listing of Quality Assured accommodation, please see directory at back of this guide.

59

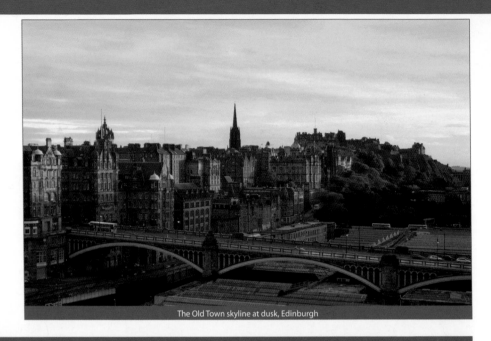

The Old Town skyline at dusk, Edinburgh

EDINBURGH AND THE LOTHIANS

Inspiring Edinburgh, where the past and present combine to give the perfect balance between all things traditional and contemporary. This World Heritage Site has been shaped by the turbulent history of days gone by with the city now a firm favourite with visitors from around the world.

Edinburgh Castle presides over the city, perched on a rocky outcrop and dominating the city skyline from every angle. Marvel at the magnificent architecture, where the lofty tenements and narrow closes of the Medieval Old Town sit in contrast with the elegance and symmetry of the Georgian New Town.

Find designer shopping and Michelin star restaurants, world-class visitor attractions and a vibrant arts scene.

But Edinburgh is also a surprisingly green place. Even in the heart of the city, you are never far from wide open spaces where you can take in an amazing view, have a picnic, or simply relax between shops. Princes Street Gardens and the Royal Botanic Garden on the north side of the city are two of Edinburgh's most popular open spaces.

As Europe's festival capital, Edinburgh has an action-packed calendar of festivals and events to keep visitors entertained all year round. The city is home to the largest International Arts Festival in the world, which can list the Fringe, Edinburgh Military Tattoo and International Book Festival amongst its impressive repertoire. The city's Hogmanay celebrations are legendary, with a packed winter programme at either side of New Year. From world class theatre and comedy to lively ceilidhs and celebrations, there is always something going on.

And foodies will not be disappointed, there's something to suit every taste and pocket. From selecting fresh, local produce at an award-winning farmers' market - where you can meet a huge range of producers and pick up invaluable preparation tips - to dining al fresco taking in the superb views.

Edinburgh and the Lothians has everything you would expect from a break and much more besides.

And with easy access to the coast and countryside, East Lothian, West Lothian and Midlothian each add their distinctive character to the city region.

Discover the stunning coastline of East Lothian, which stretches more than 40 miles, combining award-winning beaches with spectacular cliffs and boasting a fine selection of links golf courses. Home to the Scottish Seabird Centre, the National Museum of Flight, Musselburgh Racecourse and Glenkinchie Distillery, East Lothian really does have something for everyone.

Based between Edinburgh and Glasgow, offering beautiful views and some of the best shopping in Scotland, West Lothian is the ideal base from which to explore. As well as expansive valleys, wild uplands and tranquil green spaces, attractions include the magnificent ruins of Linlithgow Palace - a must for history lovers. With more country parks than any other area of Scotland, West Lothian has an array of outdoor activities on offer and an abundance of wildlife to look out for along the way.

Take some time to discover the hidden secrets of Midlothian; stroll through peaceful woodlands, explore medieval castles or tee off on beautiful country golf courses. The peace and beauty of the countryside is contrasted with award-winning visitor centres and lively towns offering every amenity a visitor could want. From tropical butterflies to the mysterious stone carvings at Rosslyn Chapel, Midlothian has it all.

A break to Edinburgh and the Lothians can provide the perfect holiday experience. From the excitement of being in a vibrant and cosmopolitan city to the treasures on offer just a few miles out of town where you can find some of the driest, sunniest weather in Scotland.

And there's an ever expanding range of quality accommodation which will suit every need.

Edinburgh, Farmers Market

What's On?

Mary King's Ghost Fest
18 - 23 March 2010
Explore Edinburgh's haunted places.
edinburghghostfest.com

Ceilidh Culture
26 March - 18 April 2010
A vibrant celebration of traditional Scottish arts.
ceilidhculture.co.uk

Edinburgh International Science Festival
3 - 17 April 2010
Stir the curiosity of inquiring minds.
sciencefestival.co.uk

Beltane Fire Festival
30 April 2010
Celebrate the start of the summer with this unique fire festival on Calton Hill.
beltane.org

Emirates Airline Edinburgh Sevens
29 + 30 May 2010
The elite international 16-team tournament returns to Murrayfield.
edinburgh7s.com

Edinburgh International Film Festival
16 - 27 June 2010
The festival where the films are the stars.
edfilmfest.org.uk

Royal Highland Show
24 - 27 June 2010
Top agricultural event at the Royal Highland Centre, Ingliston.
royalhighlandshow.org

Edinburgh Military Tattoo
6 - 28 August 2010
This military extravaganza is an international favourite.
edinburgh-tattoo.co.uk

Edinburgh Festival Fringe
6 - 30 August 2010
The largest arts festival on the planet.
edfringe.com

Edinburgh International Festival
13 August - 5 September 2010
The very best of opera, theatre, music and dance.
eif.org.uk

Edinburgh International Book Festival
14 - 30 August 2010
The world's largest public celebration of the written word.
edbookfest.co.uk

All dates correct at time of publication. Please check before booking. VisitScotland cannot be held responsible for any inaccuracies

61

DON'T MISS

1.   The UNESCO World Heritage Site at the heart of the city combines the medieval Old Town, the Georgian New Town and award winning modern architecture. Don't miss **Edinburgh's World Heritage** new House Histories trail - highlighting the stories of people who lived in historic buildings in Edinburgh. The House Histories trail focuses on six buildings which together form a journey from the Old Town through to the New Town and Dean Village.

2.   Never a month passes without a major event or **festival** in Edinburgh, whether it be Beltane, Ceilidh Culture and Science in April, Children's Theatre, the Rugby League and Rugby 7s in May, Film Festival in June, Jazz and Blues in July, Christmas or Hogmanay. And of course, there's the world's largest International Arts Festival in August, taking in the Fringe, the Tattoo, the International Book Festivals. The city buzzes with excitement no matter what season you choose to visit.

3.   Many of the area's **attractions**, museums, galleries and country parks are completely free, including the City Art Centre, Museum of Edinburgh, The Writer's Museum, John Muir and Beecraigs Country Parks. You can also enjoy entry to more than 30 top attractions with the Edinburgh Pass, which is the best value way to see the best Scotland's inspiring capital and the surrounding area has to offer. From just £24, check out www.edinburghpass.com.

4.   From high points in the city of Edinburgh, there are beguiling glimpses of the land towards **East Lothian**. A curving coastline with a hint of gold, distant red roofs, green spaces, rich fields and woods, then the hills beyond. But it's even more rewarding when you are there. The likes of North Berwick and Gullane are charming seaside communities and the beaches are superb. Beyond the dunes and the grey sea-buckthorn find golf courses - challenging, classic seaside links of championship standard. Add to that stately homes, castles, galleries, crafts and museums, and it's easy to see why East Lothian is considered a great base for all kinds of holidays and leisure breaks.

5.   In **West Lothian** you're in an area offering so much to its visitors: heritage, places to see, entertainment and great shopping. It's the sheer diversity you'll enjoy most – for example, one of the most important prehistoric sites in all of Scotland lies just a few miles from the biggest shopping centre in Europe! Long ago, Linlithgow in West Lothian thrived as a midway point between the two most important castles in the Kingdom of Scotland: Edinburgh and Stirling. Today, all of the area flourishes because it is at the centre of Scotland, midway, not just between two grand castles, but also between the two largest cities, Edinburgh and Glasgow - just one more reason to stay in West Lothian.

6.   Though you are near to the city, **Midlothian** can feel very different. Listen to the birdsong ringing out from the wooded glen by the famous Rosslyn Chapel, or explore the wide-open heathery spaces of the Pentland Hills, and it's hard to believe Scotland's bustling capital is only minutes away. Thanks to a certain Hollywood blockbuster movie, Rosslyn Chapel is now Midlothian's most famous historic site, but there are lots more places of interest. For example, discover the castle where Mary, Queen of Scots was once a wedding guest, or take a tour of a restored Victorian colliery. Midlothian is full of surprises, with plenty to entertain you from country parks to exotic butterfly displays.

WALKS/OUT AND ABOUT

7   The Lothians offer so many opportunities to get out and enjoy the **great outdoors**. Choose from a number of country parks for cycling, horse-riding or to simply take in the view. The East Lothian coast is the route for the John Muir Way, a long distance walk taking in the full coast of East Lothian from Musselburgh to Dunbar. Further inland check out the Avon River walk in West Lothian and the dramatic scenery of wooded Roslin Glen in Midlothian.

8   The impressive coastline of East Lothian means there is a great selection of award-winning **beaches** to choose from. Great for walking, picnics, fantastic sunsets and breathtaking views. Yellowcraigs Beach in Dirleton is a beautiful sandy beach with views across to Fidra – rumoured to be the inspiration for Robert Louis Stevenson's famous novel Shipwrecked. Seacliff Beach in North Berwick offers great views across to the Bass Rock. Tucked away in one corner of the beach is Scotland's smallest harbour, framed by dramatic views of Tantallon Castle.

9   The **Water of Leith Walkway** in Edinburgh is ideal for family walks. Take an afternoon stroll away from the hustle and bustle of the city along the Water of Leith, a river which once powered up to 90 water mills. The remains of these can be seen in the weirs and buildings along the river. Highlights along the way include the Gallery of Modern Art and the Dean Gallery, the Dean Village, St Bernard's Well and the Royal Botanic Garden.

10   Sitting to the south of Edinburgh, discover the tranquil beauty of the **Pentland Hills**. Their geography has shaped the success of the Lothians, playing a part in the drama of Scottish history, while poets and authors have written about them with iconic status. The range is criss-crossed by burns, cleughs and glens providing a great variety of scenery in a relatively small corner of Scotland.

FOOD & DRINK

11   Scotland is renowned for its natural larder and the Lothians are no exception. Wandering around any of the **farmers' markets** in this region is always a great experience where you can find the freshest local produce. Held every Saturday morning on Castle Terrace and the last Thursday of the month on Castle Street in Edinburgh, and the last Saturday of each month in Haddington, East Lothian, pop along early to pick up the very best supplies.

12   For the story of **whisky**, try either the Scotch Whisky Experience in Edinburgh or Glenkinchie Distillery, by Pencaitland. Recently refurbished, the former tells how the amber nectar is made and how best to enjoy it, while the latter is ideal for warming you up after exploring the East Lothian beaches.

13   Edinburgh offers a tremendous selection of all types of food, from Michelin starred restaurants like Martin Wishart to self service vegetarian fare at Henderson's on Hanover Street. **Restaurants** like Howies (of which there are a fair few in the city) offer excellent local produce served at an affordable price. George Street, the West End, the Royal Mile, the Grassmarket and Leith are just some of the areas where you'll find a range of restaurants to suit all palettes.

14   Very quickly in your travels through East Lothian, you become aware this is an area very suited to **foodies**. And it's more than the just the choice of fine dining or simple pub lunches (though, admittedly, East Lothian has more than its share of AA rosettes). There is real enthusiasm for farmers' markets and the choice of delicatessens, as well as a passion for really good produce, including seafood and organic meat.

HISTORY & HERITAGE

15 The **Scottish Mining Museum** is located at the former Lady Victoria Colliery at Newtongrange in Midlothian. This five-star attraction has turned the story of Scotland's coal into a fascinating tour and exhibition with every guide an ex-miner. You'll see and hear the authentic stories of a working mine.

16 Former floating home of the monarchy, **The Royal Yacht *Britannia*** offers a superb visitor experience that will guide you through 40 years of royal life aboard, including private quarters, state dining room, engine room and the sick bay.

17 Edinburgh is one of Europe's most haunted cities, surrounded by myth and legend. Take a journey back in time and experience the narrow underground closes at **Real Mary King's Close** or try one of the many walking ghost tours, if you dare!

18 With fantastic views over the Firth of Forth, the imposing 15th century **Blackness Castle** looks almost poised to set sail. Explore its darkened corridors, which still capture the atmosphere of a garrison fortress and state prison.

SHOPPING

19 Only a few minutes from Princes Street, visit Edinburgh's **West End** for some serious shopping in the quaint streets of Stafford Street, William Street, Randolph Place and surrounding area. This is a unique shopping quarter and home to a range of designer fashion boutiques and inspiring homeware.

20 Only a short bus ride from the city centre, take a refreshing stroll along the waterfront in **Leith**, where you'll find independent shops and galleries, alongside contemporary bars and cafes. There is a fair number of Michelin starred restaurants in Leith and of course The Royal Yacht *Britannia*.

21 **The Grassmarket** – Vintage is what The Grassmarket does brilliantly. Snap up a one-off bargain in the quirky boutiques, or splash out on a designer exclusive. There are loads of great cafes and bars if you need to refuel.

22 **Princes Street** in the city centre is Edinburgh's principal street. With only one side dedicated to shops, this stretch affords wonderful views of Edinburgh Castle. Opposite the shops and directly below the Castle, Princes Street Gardens is the perfect place to rest between shopping trips. Behind Princes Street sits George Street – the 'Bond Street' of the north. Crossing the New Town, Thistle, Frederick, Castle and Hanover Streets offer excellent boutique shopping. Don't miss Multrees Walk, just off St Andrews Square, where you can find a range of high-end designer brands.

The view over the Old Town from the Scott Monument in the city centre of Edinburgh

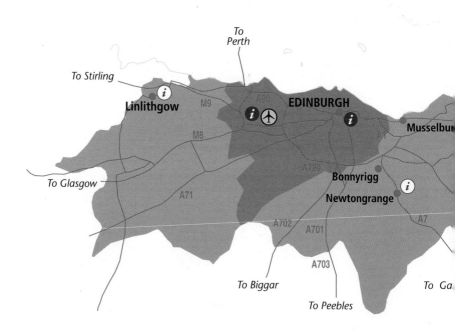

VisitScotland Information Centres

To help you plan and book your trip to Scotland email our travel experts at info@visitscotland.com. When you arrive call into one of our Information Centres where our friendly experts can offer advice on all things local as well as sharing their wider knowledge of Scotland. We don't just advise either. We can sort out your accommodation and all your travel needs, as well as tickets for events across Scotland. So if you're looking to get the most from your visit, there really is only one place to go.

Edinburgh and Lothians

Edinburgh	3 Princes Street Edinburgh, EH2 2QP
Edinburgh Airport	Main Concourse Edinburgh International Airport, EH12 9DN
North Berwick	1 Quality Street North Berwick, EH39 4HJ

North Berwick

A198

East Linton

A198

Dunbar

A1

nent

Haddington

A1

A6093

To Berwick-upon-Tweed

To Jedburgh

ls

 Open All Year

(i) Seasonal

visitscotland.com/wheretofindus

- ■ LOCAL KNOWLEDGE
- ■ WHERE TO STAY
- ■ ACCOMMODATION BOOKING
- ■ PLACES TO VISIT
- ■ THINGS TO DO
- ■ MAPS AND GUIDES
- ■ TRAVEL ADVICE
- ■ ROUTE PLANNING
- ■ WHERE TO SHOP AND EAT
- ■ LOCAL CRAFTS AND PRODUCE
- ■ EVENT INFORMATION
- ■ TICKETS

Hotels

Edinburgh
The Balmoral Hotel

Open: All year   **Map Ref: 2C5**

★★★★★ GOLD
HOTEL

1 Princes Street, Edinburgh, EH2 2EQ
T: 0131 556 2414 E: reservations.balmoral@roccofortecollection.com W: roccofortecollection.com

Indicated Prices:

Single	from £160.00 per room	Twin	from £175.00 per room
Double	from £175.00 per room	Suite	from £535.00 per room

58132

Edinburgh
Dunstane City Hotel

Open: All year   **Map Ref: 2C5**

A contemporary luxury boutique hotel, situated in Edinburgh's West End. Minutes from Edinburgh Business Centre and city attractions. The 17 bedrooms are stylish and contemporary offering a choice of standard and superior rooms. Hotel offers free wi-fi and car parking. Our friendly staff are here to help and ensure a truly memorable break.

★★★★
TOWN HOUSE HOTEL

5 Hampton Terrace, Haymarket, Edinburgh, EH12 5JD
T: 0131 337 6169 E: reservations@dunstanehotels.co.uk W: dunstanehotels.co.uk

Indicated Prices:

Single	from £95.00 per room	Twin	from £119.00 per room
Double	from £99.00 per room	Suite	from £149.00 per room

79350

Edinburgh
Dunstane House Hotel

Open: All year

Map Ref: 2C5

The friendliest hotel in Edinburgh, where you will enjoy country style tranquility of a small castle in a city setting. Located only a 10 minute walk to the city centre with free private parking. Hotel offers free wi-fi and a unique lounge bar and restaurant themed on the Scottish Isles.

★★★★
SMALL HOTEL

4 West Coates, Haymarket, Edinburgh, EH12 5JQ
T: 0131 337 6169 E: reservations@dunstanehotels.co.uk W: dunstanehotels.co.uk

Indicated Prices:
Single   from £85.00 per room   Twin   from £98.00 per room
Double   from £98.00 per room

23861

Edinburgh
Ailsa Craig Hotel

Open: All year

Map Ref: 2C4

Newly refurbished elegant Georgian Townhouse hotel. Ideal city centre location within walking distance to Waverley Station, Princes Street, Edinburgh Castle and Playhouse Theatre. Combining traditional features with modern facilities, the hotel offers superb views, private gardens and friendly atmosphere providing the perfect blend of history and hospitality. Free wi-fi internet access. Night porter.

★★★
METRO HOTEL

24 Royal Terrace, Edinburgh, EH7 5AH
T: 0131 556 6055 E: ailsacraighotel@ednet.co.uk W: townhousehotels.co.uk

Indicated Prices:
Single   from £25.00   Twin   from £25.00 per person
Double   from £25.00 per person   Family from £25.00 per person

11232

For a full listing of Quality Assured accommodation, please see directory at back of this guide.

Edinburgh
Best Western Kings Manor Hotel   Open: All year   Map Ref: 2C5

Quality accommodation in quiet suburbs of Edinburgh with easy public transport to all the city's attractions. Free on-site car parking. Family rooms available. Extensive leisure club featuring 25 metre pool –free for residents. A la carte restaurant, popular bistro and relaxing bar. Great base for touring south of Scotland.

★★★
HOTEL

100 Milton Road East, Edinburgh, EH15 2NP
T: 0131 468 8003   E: reservations@kingsmanor.com   W: kingsmanor.com

Indicated Prices:

Single	from £55.00 per room		Twin	from £95.00 per room
Double	from £95.00 per room		Suite	from £110.00 per room
			Family	from £110.00 per room

34051

Guest Houses and B&Bs

Edinburgh
Bield Bed and Breakfast   Open: All year   Map Ref: 2C4

★★★★
BED AND BREAKFAST

3 Orchard Brae West, Edinburgh, EH4 2EW
T: 0131 332 5119   E: bieldltd@hotmail.com   W: bieldbedandbreakfast.com

Indicated Prices:

Single	from £50.00 per person		Twin	from £30.00 per person
Double	from £30.00 per person			

15091

Edinburgh
Dunedin Guest House

Open: All year excl 25-26 Dec   **Map Ref: 2C5**

★★★★
GUEST HOUSE

8 Priestfield Road, Newington, Edinburgh, EH16 5HH
T: 0131 668 1949 E: reservations@dunedinguesthouse.co.uk W: dunedinguesthouse.co.uk

Indicated Prices:

Single	from £45.00 per room	Twin	from £70.00 per room
Double	from £70.00 per room	Family	from £105.00 per room

23692

Edinburgh
Frederick House

Open: All year   **Map Ref: 2C4**

Recently refurbished, Frederick House is situated amidst the Georgian elegance of Edinburgh's New Town and only five minutes walk from the world famous Princes Street. Frederick House offers a warm welcome and well-appointed accommodation in the centre of Edinburgh. Close proximity to shops, bars and cafés.

★★★★
GUEST ACCOMMODATION

42 Frederick Street, Edinburgh, EH2 1EX
T: 0131 226 1999 E: frederickhouse@ednet.co.uk W: townhousehotels.co.uk

Indicated Prices:

Single	from £35.00 per person	Twin	from £25.00 per person
Double	from £25.00 per person	Family	from £25.00 per person

26805

Edinburgh
Gil Dun Guest House

Open: All year   **Map Ref: 2C5**

★★★★
GUEST HOUSE

9 Spence Street, Edinburgh, EH16 5AG
T: 0131 667 1368 E: gildun.edin@btinternet.com W: gildun.co.uk

Indicated Prices:

Single	from £35.00 per room	Twin	from £70.00 per room
Double	from £70.00 per room	Family	from £97.50 per room

27612

For a full listing of Quality Assured accommodation, please see directory at back of this guide.

Edinburgh
Glenalmond House

Open: All year excl Xmas

Map Ref: 2C5

Luxurious accommodation in detached Victorian house, just over a mile from the main tourist attractions and centre of Edinburgh. Free private car parking and wi-fi. Ground floor rooms available. Deluxe rooms with Queen Anne four-poster and Rococco beds. Extensive breakfast menu with traditional Scottish and vegetarian options. Outdoor patio area.

★★★★
GUEST HOUSE

25 Mayfield Gardens, Edinburgh, EH9 2BX
T: 0131 668 2392 E: enquiries@glenalmondhouse.com W: www.glenalmondhouse.com

Indicated Prices:

Single	from £50.00 per room	Twin	from £65.00 per room
Double	from £65.00 per room	Family	from £80.00 per room

80429

Edinburgh
MW Townhouse Guesthouse

Open: All year

Map Ref: 2C5

 ★★★★
GUEST HOUSE

11 Spence Street, Edinburgh, EH16 5AG
T: 0131 655 1530 E: info@mwtownhouse.co.uk W: mwtownhouse.co.uk

Indicated Prices:

Single	from £49.00	Twin	from £35.00 per person
Double	from £35.00 per person	Suite	from £40.00 per person
		Family	from £32.50 per person

80832

Important: Prices stated are estimates and may be subject to amendments. Prices are per person per night unless otherwise stated.

Edinburgh
Ardenlee Guest House

Open: All year

Map Ref: 2C4

The Ardenlee is a beautiful three star guest house within a Victorian townhouse in Edinburgh's historic New Town. Ideally located half a mile from Princes Street, for exploring all of Edinburgh providing welcoming accommodation and a full cooked breakfast.

★★★
GUEST HOUSE

9 Eyre Place, Edinburgh, EH3 5ES
T: 0131 556 2838 E: info@ardenlee.co.uk W: www.ardenlee.co.uk

Indicated Prices:

Single	from £30.00 per room	Twin	from £60.00 per room
Double	from £60.00 per room	Family	from £80.00 per room

12535

Edinburgh
Ardleigh Guest House

Open: All year

Map Ref: 2C4

★★★
GUEST HOUSE

260 Ferry Road, Edinburgh, EH5 3AN
T: 0131 552 1833 E: info@ardleighhouse.com W: ardleighhouse.com

Indicated Prices:

Single	from £25.00 per room	Twin	from £45.00 per room
Double	from £45.00 per room	Family	from £90.00 per room

12599

For a full listing of Quality Assured accommodation, please see directory at back of this guide.

73

Edinburgh
Blinkbonny House

Open: All year

Map Ref: 2C4

Beautiful detached bungalow in residential area on west side of city in quiet location. Within walking distance of Prince Street, Botanic Gardens and Art Gallery. Close to airport and A90 with easy access to the Forth Road Bridge and the north. Private parking available. Two ground floor rooms with ensuite.

★★★
BED AND BREAKFAST

23 Blinkbonny Gardens, Edinburgh, EH4 3HG
T: 0131 467 1232 E: info@blinkbonnyhouse.co.uk W: blinkbonnyhouse.co.uk

Indicated Prices:

Single	from £35.00 per person	Twin	from £25.00 per person
Double	from £25.00 per person	Family	from £25.00 per person

15464

Edinburgh
Burns Guest House

Open: All year

Map Ref: 2C5

★★★
GUEST HOUSE

67 Gilmore Place, Edinburgh, EH3 9NU
T: 0131 229 1669 E: burnsbandb@talk21.com W: burnsguesthouse.co.uk

Indicated Prices:

Single	from £25.00 per room	Twin	from £50.00 per room
Double	from £50.00 per room		

16942

Edinburgh
Carrington

Open: Feb-Nov

Map Ref: 2C4

★★★
GUEST HOUSE

38 Pilrig Street, Edinburgh, EH6 5AL
T: 0131 554 4769

Indicated Prices:

Double	from £72.00 per room	Twin	from £72.00 per room
		Family	from £160.00 per room

18299

Important: Prices stated are estimates and may be subject to amendments. Prices are per person per night unless otherwise stated.

Edinburgh
Casa Buzzo Guest House

Open: All year excl Xmas Day

Map Ref: 2C5

★★★
GUEST HOUSE

8 Kilmaurs Road, Edinburgh, EH16 5DA
T: 0131 667 8998 E: l.birnie933@btinternet.com

Indicated Prices:

Single	from £38.00 per room	Suite	from £35.00 per person
Double	from £37.00 per person	Family	from £105.00 per room (3 people)
Twin	from £33.00 per person	Family	from £160.00 per room (4 people)

18348

Edinburgh
Glendevon Bed & Breakfast

Open: Apr-Oct

Map Ref: 2C5

★★★
BED AND BREAKFAST

50 Glasgow Road, Edinburgh, EH12 8HN
T: 0131 539 0491 E: simpson-glendevon@fsmail.net W: simpson-glendevon.co.uk

Indicated Prices:

Single	from £30.00 per room	Twin	from £65.00 per room
Double	from £60.00 per room		

28098

Edinburgh
Kirklea Guest House

Open: All year excl Xmas

Map Ref: 2C5

★★★
GUEST HOUSE

11 Harrison Road, Edinburgh, EH11 1EG
T: 0131 337 1129 E: kirklea11@live.co.uk W: kirklea-guest-house.co.uk

Indicated Prices:

Single	from £34.00 per room	Twin	from £62.00 per room
Double	from £58.00 per room		

34332

Edinburgh
The Laurels Guest House

Open: All year

Map Ref: 2C5

★★★
GUEST HOUSE

320 Gilmerton Road, Edinburgh, EH17 7PR
T: 0131 666 2229 E: jill@laurelsguesthouse.net W: laurelsguesthouse.net

Indicated Prices:

Single	from £25.00 per room	Twin	from £45.00 per room
Double	from £45.00 per room	Family	from £65.00 per room

70085

For a full listing of Quality Assured accommodation, please see directory at back of this guide.

Edinburgh
Panda Villa

Open: All year

Map Ref: 2C5

★★★
BED AND BREAKFAST

12 Kilmaurs Road, Edinburgh, EH16 5DA
T: 0131 667 5057 E: sichel@dircon.co.uk W: pandavilla.co.uk

Indicated Prices:

Single	from £35.00 per room	Triple	from £77.00 per room
Double	from £65.00 per room	Suite	from £68.00 per room
Twin	from £56.00 per room	Family	from £89.00 per room

49076

Edinburgh
Sonas Guest House

Open: All year excl Xmas

Map Ref: 2C5

Sonas Bed and Breakfast is a lovely Victorian terraced villa close to city centre and university. Ideal for sightseeing, Edinburgh Castle, Palace. Comfortable ensuite rooms, multichannel TVs with iPod and DVD. Complimentary tea and coffee facilities. Free parking and wi-fi. Full Scottish breakfast served every morning.

★★★
GUEST HOUSE

3 East Mayfield, Newington, Edinburgh, EH9 1SD
T: 0131 667 2781 E: info@sonasguesthouse.com W: sonasguesthouse.com

Indicated Prices:

Single	from £35.00 per room	Twin	from £55.00 per room
Double	from £55.00 per room	Family	from £60.00 per room

55185

Edinburgh
St Valery Guest House

Open: All year

Map Ref: 2C5

The St Valery offers quality accommodation in the heart of Edinburgh. Family ensuite rooms available, all with free cable TV and free broadband. Also full cooked breakfast included. For stays of two nights and more we are happy to negotiate rates. Easy walking distance to Princes Street, Castle and attractions.

★★★
GUEST HOUSE

36 Coates Gardens, Haymarket, Edinburgh, EH12 5LE
T: 0131 337 1893 E: info@stvalery.co.uk W: stvalery.com

Indicated Prices:

Single	from £36.00 per person	Twin	from £36.00 per person
Double	from £36.00 per person	Family	from £36.00 per person

56103

Edinburgh
Strathallan Guest House

Open: All year excl Xmas

Map Ref: 2C5

Elegant detached villa. Free off-street parking. Free wi-fi. Family run establishment close to Edinburgh Castle, Dynamic Earth and Arthur's Seat. As well as the two world heritage sites. Full Scottish breakfast provided with vegetarian options. Tea and coffee facilities in all rooms. No smoking in all rooms.

★★★
GUEST HOUSE

44 Minto Street, Newington, Edinburgh, EH9 2BR
T: 0131 667 6678 E: strathalan@aol.com W: strathallanguesthouse.com

Indicated Prices:

Single	from £35.00 per room	Twin	from £50.00 per room
Double	from £50.00 per room	Family	from £70.00 per room

56827

For a full listing of Quality Assured accommodation, please see directory at back of this guide.

77

Edinburgh
Mrs Linda J Allan Open: May-Oct Map Ref: 2C5

★★
BED AND BREAKFAST

10 Baberton Mains Rise, Edinburgh, EH14 3HG
T: 0131 442 3619 E: lja_bandb_edin@hotmail.com W: lindasbandb.tripod.com
Indicated Prices:
Single   from £25.00 per person
Double   from £17.00 per person

44146

Edinburgh
Averon Guest House Open: All year Map Ref: 2C5

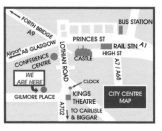

FORTH BRIDGE
A9
Airport A8 Glasgow
CONFERENCE CENTRE
WE ARE HERE
GILMORE PLACE
LOTHIAN ROAD
PRINCES ST
BUS STATION
CASTLE
HIGH ST
RAIL STN A7
A7 / A68
CLOCK
KINGS THEATRE
A702
CITY CENTRE MAP
TO CARLISLE & BIGGAR

Georgian Town House located in central Edinburgh with car park. High standard of accommodation at favourable terms.
- Full cooked breakfast
- All credit cards accepted
- 10/15 minute walk to Princes St and Castle
- AA 2 star
- Private car park

★★
GUEST HOUSE

44 Gilmore Place, Edinburgh, EH3 9NQ
T: 0131 229 9932 E: info@averon.co.uk W: www.averon.co.uk
Indicated Prices:
Single   from £26.00 per room   Twin   from £56.00 per room
Double   from £56.00 per room   Family   from £64.00 per room

13577

Edinburgh
Falcon Crest Guest House

Open: All year excl Xmas

Map Ref: 2C4

The Clark family welcome you to our three floor Victorian home in the residential area of Trinity between the Royal Botanic Gardens and the River Forth. Ideal for Edinburgh and touring. Excellent road links. Well served by buses. City centre 10 minutes (1.5 miles). Airport 8.5 miles. Free on-street parking.

★
GUEST HOUSE

70 South Trinity Road, Edinburgh, EH5 3NX
T: 0131 552 5294 E: manager@falconcrest.co.uk W: falconcrest.co.uk

Indicated Prices:

Single	from £22.00 per room	Twin	from £44.00 per room
Double	from £50.00 per room		

25545

Haddington
Orchard Guest House

Open: All year

Map Ref: 2D5

★★★
BED AND BREAKFAST

22 Letham Mains Holdings, Haddington, EH41 4HB
T: 01620 824898 E: orchardletham@aol.com W: orchardhousechalets.co.uk

Indicated Prices:

Single	from £35.00	Twin	from £27.00 per person
Double	from £27.00 per person	Family	from £65.00 per room

48547

Musselburgh
Mrs Elizabeth Aitken

Open: All year

Map Ref: 2C5

★★
BED AND BREAKFAST

18 Woodside Gardens, Musselburgh, East Lothian, EH21 7LJ
T: 0131 665 3170/3344

Indicated Prices:

Single	from £25.00 per person	Twin	from £20.00 per person
Double	from £20.00 per person	Family	from £20.00 per person

43190

For a full listing of Quality Assured accommodation, please see directory at back of this guide.

Self Catering and Camping & Caravan Parks

Edinburgh
Edinburgh Flats

Open: All year   **Map Ref: 2C4**

Beautifully renovated superbly furnished apartments in Georgian townhouses only metres from central Princes Street. Period elegance with hi-tech specifications (plasma TVs, integrated sound systems, wireless internet). Combining hotel facilities with home comforts. 24 hour on-call service.

★★★ UP TO ★★★★★★
SELF CATERING

27 Queen Street, Edinburgh, EH2 1JX
T: 07973 345559 E: info@edinburghflats.co.uk W: edinburghflats.co.uk

3 Apartments   1-2 Bedrooms   Sleeps 1-6

Prices – Apartments:
£300.00-£1250.00   Per Week

Short breaks available

10213

Edinburgh
Edinburgh Self-Catering: Square One Apartment

Open: All year   **Map Ref: 2C4**

★★★★
SELF CATERING

Edinburgh Self-Catering, 161/18 Easter Road, Edinburgh, EH7 5QB
T: 0131 553 6641 E: info@edinburghself-catering.co.uk W: edinburghself-catering.co.uk

1 Apartment   2 Bedrooms   Sleeps 1-4

Prices – Apartment:
£525.00-£875.00   Per Week

Short breaks available

24532

Important: Prices stated are estimates and may be subject to amendments. Prices are per person per night unless otherwise stated.

Edinburgh
Edinburgh Self-Catering: The Arc Apartment

Open: All year   **Map Ref: 2C4**

★★★★
SELF CATERING

Edinburgh Self-Catering, 161/18 Easter Road, Edinburgh, EH7 5QB
T: 0131 553 6641 E: info@edinburghself-catering.co.uk W: edinburghself-catering.co.uk

| 1 Apartment | 1 Bedroom | Sleeps 1-2 |

Prices – Apartment:
£385.00-£665.00   Per Week

Short breaks available

24532

Edinburgh
One O'Clock Gunn (4 York Place)

Open: All year   **Map Ref: 2C5**

★★★★
SELF CATERING

4 York Place, Edinburgh, EH1 3EP
T: 0131 441 2373 E: oneoclockgunn@aol.com W: oneoclockgunn.com

| 1 Apartment | 2 Bedrooms | Sleeps 2-4 |

Prices – Apartment:
£500.00-£995.00   Per Week

Short breaks available

66868

Edinburgh
One O'Clock Gunn (5 Coates Place)

Open: All year   **Map Ref: 2C5**

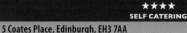

★★★★
SELF CATERING

5 Coates Place, Edinburgh, EH3 7AA
T: 0131 441 2373 E: oneoclockgunn@aol.com W: oneoclockgunn.com

| 1 Apartment | 4 Bedrooms | Sleeps 2-8 |

Prices – Apartment:
£550.00-£1600.00   Per Week

Short breaks available

66868

Edinburgh
One O'Clock Gunn (8 Woodhall Road)

Open: All year   **Map Ref: 2C5**

★★★
SELF CATERING

8 Woodhall Road, Colinton, Edinburgh, EH13 0DX
T: 0131 441 2373 E: oneoclockgunn@aol.com W: oneoclockgunn.com

| 1 Top of House | 3 Bedrooms | Sleeps up to 6 |

Prices – Top of House:
£500.00-£550.00   Per Week

Short breaks available

66868

Edinburgh and the Lothians

Edinburgh
Argyle Backpackers

Open: All year

Map Ref: 2C5

★★★
BACKPACKER

14 Argyle Place, Edinburgh, EH9 1JL
T: 0131 667 9991 E: reception@argyle-backpackers.co.uk W: argyle-backpackers.co.uk

| Hostel | 16 Bedrooms | Sleeps 2-10 |

Prices – Hostel:
£12.00-£30.00   Per Night

40604

Edinburgh
Edinburgh Lets – Rossie Place

Open: All year

Map Ref: 2C4

★★★
SELF CATERING

2 Rossie Place, Edinburgh, EH7 5SG
T: 0131 661 1934/07939 523580 E: julie@edinburghlets.org W: edinburghlets.org

| 1 Apartment | 2 Bedrooms + Boxroom | Sleeps 6-7 |

Prices – Apartment:
£588.00-£900.00   Per Week

Short breaks available

52217

Edinburgh
The Georgian Retreat

Open: All year

Map Ref: 2C4

★★★
SELF CATERING

36 Regents Street, Edinburgh, EH15 2AX
T: 0131 669 5394/07887 981401 E: x24hutchings@virginmedia.com

| 1 Apartment | 2 Bedrooms | Sleeps 1-4 |

Prices – Apartment:
£385.00   Per Week

Short breaks available

77113

Edinburgh
Morrison Circus

Open: Jun-Jul

Map Ref: 2C5

★★
SELF CATERING

Block 6 & 7, Morrison Circus, Edinburgh, EH3 8DW
T: 0131 455 3738 E: vacation.lets@napier.ac.uk W: napier.ac.uk/cca

| 24 Apartments | 4 Bedrooms | Sleeps 4 |

Prices – Apartment:
£460.00   Per Week

Short breaks available

46816

82   Important: Prices stated are estimates and may be subject to amendments. Prices are per person per night unless otherwise stated

Edinburgh
Wrights Houses Open: Jun-Aug Map Ref: 2C5

★★
SELF CATERING

Blocks 28 & 34, Wrights Houses, Bruntsfield, Edinburgh, EH10 4HR
T: 0131 455 3738 E: vacation.lets@napier.ac.uk W: napier.ac.uk/cca

| 24 Apartments | 3-5 Bedrooms | Sleeps 3-5 |

Prices – Apartment:
£420.00-£650.00 Per Week

Short breaks available

46816

North Berwick
The House at the Beach Open: All year Map Ref: 2D4

★★★
SELF CATERING

Mrs Janet McMillan, 154 Church Street, Broughty Ferry, Dundee, DD5 1AL
T: 01382 778928/07868 735895 E: mcmillanjanet@aol.com

| 1 House | 4 Bedrooms | Sleeps 10 |

Prices – House:
£620.00-£1400.00 Per Week

Short breaks available

59300

North Berwick
Kirkpatrick Self Catering Open: All year Map Ref: 2D4

★
SELF CATERING

4E Market Place, North Berwick, EH39 4JG
T: 0131 334 5951 E: ian_g_kirkpatrick@hotmail.com

| 1 Flat | 2 Bedrooms | Sleeps 1-4 |

Prices – Flat:
£180.00-£295.00 Per Week

Short breaks available

40770

For a full listing of Quality Assured accommodation, please see directory at back of this guide.

Food & Drink

Edinburgh
The Magnum

Open: All year

Map Ref: 1G6

Culinary Type:
SCOTTISH

1 Albany Street, Edinburgh, EH1 3PY
T: 0131 557 4366

Best For:
- Business lunches · Group dining
- Romantic meals · Special occasion
- Weekend brunch

Prices:
Starter from:	£4.50
Main Course from:	£13.95
Dessert from:	£4.95

Opening Times:
Lunch from 1200, last orders Mon-Sat 1430
(all day Fri-Sat; Sun from Mar onwards)
Dinner from 1730, last orders 2200

The Magnum offers you a relaxing gastro bar and restaurant in the heart of Edinburgh's New Town. Within a stone's throw of the bustling city centre, The Magnum offers a lunch and dinner menu with a focus on freshly prepared local produce, complimented with wine selected from Magnum's wine cellar.

59588

Important: Prices stated are estimates and may be subject to amendments. Prices are per person per night unless otherwise stated

Princes Street Gardens in the city centre of Edinburgh

For a full listing of Quality Assured accommodation, please see directory at back of this guide.

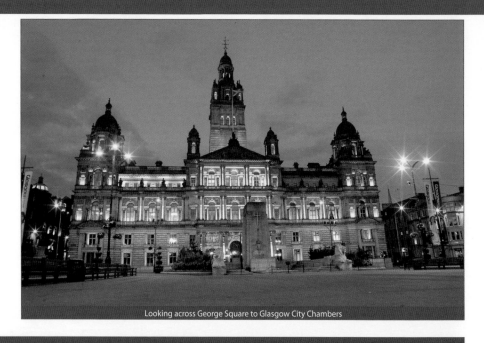

Looking across George Square to Glasgow City Chambers

GREATER GLASGOW AND CLYDE VALLEY

Glasgow is one of the most vibrant and exciting cities in Europe, which never fails to entertain with its abundance of attractions, shops, restaurants and bars.

Be inspired by stunning architecture as you visit respected attractions such as the Kelvingrove Art Gallery & Museum, the Burrell Collection and the University of Glasgow's Hunterian Museum & Art Gallery. Explore the world of one of Glasgow's most famous sons, Charles Rennie Mackintosh, with a visit to the Glasgow School of Art, the Lighthouse and stop for refreshments in the beautiful Willow Tea Rooms. There are remarkable buildings and artwork in almost every corner of Glasgow which bear the hallmarks of his style.

Scotland's largest city is home to such a varied collection of attractions, you are sure to create the perfect itinerary.

Glasgow is said to have the best shopping in the UK outside London, and has everything you need for an unforgettable weekend of retail therapy. The city centre has a fantastic array of top high street stores and the Victorianised Buchanan Street is home to Princes Square, a beautiful 19th century building housing stylish designer stores. For more unique retailers head for Glasgow's West End, with its laid back Bohemian vibe and vintage emporiums, or the Merchant City for designer labels and artist galleries.

Fondly referred to as the 'dear green place', Glasgow is home to more than 70 parks and gardens where you can collect your thoughts and relax between shopping and sightseeing. The Botanic Gardens at Kelvinside in the West End are characterised by impressive glass houses and an array of tropical plants from around the world. The beautifully restored Kibble Palace glasshouse is worth the visit alone. Take a stroll around the popular Kelvingrove Park nearby or explore the formal gardens of

To find out more go to visitscotland.com

Bellahouston Park in the south of the city, which is also home to the exquisite House for an Art Lover.

Beyond the city there is a whole world of Greater Glasgow and Clyde Valley left to explore. You can trace the river through the Clyde Valley all the way to the picturesque Falls of Clyde in Lanarkshire where you can explore New Lanark, an immaculately preserved UNESCO World Heritage Site. Take a trip on the PS Waverley, the world's last sea-going paddle steamer along the Clyde coast, explore Strathclyde Country Park in Motherwell by horseback or indulge in a spot of whisky-tasting in one of two fantastic whisky distilleries, Glengoyne and Auchentoshan.

There are endless ways to spend a day in the country, all situated in breathtaking locations and within a comfortable one-hour drive from the city centre.

After exploring you will have worked up an appetite and Glasgow's vibrant and contemporary restaurant scene is sure to impress. Visit Michelin star restaurants and laid back pubs for the very best in Scottish cuisine and complete your night with a drink in one of the cosmopolitan bars or somewhere a little more traditional. With many bars hosting live music, both traditional and the latest Scottish talent, you will be entertained long into the night in honour of Glasgow's UNESCO City of Music status.

When it comes time to rest your head, Glasgow has an impeccable choice of accommodation, from quality city centre hotels to 5-star self catering accommodation or cosy country B&Bs just outside of the city. Whatever you choose to do, wherever you stay, a visit to Glasgow and Clyde Valley will be a revelation and you're sure to return for more.

What's On?

Celtic Connections
14-31 January 2010
Glasgow's annual festival of contemporary and traditional Celtic music.
celticconnections.com

Magners Glasgow International Comedy Festival
11-28 March 2010
This hugely successful festival takes place in a variety of venues throughout the city.
glasgowcomedyfestival.com

Paisley Beer Festival
28 April - 1 May 2010
Held in Paisley Town Hall, come along and enjoy this vast selection of ales and beers from around the world.
paisleybeerfestival.org.uk

Gourock Highland Games
9 May 2010
One of the first Highland Games of the year attracting a considerable number of pipe bands, Highland dancers and Scottish heavy athletes.
gourockhighlandgames.org.uk

Glasgow River Festival
24-25 July 2010 (tbc)
A variety of both land and sea events for all the family on the banks of the River Clyde.
itsglasgowfestivaltime.com

Piping Live!
9-15 August 2010
A week of piping events held at various venues throughout the city, including the World Pipe Band Championship at the end of August.
pipingfestival.co.uk

Kirkintilloch Canal Festival
28 & 29 August 2010 (tbc)
Lively event focused on the Forth and Clyde canal including boat trips, wine tasting, street parades, farmers markets and art & craft fairs.
kirkintillochcanalfestival.org.uk

Merchant City Festival
23 - 26 September 2010
This cutting edge festival features some of the best of Scottish art and entertainment with a packed programme of theatre, music, comedy, visual art, dance, literature, markets and much more.
merchantcityfestival.com

Glasgay!
4 October - 7 November (tbc)
Scotland's annual celebration of queer culture has a superb programme of cinema, theatre, comedy and music.
glasgay.com

Winterfest
November - January 2011
Festive programme of events in Glasgow including ice-skating under the Christmas lights at George Square.
winterfestglasgow.com

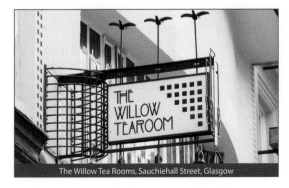
The Willow Tea Rooms, Sauchiehall Street, Glasgow

DON'T MISS

1   **Kelvingrove Art Gallery & Museum** is Scotland's most visited museum. Explore each floor and behold iconic masterpieces such as Dali's Christ of St John of the Cross and marvel at the immaculately restored spitfire.

2   Sitting cosily in the valley of the Falls of Clyde in South Lanarkshire, the **New Lanark World Heritage Site** is a beautifully restored 18th century cotton mill village. The area is a haven of tranquillity set amongst majestic rolling hills, somewhere you'll want to stand awhile and marvel at its beauty.

3   As the second most visited contemporary art gallery outside of London, be sure to visit the **Gallery of Modern Art**, an elegant neo-classical building in the heart of Glasgow city centre. With a programme of exhibitions that is constantly evolving, you're sure to find something new and exciting each time you visit.

4   Discover three floors packed with hundreds of interactive exhibits at the **Glasgow Science Centre**. This gleaming titanium crescent structure overlooks the River Clyde and is a great day out. Relax under the twinkling night sky in the Planetarium, before settling down in front of the amazing IMAX Cinema!

5   Don't miss **The Burrell Collection** at Pollok Country Park - just minutes from Glasgow City Centre - an incredible collection of art from all over the world. Here you will find everything from sculptures, medieval art and tapestries to stained glass and furniture. Sir William Burrell and his wife Constance, Lady Burrell, gifted the collection to Glasgow in 1944, and this is considered one of the most impressive art collections owned by one single person.

6   Take a trip on the last sea-going paddle steamer in the world, **PS Waverley**, which has been beautifully restored and offers unrivalled access to a stunning coastline. See the mighty steam engines at work turning the famous paddles as you explore the Lochs and Isles of the Firth of Clyde. Regular sailings depart from Glasgow Science Centre.

DISCOVER MACKINTOSH

7   A must visit is to one of Charles Rennie Mackintosh's masterpieces, the Mackintosh Building at the **Glasgow School of Art**. Be amazed by the building's stunning interior, which gives an insight into the architect's masterful attention to detail. Take advantage of an enjoyable tour of the School.

8   Step into history at the Hunterian Art Gallery and Museum and visit **Mackintosh House**, the reassembled interiors of 6 Florentine Terrace, home to Charles Rennie Mackintosh and his wife Margaret Macdonald Mackintosh from 1906 to 1914. The gallery itself is captivating, housing over 450 paintings including pieces by Rembrandt, Whistler, Chardin and the Scottish Colourists.

9   Set in the wonderful Bellahouston Park, **House for an Art Lover** is a masterpiece of modernity and an exciting example of recent research into Glasgow's most influential architect. Be dazzled by the stunning music room with its pure white walls, arched windows and iconic high-back chairs.

10   **The Lighthouse** was Mackintosh's first public commission and is now an award-winning centre for architecture and design. Scale the spiralling staircase in The Mackintosh Tower to the wonderful viewing platform and feel illuminated as you look over the entire city of Glasgow - a truly remarkable site!

BEYOND THE CITY CENTRE

11   **Summerlee, the Museum of Scottish Industrial Life** in Lanarkshire, which recently re-opened after a £10 million redevelopment, is wonderfully tactile with plenty of hands on activities. Take a ride around the site on Scotland's only working electric tramway or venture deep underground and tour an old mine.

12   Within close proximity to Glasgow's city centre you can find two **whisky distilleries**. Visit Glengoyne Distillery in Dumgoyne to explore one of Scotland's most beautiful distilleries and choose from a fantastic range of tours - including one where you can even create your very own blended whisky. Clydebank's Auchentoshan Distillery, the lowland single malt whisky distillery offers fascinating tours and great gifts to take home.

13   In Braehead just outside of the city, discover **Xscape**. This award-winning entertainment complex really does have it all; tackle the state-of-the-art aerial assault course, have a go at rock climbing, mini golf, bowling or laser games. However, without a doubt the piece-de-résistance is the incredible SNO!zone, which allows you to experience indoor skiing, snowboarding or sledging on the UK's biggest real snow slope. After working up an appetite, relax in one of the centre's many bars and restaurants.

14   **Paisley Abbey** is a former Cluniac monastery found at the banks of the White Cart River in the centre of Paisley. Now the town's parish kirk, the Abbey has been restored and boasts some beautiful examples of 19th and 20th century stained glass.

SHOPPING IN THE CITY

15 Get your fashion fix on **Glasgow's Style Mile**. Explore the stores on the pedestrianised Sauchiehall, Buchanan and Argyle Streets and find all your favourite high street brands. Buchanan Street is arguably one of the classiest major shopping thoroughfares in Britain with Buchanan Galleries at the top of the street offering a choice of more than 80 shops including John Lewis.

16 Proudly standing in the middle of the Style Mile is **Princes Square**, a beautiful 19th century building housing designer stores, exclusive boutiques and stylish bistros. Look out for the mesmerising peacock sculpture which grandly sits above the entrance.

17 The **Merchant City** is a wonderfully stylish area, east of the city centre, originally landscaped for the magnificent homes and warehouses of 18th century tobacco lairds. Today, the area is now home to stunning designer stores like Emporio Armani, Ralph Lauren, Cruise and Agent Provocateur and is perfect for an exclusive shopping trip.

18 Discover a different side to Glasgow by exploring the cobbled mews lanes which lead off the **West End's** main streets. This area is wonderfully laid back and is home to a range of cool and quirky shops. Highlights include the famous Starry Starry Night, a vintage emporium offering fabulous one-off garments. Grab some delicious nibbles in one of the West End delicatessens and relax amongst the breathtaking natural surroundings of the Botanic Gardens.

EATING & DRINKING

19 Michael Caines @ Abode on Bath Street in the **city centre** is a stylish choice with attention to fresh local produce. Enjoy a stunning setting at the delicious Grill Room, which provides the perfect vantage point to overlook the twinkling lights of Royal Exchange Square. Also try one of Glasgow's oldest and most celebrated restaurants, Two Fat Ladies at The Buttery, which can be found on Argyle Street.

20 The **West End** delivers the lovely courtyard restaurant Ubiquitous Chip, the exciting menu of Stravaigan 2 and the traditional Scottish dishes of The Bothy, all tucked away in the area's charming cobbled lanes.

21 The **Merchant City** provides the architecturally wonderful Corinthian, the mouth watering delights of Guys on Candleriggs and the luxurious City Merchant, a tasty, family run seafood restaurant.

22 Glasgow is renowned for its vibrant **bar scene** and you are always guaranteed a great night out. For the height of style and sophistication, visit one of the Merchant City bars. To enjoy a more laidback environment, wander down to the West End's relaxed Belgian Bar Brel, nestled in the cosy surroundings of Ashton Lane. For something a little more Scottish in origin, visit the Ben Nevis on Argyle Street, where traditional Scottish music sessions happen spontaneously!

Heads – the sculpture/artwork designed by Sophie Cave, in the Expression Court of the Kelvingrove Art Gallery and Museum, Glasgow

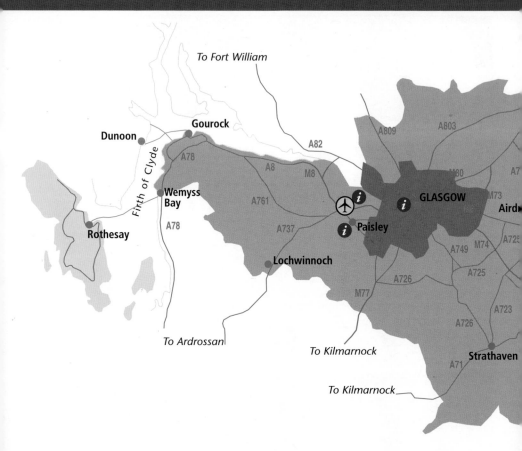

To Fort William

Dunoon

Gourock

A82

Firth of Clyde

A78

A8

M8

A809

A803

M80

A7

Wemyss
Bay

A761

GLASGOW

M73

A78

A737

Paisley

AirdⱤ

Rothesay

A749

M74

A72⁵

Lochwinnoch

A726

A725

A725

M77

A723

To Ardrossan

A726

To Kilmarnock

A71

Strathaven

To Kilmarnock

To Stirling

Caldercruix

To Edinburgh

A89   M8

A73   A71

To Edinburgh

A73

A72   A721

A721   A702

Lanark   Carstairs

To Peebles

A73

A72

A73   Biggar

M74

A73

A702

Abington

M74

To Carlisle

VisitScotland Information Centres

To help you plan and book your trip to Scotland email our travel experts at info@visitscotland.com. When you arrive call into one of our Information Centres wher our friendly experts can offer advice on all things local as well as sharing their wider knowledge of Scotland. We don't just advise either. We can sort out your accommodation and all your travel needs, as well as tickets for events across Scotland. So if you're looking to get the most from your visit, there really is only one place to go.

Greater Glasgow and Clyde Valley

Abington	Welcome Break Motorway Service Area Junction 13, M74 Abington, ML12 6RG
Glasgow	11 George Square, Glasgow G2 1DY
Glasgow Airport	International Arrivals Hall Glasgow International Airport PA3 2ST
Lanark	Horsemarket, Ladyacre Road Lanark, ML11 7QD
Paisley	9A Gilmour Street, Paisley PA1 1DD

i Open All Year

i Seasonal

Live it. Visit Scotland.
visitscotland.com/wheretofindus

■ LOCAL KNOWLEDGE
■ WHERE TO STAY
■ ACCOMMODATION BOOKING
■ PLACES TO VISIT
■ THINGS TO DO
■ MAPS AND GUIDES
■ TRAVEL ADVICE

■ ROUTE PLANNING
■ WHERE TO SHOP AND EAT
■ LOCAL CRAFTS AND PRODUCE
■ EVENT INFORMATION
■ TICKETS

Hotels

Lanark
Best Western Cartland Bridge Hotel

Open: All year

Map Ref: 2A6

An excellent venue for business meetings, conferences, weddings and all social events each catered within a varied range of suites. A stones throw from the Royal Burgh of Lanark located in the Clyde Valley. The hotel is the finest example of Sir John James Burnett's baronial style of Scottish architecture.

★★★
COUNTRY HOUSE HOTEL

Glasgow Road, Lanark, ML11 9UE
T: 01555 664426 E: sales@cartlandbridge.co.uk W: bw-cartlandbridgehotel.co.uk

Indicated Prices:

Single	from £55.00 per room		Twin	from £85.00 per room
Double	from £85.00 per room		Suite	from £105.00 per room
			Family	from £95.00 per room

18337

Important: Prices stated are estimates and may be subject to amendments. Prices are per person per night unless otherwise stated.

Strathaven
Best Western Strathaven Hotel
Open: All year   **Map Ref: 2A6**

A picturesque country house hotel set in two acres of mature gardens – the perfect setting for weddings, business or pleasure. With 22 ensuite bedrooms boasting satellite TV and mini bars there is no need to drive home after celebrations. Food served daily in Lauders Restaurant or the East Lounge.

★★★
HOTEL

Hamilton Road, Strathaven, Lanarkshire, ML10 6SZ
T: 01357 521778 E: reception@strathavenhotel.com W: strathavenhotel.com

Indicated Prices:
Single	from £56.00 per room	Twin	from £90.00 per room
Double	from £95.00 per room		

56840

Guest Houses and B&Bs

Airdrie
Craigpark House B&B
Open: All year   **Map Ref: 2A5**

★★★ GOLD
BED AND BREAKFAST

57 Airdrie Road, Caldercruix, by Airdrie, ML6 8PA
T: 01236 843211/07977 710908 E: kaymain@btinternet.com W: craigparkhouse.co.uk

Indicated Prices:
Single	from £30.00 per room	Twin	from £60.00 per room
Double	from £60.00 per room		

21053

For a full listing of Quality Assured accommodation, please see directory at back of this guide.

Glasgow
Adelaides Guest House

Open: All year excl 22 Dec 2009 - 5 Jan 2010

Map Ref: 1H5

A sensitively redeveloped 1877 Baptist Church building. Modernised and upgraded with individually controllable room heating. Rooms are attractively furnished all with direct dial telephones, colour TV and complimentary tea and coffee facilities. Adelaides is central to the attractions of this revitalised city, known for its character, hospitality and friendliness.

★★
GUEST HOUSE

209 Bath Street, Glasgow, G2 4HZ
T: 0141 248 4970 E: reservations@adelaides.co.uk W: adelaides.co.uk

Indicated Prices:

Single	from £30.00 per room	Twin	from £50.00 per room
Double	from £50.00 per room	Family	from £70.00 per room

11097

Glasgow
Amadeus Guest House

Open: All year

Map Ref: 1H5

The Amadeus is a friendly, family run guest house located in the heart of Glasgow's West End. Our rooms are contemporary, clean, bright and airy. Our breakfast is a generous continental buffet. We have rooms that range from singles to family x 4/5, mostly ensuite. We look forward to welcoming you!

★★
GUEST HOUSE

411 North Woodside Road, Glasgow, G20 6NN
T: 0141 339 8257 E: reservations@amadeusguesthouse.co.uk W: amadeusguesthouse.co.uk

Indicated Prices:

Single	from £24.00 per room	Twin	from £58.00 per room
Double	from £48.00 per room	Family	from £70.00 per room

11842

Glasgow
Craigielea House Bed & Breakfast
Open: All year **Map Ref: 1H5**

★★
BED AND BREAKFAST

35 Westercraigs, Glasgow, G31 2HY
T: 0141 554 3446 E: craigieleahouse@yahoo.co.uk W: visitscotland.com

Indicated Prices:
Single	from £30.00 per person		
Double	from £24.00 per person	Twin	from £24.00 per person

20972

Glasgow
The Kelvin
Open: All year **Map Ref: 1H5**

★★
GUEST HOUSE

15 Buckingham Terrace, 1 Great Western Road, Glasgow, G12 8EB
T: 0141 339 7143 E: enquiries@kelvinhotel.com W: kelvinhotel.com

Indicated Prices:
Single	from £31.00 per room	Twin	from £52.00 per room
Double	from £52.00 per room	Family	from £68.00 per room

33519

Lanark
Backbrae House
Open: All year **Map Ref: 2B6**

AWAITING GRADING

Carnwath Road, Braehead, Lanark, ML11 8EY
T: 01555 812777 E: catherine@zippyskipz.com W: backbraehouse.com

Indicated Prices:
Single	from £50.00 per person	Twin	from £50.00 per person
Double	from £50.00 per person	Family	from £50.00 per person

86304

For a full listing of Quality Assured accommodation, please see directory at back of this guide.

97

Self Catering and Camping & Caravan Parks

Glasgow
Kelvin Apartment
Open: All year   **Map Ref: 1H5**

★★★★
SELF CATERING

14 Buckingham Terrace, Great Western Road, Glasgow, G12 8EB
T: 0141 339 7143 E: enquiries@kelvinhotel.com W: kelvinhotel.com
| 1 Apartment | 2 Bedrooms | Sleeps 1-4 |

Prices – Apartment:
£450.00-£650.00   Per Week
£70.00-£120.00   Per Night
Short breaks available

33516

Glasgow
The White House Apartments
Open: All year   **Map Ref: 1H5**

★★★ UP TO ★★★★
SELF CATERING

11-13 Cleveden Crescent, Glasgow, G12 0PB
T: 0141 339 9375 E: info@whitehouse-apartments.com W: whitehouse-apartments.com
| 20 Studios | N/A Bedrooms | Sleeps 1-2 |
| 8 Apartments | 1-3 Bedrooms | Sleeps 1-6 |

Prices – Studio: Apartment:
£320.00-£440.00 Per Week £540.00-£900.00   Per Week
Short breaks available

64022

Lochwinnoch
East Lochhead Self-Catering Cottages
Open: All year   **Map Ref: 1G5**

★★★★
SELF CATERING

East Lochhead, Kilbirnie Road, Lochwinnoch, Renfrewshire, PA12 4DX
T: 01505 842610 E: admin@eastlochhead.co.uk W: eastlochhead.co.uk
| 4 Cottages | 1-3 Bedrooms | Sleeps 3-6 |

Prices –Cottages:
£275.00-£750.00   Per Week
Short breaks available

69844

The River Kelvin in Kelvingrove Park and the spire of the University of Glasgow

or a full listing of Quality Assured accommodation, please see directory at back of this guide.

Walkers with village of Arrochar and Ben Lomond in the distance

WEST HIGHLANDS AND ISLANDS, LOCH LOMOND, STIRLING AND TROSSACHS

Contrast is the word that best sums up an area that spans Scotland from the shores of the Forth in the east to the very tip of Tiree in the west. Here the Highlands meet the Lowlands and geography and cultures diverge.

For the visitor, the endlessly changing landscape means a rich and varied holiday experience.

There are rugged high mountains, spectacular freshwater lochs, fascinating islands and dramatic seascapes. You'll find pretty villages, mill towns, not to mention Scotland's newest city, Stirling.

Discover the birthplace of the Scots nation and visit places that witnessed some of the most dramatic scenes in Scotland's history.

On the eastern side of the country the flat plain of the Forth Valley stretches up from the River Forth towards the little towns of the Hillfoots, which enjoy the spectacular backdrop of the Ochil Hills.

Elsewhere in the Forth Valley, you can visit Scotland's smallest county, Clackmannanshire, a delightful part of the country steeped in history. Head for Dollar Glen and the magnificent Castle Campbell, once the Lowland stronghold of the Clan Campbell.

Moving to the Hillfoot towns you'll be tracing the roots of Scotland's textile industry which has thrived here for many years. Learn the history of the local woollen industry at the Mill Trail Visitor Centre in Alva.

New city, ancient history

Beyond Alva to the west lies Stirling – a city since 2002 and one of the most important places in Scottish history thanks to its strategically important location as the gateway to the Highlands.

Once, whoever controlled Stirling, controlled Scotland. Its impressive castle stands guard over all it surveys and was the capital for the Stewart Kings. It's

To find out more go to visitscotland.com

a relatively quiet spot these days but no fewer than seven battle sites can be seen from the Castle ramparts – including Stirling Bridge, a scene of triumph for William Wallace and Bannockburn where Robert the Bruce led the Scots to victory in 1314.

A National Park on your doorstep

Loch Lomond and the Trossachs National Park, Scotland's first National Park, takes advantage of the natural treasures of this area and that means 20 Munros (mountains over 3,000ft) to climb, 50 rivers to fish, 22 lochs to sail and thousands of miles of road and track to cycle. When you've had your fill of activities, head for Loch Lomond Shores for a cultural and retail experience.

You can also cruise on Loch Lomond. It's Britain's biggest freshwater expanse and there's no better way to see the surrounding countryside than from the water.

Heading west the Whisky Coast round Islay and Jura are waiting to be explored – Islay alone has eight working distilleries!

A place in history

The Cowal Peninsula with its sea lochs and deep forests is beautiful and relaxing. To get there, just jump aboard the ferry at Gourock and sail for Dunoon. While you're there, don't miss the nearby Benmore Botanic Gardens.

Explore Lochgilphead and beyond to Kilmartin where you can trace the very roots of the nation where the Scots arrived from Ireland in the 6th century.

Choosing a holiday destination in an area as diverse as this will always be difficult but the stunning array of accommodation will help firm up your thoughts.

Aberfoyle Mushroom Festival

What's On?

The Blend
March 2010 (tbc)
Traditional music festival in Stirling's celebrated Tolbooth arts venue, bringing together talent from Scotland and beyond.
stirling.gov.uk/tolbooth

Trossachs Spring Outdoor Festival
28 + 29 March 2010
Two days of fun at various venues in the Trossachs. From Scottish evenings to power kiting and paintball, there's something for everyone..
visitaberfoyle.com

Loch Lomond Dragon Boat Race
5 June 2010 (tbc)
Once again, the 40-foot dragon boats will race down the loch. A fun-filled spectacle, which raises money for charity.

Stirling Highland Games
11 July 2010
Highland games and family fun day with Highland dancing, heavyweights, tug o' war, solo piping, wrestling and haggis eating competitions.
.stirling-highland-games.co.uk

Loch Lomond Highland Games
17 July 2010
Great family day out with events including tossing the caber, putting the stone, throwing the hammer and much, much more in the beautiful village of Balloch.
llhgb.com

Trossachs Beer Festival
27 August - 6 September 2010
A celebration of the quality of real Scottish ales, with a green focus.
camra-forth-valley.co.uk

Off the Page - The Stirling Book Festival
11-18 September 2010
Stirling's popular book festival, with guest appearances from star writers and storytellers.
stirling.gov.uk/offthepage

Cowalfest
8-17 October 2010
Explore the varied landscapes of Argyll's Cowal peninsula at this annual walking festival, with a good measure of arts thrown in.
cowalfest.org

Aberfoyle International Mushroom Festival
21-24 October 2010
Four days of fungi, food, fiestas and fun for all the family.
visitaberfoyle.com

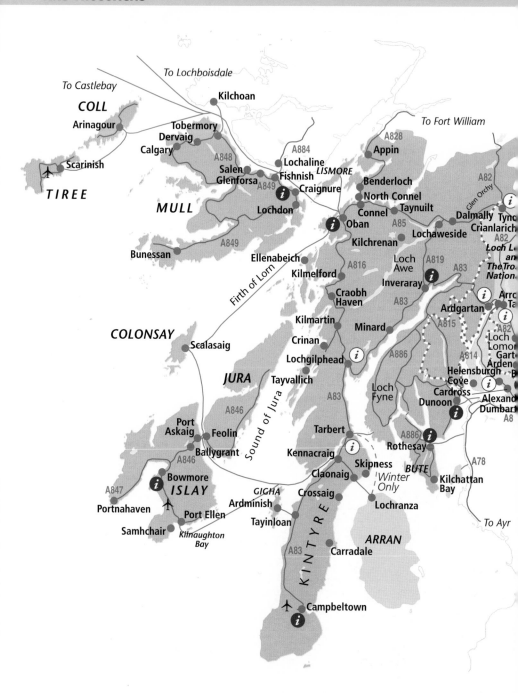

To Castlebay

To Lochboisdale

To Fort William

COLL

Arinagour

Scarinish

TIREE

Kilchoan

Tobermory
Dervaig

Calgary

A848

MULL

Salen
Glenforsa
A849
Lochdon

A849

Bunessan

COLONSAY

Scalasaig

JURA

A846

Port
Askaig
Feolin

Ballygrant

A846

A847

Bowmore
ISLAY

Portnahaven

Port Ellen

Samhchair

Kilnaughton
Bay

A884

Lochaline
Fishnish
LISMORE

Craignure

Appin

A828

Benderloch

North Connel

Connel

Oban

Kilchrenan

Taynuilt

A85

Dalmally
Lochaweside

Ellenabeich

Kilmelford

A816

Craobh
Haven

Kilmartin

Crinan

Lochgilphead

Tayvallich

A83

Minard

Loch
Awe

A819

Inveraray

A83

A886

Loch
Fyne

Tarbert

Kennacraig

Sound of Jura

GIGHA

Ardminish

Tayinloan

A83

KINTYRE

Carradale

Campbeltown

Crossaig

Claonaig

Skipness

Winter
Only

BUTE

Rothesay

A8862

Dunoon

Cardross

Helensburgh
Cove

Alexandri
Dumbart

A8

A78

To Ayr

Lochranza

ARRAN

Kilchattan
Bay

Firth of Lorn

Tyne
Crianlarich

A82

Glen Orchy

A82

Loch L
an
The Tro
Nation

Arro
Ta

Ardgartan

A815

A82

Loch
Lomo
Gart

A814

Arden

A886

Firth of Lorn

Map labels:

To Aberfeldy

Ardeonaig
Killin
A85
Lochearnhead

nd
Strathyre
hs
ark
Callander
Aberfoyle Port of Dunblane
Menteith
Causewayhead Tillicoultry
Balfron Pirnhall Blairlogie
STIRLING
Drymen Bannockburn
A81 Denny Bo'ness
A809 Falkirk Redding
A80 M9 To Edinburgh

To Perth
A9
A84
A91

M80

To Glasgow

VisitScotland Information Centres

To help you plan and book your trip to Scotland email our travel experts at info@visitscotland.com. When you arrive call into one of our Information Centres where our friendly experts can offer advice on all things local as well as sharing their wider knowledge of Scotland. We don't just advise either. We can sort out your accommodation and all your travel needs, as well as tickets for events across Scotland. So if you're looking to get the most from your visit, there really is only one place to go.

West Highlands

Bowmore	The Square, Bowmore Isle of Islay, PA43 7JP
Campbeltown	Mackinnon House, The Pier Campbeltown, PA28 6EF
Craignure	The Pier, Craignure Isle of Mull, PA65 6AY
Dunoon	7 Alexander Place Dunoon, PA23 8AB
Inveraray	Front Street Inveraray, PA32 8UY
Oban	Argyll Square Oban, PA34 4AR
Rothesay	Winter Gardens, Rothesay Isle of Bute, PA20 0AJ

Loch Lomond

Aberfoyle	Trossachs Discovery Centre Main Street, Aberfoyle, FK8 3UQ
Balloch	The Old Station Building Balloch G83 8LQ
Callander	Ancaster Square Callander, FK17 8ED

Stirling & Trossachs

Falkirk	The Falkirk Wheel, Lime Road Tamfourhill, Falkirk, FK1 4R
Stirling (Dumbarton Rd)	41 Dumbarton Road Stirling, FK8 2LQ
Stirling (Pirnhall)	Motorway Service Area Junction 9, M9

Open All Year

Seasonal

visitscotland.com/wheretofindus

- LOCAL KNOWLEDGE
- WHERE TO STAY
- ACCOMMODATION BOOKING
- PLACES TO VISIT
- THINGS TO DO
- MAPS AND GUIDES
- TRAVEL ADVICE
- ROUTE PLANNING
- WHERE TO SHOP AND EAT
- LOCAL CRAFTS AND PRODUCE
- EVENT INFORMATION
- TICKETS

Oban waterfront at night

West Highlands and Islands

There can be few experiences more satisfying than discovering deserted stretches of golden sand, crystal clear waters and inspiring landscapes at every turn. Throw in a vibrant culture, an abundance of wildlife and friendly locals, and find yourself exploring some of Scotland's most magical isles and peninsulas.

For many the pace of island life is a powerful draw and, with much of the West Highlands and Islands untouched and beautifully remote, there are endless opportunities to discover the isles and peninsulas conveniently linked together by ferries. Among the many islands to discover are Jura and Islay, known for producing some of the finest malt whisky in the world, the unspoilt beaches of Coll and Tiree and the deeply spiritual Iona, which is considered to be the birthplace of Scottish Christianity.

Try a spot of island hopping from Oban, a delightful and bustling harbour town hailed as the gateway to the isles. From here you can reach the likes of Mull, a haven for wildlife which boasts the colourful town of Tobermory, as well as Coll, Muck, Eigg, Rum, Canna and Lismore.

For a true sense of escape, explore some of these enchanting landscapes by sea kayak as you paddle around the many coves and inlets. Or perhaps sample some Kintyre Golf, where you will find five wonderful courses all boasting panoramic views of the beautiful Kintyre peninsula. If it's relaxation and stunning vistas you want from your break, you'll be spoilt for choice on the rugged west coast.

To find out more go to visitscotland.com

DON'T MISS

1   The beautiful west coast is famed for its **malt whisky** and exploring the distilleries of Islay and Jura is an experience no whisky lover should forgo. Islay alone boasts eight working distilleries, with a new addition - Kilchoman - whose first bottles only hit the shelves in September 2009. Each boasts its own distinctive peaty taste and, using methods passed down generations, discover some of the world's best-known brands, including Bruichladdich, Bowmore, Laphroaig and Lagavulin.

2   What better opportunity is there to sample some of the world's finest seafood than as you explore the idyllic shores of the rugged west coast? Discover **The Seafood Trail**, a route linked by 11 waterfront establishments in Argyll, Kintyre and around Loch Fyne, each bringing their own local delicacy to the table. From the freshest of seafood platters, to meticulously thought-out Michelin-rated menus, this is a culinary treat not to be missed.

3   Get out and try some the many **activities** on offer on these varied landscapes. At the southern end of the Kintyre Peninsula lies one of Scotland's most dramatic golf courses, Machrihanish. Visitors come from every part of the world to test its rolling links but few are prepared to negotiate the first tee. Similarly, the Machrie on Islay is a real hidden gem. Or charter a sailing boat for the day at many of the little ports along the vast coast of the West Highlands.

4   The common characteristic of the **Glorious Gardens of Argyll & Bute** is their individuality. Each garden has a variety of terrain; many are mainly level with smooth paths, while some are steep and rocky. The Gardens range from informal woodland gardens to beautiful classic examples of 18th century design, with many rare and unusual species. There are 20 in total to be found in Argyll and the islands, including Arduaine Garden, Ascog Hall Fernery, Benmore Botanic Garden and Crarae Garden.

5   **Kilmartin Glen** is home to a myriad of Neolithic and Bronze Age monuments, coupled with early Christian carved stones and ruined castles. South of Oban, this site was capital of the ancient Celtic kingdom of Dalriada, as evidenced at Dunadd Fort, where a footprint in the stone is thought to have featured in royal inauguration ceremonies.

6   With well over a hundred breeding bird species in summer, and some of Europe's largest populations of wintering wildfowl, the islands of Islay and Jura are a year round destination for ornithologists. Add to this some exceptional marine wildlife, including minke whales, common and bottlenose dolphins, basking sharks and literally thousands of seals, alongside otters, red deer and golden eagles, and you have a **natural paradise**. A particular highlight is the arrival of around 50,000 barnacle and white-fronted geese from the Arctic Circle each autumn.

West Highlands and Islands

Hotels

by Campbeltown, Carradale
Dunvalanree Hotel & Restaurant Open: All year excl Xmas **Map Ref: 1E6**

★★★★
RESTAURANT WITH ROOMS

Port Righ, Carradale, Campbeltown, Argyll, PA28 6SE
T: 01583 431226 E: book@dunvalanree.com W: dunvalanree.com

Indicated Prices:

| Single | from £100.00 per room DB&B | Twin | from £145.00 per room DB&B |
| Double | from £145.00 per room DB&B | | |

23869

Isle of Coll
Coll Hotel Open: All year **Map Ref: 1B1**

Voted Scottish Island Hotel 2008, 2009 and Scottish Hotel Restaurant 2009. This award-winning hotel ticks all the boxes. A beautiful garden for eating, drinking and relaxing with views across to Mull. Lovely rooms, most with great views. Restaurant serving the best local produce. Lobster, crab, langoustine, salad and vegetables.

★★★
INN

Arinagour, Isle of Coll, Argyll, PA78 6SZ
T: 01879 230334 E: info@collhotel.com W: collhotel.com

Indicated Prices:

| Single | from £45.00 per room | Twin | from £90.00 per room |
| Double | from £90.00 per room | Family | from £90.00 per room |

20003

Important: Prices stated are estimates and may be subject to amendments. Prices are per person per night unless otherwise stated.

Isle of Islay, Bowmore
The Harbour Inn & Restaurant

Open: All year excl Xmas/Boxing Day

Map Ref: 1C5

A destination for all seasons. This small family-run hotel is adjacent to Bowmore Harbour on the lovely Hebridean island of Islay. We offer superb accommodation, high quality award-winning food and excellent service. The hotel's location is unique with many areas of natural beauty within an easy drive.

★★★★ GOLD
RESTAURANT WITH ROOMS

The Square, Bowmore, Islay, PA43 7JR
T: 01496 810330 E: info@harbour-inn.com W: harbour-inn.com

Indicated Prices:
Double   from £120.00 per room   Twin   from £130.00 per room

29549

Isle of Mull, by Dervaig, Calgary
Calgary Hotel

Open: Apr-Oct

Map Ref: 1C1

★★★
RESTAURANT WITH ROOMS

by Dervaig, Isle of Mull, Argyll, PA75 6QW
T: 01688 400256 E: calgary.hotel.@virgin.net W: calgary.co.uk

Indicated Prices:
Single   from £46.00 B&B per room   Twin   from £92.00 B&B per room
Double   from £92.00 B&B per room   Family   from £102.00 B&B per room

17616

by Oban, Connel
Falls of Lora Hotel

Open: Feb-mid Dec

Map Ref: 1E2

★★★
HOTEL

Connel Ferry, by Oban, Argyll, PA37 1PB
T: 01631 710483 E: enquiries@fallsoflora.com W: fallsoflora.com

Indicated Prices:
Single   from £47.50 per room   Twin   from £67.00 per room
Double   from £55.00 per room   Suite   from £119.00 per room
                                         Family   from £72.50 per room

25591

For a full listing of Quality Assured accommodation, please see directory at back of this guide.

Guest Houses and B&Bs

Dunoon
Craigieburn Guest House   **Open: All year**   **Map Ref: 1F4**

★★
GUEST HOUSE

105 Alexandra Parade, Dunoon, Argyll
T: 01369 702048 E: info@craigieburnguesthouse.com W: craigieburnguesthouse.com

Indicated Prices:

Single	from £23.00 per room	Twin	from £46.00 per room
Double	from £46.00 per room	Family	from £46.00 per room

74035

Dunoon
Foxbank Guest House   **Open: All year**   **Map Ref: 1F4**

★★
BED AND BREAKFAST

141-3 Marine Parade, Hunter's Quay, Dunoon, Argyll
T: 01369 703858 E: lawther@foxbank.co.uk W: foxbank.co.uk

Indicated Prices:

Single	from £27.00	Twin	from £55.00
Double	from £55.00		

26693

Important: Prices stated are estimates and may be subject to amendments. Prices are per person per night unless otherwise stated.

Inverary
Rudha-Na-Craige

Open: All year

Map Ref: 1F3

Susan and Howard Spicer welcome you to our beautiful and historical home where the Duke of Argyll's ancestors once lived. Exceptional accommodation, great food, stunning Loch Fyne views, Inveraray centre nearby. An individual experience with a high standard of hospitality and comfort. Excellent base for touring Argyll and the Highlands.

★★★★
GUEST HOUSE

The Avenue, Inveraray, PA32 8YX
T: +44(0)1499 302668 E: enquiries@rudha-na-craige.com W: www.rudha-na-craige.com

Indicated Prices:
Single	from £60.00 per room	Twin	from £118.00 per room
Double	from £90.00 per room	Suite	from £118.00 per room

75916

Inveraray
Argyll Court Bed & Breakfast

Open: All year excl Dec 25th & Jan 1st

Map Ref: 1F1

★★★
BED AND BREAKFAST

10 Argyll Court, Inveraray, Argyll, PA32 8UT
T: 01499 302273 E: anne.macpherson1@btinternet.com W: inverarayaccommodation.co.uk

Indicated Prices:
Double	from £55.00 per room	Twin	from £55.00 per room

39651

or a full listing of Quality Assured accommodation, please see directory at back of this guide.

Isle of Islay, Bowmore
The Inns Over-By

Open: All year excl Xmas/Boxing Day

Map Ref: 1C5

Enviably situated in the centre of Bowmore yet literally a step away from the shoreline of Loch Indaal. The Inns Over-By offers the perfect environment where you can unwind and indulge your natural senses within the luxurious setting of first class accommodation. 'Rooms with a view.'

★★★★
GUEST HOUSE

The Square, Bowmore, Islay, PA43 7JP
T: 01496 810330 E: info@theinnsoverby.co.uk W: theinnsoverby.co.uk

Indicated Prices:

Double	from £120.00 per room	Twin	from £140.00 per room

70301

Isle of Islay, Kilnaughton Bay
Samhchair

Open: Apr-Oct

Map Ref: 1C6

★★★★
BED AND BREAKFAST

Kilnaughton Bay, by Port Ellen, Isle of Islay, PA42 7AX
T: 01496 302596 E: info@samhchair.co.uk W: samhchair.co.uk

Indicated Prices:

Single	from £65.00 per person	Twin	from £40.00 per person
Double	from £40.00 per person		

81290

Lochgilphead
The Corran

Open: All year

Map Ref: 1E4

★★★★
BED AND BREAKFAST

Poltalloch Street, Lochgilphead, Argyll, PA31 8LR
T: 01546 603866 E: lamonthoy@tiscali.co.uk W: lamonthoy.co.uk

Indicated Prices:

Single	from £40.00 per room	Twin	from £60.00 per room
Double	from £60.00 per room	Family	from £80.00 per room

58613

Isle of Mull, Bunessan
An Caladh Bed & Breakfast   **Open: All year excl Xmas & New Year**   **Map Ref: 1C2**

★★★★
BED AND BREAKFAST

Ardtun, Bunessan, Isle of Mull, Argyll, PA67 6DH
T: 01681 700115 E: enquiries@ancaladhmull.co.uk W: ancaladhmull.co.uk
Indicated Prices:
| Single | from £45.00 per room | Twin | from £70.00 per room |
| Double | from £60.00 per room | | |

81430

Isle of Mull, Craignure
Pennygate Lodge   **Open: All year excl Xmas/New Year**   **Map Ref: 1D2**

★★★
GUEST HOUSE

Craignure, Isle of Mull, PA65 6AY
T: 01680 812333 E: pennygatelodge@btconnect.com W: pennygatelodge.com
Indicated Prices:
| Single | from £40.00 per room | Twin | from £60.00 per room |
| Double | from £60.00 per room | | |

62200

Isle of Mull, Dervaig
Druimnacroish   **Open: Apr-Oct**   **Map Ref: 1C1**

★★★
GUEST HOUSE

Dervaig, Isle of Mull, PA75 6QW
T: 01688 400274 E: stay@druimnacroish.co.uk W: druimnacroish.co.uk
Indicated Prices:
| Double | from £64.00 per room | Twin | from £64.00 per room |

23237

Isle of Mull, Lochdon
Wild Cottage B&B   **Open: All year excl Xmas**   **Map Ref: 1D2**

★★★
BED AND BREAKFAST

Lochdon, Isle of Mull, Argyll, PA64 6AP
T: 01680 812105 E: tg2010@wildcottagemull.co.uk W: wildcottagemull.co.uk
Indicated Prices:
| Double | from £29.00 per person |

67971

For a full listing of Quality Assured accommodation, please see directory at back of this guide.

113

West Highlands and Islands

Oban
Aros Ard B&B
Open: Mar-Oct Map Ref: 1E2

★★★★
BED AND BREAKFAST

Croft Road, Oban, PA34 5JN
T: 01631 565500 E: maclean@arosard.freeserve.co.uk W: arosard.co.uk

Indicated Prices:

Single	from £70.00 per room	Twin	from £70.00 per room
Double	from £70.00 per room		

12933

Oban
Glenburnie House
Open: Mar-Nov Map Ref: 1E2

★★★★
GUEST HOUSE

Corran Esplanade, Oban, PA34 5AQ
T: 01631 562089 E: graeme.strachan@btinternet.com W: glenburnie.co.uk

Indicated Prices:

Single	from £40.00 per person	Twin	from £40.00 per person
Double	from £40.00 per person		

28018

Oban
Hawthorn
Open: All year Map Ref: 1E2

★★★★
BED AND BREAKFAST

5 Keil Croft, Benderloch, Oban, PA37 1QS
T: 01631 720452 E: june@hawthorncottages.com W: hawthorncottages.com

Indicated Prices:

Single	from £40.00 per room	Twin	from £60.00 per room
Double	from £60.00 per room	Family	from £70.00 per room

29746

Oban
Thornloe Guest House
Open: All year excl Xmas Map Ref: 1E2

★★★★
GUEST HOUSE

Albert Road, Oban, PA34 5EJ
T: 01631 562879 E: enquiries@thornloeoban.co.uk W: thornloeoban.co.uk

Indicated Prices:

Single	from £28.00 per room	Twin	from £56.00 per room
Double	from £56.00 per room	Suite	from £70.00 per room
		Family	from £90.00 per room

61013

Important: Prices stated are estimates and may be subject to amendments. Prices are per person per night unless otherwise stated.

Oban
Wellpark House

Open: Mar-end Oct

Map Ref: 1E2

GUEST HOUSE ★★★★

Esplanade, Oban, Argyll, PA34 5AQ
T: 01631 562948 E: enquiries@wellparkhouse.co.uk W: wellparkhouse.co.uk

Indicated Prices:
Single	from £45.00 per room	Twin	from £72.00 per room
Double	from £72.00 per room		

63546

Oban
Kathmore Guest House

Open: All year excl Xmas

Map Ref: 1E2

★★★
GUEST HOUSE

Soroba Road, Oban, Argyll, PA34 4JF
T: 01631 562104 E: wkathmore@aol.com W: kathmore.co.uk

Indicated Prices:
Single	from £35.00 per room	Twin	from £60.00 per room
Double	from £55.00 per room		

67995

Oban
Ulva Villa Guest House

Open: Apr-Oct

Map Ref: 1E2

★★★
GUEST HOUSE

Soroba Road, Oban, Argyll, PA34 4JF
T: 01631 563042 E: greaney@oban-guest-house.com W: oban-guest-house.com

Indicated Prices:
Single	from £32.00 per room	Twin	from £25.00 per person
Double	from £25.00 per person		

62459

---

by Oban, Connel
Ronebhal Guest House

Open: Apr-Oct

Map Ref: 1E2

★★★★
GUEST HOUSE

Connel, by Oban, Argyll, PA75 6QY
T: 01631 710310 E: info@ronebhal.co.uk W: ronebhal.co.uk

Indicated Prices:
Single	from £30.00 per room	Twin	from £60.00 per room
Double	from £60.00 per room	Family	from £90.00 per room

52032

West Highlands and Islands

by Skipness
Crossaig Lodge
Open: All year   **Map Ref: 1E6**

AWAITING GRADING

by Skipness, by Tarbert, Argyll, PA29 6YQ
T: 01880 760369 E: crossaig.lodge@virgin.net W: crossaiglodge.co.uk
Indicated Prices:
Double   from £50.00 per room

£ 🐾 V   **87605**

Taynuilt
Tanglewood Lodge
Open: All year excl Xmas week   **Map Ref: 1F2**

★★★★
BED AND BREAKFAST

Otter Creek, Taynuilt, Argyll, PA35 1HP
T: 01866 822114 E: carol@tanglewoodlodge.co.uk W: tanglewoodlodge.co.uk
Indicated Prices:

Single	from £60.00 per room	Twin	from £75.00 per room
Double	from £75.00 per room	Family	from £75.00 per room + £20.00/£25.00 per child* *Under 3s are free

                                                                     81440

A group of kayakers explore the coastline around Castle Stalker, situated on an islet on Loch Laich

Self Catering and Camping & Caravan Parks

Appin
Inver Boathouse

Open: All year

Map Ref: 1E1

Spectacular building and picturesque setting on sea loch/mountain. Private beach, slipway, spa bath, sauna, log fires. Walking, sailing, diving, wildlife, fishing, skiing. Surrounded by nature reserve, Glasdrum wood (slopes of Ben Churalain) and Loch Creran with its biogenic reefs (Special Area of Conservation). See www.inverboathouse.co.uk for activities. Sleeps 4-14 plus cot.

★★★ UP TO ★★★★
SELF CATERING

Loch Creran, Appin, Argyll, PA38 4BQ
T: 0131 550 1180 E: bookings@mackays-scotland.co.uk W: mackays-scotland.co.uk

| 1 Cottage | 2 Bedrooms | Sleeps 4 |
| 1 House | 4 Bedrooms | Sleeps 8-10 |

Prices – Cottage: House:
£272.00-£642.00   Per Week £555.00-£1998.00   Per Week

31888

Appin
Kinlochlaich House

Open: All year

Map Ref: 1E1

★★★ UP TO ★★★★
SELF CATERING

Appin, Argyll, PA38 4BD
T: 01631 730342 E: enquiries@kinlochlaich-house.co.uk W: kinlochlaich-house.co.uk

| 3 Cottages | 2 Bedrooms | Sleeps 2-5 |
| 3 Apartments | 2 Bedrooms | Sleeps 2-4 |

Prices – Cottages: Apartments:
£195.00-£560.00   Per Week £195.00-£560.00   Per Week
Short breaks available

34137

For a full listing of Quality Assured accommodation, please see directory at back of this guide.

West Highlands and Islands

Isle of Bute, Kilchattan Bay
Dykenamar

Open: All year

Map Ref: 1F6

★★★★
SELF CATERING

Dykenamar, Shore Road, Kilchattan Bay, Isle of Bute, PA20 9NW
T: 01483 772506/07712 667316 E: bookings@bute-haven.com W: bute-haven.com

| 1 Bungalow | 3 Bedrooms | Sleeps 1-6 |

Prices – Bungalow:
£450.00-£740.00   Per Week

23938

Isle of Bute, Kilchattan Bay
Daisy Bank Flats

Open: All year

Map Ref: 1F6

AWAITING GRADING

8 Roxburgh Drive, Bearsden, Glasgow, G61 3LH
T: 07974 732348 E: alanmackenzie@yahoo.co.uk

| 2 Flats | 1 Bedroom | Sleeps 4-5 |

Prices – Flat:
£225.00-£275.00   Per Week

Short breaks available

87483

Isle of Bute, Rothesay
Prospect House Holiday Complex

Open: All year

Map Ref: 1F5

The Island of Bute with palm fringed coastline is an ideal holiday destination with first-class accommodation Prospect Complex on seafront. Parking within grounds. Full central heating included in cost – both Glasgow and Prestwick airports only fifty minutes to the islands terminus with regular 35 minute passenger/car ferry journey to the island. Free brochure.

★★★
SELF CATERING

Eastbay, 21 Battery Place, Rothesay, PA20 9DU
T: 01700 503526 E: ta.shaw@zen.co.uk W: prospecthouse-bute.co.uk

| 1 Cottage | 1 Bedroom | Sleeps 3-4 |
| 6 Apartments | 1-2 Bedrooms | Sleeps 2-5 |

Prices – Cottage: **Apartments:**
£280.00-£398.00   Per Week   £280.00-£463.00   Per Week

Short breaks available

43368

Important: Prices stated are estimates and may be subject to amendments. Prices are per person per night unless otherwise stated.

West Highlands and Islands

Craobh Haven
The Deckhouse – Craobh Haven Self Catering
Open: All year   **Map Ref: 1E3**

★★★★
SELF CATERING

No 10 The Green, Craobh Haven, by Lochgilphead, Argyll, PA31 8UB
T: 07808 781464 E: info@craobhhavenselfcatering.com W: craobhhavenselfcatering.com

1 Cottage   2 Bedrooms   Sleeps 1-4

Prices – Cottage:
£330.00-£700.00   Per Week

77320

Crinan, Lochgilphead
Kilmahumaig Barn Flats
Open: All year   **Map Ref: 1E4**

★★
SELF CATERING

Kilmahumaig, Crinan, Lochgilphead, Argyll, PA31 8SW
T: 01546 830238 E: murray104@btinternet.com

3 Apartments   1-2 Bedrooms   Sleeps 1-6

Prices – Apartments:
£150.00-£425.00   Per Week

Short breaks available

33832

Dunoon
Lyall Cliff Self Catering
Open: All year excl Xmas   **Map Ref: 1F4**

★★★
SELF CATERING

141 Alexandra Parade, Dunoon, PA23 8AW
T: 01369 702041 E: info@lyallcliff.co.uk W: lyallcliff.co.uk

1 Cottage   2 Bedrooms   Sleeps 2-4
1 House   4 Bedrooms   Sleeps 2-8

Prices – Cottage: House:
£225.00-£460.00   Per Week   £435.00-£690.00   Per Week

Short breaks available

36612

Inveraray
Mr C R Elkin
Open: All year   **Map Ref: 1E4**

★★★
SELF CATERING

Inverae, Minard, Inveraray, Argyll, PA32 8YF
T: 01546 886655 E: colum.elkin@virgin.net W: brondeg.co.uk

1 Cottage   2 Bedrooms   Sleeps 2-6

Prices – Cottage:
£185.00-£420.00   Per Week

16548

Loch Awe, Inveraray
Ardbrecknish House
Open: All year **Map Ref: 1F2**

Historic house on banks of Loch Awe with ten self catering properties. Friendly licensed bar on site, bar meals. Boat hire/launch nearby, fishing, walking, bird watching. Near Oban, Mull and the Isles, Glen Coe and Fort William. Glasgow airport 1½ hours.

★★
SELF CATERING

South Lochaweside, by Dalmally, Argyll, PA33 1BH
T: 01866 833223/07767 306345 E: enquiries@loch-awe.co.uk W: loch-awe.co.uk

1 Cottage	2 Bedrooms	Sleeps 4
9 Apartments	1-5 Bedrooms	Sleeps 2-12

Prices – Cottage: **Apartments:**
£190.00-£450.00   Per Week   £175.00-£1100.00   Per Week

Short breaks available

12489

Isle of Mull, Aros
Mrs E MacPhail
Open: All year **Map Ref: 1D1**

★★★
SELF CATERING

Callachally Farm, Salen, Aros, Isle of Mull
T: 01680 300424 E: macphail@tiscali.co.uk W: holidaysonmull.co.uk

1 Cottage	3 Bedrooms	Sleeps 8

Prices – Cottage:
from £250.00   Per Week

Short breaks available

61132

Isle of Mull, Bunessan
Saorphin Cottages
Open: All year **Map Ref: 1C3**

★★
SELF CATERING

Saorphin Farm, Bunessan, Isle of Mull, Argyll, PA67 6DW
T: 01256 381275 E: estateoffice@herriardpark.com W: mull-accommodation.co.uk

3 Cottages	1-4 Bedrooms	Sleeps 2/8/10

Prices – Cottages:
£180.00-£750.00   Per Week

53048

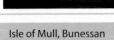

Isle of Mull, Calgary
Frachadil Farm Steadings

Open: All year excl Xmas and New Year

Map Ref: 1C1

★★★
SELF CATERING

Frachadil Farm, Calgary, Isle of Mull, Argyll, PA75 6QQ
T: 01688 400265 E: ann.frachadil@virgin.net W: accommodationsmull.co.uk/frachadil

| 1 Apartment | 2 Bedrooms | Sleeps 4-5 |

Prices – Apartment:
£250.00–£450.00 Per Week
Short breaks available

26708

Isle of Mull, Calgary
Dervaig Hall Bunkhouse

Open: All year

Map Ref: 1C1

BUNKHOUSE

Dervaig Hall, Dervaig, Isle of Mull, PA75 6QN
T: 01688 400491 E: dervaigbunkrooms@phonecoop.coop W: bunkrooms.mull-scotland.co.uk

| 1 Bunkhouse | 2 Bedrooms | Sleeps 10 |

Prices – Bunkhouse:
£14.00 Per Night

69566

Isle of Mull, Craignure
Craignure Bay House

Open: All year

Map Ref: 1D2

★★★★
SELF CATERING

Craignure, Isle of Mull, PA65 6AY
T: 07719 627500 E: enquiries@craignurebayhouse.co.uk W: www.craignurebayhouse.co.uk

| 1 House | 4 Bedrooms | Sleeps 4-8 |

Prices – House:
£500.00–£950.00 Per Week
Short breaks available

73519

Isle of Mull, Craignure
Inverlussa Caravan

Open: All year

Map Ref: 1D2

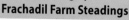

MINIMUM STANDARD HOLIDAY CARAVAN

Inverlussa, Craignure, Isle of Mull, PA65 6BD
T: 01680 812436

Arriving at ferry terminal in Craignure, turn left, drive six miles. Inverlussa on right hand side.

Holiday Caravans for Hire:
(1) £200.00 per week. Sleeps 2-6.

32021

For a full listing of Quality Assured accommodation, please see directory at back of this guide.

West Highlands and Islands

Isle of Mull, Tobermory
Oxlip Cottage

Open: All year

Map Ref: 1C1

★★★
SELF CATERING

West Street, Tobermory, Isle of Mull, PA75 6QZ
T: 07810 200310 E: lgallagher1979@yahoo.co.uk

1 Cottage   1 Bedroom   Sleeps 1-2

Prices – Cottage:
£220.00-£320.00   Per Week

Short breaks available

79189

Isle of Mull, Tobermory
Irene Young

Open: Mar-Nov

Map Ref: 1C1

A detached bungalow with private garden situated in upper Tobermory, Crosslake offers comfortable and relaxing accommodation. The property boasts a sun terrace offering views towards Ben More and the surrounding hills. An ideal base for exploring the beautiful Island of Mull. Sleeps 6 people. Sorry no pets and no smoking.

★★★
SELF CATERING

9 Strongarbh Park, Tobermory, Isle of Mull
T: 0141 944 4473 E: ireneyoung40@hotmail.com

1 Bungalow   3 Bedrooms   Sleeps 2-6

Prices – Bungalow:
£495.00   Per Week

45328

Oban
Esplanade Court Holiday Apartments

Open: Week before Easter to first week in Nov   Map Ref: 1E2

★★★ UP TO ★★★★
SELF CATERING

Corran Esplanade, Oban, Argyll, PA34 5PW
T: 01631 562067 E: enquiries@esplanadecourt.co.uk W: esplanadecourt.co.uk

45 Apartments   80 Bedrooms   Sleeps 1-6

Prices – Apartments:
£350.00-£670.00   Per Week

Short breaks available

46055

   Important: Prices stated are estimates and may be subject to amendments. Prices are per person per night unless otherwise stated.

Oban
Ulva Villa Garden Cottage

Open: All year

Map Ref: 1E2

★★★
SELF CATERING

Ulva Villa, Soroba Road, Oban, PA34 4JF
T: 01631 563042 E: greaney@oban-guest-house.com W: oban-guest-house.com

1 Bungalow   2 Bedrooms   Sleeps 2-5

Prices – Bungalow:
£350.00-£475.00   Per Week

Short breaks available

69723

by Oban, Connel
An Cladach

Open: All year

Map Ref: 1E2

★★★
SELF CATERING

North Connel, Oban, Argyll, PA37 1RD
T: 01347 878418 E: awaspa@aol.com

1 Cottage   2 Bedrooms   Sleeps 1-6
1 Bungalow   2 Bedrooms   Sleeps 1-4

Prices – Cottage: **Bungalow:**
£250.00-£500.00   Per Week   £250.00-£500.00   Per Week

Short breaks available

68208

by Oban, Lerags
An Tobar

Open: Easter-end Oct

Map Ref: 1E2

MINIMUM STANDARD HOLIDAY CARAVAN

Lerags, Oban, Argyll, PA34 4SE
T: 01631 565081 E: griffinm5@sky.com
South of Oban on Campbeltown Road turn right to Lerags Glen.

Holiday Caravans for Hire:
(1) £190.00-£220.00 per week. Sleeps 2-6.

69981

For a full listing of Quality Assured accommodation, please see directory at back of this guide.

Taynuilt
Airdeny Chalets
Open: All year   **Map Ref: 1E2**

Airdeny Chalets is situated in 3.5 acres of peaceful, natural habitat, one mile from Taynuilt. The spectacular views of Ben Cruachan and Glen Etive make it a stunning place to stay. It's a perfect venue for walking, cycling, fishing, bird watching, touring the Western Highlands & Islands or just relaxing.

★★★ UP TO ★★★★
SELF CATERING

Glen Lonan, Taynuilt, Argyll, PA35 1HY
T: 01866 822648 E: jenifer@airdenychalets.co.uk W: airdenychalets.co.uk

| 7 Chalets | 2-3 Bedrooms | Sleeps 4-6 |

Prices – Chalets:
£280.00-£725.00   Per Week

Short breaks available

11265

Taynuilt
Kirkton Cottage & Mountain View Chalet
Open: All year   **Map Ref: 1F2**

★★★ UP TO ★★★★
SELF CATERING

Dalry, Kirkton, Taynuilt, Argyll, PA35 1HW
T: 01866 822657 E: mail@kirktoncroft.co.uk W: kirktoncroft.co.uk

| 1 Cottage | 1 Bedroom | Sleeps 2-4 |
| 1 Chalet | 1 Bedroom | Sleeps 2 |

Prices – Cottage: **Chalet:**
£250.00-£435.00   Per Week   £200.00-£350.00   Per Week

Short breaks available off-season

22102

by Taynuilt, Kilchrenan
Ardabhaigh
Open: All year   **Map Ref: 1F2**

★★★★
SELF CATERING

Kilchrenan, by Taynuilt, Argyll, PA35 1HG
T: 01499 302736 E: gmoncrieff@btinternet.com

| 1 Bungalow | 4 Bedrooms | Sleeps 2-7 |

Prices – Bungalow:
£370.00-£890.00   Per Week
(10% reduction for 2-3 persons)

12459

Important: Prices stated are estimates and may be subject to amendments. Prices are per person per night unless otherwise stated.

by Taynuilt, Kilchrenan
Cuilreoch Caravans

Open: Mar-Oct

Map Ref: 1F2

MINIMUM STANDARD HOLIDAY CARAVAN

Cuilreoch, Kilchrenan, Taynuilt, Argyll, PA35 1HG
T: 01866 833236 E: joyce@cuilreoch.freeserve.co.uk W: cuilreochcaravans.co.uk

Glasgow/Edinburgh: Crianlarich – A82 Tyndrum – A85 Taynuilt – B845 Kilchrenan, bear right at Kilchrenan Inn, turn right ¼ mile – then Cuilreoch ¼ mile.

Holiday Caravans for Hire:
(3) £175.00-£200.00 per week.

21636

Tayvallich
The Steadings

Open: All year

Map Ref: 1D4

★★★★
SELF CATERING

Inchjura, Carsaig Bay, Tayvallich, Argyll, PA31 8PN
T: 01546 870294/698 E: jamesb@riddellj.freeserve.co.uk W: the-steadings-tayvallich.co.uk

1 Cottage	3 Bedrooms	Sleeps 6

Prices – Cottage:
£350.00-£575.00   Per Week

Short breaks available

60522

Looking across Oban Bay, Oban

For a full listing of Quality Assured accommodation, please see directory at back of this guide.

Food & Drink

Isle of Mull, Tobermory
Highland Cottage

Open: All year

Map Ref: 1C1

★★★★
SMALL HOTEL

Culinary Type:
SCOTTISH

Breadalbane Street, Tobermory,
Isle of Mull, PA75 6PD
T: 01688 302030
E: davidandjo@highlandcottage.co.uk
W: highlandcottage.co.uk

Best For:
• Romantic Meals
• Special Occasion

Prices:
Inclusive 3 course meal £45

Opening Times:
Dinner from 1900, last orders 2030.

30309

Highland Cottage is Mull's only two Rosette restaurant and the ideal venue for those who appreciate their food. Nothing too fancy – just quality ingredients well prepared and imaginatively presented and all designed to bring out the best of flavours and textures. Genuine hospitality and personal attention from resident owners.

Important: Prices stated are estimates and may be subject to amendments. Prices are per person per night unless otherwise stated.

Oban

Bossards Patisserie

Open: All year

Map Ref: 1E2

COFFEE & SANDWICH BAR

**Culinary Type:
SCOTTISH**

1A Gibraltar Street,
Oban, Argyll, PA34 4AY
T: 01631 564641
E: sylviabos6@aol.com

Best For:
 • Afternoon tea • Kids and families
 • Budget meals • Business lunches

Prices:
 Starter from: £2.90
 Main Course from: £4.00
 Dessert from: £1.20

Opening Times:
 0900-1700, last orders 1645.

We would like to welcome you to our lively and friendly coffee shop. At Bossards we produce and bake all our delicious cakes, bread and rolls on the premises. Freshly made soup, quiche, pizza daily. Come and enjoy lattes and Swiss hot chocolate, Eat Safe and EatScotland certificates.

68829

The Spar Cafe outside a converted church, Tobermory on the Isle of Mull

For a full listing of Quality Assured accommodation, please see directory at back of this guide.

Find Paradise

(via Oban).

Balevullin Machair, Tiree

The gateway to some of the most beautiful holiday destinations in the world is not a large airport. It's a town in Argyll.

To find out about all the Clyde and Hebridean island paradises we could transport you to, visit **calmac.co.uk** or call **08000 66 5000**.

Caledonian MacBrayne
Hebridean & Clyde Ferries

www.calmac.co.uk

Have a Caledonian MacBraynewave

Caledonian MacBrayne and CalMac are trading names of CalMac Ferries Ltd

Canoeing on Loch Lubnaig, north of Callander

Loch Lomond and The Trossachs

Whatever road you take to the bonny banks of Loch Lomond, you'll arrive at one of the most picturesque places in all of Scotland. The vast Loch Lomond & Trossachs National Park is, indeed, one of the most beautiful places in the world.

Towns like Callander, Balloch, Killin and Aberfoyle make a great base to explore different corners of the Park. And once you're there, you'll find so much to do from watersports and mountain climbing, angling to gentle strolls in stunning locations.

You can even integrate the sedate with the active - catch the SS Walter Scott from the Trossachs Pier and cruise Loch Katrine to Stronachlachar, then enjoy the 12-mile shore hike back.

This beautiful area, with its mountains, glens and rich geological environment is a haven for plants and wildlife. With 200 species of birds and more than 25% of Britain's wild plants recorded in this area, it is a naturalist's paradise.

Loch Lomond is idally situated for touring with The Highlands to the north the west coast and Islands, central Scotland and Glasgow a short drive away and Edinburgh to the East.

The River Teith at Callander, The Trossachs

DON'T MISS

1   **Loch Lomond and The Trossachs National Park** has its Gateway Centre on the southern shore of the loch in Balloch. From here and elsewhere on the loch, boat trips offer visitors the chance to explore the largest body of freshwater in Britain. To the west, Argyll Forest Park provides secluded waymarked trails, while the Trossachs to the east have provided inspiration for poets and novelists throughout the centuries.

2   At **Go Ape!** in Aberfoyle, you can take to the trees and experience a new, exhilarating course of rope bridges, tarzan swings and zip slides (including the longest in the UK) up to 37 metres above the forest floor. Hours of fun and adventure await!

3   From May to September, the **Trossachs Trundler** is a friendly country bus service throughout the Trossachs which is a great way of getting around. Linking the gateway resorts of Callander and Aberfoyle, and stopping at many points along the way, the service is also cycle friendly.

4   The dramatic scenery of the Trossachs is said to be the inspiration behind Sir Walter Scott's The Lady of the Lake. It is fitting then that the historic steamship which regularly sets sail on Loch Katrine is named after him. The **SS Sir Walter Scott** cruises up to Stronachlachar and will return you to the Trossachs Pier.

5   If you're looking for a real challenge, try one of Scotland's most popular long distance walking routes, the **West Highland Way**. Almost a third of the 95-mile trek is in the Loch Lomond area.

6   For a fun family day out, visit the **Scottish Wool Centre** in Aberfoyle, where you can enjoy a light-hearted look at 2,000 years of Scottish history portrayed by human and animal actors, plus spinning and weaving demonstrations. The live animal show features sheepdogs rounding up both sheep and Indian Runner Ducks, whilst younger visitors can enjoy the lambs and baby goats in springtime.

To find out more go to visitscotland.com

FOOD & DRINK

eatscotland.com

7 The **Coach House Coffee Shop** is situated in one of the most visited villages on the banks of Loch Lomond, the conservation village of Luss. Accompany a bumper homemade scone with a Lomond Latte or a Clyde Cappuccino and enjoy the homely and welcoming atmosphere.

8 Spectacular lochside views and a superb varied menu are just two good reasons to visit the **Cruin Bar & Restaurant**. From the windows of the restaurant, gaze across to the Island of Inchmurrin towards majestic Ben Lomond. From coffee and teas, lunches, to a beautiful dinner with wine, the choice is yours.

9 The **Village Inn** at Arrochar is a charming country inn on the edge of Loch Long. Offering traditional Scottish home-cooking, it is a great favourite with walkers exploring the adjacent 'Arrochar Alps'.

10 Visit the **Farmers Market at Loch Lomond Shores**, held several times per month, for the very best in locally-sourced, fresh Scottish produce.

WALKING

11 The village hall in Balquhidder is your starting point for one of Breadalbane's most glorious views. Head along the Kirkton Burn and upwards onto a forest road. Soon you'll reach **Creag an Tuirc** where you can absorb the beauty of Balquhidder Glen, Loch Voil and little Loch Doine. Including a short climb, this 2 ½ mile walk should take around 2 hours.

12 **Rowardennan** (B837 from Drymen) on the eastern edge of Loch Lomond is a wonderful starting and finishing point for a gentle walk along the shores, following part of the famous West Highland Way.

13 Take a dramatic and exhilarating walk from the centre of Callander to **Callander Crags and Bracklinn Fall**. The path follows a steep uphill climb to the summit cairn and the path to the falls is well worth the detour.

14 To walk along the shore of **Loch Katrine**, start at the Trossachs Pier (A821 west of Callander). Here you can choose to walk the 12-mile route to Stronachlachar and get the steamer back or you can walk as far as you like and then re-trace your steps. Cycle hire is also available here.

HISTORY & HERITAGE

15   Legend and history combine at the last resting place of the hero-outlaw, Rob Roy MacGregor. Find **Rob Roy's Grave** in the tiny, picturesque hamlet of Balquhidder, above Loch Voil. The Rob Roy Way is a 79-mile walk from Drymen to Pitlochry, linking together many of the places associated with Rob Roy MacGregor, the popular hero and outlaw who lived in these parts from 1671 to 1734.

16   There are around 60 **islands on Loch Lomond**. These vary in size and shape, with some only visible when the water is low. The main islands are rich in history and home to many ancient ruins, including Lennox Castle on Inchmurrin and a 7th-century monastery on Inchtavannach.

17   The Lake of Menteith is the only 'lake' in Scotland, all others being known as lochs. Sail from the Port of Menteith, off the A81 south of Callander, to the island that is home to **Inchmahome Priory**, an 18th century Augustinian monastery.

18   2010 will celebrate the 200th anniversary of the publication of Sir Walter Scott's **'The Lady of the Lake'**. The poem, set at Loch Katrine, was once the prime motivator in getting wealthy Victorians north and helped establish the area as a tourist destination. Look out for celebrations from June-September.

VIEWS

19   The beauty of **Loch Lomond** is undisputed but the finest vantage point is more open to debate. Everyone has their favourite spot and no doubt you will too. Take a cruise on the loch itself from Luss, Balloch or Tarbet or head to Inversnaid on the west bank for more rugged views.

20   **Conic Hill** is located just north of Balmaha on the B837. A 358m ascent, it offers superb views of Loch Lomond and its islands. From here, you can also see the dramatic changes to the landscape caused by the Highland Boundary Fault.

21   From the Stronachlachar junction on the Inversnaid road (B829), the wild landscape of **Loch Arklet** leads down towards Loch Lomond and its surrounding hills.

Hotels

Arrochar
Village Inn

Open: All year

Map Ref: 1G3

★★★
INN

Shore Road, Arrochar, Loch Long, G83 7AX
T: 01301 702279 E: villageinn@maclay.co.uk W: www.maclay.com

Indicated Prices:

Single	from £50.00 per room	Twin	from £75.00 per room
Double	from £75.00 per room	Superior double from £85.00 per room

62979

Balloch
Tullie Inn

Open: All year

Map Ref: 1G4

★★★
INN

Balloch Road, Balloch, Loch Lomond, G83 8SW
T: 01389 752052 E: tullieinn@maclay.co.uk W: www.maclay.com

Indicated Prices:

Single	from £60.00 per room	Twin	from £85.00 per room
Double	from £85.00 per room	Family	from £125.00 per room

60676

Callander
Poppies Hotel and Restaurant

Open: All year excl 24-27 Dec; 2-23 Jan

Map Ref: 1H3

★★★
SMALL HOTEL

Leny Road, Callander, FK17 8AL
T: 01877 330329 E: info@poppieshotel.com W: poppieshotel.com

Indicated Prices:

Single	from £55.00 per room	Twin	from £79.00 per room
Double	from £79.00 per room	Family	from £95.00 per room

50139

For a full listing of Quality Assured accommodation, please see directory at back of this guide.

Loch Lomond and the Trossachs

Crianlarich
The Crianlarich Hotel

Open: Mar-Oct

Map Ref: 1G2

★★★
HOTEL

Crianlarich, Perthshire, FK20 8RW
T: 01838 300272 E: info@crianlarich-hotel.co.uk W: crianlarich-hotel.co.uk

Indicated Prices:

Single	from £39.00 per room		Twin	from £39.00 per room
Double	from £39.00 per room		Family	from £39.00 per room

85535

Drymen
The Winnock Hotel

Open: All year

Map Ref: 1H4

The Winnock Hotel is a family run hotel with 73 bedrooms. It has recently been extensively and carefully refurbished whilst retaining the 18th century character of the original coaching inn. The hotel is ideally located for guests looking to explore Scotland's first national park, surrounding countryside and nearby cities.

★★★
HOTEL

The Square, Drymen, Loch Lomond, G63 0BL
T: 01360 660245 E: info@winnockhotel.com W: winnockhotel.com

Indicated Prices:

Single	from £39.00 per room		Twin	from £49.00 per room
Double	from £49.00 per room		Suite	from £89.00 per room
			Family	from £59.00 per room

64394

Luss
Lodge on Loch Lomond Hotel

Open: All year

Map Ref: 1G4

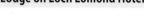

★★★★
HOTEL

Luss, Argyll, G83 8PA
T: 01436 860201 E: res@loch-lomond.co.uk W: loch-lomond.co.uk

Indicated Prices:

Single	from £89.00 per room		Suite	from £169.00 per room
Double	from £99.00 per room		Family	from £129.00 per room

36217

Important: Prices stated are estimates and may be subject to amendments. Prices are per person per night unless otherwise stated.

Loch Lomond and the Trossachs

by Luss
The Inn at Inverbeg

Open: All year

Map Ref: 1G3

★★★★
INN

Luss, Loch Lomond, G83 8PD
T: 01436 860678 E: inverbeg.reception@loch-lomond.co.uk W: innatinverbeg.co.uk

Indicated Prices:
Single	from £69.00 per room	Family	from £119.00 per room
Double	from £79.00 per room		

79429

Port of Menteith
Lake of Menteith Hotel

Open: All year

Map Ref: 1H3

★★★
SMALL HOTEL

Port of Menteith, Perthshire, FK8 3RA
T: 01877 385258 E: enquiries@lake-hotel.com W: lake-hotel.com

Indicated Prices:
Single	from £85.00 per room	Twin	from £130.00 per room
Double	from £130.00 per room	Suite	from £160.00 per room

76298

Guest Houses and B&Bs

Arrochar
Fascadail House

Open: All year excl 3 Jan-mid-Feb

Map Ref: 1G3

★★★
GUEST HOUSE

Shore Road, Arrochar, G83 7AB
T: 01301 702344 E: enquiries@fascadail.com W: fascadail.com

Indicated Prices:
Single	from £40.00 per room	King	from £60.00 per room
Double	from £50.00 per room	Triple	from £70.00 per room
Twin	from £55.00 per room	Family	from £70.00 per room

77918

For a full listing of Quality Assured accommodation, please see directory at back of this guide.

Balloch
Aird House

Open: All year excl Xmas & New Year

Map Ref: 1G4

★★★
B&B

1 Ben Lomond Walk, Balloch, G83 8RJ
T: 01389 754464/07814 730176

Indicated Prices:

Single	from £40.00	Twin	from £30.00 per person
Double	from £30.00 per person	Suite	from £60.00

TV 📶 ♿ P ☕ 🍴 ✕ 🖥 📶
V

11261

Balloch
St Blanes

Open: All year

Map Ref: 1G4

Excellent accommodation situated at quiet end of main street. Loch Lomond, restaurants and visitor attractions close by. Bus and rail station just a few minutes walk and Glasgow Airport half hour drive. Delicious breakfasts and a warm welcome awaits. We can also help with itinerary. Private off-road parking.

★★★
BED AND BREAKFAST

Drymen Road, Balloch, Dunbartonshire, G83 8HR
T: 01389 729661 E: stblanes@tiscali.co.uk W: accommodationlochlomond.com

Indicated Prices:

Single	from £30.00 per room	Twin	from £55.00 per room
Double	from £55.00 per room	Family	from £85.00 per room

TV 📶 ♿ P ☕ 🖥 (•))

55765

Balloch
Ballagan Farm

Open: All year

Map Ref: 1G4

AWAITING GRADING

Ballagan Farm, Balloch, Loch Lomond, G83 8LY
T: 01389 750092 E: sandra.gallacher@bandb-loch-lomond.co.uk W: bandb-loch-lomond.co.uk

Indicated Prices:

Double	from £60.00 per room

V

87439

Callander
Annfield Guest House

Open: Mar-Dec

Map Ref: 1H3

★★★★
GUEST HOUSE

18 North Church Street, Callander, FK17 8EG
T: 01877 330204 E: reservations@annfieldguesthouse.co.uk W: annfieldguesthouse.co.uk

Indicated Prices:
Single	from £40.00 per room	Twin	from £60.00 per room
Double	from £60.00 per room	Family	from £75.00 per room

74811

Callander
Westerton Bed & Breakfast

Open: Feb-Oct

Map Ref: 1H3

★★★★
BED AND BREAKFAST

Leny Road, Callander, Perthshire, FK17 8AJ
T: 01877 330147 E: westerton.callander@tiscali.co.uk W: westerton.co.uk

Indicated Prices:
Double   from £75.00 per room

63838

Callander
Westcot Guest House

Open: All year

Map Ref: 1H3

AWAITING GRADING

Leny Road, Callander, FK17 8AL
T: 01877 339812 E: westcotguesthouse@yahoo.co.uk W: westcotguesthouse.co.uk

Indicated Prices:
Single	from £40.00 per person	Twin	from £30.00 per person
Double	from £30.00 per person	Family	from £33.00 per person

85085

Drymen
Braeside

Open: All year

Map Ref: 1H4

AWAITING GRADING

5 Main Street, Drymen, G63 0BP
T: 01360 660989/07545 952215 E: braesidebedandbreakfast@googlemail.com

Indicated Prices:
Single	from £40.00 per room	Twin	from £60.00 per room
Double	from £60.00 per room		

87517

or a full listing of Quality Assured accommodation, please see directory at back of this guide.

Gartocharn
The Old School House   Open: All year   Map Ref: 1G4

★★★★
BED AND BREAKFAST

Gartocharn, G83 8SB   T: 01389 830373/07739 463014
E: reservations@the-old-school-house-co.uk   W: the-old-school-house.co.uk

Indicated Prices:
Single	from £37.00 per person	Twin	from £37.00 per person
Double	from £37.00 per person		

59909

Killin
Dall Lodge Country House   Open: Apr-Oct   Map Ref: 1H2

★★★★
GUEST HOUSE

Main Street, Killin, Perthshire, FK21 8TN
T: 01567 820217   E: connor@dalllodge.co.uk   W: dalllodge.co.uk

Indicated Prices:
Single	from £32.00 per person	Twin	from £30.00 per person
Double	from £27.00 per person	Suite	from £38.00 per person
		Family	from £38.00 per person

22048

Lochearnhead
Mansewood Country House   Open: All year   Map Ref: 1H2

★★★★
GUEST HOUSE

Lochearnhead, Stirlingshire, FK19 8NS   T: 01567 830213
E: stay@mansewoodcountryhouse.co.uk   W: mansewoodcountryhouse.co.uk

Indicated Prices:
Single	from £45.00 per room	Twin	from £66.00 per room
Double	from £66.00 per room		

75801

Self Catering and Camping & Caravan Parks

Arden
The Gardeners Cottages
Open: All year　　　　　　　　**Map Ref: 1G4**

★★★★
SELF CATERING

Arden House Estate, Arden, Dunbartonshire, G83 8RD
T: 01389 850601 E: amacleod@gardeners-cottages.com W: gardeners-cottages.com

3 Cottages　　　　　　　1-2 Bedrooms　　　　　　　Sleeps 2-5

Prices – Cottage:
£278.00-£609.00　　　Per Week

Short breaks available

TV 📶 🍳 🛏️ 🧺 📠 ✖ •)) †
🏊 📺 🚲

27241

Balfron Station
Ballat Smithy Cottage
Open: All year　　　　　　　　**Map Ref: 1H4**

★★★★
SELF CATERING

Balfron Station, by Loch Lomond, G63 0SE
T: 01360 440269 E: a.h.currie@btopenworld.com W: ballatsmithycottage.com

1 Cottage　　　　　　　2 Bedrooms　　　　　　　Sleeps 1-4

Prices – Cottage:
£295.00-£465.00　　　Per Week

Short breaks available

TV 🖥️ 🍳 📠 •))
☉ ◎ 🚲 🐕 🛒 🧺 🔥 ⏸️ ❄️ ① ✖ 🅿️ £ ⛽ SP 🏊 🚲 🏊

13952

Helensburgh
Pier View Self Catering
Open: All year　　　　　　　　**Map Ref: 1G4**

★★★
SELF CATERING

5 Colquhoun Street, Helensburgh, G84 9RA
T: 01436 673713 E: bookings@pier-view.co.uk W: pier-view.co.uk

1 First Floor Flat　　　　　2 Bedrooms　　　　　　　Sleeps 1-6

Prices – First Floor Flat:
£205.00-£375.00　　　Per Week

Short breaks available

TV ☎ 🖥️ 🍳 🛏️ 🧺 🎵 📠 ✖ •))

49786

Loch Lomond and the Trossachs

By Killin, Morenish
Morenish Mews

Open: All year

Map Ref: 1H2

★★★★
SELF CATERING

by Killin, Perthshire, FK21 8TX
T: 01567 820527 E: stay@morenishmews.com W: morenishmews.com

2 Cottages	1 Bedroom	Sleeps 1-2
1 Apartment	1 Bedroom	Sleeps 1-2

Prices – Cottages: **Apartment:**
£225.00-£375.00 Per Week £225.00-£375.00 Per Week
Short breaks available

72535

Lochearnhead
Earnknowe Holiday Cottages

Open: All year

Map Ref: 1H2

★★★
SELF CATERING

Earnknowe, Lochearnhead, Perthshire, FK19 8PY
T: 01567 830238 E: enquiries@earnknowe.co.uk W: earnknowe.co.uk

5 Cottages	1-2 Bedrooms	Sleeps 2-4

Prices – Cottages:
£215.00-£470.00 Per Week

44822

Lochearnhead
Lochside Cottages

Open: All year

Map Ref: 1H2

Family-run chalet and cottage business on the edge of beautiful Lochearn. Ideal centre for touring, golfing and water skiing (we have our own jetty, slipway and moorings). All chalets are kitted out for a self catering holiday made easy, and all with great views over Lochearn.

★★★
SELF CATERING

Lochearnhead, FK19 8PT
T: 01567 830268/07711 368649 E: gus.dundhu@btinternet.com W: lochsidecottages.net

1 Cottage	3 Bedrooms	Sleeps 6
9 Cabins	2-3 Bedrooms	Sleeps 1-6

Prices – Cottage: **Cabins:**
£330.00-£760.00 Per Week £180.00-£770.00 Per Week
Short breaks available

36146

Important: Prices stated are estimates and may be subject to amendments. Prices are per person per night unless otherwise state

Luss
Shegarton Farm Cottages

Open: All year

Map Ref: 1G4

★★★★
SELF CATERING

Shegarton Farm, Luss, Argyll, G83 8RH
T: 01389 850269 E: enquiries@shegartonfarmcottages.co.uk W: shegartonfarmcottages.co.uk

2 Cottages   1-2 Bedrooms   Sleeps 2-4

Prices – Cottage:
£200.00-£450.00   Per Week

Short breaks available

54426

Port of Menteith
Lochend Chalets

Open: All year

Map Ref: 1H3

On the shores of the beautiful Lake of Menteith, in the National Park, Lochend Chalets is a 38 acre, family-run estate, where Nick Nairn's Cook School is based. A perfect centre for touring or staying in to soak up the spectacular view and chat to the ducks!

★★★ UP TO ★★★★
SELF CATERING

Port of Menteith, Stirling, FK8 3JZ
T: 01877 385268 E: info@lochend-chalets.com W: lochend-chalets.com

1 Cottage	4 Bedrooms	Sleeps 2-10
1 Cabin	2-3 Bedrooms	Sleeps 2-6
3 Apartments	2-3 Bedrooms	Sleeps 2-6
3 A-Frame Chalets	3 Bedrooms	Sleeps 2-6

Prices – Cottage: **Cabin:**   **Apartments:**   **A-Frame Chalets:**
£430.00-£1250.00 pw   £165.00-£550.00 pw   £310.00-£825.00 pw   £310.00-£870.00 pw

Short breaks available

36032

For a full listing of Quality Assured accommodation, please see directory at back of this guide.

Stirling Castle

Stirling and Forth Valley

Stirling and the Forth Valley offer a huge range of visitor attractions and the beautiful rolling countryside is perfect for outdoor pursuits - just about everything is catered for, from popular cycling and horseriding trails through glorious landscapes to fantastic fishing rivers and secluded golf courses.

This region is home to one of Scotland's most popular attractions, which is considered a real triumph of modern engineering. The Falkirk Wheel is the world's only rotating boatlift and, standing an impressive 24 metres high, has reconnected the Forth & Clyde Canal with the Union Canal. Known as the Millennium Link, this project links the major cities of Edinburgh and Glasgow from coast to coast, and has opened up a world of new sailing opportunities between the two waterways.

Scotland's industrial heritage is well represented locally at Bo'Ness and Kinneil Steam Railway, Birkhill Fireclay Mine and Callendar House, while you can see traces of Scotland's woollen industry on the opposite shores of the Forth in Clackmannan.

Many visitors make Stirling their base to explore the Scotland's central belt and the Southern Highlands. This relatively new city is rich in history and has many reminders of its turbulent and often bloody past. Don't miss Stirling Castle, the National Wallace Monument, and the site of the epic Battle of Bannockburn in 1314 - one of the most historically significant battles of the Scottish Wars of Independence, which is credited with securing the nation's future with Robert the Bruce as King of Scotland.

Stirling and the Forth Valley have it all, with plenty of opportunities to experience the great outdoors and fascinating history, but remember to leave enough time to take a walk around Stirling and enjoy a spot of shopping too!

DON'T MISS

1   **Stirling Castle**, undoubtedly one of the finest in Scotland, sits high on its volcanic rock towering over the stunning countryside known as 'Braveheart Country'. A favourite royal residence over the centuries and a key military stronghold, visit the Great Hall, the Chapel Royal, and the Renaissance Palace. From the castle esplanade the sites of no less than seven historic battles can be seen, as can the majestic **National Wallace Monument** built in tribute to William Wallace.

2   Open the door to **Callendar House** in Falkirk, and you open the door to 600 years of Scottish history. Journey through time from the days of the Jacobites to the advent of the railway, and don't forget to stop at the Georgian kitchens for some refreshments prepared using authentic Georgian recipes.

3   The **Antonine Wall** dates back to the second century and once marked the northern frontier of the Roman Empire. Substantial lengths have been preserved and can still be seen at various sites around Falkirk and the site was awarded UNESCO World Heritage Status in July 2008. Follow the wall for a relaxed walk along the towpath on the north of the canal, taking you past the Falkirk Wheel to Bonnybridge.

4   **Stirling** is a shopper's dream, from its modern retail centres to its Victorian arcade, farmers' markets to elegant boutiques. Here, you'll find a fantastic selection of stylish stores and speciality shops. For a quaint shopping experience, visit **Bridge of Allan**, a small village just three miles from Stirling's centre with some stunning designer shops.

5   Formerly known as 'Castle Gloom', **Castle Campbell** sits beautifully at the head of Dollar Glen, immediately north of Dollar. Sitting in lofty isolation and overlooked by the Ochil Hills, the Castle became the chief Lowland stronghold of the Campbell clan, upon whose members the successive titles of Earl, Marquis and Duke of Arygll were bestowed. There are excellent walks through Dollar Glen to enjoy too.

6   Discover what life was like for unfortunate inmates within the authentic Victorian **Stirling Old Town Jail**. You might well run into Jock Rankin, the notorious town hangman, and even witness an attempted jail break!

FOOD & DRINK

eatscotland.com

7   After your trip to the impressive wheel, relax in the **Falkirk Wheel Café** for a delicious snack or light meal. The glass fronted café is the perfect vantage point to marvel at the panoramic views of the wheel as it rotates.

8   **Harviestoun Country Hotel and Restaurant** in Tillicoultry is the perfect place to stop, whether it is for lunch, high tea or an evening meal. The restored 18th century steading, with the backdrop of the stunning Ochil Hills, is the ideal setting for relaxing with good food and fine wine.

9   The lovely Victorian spa town of Bridge of Allan is home to the **Bridge of Allan Brewery** where you can see how traditional Scottish handcrafted ales are produced and even enjoy a free tasting.

10   The **Sheriffmuir Inn** is situated in the Ochil Hills and offers fantastic panoramic views. A family run business, which sources local produce wherever possible, this is an ideal stop for a drink or tasty meal.

HISTORY & HERITAGE

11   Situated by the banks of the River Teith, **Doune Castle** was once the ancestral home of the Earls of Moray. At one time occupied by the Jacobite troops, this castle can now be explored and makes a great picnic spot.

12   On the site of the original battlefield, the **Bannockburn Heritage Centre** on the southern outskirts of Stirling, tells the story of the greatest victory of Scotland's favourite monarch King Robert the Bruce. Walk the battlefield and then enjoy the audio-visual presentation in the centre.

13   The **Tower Trail** takes you on a tour around the amazing houses of the people who built Clackmannanshire. These buildings, created by the families who shaped the later industrial development of the county, show the changing fashions in tower architecture and are among some of the best surviving examples of the heritage of medieval Scotland.

14   Built in tribute to Scotland's national hero Sir William Wallace, the **National Wallace Monument**, by Stirling, can be seen for miles around. The Monument exhibition tells of Sir Wallace's epic struggle for a free Scotland.

ATTRACTIONS

15   Just a few miles north west of Stirling on the A84 you will find **Blair Drummond Safari Park**. Here you can drive through wild animal reserves, see the only elephants in Scotland and get close to lions, zebras and a whole host of other animals. Park and walk around the pet farm, watch a sea lion display, find out what it's like to hold a bird of prey and take a boat to Chimp Island. There is also an adventure play area, pedal boats for hire and, for the more adventurous, the flying fox!

16   An epic adventure awaits as castles, art collections, steam trains and Roman antiquities come together in **Forth's Timeline**. Unravel over 2,000 years of Scottish history and experience the rich landscape of the Forth Valley as you visit 16 attractions that showcase the region, including the Regimental Museum at Stirling Castle, Kilmadock Heritage Centre and the University of Stirling.

17   Just north of Stirling is **Argaty Red Kites** a red kite feeding station. After 130 years, Scottish Natural Heritage and the RSPB have reintroduced these exciting, acrobatic birds to central Scotland. Spend a day at the farm on the Braes of Doune and enjoy a guided walk or just watch the birds from the hide.

18   The **Stirling Smith Art Gallery and Museum** offers a fascinating introduction to the history of the area, with a popular programme of special, changing exhibitions. Make sure to sample some of the culinary delights from the café.

WALKING

19   At the heart of Clackmannanshire's 300-acre Gartmorn Dam Country Park, visitors can enjoy a short walk with gentle gradients suitable for wheelchairs or pushchairs. **Gartmorn Dam** is the oldest man-made reservoir still in use in Scotland, while the nature reserve is the winter home for thousands of migratory ducks.

20   Not far from Dollar where the A823 meets the A977 its worth stopping to explore the delightful **Rumbling Bridge**, so named because of the continuous rumbling sound of the falls and the river below. The unusual double bridge spans a narrow gorge and you'll find a network of platforms and paths that take you over the river and deep into the gorge with spectacular views of waterfalls and swirling pools.

21   Follow the **Limekilns Trail** near Stirling, a Site of Special Scientific Interest due to its beautiful ash woodland. Here you'll find some interesting flowers - look out for early purple orchids and twayblades - as well as a row of 18th century limekilns.

22   The **Darn Walk** from Bridge of Allan to Dunblane is a beautiful walk which can be enjoyed at any time of the year. Highlights include a scenic stretch alongside the River Allan and the cave which was Robert Louis Stevenson's inspiration for Ben Gunn's cave in Treasure Island. The walk can be completed in 1½ to 2 hours.

Hotels

Tillicoultry
Harviestoun Country Hotel & Restaurant

Open: All year

Map Ref: 2A3

Our award-winning sympathetically restored 18th century steading is centrally located at the foot of the stunning Ochil Hills. Privately owned and managed. Ten comfortable ensuite bedrooms, Lounge with open fire, all day dining restaurant, function suite, conferences, weddings, bus parties. Ideal for touring, golfing, business. Weekend special offers available.

★★★
SMALL HOTEL

Dollar Road, Tillicoultry, Clackmannanshire, FK13 6PQ
T: 01259 752522 E: info@harviestouncountryhotel.com W: harviestouncountryhotel.com

Indicated Prices:

Single	from £65.00 per room	Twin	from £90.00 per room
Double	from £85.00 per room	Family	from £95.00 per room

29679

Important: Prices stated are estimates and may be subject to amendments. Prices are per person per night unless otherwise stated.

Guest Houses and B&Bs

Denny
The Lodge B&B

Open: All year

Map Ref: 2A4

★★
BED AND BREAKFAST

The Lodge Home Farm, Drove Loan, Denny, Stirlingshire, FK6 5LH
T: 01324 819891 E: knowlesp4@aol.com W: visitscotland.com

Indicated Prices:

Single	from £35.00 per person	Twin	from £30.00 per room
Double	from £30.00 per room		

86009

Dunblane
Ciar Mhor

Open: All year

Map Ref: 2A3

★★★
BED AND BREAKFAST

Auchinlay Road, Dunblane, FK15 9JS
T: 01786 823371 E: jean.macgregor@btinternet.com W: ciar-mhor.co.uk

Indicated Prices:

Single	from £30.00 per room	Twin	from £44.00 per room
Double	from £44.00 per room	Family	from £50.00 per room

19246

Falkirk
Ashbank Guest House

Open: All year

Map Ref: 2A4

★★★★
GUEST HOUSE

105 Main Street, Redding, Falkirk, FK2 9UQ
T: 01324 716649 E: info@bandbfalkirk.com W: bandbfalkirk.com

Indicated Prices:

Single	from £40.00 per room	Twin	from £60.00 per room
Double	from £60.00 per room	Family	from £75.00 per room

13100

For a full listing of Quality Assured accommodation, please see directory at back of this guide.

147

Stirling
Mrs Moira Stewart

Open: All year excl 15 Dec-15 Jan

Map Ref: 2A4

★★★★
BED AND BREAKFAST

West Plean House, Denny Road, Stirling, FK7 8HA
T: 01786 812208 E: moira@westpleanhouse.com W: westpleanhouse.com

Indicated Prices:

Single	from £48.00 per room	Twin	from £75.00 per room
Double	from £75.00 per room		
		Children 12 years or under half price

63729

Stirling
Cressington B&B

Open: All year excl Xmas

Map Ref: 2A4

★★★
BED AND BREAKFAST

34 Causewayhead Road, Stirling, FK9 5EU
T: 01786 462435 E: info@cressington-bb.co.uk W: cressington-bb.co.uk

Indicated Prices:

Single	from £40.00 per room	Twin	from £50.00 per room
Double	from £50.00 per room	Family	from £75.00 per room

67429

Stirling
Laurinda B&B

Open: All year

Map Ref: 2A4

★★★
BED AND BREAKFAST

66 Ochilmount, Ochilview, Bannockburn, Stirling, FK7 8PJ
T: 01786 815612 E: paterson_e@yahoo.co.uk

Indicated Prices:

Single	from £30.00	Twin	from £25.00
Double	from £25.00	Suite	from £25.00
		Family	from £25.00

35036

Stirling
Alberts

Open: All year

Map Ref: 2A4

★
BED AND BREAKFAST

10 Hillfoots Road, Stirling, FK9 5LF
T: 01786 478728 E: albert271006@yahoo.co.uk

Indicated Prices:

Double	from £50.00	Twin	from £50.00
		Family	from £60.00

11440

Self Catering and Camping & Caravan Parks

by Stirling, Blairlogie
Witches Craig Caravan & Camping Park

Open: 1 Apr-31 Oct

Map Ref: 2A3

A warm and friendly welcome awaits you at Witches Craig. Graded excellent, this five star touring park is attractive, exceptionally well maintained and offers first class facilities. The Ochil Hills give a breathtaking backdrop and add to the relaxing holiday atmosphere. A great base for travelling and sightseeing.

★★★★★
TOURING PARK

Blairlogie, Stirling, FK9 5PX
T: 01786 474947 E: info@witchescraig.co.uk W: www.witchescraig.co.uk

3 miles north east of Stirling on the A91 Stirling to St Andrews road.

Park accommodates 60 pitches. Total touring pitches: 60.
Prices per pitch from:
(60) £14.00   (60) £14.00   (60) £14.00

64425

For a full listing of Quality Assured accommodation, please see directory at back of this guide.

149

Food & Drink

Tillicoultry
Harviestoun Country Hotel & Restaurant

Open: All year   **Map Ref: 2A3**

★★★
SMALL HOTEL

Scottish
TOURIST BOARD
EatScotland

Cullinary Type:
SCOTTISH

Dollar Road, Tillicoultry,
Clackmannanshire, FK13 6PQ
T: 01259 752522
E: info@harviestouncountryhotel.com
W: harviestouncountryhotel.com

Best For:
  • Kids and Families • Romantic Meals
  • Special Occasion • Business Lunches
  • Group Dining

Prices:
Starter from:	£4.25
Main Course from:	£9.50
Dessert from:	£4.75

Opening Times:
  Meals from 1200, last orders 2100.
  All day dining.

29679

Our award winning sympathetically restored 18th century steading is centrally located at the foot of the stunning Ochil Hills. Privately owned and managed. Ten comfortable ensuite bedrooms. Lounge wih open fire serving coffees, home baking, a la carte restaurant. All day dining. Function suite, conferences, weddings, bus parties. Ideal for touring, golfing business.

Golf course at Tillicoultry at the base of the Ochil Hills, Clackmannanshire

Perth and the River Tay

PERTHSHIRE, ANGUS & DUNDEE AND THE KINGDOM OF FIFE

There's so much to discover in Scotland's heartlands that you're sure to find something that suits you perfectly. A holiday destination that can be as active as you want it to be, from playing a round on one of the world's finest golf courses and fishing wonderful river beats to simply enjoying the great outdoors on a woodland stroll.

The varied countryside offers sights and attractions worthy of any touring itinerary. Fife has an enviable coastline with a number of charming little harbour towns, Perthshire is Big Tree Country, unspoilt and magnificent with some of Scotland's finest woodlands and stunning lochs and hills, while the Angus Glens have long been a source of inspiration for walkers. And

then there's the vibrant city of Dundee, which offers fantastic shopping, top quality visitor attractions and a variety of cosmopolitan bars and restaurants.

While Perthshire sits astride the Highland Boundary Fault, which has rewarded the area with a terrific mix of terrain suited to all manner of outdoor pursuits, from great hill walking to whitewater rafting, anglers love this region due to the sheer number and variety of fishing opportunities - be it angling for salmon and trout on the River Tay or heading to the coastal waters of Angus and Fife where the catch can be bountiful.

Of course it goes without saying that golfers love this area. This is home to the Royal and Ancient Golf Club of St Andrews and some of the world's finest courses. Find everything from the famous Old Course at St Andrews to other championship quality greats Gleneagles and Carnoustie.

If wildlife's your thing, the opportunities are endless.

In the countryside of Perthshire and the Angus Glens there are ospreys, eagles, otters and deer. Explore along the coast from Fife to Angus and spot a wide variety of seabirds – especially around the Montrose Basin where you can see thousands of migrant species.

You don't have to be escaping civilisation to enjoy these parts, however. There are towns and cities that you'll enjoy enormously, each with their own unique attractions; Perth has a fantastic mix of specialist shops and high street retailers, St Andrews is a fine university town with a fascinating history, Dunfermline was once the seat of Scotland's Kings, while Dundee, a city of many discoveries, is a great place to soak up some culture.

When it comes to accommodation, this region can offer a range of options. From self catering in former fishermen's cottages to grand Victorian mansions offering quality bed and breakfast, there is something to suit every taste and budget.

Farmers market, city of Dundee

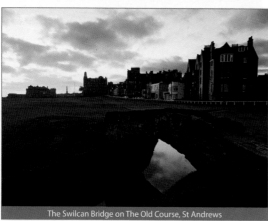
The Swilcan Bridge on The Old Course, St Andrews

What's On?

Angus Glens Walking Festival
3-6 June 2010
Explore the beauty of the Angus Glens with walks to suit all abilities.
angusahead.com/walkingfestival

Game Conservancy Scottish Fair, Scone Palace
2-4 July 2010
One of the main countryside events of the year in Scotland.
scottishfair.com

The Open Championship
15 - 18 July 2010
The tournament returns to the Home of Golf.
visitfife.com/open2010

Fife Outdoor Access Festival
31 July-9 August 2010
From walks to watersports, discover what Fife has to offer the outdoor enthusiast.
fifeoutdooraccessfestival.co.uk

Glamis Prom
Mid August 2010
The National Symphony Orchestra of Scotland performs in time to a spectacular firework finale.
glamis-castle.co.uk

Dundee Flower & Food Festival
Early September 2010
Discover the best in food and horticulture over three days in Dundee.
dundeeflowerandfoodfestival.com

RAF Leuchars Airshow
11 September 2010
Popular event with spectacular air displays.
airshow.co.uk

Angus & Dundee Roots Festival
End September-early October 2010
Research your ancestors and explore sites of historical importance.
tayroots.com

The Enchanted Forest, Faskally, by Pitlochry
Mid October-early November 2010
A spectacular journey of light and sound in Perthshire's Big Tree Country.
enchantedforest.org.uk

Dundee Mountain Film Festival
End November 2010
Celebrate epic landscapes with a programme of talks and award-winning films.
dundeemountainfilm.org.uk

Dundee Mountain Film Festival
End November 2010
Celebrate epic landscapes with a programme of talks and award-winning films.
dundeemountainfilm.org.uk

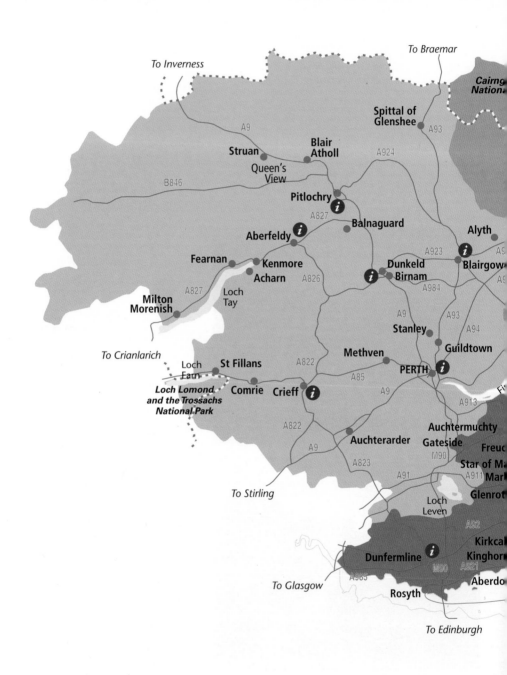

To Inverness

To Braemar

Cairng
Nationa

Spittal of
Glenshee

A93

A9

Blair
Atholl

Struan

A924

Queen's
View

B846

Pitlochry

A827

Balnaguard

Alyth

Aberfeldy

A923

Fearnan

Kenmore

Dunkeld

Blairgow

Acharn

A826

Birnam

A9

A827

Loch
Tay

A984

Milton
Morenish

A9

A93

A94

Stanley

To Crianlarich

Guildtown

St Fillans

Methven

Loch
Earn

A822

PERTH

Loch Lomond
and the Trossachs
National Park

Comrie

Crieff

A85

A9

A913

Auchtermuchty

A822

Auchterarder

Gateside

Freuc

A9

M90

Star of Ma

A823

A911

Mar

A91

Glenrot

To Stirling

Loch
Leven

A82

To Glasgow

Dunfermline

Kirkcal

Kinghor

M90

A921

Aberd o

Rosyth

A985

To Edinburgh

To Aberdeen

Brechin
Montrose
A935
A90
Kirriemuir
Letham
Forfar
A932
A930
A92
A928
Arbroath
A92
DUNDEE
Tay
A82
Strathkinness
St Andrews
Cupar
Kingsbarns
A917
A915
Crail
A916
Upper East
Largo Neuk
Anstruther
Kennoway
Lundin A917 Pittenweem
Leven Links Elie
A955
Firth of Forth
From Belgium

VisitScotland Information Centres

To help you plan and book your trip to Scotland email our travel experts at info@visitscotland.com. When you arrive call into one of our Information Centres where our friendly experts can offer advice on all things local as well as sharing their wider knowledge of Scotland. We don't just advise either. We can sort out your accommodation and all your travel needs, as well as tickets for events across Scotland. So if you're looking to get the most from your visit, there really is only one place to go.

Perthshire

Aberfeldy	The Square Aberfeldy, PH15 2DD
Blairgowrie	26 Wellmeadow, Blairgowrie PH10 6AS
Crieff	High Street, Crieff, PH7 3HU
Dunkeld	The Cross, Dunkeld, PH8 0AN
Perth	Lower City Mills, West Mill Street Perth, PH1 5QP
Pitlochry	22 Atholl Road Pitlochry, PH16 5BX

Angus and Dundee

Arbroath	Harbour Visitor Centre Fishmarket Quay Arbroath, DD11 1PS
Brechin	Pictavia Centre Haughmuir, Brechin
Dundee	Discovery Point Discovery Quay Dundee DD1 4XA

Fife

Dunfermline	1 High Street Dunfermline, KY12 7DL
Kirkcaldy	The Merchant's House 339 High Street Kirkcaldy, KY1 1JL
St Andrews	70 Market St St Andrews Fife FY16 9NU

Open All Year

Seasonal

Live it. Visit Scotland.
visitscotland.com/wheretofindus

- LOCAL KNOWLEDGE
- WHERE TO STAY
- ACCOMMODATION BOOKING
- PLACES TO VISIT
- THINGS TO DO
- MAPS AND GUIDES
- TRAVEL ADVICE
- ROUTE PLANNING
- WHERE TO SHOP AND EAT
- LOCAL CRAFTS AND PRODUCE
- EVENT INFORMATION
- TICKETS

Scottish Crannog Centre, Kenmore, Loch Tay

Perthshire

Perthshire is full of contrasts. It can be romantic yet dynamic, exciting yet tranquil, stimulating yet relaxing. Situated right in the heart of Scotland among some of the country's most varied landscapes, Perthshire offers a host of attractions - everything from history to horticulture - of which many are open all year round.

The area is perhaps best known as being Big Tree Country, boasting some of Europe's most remarkable trees and woodlands but also look out for other breathtaking attractions such as the wild expanse of Rannoch Moor, the romantic waters of Loch Leven, or the towering peak of Schiehallion - one of Scotland's best known landmarks.

The terrific mix of terrain and landscapes across the region accommodates no less than 35 outdoor activities, from the adrenaline-pumping white water rafting and canyoning to the more leisurely such as cycling and angling. Perthshire also offers some of the finest inland golf courses in the world, from the world famous Gleneagles to hidden gems just waiting to be discovered.

City lovers won't be disappointed by Perth's vibrant mix of shopping, culture and entertainment, with award-winning restaurants and markets offering the finest local produce while floral features offer a wealth of colour all year round.

Perth's history continues to hold its own whilst embracing the 21st century, especially in 2010 when the 800th anniversary of the founding of the Royal Burgh of Perth will be celebrated with a year long programme of events – www.perth800.com.

Whatever your pace or pleasure, you'll find it in Perthshire.

DON'T MISS

1   Poised above the River Tay, discover the magnificent Scone Palace and its magical gardens. Once the crowning place of Scottish kings, this was also the capital of the Picts and the rightful home of the Stone of Destiny. Today the Palace is home to the Earls of Mansfield and boasts an impressive collection of antiques, paintings and rare artefacts, which can be seen on a tour of the main State Rooms.

2   Blair Castle, the stunningly situated ancient seat of the Dukes and Earls of Atholl, is a five-star castle experience. Scotland's most visited historic house, the unmistakeable white façade is visible from the A9 just north of Blair Atholl. Dating back 740 years, the castle has played a part in some of Scotland's most tumultuous events but today is a relaxing and fascinating place. This is also the home of the Atholl Highlanders; Europe's only remaining private army.

3   The Scottish Crannog Centre at Kenmore on Loch Tay is an authentic recreation of an ancient loch-dwelling and a completely unique visitor experience. Imagine a round house in the middle of a loch with a thatched roof, on stilts. Tour the Crannog to see how life used to be 2,600 years ago. Upon your return to shore, have a go at a variety of Iron Age crafts; see if you can grind the grain, drill through stone or make fire through wood friction.

4   Among its many other attractions, Perthshire boasts some of the most remarkable trees and woodlands anywhere in Europe. Known as Big Tree Country, this is where you will find Europe's oldest tree in Fortingall Churchyard, the world's highest hedge and one of Britain's tallest trees at The Hermitage by Dunkeld. The 250 miles of waymarked paths give you an excellent opportunity to explore the area - stop at the Queen's View where the spectacular vista over Loch Tummel towards Glencoe is world famous.

5   Housed within Glenturret, Scotland's oldest malt whisky distillery, The Famous Grouse Experience is the most visited distillery in Scotland. It is an interactive attraction where visitors can familiarise themselves with this renowned tipple and the brand that accompanies it! As well as a tour of the production areas, you can enjoy a unique audio-visual presentation which gives a grouse's eye view of Scotland.

6   The Perthshire Gardens Collection, which now includes gardens in Angus & Fife, brings together eleven spectacular examples of the gardener's art. From small privately owned gardens to the more formal sumptuous variety, heather, wild woodlands and Himalayan treasures will inspire both horticultural enthusiast and novice alike.

WALKING

7 A 64 mile circular waymarked walking route through the scenic Perthshire and Angus Glens, The **Cateran Trail** follows paths used by the 15th century Caterans (cattle rustlers). Complete the whole route in a leisurely five days or simply select a section to explore in a day. Take in the soft contours of Strathardle on the Bridge of Cally to Kirkmichael section or head for the hills between Kirkmichael and the Spittal of Glenshee.

8 Revered in poetry by Scotland's national bard, Robert Burns, the **Birks of Aberfeldy** ('birks' being the old Scots for birch trees) line a short walk alongside the Moness Burn, reached from a car park on the Crieff Road. A circular path leads to a beautiful waterfall, where birds and flowers are abundant.

9 Partly accessible for wheelchairs and pushchairs, **Lady Mary's Walk** in Crieff is one of the most popular in Perthshire and provides a peaceful stroll beside the beautiful River Earn. The avenue of mature oak, beech, lime and sweet chestnut trees is particularly photogenic in the late autumn when the trees are aglow in hues of rust and gold.

10 On the A9 north of Dunkeld, you'll find **The Hermitage**. A beautiful walk along the banks of the River Braan takes you to Ossian's Hall set in a picturesque gorge and overlooking Black Linn Falls. See one of Britain's tallest trees, a stately Douglas Fir measured at 64.5 metres and keep your eyes peeled for beautiful red squirrels which can often be seen in the trees.

OUTDOOR ACTIVITIES

11 Perthshire is renowned for its stunning lochs and rivers, many of which are excellent for **white water rafting**. A truly unforgettable experience awaits you, combining rugged Highland scenery and the adrenaline rush of weaving your way down a roaring river - it's easy to understand why it's one of the most popular adventure sports in this region.

12 Perthshire is the only place in Scotland where you can try **sphereing**. This is where willing participants strap themselves safely into a 12ft inflatable ball and then take a wild and bouncy tumble down the hill. For the ultimate adrenaline rush, try eclipse sphereing - the only difference is you're in complete darkness!

13 Sample some of the finest inland golf in the world in Perthshire with a choice of two great value **golf passes**. The Perthshire Green Card offers discounted golf on 19 of Perthshire's 18-hole venues, including Crieff, Pitlochry and Murrayshall on the outskirts of Perth. Or play at a more relaxing pace with the Perthshire Highlands Golf Ticket. Suitable for all, including family groups or those who are short of time, the ticket can be used on 12 superb 9-hole layouts.

14 Within Tayside's rich territory there are many great **angling** opportunities waiting to be discovered, explored and enjoyed. The variety of fishing to be had on the mighty River Tay, Loch Tay, River Lyon and hill lochs can be matched by few areas. The salmon and trout fishing is first class and roach and pike abound. Add to this the River Tummel, River Ericht and River Earn and there's enough to satisfy even the most demanding angler.

To find out more go to visitscotland.com

FOOD & DRINK

15 Farmers' markets have seen something of a resurgence in recent years in the UK and Perth's Farmers' Market is one of the best known in Scotland. Held on the first Saturday of each month, it is something of a showcase for local producers and growers and is a rewarding visit in its own right. Look out for fish, meat and game, baked goods, fruit wines and liqueurs, honeys and preserves, fruit and vegetables, sweets and herbs. Sound tempting? Many stallholders offer free tastings and are happy to explain more about their particular specialities to visitors.

16 The area around Blairgowrie is Europe's centre for soft fruit production and you will see signs at farms inviting you to 'pick your own' juicy fruit and berries. Sample the local produce of field and hedgerow at Cairn o' Mohr Wines in Errol. A family-run business it produces Scottish fruit wines made from local berries, flowers and leaves - resulting in a truly unique end product. Explore the winery through one of the on-site tours before a tasting session!

17 Scotland's smallest malt whisky distillery, Edradour Distillery can be found in the Highland foothills just to the east of Pitlochry. Built in the early 19th century, Edradour is the only remaining 'farm' distillery in Perthshire and appears largely unchanged since it was established 170 years ago. Visitors can enjoy a guided tour of the production areas, before relaxing with a wee dram of the amber nectar.

18 In addition to outstanding restaurant facilities, Baxters at Blackford offers a fantastic Scottish showcase of inspirational fine food, gifts and much, much more. Visitors are invited to taste a variety of products, from specialist chocolate in The Chocolate Parlour to tasting what Baxters is most famous for, specialty soups, in The Baxters Hub. Whether making a quick stop or for those wishing to stay a little bit longer, Baxters is ideal for the perfect day out.

WILDLIFE

19 A National Nature Reserve since 1964, Loch Leven provides a variety of habitats for a huge range of wildlife, including thousands of migratory ducks, geese and swans every autumn and winter, the largest concentration of breeding ducks found anywhere in the UK and raptors such as osprey, buzzard and peregrine falcon. The RSPB's Vane Farm Nature Reserve and Visitor Centre can be found on the edge of the Reserve, where you can get a little closer in one of the three observation hides or by taking the wetland or woodland trails.

20 Visit Loch of the Lowes between April and August and there's every chance you'll encounter its famous nesting ospreys. The Scottish Wildlife Trust's visitor centre provides interpretation on the birds, which migrate to Scotland from their winter homes in West Africa. There are also telescopes and binoculars on hand to give you a better view. Between October and March, the nature reserve is worth visiting for the sheer numbers of wildfowl which are present.

21 Discover the rugged beauty of highland Perthshire on a wildlife tour with Highland Safaris. Covering 250,000 acres of Perthshire estate, the tours come in all shapes and sizes. Try the popular Mountain Safari and explore this amazing natural wilderness in the comfort of a 4x4 vehicle. Look out for red deer, mountain hare, golden eagles and other Highland wildlife along the way.

22 Each year between April and October an average of 5,400 salmon fight their way upstream from Atlantic feeding grounds to spawn in the upper reaches of the River Tummel. They must by-pass the Hydro-Electric dam at Pitlochry by travelling through the interconnected pools that form the Pitlochry 'fish ladder'. Witness the fish climb the height of the dam at a very special attraction.

Hotels

Blair Atholl
Atholl Arms Hotel

Open: All year excl Xmas Day

Map Ref: 4C12

Scottish Baronial style highland hotel in the centre of Blair Atholl close to the castle. Offering traditional Scottish hospitality and good base to tour the central Highlands. Enjoy the Atholl experience all year round.

★★★
HOTEL

Old North Road, Blair Atholl, Pitlochry, PH18 5SG
T: 01796 481205 E: info@athollarms.co.uk W: athollarms.co.uk

Indicated Prices:
Single	from £50.00 per room	Twin	from £65.00 per room
Double	from £65.00 per room	Family	from £80.00 per room

13304

Blairgowrie
Bridge of Cally Hotel

Open: All year

Map Ref: 2B1

★★★
SMALL HOTEL

Bridge of Cally, Blairgowrie, PH10 7JJ
T: 01250 886231 E: enquiries@bridgeofcallyhotel.com W: bridgeofcallyhotel.com

Indicated Prices:
Single	from £45.00 per room	Twin	from £70.00 per room
Double	from £70.00 per room		

72382

Crieff
Leven House Hotel

Open: Mar-Nov

Map Ref: 2A2

★★
SMALL HOTEL

Comrie Road, Crieff, Perthshire, PH7 4BA
T: 01764 652529 E: info@levenhousehotel.co.uk W: levenhousehotel.co.uk

Indicated Prices:
Single	from £35.00 per room	Twin	from £60.00 per room
Double	from £60.00 per room		

35372

For a full listing of Quality Assured accommodation, please see directory at back of this guide.

Perthshire

Dunkeld
Royal Dunkeld Hotel

Open: All year excl 25-26 Dec

Map Ref: 2B1

A friendly family run hotel located in the beautiful village of Dunkeld. Ideally situated for walking, shooting, golf and generally just relaxing. Excellent food using fresh local produce. Enjoy a dram or one of our real ales – as mentioned in the Good Beer Guide, in our convivial bar.

★★★
HOTEL

Atholl Street, Dunkeld, Perthshire, PH8 0AR
T: 01350 727322 E: reservations@royaldunkeld.co.uk W: royaldunkeld.co.uk

Indicated Prices:

Single	from £45.00 per person	Twin	from £34.00 per person
Double	from £34.00 per person	Family	from £34.00 per person

23742

Glenshee
Dalmunzie Castle Hotel

Open: All year excl part Dec

Map Ref: 4D12

Dalmunzie Castle is a stunning, quintessential Laird's mansion turreted in the Scots Baronial style and standing proudly at the head of an estate dating back to 1510. Enjoying magnificent mountain scenery, Dalmunzie is located in a hidden part of Highland Perthshire, yet is less than two hours from Edinburgh airport.

★★★
COUNTRY HOUSE HOTEL

Spittal of Glenshee, Blairgowrie, Perthshire, PH10 7QG
T: 01250 885224 E: reservations@dalmunzie.com W: dalmunzie.com

Indicated Prices:

Single	from £70.00 B&B per room	Twin	from £100.00 B&B per room
Double	from £100.00 B&B per room		

64913

Important: Prices stated are estimates and may be subject to amendments. Prices are per person per night unless otherwise stated.

Perth
The Royal George Hotel

Open: All year

Map Ref: 2B2

★★★
HOTEL

Tay Street, Perth, PH1 5LD
T: 01738 624455 E: info@theroyalgeorgehotel.co.uk W: theroyalgeorgehotel.co.uk

Indicated Prices:

Single	from £65.00	Twin	from £45.00 per person
Double	from £45.00 per person	Family	from £40.00 per person

60259

Pitlochry
Dundarach Hotel

Open: Feb-Dec

Map Ref: 2A1

★★★
HOTEL

Perth Road, Pitlochry, Perthshire, PH16 5DJ
T: 01796 472862 E: enq@dundarach.co.uk W: dundarach.co.uk

Indicated Prices:

Single	from £49.00 per room	Twin	from £96.00 per room
Double	from £96.00 per room		

23616

Pitlochry
Moulin Hotel

Open: All year

Map Ref: 4C12

310 year old inn, extended over the years to include 15 ensuite bedrooms, in the historic village square of Moulin, half a mile from Pitlochry centre. Award-winning pub with its own brewhouse open all day for food. Especially cosy in autumn/winter and spring. Attractive all year round.

★★★
HOTEL

11-13 Kirkmichael Road, Moulin, Pitlochry, Perthshire, PH16 5EH
T: 01796 472196 E: enquiries@moulinhotel.co.uk W: www.moulinhotel.co.uk

Indicated Prices:

Single	from £45.00 per room	Twin	from £60.00 per room
Double	from £60.00 per room	Family	from £75.00 per room

66021

For a full listing of Quality Assured accommodation, please see directory at back of this guide.

163

St Fillans

The Four Seasons Hotel   Open: Apr-Oct & Xmas/New Year, Mar, Nov, Dec w'ends only   Map Ref: 1H2

★★★
SMALL HOTEL

Lochside, St Fillans, Perthshire, PH6 2NF
T: 01764 685333   E: info@thefourseasonshotel.co.uk   W: thefourseasonshotel.co.uk

Indicated Prices:

Single	from £55.00 per room	Twin	from £110.00 per room
Double	from £110.00 per room	Family	from £130.00 per room

26668

Guest Houses and B&Bs

Birnam

Byways   Open: Easter-end October   Map Ref: 2B1

★★★
BED AND BREAKFAST

Perth Road, Birnam, Dunkeld, Perthshire, PH8 0DH
T: 01350 727542   E: joanne.gerrie@ukonline.co.uk   W: dunkeldaccommodation.co.uk

Indicated Prices:

Double	£30.00 per person	Twin	£30.00 per person

17142

Blair Atholl

The Firs B&B   Open: Feb-Oct   Map Ref: 4C12

★★★
GUEST HOUSE

St Andrews Crescent, Blair Atholl, Perthshire, PH18 5TA
T: 01796 481256   E: kirstie@firs-blairatholl.co.uk   W: firs-blairatholl.co.uk

Indicated Prices:

Double	from £32.50 per person	Twin	from £32.50 per person
		Family	from £32.50 per person

44075

Blairgowrie
Bankhead B&B

Open: All year excl Xmas & New Year　　　Map Ref: 2B1

★★★
FARM HOUSE

Bankhead, Clunie, Blairgowrie, PH10 6SG
T: 01250 884281　E: hilda@hwightman.orangehome.co.uk　W: bankheadbnb.co.uk

Indicated Prices:

Single	from £30.00 per room	Twin	from £50.00 per room
Double	from £50.00 per room	Family	from £70.00 per room

14200

Blairgowrie
Eildon Bank

Open: All year excl Xmas & Holidays　　　Map Ref: 2B1

★★★
BED AND BREAKFAST

118 Perth Road, Blairgowrie, PH10 6ED
T: 01250 873648　E: emurray@eildonbank.freeserve.co.uk

Indicated Prices:

Single	from £30.00 per room	Twin	from £50.00 per room
Double	from £50.00 per room		

24641

Blairgowrie
Garfield House

Open: All year excl Xmas & New Year　　　Map Ref: 2B1

★★★
BED AND BREAKFAST

Perth Road, Blairgowrie, Perthshire, PH10 6ED
T: 01250 872999　E: info@garfieldhouse.com　W: garfieldhouse.com

Indicated Prices:

Single	from £25.00 per person	Twin	from £26.00 per person
Double	from £26.00 per person		

27286

by Blairgowrie, Wester Essendy
Ridgeway B&B

Open: All year　　　Map Ref: 2B1

★★★
BED AND BREAKFAST

Ridgeway, Wester Essendy, by Blairgowrie, PH10 6RA
T: 01250 884734　E: pam.mathews@btinternet.com　W: ridgewaybandb-blairgowrie.co.uk

Indicated Prices:

Double	from £28.00	Twin	from £28.00

44837

Perthshire

Crieff
Merlindale

Open: mid Jan-mid Dec

Map Ref: 2A2

★★★★
BED AND BREAKFAST

Perth Road, Crieff, Perthshire, PH7 3EQ
T: 01764 655205/07740 873111 E: merlin.dale@virgin.net W: merlindale.co.uk

Indicated Prices:
Single	from £45.00 per room	Twin	from £70.00 per room
Double	from £70.00 per room		

38135

Perth
Achnacarry Guest House

Open: All year

Map Ref: 2B2

★★★★
GUEST HOUSE

3 Pitcullen Crescent, Perth, PH2 7HT
T: 01738 621421 E: info@achnacarry.co.uk W: achnacarry.co.uk

Indicated Prices:
Single	from £30.00 per room	Twin	from £55.00 per room
Double	from £55.00 per room	Family	from £65.00 per room

10981

Perth
Ackinnoull Guest House

Open: All year excl Xmas & New Year

Map Ref: 2B2

★★★★
GUEST HOUSE

5 Pitcullen Crescent, Perth, PH2 7HT
T: 01738 634165 E: ackinnoull@yahoo.com W: ackinnoull.com

Indicated Prices:
Single	from £30.00 per room	Twin	from £50.00 per room
Double	from £50.00 per room	Family	from £60.00 per room

11010

visitscotland.com/wildlife

WILDLIFE
SCOTLAND

To find out about watching wildlife in Europe's leading wildlife destination

log on to visitscotland.com/wildlife

Important: Prices stated are estimates and may be subject to amendments. Prices are per person per night unless otherwise stated.

Perth
Arisaig Guest House
Open: All year excl Xmas   **Map Ref: 2B2**

★★★★
GUEST HOUSE

4 Pitcullen Crescent, Perth, PH2 7HT
T: 01738 628240 E: mail@arisaigonline.co.uk W: arisaigonline.co.uk

Indicated Prices:

Single	from £30.00 per room	Twin	from £30.00 per person
Double	from £27.50 per person	Family	from £65.00 per room

12833

Perth
Clunie Guest House
Open: All year   **Map Ref: 2B2**

★★★★
GUEST HOUSE

12 Pitcullen Crescent, Perth, PH2 7HT
T: 01738 623625 E: ann@clunieguesthouse.co.uk W: clunieguesthouse.co.uk

Indicated Prices:

Single	from £30.00 per room	Twin	from £60.00 per room
Double	from £60.00 per room	Family	from £75.00 per room

19736

Perth
Halton House B&B
Open: All year   **Map Ref: 2B2**

★★★★
BED AND BREAKFAST

11 Tullylumb Terrace, Perth, PH1 1BA
T: 01738 643446 E: jody@haltonhousebandb.co.uk W: haltonhousebandb.co.uk

Indicated Prices:

Single	from £50.00 per room	Twin	from £80.00 per room
Double	from £80.00 per room		

82641

Perth
Oakwood B&B
Open: All year   **Map Ref: 2B2**

★★★★
BED AND BREAKFAST

Oakwood House, Guildtown, Perth, PH2 6DW
T: 01821 650800 E: janeydouglas@aol.com W: oakwoodhousebedandbreakfast.co.uk

Indicated Prices:

Single	from £40.00 per room
Double	from £65.00 per room

48035

Perth
Comely Bank Cottage

Open: All year excl Xmas & New Year

Map Ref: 2B2

★★★
BED AND BREAKFAST

19 Pitcullen Crescent, Perth, PH2 7HT
T: 01738 631118 E: comelybankcott@hotmail.com W: comelybankcottage.co.uk

Indicated Prices:

Single	from £30.00 per room	Twin	from £55.00 per room
Double	from £54.00 per room	Family	from £67.50 per room

20100

---

by Perth, Stanley
Mrs Ann Guthrie

Open: Jan-Nov

Map Ref: 2B2

★★★
FARM HOUSE

Newmill Farm, Stanley, Perth, PH1 4PS
T: 01738 828281 E: guthrienewmill@sol.co.uk W: newmillfarm.co.uk

Indicated Prices:

Single	from £38.00 per person	Twin	from £58.00 per room
Double	from £58.00 per room		

47290

Pitlochry
Craigroyston House

Open: All year

Map Ref: 2A1

★★★★
GUEST HOUSE

2 Lower Oakfield, Pitlochry, Perthshire, PH16 5HQ
T: 01796 472053 E: reservations@craigroyston.co.uk W: craigroyston.co.uk

Indicated Prices:

Double	from £35.00 per person	Twin	from £35.00 per person

21058

Pitlochry
Derrybeg

Open: Jan-Nov

Map Ref: 2A1

★★★★
GUEST HOUSE

18 Lower Oakfield, Pitlochry, Perthshire, PH16 5DS
T: 01796 472070 E: marion@derrybeg.fsnet.co.uk W: derrybeg.com

Indicated Prices:

Single	from £25.00 per room	Twin	from £50.00 per room
Double	from £50.00 per room		

22516

Important: Prices stated are estimates and may be subject to amendments. Prices are per person per night unless otherwise stated.

Pitlochry
Ashbank House

Open: All year

Map Ref: 2B1

★★★
BED AND BREAKFAST

14 Tomcroy Terrace, Pitlochry, PH16 5JA
T: 01796 472711 E: ashbankhouse@btinternet.com W: ashbankhouse.co.uk

Indicated Prices:
Double   from £26.00 per person   Twin   from £26.00 per person

13104

Pitlochry
The Dell

Open: All year

Map Ref: 2A1

★★★
BED AND BREAKFAST

11 Dixon Terrace, Pitlochry, Perthshire, PH16 5QX
T: 01796 470306 E: sandy307@btinternet.com W: thedellpitlochry.co.uk

Indicated Prices:
Single   from £35.00 per room   Twin   from £50.00 per room
Double   from £50.00 per room   Family   from £75.00 per room

69460

Pitlochry
Fasganeoin Country House

Open: Apr-Oct

Map Ref: 2A1

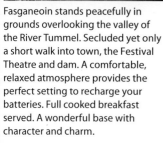

Fasganeoin stands peacefully in grounds overlooking the valley of the River Tummel. Secluded yet only a short walk into town, the Festival Theatre and dam. A comfortable, relaxed atmosphere provides the perfect setting to recharge your batteries. Full cooked breakfast served. A wonderful base with character and charm.

★★★
GUEST HOUSE

Perth Road, Pitlochry, PH16 5DJ
T: 01796 472387 E: sabrina.fasganeoin@onebillinternet.co.uk W: fasganeoincountryhouse.co.uk

Indicated Prices:
Single   from £35.00 per person   Twin   from £38.00 per person
Double   from £36.00 per person   Family   from £38.00 per person

25685

For a full listing of Quality Assured accommodation, please see directory at back of this guide.

169

Perthshire

Self Catering and Camping & Caravan Parks

Aberfeldy
Moness Resort — Open: All year — Map Ref: 2A1

Moness Resort has a selection of luxury one, two and three bedroom cottages. These cottages are beautifully furnished and equipped to Scottish Tourist Board 4 star grading. The resort is set in 35 acres of beautiful countryside and has a fully equipped leisure centre with swimming pool, two bars, two restaurants. It makes an ideal base for exploring highland Perthshire.

★★★★
SELF CATERING

Crieff Road, Aberfeldy, Perthshire, PH15 2DY
T: 0845 330 2838/01887 822100 E: info@moness.com W: moness.com

1 Cottage — 1-3 Bedrooms — Sleeps 1-8

Prices – Cottage:
£334.00-£934.00 Per Week

Short breaks available

70221

Fish IN SCOTLAND
Experience world-class fishing

For information on fishing breaks in Scotland
visitscotland.com/fish

Alyth
The Steadings

Open: All year **Map Ref: 2C1**

Four VIP cottages for dog lovers in the pastoral valley of Strathmore. 1½ hour drive Edinburgh. Glen Prosen, Glen Isla, Glen Clova (5 star) and Glen Doll (4 star) are equipped to the highest standard. Comfortable beds with Egyptian cotton linen, attention to details, fresh mountain air.

★★★★ UP TO ★★★★★
SELF CATERING

The Steadings, Auchteralyth, Alyth, Perthshire, PH11 8JT
T: 01575 530474 E: anne@auchteralythsteadings.com W: auchteralythsteadings.com

| 4 Cottages | 6 Bedrooms | Sleeps 2-12 |

Prices – Cottages:
£250.00-£700.00 Per Week

Short breaks available

72316

Alyth
Cairnleith Cottage

Open: All year **Map Ref: 2C1**

★★★
SELF CATERING

5 Cairnleith Cottage, Alyth, Perthshire, PH11 8EZ
T: 01259 218408/07794 714652 E: gordon@cairnleithcottage.co.uk W: cairnleithcottage.co.uk

| 1 Cottage | 3 Bedrooms | Sleeps 1-5 |

Prices – Cottage:
£250.00-£400.00 Per Week

Short breaks available

76760

Blairgowrie
Blairgowrie Holiday Park

Open: All year **Map Ref: 2C1**

★★★★★
HOLIDAY PARK

Rattray, Blairgowrie, Perthshire, PH10 7AL
T: 01250 876666 E: blairgowrie@holiday-parks.co.uk W: holiday-parks.co.uk
On A93 15 miles north of Perth. 1 mile north of Blairgowrie town centre turn right (park signposts). Park is on left 400 yards.
Park accommodates 20 pitches. Total touring pitches: 20.

Prices per pitch:
(100) £16.00-£18.00 (20) £16.00-£18.00
Pine lodges (9) £285.00-£775.00 sleeps 4-8.

Holiday Caravans for Hire:
(6) £195.00-£520.00 per week.
Sleeps 4-6.

Thistle

15401

For a full listing of Quality Assured accommodation, please see directory at back of this guide.

171

Perthshire

Blairgowrie
Ericht Holiday Lodges
Open: All year   Map Ref: 2C1

★★★
SELF CATERING

Balmoral Road, Rattray, Blairgowrie, PH10 7AH
T: 01250 874686 E: stay@ericht.co.uk W: www.ericht.co.uk

6 Lodges   2 Bedrooms   Sleeps 2-6

Prices – Lodge:
£260.00-£540.00   Per Week

Short breaks available

25054

by Blairgowrie
Mrs E D Church
Open: All year   Map Ref: 2B1

★★★
SELF CATERING

Rannagulzion House, Bridge of Cally, nr Blairgowrie, Perthshire, PH10 7JR
E: rannagulzion@aol.com W: rannagulzion.co.uk

1 Apartment   2 Bedrooms   Sleeps 2-4

Prices – Apartment:
£230.00-£300.00   Per Week

Short breaks available

24236

Comrie
Glenbuckie House – Comrie
Open: All year   Map Ref: 2A2

★★★★
SELF CATERING

The Estate Office, Lawers House, Comrie, Perthshire, PH6 2DX
T: 01764 670050 E: estate.office@lawers.co.uk W: lawers.co.uk

1 House   7 Bedrooms   Sleeps 12

Prices – House:
£700.00-£2000.00   Per Week

Short breaks available

74223

Comrie
Glen Cottage
Open: All year   Map Ref: 2A2

★★★
SELF CATERING

4 Aros Field East, Comrie, PH6 2EA
T: 01764 671003 E: mallan2@btopenworld.com W: glencottagecomrie.co.uk

1 House   4 Bedrooms   Sleeps 2-8

Prices – House:
£600.00-£900.00   Per Week

Short breaks available

68170

Important: Prices stated are estimates and may be subject to amendments. Prices are per person per night unless otherwise stated.

Crieff
Braidhaugh Park

Open: All year

Map Ref: 2A2

★★★
HOLIDAY PARK

South Bridgend, Crieff, PH7 4DH
T: **01764 652951** E: **info@braidhaugh.co.uk** W: **braidhaugh.co.uk**

On A822. From Stirling take A822 at Greenloaning –200 yards past visitor centre on left. From Perth A85 to end of Crieff High Street. Turn left. On right after bridge.

Park accommodates 38 pitches. Total touring pitches: 38.
Prices per pitch:
(38) £18.25–£23.00 (38) £18.25–£23.00
Wigwam (2) £20.00–£30.00 per night.

Holiday Caravans for Hire:
(3) £255.00–£450.00 per week.

16071

by Crieff, Comrie
Comrie Croft

Open: All year

Map Ref: 2A2

★★★ UP TO ★★★★
HOSTEL

by Crieff, Perthshire, PH7 4JZ
T: **01764 670140** E: **info@comriecroft.com** W: **comriecroft.com**

1 Hostel | 14 Bedrooms | Sleeps 2-8

Prices – Hostel:
from £15 Per Night (Children half price)

16081

Glenlyon
Innerwick Estate

Open: All year

Map Ref: 1H1

Three charming traditional stone cottages on a family run farm/sporting estate. Fully modernised, log fires, panoramic views and varied walks. National scenic area with special interest for botanists and bird watchers. Fishing and tennis on site. Golf, riding, watersports within 30 minutes. Weekly prices £315-£1200 inclusive of heating. Pets welcome. Brochure available.

★★★★ UP TO ★★★★★
SELF CATERING

Glenlyon, Aberfeldy, Perthshire, PH15 2PP
T: **01887 866222** E: **enquiries@innerwick.com** W: **innerwick.com**

1 Cottage | 2 Bedrooms | Sleeps 4
2 Houses | 3-4 Bedrooms | Sleeps 6-8

Prices – Cottage: | **House:** |
£315.00-£525.00 Per Week | £350.00 £1200.00 Per Week |

Short breaks available

31686

For a full listing of Quality Assured accommodation, please see directory at back of this guide.

173

Glenshee
Dalmunzie Highland Cottages

Open: All year

Map Ref: 4D12

Seven stone built traditional cottages of individual style and character on 6000 acre sporting estate. Ideal base for touring Royal Deeside and the Highlands or for a sporting holiday with our own 9-hole golf course, shooting, fishing, tennis, hillwalking.

★★★ UP TO ★★★
SELF CATERING

Spittal O'Glenshee, Blairgowrie, Perthshire, PH10 7QE
T: 01250 885226 E: enquiries@dalmunziecottages.com W: dalmunziecottages.com

7 Cottages	1-3 Bedrooms	Sleeps 2-6

Prices – Cottages:
£240.00-£550.00   Per Week

Short breaks available

22074

by Killin, Milton Morenish
Loch Tay Highland Lodges

Open: All year

Map Ref: 1H2

Pine lodges STB 3 & 4 star all with loch views. Beautifully located on Loch Tay. Balconies, private parking, landscaped grounds, marina, moorings, boat hire, fishing, boathouse, restaurant, home-cooking, activities, putting, sailing, archery, mountain biking nearby, golf, rafting, riding. Budget tepees new for 2010. Contemporary woodland cabins.

★★★ UP TO ★★★★
SELF CATERING

Milton Morenish, Killin, Perthshire, FK21 8TY
T: 01567 820323 E: info@lochtay-vacations.co.uk W: lochtay-vacations.co.uk

29 Pine Lodges	2-4 Bedrooms	Sleeps 2-8
2 Houses	4-5 Bedrooms	Sleeps 8-10
Tepees and Wigwams		

Prices – Pine Lodges: Houses:
£250.00-£730.00   Per Week   £650.00-£1400.00   Per Week

Short breaks available

72882

by Perth, Methven
Cloag Farm Cottages

Open: All year

Map Ref: 2B2

★★★
SELF CATERING

Cloag Farm, Methven, Perth, PH1 3RR
T: 01738 840239 E: info@cloagfarm.co.uk W: cloagfarm.co.uk

3 Cottages   2 Bedrooms   Sleeps 1-4

Prices – Cottages:
£250.00-£395.00   Per Week

Short breaks available

40414

Pitlochry
Milton of Fonab Caravan Site

Open: Easter-beginning Oct

Map Ref: 2B1

Quiet family run site on the banks of the River Tummel a half mile south of Pitlochry. Within easy reach of Pitlochry Festival Theatre, dam and fish ladder, excellent walks and fishing. Pitlochry is a picturesque Victorian town and an ideal location for that relaxing holiday.

★★★★
HOLIDAY PARK

Bridge Road, Pitlochry, PH16 5NA
T: 01796 472882 E: info@fonab.co.uk W: fonab.co.uk

Half mile south of Pitlochry opposite Bell's Distillery.

Park accommodates 154 pitches. Total touring pitches: 114.

Prices per pitch:
(114) £16.00-£19.00   ▲ (10) £16.00-£19.00
(30) £16.00-£19.00

Holiday Caravans for Hire:
(36) £224.00-£500.00 per week.
Sleeps 6 max.

Thistle

38495

Pitlochry
Dream Holidays

Open: All year

Map Ref: 2A1

★★★
SELF CATERING

The Old Coach House, Knockard Road, Pitlochry, PH16 5QH
T: 01847 851851 E: info@dreamholidays.org.uk W: dreamholidays.org.uk

1 House   2 Bedrooms   Sleeps 4

Prices – House:
£296.00-£478.00   Per Week

Short breaks available

84964

For a full listing of Quality Assured accommodation, please see directory at back of this guide.

175

by Pitlochry
Tummel Valley Holiday Park

Open: Mar-Nov

Map Ref: 2A1

★★★★
HOLIDAY PARK

nr Pitlochry, PH16 5SA
T: 0844 335 3728 **E:** via website **W:** parkdean.com
Follow the B8019 north of Pitlochry signed Tummel Valley.

Park accommodates 33 pitches. Total touring pitches: 33.
Prices per pitch:
(33) £12.00-£30.00
Lodges (18) £279.00-£969.00

Holiday Caravans for Hire:
(43) £199.00-£779.00 per week.

62262

Perth and the River Tay.

Important: Prices stated are estimates and may be subject to amendments. Prices are per person per night unless otherwise stated.

The award-winning Lunan Bay, south of Montrose

Angus and Dundee

Uncover a different part of Scotland, where 2,000 years of magic, mystery, and romance, are interwoven across a land rich in history, tradition and culture.

This was the heartland of the Picts and fought over by the Scots and the English - much of this early history being told at Pictavia, by Brechin - and is also where Scottish independence was declared in 1320 at Arbroath.

Enjoy a contrasting landscape, where rugged coastlines, gentle lowlands and Highland Glens, merge easily and unexpectedly, and produce world-class golf locations like Carnoustie, Montrose and Downfield set against dramatic and breathtaking scenery.

Here you can take relaxing walks in the Angus Glens, absorb the history and romance of Glamis Castle,

explore glistening beaches such as at Lunan Bay and stunning formal gardens like those in the grounds of Edzell Castle. Experience top-quality visitor attractions that inform, inspire and entertain such as at Discovery Point and in the Verdant Works; and indulge in modern, 21st century, cosmopolitan city life, which blends shopping, art, theatre and culture.

Whatever your reason for visiting Scotland, explore for yourself the legacy of ancient peoples, kings and queens, adventurers and inventors. Discover Angus and Dundee.

RRS Discovery, Dundee

DON'T MISS

1   Perhaps Scotland's finest fairytale castle, **Glamis Castle** is famed for its Macbeth connections, as well as being the birthplace of the late Princess Margaret and childhood home of the late Queen Mother. Set against the backdrop of the Grampian Mountains, Glamis is an L-shaped castle built over 5-storeys in striking pink sandstone. The grounds host the Grand Scottish Proms in August each year, complete with spectacular fireworks display.

2   Angus was the heartland of the Picts, a warrior people who lived in Scotland around 2,000 years ago and left behind many intriguing monuments. **Pictavia**, at Brechin, provides a fascinating insight including hands-on exhibits and a themed play area for all the family. The small hamlet of Aberlemno, 6 miles north-east of Forfar, is famous for its intricately sculptured Pictish cross-slab in the churchyard.

3   Dundee is the perfect place for a city break, with great shopping, restaurants and nightlife. Spend a day in Dundee's vibrant and cool **Cultural Quarter** where you can indulge in speciality shopping at the Westport, visit Sensation, Dundee's Science Centre which explores the world of the senses, take in a film or an exhibition at Dundee Contemporary Arts Centre, visit Dundee's acclaimed Rep Theatre, and round it all off with a meal at one of the many restaurants and a drink at one of the city's contemporary bars.

4   Little more than half an hour's drive north of the bustling city of Dundee, a series of five picturesque valleys runs north into the heart of the Grampians and the Cairngorms National Park. Collectively known as the **Angus Glens**, they offer the perfect escape for those seeking a walk, a spot of wildlife watching, a scenic picnic or a pub lunch. Ranging from gentle and wooded (Glen Isla) to the truly awe-inspiring (Glen Clova and neighbouring Glen Doll), there is more to discover here than you can fit into a single trip.

5   Discover Dundee's polar past at **Discovery Point**. Step aboard Captain Scott's famous ship that took Scott and Shackleton to Antarctica in 1901 and come face to face with the heroes of the ice in the award-winning visitor centre.

6   In 1178 William the Lion founded the now ruined Tironensian monastery that is **Arbroath Abbey**. The abbey is famously associated with the Declaration of Arbroath, signed here in 1320, which asserted Scotland's independence from England. See the abbey at first hand and discover its story through extensive displays and interpretations at the impressive visitor centre in Arbroath.

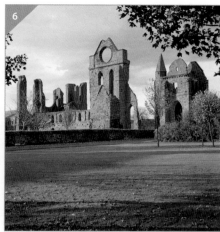

HISTORY & HERITAGE

7   **JM Barrie's Birthplace** at Kirriemuir has been carefully restored to reflect how it might have looked 150 years ago. In this anniversary year, visit the exhibition which details the life and work of the hugely talented and celebrated author, whose books include Peter Pan.

8   Learn about the great jute textile days of Dundee at **Verdant Works**. Allow the rattle and roar of the original restored machinery to take you back more than 100 years when workers toiled to create this ubiquitous product. The visitor experience is a hands-on mix of film shows, multimedia technology and interactive displays.

9   **Edzell Castle** is an elegant 16th century residence with tower house that was home to the Lindsays. The beautiful walled garden was created by Sir David Lindsay in 1604 and features an astonishing architectural framework. The 'Pleasance' is a delightful formal garden with walls decorated with sculptured stone panels, flower boxes and niches for nesting birds.

10   A journey on the **Caledonian Steam Railway** is a wonderful day out for all the family. The unique Victorian station at Brechin has lots of period charm and atmosphere, and having boarded your train, sit back and admire the views as you travel the four miles to Bridge of Dun - a frequent stopping point for royal trains.

GOLF

11   The jewel in the Angus golfing crown is the **Carnoustie Championship Course**, where Padraig Harrington made his big breakthrough in the 'Majors' when winning the 2007 British Open Championship. Tiger Woods, for one, says Carnoustie is "one of the best courses in the world if not the best".

12   **Montrose Medal Golf Course**, established in 1562, is the fifth oldest golf course in the world with a traditional links layout. At one stage in its history Montrose was the links with the greatest number of holes. When Musselburgh had only five, Montrose had five times that number. Today it has 18 and they rarely disappoint.

13   **Downfield Golf Course** is an attractive and challenging parkland course that has played host to many golfing tournaments. A final qualifying venue for the Open Championship at Carnoustie in 1999 and again in 2007, Downfield has an excellent reputation and is a golfing experience everyone should try.

14   For the perfect all round golf experience try the **Angus Golf Trail**, a collection of courses designed by James Braid. Discover some of the finest inland golf to be found anywhere in Scotland, set against a backdrop of stunning scenery.

FOOD & DRINK

15 No trip to this region would be complete without sampling a delicious Arbroath Smokie. Prepared using traditional methods dating back to the late 1800s, this unique product is safeguarded by the EU's Protected Food Name Scheme. The **But 'n Ben** in Auchmithie, just 5 miles north of Arbroath, is one of the best seafood restaurants in the area and serves as its speciality the 'smokie pancake'.

16 When visiting Angus and Dundee make sure you stop off to pick up some of the area's best local produce to take home. **Milton Haugh Farm Shop** specialises in the freshest seasonal potatoes, own reared beef and free range chickens. The Corn Kist Coffee Shop also serves up some delicious homemade meals and tempting treats.

17 Situated on the banks of the silvery Tay in the one-time fishing village of Broughty Ferry, the **Glass Pavillion** is a stunning art deco restaurant in a renovated bathing shelter from the 1930s. Whether you stop by for lunch, dinner or their famous high tea, you will be served up delicious local produce and stunning panoramic views out to the estuary.

18 **The Roundhouse Restaurant** at Lintrathen, by Kirriemuir, is an award-winning restaurant offering innovative modern menus using Angus and Perthshire produce in a peaceful rural setting. The chef is a former Master Chef of Great Britain, whose specialities include local Angus beef and game.

WILDLIFE & WALKS

19 Admire the superb panorama at **Montrose Basin**, a significant Local Nature Reserve famous for the birds that breed, feed and roost there. Learn about the wildlife and 50,000 migratory birds who visit at the Visitor Centre.

20 Take the **Seaton Cliffs Nature Trail**, a self guided trail from Arbroath into Sites of Special Scientific Interest along the top of the 400 million year old Red Sandstone cliffs - look out for striking geological formations like sea caves, natural arches and pinnacles carved by the sea, and their wealth of coastal wildlife.

21 The meadow flowers and arctic plants on the valley floor of **Glen Clova** create something of a botanist's paradise, while red deer, mountain hare, red grouse, black game, ptarmigan, peregrines and eagles all are seen regularly by wildlife watchers.

22 If you want to get out and about in the fresh air and see some of what Dundee has to offer, try out some of the themed **Dundee city centre walks** in the Dundee Walking Guide. The trails include buildings of historical significance, examples of both 19th and 20th century architecture, plus explorations of Dundee's maritime and industrial heritage. Along the routes you will pass many of Dundee's visitor attractions where you can stop en route. Pick up a guide in the VisitScotland Information Centre, Dundee.

Guest Houses and B&Bs

Arbroath
Brucefield Boutique B&B
Open: All year **Map Ref: 2E1**

★★★★★
BED AND BREAKFAST

Brucefield Boutique B&B, Cliffburn Road, Arbroath, Angus, DD11 5BS
T: +44(0)1241 875393 E: info@brucefieldbandb.com W: brucefieldbandb.com

Indicated Prices:

Single	from £85.00 per room	Twin	from £90.00 per room
Double	from £90.00 per room	Junior Suite	from £100.00 per room

86788

Brechin
Blibberhill Farmhouse
Open: All year **Map Ref: 2D1**

★★★
FARM HOUSE

Blibberhill Farm, Aberlemno, Brechin, Angus, DD9 6TH
T: 01307 830323 E: wendysstewart@aol.com W: blibberhill.co.uk

Indicated Prices:

Single	from £30.00	Twin	from £26.00 per person
Double	from £26.00 per person	Family	from £26.00 per person

15458

by Forfar, Letham
Jean Stewart
Open: All year **Map Ref: 2D1**

★★★
BED AND BREAKFAST

Woodville, 13A Guthrie Street, Letham, nr Forfar, DD8 2PS
T: 01307 818090

Indicated Prices:

Single	from £30.00 per room	Twin	from £56.00 per room

64616

Angus and Dundee

Kirriemuir
Crepto Bed and Breakfast
Open: All year **Map Ref: 2C1**

★★
BED AND BREAKFAST

1 Kinnordy Place, Kirriemuir, Angus, DD8 4JW
T: 01575 572746 E: david@jessma.wanadoo.co.uk

Indicated Prices:

Single	from £28.00 per room	Twin	from £56.00 per room
Double	from £56.00 per room		

21262

by Kirriemuir
Falls of Holm Bed & Breakfast
Open: All year **Map Ref: 2C1**

★★★★
BED AND BREAKFAST

Falls of Holm, Kingoldrum, Angus, DD8 5HY
T: 01575 575867 E: fallsofholm@btinternet.com W: fallsofholm.com

Indicated Prices:

Single	from £35.00	Twin	from £30.00 per person
Double	from £30.00 per person	Family	from £30.00 per person

25588

Montrose
Eskview Farm B&B
Open: All year **Map Ref: 4F12**

★★★★
BED AND BREAKFAST

St Cyrus, Montrose, Angus, DD10 0AQ
T: 01674 830890 E: kathsdanes@aol.com W: eskviewfarm.co.uk

Indicated Prices:

Single	from £35.00 per room	Twin	from £55.00 per room
Double	from £55.00 per room	Family	from £70.00 per room

25115

Montrose
Oaklands Guest House
Open: All year excl Xmas & New Year **Map Ref: 4F12**

★★★
GUEST HOUSE

10 Rossie Island Road, Montrose, Angus, DD10 9NN
T: 01674 672018 E: oaklands1@btopenworld.com W: nebsnow.com/oaklands

Indicated Prices:

Single	from £35.00 per room	Twin	from £60.00 per room
Double	from £60.00 per room	Family	from £75.00 per room

48017

Important: Prices stated are estimates and may be subject to amendments. Prices are per person per night unless otherwise stated.

Self Catering and Camping & Caravan Parks

Arbroath
No 8 The Shore
Open: All year Map Ref: 2D1

★★★★
SELF CATERING

Arbroath, Angus, DD11 1PB
T: 01241 879111 (Eve & wk/end 01738 621347)
E: petermacdougall@btconnect.com W: sunseafreshholidays.eu.com
1 Apartment   3 Bedrooms   Sleeps 1-6
Prices – Apartment:
£446.00-£725.00   Per Week
Short breaks available

79173

Dundee
Sanctuary Management Services
Open: July & August Map Ref: 2C2

★★
SELF CATERING

Seabraes Flats, Seabraes Court, Dundee, DD1 4LA
T: 01382 383111 E: enquiries-dundee@sanctuary-housing.co.uk W: scotland2000.com/seabraes
12 Apartments   7 Bedrooms   Sleeps 8
Prices – Apartments:
£455.00-£784.00   Per Week
Short breaks available

70027

Kirriemuir
The Crowe's Nest
Open: All year Map Ref: 2C1

★★
SELF CATERING

Annfield, 16 Woodend Drive, Northmuir, Kirriemuir, DD8 4TF
T: 01575 573604 E: ncrowe22@tiscali.co.uk
1 Guest Unit   1 Bedroom   Sleeps 1-2
Prices – Guest Unit:
£140.00-£200.00   Per Week
Short breaks available

58735

Pittenweem, East Neuk of Fife

Kingdom of Fife

The ancient Kingdom of Fife has always been at the heart of Scottish history and still cherishes its wealth of castles, palaces, cathedrals and gardens. A relaxing atmosphere prevails throughout Fife, from the delightful fishing villages of the East Neuk to St Andrews - the golfing centre of the world - and from the rolling hills of the Howe of Fife to the historic capital of Dunfermline.

If you're a golfer, the ancient Kingdom of Fife will be a powerful draw. Every serious golfer wants to play the Old Course at St Andrews at least once in a lifetime and, thanks to a public allocation of rounds each day, you can. There are also more than 45 other fantastic courses in Fife to put your game to the test.

For keen walkers, one of the great ways to explore Fife is on foot. The Fife Coastal Path takes in some truly delightful places and you'll get to relax on some of the best beaches in the country – with four of Scotland's five Blue Flag beaches on the delightful Fife coastline.

Whether you're looking for a relaxing break or an action-packed adventure, Fife has a huge variety of things to see and do. Whatever you're looking for, whenever you come, the Kingdom of Fife will live long in your memory.

Kayaking, Fife

DON'T MISS

1 Fife boasts some of Scotland's finest and cleanest sandy **beaches**, great for peaceful strolls or quiet contemplation. The area is home to four of Scotland's five Blue Flag award-winning strands; namely Aberdour, Burntisland, Elie Woodhouse and St Andrews West Sands.

2 Suitable for both recreational and serious walkers, the **Fife Coastal Path** is a 150km (93mile) walk, which weaves along the stunning coastline of Fife. Passing rugged cliffs, golden beaches, historic buildings and wildlife-rich estuaries along the way, this is a walk of great variety, from the quaint hustle and bustle of the fishing villages to the serenity of a deserted beach.

3 A prosperous university town and Mecca for golfers from across the world, **St Andrews** is one of Scotland's top attractions. Situated above two of the country's finest sandy beaches, there is a real medieval feel to the town's cobbled streets and closes, reinforced by the presence of a ruined cathedral dating from 1180 and a castle founded around 1200.

4 There's a whole host of **visitor attractions** to keep you thoroughly entertained on a trip to Fife. Experience a slice of history at Aberdour Castle or Falkland Palace or perhaps dive in to some family-favourite attractions at Deep Sea World and the St Andrews Aquarium.

5 Travel through the quaint fishing villages of the **East Neuk of Fife** and you travel back through time. This corner of Fife is filled with traditional cottages with red pantile roofs and crow-stepped gable ends which appear unchanged from a bygone age. Fishing boats lie at rest in the harbours following the bustle of unloading their catch. Between communities lie unspoilt stretches of sandy beach, perfect for walks and picnics.

6 2010 sees **The Open Championship** return to St Andrews for the 28th time. Watch some of the world's golfing greats compete for the honour of raising the Claret Jug.

WALKING

7   Dominating the skyline of central Fife, the **Lomond Hills** are one of the area's most popular walking destinations. The regional park which encompasses the hills extends over 65 square miles and provides ample opportunity for both moderate and more challenging walking experiences with spectacular vistas over the surrounding countryside.

8   Follow the Fife Coastal Path signs for an enjoyable 8km walk from **Ravenscraig to Leven**. Head past the cliff-top ruins of Ravenscraig Castle, through the picturesque fishing village of Dysart, past the fringes of Chapel Woods through the coastal villages of West and East Wemyss. Explore the wondrous Wemyss Caves with their prehistoric markings then climb the hill to reach the ruins of Macduff Castle and enjoy some excellent views of the coast to end your walk.

9   The **Isle of May**, accessible via the May Princess from Anstruther in spring and summer, provides nesting sites for 200,000 seabirds, including more than 100,000 puffins from May to July alone. In autumn, thousands of grey seals come ashore here to pup.

10   Culross and the immediate vicinity are rich in historical interest. The **Culross Town Walk**, starting west of the town, passes by a malthouse, tollbooth, mercat cross, abbeyhouse and various other points of historical interest. All are worth further exploration.

BEACHES & GOLF   **visitscotland.com/golf**

11   The long stretches of golden sandy beaches at **Elie** are undoubtedly some of the best in the East Neuk. From summer cricket matches on the beachfront to long, peaceful strolls to watch the sunset, this is an idyllic spot not to be missed.

12   The sand dunes and beach at the mouth of the Tay estuary are home to **Tentsmuir** - one of Scotland's National Nature Reserves. This dynamic coastline is important for waders and wildfowl, common and grey seals, ducks and seaduck, and colourful butterflies that light up the grassland and dunes in summer. It is truly one of Scotland's most magical coastlines and well worth a visit.

13   Recognised across the world as the Home of Golf - the **Old Course** in St Andrews is where it all began and it still remains a real test for today's champions. To play on these hallowed fairways and greens is a dream come true for golf fans and an unforgettable experience. Book well in advance to avoid disappointment.

14   As well as the iconic Old Course, the Kingdom of Fife boasts more than 45 wonderful **golf courses**, each offering something different for the visiting golfer. Try the testing challenges of the Open Qualifying courses, choose from links or parkland, 9 or 18 holes. Golf is a way of life in the Kingdom of Fife and there is something for everyone.

FOOD & DRINK

15   A great way to get a taste of Fife's finest fresh produce is to visit the weekly **Farmers' Markets**. Held at a different location every Saturday, the market is the perfect place to get a real taste of the region, from fine artisan cheese to delicious meat and fresh seafood.

16   **The Inn at Lathones**, near St Andrews, is a coaching inn with a history stretching as far back as 400 years. The restaurant continues to welcome travellers with a tempting menu featuring the best of local produce transformed into mouth-watering gourmet delights.

17   **Cairnie Fruit Farm** is a family-run business in Cupar, renowned throughout Fife for producing top quality fruit for picking. Raspberries, blackberries, redcurrants, gooseberries and tayberries are all found in abundance here. And the Cairnie Mega Maze provides entertainment for the children!

18   No trip to Fife is complete without a trip to the multi award-winning **Anstruther Fish Bar & Restaurant**. Voted Seafish Fish & Chip Shop of the Year 2008/09, they serve only the freshest prime quality seafood, offering a true taste of Scotland.

HISTORY & HERITAGE

19   **Dunfermline's** royal and monastic past dominates the town. This former capital of Scotland and birthplace of James I and Charles I, boasts a royal palace and a 12th century abbey, which is the final resting place of Robert the Bruce and the burial site of 11 other Scottish kings and queens.

20   **Aberdour Castle** was built by the Douglas Family in the 13th century and has been added to throughout the centuries, creating a wonderful mix of styles. Situated in the delightful village of the same name, the Castle boasts fine painted ceilings, galleries, a beehive shaped doocot as well as a delightful walled garden only recently uncovered.

21   The **Royal Palace of Falkland** was the countryside residence of Stuart kings and queens when they hunted deer and wild boar in the forests of Fife - and a favourite childhood playground of Mary, Queen of Scots. The Palace was built in the 1500s by James IV and James V, replacing an earlier castle from the 12th century. The current spacious garden, dating from the mid-20th century, houses the original Royal Tennis Court – the oldest in Britain still in use – built in 1539.

Kingdom of Fife

Hotels

Dunfermline
Davaar House Hotel & Restaurant
Open: All year excl 24-26 Dec   **Map Ref: 2B4**

Experience Davaar's homely atmosphere, enjoy the hospitality, comfortable rooms and excellent cooking using fresh local produce. Central location for golf in Fife, Knockhill race track, Edinburgh and St Andrews are within easy reach. Come and enjoy a relaxing break or business stay. We look forward to welcoming you to Davaar House.

★★★
SMALL HOTEL

126 Grieve Street, Dunfermline, Fife, KY12 8DW
T: 01383 721886 E: enquiries@davaar-house-hotel.com W: davaar-house-hotel.com

Indicated Prices:

Single	from £65.00 per room	Twin	from £95.00 per room
Double	from £95.00 per room	Family	from £140.00 per room

22219

Dunfermline
Holiday Inn Express Dunfermline
Open: All year excl 24-26 Dec   **Map Ref: 2B4**

★★★
METRO HOTEL

Halbeath Road, Dunfermline, KY11 8DY
T: 01383 748220 E: info@hiexpressdunfermline.co.uk W: hiexpressdunfermline.co.uk

Indicated Prices:

Single	from £49.00 per room	Twin	from £49.00 per room
Double	from £49.00 per room	Family	from £49.00 per room

68058

Important: Prices stated are estimates and may be subject to amendments. Prices are per person per night unless otherwise stated.

Freuchie
Lomond Hills Hotel & Leisure Centre

Open: All year

Map Ref: 2C3

Situated in idyllic countryside only 20 minutes from St Andrews, five minutes from Ladybank Station and 40 minutes from Edinburgh Airport. Family owned and run with 24 en-suite bedrooms. Friendly bar and lounge areas. Real ale and 50 malt whiskies. Superb food. Indoor swimming pool, sauna spa and fully equipped gym.

★★★
HOTEL

High Street, Freuchie, Cupar, Fife, KY15 7EY
T: 01337 857329 E: reception@lomondhillshotel.com W: lomondhillshotel.com

Indicated Prices:

Single	from £49.95 per room	Twin	from £79.95 per room
Double	from £79.95 per room	Family	from £89.95 per room

36274

Glenrothes
Gilvenbank Hotel

Open: All year

Map Ref: 2C3

★★★
HOTEL

Huntsman's Road, Glenrothes, Fife, KY7 6NT
T: 01592 742077 E: gilvenbankhotel@btconnect.com W: gilvenbankhotel.com

Indicated Prices:

Single	from £55.00 per room	Twin	from £55.00 per room
Double	from £55.00 per room	Family	from £55.00 per room

73135

For a full listing of Quality Assured accommodation, please see directory at back of this guide.

THE **BAY** HOTEL

Simply Breathtaking

Part of the Pettycur Bay Holiday Park

"The Bay Hotel Offers Innovative Luxurious Accommodation In A Truly Unique Setting"

MAIN HOTEL FEATURES INCLUDE

27 bedrooms all individually designed with luxurious en-suite facilities.

South facing suites accommodating up to a family of six.

Split level rooms with balconies with fabulous views over the River Forth to Edinburgh.

Widescreen LCD TVs with movies on demand.

Swimming pool with water features and jacuzzi. Steam room and sauna.

Children's soft play area. Snooker and pool tables.

The Bay Hotel, Burntisland Road, Kinghorn
Tel : 01592 892222 Fax : 01592 892206
EMail Address : thebay@pettycur.co.uk Web : www.thebayhotel.net

79438

Important: Prices stated are estimates and may be subject to amendments. Prices are per person per night unless otherwise stated.

St Andrews
The Albany Hotel

Open: All year excl Xmas & New Year

Map Ref: 2D2

★★★
METRO HOTEL

56/58 North Street, St Andrews, KY16 9AH
T: 01334 477737 E: enqu@thealbanystandrews.co.uk W: thealbanystandrews.co.uk

Indicated Prices:

Single	from £35.00 per room	Twin	from £70.00 per room
Double	from £70.00 per room	Suite	from £160.00 per room
		Family	from £125.00 per room

11413

St Andrews
West Port Bar & Kitchen

Open: All year

Map Ref: 2D2

★★★
INN

170 South Street, St Andrews, KY16 9EG
T: 01334 473186 E: westport@maclay.co.uk W: maclay.com

Indicated Prices:

Single	from £55.00 per room	Twin	from £45.00 per person
Double	from £45.00 per person		

77060

Guest Houses and B&Bs

Anstruther
Bunty Ritchie

Open: Apr-Sep

Map Ref: 2D3

★★★
BED AND BREAKFAST

32 Glenogil Gardens, Anstruther, Fife, KY10 3ET
T: 01333 310697/07826 011116

Indicated Prices:

Double	from £50.00 per room	Suite	from £100.00

60378

For a full listing of Quality Assured accommodation, please see directory at back of this guide.

191

Crail
Caiplie House

Open: All year

Map Ref: 2D3

★★★
GUEST HOUSE

53 High Street North, Crail, Fife, KY10 3RA
T: 01333 450564 E: mail@caipliehouse.co.uk W: caipliehouse.co.uk

Indicated Prices:

Single	from £35.00	Twin	from £30.00
Double	from £30.00	Family	from £30.00

17390

Dunfermline
Clarke Cottage Guest House

Open: All year

Map Ref: 2B4

Located in the ancient capital and yet only 30 minutes from Edinburgh city centre, Clarke Cottage offers private accommodation with separate guest entrance and off-street parking. All nine bedrooms have en-suite facilities, central heating, double glazing, colour television, mini-bar etc. A comfortable residents lounge and dining conservatory add to the ambience.

★★★
GUEST HOUSE

139 Halbeath Road, Dunfermline, Fife, KY11 4LA
T: 01383 735935 E: clarkecottage@ukonline.co.uk W: clarkecottageguesthouse.co.uk

Indicated Prices:

Single	from £36.00 per person	Twin	from £30.00 per person
Double	from £30.00 per person		

19522

by Glenrothes, Star of Markinch
Priory Star B&B

Open: All year excl 16 Dec-16 Jan

Map Ref: 2C3

★★★★
BED AND BREAKFAST

The Priory, East End, Star of Markinch, Glenrothes, Fife, KY7 6LQ
T: 01592 754566 E: priorystarbb@aol.com W: priorystar.com

Indicated Prices:

Single	from £26.00 per person	Twin	from £26.00 per person
Double	from £26.00 per person	Family	from £26.00 per person

60113

Important: Prices stated are estimates and may be subject to amendments. Prices are per person per night unless otherwise stated.

Lundin Links
Sandilands

Open: Mar-Nov

Map Ref: 2D3

★★★★
BED AND BREAKFAST

20 Leven Road, Lundin Links, Fife, KY8 6AH
T: 01333 329881 E: info@sandilandsfife.co.uk W: sandilandsfife.co.uk

Indicated Prices:

Single	from £40.00 per room	Twin	from £60.00 per room
Double	from £55.00 per room		

52967

Markinch
Mrs C Craig

Open: Mar-Nov

Map Ref: 2C3

★★★
BED AND BREAKFAST

Shythrum Farm, Markinch, KY7 6HB
T: 01592 758372 E: ccraig2009@hotmail.co.uk

Indicated Prices:

Single	from £30.00 per person	Twin	from £25.00 per person
Double	from £25.00 per person	Family	from £25.00 per person

57456

St Andrews
Arran House

Open: All year excl Xmas

Map Ref: 2D2

★★★
GUEST HOUSE

5 Murray Park, St Andrews, KY16 9AW
E: jmgmcgrory@btinternet.com W: arranhousestandrews.co.uk

Indicated Prices:

Single	from £45.00	Twin	from £80.00
Double	from £80.00	Family	from £90.00

74178

St Andrews
Yorkston Guest House

Open: Apr-Nov

Map Ref: 2D2

★★★
GUEST HOUSE

68 & 70 Argyle Street, St Andrews, Fife, KY16 9BU
T: 01334 472019 E: yorkstonhouse@aol.com W: yorkstonguesthouse.co.uk

Indicated Prices:

Single	from £40.00 per room	Twin	from £80.00 per room
Double	from £80.00 per room	Family	from £110.00 per room

64810

For a full listing of Quality Assured accommodation, please see directory at back of this guide.

193

St Andrews
The Humble Rowan B&B

Open: All year

Map Ref: 2D2

AWAITING GRADING

29 Irvine Crescent, St Andrews
T: 01334 475322/07979 012175 E: thehumblerowan@hotmail.co.uk W: thehumblerowan.com

Indicated Prices:

Double	from £50.00 per room	Twin/Family	from £50.00 per room

Reductions 3 nights or more

V

84387

by St Andrews, Balmullo
Hayston Farm Guest House

Open: All year

Map Ref: 2D2

★★★
BED AND BREAKFAST

Balmullo, St Andrews, KY16 0AJ
T: 01334 870210 E: info@haystonfarm.com W: haystonfarm.com

Indicated Prices:

Single	from £40.00 per person	Twin	from £27.50 per person
Double	from £27.50 per person	Family	from £27.50 per person

Children up to 5 years free; 6-15 years 50% discount

29797

by St Andrews, Strathkinness
Hilltop Bed & Breakfast

Open: All year

Map Ref: 2D2

★★★
BED AND BREAKFAST

1 Main Street, Strathkinness, Fife, KY16 9RX
T: 01334 850667/07719 533226 E: kirstiehastie@btinternet.com W: enquiries@hilltopb-b.co.uk

Indicated Prices:

Single	from £40.00 per person	Twin	from £35.00 per person
Double	from £35.00 per person		

85322

Self Catering and Camping & Caravan Parks

Crail
Sauchope Links Caravan Park
Open: Mar-Oct **Map Ref: 2D3**

★★★★★
HOLIDAY PARK

Crail, KY10 3XJ
T: 01333 450460 E: info@sauchope.co.uk W: sauchope.co.uk

Park accommodates 50 pitches. Total touring pitches: 50.
Prices per pitch:
(50) from £9.50 (50) from £9.50 (50) from £9.50

Thistle

34950

Elie
Elie Letting
Open: All year **Map Ref: 2D3**

★★★★
SELF CATERING

The Park, Bank Street, Elie, KY9 1BW
T: 01333 330219 E: elieletting@btinternet.com W: elielet.com

| 2 Cottages | 1-4 Bedrooms | Sleeps 2-8 |
| 3 Apartments | 1-4 Bedrooms | Sleeps 2-10 |

Prices – Cottages: **Apartments:**
£180.00-£900.00 Per Week £180.00-£900.00 Per Week
Short breaks available

24765

Freuchie
Creag-Ny-Baa
Open: All year **Map Ref: 2C3**

★★★
SELF CATERING

Creag-Ny-Baa, East End, Freuchie, Fife, KY15 7ET
T: 07946 304674 E: alisonsscottishcottages@btinternet.com W: alisons-scottish-cottages.com

| 1 Cottage | 2 Bedrooms | Sleeps 2-4 |

Prices – Cottage:
£310.00-£450.00 Per Week
Short breaks available

79190

For a full listing of Quality Assured accommodation, please see directory at back of this guide.

195

Lundin Links
Woodland Gardens Caravan & Camping
Open: Apr-Oct **Map Ref: 2D3**

★★★★
HOLIDAY PARK

Blindwell Road, Lundin Links, Leven, Fife, KY8 5QG
T: 01333 360319 E: enquiries@woodland-gardens.co.uk W: woodland-gardens.co.uk
Turn north off A915 (Kirkcaldy-Leven-St Andrews road) at east end of Lundin Links signposted on the A915 by international C&C signs.
Park accommodates 10 pitches. Total touring pitches: 10.
Prices per pitch:
🚐 (10) £15.00–£20.00
⛺ (5) £15.00–£20.00
🚏 (5) £15.00–£20.00

Holiday Caravans for Hire:
🚐 (2) £250.00–£395.00 per week. Sleeps 2-4.

64531

by Lundin Links
Letham Feus Park Ltd
Open: Mar-Oct **Map Ref: 2C3**

★★★★★
HOLIDAY PARK

Cupar Road, nr Lundin Links, KY8 5NT
T: 01333 351900 E: info@largoleisure.co.uk W: largoleisure.co.uk

Holiday Caravans for Hire:
🚐 (4) £149.00 per week. Sleeps 6 max.
3 nights from £105.00.

Thistle

35332

Pittenweem
Kilheugh Cottage
Open: Apr-Oct **Map Ref: 2D3**

★★
SELF CATERING

18 Bruce's Wynd, Pittenweem, KY10 2PW
T: 01357 520463 E: john.macgillivray@btopenworld.com

| 1 Cottage | 1 Bedroom | Sleeps 2/3 |

Prices – Cottage:
£235.00–£270.00   Per Week

Short breaks available

33780

Important: Prices stated are estimates and may be subject to amendments. Prices are per person per night unless otherwise stated.

St Andrews
Dron Court

Open: All year   **Map Ref: 2D2**

Dron Court is an attractive steading conversion set in two acres of gardens overlooking the Eden Valley close to St Andrews. There are six houses and cottages ranging from one to four bedrooms sleeping two to eight persons.

★★★ UP TO ★★★★
SELF CATERING

Dron Court, St Andrews, KY16 9YA
T: 0141 616 3491 E: jinglis@dron8.freeserve.co.uk W: droncourt.com

4 Cottages	1-3 Bedrooms	Sleeps 1-5
2 Houses	4 Bedrooms	Sleeps 1-8

Prices – Cottages:		Houses:	
£290.00-£510.00	Per Week	£460.00-£675.00	Per Week

Short breaks available in cottages

23207

St Andrews
Dr John Murchison Lovett

Open: Jun-mid Sept   **Map Ref: 2D2**

★★★★
SELF CATERING

The Auld Hoose, 1 Shorehead, St Andrews, KY16 9RG
T: 07748 700458/0141 943 1990 E: johnlovett@johnlovett.plus.com

1 House	3 Bedrooms	Sleeps 1-6

Prices – House:	
£650.00-£910.00	Per Week

79509

For a full listing of Quality Assured accommodation, please see directory at back of this guide.

197

St Andrews
St Andrews Country Cottages

Open: All year

Map Ref: 2C2

A super selection of high quality self-catering properties in the St Andrews area. Elegant town houses, country cottages, farmhouses or apartments in a Georgian country house. Sleeping from 4 to 14. Ideal for those who want to relax, escape or explore.

★★★ UP TO ★★★★
SELF CATERING

Mr Patrick Wedderburn, Mountquhanie Estate, by Cupar, Fife, KY15 4QJ
T: 01382 330318 E: enquiries@standrews-cottages.com W: standrews-cottages.com

18 Cottages	Bedrooms	Sleeps 4-14
2 Houses	Bedrooms	Sleeps 8
3 Apartments	Bedrooms	Sleeps 4-9

Prices – Cottages:		Houses:		Apartments:	
£195.00-£2195.00	Per Week	£295.00-£835.00	Per Week	£195.00-£695.00	Per Week

Short breaks available

55709

Looking along West Sands towards the town, St Andrews, Fife

Important: Prices stated are estimates and may be subject to amendments. Prices are per person per night unless otherwise stated.

St Andrews
Kingask Country Cottages

Open: All year

Map Ref: 2D3

★★★
SELF CATERING

**Kingask House,
St Andrews, Fife, KY16 8PN**
T: 01334 472011
E: info@kingask-cottages.co.uk
W: kingask-cottages.co.uk

Features:
- Secure private gardens
- Private parking
- Children's play areas
- Excellent walking from the doorstep
- Pets welcome – short breaks available

Indicated Prices:

18 Properties	Sleeps 2-19	Bedrooms 1-9
£275.00-£1,750.00		per week

33998

Exclusive self catering properties in and around St Andrews, Kingsbarns and Crail (sleeps 2-19 – can accommodate groups up to 26).

The houses make an ideal base from which to discover Fife, tour the rest of Scotland, play the world famous golf courses, or just relax in peaceful and welcoming surroundings.

Many are in coastal locations offering spectacular sea views.

Situated only an hour's drive from Edinburgh or Perth, and less than two hours from Glasgow, Stirling or Aberdeen.

For a full listing of Quality Assured accommodation, please see directory at back of this guide.

199

St Andrews
Cambo Estate

Open: All year

Map Ref: 2D3

★★★
SELF CATERING

116 H Market Street, St Andrews, KY16 8QD
T: 01333 450313 E: cambo@camboestate.com W: camboestate.com

1 Bungalow   2 Bedrooms   Sleeps 1-3

Prices – Bungalow:
£350.00-£610.00   Per Week
Short breaks available

78281

Food & Drink

Dunfermline
Davaar House Hotel & Restaurant

Open: All year

Map Ref: 2B4

★★★
SMALL HOTEL

**Culinary Type:
SCOTTISH**

126 Grieve Street, Dunfermline,
Fife, KY12 8DW
T: 01383 721886
E: enquiries@davaar-house-hotel.com
W: davaar-house-hotel.com

Best For:
• Kids and families • Special occasion
• Group dining

Prices:
Starter from: £4.25
Main Course from: £10.50
Dessert from: £5.25

Opening Times:
Dinner from 1800, last orders 2045.

Experience Davaar's warm welcome and homely atmosphere. Sample freshly prepared soups, pate, hand dived scallops and delicious homemade puddings. All main dishes are cooked to order using our finest fresh local produce. Relax after dinner in the comfortable lounge for coffee or sample one of our fine Scottish malts.

22219

The gardens of Falkland Palace, Falkland

For a full listing of Quality Assured accommodation, please see directory at back of this guide.

201

Gardenstown

ABERDEEN CITY AND SHIRE

There is so much to discover in Aberdeen City and Shire, whatever season you decide to visit. From exploring the region's fascinating history and heritage to getting out into the beautiful mountains and glens of the Cairngorms National Park.

A cosmopolitan and thriving city, Aberdeen strikes the perfect balance for visitors. Find yourself exploring the many museums and galleries in the morning, taking in the striking architecture and stopping along some of the many blooming gardens along the way.

When it comes to retail therapy, there is plenty to choose from. Union Street is the main city centre street with large shopping malls nearby such as The Bon Accord Centre, St Nicholas Centre, The Academy and The Mall to keep you in shopping heaven for hours. Don't miss the newly opened Union Square, which offers a cosmopolitan shopping, dining and entertainment environment in the heart of the city.

This region is renowned for its lush and fertile lands which offer the ideal conditions for growing quality produce. You'll find outstanding restaurants, cafes and pubs; their chefs proudly serving the very best in both traditional local dishes and international flavours. Sample the very best of the region's specialties, including delicious Aberdeen Angus beef, fresh seafood, organic fruit and vegetables and wonderful local dishes, such as cullen skink, butteries or rowies.

Aberdeen City and Shire is famous for its beautiful coastline; the beach is just moments from the city centre while a tour of the picturesque fishing villages, which offer a wonderful insight into the region's maritime history, is a must. The bustling city meanwhile quickly gives way to the vast open

To find out more go to visitscotland.com

landscapes of Scotland's largest national park, the Cairngorms.

Explore this beautiful countryside and find out why the wild valley of Royal Deeside has been a favourite holiday destination of the Royals for over 150 years. You can even choose to follow the Victorian Heritage Trail through the towns, landmarks, beauty spots and attractions which have a special connection to Queen Victoria. Discover for yourself the likes of Banchory, Aboyne, Ballater and Braemar, which all come with their own individual charms.

Known as Castle Country, you could spend days touring the cream of the region's many castles and historic houses and still not see them all. From Dunnottar Castle, a dramatic ruined clifftop fortress just south of Stonehaven, to the mysterious - and reputedly haunted - Fyvie Castle, each castle has a different story to tell. And don't forget to visit Slain's Castle at Cruden Bay; allegedly the inspiration behind Bram Stoker's Dracula.

No matter what time of year you decide to visit there's something exciting on. Aberdeen City and Shire has a packed programme of events all year round. Literary luminaries arrive in May for Word 2010, the University of Aberdeen Writers Festival, Scotland's proud maritime heritage is celebrated in July at the Scottish Traditional Boat Festival in Portsoy and there are Highland Games galore at the Braemar Gathering in September. And for something completely different at Hogmanay, perhaps bring in the New Year at the remarkable Stonehaven Fireball Festival.

Ornate building in Union Street, Aberdeen City

What's On?

COAST Festival of the Visual Arts
28 May-30 May 2010
An annual weekend of events taking place in the beautiful coastal towns of Banff & Macduff. Discover exhibitions, art installations, workshops, film screenings and a local food fair.
www.coastfestival.org.uk

Word 2010 - University of Aberdeen Writers Festival
14-16 May 2010
A packed programme of reading, lectures and debates as well as musical events, art exhibitions and film screenings.
abdn.ac.uk/word

The Scottish Traditional Boat Festival, Portsoy
26-27 June 2010
A great family weekend event with one of the largest collections of traditional boats in Scotland. Enjoy maritime crafts, local food, music, dance, drama, a road run and much, much more.
scottishtraditionalboatfestival.co.uk

Aberdeen International Youth Festival
28 July-7 August 2010
An energetic and colourful celebration of youthful creativity and innovation - expect a mix of entertainment showcasing the talents of young in locations across the city.
aiyf.org

Braemar Gathering
4 September 2010
Traditional Highland Games where you can witness the likes of tossing the caber, throwing the hammer, piping and highland dancing.
braemargathering.org

Stonehaven Fireball Festival
31 December 2010
A spectacular and ancient Fireball Ceremony, in which the locals parade through Stonehaven swinging flaming balls of fire before throwing them into the harbour.
stonehavenfireballs.co.uk

All dates correct at time of publication. Please check before booking. VisitScotland cannot be held responsible for any inaccuracies

203

DON'T MISS

1 Be sure to explore the ruins of **Dunnottar Castle**, a spectacular cliff-top fortress with beautiful seascape views. The castle, just south of Stonehaven, was graced by the presence of both William Wallace and Mary Queen of Scots, offers a captivating insight into Scotland's rich history.

2 **Royal Deeside** is a stunning area of natural beauty and majestic scenery combining mountains, woodland, river and quaint rural towns and villages. Home to the Royal residence of Balmoral, for over 150 years the Royal Family have chosen to holiday here and it's no surprise that visitors every year follow suit.

3 Explore the elegant marble-lined interior of **Aberdeen Art Gallery**, which hosts a varied collection of works of art, from outstanding examples of Modern Art and work by the Scottish Colourists to the exciting programme of special exhibitions and events.

4 The **David Welch Winter Garden** at Duthie Park is one of Aberdeen's top attractions. Visit at any time of year and find yourself surrounded by rare and exotic plants from around the world. Highlights include the Corridor of Perfumes, Victorian Corridor and Japanese Garden.

5 **Loch Muick** on the Balmoral Estate is a beautiful spot for walking and is perfect for spotting local wildlife, including red squirrel, red deer and capercaillie. Look out for Glas-allt Shiel, a royal bothy built by Queen Victoria, which sits in a small pine plantation and can be accessed via the footpath that runs around the loch.

6 From its days as a lively fishing port to its current status as Europe's North Sea oil capital, Aberdeen's historic relationship with the sea is brought to life at the five-star **Aberdeen Maritime Museum**. Located in the city's historic Shiprow area, this attraction enjoys spectacular views over the busy harbour.

WALKING

7   **Bennachie** is one of the most popular hill ranges in the north east of Scotland, which guarantees magnificent panoramic views of Aberdeenshire and beyond. Starting at the Bennachie Visitor Centre, there are several marked paths, including the fairly easy ascents to the peaks of Oxen Craig and Mither Tap.

8   Park at Kirkhill Forest car park on the outskirts of Aberdeen city and take a woodland walk up **Tyrebagger Hill**. There are two waymarked walks - one short trail through a beautiful set of beech trees and another longer trail taking in a range of woodland sculptures along the way. This area is also very popular with mountain bikers.

9   Follow the **Deeside Railway Line** from Ballater to Dinnet through changing scenery of birch, pine and heather for wonderful views of River Dee and the elegant white suspension bridge at Cambus O'May. The beautiful, flat walk starts at the Old Royal Station in Ballater, where you can find information on its 100 year history of Royal use, including a unique royal waiting room built for Queen Victoria.

10   To discover some of the famous Aberdeenshire coast and a huge diversity of both bird and plant life, take a walk from **Forvie Sands to Collieston**. This starts at the estuary of the River Ythan and over sand dunes to the seashore, before following a cliff path to the old village of Collieston. The inland return route passes through the Forvie National Nature Reserve.

HISTORY & HERITAGE

11   **Provost Skene's House** is an elegant 16th century town house which contains an attractive series of period room settings, recalling the graceful furnishings of earlier times. The displays include a suite of 17th century rooms, a Regency Parlour and an Edwardian Nursery.

12   The historic north east of Scotland is home to around a thousand castles or castle ruins, providing a wealth of history to explore. Aberdeenshire is home to Scotland's only **castle trail**. Follow the signs and discover 13 unique castles, explore walled gardens and perhaps stop at a traditional tearoom along the way.

13   Deep in the heart of north-east Scotland, in the beautiful former home of prominent Scottish artist, Sir George Reid, discover the **The Gordon Highlanders Museum**. Preserving the 200-year legacy of this regiment, the Museum hosts a huge selection of artefacts, from armoury and regimental treasures to photographs and sketches.

14   The **Museum of Scottish Lighthouses**, in Fraserburgh, celebrates the first lighthouse built on mainland Scotland. The highlight of a visit is a guided tour to Kinnaird Head lighthouse.

FOOD & DRINK

15 Learn about the history of **Dean's of Huntly** shortbread through storyboards and a video presentation. See the factory at work, relax and savour home baking delights in the café and pick up some 'melt in the mouth' shortbread in the 5-star gift shop.

16 Aberdeenshire is famous for its **distilleries** and makes much of this rich legacy. Visit Glen Garioch Distillery in the village of Old Meldrum, one of the oldest working distilleries in the region, which takes its name from the valley of the Garioch - traditionally the finest barley growing area of Scotland. Another must-see is Royal Lochnagar Distillery, which is nestled beautifully on the north side of the Dee next to Balmoral Castle.

17 **Taste of Grampian**, a one-day food and drink festival on Saturday 5 June 2010, is a great day out for all the family. This popular annual event allows visitors to discover and sample the wide range of high quality food and drink products from the Grampian larder, with demonstrations by local and celebrity chefs.

18 This region is renowned for the variety and quality of its food and drink. Meet a huge range of local producers at one of the many **farmers' markets** and discover fresh, seasonal produce. Each has their own story to tell - a new recipe, organic produce, artisan food and crafts and, of course, a passion for these fine products.

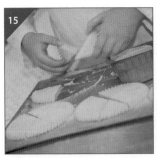

ADVENTURE

19 The ski centres at **Glenshee** and **The Lecht** are in some of Scotland's most inspiring scenery. The largest resort in the UK, Glenshee straddles the Aberdeenshire/Perthshire border and covers an area of more than 2,000 acres, four mountains and three valleys. Offering some of the most consistent snow in Scotland and a range of outdoor activities during the summer months, The Lecht is based in the eastern Cairngorms.

20 With its unspoilt, rugged seascape, big waves, winding rivers and lochs, Aberdeenshire is the ideal location for a variety of **watersports**. Try sailing around the beautiful coastline, windsurfing at Aberdeen's beachfront or even surfing at Banff.

21 For hillwalking and climbing discover **Lochnagar**, a majestic mountain found in the royal estate of Balmoral, where the great north-east corrie with its 200-metre high cliffs overlooking a little loch offers unparalleled views. Meanwhile, the **Cairngorms National Park** is the largest in Britain, covering 3,800 kilometres of beautiful and unspoilt countryside. This is a wild, fascinating and remote area characterised by wide spaces, stony tundra, long glacially carved lochs and craggy peaks.

22 Of course you don't need to leave the city for adventure ... **Transition Extreme** near Aberdeen's Beach Boulevard has something for everyone, including a skate park and climbing centre. For skiing and snowboarding try the **Aberdeen Snowsports Centre** in Garthdee, where thrill seekers can also try the tubing slope.

His Majesty's Theatre illuminated at dusk, Aberdeen city centre

To help you plan and book your trip to Scotland email our travel experts at info@visitscotland.com. When you arrive call into one of our Information Centres where our friendly experts can offer advice on all things local as well as sharing their wider knowledge of Scotland. We don't just advise either. We can sort out your accommodation and all your travel needs, as well as tickets for events across Scotland. So if you're looking to get the most from your visit, there really is only one place to go.

Aberdeen City and Shire

Aberdeen	23 Union Street, Aberdeen AB11 5BP
Ballater	The Old Royal Station Station Square Ballater, AB35 5QB
Braemar	Unit 3, The Mews, Mar Road Braemar, AB35 5YL

Map labels:

Fraserburgh
cduff
A98
New Leeds
A90
A950
A952
norman
To Kirkwall and Lerwick
Oldmeldrum
A90
rie
A96
Craibstone
Bucksburn
ABERDEEN
Altens
A957
Stonehaven
A90
A92
IS

i Open All Year

i Seasonal

Live it. Visit Scotland.
visitscotland.com/wheretofindus

- LOCAL KNOWLEDGE
- WHERE TO STAY
- ACCOMMODATION BOOKING
- PLACES TO VISIT
- THINGS TO DO
- MAPS AND GUIDES
- TRAVEL ADVICE
- ROUTE PLANNING
- WHERE TO SHOP AND EAT
- LOCAL CRAFTS AND PRODUCE
- EVENT INFORMATION
- TICKETS

Hotels

Aberdeen
Chapel Apartments

Open: All year　　　　　**Map Ref: 4G10**

Chapel Apartments are conveniently located in the west end of Aberdeen's city centre. There are seven luxury one bedroom apartments, each boasting modern design with a homely touch. Each apartment comprises a spacious lounge, fully-fitted open plan kitchen, bedroom and bathroom with built in shower. The apartments are fully serviced.

★★★ UP TO ★★★★
SERVICED APARTMENTS

44 Chapel Street, Aberdeen, AB10 1SP
T: 07824 666321　E: melissaross05@aol.com　W: chapelapartments.com

| 7 Apartments | 1 Bedroom | Sleeps 1-4 |

Prices – Apartments:
£560.00-£850.00　Per Week

Short breaks available

76210

Aberdeen
The Craibstone Suites

Open: All year　　　　　**Map Ref: 4G10**

★★★★
SERVICED APARTMENTS

15 Bon Accord Square, Aberdeen, AB11 6DJ
T: 01224 857950　E: reception@craibstone-suites.co.uk　W: craibstone-suites.co.uk

Indicated Prices:
Suite　　from £66.50 per room

86048

Aberdeen
Hilton Aberdeen Treetops

Open: All year

Map Ref: 4G10

★ ★ ★ ★
HOTEL

161 Springfield Road, Aberdeen, AB15 7AQ
T: 01224 313377 E: reservations.aberdeen@hilton.com W: hilton.co.uk/aberdeen

Indicated Prices:

Single	from £65.00 per room	Twin	from £65.00 per room
Double	from £65.00 per room	Suite	from £100.00 per room
		Family	from £65.00 per room

30604

Union Terrace Gardens in the city centre of Aberdeen

SKENE HOUSE

HOTELSUITES

ABERDEEN • SCOTLAND

Everywhere

minutes away

Relax into the warm *welcoming* atmosphere of Aberdeen's unique Skene House HotelSuites and enjoy the *luxury* of our home from home comforts.

Skene House HotelSuites not only provide *superb accommodation* but can help plan sight seeing itineraries, golf itineraries, coach transportation, car hires and *much more*.

Rates range from **£33.00** per person per night based upon 6 sharing a 3 bedroom suite.

Presentation of this advert entitles the bearer to a complimentary

Full Scottish Breakfast

for every person staying in the suite.

Please quote VisitScotland Touring Guide when booking

See our latest offers at:
www.skene-house.co.uk

Central Reservations
T: +44 (0) 1224 659392
E: reservations@skene-house.co.uk

A suite for the price of a hotel room

54826

Aberdeen
Skene House Holburn

Open: All year

Map Ref: 4G10

★★★★
SERVICED APARTMENTS

6 Union Grove, Aberdeen, AB10 6SY
T: 01224 659392 E: reservations@skene-house.co.uk W: skene-house.co.uk

Indicated Prices:

Single suites	from £102.00 per suite	Twin suites	from £102.00 per suite
Double suites	from £102.00 per suite	Two bedroom suites	from £128.00 per suite
		Three bedroom suites	from £237.00 per suite

54826

Aberdeen
Skene House Rosemount

Open: All year

Map Ref: 4G10

★★★ UP TO ★★★★
SERVICED APARTMENTS

94 Rosemount Viaduct, Aberdeen, AB25 1NX
T: 01224 659392 E: reservations@skene-house.co.uk W: skene-house.co.uk

Indicated Prices:

Single suites	from £86.00 per suite	Twin suites	from £86.00 per suite
Double suites	from £86.00 per suite	Two bedroom suites	from £137.00 per suite
		Three bedroom suites	from £186.00 per suite

54826

Aberdeen
Skene House Whitehall

Open: All year

Map Ref: 4G10

★★★★
SERVICED APARTMENTS

2 Whitehall Place, Aberdeen, AB25 2NX
T: 01224 659392 E: reservations@skene-house.co.uk W: skene-house.co.uk

Indicated Prices:

Single suites	from £102.00 per suite	Twin suites	from £102.00 per suite
Double suites	from £102.00 per suite	Two bedroom suites	from £128.00 per suite
		Three bedroom suites	from £182.00 per suite

54826

For a full listing of Quality Assured accommodation, please see directory at back of this guide.

213

Aberdeen
Craighaar Hotel

Open: All year excl 25-26 Dec

Map Ref: 4G10

Charming hotel five minutes from airport in a quiet location. 15 mins from city centre. 55 bedrooms, 6 split-level suites. All rooms en-suite, tea/coffee, flat screen, Freeview TV, trouser-press, wi-fi access. Renowned for quality cuisine in the informal restaurant. Extensive wine list and vintage selection. Relaxed and friendly atmosphere.

★★★
HOTEL

Waterton Road, Bucksburn, Aberdeen, AB21 9HS
T: 01224 712275 E: info@craighaar.co.uk W: craighaarhotel.com

Indicated Prices:

Single	from £55.00 per room	Twin	from £75.00 per room
Double	from £75.00 per room	Suite	from £79.00 per room
		Family	from £85.00 per room

20936

Aberdeen
Express by Holiday Inn

Open: All year

Map Ref: 4G10

★★★
METRO HOTEL

Chapel Street, Aberdeen, AB10 1SQ
T: 01224 623500 E: info@hieaberdeen.co.uk W: hieaberdeen.co.uk

Indicated Prices:

Single	from £55.00 per room	Twin	from £55.00 per room
Double	from £55.00 per room	Family	from £55.00 per room

25386

Aberdeen
Jurys Inn Aberdeen

Open: All year excl 24, 25 & 26 Dec

Map Ref: 4G10

Jurys Inn Aberdeen is the perfect choice for a stay in Aberdeen. Newly built. Modern comfortable rooms, excellent central location and easily accessible to all transport links. Part of the Union Square shopping centre. Jurys Inn Aberdeen offers excellent value for money.

★★★
HOTEL

Union Square, Guild Street, Aberdeen, AB11 5RG
T: 01224 381200 E: jurysinnaberdeen@jurysinns.com W: jurysinns.com

Indicated Prices:
Single	from £49.00 per room	Twin	from £49.00 per room
Double	from £49.00 per room		

86723

Aberdeen
Thistle Aberdeen Altens

Open: All year

Map Ref: 4G10

★★★
HOTEL

Souterhead Road, Aberdeen, AB12 3LF
T: 01224 877000 E: reservations.aberdeenaltens@thistle.co.uk W: thistle.com

Indicated Prices:
Double	from £70.00 per room	Twin	from £70.00 per room
		Family	from £90.00 per room

60890

Ballater
Cambus O'May Hotel

Open: All year

Map Ref: 4E11

★★★
COUNTRY HOUSE HOTEL

Cambus O'May, Ballater, Aberdeenshire, AB35 5SE
T: 013397 55428 E: mckechnie@cambusomay.freeserve.co.uk W: cambusomayhotel.co.uk

Indicated Prices:
Single	from £45.00 per person	Twin	from £45.00 per person
Double	from £45.00 per person	Family	from £45.00 per person

17716

For a full listing of Quality Assured accommodation, please see directory at back of this guide.

215

by Ballater, Dinnet

Loch Kinord Hotel

Open: All year **Map Ref: 4E11**

In the heart of Royal Deeside, the Victorian Loch Kinord Hotel makes an ideal base to explore this historic and beautiful area. Fine dining rosette restaurant. Fine selection of malt whisky and cosy bedrooms and lounges to relax. Golf, fishing, walking, shooting, mountaineering, cycling etc all available nearby.

★★★
HOTEL

Dinnet, nr Ballater, Royal Deeside, Aberdeenshire, AB34 5LW
T: 01339 885229 E: stay@lochkinord.com W: lochkinord.com

Indicated Prices:

Single	from £65.00 per room	Twin	from £90.00 per room
Double	from £90.00 per room	Suite	from £140.00 per room
		Family	from £90.00 per room

35851

Banchory

The Best Western Burnett Arms Hotel

Open: All year **Map Ref: 4F11**

A historic coaching inn 'The Burnett' is ideally situated for touring Royal Deeside and the north-east of Scotland. The hotel sits in the centre of Banchory on the A93 Braemar road. Facilities include two function suites, a restaurant and two bars. Ample parking to rear.

★★★
SMALL HOTEL

25 High Street, Banchory, Kincardineshire, AB31 5TD
T: 01330 824944 E: theburnett@btconnect.com W: bw-burnettarms.co.uk

Indicated Prices:

Single	from £69.00 per room	Twin	from £86.00 per room
Double	from £86.00 per room	Family	from £120.00 per room

16913

Important: Prices stated are estimates and may be subject to amendments. Prices are per person per night unless otherwise stated.

Braemar
Braemar Lodge
Open: All year   **Map Ref: 4D11**

★★★
SMALL HOTEL

6 Glenshee Road, Braemar, Aberdeenshire, AB35 5YQ
T: 01339 741627   E: mail@braemarlodge.co.uk   W: braemarlodge.co.uk

Indicated Prices:

Single	from £30.00 per room	Twin	from £60.00 per room
Double	from £60.00 per room	Family	from £75.00 per room

16019

Inverurie
Strathburn Hotel
Open: All year excl Xmas & New Year   **Map Ref: 4G9**

Strathburn Hotel can provide visitor packages by arrangement. The hotel owned and managed by my wife and myself since 1985 along with loyal and capable staff take pride in quality and care of service we offer. Please contact myself, David Barrack, to discuss your requirements – example golf, walking, fishing, castles etc.

★★★
HOTEL

Burghmuir Drive, Inverurie, Aberdeenshire, AB51 4GY
T: 01467 624422   E: strathburn@btconnect.com   W: strathburn-hotel.co.uk

Indicated Prices:

Single	from £65.00 per room	Twin	from £95.00 per room
Double	from £95.00 per room	Family	from £120.00 per room

56854

Rothienorman
Rothie Inn
Open: All year excl Xmas & New Year   **Map Ref: 4F9**

★★★
INN

Main Street, Rothienorman, Aberdeenshire, AB51 8UD
T: 01651 821206   E: rothieinn@fsmail.net

Indicated Prices:

Single	from £40.00	Twin	from £30.00 per person
		Family	from £70.00 per room

52263

Stonehaven
The Ship Inn

Open: All year but only drinks at Xmas

Map Ref: 4G11

The Ship Inn (est 1771), situated on the edge of Stonehaven's picturesque and historic harbour, is an ideal base to explore the Grampian region and Royal Deeside. Aberdeen – the Oil Capital of Europe – is only a 20 minute drive away.

★ ★
INN

5 Shorehead, Stonehaven, Kincardineshire, AB39 2JY
T: 01569 762617 E: enquiries@shipinnstonehaven.com W: shipinnstonehaven.com

Indicated Prices:

Single	from £55.00 per room	Twin	from £85.00 per room
Double	from £85.00 per room	Family	from £115.00 per room

60406

Castle Fraser, near Inverurie

Important: Prices stated are estimates and may be subject to amendments. Prices are per person per night unless otherwise stated.

Guest Houses and B&Bs

Aberdeen
Aldridge B&B

Open: All year excl Xmas & New Year   **Map Ref: 4G10**

This newly refurbished B&B offers warm friendly and attentive hospitality. Guest rooms are bright, airy and furnished to a very high standard. Set in a quiet residential area yet very convenient for Aberdeen Royal Infirmary, Aberdeen University, the city centre and a variety of sports and cultural centres.

★★★
BED AND BREAKFAST

60 Hilton Drive, Aberdeen, AB24 4NP
T: 01224 485651

Indicated Prices:
Single   from £40.00 per room
Double   from £60.00 per room

TV 🛏 P 🍵 🔌

79183

Aberdeen
Armadale Guest House

Open: All year   **Map Ref: 4G10**

★★★
GUEST HOUSE

605 Holburn Street, Aberdeen, AB10 7JN
T: 01224 580636 E: armadaleguesthouse@tiscali.co.uk W: armadaleguesthouse.co.uk

Indicated Prices:
Single   from £30.00 per room   Twin   from £60.00 per room
Double   from £60.00 per room   Family   from £70.00 per room

TV 🛏 P 🍵 •))
🍴✕ C £ V

12869

Aberdeen City and Shire

Aberdeen
Furain Guest House

Open: All year excl Xmas & New Year　　**Map Ref: 4G10**

Late Victorian house built of red granite. Family run. Convenient for town, Royal Deeside and Castle Trail. Private car parking. Close to River Dee. Well located for fishing, golf and walking.

★★★
GUEST HOUSE

92 North Deeside Road, Peterculter, Aberdeen, AB14 0QN
T: 01224 732189　E: furain@btinternet.com　W: furain.co.uk

Indicated Prices:

Single	from £44.00	Twin	from £29.00
Double	from £29.00	Family	from £75.00 per room

26933

Aberdeen
Scottish Agricultural College

Open: 22 Mar-16 Apr, 5 Jul-24 Sep　　**Map Ref: 4G10**

Set in an 800 acre estate with glorious surroundings away from the hustle and bustle of city life, free from busy roads. Craibstone is the ideal setting for a truly relaxing holiday and the perfect base for touring north east Scotland.

★★
CAMPUS ACCOMMODATION

Facilities Office, Hunter Annexe, Craibstone Estate, Bucksburn, Aberdeen, AB21 9TR
T: 01224 711012　E: gwen.bruce@sac.co.uk　W: www.sac.ac.uk/holidayletsaberdeen

60 Ensuite rooms　　Sleeps 1-2

Indicated Prices:
from £135.00 per week

53468

Alford
Bydand Bed & Breakfast

Open: All year   Map Ref: 4F10

★★★ GOLD
BED AND BREAKFAST

18 Balfour Road, Alford, Aberdeenshire, AB33 8NF
T: 01975 563613   E: info@alfordaccommodation.com   W: alfordaccommodation.com

Indicated Prices:
Single   from £30.00 per room   Twin   from £54.00 per room
Double   from £54.00 per room

17128

Ballater
Glenernan Guest House

Open: All year   Map Ref: 4E11

★★★★
GUEST HOUSE

37 Braemar Road, Ballater, AB35 5RQ
T: 01339 753111   E: enquiries@glenernanguesthouse.com   W: glenernanguesthouse.com

Indicated Prices:
Single   from £40.00 per room   Twin   from £60.00 per room
Double   from £60.00 per room   Family   from £80.00 per room

73409

Braemar
Clunie Lodge Guest House

Open: All year   Map Ref: 4D11

★★★
GUEST HOUSE

Clunie Bank Road, Braemar, Aberdeenshire, AB35 5ZP
T: 01339 741330   E: karen@clunielodge.com   W: clunielodge.com

Indicated Prices:
Single   from £45.00 per room   Twin   from £60.00 per room
Double   from £60.00 per room   Family   from £90.00 per room

19737

Scotland.
The Home of Golf

For everything you need to know about golfing in Scotland

visitscotland.com/golf

Huntly
Coynachie Guest House

Open: All year excl Xmas

Map Ref: 4E9

Coynachie –a large period house in a tranquil valley, peace and relaxation. Luxurious bedrooms and bathrooms. We invite you to come and slow down with us! This is the perfect base to explore the North East of Scotland from Mountain to Sea, Castle to Distillery. Touring is easy from here.

★★★★
GUEST HOUSE

Gartly, Huntly, Aberdeenshire, AB54 4SD
T: 01466 720383 E: info@coynachieguesthouse.com W: coynachieguesthouse.com

Indicated Prices:

Double	from £34.00 per person	Twin	from £34.00 per person
		Family	from £90.00 per room

84270

Huntly
Drumdelgie House B&B

Open: All year excl Xmas & New Year

Map Ref: 4E8

★★★★
BED AND BREAKFAST

Cairnie, Huntly, Aberdeenshire, AB54 4TH
T: 01466 760346 E: info@drumdelgiecottages.co.uk W: drumdelgiecottages.co.uk

Indicated Prices:

Single	from £30.00 per room	Twin	from £55.00 per room
Double	from £55.00 per room		

79809

Huntly
Greenmount Guest House

Open: All year excl Xmas & New Year

Map Ref: 4F9

★★★
GUEST HOUSE

43 Gordon Street, Huntly, AB54 8EQ
T: 01466 792482 E: greenmountguest@btconnect.com W: deveronfishing.com

Indicated Prices:

Single	from £23.00 per person	Double/Twin	from £25.00 per person

29032

Inverurie
Breaslann Guest House

Open: All year excl Xmas & New Year

Map Ref: 4G9

★★★
GUEST HOUSE

Old Chapel Road, Inverurie, Aberdeenshire, AB51 4QN
T: 01467 621608 E: breaslann@btconnect.com W: breaslann.co.uk

Indicated Prices:
Double	from £55.00 per room	Twin	from £55.00 per room
		Family	from £82.50 per room

16155

Macduff
Monica and Martin's B&B

Open: All year

Map Ref: 4F7

★★★★
BED AND BREAKFAST

21 Gellymill Street, Macduff, Aberdeenshire, AB44 1TN
T: 01261 832336 E: gellymill@talktalk.net

Indicated Prices:
Single	from £25.00 per person	Twin	from £23.00 per person
Double	from £23.00 per person		

38842

Oldmeldrum
Cromlet Hill Guest House

Open: All year

Map Ref: 4G9

★★★★
BED AND BREAKFAST

South Road, Oldmeldrum, Aberdeenshire, AB51 0AB
T: 01651 872315 E: johnpage@cromlethill.co.uk W: cromlethill.co.uk

Indicated Prices:
Single	from £40.00	Twin	from £56.00 per room
Double	from £56.00 per room	Family	from £70.00 per room

21414

Peterhead
Rose Lodge Bed & Breakfast

Open: All year

Map Ref: 4G8

★★★★
BED AND BREAKFAST

New Leeds, Peterhead, AB42 4HX
T: 01346 531148 E: lucinda@roselodge.fsworld.co.uk W: roselodge.fsworld.co.uk

Indicated Prices:
Single	from £27.00	Twin	from £26.00 per person
Double	from £26.00 per person	Suite	from £26.00 per person

52070

For a full listing of Quality Assured accommodation, please see directory at back of this guide.

Stonehaven
Cardowan B&B

Open: All year excl Xmas & New Year

Map Ref: 4G11

★★★★
BED AND BREAKFAST

31 Slug Road, Stonehaven, AB39 2DU
T: 01569 762759 E: thelmaritchie@btinternet.com W: stonehavenaccommodation.co.uk

Indicated Prices:
Single	from £55.00 per room	Twin	from £65.00 per room
Double	from £65.00 per room		

78617

Stonehaven
Ambleside B&B

Open: All year

Map Ref: 4G11

★★★
BED AND BREAKFAST

Netherley, Stonehaven, AB39 3RB
T: 01569 731105 E: helensbb@ambleside350.fslife.co.uk W: amblesidebb.co.uk

Indicated Prices:
Single	from £50.00 per room	Twin	from £65.00 per room
Double	from £65.00 per room		

11874

Stonehaven
Tewel Farmhouse B&B

Open: All year

Map Ref: 4G11

★★
FARM HOUSE

Tewel Farm, Stonehaven, South Aberdeenshire, AB39 3UU
T: 01569 762306

Indicated Prices:
Single	from £27.00 per person	Twin	from £24.00 per person
Double	from £24.00 per person	Family	from £74.00 per room

57963

by Strathdon, Glenkindie
The Smiddy House

Open: Mar-Nov

Map Ref: 4E10

★★★
BED AND BREAKFAST

Glenkindie, Aberdeenshire, AB33 8SS
T: 01975 641216 E: jones.thesmiddy@btinternet.com W: thesmiddyhouse.co.uk

Indicated Prices:
Single	from £30.00 per room	Twin	from £50.00 per room
Double	from £50.00 per room		

60431

Important: Prices stated are estimates and may be subject to amendments. Prices are per person per night unless otherwise stated.

Self Catering and Camping & Caravan Parks

Aboyne
Royal Deeside Holiday Cottages

Open: mid Mar-Oct   **Map Ref: 4E11**

★★★
SELF CATERING

Estate Office, Dinnet, Aboyne, Aberdeenshire, AB34 5LL
T: 013398 85341 E: office@dinnet-estate.co.uk W: royaldeesideholidaycottages.co.uk

| 1 Cottage | 2 Bedrooms | Sleeps 4 |
| 3 Houses | 3 Bedrooms | Sleeps 6 |

Prices – Cottage: **Houses:**
from £350.00   **Per Week**   from £350.00   **Per Week**

22688

Alford
Craich Cottage

Open: All year   **Map Ref: 4F10**

★★★
SELF CATERING

J & A Wright, Craich, Tough, Alford, Aberdeenshire, AB33 8EN
T: 01975 562584 E: john.f.wright237@btinternet.com W: craichcottage.co.uk

| 1 Cottage | 3 Bedrooms | Sleeps 1-6 |

Prices – Cottage:
£325.00-£425.00   **Per Week**
Short breaks available

20826

Archiestown
Ivy Cottage

Open: All year   **Map Ref: 4D8**

★★
SELF CATERING

Souters Lane, Archiestown, Moray, AB38 7QX T: 01463 791714
E: mbmansfield@mansfieldhighlandholidays.com W: mansfieldhighlandholidays.com

| 1 Cottage | 3 Bedrooms | Sleeps 4 |

Prices – Cottage:
£130.00-£280.00   **Per Week**

Short breaks available

32377

Ballater
Invercauld Lodges
Open: All year   **Map Ref: 4E11**

Beautifully set in a secluded garden only 400 yards from the centre of the village, Invercauld Lodges offer a peaceful, quiet location where guests of all ages return year after year. Our policy of continually investing in the lodges means you will thoroughly enjoy your relaxing break.

★★★★
SELF CATERING

12 Invercauld Road, Ballater, Royal Deeside, Aberdeenshire, AB35 5RP
T: 01339 755015 E: info@invercauldlodges.co.uk W: invercauldlodges.co.uk

| 6 Cabins | 2 Bedrooms | Sleeps 3-5 |

Prices – Cabins:
£250.00-£495.00   Per Week

Short breaks available

79176

---

by Ballater, Dinnet
Royal Deeside Woodland Lodges
Open: All year   **Map Ref: 4E11**

★★★
SELF CATERING

Dinnet, nr Ballater, Royal Deeside, Aberdeenshire, AB34 5LW
T: 01339 885229 E: stay@lochkinord.com W: woodland-lodges.com

| 2 Cabins | 2 Bedrooms | Sleeps 1-4 |

Prices – Cabins:
£250.00-£700.00   Per Week

Short breaks available

77039

Banchory
Woodend Chalet Holidays
Open: All year   **Map Ref: 4F11**

★★★ UP TO ★★★★★
SELF CATERING

Glassel, Banchory, Aberdeenshire, AB31 4DB
T: 01339 882562 E: info@woodendchalets.co.uk W: woodendchalets.co.uk

| 7 Chalets | 1-2 Bedrooms | Sleeps 1-4 |
| 2 Lodges | 3 Bedrooms | Sleeps 1-6 |

Prices – Chalets: Lodges:
£160.00-£450.00   Per Week   £460.00-£695.00   Per Week

Short breaks available

64499

Braemar
Braemar Holiday Lodges & Bunkhouse
Open: All year　　　　　**Map Ref: 4D11**

★★★★
HOSTEL

6 Glenshee Road, Braemar, AB35 5YQ
T: 013397 41627　E: mail@braemarlodge.co.uk

8 Cabins	1-3 Bedrooms	Sleeps 2-6
1 Hostel		Sleeps 12

Prices – Cabins:　　　**Hostel:**
£250.00-£700.00　**Per Week**　from £13.00　　**Per Night**
Short breaks available

68390

by Laurencekirk
Dovecot Caravan Park
Open: Apr-mid Oct　　　　**Map Ref: 4F12**

★★★★
HOLIDAY PARK

Northwaterbridge, by Laurencekirk, Aberdeenshire, AB30 1QL
T: 01674 840630　E: adele@dovecotcaravanpark.co.uk　W: dovecotcaravanpark.co.uk
From Brechin (A90) 5 miles north, at Northwaterbridge, turn left to Edzell Woods. Site is 300m on left. Signposted.

Park accommodates 25 pitches. Total touring pitches: 25.
Prices per pitch:
🚐 (25) £11.50-£12.50　　⛺ (25) £7.50-£9.50
🚍 (25) £11.50-£12.50

Holiday Caravans for Hire:
(1) £220.00-£250.00 per week.

23038

Aberdeen, Scotland's third largest city

For a full listing of Quality Assured accommodation, please see directory at back of this guide.

Food & Drink

Stonehaven
The Ship Inn

Open: All year

Map Ref: 4G11

★★
INN

**Culinary Type:
SCOTTISH**

5 Shorehead,
Stonehaven, AB39 2JY
T: 01569 762617
E: enquiries@shipinnstonehaven.com
W: shipinnstonehaven.com

Best For:
- Kids and families • Romantic meals
- Outstanding views • Special occasion
- Business lunches

Prices:

Starter from:	£2.95
Main Course from:	£7.95
Dessert from:	£4.95

We offer a wide range of freshly cooked dishes using the finest and freshest ingredients. Fresh, locally caught fish and seafood are a speciality but we also offer fine steaks, chicken dishes, pasta, vegetarian options, home-made burgers – something for everybody in fact! In the bar, a wide range of draught beers is served – including real ales which are changed regularly for variety –and more than 100 different malt whiskies are available. We also offer a range of bottled beers, wines and soft drinks.

Opening Times:
Lunch from 1200, last orders 1415.
Dinner from 1730, last orders 2130.

60406

Important: Prices stated are estimates and may be subject to amendments. Prices are per person per night unless otherwise stated.

River Spey, Aberdeenshire

Plockton, looking across Loch Kishorn towards the Bealach na Ba, Highlands

THE HIGHLANDS, MORAY AND OUTER HEBRIDES

If you're searching for tranquillity, you'll find that the Highlands moves at a refreshingly relaxed pace.

This region is home to some of Scotland's most enduring scenery. The rugged majesty of the mountainous north never fails to impress, while the coastal and hill scenery found on the legendary Road to the Isles is breathtaking. And Moray is Malt Whisky Country, where you can explore the lush countryside as you take in some of Scotland's best-loved drams.

There is so much to experience on your travels, from the eerie silence of Glen Coe to the mysterious Loch Ness; the diverse wildlife habitats of the Cairngorms to the poignant Culloden battlefield; the wild flatlands of the Flow Country to the golden beaches of the west and north coast; and the remote wildernesses of Knoydart and Ardnamurchan to the

thriving city of Inverness, the choice is endless.

Wildlife flourishes here: you'll see red squirrels and tiny goldcrests in the trees, otters feeding by the waterside, deer coming down from the hill to the forest edge, dolphins and whales off the coast, ospreys and eagles soaring overhead.

With such a variety of terrain, this is nature's playground. Climbers, walkers and mountain bikers take to the hills. Surfers, sailors, canoeists and fishermen enjoy the beaches, rivers and lochs. And for the more adventurous, there's skiing, canyoning and white water rafting. Whatever outdoor activity you like to pursue, you'll find experienced, professional experts on hand to ensure you enjoy it to the full.

Once you've had enough exercise and fresh air, you can be assured of some fine Highland hospitality – whether you're enjoying a culinary tour of Skye, hitting a thriving activity centre like Aviemore or exploring the rapidly expanding city of Inverness. In the pubs and hotels, restaurants and other venues around the community, you'll find music and laughter. Perhaps a riotous ceilidh in full fling and unforgettable nights of eating and drinking into the wee small hours.

Every year people come to discover the traditional homeland of their clan and witness the locations where the history of their ancestors was played out; from the unknown highlander on the Glenfinnan Monument where Bonnie Prince Charlie raised the standard in 1745 to the Jacobite army's last stand in Culloden less than a year later.

And history lovers can't resist the Outer Hebrides, a 150-mile long island chain off Scotland's west coast characterised by beautiful landscapes and a rich heritage. Discover the iconic 5,000-year-old Calanais Standing Stones on Lewis, the medieval Kisimul Castle on Barra and so much more besides. Whether you fancy sea kayaking around the coastline on the lookout for wildlife, relaxing on sandy white beaches or savouring some of the region's delicious local produce on a food trail, the islands really do have something for everyone.

Wherever you choose to explore in this endlessly inspiring region, you are sure to find quality accommodation that suits your needs perfectly. Expect to return time and again.

O'Neill Cold Water Classic, Brim's Ness, Thurso

What's On?

Glen Affric Winterfest 2010
29 Jan - 1 Feb 2010
Opportunity to see some of the most breathtaking winter scenery in the world.
naturalhighguiding.co.uk/winterfest.htm

O'Neill Cold Water Classic
29 April - 6 May 2010
The classic surf contest takes on the swell in Thurso.
oneill.com/cwc/scotland

UCI Mountain Bike World Cup, Fort William
5-6 June 2010
Iconic event returns to the slopes of Aonach Mor.
fortwilliamworldcup.co.uk

Harris Arts Festival
12-16 July 2010
Experience the rich culture and traditions on the island.

Hebridean Maritime Festival
12-17 July 2010
A sailing event with entertainment for the novice and proficient sailor alike.
sailhebrides.com

Hebridean Celtic Festival
14 -17 July 2010
A lively four day music festival located amidst beautiful scenery.
www.hebceltfest.com

Lewis Highland Games
17 July 2010
Visit the village of Tong in Lewis for some traditional and strong-man events.
lewishighlandgames.co.uk

Inverness Highland Tattoo
26-31 July 2010
Be captivated by the skirl of the pipes at this popular week-long event.
tattooinverness.org.uk

Belladrum Tartan Heart Festival
6-7 August 2010
Family-friendly festival held in the beautiful Italian Gardens at Belladrum.
tartanheartfestival.co.uk

Blas Festival
3-11 September 2010
Traditional music and Gaelic culture.
blas-festival.com

All dates correct at time of publication. Please check before booking. VisitScotland cannot be held responsible for any inaccuracies

231

VisitScotland Information Centres

To help you plan and book your trip to Scotland email our travel experts at info@visitscotland.com. When you arrive call into one of our Information Centres where our friendly experts can offer advice on all things local as well as sharing their wider knowledge of Scotland. We don't just advise either. We can sort out your accommodation and all your travel needs, as well as tickets for events across Scotland. So if you're looking to get the most from your visit, there really is only one place to go.

North Highlands, Inverness, Loch Ness and Nairn

Inverness	Castle Wynd, Inverness, IV2 3BJ
Drumnadrochit	The Car Park, Drumnadrochit, Inverness-shire, IV63 6TX

Fort William and Lochaber, Skye and Lochalsh

Fort William	15 High Street Fort William, PH33 6DH
Portree	Bayfield Road, Portree Isle of Skye, IV51 9EL
Dunvegan	2 Lochside, Dunvegan Isle of Skye, IV55 8WB

Moray, Aviemore and the Cairngorms

Aviemore	Grampian Road Aviemore, PH22 1PP
Elgin	17 High Street, Elgin, IV30 1EG

Outer Hebrides

Stornoway	26 Cromwell Street, Stornoway Isle of Lewis, HS1 2DD

(Map of northern Scotland showing locations including To Stromness (Orkney), To St Margaret's Hope, Strathy Point, Scrabster, Thurso, Gills Bay, John o'Groats, Canisbay, Melvich, Weydale, Bettyhill, Tongue, Forsinard, Wick, Lybster, Altnaharra, Loch Shin, Lairg, Backies, Golspie, Embo, Dornoch, Tain, Fearn, Lossiemouth, Cullen, Alness, Invergordon, Culbokie, Dingwall, North Kessock, Elgin, Urquhart, Fortrose, Nairn, Forres, Keith, Beauly, Dalcross, Culloden, Aberlour, Dufftown, To Aberdeen, INVERNESS, Smithton, Culloden Moor, Archiestown, Dulnain Bridge, Grantown-on-Spey, Drumnadrochit, Carrbridge, Nethy Bridge, Loch Ness, Aviemore, Boat of Garten, Fort Augustus, Kincraig, Cairngorm Mountains, To Aberdeen, invergarry, Kingussie, Insh, Cairngorms National Park, Laggan, Newtonmore, Dalwhinnie, verroy, leven, To Perth, A82, sgow)

©Collins Bartholomew Ltd 2009

i Open All Year

(i) Seasonal

Live it. Visit Scotland.
visitscotland.com/wheretofindus

Cawdor Castle, near Nairn, home to the legends of Macbeth

Northern Highlands, Inverness, Loch Ness and Nairn

The north of the Scottish Highlands offers a great diversity of landscapes, where wildlife thrives and every turn is greeted by iconic scenery.

Home to Scotland's first Geopark, the geology of this region is impressive. Loch Ness and the Great Glen cut a trench across the Highlands, there are magnificent stand-alone mountains such as Ben Wyvis and Ben Hope, while the rolling green hills of Caithness in the east give way to Sutherland's hills and mountains in the west. And there are a number of coastal delights, from formidable cliffs to fringes of sparkling white sand.

When it comes to adventure, you can always go the extra mile in the North Highlands. Relax with a little golf and fishing, or for those who prefer walking, trekking or cycling, exploring these wild and remote landscapes can offer a truly exhilarating experience.

This region is home to an abundance of wildlife, with dolphins and famous seabird colonies along the coast and red squirrel, pine marten and roe deer in the woodlands. Get a little closer on a wildlife tour.

Whether you want to explore rich archaeological sites, discover delicious local produce, sample a fine malt whisky or simply relax in the picturesque city of Inverness, everything you need for the perfect Highland escape is right here on your doorstep.

Handa Island, north west Highlands

To find out more go to visitscotland.com

DON'T MISS

1   Stretching from the Summer Isles in Wester Ross northwards through west Sutherland to the north coast, The **Northwest Highlands Geopark** extends to the east of Durness, beyond Loch Eriboll, and on to The Moine. This is Scotland's first Geopark and home to some fascinating geological features, from the classic peaks of Suilven and Stac Pollaidh to endless deserted beaches and seashores. This landmark wilderness is one of the best places to explore in Europe.

2   Explore the myth that surrounds Loch Ness - and its infamous monster - and uncover some of the hoaxes and illusions that make this such a fascinating and mysterious location. Learn more about Scotland's deepest freshwater loch at the **Loch Ness Centre and Exhibition Experience** and explore the picturesque village of Drumnadrochit.

3   Situated on the north coast of Caithness, the **Castle of Mey** proudly overlooks the Pentland Firth and the Orkney Islands. Restored and renovated by the Queen Mother, this striking Castle stands as the most northerly on the mainland. Walled gardens flourish in the unlikely location and the castle kitchen benefits from the home grown fruit and vegetables.

4   Visit **Hugh Miller's Cottage** in the historic coastal town of Cromarty on the Black Isle, north of Inverness. As the birthplace of renowned geologist Hugh Miller, the three-story Georgian villa exhibits works from his life and is a hands on family-friendly opportunity to study an outstanding display of fossils.

5   Explore the myths and legends of Loch Ness on a **Jacobite** cruise. Get close up to Urquhart Castle from the water and take a look at the loch from a different and more calming perspective. You'll have an opportunity to get off and explore the exhibition and castle ruins.

6   Between April and September, take a boat trip over to **Handa Island** from Tarbet and with the aid of a ranger explore the precipitous sea cliffs and the famous stack that provides sanctuary to thousands of breeding seabirds. More than 200,000 seabirds, including skuas, puffins, guillemots and razorbills, gather to breed each year on the Torridonian sandstone cliffs.

WALKING

7   The **Glen Affric Walking Festival** is a sociable event based in the stunningly picturesque setting of deciduous woodland and sparkling freshwater lochs. Held in June, spring will have reached the upper glen while the last of the snow lingers on the highest tops and animals work hard to rear their young. Although the festival is held over a long weekend, the walks are enjoyable at any time of the year.

8   Although within the city, the **Ness Islands** walk could be a million miles from it. The islands, linked by several old bridges, offer a quiet, scenic walk through tall, native and imported trees. A popular spot with locals, expect to encounter joggers and dog walkers, while you can also witness fly fishing on the excellent salmon pools. This is an enjoyable family walk which accommodates wheelchairs.

9   Near John o'Groats see a dramatic coastline where thousands of seabirds nest in vast colonies. A walk across the clifftop fields will reward you with a stunning view south to Thirle Door and the **Stacks of Duncansby**. The first is a rocky arch, the second a group of large jagged sea stacks. This is a spot you will want to savour, with a view that varies as you move along the clifftop path and bring into play different alignments of the stacks and arch.

10   **Culloden Battlefield** is the site of the last major battle fought on mainland Britain in 1746. Bonnie Prince Charlie's Jacobite troops were defeated here by the Duke of Cumberland and the Hanoverian government forces. The new visitor centre – opened in 2007 – features a battle immersion cinema and handheld multi-lingual audio devices to bring the battle to life as you walk around the battlefield and clan graves.

WILDLIFE

11   Based in the small west coast fishing community of Gairloch, **Hebridean Whale Cruises** closely monitors the feeding grounds for a variety of marine wildlife. Explore the offshore waters of the North Minch - the stretch of water between the mainland and the Outer Hebrides - which is a hotspot for whales and dolphins. Or opt for a tour of the coastline around Loch Gairloch, where you can get up close to seals, otters and seabirds, all under the stunning backdrop of the Torridon mountains.

12   Take the Greengates walkway in Fortrose for a gentle stroll out to Chanonry Point where you can look across to Fort George, an 18th century artillery fortification. **Dolphins** are often seen from the shoreline; the best time is apparently two hours after the low tide.

13   Visit Brahan Estate near Dingwall, where a new **red kite** feeding station has been introduced at Tollie. A small amount of carrion is put out to feed the red kites, allowing visitors to view these magnificent birds up close. These are the major success story as conservationists have worked hard to re-introduce the birds to the Scottish countryside.

14   Get away from it all on the Moray coast and discover **Culbin Sands** just east of the Victorian town of Nairn. This beautiful and unspoilt reserve is home to long-tailed ducks and velvet scooters, while ospreys fish during the summer months, giving way to wintering wildfowl. See a variety of birds and butterflies among the tall pines of Culbin Forest; Hill 99, a tall wooden structure, provides an excellent viewing station with views over the Moray Firth.

GOLF

15   Opened in July 2009, **Castle Stuart Golf** has proven an immediate success with many golfers complimenting the course's unique design features. These include the infinity edges that draw the eye across to classic views of the Kessock Bridge, Chanonry Lighthouse and Fort George, the use of sleepers to add details around the course and revetted bunkers that provide a challenge to the seasoned golfer and waste sand areas that are much more in keeping with the links environment.

16   **Royal Dornoch Golf Course** is thought to be one of the great outposts of world golf. A magnificent links course in remote corner of Sutherland, 45 miles north of Inverness, this has been lauded by golf luminaries the world over. Tom Watson famously remarked it was 'the most fun I've ever had on a golf course'.

17   Considered one of the best courses in Scotland, **Nairn West Golf Club** offers a challenge for all abilities. Situated on the shores of the Moray Firth, a 20 minute drive from Inverness, this 18-hole favourite is perfect for the discerning golfer looking to experience a traditional links course.

18   **Strathpeffer Spa** is one of the oldest courses in the North of Scotland - having first opened for play in 1888. In its early years, it existed as a nine-hole course before being extended to 18 holes in 1896 with a little help from old Tom Morris. The scenery is just remarkable with panoramic views to enjoy across the Black Isle and down towards Peffery Valley whilst the opening hole is spectacular, with the highest tee to green drop in Scottish golf.

TOURING

19   Tour the **Applecross** peninsula where you'll be amazed by the Bealach na Ba (Pass of the Cattle) which rises from sea level to over 2000ft after a series of switchbacks and hairpin bends. It boasts the greatest ascent of any road climb in the UK and you'll be rewarded with outstanding views back across Kishorn and then out towards Applecross. Taking this route north will reward you with views out across to the Cuillin of Skye and the picturesque village of Sheildaig. Stop off and take nourishment at the Applecross Inn, which is renowned for its food.

20   **The North & West Highlands Tourist Route** (140 miles) boasts some of the most magnificent scenery in Europe. Starting at the thriving fishing village of Ullapool, the route winds its way north through magnificent mountain country, passing the picturesque villages of Achiltibuie, Lochinver and Kinlochbervie as it makes for Durness in the north-west corner of Scotland. From Durness, the route heads east through gradually softening scenery to John o'Groats, taking you from one end of Scotland's north coast to the other.

21   The **Moray Firth Coastal Route** (80 miles) takes you in a semi-circle around three of the most beautiful inlets on the east coast of Britain - the Beauly, Cromarty and Dornoch Firths - as it heads north from Inverness into the heart of the northern Highlands. Highlights include the Struie viewpoint over the Dornoch Firth, seals and clan history at Foulis Ferry and whisky at Glen Ord.

22   Find yourself at the heart of whisky country on the **Highland Tourist Route** (118 miles) from Aberdeen to Inverness. On the way you can visit the Grampian Transport Museum at Alford, explore the lovely valley of Upper Donside and on up the heather-clad slopes of the Lecht to Tomintoul in the fringes of the Cairngorms. The last part of the journey before Inverness takes you through through Grantown-on-Spey, a popular salmon-fishing centre.

Hotels

Beauly
Priory Hotel   Open: All year   Map Ref: 4A8

★★★
HOTEL

The Square, Beauly, IV4 7BX
T: 01463 782309 E: reservations@priory-hotel.com W: priory-hotel.com

Indicated Prices:

Single	from £55.00 per room	Twin	from £75.00 per room
Double	from £75.00 per room	Suite	from £100.00 per room
		Family	from £75.00 per room

50521

Contin
Coul House Hotel   Open: All year excl 24-26 Dec   Map Ref: 4A8

Seventeen miles north west of Inverness in the village of Contin, Ross-shire. Some know Contin for its salmon fishing on the Conon River and others for Rogie Waterfalls and the Achilty Forest. The perfect place to base oneself to explore both the east and west coasts of the Highlands often being able to choose the best of the weather.

★★★
COUNTRY HOUSE HOTEL

Contin, IV14 9ES
T: 01997 421487 E: stay@coulhouse.com W: coulhouse.com

Indicated Prices:

Single	from £80.00 per room	Twin	from £170.00 per room
Double	from £150.00 per room	Suite	from £190.00 per room
		Family	from £170.00 per room

20630

Dornoch
Dornoch Castle Hotel

Open: All year excl 25-26 Dec, 10-17 Jan 2010

Map Ref: 4B6

★★★
HOTEL

Castle Street, Dornoch,
Sutherland, IV25 3SD
T: **01862 810216**
E: **enquiries@dornochcastlehotel.com**
W: **www.dornochcastlehotel.com**

Features:
- Minutes from Royal Dornoch Golf Course
- AA ❀ Restaurant
- 24 Bedrooms Deluxe, Superior or Standard

Indicated Prices:

Single	from £60.00 per room
Double	from £90.00 per room
Twin	from £90.00 per room
Family	from £105.00 per room
Suite	from £190.00 per room

AA ❀

22964

Steeped in Scottish history and fascinating legends, the 15th century Dornoch Castle Hotel firmly stands its ground opposite the inspiring 12th century Dornoch Cathedral. Set in private and beautifully manicured gardens, this Scottish castle still bears an air of magnificence and grace. Dornoch Castle Hotel is the perfect venue for your Scottish Highland luxury castle hotel break or as one of the most stunning Scottish wedding venues in the UK.

For a full listing of Quality Assured accommodation, please see directory at back of this guide.

239

by Drumnadrochit, Balnain
Glenurquhart House

Open: 1 Mar-14 Nov

Map Ref: 4A9

★★★★
RESTAURANT WITH ROOMS

Balnain, Drumnadrochit, Inverness, IV63 6TJ
T: 01456 476234 E: info@glenurquhart-house-hotel.co.uk W: glenurquhart-house-hotel.co.uk

Indicated Prices:
Single	from £55.00 per room	Twin	from £90.00 per room
Double	from £90.00 per room	Family	from £110.00 per room

28370

Fort Augustus
Caledonian Hotel

Open: 1 Apr-1 Nov

Map Ref: 4A10

★★★
SMALL HOTEL

Main Road (A82), Fort Augustus, PH32 4BQ
T: 01320 366256 E: johanna.maclellan@thecaledonianhotel.com W: caledonian-hotel.co.uk

Indicated Prices:
Single	from £60.00 per room	Twin	from £80.00 per room
Double	from £80.00 per room		

17592

Gairloch
The Old Inn

Open: All year

Map Ref: 3F7

★★★
SMALL HOTEL

Gairloch, IV21 2BD
T: 01445 712006 E: enquiries@theoldinn.net W: theoldinn.net

Indicated Prices:
Single	from £35.00 per room	Twin	from £65.00 per room
Double	from £65.00 per room	Family	from £75.00 per room

59848

WALKING IN SCOTLAND

For everything you need to know about walking in Scotland
Scotland. Created for Walking visitscotland.com/walking

Important: Prices stated are estimates and may be subject to amendments. Prices are per person per night unless otherwise stated.

Inverness
Culloden House

Open: All year excl Xmas

Map Ref: 4B8

Steeped in history, this award winning 18th century country house offers luxury accommodation and fine dining cuisine. Set in 40 acres of private grounds and gardens three miles east of Inverness. Easy access to Inverness airport, visitor attractions and touring.

★★★★
COUNTRY HOUSE HOTEL

Culloden, Inverness, IV2 7BZ
T: 01463 790461 E: reservations@cullodenhouse.co.uk W: cullodenhouse.co.uk

Indicated Prices:
Single	from £95.00 per room		Twin	from £190.00 per room
Double	from £190.00 per room		Suite	from £300.00 per room
			Family	from £240.00 per room

21689

Inverness
Glenmoriston Town House

Open: All year

Map Ref: 4B8

Situated on the banks of the River Ness, with its majestic setting, the Glenmoriston Town House has everything to meet your needs whether your stay is for business or leisure. With an award winning French Restaurant Abstract, a riverside Brasserie Contrast, 30 luxurious bedrooms and a Piano bar with live music every Friday and Saturday.

★★★★
HOTEL

20 Ness Bank, Inverness, IV2 4SF
T: 01463 223777 E: reception@glenmoristontownhouse.com W: glenmoristontownhouse.com

Indicated Prices:
Single	from £95.00 per room	Twin	from £130.00 per room
Double	from £130.00 per room		

28283

For a full listing of Quality Assured accommodation, please see directory at back of this guide.

241

Inverness
MacDougall Clansman Hotel
Open: All year excl Xmas & New Year   **Map Ref: 4B8**

★★
METRO HOTEL

103 Church Street, Inverness, IV1 1ES
T: 01463 713702 E: info@invernesscentrehotel.co.uk W: invernesscentrehotel.co.uk

Indicated Prices:

Single	from £38.00 per room	Twin	from £58.00 per room
Double	from £58.00 per room	Family	from £68.00 per room

36871

Inverness
The Chieftain Hotel
Open: All year excl 25-26 Dec   **Map Ref: 4B8**

Restaurant, sports bar, lounge bar. Free wi-fi. 24 hour reception. Conferencing. Five pool tables, two dart boards, Sky Sports, big screen TV, five minute walk from city centre. All rooms en-suite.

AWAITING GRADING

2 Millburn Road, Inverness, IV2 3PS
T: 01463 232241 E: admin@chieftainhotel.co.uk W: chieftainhotel.co.uk

Indicated Prices:

Single	from £60.00 per room	Twin	from £80.00 per room
Double	from £80.00 per room	Triple	from £90.00 per room
		Family	from £90.00 per room

87451

Important: Prices stated are estimates and may be subject to amendments. Prices are per person per night unless otherwise stated.

by Lairg, Loch Shin
The Overscaig House Hotel

Open: May-Sept

Map Ref: 4A5

Spend time amidst the peace and tranquility of this wonderful location in Sutherland overlooking Loch Shin. Enjoy the locally sourced cuisine in our loch view dining room, read a book in our comfortable lounge or simply have a drink in the bar. A perfect base for exploring the North Highlands.

★★★
SMALL HOTEL

Loch Shin, by Lairg, Sutherland, IV27 4NY
T: 01549 431203 E: visits@overscaig.com W: overscaig.com

Indicated Prices:

Single	from £48.00 per person	Twin	from £48.00 per person
Double	from £48.00 per person	Family	from £140.00 per room

48851

Lochinver
Inver Lodge Hotel

Open: Easter-Oct

Map Ref: 3G5

★★★★
HOTEL

Iolaire Road, Lochinver, Sutherland, IV27 4LU
T: 01571 844496 E: stay@inverlodge.com W: inverlodge.com

Indicated Prices:

Single	from £110.00 per room	Twin	from £200.00 per room
Double	from £200.00 per room		

66454

Muir of Ord
Ord House Hotel

Open: Apr-Oct

Map Ref: 4A8

★★
COUNTRY HOUSE HOTEL

Muir of Ord, Highlands, IV6 7UH
T: 01463 870492 E: admin@ord-house.co.uk W: ord-house.co.uk

Indicated Prices:

Single	from £45.00 per room	Twin	from £90.00 per room
Double	from £90.00 per room	Family	from £130.00 per room

48572

For a full listing of Quality Assured accommodation, please see directory at back of this guide.

243

Scourie
Eddrachilles Hotel

Open: All year excl Oct-mid Mar

Map Ref: 3H4

Escape to the peace and tranquillity of Eddrachilles Hotel, magnificently situated at the head of the island studded Badcall Bay. All bedrooms are en-suite. The restaurant serves fresh local produce. We have an extensive wine list of over 70 bins and a selection of over 130 single malt whiskys.

★★★
SMALL HOTEL

Badcall Bay, Scourie, Sutherland, IV27 4TH
T: 01971 502080   E: info@eddrachilles.com   W: eddrachilles.com

Indicated Prices:

Single	from £70.00	Twin	from £47.00 per person
Double	from £47.00 per person	Family	from £127.00 per room

24356

Guest Houses and B&Bs

Beauly
Broomhill

Open: All year

Map Ref: 4A9

★★★
BED AND BREAKFAST

Kiltarlity, Beauly, Inverness-shire, IV14 7JH
T: 01463 741447   E: broom.hill@tiscali.co.uk   W: myweb.tiscali.co.uk/broomhill1

Indicated Prices:

Double	£19.50 per person	Twin	£19.50 per person

16576

Canisbay
Bencorragh House

Open: All year excl Xmas & New Year   Map Ref: 4D2

★★★
FARM HOUSE

Upper Gills, Canisbay, by John O'Groats, Caithness, KW1 4YD
T: 01955 611449 E: bartonsandy@hotmail.com W: bencorraghhouse.com

Indicated Prices:

Single	from £45.00 per room	Twin	from £54.00 per room
Double	from £54.00 per room	Family	from £72.00 per room

14913

Dornoch
Hillview

Open: All year excl Xmas/New Year   Map Ref: 4B6

★★★★
BED AND BREAKFAST

Evelix Road, Dornoch, IV25 3RD
T: 01862 810151 E: hillviewbb@talk21.com W: milford.co.uk/go/hillviewbb.html

Indicated Prices:

Single	from £45.00 per room	Twin	from £60.00 per room
Double	from £60.00 per room	Family	from £90.00 per room

30587

by Dornoch, Embo
Corven B&B

Open: Apr-Oct   Map Ref: 4B6

★★
BED AND BREAKFAST

Station Road, Embo, by Dornoch, Sutherland, IV25 3PR
T: 01862 810128 E: dotdon@zacarius.orangehome.co.uk

Indicated Prices:

Single	from £40.00 per room	Twin	from £50.00 per room
Double	from £50.00 per room		

20577

For a full listing of Quality Assured accommodation, please see directory at back of this guide.

Drumnadrochit
Great Glen B&B

Open: All year excl Xmas

Map Ref: 4A9

'Absolute paradise' in the heart of the Highlands/Loch Ness. Candle-lit dinners, BBQs and so much more with luxury leisure facilities. Nessie hunting to hill walking through some of the world's most breathtaking, raw countryside. We are the perfect base for your historic adventure to begin whilst enjoying real Highland pampering.

★★★★
BED AND BREAKFAST

Anderson Farm House, The Jennings, Drumnadrochit, Inverness, IV63 6XT
T: 01456 450114/07812 576152 E: sonia@greatglenbandb.co.uk W: greatglenbandb.co.uk

Indicated Prices:

Single	from £50.00 per room	Twin	from £70.00 per room
Double	from £60.00 per room	Suite	from £100.00 per room
		Family	from £75.00 per room

85984

Drumnadrochit
Rowan Cottage Bed & Breakfast

Open: Mar-Nov

Map Ref: 4A9

★★★★
BED AND BREAKFAST

10 West Lewiston, Drumnadrochit, Inverness, IV63 6UW
T: 01456 450944 E: rowanbandb@aol.com W: rowancottagebedandbreakfast.co.uk

Indicated Prices:

Double	from £82.00 per room	Twin	from £82.00 per room

78899

Dunbeath
Tormore Farm

Open: May-Oct

Map Ref: 4D4

★★
FARMHOUSE

Dunbeath, Caithness, KW6 6EH
T: 01593 731240 W: visithighlands.com

Indicated Prices:
Double   from £19.00 per person

44650

Fortrose
Waters Edge
Open: All year

Map Ref: 4B8

★★★★★
BED AND BREAKFAST

Canonbury Terrace, Fortrose, IV10 8TT
T: 01381 621202 E: gill@watersedge.uk.com W: watersedge.uk.com

Indicated Prices:
Single   from £45.00 per person
Double   from £50.00 per person

76567

Gairloch
Gairloch View Guest House and B&B
Open: All year

Map Ref: 3F7

★★★★
BED AND BREAKFAST

Auchtercairn, Gairloch, Ross-shire, IV21 2BN
T: 01445 712666 E: enquiries@gairlochview.com W: gairlochview.com

Indicated Prices:
Single   from £42.00 per room   Twin   from £70.00 per room
Double   from £70.00 per room

77101

Garve
Inchbae Lodge Guest House
Open: All year excl Nov

Map Ref: 4A7

★★
GUEST HOUSE

Garve, Ross-shire, IV23 2PH
T: 01997 455269 E: contact@inchbae.co.uk W: inchbae.co.uk

Indicated Prices:
Single   from £35.00 per room   Twin   from £59.95 per room
Double   from £59.95 per room   Family   from £59.95 per room

31528

Inverness
Ballifeary Guest House
Open: All year excl 24-28 Dec

Map Ref: 4B8

AA ★★★★ GUEST HOUSE

10 Ballifeary Road, Inverness, IV3 5PJ
T: 01463 235572 E: info@ballifearyguesthouse.co.uk W: ballifearyguesthouse.co.uk

Indicated Prices:
Single   from £40.00 per room   Kingsize Double from £80.00 per room
Double   from £70.00 per room   Twin   from £70.00 per room

13974

For a full listing of Quality Assured accommodation, please see directory at back of this guide.

Inverness
Craig Villa

Open: All year excl Xmas

Map Ref: 4B8

★★★★
BED AND BREAKFAST

42 Kenneth Street, Inverness, IV3 5DH
T: 01463 237568 E: info@craig-villa.co.uk W: craig-villa.co.uk

Indicated Prices:
Single   from £30.00 per room   Twin   from £60.00 per room
Double   from £60.00 per room

78424

Inverness
Abermar Guest House

Open: All year excl Xmas & New Year

Map Ref: 4B8

★★★
GUEST HOUSE

25 Fairfield Road, Inverness, IV3 5QD
T: 01463 239019 E: abermar@talk21.com W: abermar.co.uk

Indicated Prices:
Single   from £30.00   Twin   from £26.00 per person
Double   from £26.00 per person

10835

Inverness
Ardross and Glencairn Guest House

Open: All year

Map Ref: 4B8

Glencairn and Ardross Guest House is a family run guest house with a 3 star tourist board rating. The building is an elegant detached listed Victorian house situated in a quiet street close to the scenic River Ness and only a few minutes walk from Inverness town centre.

★★★
GUEST HOUSE

19 Ardross Street, Inverness, IV3 5NS
T: 01463 232965 E: ardrossglencairn@aol.com W: glencairnardross.co.uk

Indicated Prices:
Single   from £35.00 per person   Twin   from £30.00 per person
Double   from £30.00 per person   Family   from £25.00 per person

28023

Inverness
Bayview

Open: Apr-Oct

Map Ref: 4B8

★★★
BED AND BREAKFAST

West Hill, Inverness, IV2 5BP
T: 01463 790386 E: bayview.guest@lineone.net

Indicated Prices:
Single	from £35.00	Twin	from £54.00 per room
Double	from £54.00 per room		

14476

Inverness
Fairfield Villa

Open: All year

Map Ref: 4B8

★★★
BED AND BREAKFAST

34 Fairfield Road, Inverness, IV3 5QD
T: 01463 242243 E: macdonald631@btinternet.com

Indicated Prices:
Single	from £25.00	Twin	from £50.00 per room
Double	from £50.00 per room	Family	from £70.00 per room

73387

Inverness
Fraser House

Open: All year excl Feb-Mar

Map Ref: 4B8

★★★
GUEST HOUSE

49 Huntly Street, Inverness, IV3 5HS
T: 01463 716488 E: fraserlea@btopenworld.com W: fraserhouse.co.uk

Indicated Prices:
Single	from £30.00	Twin	from £50.00 per room
Double	from £50.00 per room	Family	from £65.00 per room

26777

Inverness
Glendoune B&B

Open: All year excl Xmas & New Year

Map Ref: 4B8

★★★
BED AND BREAKFAST

24 Perceval Road, Inverness, IV3 5QE
T: 01463 231493 E: angusnoble@aol.com W: glendoune.co.uk

Indicated Prices:
Double	from £27.50 per person	Twin	from £27.50 per person
		Family	from £27.50 per person

28111

For a full listing of Quality Assured accommodation, please see directory at back of this guide.

249

Inverness
Heronwood Bed and Breakfast

Open: All year excl Xmas & New Year   Map Ref: 4B9

★★★
BED AND BREAKFAST

16A Island Bank Road, Inverness, IV2 4QS
T: 01463 243275 E: heronwood@talk21.com W: heronwood-bed-and-breakfast.co.uk

Indicated Prices:
Double   from £28.00 per person   Twin   from £28.00 per person

30152

Inverness
MacDonald House

Open: All year excl 25-26 Dec   Map Ref: 4B8

★★★
GUEST HOUSE

1 Ardross Terrace, Inverness, IV3 5NQ
T: 01463 232878 E: f.blair@homecall.co.uk

Indicated Prices:
Single   from £45.00 per room   Twin   from £60.00 per room
Double   from £60.00 per room   Family   from £75.00 per room

36855

Inverness
Royston Guest House

Open: All year   Map Ref: 4B8

★★★
GUEST HOUSE

16 Millburn Road, Inverness, IV2 3PS
T: 01463 231243 E: roystonguesthouse@btinternet.com W: roystonguesthouse.com

Indicated Prices:
Single   from £35.00 per room   Twin   from £70.00 per room
Double   from £70.00 per room   Family   from £40.00 per person

52571

by Inverness
Eiland View Bed & Breakfast

Open: All year excl Xmas & New Year   Map Ref: 4B8

★★★★
BED AND BREAKFAST

Woodside of Culloden, Westhill, Inverness, IV2 5BP
T: 01463 798900 E: info@eilandview.com W: eilandview.com

Indicated Prices:
Single   from £35.00 per room   Twin   from £58.00 per room
Double   from £58.00 per room

24639

by Inverness
Stonea

Open: All year excl Xmas & New Year

Map Ref: 4B8

★★★
BED AND BREAKFAST

3A Resaurie, Smithton, by Inverness, IV2 7NH T: 01463 791714
E: mbmansfield@mansfieldhighlandholidays.com W: mansfieldhighlandholidays.com

Indicated Prices:

Single	from £33.00 per person	Twin	from £22.00 person
Double	from £22.00 per person		

56701

by Inverness
Westhill House

Open: Easter-Oct

Map Ref: 4B8

★★
BED AND BREAKFAST

Westhill, Inverness, Inverness-shire, IV2 5BP
T: 01463 793225 E: j.honnor@bigfoot.com W: scotland-info.co.uk/westhill.htm

Indicated Prices:

Single	from £30.00 per person	Twin	from £30.00 per person
Double	from £30.00 per person	Family	from £30.00 per person

63857

Lairg
Park House

Open: All year

Map Ref: 4A6

★★★★
GUEST HOUSE

Station Road, Lairg, Sutherland, IV27 4AU
T: 01549 402208 E: david-walker@park-house.freeserve.co.uk W: parkhousesporting.com

Indicated Prices:

Single	from £40.00 per room	Twin	from £70.00 per room
Double	from £70.00 per room	Family	from £95.00 per room

49185

Lochinver
Polcraig

Open: All year

Map Ref: 3G5

★★★★
GUEST HOUSE

Cruamer, Lochinver, Sutherland, IV27 4LD
T: 01571 844429 E: cathelmac@aol.com W: smoothhound.co.uk/hotels/polcraig.html

Indicated Prices:

Single	from £40.00	Twin	from £30.00 per person
Double	from £30.00 per person		

50075

For a full listing of Quality Assured accommodation, please see directory at back of this guide.

251

Lybster
Croft House
Open: All year   **Map Ref: 4D4**

★★★
BED AND BREAKFAST

Swiney, Lybster, KW3 6BT
T: 01593 721342 E: reservations@crofthouse.biz W: crofthouse.biz

Indicated Prices:
Single	from £32.00 per room	Twin	from £52.00 per room
Double	from £52.00 per room		

58725

Nairn
Greenlawns
Open: Mar-Nov, New Year   **Map Ref: 4C8**

★★★★
GUEST HOUSE

13 Seafield Street, Nairn, IV12 4HG
T: 01667 452738 E: greenlawns@cali.co.uk W: greenlawns.uk.com

Indicated Prices:
Single	from £32.00 per room	Twin	from £46.00 per room
Double	from £44.00 per room	Family	from £77.00 per room

29027

Nairn
Inveran Lodge
Open: All year   **Map Ref: 4C8**

★★★★
BED AND BREAKFAST

Seafield Street, Nairn, IV12 4HG
T: 01667 455666 E: info@inveranlodge.co.uk W: inveranlodge.co.uk

Indicated Prices:
Double	from £65.00 per room	Twin	from £65.00 per room

31909

Strathy Point
Sharvedda
Open: All year excl Xmas & New Year   **Map Ref: 4B3**

★★★★
BED AND BREAKFAST

Strathy Point, Strathy, Thurso, Sutherland, KW14 7RY
T: 01641 541311 E: patsy@sharvedda.co.uk W: sharvedda.co.uk

Indicated Prices:
Single	from £40.00	Twin	from £30.00 per person
Double	from £30.00 per person		

54321

Tain
Mrs K M Roberts
Open: All year **Map Ref: 4B7**

★★★
BED AND BREAKFAST

Carringtons, Morangie Road, Tain, IV19 1PY
T: 01862 892635 E: mollie1@btinternet.com W: stelogic.com/carringtons

Indicated Prices:

Single	from £25.00 per person	Twin	from £25.00 per person
Double	from £25.00 per person	Suite	from £25.00 per person
		Family	from £25.00 per person

18300

Thurso
Pentland Lodge House
Open: All year **Map Ref: 4D3**

★★★★
GUEST HOUSE

Granville Street, Thurso, Caithness, KW14 7XU
T: 01847 895103 E: info@pentlandlodgehouse.co.uk W: pentlandlodgehouse.co.uk

Indicated Prices:

Single	from £48.00 per room	Twin	from £84.00 per room
Double	from £80.00 per room	Family	from £90.00 per room

68291

Ullapool
Ardvreck Guest House
Open: Mar-Nov **Map Ref: 3G6**

★★★★
GUEST HOUSE

Morefield, Ullapool, Ross-shire, IV26 2TH
T: 01854 612028 E: ardvreck@btconnect.com W: www.SmoothHound.co.uk/hotels/ardvreck

Indicated Prices:

Single	from £35.00 per room	Twin	from £70.00 per room
Double	from £70.00 per room	Family	from £85.00 per room

12714

Ullapool
Dromnan Guest House
Open: Mar-Oct **Map Ref: 3G6**

★★★★
GUEST HOUSE

Garve Road, Ullapool, Ross-shire, IV26 2SX
T: 01854 612333 E: info@dromnan.com W: dromnan.co.uk

Indicated Prices:

Single	from £40.00 per room	Twin	from £78.00 per room
Double	from £75.00 per room	Family	from £80.00 per room

23205

For a full listing of Quality Assured accommodation, please see directory at back of this guide.

253

Ullapool
Broombank
Open: All year excl Xmas   Map Ref: 3G6

★★★
BED AND BREAKFAST

4 Castle Terrace, Ullapool, Ross-shire, IV26 2XD
T: 01854 612247 E: rj4broombank@btinternet.com W: broombankullapool.com

Indicated Prices:
Double   from £27.50 per person   Twin   from £27.50 per person

16566

Ullapool
Mrs P F R Browne
Open: Apr-mid Oct   Map Ref: 3G6

★★★
BED AND BREAKFAST

3 Castle Terrace, Ullapool, Ross-shire, IV26 2XD
T: 01854 612409 W: freewebs.com/pennybrowne

Indicated Prices:
Single   from £28.00 per person   Twin   from £27.00 per person
Double   from £28.00 per person

13701

by Ullapool
Torran
Open: All year excl Xmas & New Year   Map Ref: 3H6

★★★
BED AND BREAKFAST

Loggie, Lochbroom, Ullapool, Ross-shire, IV23 2SG
T: 01854 655227/07753 854281 E: mairi@torranloggie.co.uk W: torranloggie.co.uk

Indicated Prices:
Single   from £50.00 per room   Twin   from £60.00 per room
Double   from £60.00 per room

61575

Wick
The Clachan Bed and Breakfast
Open: All year excl Xmas & New Year   Map Ref: 4E3

★★★★ GOLD
BED AND BREAKFAST

13 Randolph Place, South Road, Wick, Caithness, KW1 5NJ
T: 01955 605384 E: enquiry@theclachan.co.uk W: theclachan.co.uk

Indicated Prices:
Single   from £50.00 per room   Twin   from £60.00 per room
Double   from £60.00 per room

58504

Self Catering and Camping & Caravan Parks

Invermudale Annexe

Open: All year

Map Ref: 4A4

★★★★
SELF CATERING

Invermudale, Altnaharra, by Lairg, Sutherland, IV27 4VE
T: 01549 411250 E: invermudale@btopenworld.com W: invermudale.co.uk

| 1 Cottage | 1 Bedroom | Sleeps 2 |

Prices – Cottage:
£300.00-£350.00   Per Week

Short breaks available

32029

Lower Inchlumpie

Open: All year

Map Ref: 4A7

★★★★
SELF CATERING

Strathrusdale, Ardross, Ross-shire, IV17 0YQ
T: 01903 260334 E: margaret@lowerinchlumpie.co.uk W: www.lowerinchlumpie.co.uk

| 1 House | 5 Bedrooms | Sleeps 2-8 |

Prices – House:
£650.00-£1250.00   Per Week

83023

For a full listing of Quality Assured accommodation, please see directory at back of this guide.

255

Beauly
Aigas Holiday Cottages

Open: Mar-Nov

Map Ref: 4A9

Aigas nestles spectacularly between the Aigas Forest and the peaceful river Beauly. Our holiday cottages, golf course and farm are the ideal base from which to enjoy the complete Highland holiday experience. Ten minutes drive from Beauly, 20 minutes drive from Inverness and Loch Ness, 40 minutes from Inverness Airport.

★★★
SELF CATERING

Mains of Aigas, Beauly, Inverness-shire, IV4 7AD
T: 01463 782423/782942 E: info@aigas-holidays.co.uk W: aigas-holidays.co.uk

3 Cottages	7 Bedrooms	Sleeps 4-5

Prices – Cottages:
£230.00-£590.00 Per Week

Short breaks available

37138

Beauly
Culligran Cottages

Open: Mid Mar-Mid Nov

Map Ref: 3H9

★★ UP TO ★★★
SELF CATERING

Glen Strathfarrar, Struy, Beauly, Inverness-shire, IV4 7JX
T: 01463 761285 E: info@culligrancottages.co.uk W: culligrancottages.co.uk

1 Cottage	3 Bedrooms	Sleeps 6 + sofabed
4 Cabins	2-3 Bedrooms	Sleeps 4-6 + sofabed

Prices – Cottage: Cabin:
£289.00-£529.00 Per Week   £199.00-£499.00 Per Week

Short breaks available

21682

by Beauly
Mrs C M Guthrie

Open: Apr-Oct

Map Ref: 4A9

★
SELF CATERING

41 Barrow Point Avenue, Pinner, Middlesex, HA5 3HD
T: 0208 866 5026

1 Cottage	2 Bedrooms	Sleeps 4

Prices – Cottage:
£190.00-£260.00 Per Week

38725

Important: Prices stated are estimates and may be subject to amendments. Prices are per person per night unless otherwise stated.

Bettyhill
Mrs Ola Todd

Open: All year

Map Ref: 4D3

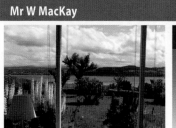

★★★★
SELF CATERING

Contact: Mrs Ola Todd, 6 Hoy Farm, Halkirk, Caithness, KW12 6UU
T: 01847 831544 E: olatodd@tiscali.co.uk W: visithighlands.com

| 1 House | 3 Bedrooms | Sleeps 6 |

Prices – House:
from £400.00   Per Week

Short breaks available

44774

Black Isle
Mr W MacKay

Open: Apr-Oct

Map Ref: 4B8

★★★
SELF CATERING

Fernvilla, Halebank Road, Widnes, Cheshire, WA8 8NP
T: 0151 425 2129/07795 202718 E: billandalisonmackay@yahoo.co.uk

| 1 Cottage | 3 Bedrooms | Sleeps 2-5 |

Prices – Cottage:
from £350.00   Per Week

50019

Cannich
Tomich Holidays

Open: All year

Map Ref: 3H9

★★★ UP TO ★★★★
SELF CATERING

Guisachan Farm, Tomich, Cannich, IV4 7LY
T: 01456 415332 E: admin@tomich-holidays.co.uk W: tomich-holidays.co.uk

| 6 Cottages | 2 Bedrooms | Sleeps 1-5 |
| 6 Wooden Chalets | 3 Bedrooms | Sleeps 1-6 |

Prices – Cottages: Wooden Chalets:
£260.00-£650.00   Per Week   £270.00-£630.00   Per Week

Short breaks available

48242

For a full listing of Quality Assured accommodation, please see directory at back of this guide.

Dalcross, Inverness
Easter Dalziel Farm Cottages

Open: All year　　　　　**Map Ref: 4B8**

Set amidst farmland with its abundant wildlife and our hairy Highland cattle, these three traditional stone cottages provide a superb base. Panoramic views, central location for castle and whisky trails, golfing, touring and family holidays. Mostly ground floor accommodation. All linen provided. Long or short breaks? You're welcome all year.

★★★ UP TO ★★★★
SELF CATERING

Easter Dalziel Farm, Dalcross, Inverness, IV2 7JL
T: 01667 462213　**E:** enquiries@easterdalzielfarm.co.uk　**W:** easterdalzielfarm.co.uk

3 Cottages	3 Bedrooms	Sleeps 2-6

Prices – Cottage:
£180.00-£520.00　　**Per Week**

Short breaks available

69716

by Dingwall
Fodderty Lodge

Open: All year　　　　　**Map Ref: 4A8**

★★★ UP TO ★★★★
SELF CATERING

Fodderty, by Dingwall, IV15 9UE
T: 01997 421393　**E:** lee@foddertylodge.com　**W:** foddertylodge.com

2 Cottages	2-3 Bedrooms	Sleeps 1-6
1 Apartment	1 Bedroom	Sleeps 1-2

Prices –Cottages:　　　**Apartment:**
£350.00-£620.00　**Per Week**　£215.00-£295.00　　**Per Week**

Short breaks available

40774

by Dingwall, Culbokie
Wester Brae Highland Lodges

Open: All year　　　　　**Map Ref: 4B8**

★★★★
SELF CATERING

Culbokie, Dingwall, Ross-shire, IV7 8JU
T: 01349 877609　**E:** westerbrae@btconnect.com　**W:** westerbraehighlandlodges.co.uk

4 Cottages	2-3 Bedrooms	Sleeps 2-6

Prices –Cottages:
£270.00-£510.00　　**Per Week**

Short breaks available

63804

Dornoch
Dornoch Caravan Park

Open: 1 Apr-26 Oct

Map Ref: 4B6

★★★★
HOLIDAY PARK

The Links, River Street, Dornoch, Sutherland, IV25 3LX
T: 01862 810423 E: info@dornochcaravans.co.uk W: dornochcaravans.co.uk
6 miles north of Tain, turn right for 2 miles to Dornoch. At bottom of square turn right for 450 yards.

Park accommodates 138 pitches. Total touring pitches: 120.
Prices per pitch:
🚐 (120) £9.50 ⛺ (120) £9.50 🚎 (120) £9.50

Holiday Caravans for Hire:
🏠 (18) £140.00-£360.00 per week.

Thistle

22963

by Dornoch, Embo
Grannies Heilan Hame Holiday Park

Open: Mar-Nov

Map Ref: 4B6

★★★★
HOLIDAY PARK

Embo, Dornoch, Sutherland, IV25 3QD
T: 0844 335 3728 E: via website W: parkdean.com
Follow A9 from Inverness, exit on to A949 for Dornoch and follow road for 3 miles then take right for Embo.

Park accommodates 237 pitches. Total touring pitches: 237.
Prices per pitch:
🚐 (237) £11.00-£29.00

Holiday Caravans for Hire:
🏠 (163) £199.00-£809.00 per week.

Thistle

68938

Drumnadrochit
Drumnadrochit Lodges

Open: All year

Map Ref: 4A9

★★★ UP TO ★★★★
SELF CATERING

Upper Achmony, Drumnadrochit, Inverness-shire, IV63 6UX
T: 01456 450467 E: drumnadrochit-lodges@tiscali.co.uk W: drumnadrochit-lodges.com
5 Lodges   3 Bedrooms   Sleeps 1-6

Prices – Lodge:
£300.00-£725.00   Per Week

Short breaks available

23328

by Drumnadrochit, Balnain
Glenurquhart Lodges

Open: All year

Map Ref: 4A9

Four lodges set in six acres of wooded grounds with scenic views of Loch Meikle and Glen Urquhart. Situated between Loch Ness and Glen Affric and ideal for touring the Scottish Highlands. Well equipped and furnished for six people. Owners hotel with welcoming restaurant and bar nearby.

★★ UP TO ★★★
SELF CATERING

Balnain, nr Drumnadrochit, Inverness-shire, IV63 6TJ
T: 01456 476234 E: carol@glenurquhartlodges.co.uk W: glenurquhart-lodges.co.uk

1 Bungalow	3 Bedrooms	Sleeps 2-6
3 Cabins	3 Bedrooms	Sleeps 2-6

Prices – Bungalow: **Cabin:**
£350.00-£850.00   Per Week   £230.00-£495.00   Per Week
Short breaks available

70432

Dundonnell
Badrallach DB&B, Bothy, Cottage & Campsite

Open: All year

Map Ref: 3G6

★★★★
SELF CATERING

Croft 9, Badrallach, Dundonnell, Ross-shire, IV23 2QP
T: 01854 633281 E: mail@badrallach.com W: badrallach.com

1 Cottage	2 Bedrooms	Sleeps 4
1 Hostel	1 Bedroom	Sleeps 12
2 Caravans	1 Bedroom	Sleeps 4
1 Camp Site	n/a	Sleeps 40

Prices – Cottage: **Hostel:**   **Caravans:**   **Camp Site:**
£230.00-£350.00   Per Week   £28.00-£420.00   Per Week   £200.00-£450.00   Per Week   £42.00-£52.00   Per Week
Short breaks available

50304

Durness
Norsehaven Cottages

Open: All year

Map Ref: 4A3

Three quality cottages in a land that is majestic, remote and unchanged. Ceannabeinne lies high above a superb sandy bay. A cosy croft converted in harmony with its dramatic location (sleeps 4). Craigmor and Cranstackie, in the village a short walk from Sango Bay, blend modern comforts with a mellow atmosphere of antique pine and natural stone (sleep 8 and 4).

★★★
SELF CATERING

Norsehaven Cottages, Oldbury House, Ightham, Sevenoaks, Kent, TN15 9DE
T: 01732 882320 E: info@norsehaven.com W: norsehaven.com

3 Cottages	1-4 Bedrooms	Sleeps 2-8

Prices – Cottage:
£295.00-£595.00   Per Week

Short breaks available

47617

Forsinard
Corn Mill Bunkhouse

Open: All year

Map Ref: 4C3

★★★★
HOSTEL

Achumore, Forsinard, Sutherland, KW13 6YT
T: 01641 571219/07808 197350 E: sandy.murray2@btinternet.com W: achumore.co.uk

1 Hostel	2 Bedrooms	Sleeps 14

Prices – Hostel:
£14.00   per bed per night

85001

Forsinard
Strath Halladale Partnership

Open: All year

Map Ref: 4C3

★★★ UP TO ★★★★
SELF CATERING

Estate Office, Forsinard, Sutherland, KW13 6YT
T: 01641 571271 E: info@strathhalladale.com W: strathhalladale.com

1 Cottage	2 Bedrooms	Sleeps 4
1 House	3 Bedrooms	Sleeps 6 adults +2 children
1 Bungalow	2 Bedrooms	Sleeps 4

Prices – Cottage:		**House:**		**Bungalow:**	
£300.00-£550.00	Per Week	£950.00-£1350.00	Per Week	£245.00-£450.00	Per Week

60534

For a full listing of Quality Assured accommodation, please see directory at back of this guide.

261

Fort Augustus
Morag's Lodge

Open: All year

Map Ref: 4A10

★★★★
HOSTEL

Bunoich Brae, Fort Augustus, Inverness-shire, PH32 4DG
T: 01320 366289 **E:** info@moragslodge.com **W:** moragslodge.com

| 1 Hostel | 18 Bedrooms | Sleeps 1-80 |

Prices – Hostel:
£17.00   Per Night

Short breaks available

38950

Fort Augustus
Bon Accord/Caledonian Cottages

Open: All year

Map Ref: 4A10

★★★
SELF CATERING

Canalside, Fort Augustus, PH32 4BA
T: 01925 740061/07896 577375 **E:** enquiries@caledoniancottages.co.uk **W:** caledoniancottages.co.uk

| 1 Cottage | 2 Bedrooms | Sleeps 2-4 |

Prices – Cottage:
£290.00-£600.00   Per Week

Short breaks available

81106

Glen Urquhart
Millness Croft Luxury Cottages

Open: All year

Map Ref: 4A9

★★★★★
SELF CATERING

Millness Croft, Glen Urquhart, Inverness, IV63 6TW
T: 01456 476761 **E:** info@millnesscroft.co.uk **W:** millnesscroft.co.uk

| 3 Cottages | 2 Bedrooms | Sleeps 1-4 |

Prices – Cottage:
£550.00-£970.00   Per Week

Short breaks available

68161

WALKING IN SCOTLAND

For everything you need to know about walking in Scotland
Scotland. Created for Walking visitscotland.com/walking

Northern Highlands, Inverness, Loch Ness and Nairn

Golspie
The Log Cabin
Open: Apr-Nov inclusive · Map Ref: 4B6

Very comfortable, fully equipped, ideal for family holiday. Situated on high ground in crofting district facing south. Lovely views over hills and woodland to the sea and Dornoch Firth. Semi wild garden merging into surrounding birch woods. Golspie 1½ miles with excellent shops, wonderful walks. Peaceful and quiet surroundings.

★★
SELF CATERING

Mr Scott, The Old School, Ann Street, Gatehouse of Fleet, Kirkcudbrightshire, DG7 2HU
T: 01557 814058

| 1 Log Cabin | 3 Bedrooms | Sleeps 5 |

Prices – Log Cabin:
£250.00-£400.00 Per Week

59556

Inverness
Mrs S Schwarzensteiner
Open: All year · Map Ref: 4B9

★★★
SELF CATERING

38 Glenburn Drive, Inverness, IV2 4ND
T: 01463 234817 E: douglas.burns@virgin.net

| 1 House | 3 Bedrooms | Sleeps 1-8 |

Prices – House:
£350.00-£500.00 Per Week

Short breaks available

42994

John O'Groats
John O'Groats Caravan & Camping Site
Open: 1 Apr-30 Sep · Map Ref: 4E2

★★★
TOURING PARK

John O'Groats, Caithness, KW1 4YR
T: 01955 611329/744 E: info@johnogroatscampsite.co.uk W: johnogroatscampsite.co.uk
At end of A99 beside last house in Scotland.

Park accommodates 90 pitches. Total touring pitches: 90.
Prices per pitch:
(90) £14.00-£15.00 (90) £11.00-£13.00
(90) £14.00-£15.00

33079

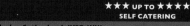
Northern Highlands, Inverness, Loch Ness and Nairn

Kylesku
Unapool House Cottages
Open: All year — **Map Ref: 3H4**

★★★ UP TO ★★★★★
SELF CATERING

Kylesku, Sutherland, IV27 4HW
T: 01971 502344 E: mail@unapoolhouse.co.uk W: unapoolhouse.co.uk
3 Cottages — 1-2 Bedrooms — Sleeps 1-3
Prices – Cottages:
£185.00-£385.00 Per Week
Short breaks available

80575

Lairg
Mrs Johan Reid
Open: Apr-Nov — **Map Ref: 4A6**

★★★
SELF CATERING

'Brown Villa', Lairg, Sutherland, IV27 4DD
T: 01779 473116/07732 545123 E: shona.reid@hotmail.co.uk W: visithighlands.com
1 House — 4 Bedrooms — Sleeps 6
Prices – House:
£290.00-£390.00 Per Week

16619

Lochinver
Cathair Dhubh Estate
Open: All year — **Map Ref: 3G5**

★★★★
SELF CATERING

Lochinver, IV27 4JB
T: 01571 855277 E: cathairdhubh@btinternet.com W: cathairdhubh.co.uk
5 Cottages — 2-3 Bedrooms — Sleeps 4-6
Prices – Cottage:
£287.00-£896.00 Per Week
Short breaks available

18551

Nairn
Nairn Lochloy Holiday Park
Open: Mar-Nov — **Map Ref: 4C8**

★★★★
HOLIDAY PARK

East Beach, Nairn, IV12 6PH
T: 0844 335 3728 E: via website W: parkdean.com

Park accommodates 13 pitches. Total touring pitches: 13.
Prices per pitch:
(89) £10.00-£32.00

Holiday Caravans for Hire:
(71) £219.00-£739.00 per week.

Thistle

46797

264   Important: Prices stated are estimates and may be subject to amendments. Prices are per person per night unless otherwise stated.

Scourie
Cnoclochan

Open: All year excl end Oct-Easter

Map Ref: 3G5

Cnoclochan stands on open ground in Scourie village with a footpath to the beach. There is excellent walking in the Northern Highlands. The Handa Bird Sanctuary is close for bird watching. These activities can also be enjoyed in the hills and on other magnificent sandy beaches.

★★
SELF CATERING

Cnoclochan, Scourie, by Lairg, Sutherland, IV27 4TE
T: 01483 274846 E: jmwqc@dial.pipex.com W: visitscotland.com

| 1 Bungalow | 3 Bedrooms | Sleeps up to 6 |

Prices – Bungalow:
£310.00-£440.00 **Per Week**

40930

Strathpeffer
Ross Holiday Homes

Open: Mar-Nov

Map Ref: 4A8

★★★
SELF CATERING

Eagle & Otter Lodges, Blackmuir Wood, Strathpeffer, Ross-shire, IV14 9BT
T: 01224 318520 E: enquiries@rossholidayhomes.co.uk W: rossholidayhomes.co.uk

| 2 Chalets | 2 Bedrooms | Sleeps 4 |

Prices – Chalets:
£250.00-£450.00 **Per Week**

Short breaks available

39704

by Tain, Fearn
Sycamore Country Lettings

Open: All year

Map Ref: 4C7

★★★★
SELF CATERING

Sandpiper Cottage, Fearn, Tain, Ross-shire, IV20 1TR
T: 01282 700425 E: enquiries@sycamorecountrylettings.co.uk W: sycamorecountrylettings.co.uk

| 1 Cottage | 3 Bedrooms | Sleeps 8 |

Prices – Cottage:
£500.00-£600.00 **Per Week**

Short breaks available

85164

For a full listing of Quality Assured accommodation, please see directory at back of this guide.

Thurso
Curlew Cottage

Open: All year

Map Ref: 4D3

★★★★
SELF CATERING

Hilliclay, Weydale, Thurso, Caithness, KW14 8YN
T: 01847 895638 E: macgregor@curlewcottage.com W: curlewcottage.com

1 Cottage   2 Bedrooms   Sleeps 1-4

Prices – Cottage:
£300.00-£485.00   Per Week

Short breaks available

21775

Torridon
Alt Na Criche

Open: All year

Map Ref: 3F8

A fully modernised cottage offering comfort and tranquility in a location of exceptional beauty on the shore of Loch Torridon. Newly fitted kitchen and bathrooms, one en-suite. Open fire and large picture window in lounge. Ideal touring base.

★★★
SELF CATERING

Alma House, 12 William Street, Torphins, Kincardineshire, AB31 4FR
T: 07872 387274/07885 363001 E: altnacriche@yahoo.co.uk

1 Cottage   3 Bedrooms   Sleeps 6

Prices – Cottage:
from £550.00   Per Week

69036

Ullapool
Mrs A L MacKenzie

Open: All year

Map Ref: 3G6

★★★
SELF CATERING

7 and 8 Mill Street, Ullapool, Ross-shire
T: 01854 666217 E: netta@mackenzieelphin.co.uk W: mackenzie-elphin.co.uk

2 Houses   2-3 Bedrooms   Sleeps 2-6

Prices – House:
£300.00-£400.00   Per Week

Short breaks available

60817

Important: Prices stated are estimates and may be subject to amendments. Prices are per person per night unless otherwise stated.

Ullapool
The Chalet & The Cottage

Open: All year

Map Ref: 3H6

Comfortable and well-equipped, our traditional croft cottage and chalet are sited in the peaceful area of Braes, about a mile south of Ullapool, with lovely views to the hills across Lochbroom. Ideal centre for exploring the beautiful north-west Highlands. Private parking.

★ ★
SELF CATERING

Sandy & Molly MacLennan, Invercorrie, Braes, Ullapool, Wester Ross, IV26 2TB
T: 01854 612272 E: mlas@globalnet.co.uk W: invercorrie.co.uk

1 Cottage	4 Bedrooms	Sleeps 6
1 Cabin	2 Bedrooms	Sleeps 4

Prices – Cottage: **Chalet:**
from £265.00   Per Week   from £255.00   Per Week

Short breaks available

31966

Inverness Castle and the River Ness

For a full listing of Quality Assured accommodation, please see directory at back of this guide.

267

Food & Drink

Contin
Coul House Hotel

Open: All year

Map Ref: 4A8

★★★
COUNTRY HOUSE HOTEL

Culinary Type:
SCOTTISH

Contin,
Ross-shire, IV14 9ES
T: 01997 421487
E: stay@coulhouse.com
W: coulhouse.com

Best For:
- Afternoon tea · Romantic meals
- Special occasion · Late dining · Group dining

Prices:

Starter from:	£4.00
Main Course from:	£16.00
Dessert from:	£6.00

Opening Times:
Lunch from 1200, last orders 1430.
Dinner from 1830, last orders 2100.
Soup and sandwiches all day

Seventeen miles north west of Inverness in the village of Contin, Ross-shire. Some know Contin for its salmon fishing on the Conon River and others for Rogie Waterfalls and the Achilty Forest. The perfect place to base oneself to explore both the east and west coasts of the Highlands often being able to choose the best of the weather.

20630

Important: Prices stated are estimates and may be subject to amendments. Prices are per person per night unless otherwise stated.

Dornoch
Dornoch Castle Hotel

Open: All year

Map Ref: 4B6

★★★
HOTEL

❀

Culinary Type:
SCOTTISH

Castle Street, Dornoch,
Sutherland, IV25 3SD

T: 01862 810216
E: enquiries@dornochcastlehotel.com
W: www.dornochcastlehotel.com

Best For:
- Afternoon tea • Romantic meals
- Special occasion • Late dining
- Lunch deals

Prices:

Starter from:	£5.50
Main Course from:	£10.50
Dessert from:	£5.50

Opening Times:
Lunch from 1200, last orders 1430.
Dinner from 1730, last orders 2130.
Snacks and platters all day

Dornoch Castle Hotel is a 15th century ecclesiastical keep and tower which is situated in the middle of the pretty village of Dornoch. Our head chef Mikael Helies and his team create seasonal, stylish menus which utilise the best local Scottish produce. AA Rosette for culinary excellence.

🅿 🚶

22964

Urquhart Castle, beside Loch Ness

For a full listing of Quality Assured accommodation, please see directory at back of this guide.

269

A steam train on the West Highland Line as it skirts Loch Eilt

Fort William, Lochaber, Skye and Lochalsh

This region is home to some of Scotland's most spectacular landscapes; imposing and dramatic mountains on the approach from Glencoe over to Rannoch Moor, breathtaking views across Loch Duich, the wild isolation of Ardnamurchan Point and the beautiful Small Isles. There are so many amazing places to discover, it's difficult to know where to begin.

Known as the Outdoor Capital of the UK, Fort William and Lochaber can be found next to Scotland's highest mountain, Ben Nevis and plays host to the Mountain Biking World Cup each year. Boasting a variety of terrain, from beaches and lochs to mountains and glens, find anything from low level hiking to adrenaline-filled gorge walking or canoeing.

For magnificent views, follow the legendary Road to the Isles from Fort William to Mallaig. A short trip by ferry from Mallaig will take you to the serenely beautiful Small Isles - Eigg, Rum, Canna and Muck - and the Isle of Skye. Ardnamurchan Point, meanwhile, is the most westerly point on the British mainland and a favourite spot for geologists and wildlife enthusiasts.

The turbulent history and majestic scenery of Skye and Lochalsh make the area one of Scotland's most romantic destinations. From the picture postcard Eilean Donan Castle to the soaring craggy heights of the Cuillin, walkers love to explore this region. And foodies are equally well catered for, with a wonderful natural larder and the likes of the world-famous Three Chimneys restaurant and the Talisker Distillery.

DON'T MISS

1   Voted 'Top Railway Journey in the World 2009' by Wanderlust Magazine, travel the whole length of the Road to the Isles on the **Jacobite Steam Train**. The journey between Fort William and Mallaig takes in some truly magnificent scenery, including views of Ben Nevis, Britain's highest mountain, the glorious coastline of Arisaig and Morar and the 21-arch Glenfinnan Viaduct made famous by the Harry Potter films. Use it as a way to visit Mallaig or en-route to Skye or the Small Isles.

2   Reintroduced from 1975, sea eagles have been a success story on Skye with many of the bold headlands providing refuge to at least one pair. The **Aros Centre** in Portree provides live nest-cams of the sea eagles - not to mention herons, owls and sparrow hawks - where you can watch as the birds feed and nurture their young. RSPB officers are on hand at the centre to answer any questions. Twice daily tours round Skye, a restaurant and cinema, ensures there is plenty of entertainment on offer.

3   Take to the open seas with **Rockhopper Sea Kayaking** and explore the spectacular coastal, mountain and island scenery around the west coast of Scotland. Rockhopper is based in Corpach near Fort William and offers half, full or multi-day trips, where you can expect to spot a variety of wildlife, including seals, dolphins, porpoise, otters, a huge variety of coastal birds - and perhaps even the white tailed sea eagle.

4   Accessible only by boat from Mallaig, or a 20-mile walk from Kinlochhourn, **Knoydart** is recognised as the last wilderness area of mainland Britain and is the perfect location for outdoor enthusiasts. Set up camp and explore one of the best hiking spots in the country, try some canoeing and fishing, and take in the breathtaking views. And don't forget to stop along the Old Forge - the most remote pub on mainland Britain according to the Guinness Book of Records - which takes pride in serving up a delicious seafood platter and pint of real ale to guests.

5   Take the opportunity to explore a little off the beaten track and visit **Glenelg**, which is accessed by an impressive pass offering views back across Loch Duich towards the 5 Sisters of Kintail. When in Glenelg, explore the three ancient brochs and Bernera Barracks (a fortification built in 1723 by the Government following the 1715 Jacobite uprising) before taking the small ferry across to Kylerhea on Skye. At Kylerhea visit the Forestry Commission otter haven and the Bright Water Visitor Centre - which tells the story of renowned naturalist and author Gavin Maxwell.

6   Take a boat trip from Elgol (B8083 from Broadford) to isolated and inspiring **Loch Coruisk**. Found at the very heart of the Cuillin, the walk around this magnificent loch's shores gives unrivalled views into the mountains. You will get up close to Britain's most dramatic landscapes, while your local guide will make sure you don't miss out on seeing the abundant wildlife – including the famous seal colony on the banks of the loch.

SHORT WALKS

7   Glencoe is one of the most popular hiking destinations in Scotland - and rightly so. For a beautiful walk through mixed woodland and views towards the distinctive peak of the Pap of Glencoe, follow the easy waymarked trails around the **Glencoe Lochans**. The 1.5 mile lochside walk is accessible to wheelchairs and will take around an hour - after which you can take advantage of the picnic tables and enjoy the view..

8   Follow the canal-side path from the entrance of the Caledonian Canal at Loch Linnhe and admire the famous **Neptune's Staircase**, a series of eight lock gates that lift boats 64 feet towards the Great Glen. Overlooked by Ben Nevis, all kinds of vessels use the busy staircase, including yachts, pleasure craft and boats.

9   The **Mallaig Circuit** is a well constructed network of paths leading up from the East Bay carpark in Mallaig through a hidden valley and up a minor detour to a hilltop viewpoint. Some way along, marvel at views of the remotest part of the British mainland, Knoydart over Loch Nevis. This hour-long walk offers a good opportunity to explore the harbour and small shops and galleries in Mallaig.

10   Explore the **Sunart Oakwoods** in Ardamurchan for great wildlife spotting opportunities. Park at the Ard Airigh car park and begin the walk along the wide path signposted 'Garbh Eilean wildlife hide - 780m'. Woodland paths give way to beautiful ancient oak birches and hazel trees, nestled amongst which is an excellent wildlife hide on the banks of Loch Sunart. Thanks to the oakwoods that provide shelter to the shore, this is a great place to see otters. Wheelchair access to the hide is available from the A861.

OUTDOOR ACTIVITIES

11   **Nevis Range** is a year round destination, offering everything from cross country and downhill mountain biking in the summer to skiing and snowboarding in the winter. Take Britain's only mountain gondola 650m up the slopes of Aonach Mor; enjoy panoramic Highland views, explore the Mountain Discovery Centre and relax in the Snowgoose Restaurant.

12   The biggest indoor ice climbing facility in the world, **The Ice Factor** is situated in a former aluminium works in Kinlochleven. With rock climbing walls, a gym, sauna, and plunge pool, this is a great day out for the whole family. As the National Centre for Indoor Ice Climbing, experts can try out new techniques whilst novices can get to grips with the basics in a safe and secure environment.

13   The award winning **Seaprobe Atlantis**, based at Kyle of Lochalsh, is the only semi-submersible glass bottom boat in Scotland, which allows passengers to explore the local marine environment, both above and below the waves. Enjoy the spectacular scenery of Skye and Lochalsh and superb close-up views of seals, otters and even sharks. Atlantis has a large underwater viewing gallery, where you can experience for yourself the rich diversity of marine wildlife in this European designated Special Area of Conservation.

14   Led by experienced, qualified guides, **Skyak Adventures** can guide novices and experts of any age around the spectacular scenic coastline of Skye. Many of the places on route can only be accessed by kayak - so expect to find some real hidden gems, from secluded beaches to rare wildlife.

OUTSTANDING VIEWS

15 Drive in either direction through the dramatic valley of Glencoe and you will be rewarded with inspiring views of the **Bidean nam Bian** range. Its dramatic northern ridges are known as the Three Sisters of Glencoe, which stand as imposing sentinels rising steeply from the floor of the glen. There are various walks up into the hills, but for those keen to avoid the rocky terrain, the view can just as easily be admired from the comfort of the carpark on the A82.

16 There are many classic views of the **Cuillin Ridge**. However, for sheer drama, few views in all of Scotland compare with the sight of Sgurr Nan Gillean rearing up behind Sligachan bridge, or the full mountain range rising almost sheer from Loch Scavaig, opposite the tiny village of Elgol, west of Broadford.

17 For an elevated view of Eilean Donan Castle and Loch Duich, take the road towards the village of Dornie. Follow the tiny road to the right signposted as **Carr Brae scenic viewpoint**, which leads you up the hillside. As well as fantastic views down to the castle, you can also see the mountains on the Isle of Skye to the west and Kintail to the east. The road continues along the hillside and eventually joins up with the main road at Inverinate.

18 **Camusdarach, Traigh** and the **Silver Sands of Morar** are just a selection of exquisite beaches along the shoreline between Arisaig and Mallaig. Spend some time picnicking, with the breathtaking backdrop of the Small Isles of Eigg and Rum rising out of the sea in front of you, and admire the changing light on the sea as it catches the numerous skerries that pepper the coast.

HERITAGE

19 Set at the head of Loch Sheil, the **Glenfinnan Monument** is a memorial to those who fought and died in the Jacobite uprising of 1745. Take in the views down Loch Sheil, as well as back towards the Glenfinnan Viaduct, both of which are stunning. There are some good short walks in the area, as well as a coffee shop and visitor centre, where you can find information and exhibitions.

20 The multi award-winning **Glencoe Visitor Centre** can be found nestled in the heart of Glencoe, just off the A82. Exciting interactive displays and video presentations tell the story of this fascinating part of the Highlands, from how the glen was formed millions of years ago to the massacre of Glencoe in 1692.

21 One of the most picturesque castles in Scotland, **Eilean Donan Castle**, sits on Loch Duich beside the tiny village of Dornie. Stroll across the causeway that links it to the shore and explore it for yourself. You can explore almost every part of the castle - from the Banqueting Hall to the bedrooms.

22 Located at Orbost on Skye, **Orbost Gallery** celebrates the beautiful art inspired by the impressive surroundings of Skye and the Hebrides. Pieces on display range from engravings and calligraphy to watercolours and prints from local artists. The gallery is open from April to September.

Hotels

The view to Portree

Important: Prices stated are estimates and may be subject to amendments. Prices are per person per night unless otherwise stated.

Fort William
Clan Macduff Hotel

Open: Apr-Oct 2010

Map Ref: 3G12

★★★
HOTEL

**Achintore Road,
Fort William, PH33 6RW**
T: 01397 702341
E: reception@clanmacduff.co.uk
W: clanmacduff.co.uk

Features:
- Excellent touring location for West Highlands
- All bedrooms ensuite, wireless internet, telephone
- Large free car park, passenger lift
- Ben Nevis 4 miles Glencoe 15 miles
- Spring and autumn special offers

Indicated Prices:

Single	from £38.50 per room
Double	from £27.50 per person
Twin	from £27.50 per person
Family	price on application

Overlooking Loch Linnhe only two miles south of Fort William. Our friendly helpful staff will soon put you at ease enabling you to enjoy magnificent views of the mountains and loch from the restaurant or lounges. Traditional restaurant menu or delicious bar suppers complemented by our wine list and numerous malt whiskies. Large selection of bedroom types to suit most requirements. This friendly family managed hotel is dedicated to providing good quality and value hospitality.

19453

or a full listing of Quality Assured accommodation, please see directory at back of this guide.

275

Fort William – Banavie
Moorings Hotel
Open: All year excl 23-26 Dec   **Map Ref: 3H12**

★★★
HOTEL

Banavie, Fort William, PH33 7LY
T: 01397 772797 E: reservations@moorings-fortwilliam.co.uk W: moorings-fortwilliam.co.uk

Indicated Prices:

Single	from £70.00 per room	Twin	from £98.00 per room
Double	from £98.00 per room	Suite	from £116.00 per room
		Family	from £120.00 per room

66659

Glenfinnan
The Prince's House Hotel
Open: Mar-Dec (closed 2 weeks in October & Xmas)   **Map Ref: 3G12**

★★★
SMALL HOTEL

Glenfinnan, Inverness-shire, PH37 4LT
T: 01397 722246 E: princeshouse@glenfinnan.co.uk W: glenfinnan.co.uk

Indicated Prices:

Single	from £60.00 per room	Twin	from £95.00 per room
Double	from £95.00 per room	Suite	from £130.00 per room

50489

Glenmoriston
Cluanie Inn
Open: All year   **Map Ref: 3G10**

★★★
SMALL HOTEL

Glenmoriston, Inverness-shire, IV63 7YW
T: 01320 340238 E: stay@cluanieinn.com W: cluanieinn.com

Indicated Prices:

Single	from £52.00	Twin	from £37.50 per person
Double	from £52.00 per person	Suite	from £67.50 per person

85224

Invergarry
Glengarry Castle Hotel

Open: 19 Mar-8 Nov 2010

Map Ref: 3H11

★★★★
COUNTRY HOUSE HOTEL

Invergarry,
Inverness-shire, PH35 4HW
T: 01809 501254
E: castle@glengarry.net
W: glengarry.net

Features:
- Eilean Donan Castle
- Isle of Skye
- Loch Ness
- Fort William
- Great Glen Way walks

Indicated Prices:

Single	from £62.00 per room
Double	from £90.00 per room
Twin	from £90.00 per room
Family room	from £140.00 per room

28180

Situated in the heart of the Great Glen overlooking Loch Oich, this is a perfect centre for day trips. To the north are Eilean Donan Castle and the Isle of Skye. Urquhart Castle, Loch Ness and Inverness can be toured on an outing east.

Fort William, Ben Bevis and the Road to the Isles make a good trip to the west coast. Also a great range of river, loch side and Great Glen Way walks all starting from the hotel.

For a full listing of Quality Assured accommodation, please see directory at back of this guide.

277

Kinlochleven
Tailrace Inn

Open: 09 - open all year

Map Ref: 3H12

★★★
INN

Riverside Road, Kinlochleven, Argyll, PH50 4QH
T: 01855 831777 E: tailrace@btconnect.com W: tailraceinn.co.uk

Indicated Prices:

Single	from £50.00 per room	Twin	from £70.00 per room
Double	from £70.00 per room	Family	from £70.00 per room

66920

Mallaig
West Highland Hotel

Open: Apr-Oct

Map Ref: 3F11

★★★
HOTEL

Mallaig, Inverness-shire, PH41 4QZ
T: 01687 462210 E: westhighland.hotel@virgin.net W: westhighlandhotel.co.uk

Indicated Prices:

Single	from £46.00 per room	Twin	from £85.00 per room
Double	from £85.00 per room	Family	from £110.00 per room

63661

Onich
Lodge on the Loch Hotel

Open: All year

Map Ref: 1F1

★★★
SMALL HOTEL

Onich, Fort William, PH33 6RY
T: 01855 821238 E: info@lodgeontheloch.com W: lodgeontheloch.com

Indicated Prices:

Double	from £86.00 per room	Twin	from £86.00 per room
		Suite	from £148.00 per room

59550

Important: Prices stated are estimates and may be subject to amendments. Prices are per person per night unless otherwise stated.

Isle of Raasay
Raasay House Hotel and Activities

Open: All year

Map Ref: 3E9

Based on the unique and unspoilt Isle of Raasay, we offer spacious accommodation with fantastic views of the Sound of Raasay, fabulous food using local produce, a licensed bar with Scottish ales and whiskys, an exciting range of activities for all ages, bike hire, amazing location for walking and wildlife.

★★★
SMALL HOTEL

Isle of Raasay, IV40 8PB
T: 01478 660266 E: info@raasay-house.co.uk W: raasay-house.co.uk

Indicated Prices:

Single	from £40.00 per room	Twin	from £65.00 per room
Double	from £65.00 per room	Family	from £80.00 per room

50965

Isle of Skye, Ardvasar
Ardvasar Hotel

Open: All year

Map Ref: 3E11

Set in a stunning location overlooking the Sound of Sleat and the magnificent Knoydart Mountains. Situated only 800 metres from Armadale, here the ferry from Mallaig brings you 'over the sea to Skye'. All rooms have been recently renovated offering a very high standard of accommodation. Excellent local seafood is served.

★★★
SMALL HOTEL

Ardvasar, Sleat, Isle of Skye, IV45 8RG
T: 01471 844223 E: richard@ardvasar-hotel.demon.co.uk W: ardvasarhotel.com

Indicated Prices:

Single	from £80.00	Twin	from £45.00 per person
Double	from £45.00 per person	Family	from £50.00 per person

12706

For a full listing of Quality Assured accommodation, please see directory at back of this guide.

279

Isle of Skye, Portree
Rosedale Hotel

Open: All year excl Nov-mid Mar

Map Ref: 3E9

The Rosedale Hotel is a small family run establishment with an eclectic mix of rooms spread over three buildings in a maze of corridors. All the rooms are different in size and decoration with most enjoying beautiful views over Portree Harbour. Come and enjoy some genuine Highland hospitality and relaxation.

★★★
HOTEL

Beaumont Crescent, Portree, Isle of Skye, IV51 9DF
T: 01478 613131 E: rosedalehotelsky@aol.com W: rosedalehotelskye.co.uk

Indicated Prices:

Single	from £30.00 per room		Twin	from £70.00 per room
Double	from £70.00 per room		Family	from £80.00 per room

52112

Isle of Skye, Portree
Royal Hotel

Open: All year excl 25 & 26 Dec

Map Ref: 3E9

Family run hotel in central position overlooking Portree Bay with all rooms ensuite and free use of the fitness centre. Tianavaig restaurant overlooking the Portree harbour serving home cooked local produce. Relax in MacNabs where you can sample our exclusive 'Macnabs ale' or malt whiskies and live entertainment. Well Plaid is our family friendly restaurant and caters to all tastes.

★★★
HOTEL

Bank Street, Portree, Isle of Skye, IV51 9BU
T: 01478 612525 E: info@royal-hotel-skye.com W: royal-hotel-skye.com

Indicated Prices:

Single	from £80.00	Twin	from £115.00 per room
Double	from £115.00 per room		

52487

Important: Prices stated are estimates and may be subject to amendments. Prices are per person per night unless otherwise stated.

Isle of Skye, Sleat
Duisdale House Hotel

Open: All year

Map Ref: 3F10

Duisdale House Hotel is a small, wildly romantic, luxury hotel, located on the Isle of Skye. Totally transformed over recent years it is a perfect base for touring the island's world famous sites of interest. Our award-winning chef showcases fresh island produce in delicious a la carte menus. Daily sailing trips.

★★★★
COUNTRY HOUSE HOTEL

Sleat, Isle of Skye, IV43 8QW
T: 01471 833202 E: info@duisdale.com W: duisdale.com

Indicated Prices:

Single	from £70.00	Twin	from £65.00 per person
Double	from £65.00 per person	Suite	from £100.00 per person

67064

Isle of Skye, Sleat
Toravaig House Hotel

Open: All year

Map Ref: 3F10

Toravaig House Hotel is an intimate, luxury hotel, located on the Isle of Skye ideally located for exploring the island and its beautiful coastline, mountains and historic castles. Beautiful contemporary bedrooms each individually designed. Award-winning fine dining showcases fresh local produce. Daily sailing trips on board luxury yacht May-September.

★★★★
SMALL HOTEL

Knock Bay, Sleat, Isle of Skye, IV44 8RE
T: 01471 820200 E: info@skyehotel.co.uk W: skyehotel.co.uk

Indicated Prices:

Single	from £70.00	Twin	from £65.00 per person
Double	from £65.00 per person	Suite	from £100.00 per person

61518

For a full listing of Quality Assured accommodation, please see directory at back of this guide.

281

Isle of Skye, Staffin
Flodigarry Country House Hotel

Open: All year excl 3 Nov-14 Dec and Jan

Map Ref: 3E7

Flodigarry is a sheltered haven amidst the dramatic scenery of Northern Skye and is magnificently situated with panoramic views across the sea to the Torridon Mountains. The hotel offers an excellent choice of 18 comfortable ensuite rooms both in the main house and Flora MacDonald Cottage.

★★★
COUNTRY HOUSE HOTEL

Flodigarry, Staffin, Isle of Skye, IV51 9HZ
T: 01470 552203 E: info@flodigarry.co.uk W: flodigarry.co.uk

Indicated Prices:

Single	from £80.00	Twin	from £50.00 per person
Double	from £60.00 per person	Family	from £80.00 per person

82783

Isle of Skye, Uig
Ferry Inn

Open: All year excl Xmas Day & New Year's Day

Map Ref: 3D8

★★★
INN

Uig, Isle of Skye, IV51 9XP
T: 01478 611216 E: info@ferryinn.co.uk W: ferryinn.co.uk

Indicated Prices:

Single	from £42.00 per room	Twin	from £74.00 per room
Double	from £74.00 per room		

25841

WALKING IN SCOTLAND

For everything you need to know about walking in Scotland
Scotland. Created for Walking visitscotland.com/walking

by Spean Bridge, Loch Lochy
Corriegour Lodge Hotel

Open: Mar-Nov & New Year; closed Dec & Jan

Map Ref: 3H11

★★★★
SMALL HOTEL

Loch Lochy,
by Spean Bridge, PH34 4CA
T: 01397 712685
E: info@corriegour.com
W: corriegour.com

Features:
• Views – stunning and panoramic loch vistas
• Food – fine dining – exquisite taste and texture
• Family – charming small hotel
• Peace – and tranquillity for discerning guests
• Location – walking, scenery and touring

Indicated Prices:

Single	from £79.00
Double	from £79.00 per person
Twin	from £79.00 per person
Family room	from £200.00 per room

20535

Corriegour Lodge Hotel has been lovingly restored to reflect the quality and furnishings of a bygone shooting lodge, whilst providing comfort and style. All 12 refurbished rooms provide the perfect blend of modern sophistication with traditional décor.

Corriegour is passionate about good food and doesn't compromise, sourcing all the freshest ingredients from the best suppliers. Good food and an extensive wine list to complement your meal and stunning views from the conservatory restaurant make this a dining pleasure.

For a full listing of Quality Assured accommodation, please see directory at back of this guide.

283

Strontian
Kilcamb Lodge
Open: 1 Feb-31 Dec — Map Ref: 1E1

★★★ GOLD
COUNTRY HOUSE HOTEL

Strontian, Argyll, PH36 4HY
T: 01967 402257 E: enquiries@kilcamblodge.co.uk W: kilcamblodge.co.uk

Indicated Prices:
Single	from £103.00 per room	Twin	from £168.00 per room
Double	from £168.00 per room	Suite	from £238.00 per room

33727

Guest Houses and B&Bs

Ballachulish
Craiglinnhe House
Open: All year excl Xmas — Map Ref: 1F1

★★★★
GUEST HOUSE

Lettermore, Ballachulish, PH49 4JD
T: 01855 811270 E: info@craiglinnhe.co.uk W: craiglinnhe.co.uk

Indicated Prices:
Double	from £56.00 to £85.00 per room	Twin	from £56.00 to £85.00 per room

73699

Important: Prices stated are estimates and may be subject to amendments. Prices are per person per night unless otherwise stated.

Ballachulish
Lyn-Leven Guest House   Open: All year excl Xmas   Map Ref: 1F1

Family-run award winning guest house with the freedom and comfort of a hotel at guest house prices, situated on the shores of Loch Leven- Glencoe one mile. Magnificent scenery with spectacular views of Glencoe and Mamore Hills. Ideal for all types of countryside activities. AA Selected 4 Stars.

★★★★
GUEST HOUSE

West Laroch, Ballachulish, Argyll, PH49 4JP
T: 01855 811392 W: lynleven.co.uk

Indicated Prices:
Single   from £35.00 per room   Twin   from £64.00 per room
Double   from £64.00 per room   Family from £80.00 per room

36649

Ballachulish
Dunire Guest House   Open: Feb-beginning Dec   Map Ref: 1F1

★★★
GUEST HOUSE

Glencoe, Ballachulish, Argyll, PH49 4HS
T: 01855 811305 E: dunire.glencoe@hotmail.co.uk W: www.dunireglencoe.co.uk

Indicated Prices:
Double   from £24.00 per person   Family from £24.00 per person
Twin   from £24.00 per person

23731

Ballachulish
Parkview Bed and Breakfast   Open: All year excl Xmas & New Year   Map Ref: 1F1

★★★
BED AND BREAKFAST

18 Park Road, Ballachulish, Argyll, PH49 4JS
T: 01855 811560 E: db.macaskill@talk21.com W: glencoe-parkview.co.uk

Indicated Prices:
Single   from £25.00 per room   Twin   from £20.00 per person
Double   from £20.00 per person

49238

Ballachulish
Strathassynt Guest House

Open: All year · Map Ref: 1F1

★★★
GUEST HOUSE

Loanfern, nr Glencoe, Ballachulish, PH49 4JB
T: 01855 811261 E: info@strathassynt.com W: strathassynt.com

Indicated Prices:

Single	from £25.00 per room	Twin	from £40.00 per room
Double	from £40.00 per room	Family	from £50.00 per room

56833

Dornie
Sealladh Mara

Open: All year · Map Ref: 3F9

Sealladh Mara is situated in the quiet Ross-shire village of Ardelve, overlooking the beautiful and historic Eilean Donan Castle, and within walking distance of the picturesque village of Dornie. The proprietor, Mrs Phyllis Peterkin, is friendly and helpful to her guests. Bikers welcome.

★★★
BED AND BREAKFAST

Ardelve, Dornie, Kyle of Lochalsh, IV40 8EY
T: 01599 555296 E: phyllis@sealladhmara.co.uk W: sealladhmara.co.uk

Indicated Prices:

Double	from £50.00 per room	Twin	from £50.00 per room
		Family	from £65.00 per room

54009

Important: Prices stated are estimates and may be subject to amendments. Prices are per person per night unless otherwise stated.

Fort William, Lochaber, Skye and Lochalsh

Fort William
The Gantocks

Open: All year excl Xmas & New Year

Map Ref: 3G12

The Gantocks overlooking Loch Linnhe is the perfect place to have a relaxing break. With three tastefully decorated bedrooms, all with power showers, two baths, attention to detail by your Highland hosts is guaranteed. The imaginative breakfast is individually prepared and based round fresh local produce and home baking.

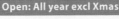
★★★★★
BED AND BREAKFAST

Achintore Road, Fort William, PH33 6RN
T: 01397 702050 E: thegantocks@hotmail.co.uk W: fortwilliam5star.co.uk

Indicated Prices:
Double   from £90.00 per room

78946

Fort William
Argyll House

Open: All year excl Xmas

Map Ref: 3G12

Located in Fort William town centre and with views of Loch Linnhe and the Ardgour Hills, Argyll House is ideally located for hill walking and sight seeing. Conveniently placed for train and bus stations with ample private parking. All rooms very comfortable, fully ensuite and finished to a high standard.

★★★★
BED AND BREAKFAST

Hillside Estate, Fort William, PH33 6RS
T: 01397 700004 E: mairi@argyllhouse-bnb.co.uk W: argyllhouse-bnb.co.uk

Indicated Prices:
Single   from £45.00 per room   Twin   from £60.00 per room
Double   from £60.00 per room

82550

For a full listing of Quality Assured accommodation, please see directory at back of this guide.   287

Fort William, Lochaber, Skye and Lochalsh

Fort William
Carna B&B

Open: All year excl Xmas

Map Ref: 3G12

★★★★
BED AND BREAKFAST

Carna, Achintore Road, Fort William, PH33 6RQ
T: 01397 708995 E: stay@carnabandb.co.uk W: carnabandb.co.uk

Indicated Prices:

Double	from £40.00 per person	Twin	from £40.00 per person

83178

Fort William
Lawriestone Guest House

Open: All year excl Xmas & New Year

Map Ref: 3G12

A warm welcome awaits you at Lawriestone. The beautifully furnished rooms are all en-suite with TV, tea and coffee etc. At breakfast a varied selection including Scottish and vegetarian is available. Experience our hospitality and beautiful location by Loch Linnhe and the surrounding hills. Only 5 minutes walk to town.

★★★★
BED AND BREAKFAST

Achintore Road, Fort William, PH33 6RQ
T: 01397 700777 E: susan@lawriestone.co.uk W: lawriestone.co.uk

Indicated Prices:

Double	from £30.00 per person	Twin	from £30.00 per person
		Family	from £30.00 per person

68003

Fort William
Mayfield Bed & Breakfast

Open: Mar-Oct

Map Ref: 3H12

★★★★
BED AND BREAKFAST

Happy Valley, Torlundy, Fort William, PH33 6SN
T: 01397 703320 E: mayfield@torlundy.co.uk W: torlundy.co.uk

Indicated Prices:

Single	from £35.00 per room
Double	from £60.00 per room

37718

---

288   Important: Prices stated are estimates and may be subject to amendments. Prices are per person per night unless otherwise stated.

Fort William, Lochaber, Skye and Lochalsh

Fort William
Alt-An Lodge
Open: All year excl Xmas & New Year   **Map Ref: 3G12**

★★★
BED AND BREAKFAST

Achintore Road, Fort William, Inverness-shire, PH33 6RN
T: 01397 704546   E: altanlodge@googlemail.com   W: bedandbreakfastfortwilliam.co.uk

Indicated Prices:
Single	from £36.00 per room	Twin	from £50.00 per room
Double	from £50.00 per room		

11780

Fort William
Ben Nevis View B&B
Open: Feb-end Oct   **Map Ref: 3G12**

★★★
BED AND BREAKFAST

Station Road, Corpach, Fort William, PH33 7JH
T: 01397 772131   E: info@bennevisview.co.uk   W: bennevisview.co.uk

Indicated Prices:
Single	from £30.00 per room	Twin	from £25.00 per person
Double	from £25.00 per person	Family	from £75.00 per room

14886

Fort William
Ben View Guest House
Open: Easter-Oct   **Map Ref: 3H12**

★★★
GUEST HOUSE

Belford Road, Fort William, PH33 6ER
T: 01397 702966   E: jim@gowanbraes.freeserve.co.uk

Indicated Prices:
Single	from £30.00 per room	Twin	from £55.00 per room
Double	from £52.00 per room		

14895

Fort William
Guisachan House
Open: All year   **Map Ref: 3H12**

★★★
GUEST HOUSE

Alma Road, Fort William, Inverness-shire, PH33 6HA
T: 01397 703797   E: guisachanhouse@aol.com   W: fortwilliamholidays.co.uk

Indicated Prices:
Single	from £30.00 per room	Twin	from £60.00 per room
Double	from £60.00 per room	Family	from £75.00 per room

29247

For a full listing of Quality Assured accommodation, please see directory at back of this guide.

289

Fort William
The Neuk Guest House
Open: All year excl Xmas & New Year Map Ref: 3G12

★★★
BED AND BREAKFAST

Corpach, Fort William, PH33 7LR
T: 01397 772244 E: norma.mccallum@theneuk.fsbusiness.co.uk W: theneuk.fsbusiness.co.uk

Indicated Prices:
Single	from £40.00 per room	Twin	from £58.00 per room
Double	from £52.00 per room	Family	from £75.00 per room

59765

Fort William
Craig Nevis Guest House
Open: All year Map Ref: 3H12

★★
GUEST HOUSE

Belford Road, Fort William, Inverness-shire, PH33 6BU
T: 01397 702023 E: craigdon42@hotmail.com W: craignevis.co.uk

Indicated Prices:
Double	from £25.00 per person	Twin	from £25.00 per person

21033

Fort William – Banavie
Rhiw Goch Guest House
Open: Apr-Oct Map Ref: 3H12

★★★
BED AND BREAKFAST

Banavie, Fort William, PH33 7LY
T: 01397 772373 E: kay@rhiwgoch.co.uk W: rhiwgoch.co.uk

Indicated Prices:
Twin	from £28.00 per person	Single	from £38.00

51545

Fort William – Banavie
Taormina
Open: Apr-Sept Map Ref: 3H12

★
BED AND BREAKFAST

Banavie, Fort William, PH33 7LY
T: 01397 772217

Indicated Prices:
Single	from £22.00 per room	Twin	from £42.00 per room
Double	from £42.00 per room	Family	from £56.00 per room

42183

Glencoe
Highland View B&B

Open: All year

Map Ref: 1F1

★★★★
BED AND BREAKFAST

Creag Dhu House, North Ballachulish, PH33 6RY
T: 01855 821555 E: highlandviewbb@btinternet.com W: highlandviewbandb.co.uk

Indicated Prices:

Single	from £60.00 per room	Twin	from £60.00 per room
Double	from £60.00 per room	Family	from £60.00 per room

72867

Glencoe
Scorrybreac Guest House

Open: All year excl Xmas

Map Ref: 1F1

Scorrybreac sits on the edge of Glencoe village in an elevated tranquil spot surrounded by trees and mountains with a spectacular view across Loch Leven and the mountains beyond. The house has been upgraded and modernised over the years and offers well appointed bedrooms. A perfect base for exploring.

★★★★
GUEST HOUSE

Glencoe, Argyll, PH49 4HT
T: 01855 811354 E: info@scorrybreac.co.uk W: scorrybreac.co.uk

Indicated Prices:

Single	from £44.00 per room	Twin	from £54.00 per room
Double	from £54.00 per room	Family	from £90.00 per room

53242

For a full listing of Quality Assured accommodation, please see directory at back of this guide.

291

Fort William, Lochaber, Skye and Lochalsh

Kinlochleven
Edencoille Guest House
Open: All year   **Map Ref: 3H12**

This is a warm and welcoming 4 star familiy run guest house with comfortably appointed rooms complete with their own television, coffee and tea facilities, hairdryers and foot spas and separate guest lounge. Renowned for our quality of breakfasts with an extensive selection of dishes which will start your day properly.

★★★★
GUEST HOUSE

Garbhein Road, Kinlochleven, Argyll, PH50 4SE
T: 01855 831358 E: edencoille@tiscali.co.uk W: kinlochlevenbedandbreakfast.co.uk

Indicated Prices:

Single	from £34.00	Twin	from £34.00 per person
Double	from £34.00 per person	Family	from £34.00 per person

24382

by Kyle of Lochalsh, Balmacara
Balmacara Lodge Bed and Breakfast
Open: All year excl Xmas   **Map Ref: 3F9**

★★★
BED AND BREAKFAST

Balmacara Square, Balmacara, by Kyle of Lochalsh, Ross-shire, IV40 8DP
T: 01599 566282 E: angela@balmacaralodge.com W: balmacaralodge.com

Indicated Prices:

Double	from £27.50 per person	Twin	from £27.50 per person

83346

Mallaig
Seaview Guest House
Open: Mar-Oct   **Map Ref: 3F11**

★★★
GUEST HOUSE

Main Street, Mallaig, Inverness-shire
T: 01687 462059 E: info@seaviewguesthousemallaig.com W: seaviewguesthousemallaig.com

Indicated Prices:

Double	from £27.50 per person	Twin	from £27.50 per person

54062

   Important: Prices stated are estimates and may be subject to amendments. Prices are per person per night unless otherwise stated.

Onich
Cuilcheanna House

Open: All year excl Xmas & New Year

Map Ref: 1F1

★★★★
GUEST HOUSE

Onich, Fort William, Inverness-shire, PH33 6SD
T: 01855 821226 E: kirstienblack@yahoo.co.uk W: cuilcheanna.co.uk

Indicated Prices:

Single	from £37.50 per room	Twin	from £75.00 per room
Double	from £75.00 per room		

80509

Onich
The Woolly Rock Bed & Breakfast

Open: All year

Map Ref: 1F1

★★★
BED AND BREAKFAST

North Ballachulish, Inverness-shire, PH33 6SA
T: 01855 821338 E: rogerlucas@woollyrock.co.uk W: woollyrock.co.uk

Indicated Prices:

Single	from £40.00 per room	Twin	from £55.00 per room
Double	from £55.00 per room		

75969

by Plockton
Soluis Mu Thuath Guest House

Open: All year

Map Ref: 3F9

Situated near Plockton in peaceful Strath Ascaig. Soluis Mu Thuath is set in open countryside with stunning mountain views. All rooms are spacious with ensuite facilities. Excellent centre for north west of Scotland including Skye, Applecross and Torridon. No smoking. Evening meal available. Suitable for accompanied disabled visitors.

★★★
GUEST HOUSE

Braeintra, by Achmore, Plockton, IV53 8UP
T: 01599 577219 E: soluismuthuath@btopenworld.com W: highlandsaccommodation.co.uk

Indicated Prices:

Single	from £35.00 per room	Twin	from £50.00 per room
Double	from £50.00 per room	Family	from £75.00 per room

43723

For a full listing of Quality Assured accommodation, please see directory at back of this guide.

Crossal House
Isle of Skye, by Carbost

Open: All year excl Xmas & New Year

Map Ref: 3E9

★★★
BED AND BREAKFAST

Crossal, by Carbost, Isle of Skye, IV47 8SP
T: 01478 640745 E: andrea@richardson9031.freeserve.co.uk W: crossal.co.uk

Indicated Prices:
Double   from £55.00 per room   Twin   from £55.00 per room

21453

Roskhill House
Isle of Skye, Dunvegan

Open: Mar-Dec

Map Ref: 3D9

★★★★
GUEST HOUSE

Roskhill, Dunvegan, Isle of Skye, IV55 8ZD
T: 01470 521317 E: stay@roskhillhouse.co.uk W: roskhillhouse.co.uk

Indicated Prices:
Single   from £42.00 per room   Twin   from £66.00 per room
Double   from £64.00 per room

82999

Dalriada Guest House
Isle of Skye, Portree

Open: All year excl Xmas & New Year

Map Ref: 3E9

Enjoy a warm welcome and tasty breakfast in our comfortable home with relaxing guest lounge. All rooms ensuite. We are situated in a peaceful rural location with panoramic views, just 1½ miles from Portree. Dalriada makes an ideal base to explore the island and experience its many delights.

★★★
GUEST HOUSE

Dalriada, Achachork, Portree, Isle of Skye, IV51 9HT
T: 01478 612397 E: duncan.brown1@tiscali.co.uk W: dalriadaguesthouse.co.uk

Indicated Prices:
Single   from £25.00 per person   Twin   from £25.00 per person
Double   from £25.00 per person   Family   from £25.00 per person

22096

Isle of Skye, Portree
Mrs Elizabeth MacDonald
Open: All year

Map Ref: 3E9

★★★
BED AND BREAKFAST

25 Urquhart Place, Portree, Isle of Skye, IV51 9HJ
T: 01478 612374/07738 709924 E: lizmacdonald118@btinternet.com

Indicated Prices:

Single	from £25.00 per person	Twin	from £25.00 per person
Double	from £25.00 per person	Family	from £22.00 per person

43206

Isle of Skye, Uig
Cnoc Preasach
Open: Mar-Oct

Map Ref: 3D8

★★★
BED AND BREAKFAST

2 Peinlich, Glenhinnisdale, by Uig, Isle of Skye, IV51 9UY
T: 01470 542406

Indicated Prices:

Single	from £25.00	Twin	from £25.00 per person
Double	from £25.00 per person		

19855

Isle of Skye, Uig
Mrs Mary MacLeod
Open: Mar-Oct

Map Ref: 3D8

★★★
BED AND BREAKFAST

11 Earlish, Uig, by Portree, Isle of Skye, IV51 9XL
T: 01470 542319

Indicated Prices:

Single	from £23.00	Twin	from £23.00 per person
Double	from £23.00 per person	Family	from £23.00 per person

44654

Isle of Skye, Upper Breakish
Tir Alainn
Open: Mid Mar-Oct

Map Ref: 3F10

★★★★
BED AND BREAKFAST

8 Upper Breakish, Isle of Skye, IV42 8PY
T: 01471 822366 E: tiralainn@btinternet.com W: visitskye.com

Indicated Prices:

Single	from £40.00 per room
Double	from £75.00 per room

61323

For a full listing of Quality Assured accommodation, please see directory at back of this guide.

295

Spean Bridge
Faegour House

Open: All year

Map Ref: 3H12

★★★★
BED AND BREAKFAST

Tirindrish, Roybridge Road, Spean Bridge, PH34 5EU
T: 01397 712903 E: enquiry@faegour.co.uk W: faegour.co.uk
Indicated Prices:
Double   from £32.50 per person   Double/Family   from £32.50 per person

25454

Spean Bridge
Riverside Lodge Gardens B&B

Open: Apr-Oct

Map Ref: 3H12

Set back at the end of a beautiful
tree lined cul-de-sac with the river
flowing past the garden. Quality,
spacious accommodation awaits you
in a relaxing, friendly atmosphere.
Breakfast is served overlooking
the Nevis mountain range whilst
indulging in the wide choices
available. Easy walking distance to
excellent eating opportunities.

★★★★
BED AND BREAKFAST

Spean Bridge, Inverness-shire, PH34 4EN
T: 01397 712702/07789 517833 E: colincfindlay@aol.com W: visitscotland-spean.co.uk
Indicated Prices:
Single   from £45.00 per room   Twin   from £70.00 per room
Double   from £70.00 per room   Family   from £80.00 per room

67874

Spean Bridge
Riverside House

Open: Mar-Nov

Map Ref: 3H11

★★★★
BED AND BREAKFAST

Invergloy, Spean Bridge, Inverness-shire, PH34 4DY
T: 01397 712684 E: enquiries@riversidelodge.org.uk W: riversidelodge.org.uk
Indicated Prices:
Family   from £35.00 per person

51706

Spean Bridge
Coire Glas Guest House

Open: All year excl Xmas   **Map Ref: 3H12**

★★★
GUEST HOUSE

Roybridge Road, Spean Bridge, PH34 4EU
T: 01397 712272 E: enquiry@coireglas.co.uk W: coireglas.co.uk

Indicated Prices:

Single	from £40.00 per room		Twin	from £60.00 per room
Double	from £60.00 per room		Triple	from £80.00 per room
			Family	from £90.00 per room

19970

Spean Bridge
Inverour Guest House

Open: All year   **Map Ref: 3H12**

★★★
GUEST HOUSE

Roy Bridge Road, Spean Bridge, PH34 4EU
T: 01397 712218 E: enquiries@inverourguesthouse.co.uk W: inverourguesthouse.co.uk

Indicated Prices:

Single	from £27.50 per room		Twin	from £55.00 per room
Double	from £55.00 per room		Family	from £75.00 per room

32084

Self Catering and Camping & Caravan Parks

Arisaig
Ach na skia Croft

Open: All year   **Map Ref: 3F11**

★★★ UP TO ★★★★
SELF CATERING

Arisaig, Inverness-shire, PH39 4NS
T: 01687 450606 E: achnaskia@aol.com W: achnaskiacroft.co.uk

1 Cottage	2 Bedrooms	Sleeps 1-4+baby
3 Wooden Lodges	2 Bedrooms	Sleeps 1-5+baby

Prices – Cottage: **Wooden Lodges:**
£320.00-£575.00 Per Week   £345.00-£625.00 Per Week

Short breaks available

10998

Ballachulish
Red Squirrel Campsite

Open: All year

Map Ref: 1F1

Natural, happy and clean site with small camp fires until 11pm. Swim in river. Simple showers. WCs with hot and cold water. Mountains all round. Inn with weekend music and meals 2 miles. Choose own pitch, tree lined or riverside. Historic area. Good location for day trips by car or bike. Walks, fishing, boats etc 3 miles.

★★
CAMPING PARK

Leacantuim Farm, Glencoe, Argyll, PH49 4HX
T: **01855 811256**

On loop road 2 miles from Glencoe village on A82, turn right after small loch or, up village street and on 1½ miles.

Park accommodates 250 pitches. Total touring pitches: 250.   Kids under 12 years 50p
Prices per pitch:
🏕 £7.50   🚐 £7.50

51261

Balmacara
Reraig Caravan Site

Open: May-Sep

Map Ref: 1F1

★★★★
TOURING PARK

Balmacara, Kyle of Lochalsh, IV40 8DH
T: **01599 566215** E: **warden@reraig.com** W: **reraig.com**
On A87 2 miles west of junction with A890. 4 miles east of bridge to Isle of Skye.

Park accommodates 40 pitches. Total touring pitches: 40.
Prices per pitch:
🚐 (40) See website for prices   🏕 (5) See website for prices
🚐 (40) See website for prices

51469

Fort William
Glen Nevis Caravan & Camping Park

Open: Mar-Oct   **Map Ref: 3H12**

★★★★★
HOLIDAY PARK

Glen Nevis, Fort William, Inverness-shire, PH33 6SX
T: 01397 702191 E: holidays@glen-nevis.co.uk W: glen-nevis.co.uk

On A82 proceed to mini roundabout at northern outskirts of Fort William, exit for Glen Nevis Park 2½ miles on right.

An award-winning 5 star touring park offering excellent facilities and separate areas for caravans/motor-homes and tents with a purpose built motor-home service point. Set amidst magnificent scenery at the foot of mighty Ben Nevis, this is an ideal tour location for the Western Highlands and beyond.

Park accommodates 250 pitches. Total touring pitches: 250.
Prices per pitch:
(250) £11.20-£17.00 (130) £7.60-£16.00
(250) £11.20-£17.00 Cottages (12) sleeps 2-4

Holiday Caravans for Hire:
(22) £315.00-£540.00 per week. Sleeps 2-6.

27935

Fort William
The Logs

Open: All year   **Map Ref: 3H12**

★★★★
SELF CATERING

24 Zetland Avenue, Fort William, Inverness-shire, PH33 6LL
T: 01397 702532 E: thelogs@scotland-info.co.uk W: scotland-info.co.uk/thelogs

1 House   6 Bedrooms   Sleeps 2-10
Prices – House:
£550.00-£1350.00   Per Week
Short breaks available

59558

Fort William
Taigh Nan Chleirich

Open: All year   **Map Ref: 3G12**

★★★
SELF CATERING

14 Perth Place, Fort William, PH33 6UL
T: 01397 702444 E: neil.m.clark@hotmail.co.uk W: taighnanchleirich.website.orange.co.uk

1 Self-Contained Flat   1 Bedroom   Sleeps 2-4
Prices – Self-Contained Flat:
£135.00-£195.00   Per Week
Short breaks available

43091

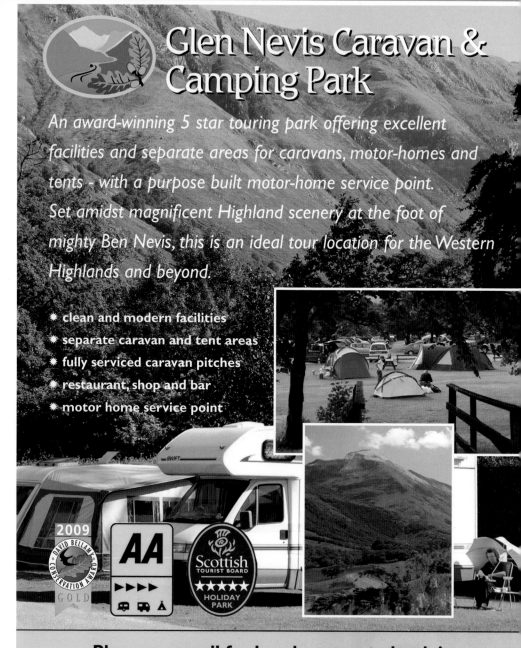

Glen Nevis Caravan & Camping Park

An award-winning 5 star touring park offering excellent facilities and separate areas for caravans, motor-homes and tents - with a purpose built motor-home service point. Set amidst magnificent Highland scenery at the foot of mighty Ben Nevis, this is an ideal tour location for the Western Highlands and beyond.

* clean and modern facilities
* separate caravan and tent areas
* fully serviced caravan pitches
* restaurant, shop and bar
* motor home service point

Phone or email for brochures or to book !
Tel: 0044 (0)1397 702191
holidays@glen-nevis.co.uk   www.glen-nevis.co.uk

27935

Fort William
Cruachan Caravans
Open: Feb-Nov **Map Ref: 3G12**

MINIMUM STANDARD HOLIDAY CARAVAN

Cruachan, 19 Badabarie, Corpach, Fort William, PH33 7JG
T: 01397 772573 W: visitscotland.com
Situated on the A830, before Corpach village on the right hand side of main road.

Holiday Caravans for Hire:
(3) £210.00–£255.00 per week.

21532

Fort William – Banavie
Christine Donnachie
Open: Feb-Nov **Map Ref: 3H12**

Three bedroom (two ensuite) bungalow three miles from Fort William. Quiet rural setting. Living room, dining room and kitchen to front. Wonderful views of Ben Nevis and surrounding hills. Full oil central heating and open coal fire. Large patio and garden. Fully equipped. Very comfortable.

★★★
SELF CATERING

Mount Alexander, Banavie, Fort William, PH33 7NF
T: 01397 704466 E: christine@donnachie5987.freeserve.co.uk W: benneviscottage.co.uk
1 Bungalow 3 Bedrooms Sleeps 6
Prices – Bungalow:
£300.00–£480.00 Per Week
Short breaks available

39172

Glencoe
Glencoe Hideaway Lochview
Open: All year **Map Ref: 1F1**

★★★
SELF CATERING

9 Tighphuirt, Glencoe, Argyll, PH49 4HN
T: 01895 675662 E: stay@glencoe-hideaway.co.uk W: glencoe-hideaway.co.uk
1 Cottage 2 Bedrooms Sleeps 2-6
Prices – Cottage:
£300.00–£550.00 Per Week
Short breaks available

28045

Invercoe
Invercoe Caravan & Camping Park

Open: All year

Map Ref: 1F1

A family run park set amidst spectacular scenery with magnificent views over Loch Leven. Covered picnic/BBQ area, children's playpark, laundrette, shop, slipway access available. A great base to explore Fort William, Oban, Skye and Mull. Wi-fi available (chargeable).

★★★★★
HOLIDAY PARK

Invercoe, Glencoe, PH49 4HP
T: **01855 811210** E: **holidays@invercoe.co.uk** W: **invercoe.co.uk**

Park accommodates 60 pitches. Total touring pitches: 60.
Prices per pitch:
🚐 (60) £20.00–£25.00 ⛺ (60) £18.00–£25.00
🚌 (60) £20.00–£25.00

Holiday Caravans for Hire:
(4) £325.00–£500.00 per week.
Sleeps 1-4.

Thistle

71207

Knoydart
Creag Eiridh

Open: All year excl New Year

Map Ref: 3F11

Situated loch side, this lovely house has spacious accommodation, equipped and furnished to a high standard, offering a very comfortable holiday home for large families or small groups wanting an unforgettable holiday amid the hills and rivers of this fantastic area.

★★★
SELF CATERING

Geoff & Ginny Hayward, Blynfield, Stour Row, Shaftesbury, Dorset, SP7 0QW
T: **01747 852289** E: **creageiridh@virginiahayward.com** W: **creageiridh.co.uk**

1 House   5 Bedrooms   Sleeps 2-10

Prices – House:
£1000.00–£1500.00   Per Week

Short breaks available

15522

Important: Prices stated are estimates and may be subject to amendments. Prices are per person per night unless otherwise stated.

Fort William, Lochaber, Skye and Lochalsh

Kyle of Lochalsh
Lamont Holiday Homes
Open: All year — Map Ref: 3F10

★★★
SELF CATERING

Creagmhor, Glenelg, Kyle of Lochalsh, IV40 8LA
T: 01599 522231 E: lamont@creagmhor.plus.com W: creagmhor.plus.com

1 Bungalow — 3 Bedrooms — Sleeps 2-6
Prices – Bungalow:
£235.00-£420.00 Per Week

Short breaks available

21199

Letterfearn
Sealoch Cottages
Open: All year — Map Ref: 3G10

★★★★★
SELF CATERING

Lochside House, Letterfearn, by Kyle of Lochalsh, IV40 8HT
T: 0844 815 9967 (Quote 54532) W: hoseasons.co.uk/cottages

1 House — 4 Bedrooms — Sleeps 8

Prices – House: £500.00-£1100.00 Per Week

Short breaks available

85103

Onich
Springwell Holidays
Open: All year — Map Ref: 1F1

★★★ UP TO ★★★★
SELF CATERING

Onich, Fort William, PH33 6RY
T: 07977 981370 E: rc@springwellholidays.co.uk W: springwellholidays.co.uk

6 Cottages — 2-4 Bedrooms — Sleeps 4-8
Prices – Cottages:
£300.00-£950.00 Per Week

Short breaks available

79605

Onich
Bunree Holiday Cottages
Open: All year — Map Ref: 3G12

★★★
SELF CATERING

Janika, Bunree, Onich, Fort William, PH33 6SE
T: 01855 821359 E: janika@btinternet.com W: holiday-homes.org

2 Cottages — 2 Bedrooms — Sleeps 4
2 Apartments — 2 Bedrooms — Sleeps 4
Prices – Cottages: £285.00-£465.00 Per Week
Apartment: £285.00-£465.00 Per Week
Short breaks available Oct-Apr

32769

Isle of Skye, Armadale
Clan Donald Skye Lodges

Open: All year   **Map Ref: 3E11**

Six purpose built lodges situated on the hillside above Armadale, opposite Knoydart, with outstanding views over the Sound of Sleat. We also offer the Foresters Cottage that nestles in a clearing and the tasteful Flora MacDonald Suite situated within the restored Stable building.

★★★ UP TO ★★★★
SELF CATERING

Sleat, Isle of Skye, IV45 8RS
T: 01471 844305 E: office@clandonald.com W: clandonald.com

6 Cottages	2-3 Bedrooms	Sleeps 4-6
1 House	2 Bedrooms	Sleeps 4
1 Apartment	2 Bedrooms	Sleeps 4

Prices –Cottages:		House:		Apartment:	
£310.00-£585.00	Per Week	£310.00-£550.00	Per Week	£410.00-£670.00	Per Week

Short breaks available

19449

Isle of Skye, Carbost
Mrs J M Brown

Open: All year excl Xmas & New Year   **Map Ref: 3D9**

Detached bungalow in enclosed garden ground overlooks Loch Harport and within one mile of Talisker Distillery. Viewing Cuillin Ridge within eight miles of Sligachan and Glenbrittle. Glenbrittle has safe sandy beach and camp site shop. Level walks and off-road cycling on forest roads. Sky TV, double and twin, electric heating included.

★★
SELF CATERING

11 Laggan Road, Inverness, IV2 4EH
T: 01463 235793 E: j.brown793@btinternet.com *or* browns.glenbrittle@virgin.net

1 Bungalow	2 Bedrooms	Sleeps 4-6

Prices – Bungalow:	
£280.00-£320.00	Per Week

Short breaks available

35966

# Fort William, Lochaber, Skye and Lochalsh

Isle of Skye, Portree
Coolin Lodge
Open: All year   **Map Ref: 3E9**

★★★★★
SELF CATERING

Coolin Hills Estate, Portree, Isle of Skye, IV51 9LU
T: 01478 613240   E: info@coolinlodge.co.uk   W: coolinlodge.co.uk

| 1 House | 2 Bedrooms | Sleeps 4 |

Prices – House:
£800.00   Per Week

85441

Isle of Skye, Portree
Gleniffer House
Open: All year   **Map Ref: 3E9**

★★★★
SELF CATERING

Beaumont Crescent, Portree, Isle of Skye, IV51 9DF
T: 01478 612048   E: rohwersafaris@hotmail.com   W: selfcatering-isleofskye-scotland.com

| 1 House | 3 Bedrooms | Sleeps 2-6 |

Prices – House:
£350.00-£750.00   Per Week

Short breaks available

28215

Isle of Skye, by Portree
Lawries Thatched Cottage
Open: All year   **Map Ref: 3D8**

★★★
SELF CATERING

8 Totescore, Kilmuir, by Portree, Isle of Skye, IV51 9UW
T: 01470 542409   E: macinnes_83@msn.com

| 1 Cottage | 1 Bedroom | Sleeps 2 |

Prices – Cottage:
£270.00-£390.00   Per Week

69701

Isle of Skye, Skinidin
Mr A MacFarlane
Open: All year   **Map Ref: 3D9**

★★★
SELF CATERING

11 Elm Road, Hale, Altrincham, Cheshire, WA15 9QW
T: 0161 941 3440   E: aa_sa@mcfarlane7789.freeserve.co.uk

| 1 Bungalow | 3 Bedrooms | Sleeps 5 |

Prices – Bungalow:
£280.00-£560.00   Per Week

14703

For a full listing of Quality Assured accommodation, please see directory at back of this guide.

305

Spean Bridge
Corrieview Lodges

Open: All year   Map Ref: 3H11

Fully equipped lodges with two downstairs bedrooms and upstairs living area. Patio doors lead from the lounge to a small wooden balcony with panoramic views across the glen to the Nevis Mountain Range. Village shops and pubs within a few minutes walk.

★★★★
SELF CATERING

Grey Corries, Spean Bridge, Inverness-shire, PH34 4DX
T: 01397 712395 E: fantasticviews@corrieviewlodges.com W: corrieviewlodges.com

| 2 Lodges | 2 Bedrooms | Sleeps 2-5 |

Prices – Lodges:
£295.00-£550.00   Per Week

Short breaks available

29091

Spean Bridge
Gairlochy Holiday Park

Open: Dec-Oct   Map Ref: 3H11

★★★★
SELF CATERING

Spean Bridge, Inverness-shire, PH34 4EQ
T: 01397 712711 E: theghp@talk21.com W: theghp.co.uk

| 3 Lodges | 2 Bedrooms | Sleeps 4 |
| 4 Caravans | 2 Bedrooms | Sleeps 4 |

Prices – Lodges: Caravans:
£285.00-£615.00   Per Week   £225.00-£465.00   Per Week

Short breaks available

69782

Spean Bridge
Riverside Lodges

Open: All year   Map Ref: 3H11

★★★★
SELF CATERING

Invergloy, Spean Bridge, Inverness-shire, PH34 4DY
T: 01397 712684 E: enquiries@riversidelodge.org.uk W: riversidelodge.org.uk

| 3 Chalets | 3 Bedrooms | Sleeps 6 |

Prices – Chalets:
£450.00-£760.00   Per Week

Short breaks available

70348

Food & Drink

Fort William
Glen Nevis Restaurant & Bar

Open: All year

Map Ref: 3H12

★★★★★
HOLIDAY PARK

Culinary Type:
SCOTTISH

Glen Nevis,
Fort William, PH33 6SX
T: 01397 705459
E: restaurant@glen-nevis.co.uk
W: glennevisrestaurant.co.uk

Best For:
- Afternoon tea • Kids and families
- Outstanding views • Special occasion
- Group dining

Prices:
Starters from	£3.50
Main courses from	£8.50
Desserts from	£5.50

Opening Times:
Lunch from 1200, last orders by 1700
Dinner from 1800, last orders by 2130
Food served all day

Located in one of Scotland's most beautiful glens at the foot of Ben Nevis and only minutes from Fort William. Glen Nevis Restaurant and Lounge Bar offers a good Scottish menu from teas, light meals and snacks to full meals and refreshments all in a friendly, relaxing and pleasant environment.

27935

For a full listing of Quality Assured accommodation, please see directory at back of this guide.

307

by Spean Bridge, Loch Lochy
Corriegour Lodge Hotel

Open:

Map Ref: 3H11

★★★★
SMALL HOTEL

**Culinary Type:
SCOTTISH**
Loch Lochy, by Spean Bridge,
Inverness, PH34 4EA
T: 01397 712685
E: info@corriegour.com
W: corriegour.com

Best For:
- Romantic meals • Outstanding views
- Special occasion • Breakfast
- Group dining

Prices:
From   £47.50

Opening Times:
Dinner from 18:30, last orders 20:30.

Corriegour is passionate about good food and does not compromise sourcing all the freshest ingredients from the best of suppliers. Good food costs more but when delivered in style in a restaurant with views and an extensive wine list to complement your meal – you know it is worth it.

20535

Blackboard sign, Isle of Skye

Important: Prices stated are estimates and may be subject to amendments. Prices are per person per night unless otherwise stated.

Approaching The Lairig Ghru by mountain bike, Cairngorms National Park

Moray, Aviemore and the Cairngorms

If you love the great outdoors, you'll be impressed by the range of activities on offer around Moray, Aviemore and the Cairngorms.

For watersports, including canoeing, sailing and windsurfing, head for Loch Insh or Loch Morlich. Hillwalkers will find the Cairngorm range offers a challenge while the more leisurely can wander to their heart's content in Rothiemurchus Estate, Inshriach Forest, Craigellachie National Nature Reserve, Glenlivet Estate and many other hidden gems.

Discover wildlife abound in these spectacular and varied landscapes. Spot crested tits and red squirrels in pine forests, ptarmigan in the mountains and, for a chance to see the rarer pine martens and capercaillie, join a ranger guided walk or spend an evening in a nature hide. Explore the Moray coastline for bottlenose dolphin and the occasional minke whale.

There are plenty of exciting ways to get around. Travel by steam train from Aviemore to Boat of Garten and Broomhill, ascend Cairn Gorm on the funicular railway or even charter a yacht to explore the Moray coast.

Moray is whisky country and is home to more than 50 distilleries - around half the total distilleries in Scotland. With some of the world's biggest names in whisky within a relatively short distance, any visit to this region would not be complete without exploring the waymarked Malt Whisky Trail through beautiful Speyside.

Bow Fiddle Rock, Portnockie, Moray

DON'T MISS

1 **Cairngorms National Park** is home to 25% of the UK's threatened bird, animal and plant species. The Cairngorms is the best place to see the Scottish crossbill, the only bird unique to Britain. Golden eagle, osprey, dotterell, capercaillie, and crested tit are just a few of the bird species found here. The National Park is home to a wide variety of animals - including pine martens, red squirrels, badgers, wildcats, water vole and otters.

2 Throughout Badenoch and Strathspey Highland Council hold a wide ranging programme of **ranger guided walks** with an emphasis on exploring the local area, flora and fauna. Join other likeminded walkers on these tours and share the experience of seeing some of Britain's rarest wildlife and plant species in outstanding scenery that distinctly changes character with the light.

3 Scotland's whisky trail signposts lead you through the picturesque lush countryside of Speyside, the world's favourite malt whisky region. Discover eight distilleries on the **Malt Whisky Trail** and enjoy the wide-ranging flavour of malts whisky as you wind your way through Speyside sampling each one. Also on the trail is the family owned Speyside Cooperage where you can watch oak whisky barrels being constructed using traditional methods.

4 Elgin boasts a number of remarkable **historical sites**. Elgin Cathedral is a well-preserved 13th century ruin with many architectural features, including the country's finest octagonal chapter house. Discover a thousand years of Scottish history with a Moray perspective at Elgin Museum and visit Spynie Palace, which, until 1686, was the residence of the bishops of Moray for five centuries. A mighty tower, named David's Tower, dominates the south west corner of the palace - at 22m this was one of the largest tower houses ever built in Scotland.

5 When **ospreys** returned to breed in Scotland, the ancient Caledonian pinewood of Loch Garten was their first choice. Watch these magnificent birds bring fish to their chicks from the RSPB hide or on non-invasive CCTV. The reserve also has some excellent walks where you can spot red squirrels, crested tits and dragonflies. The ospreys are in residence from April till August but birds like capercaillie, redstart and goldeneye fill the calendar.

6 At the heart of the beautiful Cairngorms National Park is the **Cairngorm Mountain Railway**. As the UK's highest funicular railway, it takes eight minutes from bottom to top. Enjoy the stunning panoramic views of the National Park and visit the interactive exhibition, which tells the history and ecology of the surrounding area. Have a bite to eat and take in the view stretching from the Cairngorm plateau to the Monadliath Mountains and beyond.

SHORT WALKS

7   The attractions from **Cullen to Portknockie** start with the superb viaducts of a former railway line built in the late 19th century, and takes in the broad stretches of sand at Cullen Bay, Bow Fiddle Rock (a curiously shaped rock formation) and the Preacher's Cave. Look out for a variety of birdlife and even dolphins, which are known to be frequent visitors to the Moray coastline. This 6km walk loops back to Cullen, where you can try some of the town's delicious namesake soup, Cullen Skink.

8   **Coire an Lochain** makes a quieter, longer alternative to the popular Coire an t-Sneachda walk, and is a fine challenge for seasoned hillwalkers. The paths give way to an exposed walk, so a full kit is required. This route has views across to some popular climbs, the most famous being Savage Slit, a rock-climb which follows a crack all the way up the large western buttress. The summit offers great views over Strathspey.

9   Covering around 65 miles, **The Speyside Way** runs from Buckie on the shore of the Moray Firth coast, south westwards towards Aviemore on the edge of the Cairngorm Mountains. Walkers can appreciate diverse landscapes from the heart of the Cairngorms National Park through to the coastal scenery of Spey Bay.

10   The walk around **Loch an Eilein** is a popular route and, after you've completed the 7km circuit, you'll understand why. There are good footpaths around this beautiful loch, surrounded by the magnificent pines of Rothiemurchus Forest. This route can be extended to take in the quieter Loch Gamhna. The centre of Loch an Eilein has an island with a castle on it. Formerly a stronghold of the Wolf of Badenoch the castle was once connected to the shore by a causeway but that was lost when the water level was raised in the 18th century.

ACTIVITIES

11   Based on the sandy shore of Loch Morlich at the foot of Cairngorm, **Loch Morlich Watersports** caters for all abilities with a range of activities, including sailing, kayaking, and windsurfing. A range of hire is available, while lessons from qualified instructors will make sure you really get the most from your visit. This beautiful loch recently made history as the first fresh water loch to receive Blue Flag status for its beach.

12   Up to 30km of fun-packed mountain biking awaits at the **Moray Monster Trails**. Find three independent sites within easy distance of one other. So for those with a truly monster appetite and stamina to match, try all three sites end to end, from Fochabers to Craigellachie. For the more leisurely try the green-graded trail at Quarrelwood, by Elgin. There are also plenty of waymarked walking routes around the woodlands.

13   Enjoy year-round outdoor fun and action at the **Lecht Multi-Activity Centre**. With summer action on quad bikes, fun karts, dévalkarts and chairlift rides, winter is covered by skiing, snowboarding and tubing. A new mountain bike trail at the top of the hill can also be accessed by a three-man chairlift. The 'Red Fox' trail, a red run with a length of 1,600m, boasts an assortment of dirt jumps, bomb holes and riding features built from rock. The second mountain cross trail, 'Blue Hare' (1,900m), is a blue single track complete with easy jumps, bermed corners, avoidance lanes and passing places. .

14   **Glenlivet Estate** is a large Highland estate in the foothills of the Cairngorms offering more than 100 miles of way-marked trails which can be accessed for walking, cycling or horse riding. There are a number of pursuits to enjoy, from Landrover tours and ranger guided walks to stocked trout lochs for fishing enthusiasts. An important habitat for a diverse range of wildlife, the estate boasts no less than five Sites of Special Scientific Interest (SSSI).

WILDLIFE

15 **Speyside Wildlife** run fully guided, bird, mammal watching holidays, in Scotland, for enthusiasts of every ability, plus tailor-made wildlife watching tours of any length to suit your requirements. Their comfortable wildlife hides in the Cairngorms National Park offer a close up and personal view of pine martens, badgers and more.

16 When **ospreys** returned to breed in Scotland the ancient Caledonian pinewood of Loch Garten was their first choice. Watch from the RSPB hide or on non-invasive CCTV as these magnificent birds bring fish to their chicks. The reserve also has some excellent walks where you can spot red squirrels, crested tits and dragonflies. The ospreys are in residence from April till August but birds like capercaillie, redstart and goldeneye fill the calendar.

17 **Insh Marshes Bird Reserve** is a birdwatcher's paradise! Considered one of the most important wetlands in Europe, early spring is best for breeding waders, including lapwings, curlews, snipe and redshank, while ospreys fish in the loch. In autumn and winter, the marshes host flocks of whooper swans and greylag geese with roe deer and wildcat at the marsh edges. There are also three woodland trail areas to explore: Invertromie (4.5 km), Lynachlaggan (2.5 km) and Loch Insh Woods (2 km).

18 **Culbin Forest** meets the Moray coast between Nairn and Forres and offers cycling and walking on gentle paths with junction markers so you can make it up as you go along. Look out for notoriously furtive creatures such as otters, roe deer, badger and heron at Otter Pool, trace the human legacy at Cublin at the Hidden History stopping point and enjoy the magnificent view from the 20m viewing tower at Hill 99 – a 99ft sand dune.

VISITOR ATTRACTIONS

19 Find fun for all the family at the **Landmark Forest Adventure Park** - a haven for adventure activities. Water slides, zip line, climbing poles, high-wires and a climbing wall make this a place to explore and great fun for children. There's an opportunity to see red squirrels up close at the wildlife feeding area and pinewood birds as you make your way through the tree top trail. Climb the 105 steps to the top of the Fire Tower and watch the Funicular Railway climb Cairngorm 12 miles away!

20 In the heart of Malt Whisky Country lies **Speyside Cooperage**, the only working cooperage in the UK where you can experience the ancient art of producing whisky barrels. The Acorn to Cask exhibition will take you on a journey through the lifecycle of the cask, where you will learn why, in years gone by, every household and every business depended on a Cooper.

21 The **Cairngorm Reindeer Centre** is home to the only reindeer herd in the country and, living in their natural environment out on the Cairngorm Mountains and the Cromdale Hills, this is a fantastic opportunity to encounter the animals living freely. During a guided tour, wander freely among the reindeer, stroking and feeding them. These friendly deer are a delight to all ages.

22 Independently run since 1797, Scottish woollen mill Johnstons has been making beautiful knitwear, clothing and accessories from luxurious wools for more than 200 years. Visit the **Johnstons Cashmere Heritage Centre** in Elgin, where you can learn the story of the only Scottish mill to transform cashmere from fibre to garment. Take the engaging tour, before stopping in the tempting food hall for refreshments.

Hotels

Aberlour
Dowans Hotel

Open: All year

Map Ref: 4D9

Set above the village of Aberlour with views over the Spey Valley and the river below, the Dowans Hotel offers the opportunity for guests to relax and enjoy the friendly ambience of a Scottish country house hotel. The attractive building provides comfortable accommodation including whisky themed rooms with complimentary drams.

★★★
SMALL HOTEL

Aberlour, AB38 9LS
T: 01340 871488 E: enquiries@dowanshotel.com W: dowanshotel.com

Indicated Prices:

Single	from £68.00 per room		Twin	from £110.00 per room
Double	from £110.00 per room		Suite	from £150.00 per room
			Family	from £160.00 per room

79270

Carrbridge
The Cairn Hotel

Open: All year excl Xmas

Map Ref: 4C9

★★★
INN

Main Road, Carrbridge, Inverness-shire, PH23 3AS
T: 01479 841212 E: info@cairnhotel.co.uk W: cairnhotel.co.uk

Indicated Prices:

Single	from £28.00		Twin	from £28.00 per person
Double	from £28.00 per person		Family	from £70.00 per room

17400

For a full listing of Quality Assured accommodation, please see directory at back of this guide.

Carrbridge
Dalrachney Lodge Hotel

Open: All year

Map Ref: 4C9

Situated within the Cairngorm National Park in the heart of the Scottish Highlands, Dalrachney is an ideal base for a memorable holiday. Enjoy breathtaking scenery, abundant wildlife and numerous outdoor activities. Spacious, well-appointed rooms. Emphasis on good food and wine served in a relaxed and friendly setting.

★★★
COUNTRY HOUSE HOTEL

Grantown Road, Carrbridge, Inverness-shire PH23 3AT
T: 01479 841252 E: dalrachney@aol.com W: dalrachney.com

Indicated Prices:

Single	from £65.00 per room	Twin	from £83.00 per room
Double	from £83.00 per room	Family	from £100.00 per room

22083

Cullen
The Seafield Arms Hotel

Open: All year excl 1 day between Xmas & New Year

Map Ref: 4E7

★★★
HOTEL

17-19 Seafield Street, Cullen, Moray, AB56 4SG
T: 01542 840791 E: info@theseafieldarms.co.uk W: theseafieldarms.co.uk

Indicated Prices:

Single	from £63.00 per room	Twin	from £94.00 per room
Double	from £94.00 per room	Suite	from £139.00 per room
		Family	from £119.00 per room

60356

Important: Prices stated are estimates and may be subject to amendments. Prices are per person per night unless otherwise stated.

Forres
Knockomie Hotel

Open: All year excl 25-26 Dec

Map Ref: 4C8

Set back in four acres of garden and woodland, Knockomie is a new generation of hotel in the country providing friendly, honest and unstuffy service. With the Grill Room offering the finest local produce and well stocked Malt Library bar, you're assured of a great time. Local attractions include Brodie Castle, Cawdor Castle, Loch Ness, Johnston's Cashmere Centre in Elgin and Benromach Distillery.

★★★★
SMALL HOTEL

Grantown Road, Forres, IV36 2SG
T: 01309 673146 E: stay@knockomie.co.uk W: knockomie.co.uk

Indicated Prices:

Single	from £149.00 per room	Twin	from £149.00 per room
Double	from £149.00 per room	Family	from £169.00 per room

34487

Grantown on Spey
Culdearn House

Open: All year

Map Ref: 4C9

★★★★★
SMALL HOTEL

Woodlands Terrace, Grantown on Spey, Moray, PH26 3JU
T: 01479 872106 E: enquiries@culdearn.com W: culdearn.com

Indicated Prices:

Single	from £100.00 per room	Twin	from £130.00 per room
Double	from £130.00 per room	Suite	from £150.00 per room

21664

Kingussie
Duke of Gordon Hotel

Open: All year

Map Ref: 4B11

★★★
HOTEL

Newtonmore Road, Kingussie, PH21 1HE
T: 01540 661302 E: reception@dukeofgordonhotel.co.uk W: dukeofgordonhotel.co.uk

Indicated Prices:

Single	from £69.00 per room	Twin	from £138.00 per room
Double	from £138.00 per room	Family	from £207.00 per room

17444

For a full listing of Quality Assured accommodation, please see directory at back of this guide.

Guest Houses and B&Bs

Aviemore
Ardlogie Guest House

Open: All year

Map Ref: 4C10

★★★
GUEST HOUSE

Dalfaber Road, Aviemore, Inverness-shire, PH22 1PU
T: 01479 810747 E: ardlogie@btinternet.com W: ardlogie.co.uk

Indicated Prices:

Double	from £60.00 per room	Twin	from £60.00 per room
		Family	from £78.00 per room

76065

Aviemore
Cairn Eilrig

Open: All year

Map Ref: 4C10

★★★
BED AND BREAKFAST

Glenmore, Aviemore, PH22 1QU
T: 01479 861223 E: mary@cairneilrig.com W: bedandbreakfast-aviemore-glenmore.com

Indicated Prices:

Single	from £25.00	Twin	from £25.00 per person
Double	from £25.00 per person	Family	from £25.00 per person

17397

Aviemore
Cairngorm Guest House

Open: All year excl Xmas

Map Ref: 4C10

★★★
GUEST HOUSE

139 Grampian Road, Aviemore, PH22 1RP
T: 01479 810630 E: enquiries@cairngormguesthouse.com W: cairngormguesthouse.com

Indicated Prices:

Single	from £40.00 per room	Twin	from £60.00 per room
Double	from £60.00 per room	Family	from £80.00 per room

17434

Important: Prices stated are estimates and may be subject to amendments. Prices are per person per night unless otherwise stated.

Moray, Aviemore and the Cairngorms

Aviemore
Carn Mhor Bed & Breakfast
Open: All year **Map Ref: 4C10**

★★★
BED AND BREAKFAST

The Shieling, Aviemore, PH22 1QD
T: 01479 811004 E: info@carnmhor.co.uk W: carnmhor.co.uk

Indicated Prices:

Single	from £40.00 per room	Twin	from £55.00 per room
Double	from £55.00 per room	Family	from £70.00 per room

69293

Aviemore
Eriskay B&B
Open: All year **Map Ref: 4C10**

AWAITING GRADING

Craig-na-Gower Avenue, Aviemore, Inverness-shire, PH22 1RW
T: 01479 810717 E: enquiry@eriskay-aviemore.co.uk W: eriskay-aviemore.co.uk

Indicated Prices:

Single	from £30.00 per room	Twin	from £55.00 per room
Double	from £55.00 per room		

88182

Boat of Garten
Moorfield House
Open: All year excl Nov & Xmas **Map Ref: 4C10**

★★★★
GUEST HOUSE

Deshar Road, Boat of Garten, Inverness-shire, PH24 3BN
T: 01479 831646 E: enquiries@moorfieldhouse.com W: moorfieldhouse.com

Indicated Prices:

Single	from £50.00 per room	Twin	from £76.00 per room
Double	from £76.00 per room		

38931

For a full listing of Quality Assured accommodation, please see directory at back of this guide.

A family run guest house located near Aviemore in the Cairngorm National Park. A perfect base for numerous outdoor activities such as skiing/boarding, climbing, fishing, cycling, water-sports, bird-watching, wildlife – including animal attractions, steam train, golfing holidays, sightseeing, walking, munro bagging etc. Warm friendly welcome always assured, hearty breakfast included. Open all year.

★★★
GUEST HOUSE

Deshar Road, Boat of Garten, nr Aviemore, Inverness-shire, PH24 3BN
T: 01479 831484 E: theboathouse4u@yahoo.co.uk W: www.theboathouse4u.com

Indicated Prices:

Single	from £27.50 per room	Twin	from £55.00 per room
Double	from £55.00 per room	Family	from £55.00 per room

80970

Dalwhinnie
Balsporran Cottages

Open: All year excl Xmas

Map Ref: 4B11

★★★
BED AND BREAKFAST

Drumochter Pass, Dalwhinnie, Highland, PH19 1AF
T: 01528 522389 E: ann@balsporran.fsbusiness.co.uk W: balsporran.com

Indicated Prices:

Single	from £32.50 per person	Twin	from £30.00 per person
Double	from £30.00 per person		

14107

Elgin
Ardvorlich Guest House

Open: All year

Map Ref: 4D8

★★★
BED AND BREAKFAST

125 South Street, Elgin, Moray, IV30 1JB
T: 01343 556064 E: lynnfyvie@hotmail.com W: ardvorlich.com

Indicated Prices:

Single	from £40.00 per room	Twin	from £60.00 per room
Double	from £60.00 per room	Suite	from £75.00 per room
		Family	from £85.00 per room

71006

Important: Prices stated are estimates and may be subject to amendments. Prices are per person per night unless otherwise stated.

Forres
Springfield B&B
Open: All year – Xmas & New Year by arrangement   **Map Ref: 4C8**

★★★★
BED AND BREAKFAST

Croft Road, Forres, IV36 3JS
T: 01309 676965 E: catherinebain@tinyworld.co.uk W: springfieldb-b.co.uk

Indicated Prices:
Single   from £40.00 per room   Twin   from £30.00 per person
Double   from £30.00 per person

55616

Grantown-on-Spey
An Cala Guest House
Open: All year excl Xmas   **Map Ref: 4C9**

★★★★★
GUEST HOUSE

Woodlands Terrace, Grantown-on-Spey, PH26 3JU
T: 01479 873293 E: ancala@globalnet.co.uk W: www.ancala.info

Indicated Prices:
Double   from £78.00 per room   Twin   from £78.00 per room

11944

Kincraig
Braeriach Guest House
Open: All year   **Map Ref: 4C10**

★★★★
GUEST HOUSE

Braeriach Road, Kincraig, by Kingussie, Inverness-shire, PH21 1QA
T: 01540 651369 E: fiona@braeriachgh.com W: braeriachgh.com

Indicated Prices:
Single   from £40.00 per room   Twin   from £70.00 per room
Double   from £75.00 per room   Family   from £90.00 per room

16028

Kincraig
Insh House Guesthouse
Open: Jan-Oct   **Map Ref: 4C10**

★★★
GUEST HOUSE

Kincraig, by Kingussie, PH21 1NU
T: 01540 651377 E: inshhouse@btinternet.com W: kincraig.com/inshhouse

Indicated Prices:
Single   from £28.00   Twin   from £56.00 per room
Double   from £56.00 per room   Family   from £70.00 per room

26768

Moray, Aviemore and the Cairngorms

Kingussie
The Hermitage Guest House
Open: All year   **Map Ref: 4B11**

★★★★
GUEST HOUSE

Spey Street, Kingussie, Inverness-shire, PH21 1HN
T: 01540 662137   E: thehermitage@clara.net   W: thehermitage-scotland.com

Indicated Prices:

Single	from £40.00 per room	Twin	from £60.00 per room
Double	from £60.00 per room	Family	from £75.00 per room

59243

Kingussie
Allt Gynack Guest House
Open: All year excl Xmas Day   **Map Ref: 4B11**

★★★
GUEST HOUSE

1 High Street, Kingussie, PH21 1HS
T: 01540 661081   E: alltgynack@tiscali.co.uk   W: alltgynack.com

Indicated Prices:

Single	from £28.00 per room	Twin	from £52.00 per room
Double	from £52.00 per room	Suite	from £54.00 per room
		Family	from £74.00 per room

77326

Kingussie
Ardselma
Open: All year   **Map Ref: 4B11**

★★★
BED AND BREAKFAST

The Crescent, Kingussie, Inverness-shire, PH21 1JZ
T: 07786 696384   E: valerieardselma@aol.com   W: kingussiebedandbreakfast.co.uk

Indicated Prices:

Double	from £30.00 per person	Twin	from £30.00 per person
		Family	from £70.00 per room

12674

Newtonmore
Alvey House
Open: All year excl 24-26 Dec   **Map Ref: 4B11**

★★★
GUEST HOUSE

Golf Course Road, Newtonmore, PH20 1AT
T: 01540 673260   E: enquiries@alveyhouse.co.uk   W: alveyhouse.co.uk

Indicated Prices:

Single	from £27.50	Twin	from £55.00 per room
Double	from £55.00 per room	Family	from £70.00 per room

11819

Important: Prices stated are estimates and may be subject to amendments. Prices are per person per night unless otherwise stated.

by Newtonmore, Laggan
The Rumblie Guest House

Open: end Jan-end Nov; 27th Dec-3rd Jan

Map Ref: 4B11

★★★★
GUEST HOUSE

Gergask Avenue, Laggan, PH20 1AH
T: 01528 544766 E: mail@rumblie.com W: rumblie.com
Indicated Prices:
Double   from £30.00 per person   Twin   from £30.00 per person

TV 🐕 🖥️ P 🅿️ 🍴 ✕ 🔌•))
♿ V 🚫 🖼️ ♪♪♪

60279

Self Catering and Camping & Caravan Parks

Aviemore
A & J Burns-Smith

Open: All year

Map Ref: 4C10

★★★ UP TO ★★★★
SELF CATERING

Pine Bank Chalets, Dalfaber Road, Aviemore, Inverness-shire, PH22 1PX
T: 01479 810000 E: pinebankchallets@btopenworld.com W: pinebankchalets.co.uk

5 Log Cabins	1-2 Bedrooms	Sleeps 2-6
2 Apartments	2 Bedrooms	Sleeps 2-6
8 Chalets	1-3 Bedrooms	Sleeps 2-6

| **Prices – Log Cabins:** | **Apartments:** | | **Chalets:** | |
| £350.00-£725.00 | **Per Week** | £350.00-£725.00 | **Per Week** | £350.00-£725.00 | **Per Week** |

TV 🐕 🖥️ ((🗄️ 🖼️ 🍴 🛏️ 📺 ♪ 🔌 📷 🗑️
M ◎ ⊚ 🖐️ 🐾 📷 🍴 ⚡ 🛏️ ❄️ 🐕 ① 💪 P 🏃 🧗 🚲 ⛷️ 🚤 ⛳

49818

Aviemore
Cairngorm Highland Bungalows

Open: All year

Map Ref: 4C10

★★★ UP TO ★★★★
SELF CATERING

29 Grampian View, Aviemore, PH22 1TF
T: 01479 810653 E: linda.murray@virgin.net W: cairngorm-bungalows.co.uk

| 3 Bungalows | 2-4 Bedrooms | Sleeps 2-8 |

Prices – Bungalows:
£195.00-£850.00   **Per Week**

Short breaks available

TV 🗄️ 🖼️ 🍴 🛏️ ⚡ 🔌 ♪ 📺 📷
◎ 🖐️ 🐾 📷 🍴 ⚡ 🛏️ 🐾 ❄️ 🐕 ① 💪 R 🏃 P 🗑️

27905

For a full listing of Quality Assured accommodation, please see directory at back of this guide.

321

Aviemore
Lairig Vue Holiday House
Open: All year **Map Ref: 4C10**

★★★
SELF CATERING

5 Dalnabay, Aviemore, Inverness-shire, PH22 1RE
T: 07746 608065 E: lairigvuedalnabay@btinternet.com W: lairigvue.co.uk

| 1 Cottage | 2 Bedrooms | Sleeps 5+baby |

Prices – Cottage:
£325.00-£450.00 Per Week

Short breaks available

77601

Aviemore
20 Munro Place
Open: All year **Map Ref: 4C10**

★★★
SELF CATERING

Aviemore, PH22 1TE
T: 07973 444519/01698 360823 E: info@selfcatering-aviemore.co.uk W: selfcatering-aviemore.co.uk

| 1 Bungalow | 3 Bedrooms | Sleeps 2-6 |

Prices –Bungalow:
£460.00-£560.00 Per Week

Short breaks available

67772

Boat of Garten
3 High Terrace
Open: Mar-Oct **Map Ref: 4C10**

★★
SELF CATERING

3 High Terrace, Boat of Garten, Inverness-shire, PH24 3BW
T: 01479 831262 E: dodo.keir@btinternet.com

| 1 Flat | 2 Bedrooms | Sleeps 4 |

Prices – Flat:
£155.00-£200.00 Per Week

40615

Kincraig
Balbeag
Open: Mar-Dec **Map Ref: 4C11**

★★★
SELF CATERING

Kincraig, Kingussie, Inverness-shire, PH21 1NX
T: 01963 220250 E: camacg@talk21.com W: balbeag.co.uk

| 1 Cottage | 4 Bedrooms | Sleeps 8 |

Prices – Cottage:
£455.00-£680.00 Per Week

Short breaks available

58750

Kincraig
Fraser and Telford Cottages Open: All year Map Ref: 4C10

★★★
SELF CATERING

Insh House, Kincraig, Kingussie, Inverness-shire, PH21 1NU
T: 01540 651377 E: inshhouse@btinternet.com W: kincraig.com/inshhouse

2 Cottages 2 Bedrooms Sleeps 4

Prices –Cottages:
£250.00-£400.00 Per Week

54152

by Kingussie
Aonach Open: All year Map Ref: 4B11

★★★
SELF CATERING

Drumguish, by Kingussie, Inverness-shire, PH21 1HD
T: 01540 661636 E: mail@aonach.ukf.net W: aonach.ukf.net

1 Bungalow 3 Bedrooms Sleeps 6

Prices – Bungalow:
£495.00-£650.00 Per Week

52610

by Kingussie
Mrs Ann Mackintosh Open: All year Map Ref: 4B11

★★★
SELF CATERING

Annandale, Gordonhall, Kingussie, PH21 1NR
T: 01540 661560

1 Cabin 2 Bedrooms Sleeps 4-6

Prices – Cabin:
£180.00-£300.00 Per Week
Short breaks available

12192

Nethy Bridge
Woodbridge Open: Mar-Nov Map Ref: 4C10

★★★
SELF CATERING

Miss K M Grant, Tombae, West Cullachie, Boat of Garten, Inverness-shire, PH24 3BY
T: 01479 821226

1 Bungalow 3 Bedrooms Sleeps 5

Prices – Bungalow:
£250.00-£400.00 Per Week

61445

For a full listing of Quality Assured accommodation, please see directory at back of this guide.

Lorien

Open: All year   Map Ref: 4C10

★★★
SELF CATERING

Dell Road, Nethybridge, Inverness-shire, PH25 3DA
T: 0141 563 7830 E: lornethy@ntlworld.com W: lorien.org.uk

| 1 Bungalow | 4 Bedrooms | Sleeps 8-11 |

Prices – Bungalow:
£297.00-£654.00   Per Week

Short breaks available

36386

---

by Newtonmore, Laggan

Gaskbeg Holidays – Bail-Nan-Cnoc – Gaskbeg Cottages

Open: All year   Map Ref: 4B11

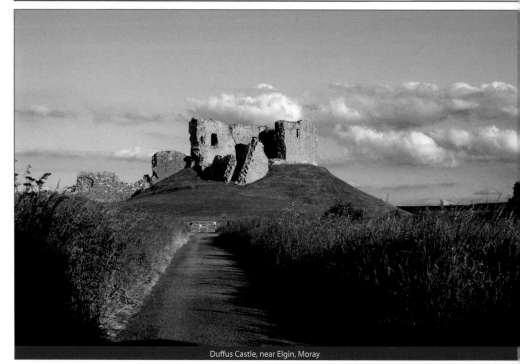

★★★ UP TO ★★★★
SELF CATERING

Gaskbeg Farm, Laggan, by Newtonmore, PH20 1BS
T: 01528 544336 E: gaskbeg@btinternet.com W: gaskbeg.co.uk

| 2 Cottages | 2 Bedrooms | Sleeps 1-4 |
| 1 House | 3 Bedrooms | Sleeps 1-6 |

Prices – Cottage: Prices – House:
£260.00-£680.00 Per Week £260.00-£680.00 Per Week

Short breaks available

27369

Duffus Castle, near Elgin, Moray

Festival revellers during the Hebridean Celtic Festival in the grounds of Lews Castle, Stornoway, Isle of Lewis

Outer Hebrides

Located 40 miles off the west coast of Scotland, the 150 mile long island chain of the Outer Hebrides are synonymous with tranquillity, beauty and warm hospitality.

The Hebridean Gaels always provide a friendly welcome, making sure visitors enjoy a sense of belonging and freedom - one of the great traits of the local heritage. Nowhere else will you find such diversity of landscapes and species, arts, crafts and music. The islands have an abundance of beautiful habitats, which are at once peaceful, unspoilt and natural.

For the wildlife enthusiast, these islands are teeming with bird and sea life. The hills and moors are filled with native wildlife in their natural setting. Similarly those who enjoy the great outdoors can find plenty of activities to choose from including walking, surfing, cycling and kayaking. Few places can offer such variety for a holiday or short break.

You can get to the Outer Hebrides by plane. Why not fly to Barra and experience landing on the beach at low tide? Or make your way by ferry through the scattering of islands on Scotland's western edge from Oban or from Uig on Skye. With all ferry fares to the Outer Hebrides starting at £65 there has never been a better time to visit the Outer Hebrides.

Camping above Horgabost Beach (Traig Nisabost) on the Isle of Harris, with a view to the Isle of Taransay beyond, Outer Hebrides

DON'T MISS

1. On the Isle of Lewis a must visit is the **archaeological route** around the Westside. The famous Calanais Standing Stones, Arnol Blackhouse and the Broch, are among more than 20 historical sites dotted throughout the islands. The 5,000 year-old Calanais Standing Stones on the west side of Lewis are a spectacular sight - the meaning of their cross-shaped layout continues to fascinate and mystify archaeologists.

2. If you have the time and are looking for the ultimate experience, consider a day trip to **St Kilda**. Due west and into the Atlantic Ocean, these volcanic islands are incredibly dramatic and boast the highest sea cliffs in Britain. St Kilda is also the most important sea bird breeding station in north west Europe. Once home to Europe's most remote community, this archipelago is a double World Heritage Site and there are boat trips available to ensure you have a fantastic experience.

3. Nature lovers and bird watchers love the **Uists**. With two nature reserves and the largest breeding grounds for the Greylag Goose amongst others, together with excellent fishing well into the autumn, and the wild flowers like a blanket on the machair, there is no comparison to these islands.

4. For a truly diverse landscape, the most awe-inspiring beaches, and some of the friendliest people in the world, **Harris** is a unique and very popular destination and definitely one not to be missed. Visitor attractions such as Seallam!, the geneaology centre in Northton, and St Clements Church in Rodel, where the MacLeod Chiefs used to worship in the 1500s, are but a taste of what is available in this lovely island.

5. Only five miles across and eight miles long, with one ring road all the way round, **Barra** is a petite paradise for visitors. Kisimul Castle sits majestically out from Castlebay, as if watching over the village and its residents. If you decide to fly to Barra a real experience awaits - this is the world's only scheduled flight which lands on a beach, at low tide of course.

6. With **ferry fares to the Outer Hebrides starting at £65 return** for a car and two passengers, it's now much more affordable to come to the islands. To experience the unique culture, hospitality and absolute freedom, welcome to paradise made affordable.

WALKING

7. With more than 30 waymarked walks available in the Outer Hebrides, there's something to suit every level and ability. The **Clisham** is the highest hill in the Outer Hebrides at 799 metres and offers exceptional views. At seven hours this is a climb which requires a little effort but the panorama at the summit more than makes up for it.

8. Whatever the weather, whatever your interest or whatever your age, there is something for you in the **Lews Castle** grounds. Pathways are designed to highlight the main features found in the grounds - shoreline, woodland, river and moorland. There are a number of vantage points which give excellent views of the town of Stornoway, the harbour and surrounding area.

9. The **Eriskay Walk** in South Uist takes in a variety of terrain and offers a great opportunity to spot some local wildlife. Taking in Coilleag a' Phrionnsa, the beach where Bonny Prince Charlie first stepped ashore in Scotland, continue towards Acarsaid Harbour, climb the rock face uphill for a views of Skye, Soay, Canna, Rum, Eigg and Muck, and on a clear day, Mull, Tiree and Coll. At the end of the walk is a secluded little bay where you might catch sight of otters.

To find out more go to visitscotland.com

Hotels

Lochcarnan, South Uist
Orasay Inn
Open: All year   **Map Ref: 3B9**

★★★
SMALL HOTEL

Lochcarnan, Isle of South Uist, HS8 5PD
T: 01870 610298 E: orasayinn@btinternet.com W: orasayinn.co.uk

Indicated Prices:

Single	from £55.00 per room	Twin	from £79.00 per room
Double	from £79.00 per room	Family	from £104.00 per room

48527

Guest Houses and B&Bs

Isle of Lewis, Point
Ceol-na-Mara
Open: All year   **Map Ref: 3E4**

★★★
BED AND BREAKFAST

1A Aignish, Isle of Lewis, HS2 0PB
T: 01851 870339 E: sarah@ceol-na-mara.co.uk W: www.ceol-na-mara.co.uk

Indicated Prices:

Single	from £30.00 per room	Twin	from £26.00 per person
Double	from £26.00 per person	Family	from £25.00 per person

66940

Lochmaddy, North Uist
Rushlee House
Open: All year excl Xmas & New Year   **Map Ref: 3B8**

★★★★
BED AND BREAKFAST

Lochmaddy, North Uist, HS6 5AE
T: 01876 500274 E: rushleehouse@hebrides.net W: rushleehouse.co.uk
Indicated Prices:
Single   from £43.00 per room
Double   from £66.00 per room

52644

Self Catering and Camping & Caravan Parks

Isle of Lewis, Uig
11B Riof
Open: All year   **Map Ref: 3C4**

★★★
SELF CATERING

Uig, Isle of Lewis, HS2 9HU
T: 07904 024611 E: janepaton@hebridescottage.com W: hebridescottage.com
1 Cottage   2 Bedrooms   Sleeps 4-6
Prices – Cottage:
£400.00-£500.00   Per Week
Short breaks available

69268

Claddach Kirkibost, North Uist
John MacIsaac
Open: All year   **Map Ref: 3B8**

★★★★★
SELF CATERING

An Airigh, 2 Claddach, Kirkibost, North Uist, HS6 5EP
T: 01224 825509/07990 975566 E: john@qestuk.com
1 House   4 Bedrooms   Sleeps 7
Prices – House:
£700.00-£1200.00   Per Week

77752

Locheport, North Uist
The Moorings

Open: All year

Map Ref: 3B8

★★★
SELF CATERING

Sidinish, North Uist, HS6 5EX
T: 01505 614660 **E:** lysbe@aol.com **W:** the-moorings.org

1 Bungalow   3 Bedrooms   Sleeps 6

Prices – Bungalow:
£280.00-£450.00   Per Week

44102

Lochmaddy, North Uist
Trinity Factors

Open: All year

Map Ref: 3B7

★★★
SELF CATERING

209-211 Bruntsfield Place, Edinburgh, EH10 4DH
T: 0131 447 9911 **E:** admin@trinityfactors.co.uk **W:** trinityfactors.co.uk

1 Cottage   3 Bedrooms   Sleeps 6

Prices – Cottage:
£300.00-£475.00   Per Week

Short breaks available

35947

Stornoway harbour, Stornoway

For a full listing of Quality Assured accommodation, please see directory at back of this guide.

The Sands of Breckon (an award-winning white sand beach), North Yell, Shetland

NORTHERN ISLES
Orkney, Shetland

Discover Scotland's most northerly islands, where ancient history intertwines with striking landscapes, rich wildlife habitats and a fascinating culture and heritage.

These stunning archipelagos offer an array of beautiful scenery, from rugged coastlines and dramatic cliffs to serene sandy beaches and quiet inland lochs. Add to this an abundance of wildlife and rare flora and fauna; there are endless opportunities to explore the great outdoors.

The islands are also home to a wealth of archaeological sites and evidence of the Vikings is everywhere. Orcadians spoke Old Norse until the mid 1700s and the ancient Viking Parliament used to meet at Scalloway in Shetland. Nowhere else will you find the distant past so alive. Boasting some of the best-preserved archaeological sites in Europe,

find the Ring of Brodgar, the Standing Stones of Stenness and the Neolithic village of Skara Brae in Orkney, while Shetland is home to Mousa Broch and the archaeological dig at Old Scatness.

The northern isles are considered something of a haven for outdoor enthusiasts. A coastline characterised by sea caves, skerries, inland sea lochs, beautiful beaches and crystal clear waters is great for all kinds of watersports, from sailing and sea kayaking to scuba diving. Or discover some of the hidden gems, landmarks and remarkable views the islands have to offer by following one of the waymarked walking or cycling routes. When it comes to stunning views, the likes of the black volcanic cliffs at Eshaness in Shetland, or Orkney's solitary sea stack the Old Man of Hoy, continue to enthral locals and visitors alike.

Thanks to a rich variety of landscapes, the islands also boast wonderful culinary specialties. Livestock graze over wide open spaces, from the shore to heather-clad hills, while the clear northern waters yield an abundance of fresh and flavoursome seafood. For a real taste of the islands, sample Orkney's famous seaweed-eating North Ronaldsay lamb or the delicious plump Shetland mussels served up in restaurants across Scotland. Order a seafood platter in a cosy harbour-side restaurant and watch the world go by as you enjoy.

Shetland can also lay claim to the UK's most northerly brewery, which benefits from the natural environment and pure waters around the island of Unst. And while Valhalla Brewery serves up real ales inspired by the island, Orkney boasts the most northerly distillery, producing the award-winning Highland Park malt whisky.

And you can expect a warm reception from the famously friendly locals. Both islands have their own time-honoured customs and traditions - be it Up Helly Aa, Shetland's spectacular winter fire festival, or the highly competitive Ba' game in Orkney - the islanders always seem to find something to celebrate. And for those keen on traditional music, Scotland's northern isles are a must, with the acclaimed Shetland and Orkney folk festivals attracting visitors far and wide every year.

These islands are truly irresistible. Whether it's to try a spot of island hopping, or to simply relax and mingle with the locals, a visit to Shetland and Orkney is an experience to remember.

A member of the "Shetland Fiddlers" enjoys performing in a concert at Lerwick, Shetland

What's On?

Up Helly Aa
Last Tuesday in January
Warm up on a chilly winter night at the Viking inspired Up Helly Aa, the world's largest annual fire festival.
visitshetland.com/major-events/up-helly-aa

Orkney Jazz Festival
23 - 25 April 2010
Weekend of mainly traditional jazz by visiting and local performers.
stromnesshotel.com

Shetland Folk Festival
29 April - 2 May 2010
Check out the very best of local and international talent at the UK's most northerly folk festival.
shetlandfolkfestival.com

Orkney Folk Festival
27 -30 May 2010
The Festival features mainly traditional music with visiting musicians and local talent in concerts, ceilidhs, stomps, festival clubs, workshops and informal sessions.
orkneyfolkfestival.com

Orkney Wine Festival
5 - 13 June 2010
Expect dinners and tastings with leading international winemakers, as well as informative and casual tasting events.
thelongship.co.uk

Shetland Hamefarin
14-27 June 2010
Shetland will host a 'Hamefarin' (homecoming), welcoming Shetlanders from all around the world back to their home islands.
shetlandhamefarin.com

Flavour of Shetland
18-21 June 2010
Experience some true hospitality and 'get a flavour of' Shetland music, food, drink and crafts.
flavourofshetland.com

St Magnus Festival
18 - 23 June 2010
Orkney's midsummer celebration of the arts, renowned for its unique blend of world-class artists and community participation.
stmagnusfestival.com

Shetland Festival of Nature
3-11 July 2010
Don't miss an opportunity to join a variety of specialised wildlife tours with local rangers, photography sessions and expert talks.
visitshetland.com/major-events/shetland-nature-festival

Annual Agricultural Shows
6 - 14 August 2010
Stock showing, judging and show jumping, a wide variety of trade stands and stalls, and sporting events, find entertainment all day for all tastes.
visitorkney.com

DON'T MISS

1   Following a major renovation, the Pier Arts Centre is now considered one of the most striking buildings in the north of Scotland. Found at the harbour's edge in the historic town of Stromness, the Centre has a permanent collection of exemplary paintings and sculptures.

2   The impressive Isbister Chambered Cairn was discovered by a local farmer in the south-eastern tip of South Ronaldsay more than 50 years ago, offering a fascinating insight into Stone Age life. Dating from around 3000 BC the site was later named Tomb of the Eagles after talons and claws of sea-eagles were found among the burials. Explore the visitor centre and interpretation centre before heading out to the site.

3   Take some time to visit the Highland Park whisky distillery, which boasts traditional working floor maltings and peat kilns and is heavily influenced by Orkney's Viking heritage. This splendid single malt whisky has received praise from enthusiasts around the world, which, with 200 years of distilling tradition behind it, shows no sign of abating.

4   Maeshowe is the finest chambered tomb in Western Europe. Built before 2700 BC, it was raided by the Vikings in the mid-12th century and plundered of its treasures. Maeshowe is interesting because of the various inscriptions carved into the walls. This is one of the best known collections and includes the Maeshowe Dragon - a very well known Orkney icon. During the winter solstice every year the sun shines down the long entrance passage and lights up the back wall.

5   Founded in 1137 by Norse Earl Rognvald Kolson in memory of his uncle Saint Magnus, the St Magnus Cathedral belongs to the people of Orkney and its doors are open to all. Set in the heart of Kirkwall, the Cathedral boasts marvellous medieval grave markers and noted stained glass. Tours of the upper floor are available.

6   One of the most famous Neolithic sites in Northern Europe, Skara Brae is an incredibly well preserved village containing an intricate maze of eight separate dwellings linked by covered passages, with stone beds, lintels and cupboards all intact. The site, which stands by the shore of the Bay o' Skaill in Sandwich, was revealed by a violent storm in 1850 and dates back some 5,000 years.

HISTORY AND HERITAGE

7   Another Neolithic treasure in Orkney's west mainland is The Ring of Brodgar, a ring of enormous stone pillars thought to have been erected between 2500 BC and 2000 BC. Of the 60 original stones, 27 remain standing today, varying 2m and 4.5m in height. This ancient site is eerily beautiful, especially so at dawn or sunset.

8   The Broch of Gurness is an Iron Age 'Broch Village' on the north eastern shore of the Orkney mainland. It is thought to have been built between 200 and 100BC and would probably have housed up to 40 families within the Broch and the outer defences.

9   Scapa Flow is one of most historically significant stretches of water in Britain, playing an important role in travel, trade and conflict throughout the centuries - especially during both World Wars. Find out more about the role of the Royal Navy in Orkney during this time at the Scapa Flow Visitor Centre on the island of Hoy, where you can see artefacts and photographs documenting this fascinating history

10   The astonishingly beautiful Italian Chapel is a work of art created by Domenico Chiocchetti and his fellow prisoners who worked on the construction of the Churchill Barriers during World War 2. Found on the north side of Lamb Holm island, few can believe it is based on a basic Nissen hut, with fittings made of concrete and enhanced only by items of apparently worthless scrap.

DON'T MISS

1   Shetland has gained a reputation over the years for attracting rare migrant birds, but it is the vast **seabird colonies** which attract birdwatchers to the islands in their droves. Visit Sumburgh Head, Noss or Hermaness Nature Reserves where the deafening racket of thousands of nesting seabirds, including guillemots, razorbills, kittiwakes and fulmars, is an experience to behold. Shetland is also home to thousands of the wonderful parrot-like puffins - or tammy norries as they are known locally.

2   Shetland really comes alive during the long summer days from mid-May until mid-July (known locally as the 'Simmer Dim'). With beautiful sunsets and sunrises throughout the summer months, this is a great time to really appreciate the stunning landscapes. At **midsummer**, when it never really gets dark, the islands enjoy 19 hours of daylight and you can even play a round of 'midnight golf'!

3   Take a fascinating journey through Shetland's geological beginnings to the present day at the **Shetland Museum and Archives**. This purpose built museum, complete with its impressive three-storey Boat Hall, houses thousands of fascinating objects and documents. There is also a cafe/restaurant where you can stop for refreshments.

4   A visit to the **Eshaness Cliffs** in the North Mainland is a must on any touring itinerary. The journey to Eshaness alone is unforgettable, as the winding road gives way to spectacular views of sea stacks and craggy inlets; look out for rock formations such as the Drongs and the Dore Holm out at sea along the way. When you reach the Eshaness Lighthouse, take a wander along the coast, taking care along the cliff edges. The views of the black volcanic rock jutting out of the shoreline are simply awe-inspiring. Stop along the Tangwick Haa Museum on the way back for a beautifully presented snapshot of life in the local area.

5   One of world's finest examples of an Iron Age broch is something of a solitary figure on the uninhabited island of Mousa, which lies a mile or so off the east coast of Shetland's mainland. **Mousa Broch** is incredibly well preserved, standing at a height of more than 13 metres, and visitors can climb the narrow steps to the top for fantastic views out to Mousa Sound. The island is home to a RSPB bird sanctuary, while breeding storm petrels actually nest in the broch itself.

6   Shetland boasts more than 1,500km of winding coastline, so there are endless secluded inlets to explore and miles of beautiful stretches of sand. St Ninian's Ayre is one of the finest examples, where the fine sand tombolo beach links **St Ninian's Isle** with the mainland. St Ninian's Isle is rich in Viking relics and is a popular spot for picnics.

ATTRACTIONS

7   **Jarlshof** is an extraordinary archaeological site which, like so many examples in Scotland, was only brought to light after a storm washed away the ground hiding the ancient dwellings below. The unique element to this site near Sumburgh is that it contains examples of settlements from the Stone Age, Bronze Age and Iron Age, right through to the 16th century. Here you can find a Viking village, medieval farmstead and Iron Age broch within close proximity. Spend some time at the visitor centre.

8   The **Shetland Crofthouse**, Boddam is a typical thatched crofthouse of the 19th century restored with traditional materials. The layout of the house is similar to Norse houses from 1,000 years earlier and the sweet smell of peat smoke, thick walls and cramped living space will instantly take you back to life in the 1870s.

9   **Clickimin Broch** was excavated partly in the 1850s and then again in the 1950s to reveal what can be seen today. The broch would have originally stood approximately 12-15m high. Although the site has lost some height it still possesses many original characteristics, including the rooms which would have been used for shelter and part of the stairs between the two outer walls.

10 Built by Earl Patrick Stewart around 1600, **Scalloway Castle** stands three storeys high and still has many of its original rooms, including the banqueting hall and kitchens. This grand structure overlooks the Scalloway harbour and is open to the public.

The beach at the Bay of Skaill, Orkney, adjacent to Skara Brae

VisitScotland Information Centres

To help you plan and book your trip to Scotland email our travel experts at info@visitscotland.com. When you arrive call into one of our Information Centres where our friendly experts can offer advice on all things local as well as sharing their wider knowledge of Scotland. We don't just advise either. We can sort out your accommodation and all your travel needs, as well as tickets for events across Scotland. So if you're looking to get the most from your visit, there really is only one place to go.

Orkney

Kirkwall The Travel Centre
West Castle Street, Kirkwall
Orkney KW15 1GU

Shetland

Lerwick Market Cross, Lerwick
Shetland, ZE1 0LU

**Sumburgh
(Airport)** Wilsness Terminal
Sumburgh Airport
Shetland ZE3 9JP

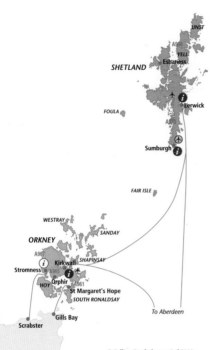

UNST
A968
YELL
Eshaness
SHETLAND
FOULA
Lerwick
A970
Sumburgh
FAIR ISLE
WESTRAY
SANDAY
ORKNEY
A967
Kirkwall
SHAPINSAY
Stromness A965
HOY Orphir A961
St Margaret's Hope
SOUTH RONALDSAY
Gills Bay
To Aberdeen
Scrabster

©Collins Bartholomew Ltd 2009

 Open All Year

(i) Seasonal

Live it. Visit Scotland.
visitscotland.com/wheretofindus

Orkney

Hotels

Kirkwall
Orkney Hotel   **Open: All year**   **Map Ref: 5B11**

★★★
HOTEL

40 Victoria Street, Kirkwall, Orkney, KW15 1DN
T: 01856 873477 E: info@orkneyhotel.co.uk W: orkneyhotel.co.uk

Indicated Prices:

Single	from £65.00	Twin	from £39.50 per person
Double	from £39.50 per person	Superior	from £49.50 per person

52470

Guest Houses and B&Bs

Kirkwall
Sanderlay Guest House   **Open: All year**   **Map Ref: 5B11**

★★★
GUEST HOUSE

2 Viewfield Drive, Kirkwall, Orkney, KW15 1RB
T: 01856 875587 E: enquiries@sanderlay.co.uk W: sanderlay.co.uk

Indicated Prices:

Single	from £38.00 per room	Twin	from £60.00 per room
Double	from £60.00 per room	Family	from £75.00 per room

52953

Important: Prices stated are estimates and may be subject to amendments. Prices are per person per night unless otherwise stated.

Orphir
The Quoy of Houton

Open: All year

Map Ref: 5B11

★★★★
BED AND BREAKFAST

The Quoy of Houton, Orphir, Orkney, KW17 2RD
T: 01856 811237 E: c.kritchlow258@btinternet.com W: orkneybedandbreakfast.org.uk
Indicated Prices:
Room (B&B) £66.00-£75.00

84766

Orphir
Mr & Mrs E B Clouston

Open: All year

Map Ref: 5B11

★★★
BED AND BREAKFAST

Scorralee, Orphir, Orkney, KW17 2RF
T: 01856 811268 E: ebclouston@aol.com W: scorralee.co.uk

Indicated Prices:
Single	from £30.00 per person	Twin	from £25.00 per person
Double	from £25.00 per person		

53240

Stromness
Venus Hourston

Open: All year excl Xmas & New Year

Map Ref: 5B11

★★★★
BED AND BREAKFAST

Ferrybank, 2 North End Road, Stromness, Orkney, KW16 3AG
T: 01856 851250

Indicated Prices:
Double	from £28.00 per person	Family	from £28.00 per person

45250

For a full listing of Quality Assured accommodation, please see directory at back of this guide.

Self Catering and Camping & Caravan Parks

Orphir
Clouston Lodges   **Open: All year**   **Map Ref: 5B11**

★★★★
SELF CATERING

Scapa Flow Lodges, Scorralee, Scorradale Road, Orphir, Orkney, KW17 2RF
T: 01856 811268 E: ebclouston@aol.com W: scapaflow-lodges.co.uk

3 Cottages   2 Bedrooms   Sleeps 4

Prices – Cottages:
£290.00–£490.00   Per Week

Short breaks available

74218

The Earl's Palace, Kirkwall, Orkney

The Ring of Brodgar Stone Circle and Henge, Orkney

For a full listing of Quality Assured accommodation, please see directory at back of this guide.

339

Guest Houses and B&Bs

Lerwick
Fort Charlotte Guest House

Open: All year

Map Ref: 5G5

★★★
GUEST HOUSE

1 Charlotte Street, Lerwick, Shetland, ZE1 0JL
T: 01595 692140 E: fortcharlotte@btconnect.com W: fortcharlotte.co.uk

Indicated Prices:

Single	from £30.00 per room	Twin	from £60.00 per room
Double	from £60.00 per room	Family	from £60.00 per room

26569

Lerwick
Glen Orchy House

Open: All year

Map Ref: 5G5

Situated on the south side of Lerwick adjoining 9-hole golf course free to the public. Close to the town centre and harbour. Licensed. Evening meals from 6.30pm-9pm. Freeview TV, underfloor heating, air conditioning, tea and coffee making facilities in all bedrooms.

★★★
GUEST HOUSE

20 Knab Road, Lerwick, Shetland, ZE1 0AX
T: 01595 692380 E: glenorchy.house@virgin.net W: guesthouselerwick.com

Indicated Prices:

Single	from £60.00 per room	Twin	from £85.00 per room
Double	from £85.00 per room	Family	from £85.00 per room

27943

Self Catering and Camping & Caravan Parks

Eshaness
Braewick Cafe & Caravan Park

Open: Mar-Oct

Map Ref: 5F3

★★★★
TOURING PARK

Braewick, Eshaness, Shetland, ZE2 9RS
T: 01806 503345 E: braewick@hotmail.co.uk W: eshaness.shetland.co.uk
Drive north on the A970 to Hillswick, take the B9078 to Eshaness.

Park accommodates 30 pitches. Total touring pitches: 10.
Prices per pitch:
🚐 (10) £12.50   ⛺ (20) £6.50
Wigwam (4) £30.00 per night. Sleeps up to 6.

66629

Lerwick
Blydest Self Catering

Open: All year

Map Ref: 5G5

★★★
SELF CATERING

19c St Magnus Street, Lerwick, Shetland
T: 01950 431496 E: cairnlea.smith@btinternet.com

1 Apartment   2 Bedrooms   Sleeps 1-6

Prices – Apartment:
£210.00-£406.00   Per Week

77203

For a full listing of Quality Assured accommodation, please see directory at back of this guide.

White water raft group on River Moriston near Invermoriston, by Loch Ness, Highlands of Scotland

Location	Property Name	Postcode	Telephone	Classification	Star Rating	
Aberdeen	20 Louisville Avenue	AB10 6TX	01224 319812	Bed & Breakfast	★★★	
	4 The Orchard		01779 476411	Self Catering	★★★	
	5 Monaltrie		01224 734800	Self Catering	★★★★	
	64 Cromwell Road		07966 026164	Self Catering	★★★	
	66 Great Northern Road		01224 646912	Self Catering	★★★	
	Abbotswell Guest House	AB12 5AR	01224 871788	Guest House	★★★	
	Aberdeen Central West Premier Inn	AB15 6DW	0870 9906430	Budget Hotel		
	Aberdeen City Centre Hotel	AB10 1JR	01224 658406	Metro Hotel	★★★	♿
	Aberdeen City Centre Premier Inn	AB24 5AR	0870 990 6300	Budget Hotel		
	Aberdeen Douglas Hotel	AB11 5EL	01224 582255	Hotel	★★★	
	Aberdeen Guest House	AB10 6PD	01224 211733	Guest House	★★★	
	Aberdeen Marriott Hotel	AB21 7AZ	01224 763738	Awaiting Grading		♿
	Aberdeen South Premier Inn	AB12 4QS	0870 197 7013	Budget Hotel		
	Aberdeen Youth Hostel	AB10 4ZT	0870 0041100	Hostel	★★★★	🌿
	Adelphi Guest House	AB11 7XH	01224 583078	Guest House	★★★	
	Aldersyde Guest House	AB11 6TX	01224 580012	Guest House	★★★	
	Aldridge	AB24 4NP	01224 485651	Bed & Breakfast	★★★	
	Antrim Guest House	AB11 6HT	01224 590987	Guest House	★★	
	Apartment 13	AB10 1RB	01224 663300	Awaiting Grading		
	Apt 5 (19-21 Regent Quay) and Apts 2 & 3 (57 Regent Quay)	AB11 5BE	08450 942424	Serviced Apartments	★★★ to ★★★★	♿
	Arden Guest House	AB10 2EE	01224 580700	Guest House	★★★	
	Ardo Mains House & Garden Cottage		01358 742276	Self Catering	★★★	
	Ardoe House Hotel	AB12 5YP	01224 860600	Hotel	★★★★	♿
	Arkaig Guest House	AB25 3PP	01224 638872	Guest House	★★★	
	Armadale Guest House	AB10 7JN	01224 580636	Guest House	★★★	
	Ashgrove Guest House	AB25 3AD	01224 484861	Guest House	★★★	
	Atholl Hotel	AB15 4DA	01224 323505	Hotel	★★★★	
	Aurora Guest House	AB10 6NJ	01224 311602	Guest House	★★★	
	Avalon B&B	AB23 8UA	01358 742619	Bed & Breakfast	★★★	
	Beeches	AB10 6PS	01224 586413	Guest House	★★★	
	Bimini Guest House	AB24 5ET	01224 646912	Guest House	★★★	
	Brentwood Hotel	AB11 6HH	01224 595440	Hotel	★★★	
	Brentwood Villa	AB24 5SR	01224 480633	Guest House	★★★	
	Britannia Hotel	AB21 9LN	01224 409988	Hotel	★★★	🚶
	Broomhill Apartments		01224 322518	Self Catering	★★★	
	Burnetts Guest House	AB24 5ET	01224 647995	Guest House	★★★	
	Cedars Guest House	AB10 6NW	01224 583225	Guest House	★★★	
	Chapel Apartments	AB10 1SP	07824 666321	Serviced Apartments	★★★ to ★★★★	
	Cloverleaf Hotel	AB21 9DG	01224 714294	Small Hotel	★	
	Copthorne Hotel	AB10 1SU	01224 630404	Hotel	★★★★	♿
	Craibstone Estate	AB21 9YA	01224 711012	Campus	★★	♿
	Craighaar Hotel	AB21 9HS	01224 712275	Hotel	★★★	
	Crombie House	AB24 3TS	01224 273444	Campus	★	
	Cults Hotel	AB15 9SE	01224 867632	Hotel	★★★	
	Dee Street	AB11 6DQ	01224 213000	Serviced Apartments	★★★★	
	Deeside Holiday Park	AB12 5FX	01250 876666	Holiday Park	★★★★★	
	Deskford House		01651 891605	Self Catering	★★★	

♿ Unassisted wheelchair access   ♿ Assisted wheelchair access   🚶 Access for visitors with mobility difficulties
🌿 Bronze Green Tourism Award   🌿🌿 Silver Green Tourism Award   🌿🌿🌿 Gold Green Tourism Award
For further information on our Green Tourism Business Scheme please see page 7.

Advertisers' locations have been sorted by postcode. In Scotland, postcodes can cover fairly large geographical areas.
Please check distance of property from specified location with the individual provider. VisitScotland cannot take any responsibility for this.

343

Location	Property Name	Postcode	Telephone	Classification	Star Rating	
Aberdeen	Dunrovin Guest House	AB11 6TX	01224 586081	Guest House	★★★	
	Ellenville Guest House	AB11 6LR	01224 213334	Guest House	★★★	
	Express by Holiday Inn	AB10 1SQ	01224 623500	Metro Hotel	★★★	♿
	Flat 1		01224 722243	Self Catering	★★★★	⒫
	Forest Apartment	AB15 4TW	01224 315992	Serviced Apartments	★★★ to ★★★★	
	Forest Bank Apartment		01224 693743	Self Catering	★★★★	
	Granville Guest House	AB10 6NY	01224 313043	Guest House	★★★	
	Hayfield House		01224 315703	Self Catering	★★★	
	Hillhead Halls		01224 274000	Self Catering	★	
	Hilton Aberdeen Treetops	AB15 7AQ	01224 313377	Hotel	★★★★	♿
	Hilton Double Tree Hotel	AB24 5EF	01224 633339	Hotel	★★★★	♿
	Holiday Inn	AB23 8GP	0870 4009046	Hotel	★★★	♿
	Holiday Inn Express Aberdeen Exhibition Centre	AB23 8AJ	01224 227250	Metro Hotel	★★★	♿
	Jurys Inn Aberdeen	AB11 6NE	01224 381200	Awaiting Grading		
	Kildonan Guest House	AB10 6NR	01224 316115	Guest House	★★★	
	King's Hall	AB24 3FX	01224 272660	Campus	★★	♿
	Lewisville	AB12 5GB	01224 735798	Bed & Breakfast	★★★★	
	Malmaison	AB15 4YP	01224 327370	Awaiting Grading		
	Mariner Hotel	AB10 6NW	01224 588901	Hotel	★★★	
	Maryculter House Hotel	AB12 5GB	01224 732124	Country House Hotel	★★★★	⒫⒫
	Merkland Guest House	AB24 5PR	01224 634451	Guest House	★★★	
	Micasa Aparthotel Ltd	AB11 5PD	01224 565950	Serviced Apartments	★★★★	
	Middle Hill		01651 869059	Self Catering	★★★★	
	Middle Hill		01651 869059	Self Catering	★★★★	
	No 21 Hilton		01224 867184	Self Catering	★★★ to ★★★★	
	Noble Guest House	AB10 6PH	01224 313678	Guest House	★★★	
	Northern Hotel	AB24 3PS	01224 483342	Hotel	★★★	⚲
	Norwood Hall Hotel	AB15 9NX	01224 868951	Hotel	★★★★	
	Oakhill Apartments – 47 Morningfield Mews	AB12 5XN	01224 895545	Serviced Apartments	★★★★ to ★★★★★	
	Old Mill Inn	AB12 5FX	01224 733212	Inn	★★★	
	Open Hearth Guest House	AB10 7FQ	01224 591675	Awaiting Grading		
	Palm Court Hotel	AB15 7YX	01224 310351	Hotel	★★★★	
	Parkview	AB23 8UY	01358 743299	Bed & Breakfast	★★★	
	Penny Meadow	AB10 6PS	01224 588037	Guest House	★★★★	
	Premier Inn Aberdeen North (Murcar)	AB23 8BP	0870 1977012	Budget Hotel		
	Rosebank House	AB21 0QE	01651 862397	Bed & Breakfast	★★★★	
	Roselea House	AB10 2LS	01224 583060	Guest House	★★★	
	Royal Crown Guest House	AB11 2HN	01224 586461	Guest House	★★★	
	Royal Hotel	AB11 6BJ	01224 585152	Hotel	★★	
	Simpson's Hotel	AB15 4YP	01224 327777	Hotel	★★★★	
	Skene House – Gilcomston Park	AB25 1NX	01224 645971	Serviced Apartments	★★★ to ★★★★	
	Skene House Holburn	AB10 6SY	01224 645971	Serviced Apartments	★★★★	
	Skene House Whitehall	AB25 2NX	01224 645971	Serviced Apartments	★★★★	
	Speedbird Inn	AB21 0AF	01224 772884	Hotel	★★★	♿
	St Elmo	AB24 4NP	01224 483065	Guest House	★★★★	
	St Machar B&B	AB24 3RY	01224 488646	Awaiting Grading		
	The Bothy		01224 869960	Self Catering	★★★	

♿ Unassisted wheelchair access   ♿ Assisted wheelchair access   ⚲ Access for visitors with mobility difficulties
⒫ Bronze Green Tourism Award   ⒫⒫ Silver Green Tourism Award   ⒫⒫⒫ Gold Green Tourism Award
For further information on our Green Tourism Business Scheme please see page 7.

344   To find out more go to visitscotland.com

Location	Property Name	Postcode	Telephone	Classification	Star Rating	
Aberdeen	The Byre		01358 742673	Self Catering	★★★	℟
	The Craibstone Suites	AB11 6DJ	01224 857950	Serviced Apartments	★★★★	
	The Globe Inn	AB10 1RJ	01224 624258	Inn	★★★	
	The Jays Guest House	AB24 3BR	01224 638295	Guest House	★★★★	
	The Marcliffe Hotel and Spa	AB15 9YA	01224 861000	Hotel	★★★★★	♿
	The School House	AB21 0WB	01651 862970	Bed & Breakfast	★★★★	
	Thistle Aberdeen Airport Hotel	AB21 0AF	08703 3339150	Hotel	★★★★	♿
	Thistle Aberdeen Altens	AB12 3LF	0870 3339150	Hotel	★★★	♿
	Thistle Aberdeen Caledonian	AB10 1WE	0870 3339150	Hotel	★★★★	
	Travelodge Aberdeen	AB11 6JL	01224 584555	Budget Hotel		
	Travelodge Aberdeen Aiport	AB21 0HW	08719 846309	Budget Hotel		
	Travelodge Aberdeen Bucksburn	AB21 0HW		Budget Hotel		
	Viewfield	AB23 8UG	01358 742605	Bed & Breakfast	★★★	
	White Horse Inn	AB23 8XR	01358 742404	Small Hotel	★★★	
	Woodhill Bed & Breakfast	AB21 0RZ	01224 791699	Awaiting Grading		
	Woolmanhill Flats		01224 262134	Self Catering	★★	℟
	Woolmanhill Flats		01224 262134	Self Catering	★★	℟
			01224 734800	Self Catering	★★★★	
Aberfeldy	6 The Beeches	PH15 2BZ	01887 829490	Bed & Breakfast	★★★★	
	Aberfeldy Caravan Park	PH15 2AQ	01738 476476	Touring Park	★★★★	
	Aberfeldy Weem Hotel	PH15 2LD	01887 820381	Small Hotel	★★★	
	Ailean Chraggan Hotel	PH15 2LD	01887 820346	Inn	★★★	
	Appletree Cottage		0131 3396548	Self Catering	★★★ to ★★★★	
	Ardchoille		01887 830503	Self Catering	★★★	
	Ardtalnaig Lodge	PH15 2HX	01567 820771	Bed & Breakfast	★★★	
	Ardtornish	PH15 2BL	01887 820629	Bed & Breakfast	★★★	
	Balbeg Farm		01567 820642	Self Catering	★★★★	
	Balnearn House	PH15 2BJ	01887 820431	Guest House	★★★	
	Balnearn House	PH15 2BJ	01887 820431	Guest House	★★★	
	Ben Lawers at Ardtalnaig Estate	PH15	01567 820400	Awaiting Grading		
	Bracken Lodges		01567 820169	Self Catering	★★★★	
	Brae House	PH15 2BF	01887 820081	Bed & Breakfast	★★★★	
	Briar Croft		01738 622336	Self Catering	★★★	
	Burn Cottage	PH15 2NF	01314 469854	Awaiting Grading		
	Burnbank		01764 656233	Self Catering	★★★	
	Callwood Smiddy		01887 830543	Self Catering	★★★★	
	Capercaillie Cottage		01363 877676	Self Catering	★★★★	
	Castle Menzie Farm Holiday Cottages – West Lodge		01887 820260	Self Catering	★★★ to ★★★★	
	Clachmhor		0141 6382643	Self Catering	★★★	
	Coshieville House	PH15 2NE	01887 830319	Guest House	★★★★	
	Croftness Bothy		01887 822789	Self Catering	★★★★	
	Cruck Cottage		01887 820071	Self Catering	★★★★	
	Culdees Bunkhouse	PH15 2PG	01887 830519	Hostel	★★★	
	Drumcroy Lodges		01887 820978	Self Catering	★★★★	℟ 🏵🏵
	Dunskiag Farmhouse		01887 829111	Self Catering	★★★★	
	Fernbank House	PH15 2BL	01887 820486	Bed & Breakfast	★★★★	
	Fortingall Hotel	PH15 2NQ	01887 830367	Small Hotel	★★★★	🏵🏵🏵

♿ Unassisted wheelchair access ℟ Assisted wheelchair access ☥ Access for visitors with mobility difficulties
🏵 Bronze Green Tourism Award 🏵🏵 Silver Green Tourism Award 🏵🏵🏵 Gold Green Tourism Award
For further information on our Green Tourism Business Scheme please see page 7.

Advertisers' locations have been sorted by postcode. In Scotland, postcodes can cover fairly large geographical areas.
Please check distance of property from specified location with the individual provider. VisitScotland cannot take any responsibility for this.

345

Location	Property Name	Postcode	Telephone	Classification	Star Rating
Aberfeldy	Grandpa's Cottage		01887 830315	Self Catering	★★★★
	Hawthorn Cottage		01887 830615	Self Catering	★★★
	Hideaway Cottage		01887 829008	Self Catering	★★★★
	Innerwick Estate		01887 866222	Self Catering	★★★★ to ★★★★★
	Keepers Cottage		01887 830689	Self Catering	★★★★★
	Kenmore Hotel	PH15 2NU	01887 830205	Hotel	★★★ 🅟
	Laurelbank Cottage		01313 396548	Self Catering	★★★★
	Loch Tay Lodges		01887 830209	Self Catering	★★★ 🦽
	Lurgan Farm	PH15 2JX	01887 840451	Farm House	★★
	Machuim Farm Cottages – Tulloch Cottage		01567 820670	Self Catering	★★★
	Mains of Murthly Cottages – Hill Cottage		01887 820427	Self Catering	★★★★
	Moness Country Club – Gate Lodge		0870 4431499	Self Catering	★★★★
	Moness House Hotel & Country Club	PH15 2DY	0870 4431466	Country House Hotel	★★★
	No 3 The Beeches		01622 764765	Self Catering	★★★★
	Novar		01721 720292	Self Catering	★★★★
	Old Police Station	PH15 2AS	01887 822980	Bed & Breakfast	★★★
	Riverview Cottage		01887 820754	Self Catering	★★★★
	Sky & Waterfall Cottages		01887 830336	Self Catering	★★★ to ★★★★★
	Stablefield		0131 6624528	Self Catering	★★★★
	Struan House	PH15 2DD	0208 3084951	Awaiting Grading	
	Taronga		01796 470100	Self Catering	★★★★
	The Cottage		01887 820992	Self Catering	★★★
	The Cottage		01887 829490	Self Catering	★★★★
	The Ghillies Cottage		01887 829553	Self Catering	★★★★ 🚶
	The Stables		01887 830226	Self Catering	★★★★ to ★★★★★
	The Turret House		0773 9777117	Self Catering	★★★★
	The White Tower		01887 829244	Self Catering	★★★★★
	Tigh Na Clachan		01670 772234	Self Catering	★★★★
	Tigh'n Eilean	PH15 2BP	01887 820109	Bed & Breakfast	★★★★
	Tomvale	PH15 2JT	01887 820171	Farm House	★★★ 🦽
	Tomvale		01887 820171	Self Catering	★★★ 🦽
	Wester Camusvrachan	PH15 2NL	01887 866230	Awaiting Grading	
Aberlour	Aberlour Gardens	AB38 9LD	01340 871586	Holiday Park	★★★★★
	Allachy House		01224 797946	Self Catering	★★★
	Archiestown Hotel	AB38 7QL	01340 810218	Small Hotel	★★★
	Craigellachie Hotel	AB38 9SR	01340 811204	Awaiting Grading	🦽
	Dowans Hotel	AB38 9LS	01340 871488	Small Hotel	★★★
	Highlander Inn	AB38 9SR	01340 881446	Inn	★★★
	Ivy Cottage		01463 791714	Self Catering	★★
	Lynwood Bed and Breakfast	AB38 9SQ	01340 871801	Bed & Breakfast	★★★★
	Milton Cottage		01340 810389	Self Catering	★★★★
	Norlaggan	AB38 9QD	01340 871270	Bed & Breakfast	★★★
	Rhynagarrie Mill		01544 230218	Self Catering	★★★★★
	Spey Burn House B&B	AB38 7QZ	01340 810543	Bed & Breakfast	★★★★
	Speybank	AB38 9SY	01340 871888	Bed & Breakfast	★★★
	Speyside Camping & Caravanning Club Site	AB38 9SL	02476 475318	Touring Park	★★★★

♿ Unassisted wheelchair access 🦽 Assisted wheelchair access 🚶 Access for visitors with mobility difficulties
🅟 Bronze Green Tourism Award 🅟🅟 Silver Green Tourism Award 🅟🅟🅟 Gold Green Tourism Award
For further information on our Green Tourism Business Scheme please see page 7.

346 To find out more go to visitscotland.com

Location	Property Name	Postcode	Telephone	Classification	Star Rating	
Aboyne	9 Strachan Cottages		01339 881401	Self Catering	★★	
	Chesterton House	AB34 5HF	01339 886740	Bed & Breakfast	★★	🧍
	Deeside Lodge B&B	AB34 5EL	01339 885566	Bed & Breakfast	★★★★	
	Dinnet House	AB34 5LN	01339 885332	Bed & Breakfast	★★★★	
	East Wing Dorevay		01339 886232	Self Catering	★★★★	
	Glen Tanar – Butler's Lodge		01339 886451	Self Catering	★★★★	🅿
	Glendavan House	AB34 5LU	01339 881610	Bed & Breakfast	★★★★★	
	Huntly Arms Hotel	AB34 5HS	01339 886101	Hotel	★★★	
	Loch Kinord Hotel	AB34 5JY	01339 885229	Hotel	★★★	🅿🅿
	Newton of Drumgesk	AB34 5BL	01339 886203	Bed & Breakfast	★★	
	Royal Deeside Log Cabins	AB34 5LW	01339 885229	Holiday Caravan		
	Royal Deeside Log Cabins		01339 885229	Self Catering	★★★	
	St Katherine's Cottage		01339 86551	Self Catering	★★★★	
	Tanar View		01339 885764	Self Catering	★★★★	
	Tarland Camping & Caravanning Club Site	AB34 4UP	02476 475318	Touring Park	★★★★★	
	The Commercial Hotel	AB34 4TX	01339 881922	Inn	★★★	
	Wisdomhowe		01339 885341	Self Catering	★★★	
Acharacle	Ariundle Bunkhouse	PH36 4JA	01967 402279	Hostel	★★★★	♿
	Balnaha Cottage		01972 510262	Self Catering	★★★	
	Ben View Hotel	PH36 4HY	01967 402333	Small Hotel	★★	
	Ben View Hotel Holiday Cottage – Mossvale		01967 402333	Self Catering	★★★	
	Borve House		01972 510262	Self Catering	★★★	
	Braeriach		01972 510262	Self Catering	★★★	
	Branault Croft Caravans	PH36 4LG	01972 510284	Holiday Caravan		
	Bruadar Iain		01538 385853	Self Catering	★★★★	
	Burnbank	PH36 4JL	01967 431223	Holiday Caravan		
	Burnbank Croft Cottage		01967 431223	Self Catering	★★★	
	Ceol Na Mara		01972 510262	Self Catering	★★★	
	Coiresgeir		01972 510262	Self Catering	★★★	
	Dalilea Bungalow		01388 537728	Self Catering	★★★	
	Doire An Daimh	PH36 4JL	01967 431563	Awaiting Grading		
	Dondies House		01972 510262	Self Catering	★★★	
	Eilean Feoir		01972 510262	Self Catering	★★★	
	Glenmore Holidays – Otter Lodge		01972 500263	Self Catering	★★★★ to ★★★★★	
	Grigadale House		01972 510262	Self Catering	★★★★	
	Honeysuckle		01967 402226	Self Catering	★★★★★	♿ 🅿🅿🅿
	Ian's A Lodge		01206 262064	Self Catering	★★	
	Kilcamb Lodge Hotel	PH36 4HY	01967 402257	Country House Hotel	★★★	
	Loch Shiel House Hotel	PH36 4JL	01967 431224	Small Hotel	★★	
	Lochside Follies (Ruin)		01972 500201	Self Catering	★★★★	
	Meadow Lodge		0131 6203081	Self Catering	★★★★	
	Mull View		01972 510262	Self Catering	★★	
	Ockle Holidays – Struthan Ruadh		01972 510 321	Self Catering	★★ to ★★★	
	Otterburn B&B	PH36 4HZ	01967 402138	Bed & Breakfast	★★★★	
	Resipole Farm Caravan Park	PH36 4HX	01967 431235	Holiday Park	★★★★	
	Resipole Farm Self Catering – Hazel & Aspen		01967 431235	Self Catering	★★★	

♿ Unassisted wheelchair access   ♿ Assisted wheelchair access   🧍 Access for visitors with mobility difficulties
🅿 Bronze Green Tourism Award   🅿🅿 Silver Green Tourism Award   🅿🅿🅿 Gold Green Tourism Award
For further information on our Green Tourism Business Scheme please see page 7.

Advertisers' locations have been sorted by postcode. In Scotland, postcodes can cover fairly large geographical areas.
Please check distance of property from specified location with the individual provider. VisitScotland cannot take any responsibility for this.

347

Location	Property Name	Postcode	Telephone	Classification	Star Rating
Acharacle	Rowanhill		0780 3499322	Self Catering	★★★
	Shoreline Cottages		01972 500248	Self Catering	★★★★★
	Somerled		01967 431456	Self Catering	★★★★ to ★★★★★
	Strathconon			Self Catering	★★ to ★★★
	Strathconon			Self Catering	★★ to ★★★
	The Bield		01823 413840	Self Catering	★★★
	The Bield		01823 413840	Self Catering	★★★
	The Bungalow		01972 500262	Self Catering	★★
	The Byre		01972 510262	Self Catering	★★★
	The Saltings		01972 510262	Self Catering	★ to ★★
	Tigh A'Ghobhainn	PH36 4LH	01972 510771	Bed & Breakfast	★★★
	Tom An Sighean	PH36 4JB	01967 402464	Bed & Breakfast	★★★
	Tom Fraoich		01967 402470	Self Catering	★★★
	Torr Solais	PH36 4LH	01972 510389	Bed & Breakfast	★★★★
Achnasheen	31 Mellon Charles		01445 731382	Self Catering	★★★★
	Alt Na Criche		01339 882711	Self Catering	★★★
	Annat Lodge		0131 4475276	Self Catering	★★★★
	Aultbea Highland Lodges		01408 621041	Self Catering	★★★★
	Bayview Bungalows		01445 731151	Self Catering	★★★★
	Beinn Eighe and Slioch		01539 433205	Self Catering	★★★
	Brentwood		01445 781241	Self Catering	★★★
	Bruach Ard	IV22 2LN	01445 781765	Bed & Breakfast	★★★
	Burnside	IV22 2JL	01445 731270	Bed & Breakfast	★★★
	Cairn Shiel		01445 771225	Self Catering	★★★★
	Caladh		01349 877762	Self Catering	★★★
	Cartmel Guest House	IV22 2HU	01445 731375	Bed & Breakfast	★★★★
	Corriness House	IV22 2JU	01445 781785	Guest House	★★★★
	Crofter's Cottages		01445 781268	Self Catering	★★
	Crofter's Cottages		01445 781268	Self Catering	★★
	Drumchork Lodge Hotel	IV22 2HU	01445 731242	Small Hotel	★★
	Eilean View Bungalow and Apartment		01445 731546	Self Catering	★★★★
	Ewe View		01445 731394	Self Catering	★★★
	Ferroch	IV22 2EU	01445 791451	Bed & Breakfast	★★★★
	Fionn Cottage		0797 0574037	Self Catering	★★★
	Innes Maree Bungalows		01445 781454	Self Catering	★★★
	Inverewe Gardens Camping & Caravanning Club Site	IV22 2LF	02476 475318	Touring Park	★★★★
	Kildonan		01349 864317	Self Catering	★★★
	Kildonan		01349 864317	Self Catering	★★★
	Kinlochewe Bunkhouse	IV22 2PA	01445 760253	Bunkhouse	
	Kinlochewe Caravan Club Site	IV22 2PA	01342 336842	Touring Park	★★★★★
	Kinlochewe Hotel	IV22 2PA	01445 760253	Small Hotel	★★★
	Ledgowan Lodge Hotel	IV22 2EJ	01445 720252	Country House Hotel	★★★
	Mansefield		0151 6482454	Self Catering	★★★★
	Mellondale Bungalow		01445 731326	Self Catering	★★★★
	Mellondale Guest House	IV22 2JL	01445 731326	Guest House	★★★★
	Old Smiddy Guest House	IV22 2NB	01445 731696	Bed & Breakfast	★★★★
	Pool House	IV22 2LD	01445 781272	Guest Accommodation	★★★★★

♿ Unassisted wheelchair access   Assisted wheelchair access   Access for visitors with mobility difficulties
P Bronze Green Tourism Award   PP Silver Green Tourism Award   PPP Gold Green Tourism Award
For further information on our Green Tourism Business Scheme please see page 7.

Location	Property Name	Postcode	Telephone	Classification	Star Rating	
Achnasheen	Poolewe Hotel	IV22 2JX	01445 781241	Inn	★★★	
	Rocklea Little Gruinard		0131 4416053	Self Catering	★★★★	ⓖ
	Shore Croft		01514 941488	Self Catering	★★★★★	
	Stalkers Cottage		0131 243331	Self Catering	★★★	
	The Narrows		01445 781231	Self Catering	★★★★	
	The New Lodge		01241 830258	Self Catering	★ to ★★★	
	The Old Nurses Cottage		0131 4419318	Self Catering	★	
	The Sheiling	IV22 2NS	01445 731487	Holiday Caravan		
	The Sheiling	IV22 2NS	01445 731487	Bed & Breakfast	★★★★	
	The Sheiling		01445 731487	Self Catering	★★★★	
	The Torridon	IV22 2EY	01445 791242	Country House Hotel	★★★★	♿ 🍃🍃
	Torridon Inn	IV22 2EY	01445 791242	Inn	★★★	
	Torridon Youth Hostel	IV22 2EZ	0870 0041154	Hostel	★★★★	🍃🍃
	Wavecrest		01225 766379	Self Catering	★★★	
	Wavecrest		01225 766379	Self Catering	★★★	
	Willow Cottage Flat		01445 731263	Self Catering	★★★	
Airdrie	Acorn Cottage		01236 830243	Self Catering	★★★★	♄ 🍃🍃
	Craigpark House B&B	ML6 8PA	01236 843211	Bed & Breakfast	★★★	
	Easter Glentore Farm	ML6 7TJ	01236 830243	Farm House	★★★★	🍃🍃
	Knight's Rest	ML6 6DZ	01236 606193	Guest House	★★★	
	Shawlee Cottage	ML6 8SW	01236 753774	Bed & Breakfast	★★★	
Alexandria	11 Lomond Castle	G83 8EE	0141 9423399	Awaiting Grading		
	Aird House	G83 8RJ	01389 754464	Bed & Breakfast	★★★	
	Alba Bed & Breakfast Accommodation	G83 8LY	01389 758755	Bed & Breakfast	★★★	
	Alba Self Catering Accommodation		01389 758755	Self Catering	★★★★	
	Albannach	G83 0NU	01389 603345	Bed & Breakfast	★★★★	
	Ardoch Cottage	G83 8NE	01389 830452	Bed & Breakfast	★★★★	
	Auchendennan Farm Cottage		01389 850606	Self Catering	★★★★	
	Ballagan Farm	G83 8LY	01389 750092	Awaiting Grading		
	Barton Bed and Breakfast	G83 8SR	01389 759653	Bed & Breakfast	★★★	♄
	Blairhosh Cottage		01389 758267	Self Catering	★★	
	Braeburn Cottage	G83 9LU	01389 710998	Bed & Breakfast	★★★	
	Cameron House Lodges		01389 755625	Self Catering	★★★★★	
	Castle Steadings Self Catering Unit		07866 713438	Self Catering	★★★★	
	Cloudside	G83 0LJ	01389 601588	Bed & Breakfast	★★★★	
	Craigton Cottages	G83 8NX	01389 850289	Awaiting Grading		
	Culag Lochside Guest House	G83 8PD	01436 860248	Guest House	★★★★	♄
	Cundy Lodge	G83 8RB	01389 850688	Awaiting Grading		
	De Vere Cameron House	G83 8QZ	01389 755565	Hotel	★★★★★	♿
	Doune of Glen Douglas Farm	G83 8PD	01301 702312	Farm House	★★★	
	Drumkinnon Apartment		01389 756004	Self Catering	★★★ to ★★★★★	
	Duck Bay Hotel & Marina	G83 8QZ	01389 751234	Hotel	★★★	
	Dumbain Farm	G83 8DS	01389 752263	Bed & Breakfast	★★★	
	Glenview	G83 8PA	01436 860606	Bed & Breakfast	★★★★	
	Glyndale	G83 8HL	01389 758238	Bed & Breakfast	★★★	
	Gowanlea	G83 8HS	01389 752456	Bed & Breakfast	★★★★	
	Greystonelea Lodge		01389 830419	Self Catering	★★★★	ⓖ 🍃🍃
	Inverbeg Holiday Park	G83 8PD	01436 860267	Holiday Park	★★★★★	

♿ Unassisted wheelchair access　ⓖ Assisted wheelchair access　♄ Access for visitors with mobility difficulties
🍃 Bronze Green Tourism Award　🍃🍃 Silver Green Tourism Award　🍃🍃🍃 Gold Green Tourism Award
For further information on our Green Tourism Business Scheme please see page 7.

Advertisers' locations have been sorted by postcode. In Scotland, postcodes can cover fairly large geographical areas.
Please check distance of property from specified location with the individual provider. VisitScotland cannot take any responsibility for this.

349

Location	Property Name	Postcode	Telephone	Classification	Star Rating		
Alexandria	Inverbeg Holiday Park – Units 114/116		01436 860267	Self Catering	★★★★ to ★★★★★		
	Laudervale Gardens		07918 142090	Self Catering	★★★★		
	Loch Lomond Haven – Bramble Cottage		01436 860252	Self Catering	★★★★		
	Loch Lomond Youth Hostel	G83 8RB	0870 1553255	Hostel	★★★		🅟
	Lomond Fairways		07855 769338	Self Catering	★★★★		
	Lomond Woods Holiday Park		01389 755000	Self Catering	★★★★		
	Lomond Woods Holiday Park	G83 8QP	01389 755000	Holiday Park	★★★★★		
	Luss Camping & Caravanning Club Site	G83 8NT	02476 475318	Touring Park	★★★★		
	MacFarlane's Chalet	G83 8NQ	01389 830281	Awaiting Grading			
	Millhall	G83 8QP	01389 750451	Bed & Breakfast	★★★		
	Monday Cottage	G83 8JL	01389 759932	Bed & Breakfast	★★★		
	Norwood Guest House	G83 8LE	01389 750309	Guest House	★★★		
	Oakvale	G83 8JY	01389 751615	Bed & Breakfast	★★★		
	Palombo's of Balloch	G83 8LE	01389 753501	Restaurant With Rooms	★★★		
	Park View Apartment		01389 755792	Self Catering	★★★★		
	Polnaberoch	G83 8RQ	01389 850593	Bed & Breakfast	★★★		
	Restil	G83 8LF	01389 753105	Bed & Breakfast	★★		
	River Cottage		01436 860666	Self Catering	★★★★ to ★★★★★	🦽	
	Shantron Farm House	G83 8RH	01389 850231	Bed & Breakfast	★★★		🅟
	Shegarton Farm Cottages		01389 850269	Self Catering	★★★★		
	Shemore Farm Cottage		01389 850231	Self Catering	★★★		🅟
	St Blanes	G83 8JY	01389 729661	Bed & Breakfast	★★★		
	Sunnyside B & B	G83 9JX	01389 750282	Bed & Breakfast	★★★		
	The Corries	G83 8PD	01436 860275	Bed & Breakfast	★★★		
	The Gardener's Cottages		01389 850601	Self Catering	★★★★		🅟🅟
	The Hungry Monk	G83 8RX	01389 830448	Inn	★★★		
	The Inverbeg Inn	G83 8PD	01436 860678	Inn	★★★★		
	The Lodge on Loch Lomond	G83 8NT	01436 860201	Hotel	★★★★		🅟🅟
	The Loft Apartment		07747 181494	Self Catering	★★★★		
	The Lorn Mill Cottages		01389 753074	Self Catering	★★★★		
	The Old School House	G83 8SB	01389 830373	Bed & Breakfast	★★★★		
	The Old Smiddy Cottage		01389 750767	Self Catering	★★★		
	The Smiddy		0141 5781039	Self Catering	★★★		
	Tullichewan Farm	G83 8QY	01389 711190	Bed & Breakfast	★★★★		
	Tullie Inn	G83 8SW	01389 752052	Inn	★★★		
	Waters Edge Cottage	G83 8QZ	01389 850629	Bed & Breakfast	★★★★		
	Woodvale	G83	01389 755771	Bed & Breakfast	★★★★		
Alford	Balfluig Castle		020 76243200	Self Catering	★★★		
	Bydand Bed & Breakfast	AB33 8NF	01975 563613	Bed & Breakfast	★★★		
	Craich Cottage		01975 562584	Self Catering	★★★	🚶	🅟
	Forbes Arms Hotel	AB33 8QJ	01975 562108	Small Hotel	★★		
	Haughton Caravan Park	AB33 8NA	01975 562107	Holiday Park	★★★★		
	Haughton Country Park – Apartment 1		01467 627622	Self Catering	★ to ★★		
	The Smiddy House	AB33 8SS	01975 641216	Bed & Breakfast	★★★		
	Steading Cottage		0131 2439335	Self Catering	★★★		
	The Hayloft	AB33 8LL	01975 581149	Awaiting Grading			
	North Mains Cottage		0131 2439335	Self Catering	★★★		

  ♿ Unassisted wheelchair access   🦽 Assisted wheelchair access   🚶 Access for visitors with mobility difficulties
  🅟 Bronze Green Tourism Award   🅟🅟 Silver Green Tourism Award   🅟🅟🅟 Gold Green Tourism Award
For further information on our Green Tourism Business Scheme please see page 7.

Location	Property Name	Postcode	Telephone	Classification	Star Rating
Alloa	7 McAlpine Court		01764 652211	Self Catering	★★★
	Breacan House	FK10 1LN	01259 724786	Bed & Breakfast	★★★★
	Devon Valley Drive		01259 725986	Self Catering	★★★
	The Royal Oak Hotel	FK10 1LJ	01259 722423	Inn	★★
Alloa/ Clackmannan	Tower House	FK10 4JA	01259 213889	Bed & Breakfast	★★★
Alness	Kildermorie Estate	IV17 0YH	0207 3526248	Exclusive Use Venue	★★★★
	Lower Inchlumpie		01903 260334	Self Catering	★★★★
	Teaninich Castle	IV17 0XB	01349 883231	Country House Hotel	★★★
	Tullochard Guest House	IV17 0TU	01349 882075	Guest House	★★★
	34 Henry Street	FK12 5LQ	07947 184259	Awaiting Grading	
	Balquharn Farm		01259 763378	Self Catering	★★★★
Alva	Mill Glen & Ben Ever		01259 769638	Self Catering	★★★ to ★★★★ ⬩🚶
	Bella Vista	DG12 5PH	07834 518566	Awaiting Grading	
	Cormorant & Dunlin Cottages		01461 40873	Self Catering	★★★
	Dumbretton Farm		01461 500345	Self Catering	★★★
Annan	East Upper Priestside	DG12 5PX	01387 870668	Farm House	★★★
	Galabank Caravan & Camping Site	DG12 5DQ	01461 203539	Touring Park	★★
	Kinmount Court		01461 700406	Self Catering	★★★
	Queensberry Bay Caravan Park	DG12 5PU	01461 700205	Holiday Park	★★★★
	Rowanbank	DG12 5AW	01461 204200	Guest House	★★
	The Graham Arms Guest House	DG12 6NL	01461 40031	Guest House	★★★ 🚶
	The Old Rectory Guest House	DG12 6AW	01461 202029	Guest House	★★★
	The Powfoot Golf Hotel	DG12 5PN	01461 700254	Hotel	★★★ ♿
Anstruther	1 Midshore		0131 5388300	Self Catering	★★★★ to ★★★★★
	2 The Gyles		01333 310695	Self Catering	★★★★
	21 Shoregate		0207 2660801	Self Catering	★★★★
	3 Nethergate North		0131 476 4011	Self Catering	★★★★
	43 Shoregate		0131 6672175	Self Catering	★★★
	6 Chalmers Brae		0156 4782428	Self Catering	★★★★
	6 Westgate South	KY10 3RF	07950 652473	Awaiting Grading	
	63 Abbey Wall Road	KY10 2NE	01382 668347	Awaiting Grading	
	8 and 9 East Shore		01333 310421	Self Catering	★★★★
	8 Melville Terrace	KY10 3EW	01333 310 453	Bed & Breakfast	★★★
	9 Westgate North		0141 5545281	Self Catering	★★★
	Alton Garden Apartment		01333 451483	Self Catering	★★
	Arradoul		001 530 713 2486	Self Catering	★★★★
	Bakerswell House	KY10 3AY	07946 633002	Awaiting Grading	
	Balcomie Links Hotel	KY10 3TN	01333 450237	Small Hotel	★★
	Barnsmuir Farmhouse	KY10 3XB	01333 450342	Bed & Breakfast	★★★
	Beaumont Lodge	KY10 3DT	01333 310315	Bed & Breakfast	★★★★
	Bishop Cottage		01786 821702	Self Catering	★★★★
	Bishop Cottage		01786 821702	Self Catering	★★★★
	Caiplie Guest House	KY10 3RA	01333 450564	Guest House	★★★
	Craighead Farm		01383 820397	Self Catering	★★★★
	Crichton House	KY10 3DJ	01333 310219	Bed & Breakfast	★★★

Advertisers' locations have been sorted by postcode. In Scotland, postcodes can cover fairly large geographical areas.
Please check distance of property from specified location with the individual provider. VisitScotland cannot take any responsibility for this.

351

Location	Property Name	Postcode	Telephone	Classification	Star Rating
Anstruther	East and West Barns		01333 310527	Self Catering	★★★★
	East Haven		01505 862398	Self Catering	★★★
	Far Reaches B&B	KY10 3AL	01333 310448	Bed & Breakfast	★★★★
	Flat 2		01333 450270	Self Catering	★★★ to ★★★★
	Garden Cottage (East Cottage)	KY10 3TQ	0141 6386148	Awaiting Grading	
	Glenapp	KY10 3EL	07796 133377	Awaiting Grading	
	Invermay Cottage	KY10 3JQ	01333 312314	Bed & Breakfast	★★★
	Kilheugh Cottage		01357 520463	Self Catering	★★
	Kilrenny Mill Farmhouse	KY10 3JW	01333 311272	Bed & Breakfast	★★★
	Laggan House	KY10 3AW	01333 311170	Bed & Breakfast	★★★★
	Lobster Pot		07812 663854	Self Catering	★★★ to ★★★★
	Lobster Pot Cottage		01333 340640	Self Catering	★★★★ ♿
	Marie Philp	KY10 2LT	01333 311964	Bed & Breakfast	★★★
	Marine Hotel	KY10 3TZ	01333 450207	Guest House	★★★
	Newark Farm Cottages	KY10 2DB	01333 739003	Awaiting Grading	
	No 6 Urquhart Wynd	KY10 3BN	01333 310939	Bed & Breakfast	★★★★
	Old Coach House		01207 583612	Self Catering	★★★
	Pebbles	KY10 3RF	01333 312321	Awaiting Grading	
	Periwinkle		01206 547835	Self Catering	★★★★
	Periwinkle		01206 547835	Self Catering	★★★★
	Rooms@25	KY10 2QH	01333 313306	Bed & Breakfast	★★★
	Sauchope Links Caravan Park	KY10 3XJ	01333 450460	Holiday Park	★★★★★
	Seaview		01738 583705	Self Catering	★★★
	Seaview Cottage		01383 723366	Self Catering	★★★★
	Second Floor West		01333 313997	Self Catering	★★★★
	Shore Holidays			Self Catering	★★★
	Spalefield Lodge	KY10 3LB	01333 313659	Bed & Breakfast	★★★★
	Spindle Cottage		01202 257914	Self Catering	★★★★★
	St Monans Caravan Park	KY10 2DN	01334 474250	Holiday Park	★★★
	Sunny Patch		01324 563787	Self Catering	★★★
	Symphony Craws Nest Hotel	KY10 3DA	01333 310691	Hotel	★★★
	The Bakehouse & The Granary	KY10 3EA	01333 312200	Restaurant With Rooms	★★★
	The Coach House		01333 311255	Self Catering	★★★★
	The Cooperage		01333 310864	Self Catering	★★★★
	The Gables		0131 4412006	Self Catering	★★★
	The Gables		0131 4412006	Self Catering	★★★
	The Garden Flat		01333 312389	Self Catering	★★★★
	The Gatehouse		0131 4469011	Self Catering	★★★★
	The Hazelton	KY10 3TH	01333 450250	Guest House	★★★
	The Honeypot Guest House	KY10 3TD	01333 450935	Guest House	★★★
	The Old Barn		01333 720235	Self Catering	★★★★
	The Sheiling	KY10 3ET	01333 310697	Bed & Breakfast	★★★
	The Spindrift	KY10 3DT	01333 310573	Guest House	★★★★ 𝄞𝄞
	Tigh Na Mara		01333 310307	Self Catering	★★★
	Appin Holiday Homes	PA38 4BQ	01631 730287	Holiday Park	★★★★
	Ardselma		07711 541970	Self Catering	★★★
	Bealach House	PA38 4BW	01631 740298	Bed & Breakfast	★★★★

♿ Unassisted wheelchair access   ♿ Assisted wheelchair access   ♿ Access for visitors with mobility difficulties
ⓟ Bronze Green Tourism Award   𝄞𝄞 Silver Green Tourism Award   𝄞𝄞𝄞 Gold Green Tourism Award
For further information on our Green Tourism Business Scheme please see page 7.

352   To find out more go to visitscotland.com

Location	Property Name	Postcode	Telephone	Classification	Star Rating	
Anstruther	Bothan Darach		0141 4270814	Self Catering	★★★★	🅟
	Fasgadh Guest House	PA38 4DE	01631 730374	Bed & Breakfast	★★★	
	Gate Lodge		01631 730207	Self Catering	★★★★	♿ 🅟
	Holly Tree Hotel	PA38 4BY	01631 740292	Hotel	★★★	
	Inver Cottage		0208 9816996	Self Catering	★★★ to ★★★★	
	Kinlochlaich House – Laich Cottage		01631 730342	Self Catering	★★★ to ★★★★	🅟🅟🅟
	Lagnaha	PA38 4BS	01631 740282	Bed & Breakfast	★★★	
	Linnhe Croft Holiday Cottages		01631730513	Self Catering	★★★	
	Loch Linnhe Lodges		01631 740292	Self Catering	★★★	
	Pineapple House	PA38 4BP	01631 740557	Guest House	★★★★	
	Squirrel, Fox, Badger & Otter		01631 730287	Self Catering	★★★	
	Stable Bothy & Shepherds Bothy		01631 740282	Self Catering	★★★	♸
Appin	The Airds Hotel	PA38 4DF	01631 730236	Small Hotel	★★★★	
	The Cottage		01631 740318	Self Catering	★★★	
	The Pierhouse Hotel	PA38 4DE	01631 730302	Small Hotel	★★★	
Arbroath	5 Hill Terrace	DD11 1AH	0141 9420164	Awaiting Grading		
	Ashwell B&B	DD11 1TU	01241 874258	Bed & Breakfast	★★★	
	Balnabrechan Lodge	DD11 5SS	01241 830462	Awaiting Grading		
	Blairdene Guest House	DD11 1HY	01241 872380	Guest House	★★★	
	Brambles	DD11 2BT	01241 874601	Bed & Breakfast	★★★	
	Brucefield Boutique B&B	DD11 5BS	0845 2802686	Bed & Breakfast	★★★★★	♸
	Chance Inn		01241 830562	Self Catering	★★	
	Copper Dell B&B	DD11 4QD	01241 890546	Bed & Breakfast	★★★	
	Croftsmuir Steading	DD11 2RQ	01241 860245	Bed & Breakfast	★★★	
	Fins B&B	DD11 1AB	01241 872921	Awaiting Grading		
	Five Gables House	DD11 2PE	01241 871632	Bed & Breakfast	★★★	
	Gordon's Restaurant With Rooms	DD11 5RN	01241 830364	Restaurant With Rooms	★★★★	
	Grieve's Cottage		01241 830202	Self Catering	★★★	
	Harbour Nights Guest House	DD11 1PB	01241 434343	Guest House	★★★★	
	Inishowen Guest House	DD11 2PE	01241 871922	Bed & Breakfast	★★★★	
	Lawton House	DD11 4RU	01241 830217	Bed & Breakfast	★★	
	Letham Grange Golf Hotel and Country Estate	DD11 4RL	01241 890459	Awaiting Grading		
	Muckle Backit Guest House	DD11 5SQ	01241 437353	Bed & Breakfast	★★★	
	No 8 Shore		01241 879000	Self Catering	★★★★	
	Ogstons Arbroath	DD11 1DP	01241 431577	Awaiting Grading		
	Rosely Country House Hotel	DD11 3RB	01241 876828	Small Hotel	★★	
	Saughmont Cottage		01241 890743	Self Catering	★★★	
	The Chauffeurs Cottage & The Studio		01241 890204	Self Catering	★★★★	
	The Old Vicarage B & B	DD11 5DX	01241 430475	Bed & Breakfast	★★★★★	🅟
	Towerbank Guest House	DD11 1JP	01241 431343	Guest House	★★	
	Wee Anchor (Surf N Turf Cottages)		01241 430477	Self Catering	★★★ to ★★★★	
	Woodfield Cottage		01241 437456	Self Catering	★★★	
Ardgay	Achue Croft Cottage		01863 766144	Self Catering	★★★	
	Alladale Wilderness Lodge & Reserve	IV24 3BS	01863 755338	Hotel	★★★★★	
	Carbisdale Castle Youth Hostel	IV24 3DP	0870 1553255	Hostel	★★★★	♿ 🅟🅟

♿ Unassisted wheelchair access   ♿ Assisted wheelchair access   ♸ Access for visitors with mobility difficulties
🅟 Bronze Green Tourism Award   🅟🅟 Silver Green Tourism Award   🅟🅟🅟 Gold Green Tourism Award
For further information on our Green Tourism Business Scheme please see page 7.

Advertisers' locations have been sorted by postcode. In Scotland, postcodes can cover fairly large geographical areas.
Please check distance of property from specified location with the individual provider. VisitScotland cannot take any responsibility for this.

353

Location	Property Name	Postcode	Telephone	Classification	Star Rating
Ardgay	Ceannloch		0141 5789121	Self Catering	★★
	Corvost	IV24 3BP	01863 755317	Bed & Breakfast	★★
	The Lower Apartment		0131 2439335	Self Catering	★★★
	The Steading		07889 143962	Self Catering	★★★★
	The Upper Apartment		0131 2439335	Self Catering	★★★
Ardrossan	Edenmore	KA22 8AN	01294 462306	Bed & Breakfast	★★
Arisaig	Achnaskia Croft – Craig Mhor		01687 450606	Self Catering	★★★ to ★★★★ 🄿🄿
	Caimberidge House		01687 450375	Self Catering	★★★ to ★★★★
	Camusdarach	PH39 4NT	01687 450221	Touring Park	★★★★
	Cnoc-Na-Faire	PH39 4NS	01687 450249	Inn	★★★★
	Derryfad House		01687 450667	Self Catering	
	Kilmartin Farm Guesthouse	PH39 4NS	01687 450366	Bed & Breakfast	★★★
	Kinloid Caravans	PH39 4NS	01687 450366	Holiday Caravan	
	Kinloid Cottages		01687 450366	Self Catering	★★★
	Leven House	PH39 4NR	01687 450238	Bed & Breakfast	★★★★
	Loch Morar		01343 814845	Self Catering	★★ to ★★★
	Sunnyside Croft Touring Caravan & Camping Site	PH39 4NT	01687 450643	Awaiting Grading	
	The Old Library Lodge	PH39 4NH	01687 450651	Restaurant With Rooms	★★★
	Traigh Lodges – Golden Eagle and Sea Eagle		01687 450645	Self Catering	★★ to ★★★
Arrochar	Ardgartan Camping & Caravanning Club Site	G83 7AR	02476 475318	Touring Park	★★★
	Ardgarten Caravan & Campsite	G83 7AR	01283 228607	Touring Park	★★★★
	Ardlui Holiday Home Park	G83 7EB	01301 704243	Holiday Park	★★★★
	Ardlui Hotel	G83 7EB	01301 704243	Small Hotel	★★★
	Argyll View	G83 7AA	01301 702932	Bed & Breakfast	★★★★
	Argyll View Cottage		01301 702932	Self Catering	★★★
	Arrochar Hotel	G83 7AU		Awaiting Grading	
	Aye Servus	G83 7DD	01301 702819	Bed & Breakfast	★★★
	Ballyhennan Old Toll House	G83 7DA	01301 702203	Bed & Breakfast	★★★
	Beinglas Farm Campsite	G83 7DX	01301 704281	Inn	★★★
	Ben Bheula	G83 7AL	01301 702184	Bed & Breakfast	★★★
	Ben Dubthcriag & Cnap Mor		01301 704243	Self Catering	★★★★
	Bon-Etive	G83 7DF	01301 702219	Bed & Breakfast	★★★
	Braemor B&B	G83 7AA	01301 702535	Bed & Breakfast	★★★★
	Burnbrae	G83 7AG	01301 702988	Bed & Breakfast	★★★★
	Claymore Hotel	G83 7BB	01301 702238	Hotel	★★
	Clisham Cottage Bed and Breakfast	G83 7DX	01301 704339	Bed & Breakfast	★★
	Cruach View Lodge		01301 704243	Self Catering	★★★★
	Cruachan B&B	G83 7BB	01301 702521	Bed & Breakfast	★★★★
	Dalkusha House	G83 7AA	01301 702234	Bed & Breakfast	★★★★
	Fascadail Country Guest House	G83 7AB	01301 702344	Guest House	★★★
	Inneranjay Cottage 1-4		01301 702133	Self Catering	★★★★
	Inveruglas Farm	G83 7DP	01301 704210	Awaiting Grading	
	Loch Lomond Holiday Park	G83 7DW	01301 704224	Holiday Park	★★★★★
	Loch Lomond Holiday Park – Island Lodge. No1		01301 704224	Self Catering	★★★★ to ★★★★★

♿ Unassisted wheelchair access   ♿ Assisted wheelchair access   ♿ Access for visitors with mobility difficulties
🄿 Bronze Green Tourism Award   🄿🄿 Silver Green Tourism Award   🄿🄿🄿 Gold Green Tourism Award
For further information on our Green Tourism Business Scheme please see page 7.

354   To find out more go to visitscotland.com

Location	Property Name	Postcode	Telephone	Classification	Star Rating		
Arrochar	Loch Long Hotel	G83 7AA	01389 713713	Hotel	★★★		🅿🅿
	Lochview	G83 7DD	01301 702200	Bed & Breakfast	★★		
	Lomond View	G83 7DG	01301 702477	Bed & Breakfast	★★★★		
	Mansefield House		01301 702956	Self Catering	★★★★		
	Stewart House	G83 7DE	01301 702230	Bed & Breakfast	★★★	🚶	
	Stuckgowan Cottage	G83 7DH	01301 702451	Bed & Breakfast	★★★		
	Tarbet Hotel	G83 7DE	01301 702346	Hotel	★★		
	Village Inn	G83 7AX	01301 702279	Inn	★★★	🚶	
Auchterarder	17 Guthrie Court		01764 684633	Self Catering	★★★★		
	9 Windsor Gardens		01764 684100	Self Catering	★★★★		
	Alma House	PH3 1PA	01764 662894	Bed & Breakfast	★★★★		
	Blackford Hotel	PH4 1QF	01764 682497	Small Hotel	★★★	🚶	
	Cairn Lodge Hotel	PH3 1LX	01764 662634	Small Hotel	★★★		
	Duchally Country Estate	PH3 1PN	01764 660313	Country House Hotel	★★★★		🅿🅿
	Duchally Country Estate		01764 660313	Self Catering	★★★★★	♿	
	Easterton Farm	PH4 1RQ	01764 682268	Bed & Breakfast	★★★		
	GlenMhor		01764 664575	Self Catering	★★★★		
	Greystanes	PH3 1JJ	01764 664239	Bed & Breakfast	★★★★	🚶	
	Kilrymont	PH3 1JF	01764 662660	Bed & Breakfast	★★★★		
	Lang Toon Bed & Breakfast	PH3 1BJ	01764 662928	Bed & Breakfast	★★★		
	Mountwood Lodges		01764 662609	Self Catering	★★★★★		
	Retreat@trinitygask		07889 492162	Self Catering	★★★★★		
	Smiddy Haugh Hotel	PH3 1HE	01764 662013	Inn	★★		
	The Gleneagles Hotel	PH3 1NF	01764 662231	Hotel	★★★★★	♿	🅿🅿🅿
	The Old Dairy Cottage		01764 662369	Self Catering	★★★		
	The Parsonage Guest House	PH3 1AA	01764 662392	Bed & Breakfast	★★★		
Aviemore	10 Spey Avenue		01505 613665	Self Catering	★★★		
	14 Johnstone Road	PH22 1TY	01314 764914	Awaiting Grading			
	3 Dalfaber Park		0131 4666917	Self Catering	★★★★		
	45 Dalnabay		01592 641743	Self Catering	★★★		
	64 Dalnabay		01773 510 041	Self Catering	★★★		
	7 Morlich Place		01236 879390	Self Catering	★★★ to ★★★★		
	81 Dalnabay		01475 632779	Self Catering	★★★★		
	83 Dalnabay		01479 810499	Self Catering	★★★ to ★★★★	🚶	
	Achlean		01313 314941	Self Catering	★★★★		
	Alvie & Garten Lodges		01479 811244	Self Catering	★★ to ★★★★		
	Appintree Cottage		01382 480619	Self Catering	★★★		
	Ard Tigh		01475 673885	Self Catering	★★★★		
	Ardlogie Guest House	PH22 1PU	01479 810747	Guest House	★★★		
	Avielochan Farm Holiday Cottages		01479 810846	Self Catering	★★★	🚶	🅿🅿
	Aviemore Bunkhouse	PH22 1PU	01479 811181	Hostel	★★★★	♿	🅿
	Aviemore Four Seasons	PH22 1PJ	01479 815200	Hotel	★★★		
	Aviemore SYHA	PH22 1PR	01479 810345	Hostel	★★★★	♿	🅿
	Avonglen		07999 819762	Self Catering	★★★★		
	Badaguish		01479 861285	Self Catering	★★★	♿	
	Beaver Creek		0870 2416970	Self Catering	★★★★ to ★★★★★		
	Ben Bheag		0141 5870451	Self Catering	★★★		

♿ Unassisted wheelchair access   ♿ Assisted wheelchair access   🚶 Access for visitors with mobility difficulties
🅿 Bronze Green Tourism Award   🅿🅿 Silver Green Tourism Award   🅿🅿🅿 Gold Green Tourism Award
For further information on our Green Tourism Business Scheme please see page 7.

Advertisers' locations have been sorted by postcode. In Scotland, postcodes can cover fairly large geographical areas.
Please check distance of property from specified location with the individual provider. VisitScotland cannot take any responsibility for this.

355

Location	Property Name	Postcode	Telephone	Classification	Star Rating		
Aviemore	Birchwood		01296 713849	Self Catering	★★★		
	Braeriach		0141 5865024	Self Catering	★★★★		
	Braeriach		01479 810636	Self Catering	★★★ to ★★★★	♿	
	Caberfeidh Log Cabin		01540 660024	Self Catering	★★★		
	Cairn Eilrig	PH22 1QU	01479 861223	Bed & Breakfast	★★★		
	Cairngorm Guest House	PH22 1RP	01479 810630	Guest House	★★★		🅿
	Cairngorm Highland Bungalows – Coire Cas		01479 810653	Self Catering	★★★ to ★★★★		
	Cairngorm Holiday Bungalows		01479 810653	Self Catering	★★★		
	Cairngorm Hotel	PH22 1PE	01479 810233	Hotel	★★★		
	Cairngorm Lodge (Loch Morlich)	PH22 1QY	01479 861238	Hostel	★★★	♟	🅿🅿
	Caledonia Holiday & Leisure		01479 811326	Self Catering	★★★		
	Carn Mhor B&B	PH22 1QD	01479 811004	Bed & Breakfast	★★★		
	Claymore		01346 582035	Self Catering	★★		
	Cooks Cottage		01479 811685	Self Catering	★★★★		
	Corrour House	PH22 1QH	01479 810220	Guest House	★★★★		
	Craigellachie View		01479 810694	Self Catering	★★★		
	Culduthel		0141 6382224	Self Catering	★★★★		
	D&K Charnley		01698 360823	Self Catering	★★★		
	Dalraddy Holiday Park	PH22 1QB	01479 810330	Holiday Park	★★★★		
	Dunroamin	PH22 1RW	01479 810698	Bed & Breakfast	★★★		
	Eagle (Standard)		01479 810165	Self Catering	★★★ to ★★★★	♿	
	Eriskay	PH22 1RW	01479 810717	Bed & Breakfast	★★★		
	Eriskay Bed & Breakfast	PH22 1RW	01479 810717	Awaiting Grading			
	Falcon Lodge		01479 811463	Self Catering	★★★		
	Glenmore Caravan & Campsite	PH22 1QU	01283 228607	Touring Park	★★★★		🅿
	Glenrothay		01343 540608	Self Catering	★★★		
	Glenrothay		01343 540608	Self Catering	★★★		
	Hilton Coylumbridge		01479 813066	Self Catering	★★★★		
	Hilton Coylumbridge Hotel	PH22 1QN	01479 811811	Hotel	★★★		🅿🅿🅿
	Junipers	PH22 1QW	01479 810405	Guest House	★★★		
	Lairig Vue		01479 810212	Self Catering	★★★		
	Locha'an		01479 810735	Self Catering	★★★		
	Lochan		01357 522325	Self Catering	★★★		
	Lochan Mhor Apartment		01381 622461	Self Catering	★★★★		
	Macdonald Academy	PH22 1PF	01479 810781	Guest Accommodation	★★★	♿	
	Macdonald Highland Lodges	PH22 1PJ	01479 815100	Serviced Apartments	★★★★		
	Macdonald Highlands Hotel	PH22 1PV	01479 815100	Hotel	★★★★		
	MacKenzies Highland Inn	PH22 1RL	01479 810672	Inn	★★		
	McAndrew House		07725 420765	Self Catering	★★★★	♟	
	Pine Bank Chalets – Cairn Lochan		01479 810000	Self Catering	★★★ to ★★★★	♟	🅿
	Pityoulish Estate Cottages		01667 493312	Self Catering	★★		
	Ravenscraig Guest House	PH22 1RP	01479 810278	Guest House	★★★★	♟	🅿🅿
	Rothiemurchus Camping & Caravan Park	PH22 1QU	01479 812800	Touring Park	★★★★		
	Silver Birch Cottage		0870 246970	Self Catering	★★★★		
	Speyside Highland Leisure Park	PH22 1PX	01479 810694	Holiday Caravan			
	Speyside Leisure Park	PH22 1PX	01479 810236	Holiday Park	★★★★		

♿ Unassisted wheelchair access　♿ Assisted wheelchair access　♟ Access for visitors with mobility difficulties
🅿 Bronze Green Tourism Award　🅿🅿 Silver Green Tourism Award　🅿🅿🅿 Gold Green Tourism Award
For further information on our Green Tourism Business Scheme please see page 7.

Location	Property Name	Postcode	Telephone	Classification	Star Rating	
Aviemore	Speyside Leisure Park – Chalet No. 87		01479 810236	Self Catering	★★ to ★★★	
	Steamview Holiday Home		01479 811619	Self Catering	★★★	
	Strathspey House	PH22 1RP	01479 812453	Bed & Breakfast	★★★★	
	Struan		01294 463654	Self Catering	★★★	
	Sunbury		07753 622959	Self Catering	★★★★	
	The Garden Suite	PH22 1TA	01479 812293	Bed & Breakfast	★★★★	
	The Highland Council @ Badaguish		01463 870797	Self Catering	★★★	&.
	The Old Ministers House	PH22 1QH	01479 812181	Guest House	★★★★	
	The Retreat		01479 812453	Self Catering	★★★★	
	The Rowan Tree Country Hotel	PH22 1QB	01479 810207	Inn	★★★	
	Tigh na Lochan		0141 2485051	Self Catering	★★★★	
	Vermont Guest House	PH22 1RP	01479 810470	Guest House	★★★	
	Waverley	PH22 1SN	01479 811226	Bed & Breakfast	★★★	🕇
Avoch	Ardvreckan	IV9 8RD	01381 621523	Bed & Breakfast	★★★★	
	Roebuck Cottage/Swallow Cottage		01463 811205	Self Catering	★★★★	
Ayr	12 Marlborough Court		01290 550483	Self Catering	★★★	
	5A Park Circus		01292 619373	Self Catering	★★★	
	Abbotsford Hotel	KA7 2ST	01292 261506	Small Hotel	★★★	
	Acorn Cottage		01292 474642	Self Catering	★★★ to ★★★★	
	Alt-Na-Craig	KA6 7EB	01292 560555	Bed & Breakfast	★★★★	🕇
	Auldbyres Bungalow		01292 570301	Self Catering	★★★	
	Ayr Gatehouse	KA8 8LE	01292 284065	Awaiting Grading		
	Ayrs & Graces	KA7 4EE	01292 440028	Bed & Breakfast	★★★★	
	Ayrshire & Galloway Hotel	KA7 2EA	01292 262626	Hotel	★★	
	Belmont	KA7 2DJ	01292 290303	Guest House	★★★	
	Berkeley House	KA7 1XB	01292 287888	Awaiting Grading		
	Bothy Cottage		01292 500225	Self Catering	★★★	
	Bothy Cottage		01292 500225	Self Catering	★★★	
	Brig O' Doon Hotel	KA7 4PQ	01292 442466	Small Hotel	★★★★	
	'Bright & Beautiful'	KA7 4GZ	01555 820013	Awaiting Grading		
	Burnside Guest House	KA7 1DU	01292 263912	Guest House	★★★★	
	Bythesea Guest House	KA7 1DU	01292 282365	Guest House	★★★★	
	Canter Holm Guest House	KA7 2DG	01292 880919	Bed & Breakfast	★★★	
	Carrick Lodge Hotel	KA7 2RE	01292 262846	Small Hotel	★★★	
	Citadel Penthouse		01292 264246	Self Catering	★★★★	
	Coila Guest House	KA7 3BB	01292 262642	Guest House	★★★★	
	Country Courtyard Cottages		01292 570251	Self Catering	★★★★	
	Craig Holm Guest House	KA7 1DU	01292 261470	Guest House	★★★	
	Craig Tara	KA7 4LB	01292 265141	Holiday Park	★★★★	🅿🅿
	Craig Tara Holiday Park		01292 294532	Self Catering	★★★	
	Craigie Gardens Caravan Club Site	KA8 0SS	01342 336842	Touring Park	★★★★★	
	Croft Head Caravan Park	KA6 6EN	01292 263516	Holiday Park	★★★★	
	Dalmellington House	KA6 7QL	01563 571533	Awaiting Grading		
	Daviot House	KA7 1DU	01292 26978	Guest House	★★★★	
	Dunn Thing Guest House	KA7 2DJ	01292 284531	Bed & Breakfast	★★★	
	Eglinton Guest House	KA7 1JJ	01292 264623	Guest House	★★	
	Ellisland	KA7 2TD	01292 260111	Small Hotel	★★★	

Advertisers' locations have been sorted by postcode. In Scotland, postcodes can cover fairly large geographical areas.
Please check distance of property from specified location with the individual provider. VisitScotland cannot take any responsibility for this.

357

Location	Property Name	Postcode	Telephone	Classification	Star Rating	
Ayr	Elms Court Hotel	KA7 2AX	01292 264191	Small Hotel	★★★	
	Enterkine Country House	KA6 5AL	01292 520580	Country House Hotel	★★★	
	Express by Holiday Inn Ayr	KA8 9RT	01292 272300	Metro Hotel	★★★	
	Failte	KA8 8LD	01292 265282	Bed & Breakfast	★★★	
	Fairfield House Hotel	KA7 2AS	01292 267461	Hotel	★★★★	🚶
	Gadgirth Estate Lodges		01292 520721	Self Catering	★★★★	
	Garth Madryn	KA7 4TB	01292 443346	Bed & Breakfast	★★	
	Grange View Bed & Breakfast	KA7 2RA	01292 266680	Bed & Breakfast	★★★	
	Greenan Lodge	KA7 4HR	01292 443939	Bed & Breakfast	★★★★	
	Heads of Ayr Caravan Park	KA7 4LD	01292 442269	Holiday Park	★★★★	
	Horizon Hotel	KA7 1DT	01292 264384	Hotel	★★★	♿
	Kensington House	KA7 2AX	01292 266301	Bed & Breakfast	★★★	
	Kilkerran Guest House	KA8 8LD	01292 266477	Guest House	★★	
	Langley Bank Guest House	KA7 2RD	01292 264246	Guest House	★★★★	
	Leslie Anne Guest House	KA7 2HX	01292 265666	Bed & Breakfast	★★★	
	Lochinver	KA7 2DL	01292 265086	Bed & Breakfast	★★★	
	Miller House	KA7 2AY	01292 282016	Guest House	★★★	
	Muirburn House B&B	KA6 5AG	01292 521430	Bed & Breakfast	★★★★	
	No. 26 The Crescent	KA7 2DR	01292 287329	Guest House	★★★★★	
	Queen's Guest House	KA7 1DU	01292 265618	Guest House	★★★	
	Ramada Jarvis	KA7 1UG	01292 269331	Hotel	★★★	♿ 🅿
	Richmond Guest House	KA7 2DL	01292 265153	Guest House	★★★	
	South Lodge		01292 441313	Self Catering	★★★	♿
	Springwater Chalets Ltd		01463 226990	Self Catering	★★★	🚶
	St Andrews Hotel	KA8 8LD	01292 263211	Inn	★★	
	Stewartlea Stables		01540 673447	Self Catering	★★★	
	Sundrum Castle Holiday Park	KA6 6HX	01292 570057	Holiday Park	★★★★★	
	Sunnyside	KA7 4HR	01292 441234	Bed & Breakfast	★★★★	
	The Beechwood Guest House	KA8 8LE	01292 262093	Guest House	★★★	
	The Coach House		01292 285033	Self Catering	★★★★	
	The Ivy Rooms	KA7 2AX	01292 262474	Hotel	★★★	
	The Kirkton Inn	KA6 6OF	01292 560241	Inn	★★	
	The Kyle Hotel	KA6 6JW	01292 570312	Inn	★★★	
	The Windsor	KA7 2AA	01292 264689	Guest House	★★★	
	The Wytchery	KA6 6FD	01292 442070	Bed & Breakfast	★★★★	
	Travelodge Ayr	KA8 9SH	0871 9846321	Budget Hotel		
	Turnberry House		07919 174484	Self Catering	★★★	
	Woodcroft Cottage		01292 264383	Self Catering	★★★	
	Woodside Farmhouse	KA6 6HQ	01292 570254	Bed & Breakfast	★★★	
Balerno	Haughhead Farm	EH14 7JH	0131 4493875	Farm House	★★★	
Balerno/Currie/ Juniper Green	Riccarton Arms	EH14 5NX	0131 4492230	Inn	★★	
	Violet Bank House	EH14 5NZ	0131 4515103	Bed & Breakfast	★★★★★	
Ballachulish	Alltbeag	PH49 4HN	01855 811719	Bed & Breakfast	★★★★	
	An Darag	PH49 4HU	01855 811643	Bed & Breakfast	★★★	
	Ardno House	PH49 4JD	01855 811830	Bed & Breakfast	★★★★	
	Ben Vheir Cottage		01855 811200	Self Catering	★★★★	

♿ Unassisted wheelchair access   ♿ Assisted wheelchair access   🚶 Access for visitors with mobility difficulties
🅿 Bronze Green Tourism Award   🅿🅿 Silver Green Tourism Award   🅿🅿🅿 Gold Green Tourism Award
For further information on our Green Tourism Business Scheme please see page 7.

Location	Property Name	Postcode	Telephone	Classification	Star Rating		
Ballachulish	Callart View B&B	PH49 4HP	01855 811259	Bed & Breakfast	★★★		
	Callart View Cottage		01516 482454	Self Catering	★★★		
	Ceol Mara		01434 606512	Self Catering	★★★		
	Cherry Cottage		01631 740556	Self Catering	★★★★		
	Clachaig Inn	PH49 4HX	01855 811252	Inn	★★		🄿
	Craiglinnhe House	PH49 4JD	01855 811270	Guest House	★★★★		
	Dalcraig House		01855 811608	Self Catering	★★★★ to ★★★★★		
	Dorrington Lodge	PH49 4HN	01855 811653	Guest House	★★★		
	Dunire	PH49 4HS	01855 811305	Guest House	★★★		
	Fern Villa Guest House	PH49 4JE	01855 811393	Guest House	★★★		
	Glencoe Camping & Caravanning Club Site	PH49 4LA	02476 475318	Touring Park	★★★★		
	Glencoe Youth Hostel	PA39 4HX	01855 811219	Hostel	★★★		🍃🍃
	Glencoe Cottages		01855 811207	Self Catering	★★★	🏃	🍃🍃🍃
	Glencoe Hideaway Lochview		01895 675662	Self Catering	★★★		
	Glencoe Independent Hostel	PH49 4HX	01855 811906	Bunkhouse			
	Glencoe Mountain Cottages		01855 811598	Self Catering	★★★★		
	Holly Cottage		01855 811419	Self Catering	★★★★		
	Invercoe Caravan & Camping Park	PH49 4HP	01855 811210	Holiday Park	★★★★★		
	Invercoe Highland Holidays		01855 811210	Self Catering	★★★★		
	Isles of Glencoe Hotel & Leisure Centre	PH49 4HL	01855 811602	Hotel	★★★	♿	🍃🍃🍃
	Kings House Hotel	PH49 4HY	01855 851259	Inn	★★		
	Lia-Fail		07974 330861	Self Catering	★★★★		
	Lyn-Leven Guest House	PH49 4JP	01855 811392	Guest House	★★★★		
	Parkview B&B	PH49 4JS	01855 811560	Bed & Breakfast	★★★		
	Red Peak		01424 813249	Self Catering	★★★★		
	Red Squirrel Camp Site	PH49 4HX	01855 811256	Camping Park	★★		
	Scorry Breac Guest House	PH49 4HT	01855 811354	Guest House	★★★★		
	Signal Rock Cottage B&B	PH49 4HX	01855 811207	Bed & Breakfast	★★★		🍃🍃🍃
	Sorcha		07751 105345	Self Catering	★★★		
	Stone Cottage Unit 1	PH49 4HW	01539 624194	Awaiting Grading			
	Strathassynt Guest House	PH49 4JB	01855 811261	Guest House	★★★		
	The Ballachulish Hotel	PH49 4JY	01855 811606	Hotel	★★★	♿	
Ballater	13 The Monaltrie			Self Catering	★★★★		
	4 the Monaltrie		01569 731725	Self Catering	★★★★		
	6 Braichlie Buildings		01569 731831	Self Catering	★★★		
	7 Old Stables Courtyard		01224 316876	Self Catering	★★★		
	7 The Monaltrie		01224 855296	Self Catering	★★★		
	Alexandra Hotel	AB35 5QJ	01339 755376	Small Hotel	★★★		
	Arisaig Cottage		01339 755177	Self Catering	★★★★		
	Averill		01698 811932	Self Catering	★★★		
	Ballater Caravan Park	AB35 5QR	01467 627622	Holiday Park	★★★		
	Ballater Lodge		0141 3533839	Self Catering	★★★★		
	Balmoral Estates		01339 742534	Self Catering	★★★ to ★★★★		
	Birch Cottage		01224 649814	Self Catering	★★★★		
	Braemar Lodge	AB35 5YQ	01339 741627	Small Hotel	★★★		
	Braemar Lodge Bunkhouse	AB35 5YQ	01339 741627	Hostel	★★★★		
	Braemar Lodge Hotel		01339 741627	Self Catering	★★★	🏃	
	Braemar Youth Hostel	AB35 2QL	0870 1553255	Hostel	★★★		🍃🍃

♿ Unassisted wheelchair access   ♿ Assisted wheelchair access   🏃 Access for visitors with mobility difficulties
🄿 Bronze Green Tourism Award   🍃🍃 Silver Green Tourism Award   🍃🍃🍃 Gold Green Tourism Award
For further information on our Green Tourism Business Scheme please see page 7.

Advertisers' locations have been sorted by postcode. In Scotland, postcodes can cover fairly large geographical areas.
Please check distance of property from specified location with the individual provider. VisitScotland cannot take any responsibility for this.

359

Location	Property Name	Postcode	Telephone	Classification	Star Rating		
Ballater	Braeriach		0131 2439335	Self Catering	★★★		
	Broom Cottage		01330 820740	Self Catering	★★★		
	Bruach Mhor		01224 315607	Self Catering	★★★		
	Bynack		0131 2439335	Self Catering	★★★		
	Callater Lodge Guest House	AB35 5YQ	01339 741275	Guest House	★★★★		
	Cambus O'May Hotel	AB35 5SE	01339 755428	Country House Hotel	★★★		
	Celicall	AB35 5RL	01339 755699	Bed & Breakfast	★★★		
	Claybokie		0131 2439331	Self Catering	★★★★		
	Clunie Lodge Guest House	AB35 5ZP	01339 741330	Guest House	★★★		
	Craig Vallich		01224 317713	Self Catering	★★★★		
	Craiglea	AB35 5YU	01339 741641	Guest House	★★★		
	Crathie Opportunity Holidays		01339 742100	Self Catering	★★★★	♿	𝒫𝒫𝒫
	Crathie Opportunity Holidays		01339 742100	Self Catering	★★★★	♿	𝒫𝒫𝒫
	Creag Bhalg		0131 2439335	Self Catering	★★★★★		
	Creag Meggan	AB35 5UD	01339 755767	Bed & Breakfast	★★★		
	Croft Muicken		0131 5523866	Self Catering	★★★		
	Dalmore House	AB35 5NS	01339 741225	Bed & Breakfast	★★★		
	Dalvorar		0131 2439335	Self Catering	★★★		
	Darroch Learg Hotel	AB35 5UX	01339 755443	Small Hotel	★★★	♀	
	Deeside Hotel	AB35 5RQ	01339 755420	Small Hotel	★★★		𝒫
	Derry		0131 2439335	Self Catering	★★★		
	Elvenstones		01334 476679	Self Catering	★		
	Fairdene B&B	AB35 5RJ	01339 755929	Bed & Breakfast	★★★★		
	Fairdene Cottage		01339 755929	Self Catering	★★★★		
	Gairnshiel		0131 3346473	Self Catering	★★★★		
	Gairnshiel		0131 3346473	Self Catering	★★★★		
	Glen Lui Hotel	AB35 5PP	01339 755402	Small Hotel	★★★		𝒫𝒫
	Glenernan Guest House	AB35 5RQ	01339 753111	Guest House	★★★★	♿	
	Habitat @ Ballater	AB35 5QJ	01339 753752	Hostel	★★★★★		
	Havelock		01224 649101	Self Catering	★★★		
	Hilton Craigendarroch – Ballater Lodge		01339 755858	Self Catering	★★★★ to ★★★★★		𝒫
	Hilton Craigendarroch Hotel	AB35 5RQ	01339 755858	Hotel	★★★		𝒫
	Invercauld Lodges		07778 210767	Self Catering	★★★★		
	Lary Cottage		0131 3370617	Self Catering	★★★		
	Macdui		0131 2439335	Self Catering	★★★		
	Moorfield House	AB35 5YT	01339 741244	Restaurant With Rooms	★★★		
	Moorside Guest House	AB35 5RL	01339 755492	Guest House	★★★★	♀	
	Morvada House	AB35 5RL	01339 756334	Guest House	★★★★		
	Myrtle Cottage		01330 833557	Self Catering	★★★★		
	Netherley Guest House	AB35 5QE	01339 755792	Guest House	★★★★		
	No 3 Knocks Cottages		01372 459123	Self Catering	★★★★		
	Pine Trees Cottage		01224 585500	Self Catering	★★★★	♿	
	Rosedale Cottage		01224 867975	Self Catering	★★★		
	Schiehallion Guest House	AB35 5YQ	01339 741679	Guest House	★★★		
	School House	AB35 5QW	01339 756333	Bed & Breakfast	★★★★	♀	𝒫
	Tangley House	AB35 5RQ	01339 755624	Bed & Breakfast	★★★★		
	The Attic Apartment		01224 486929	Self Catering	★★★★		

♿ Unassisted wheelchair access   ♿ Assisted wheelchair access   ♀ Access for visitors with mobility difficulties
𝒫 Bronze Green Tourism Award   𝒫𝒫 Silver Green Tourism Award   𝒫𝒫𝒫 Gold Green Tourism Award
For further information on our Green Tourism Business Scheme please see page 7.

360   To find out more go to visitscotland.com

Location	Property Name	Postcode	Telephone	Classification	Star Rating		
Ballater	The Auld Kirk	AB35 5RQ	01339 755762	Restaurant With Rooms	★★★★		
	The Coach House		01339 755482	Self Catering	★★★★		
	The Firs		01224 312069	Self Catering	★★★★		
	The Gordon Guest House	AB35 5QB	01339 755996	Guest House	★★★★		
	The Green Inn	AB35 5QQ	01339 755701	Restaurant With Rooms	★★★★		
	The Inver Hotel	AB35 5XN	01339 742345	Inn	★★★		
	The Invercauld Arms Hotel	AB35 5YR	01339 741605	Hotel	★★★		
	The Invercauld Caravan Club Site	AB35 5YQ	01342 336842	Touring Park	★★★★		
	Tigh-Na-Croabh		01224 318257	Self Catering	★★★★		
	Woodside	AB35 5UT	01339 756351	Bed & Breakfast	★★★		
Ballindalloch	Altnavoir		01807 580336	Self Catering	★★★		
	Argyle Guest House	AB37 9EX	07974 355086	Guest House	★★★		
	Benavon		01807 580221	Self Catering	★★★		
	Cragganmore Lodge		07887 621443	Self Catering	★★★		
	Croughly Cottage		01807 580476	Self Catering	★★★		
	Delnalyne		01324 712415	Self Catering	★★★★		
	Deskie Cottage		01807 590207	Self Catering	★★★		
	Enoch Dhu		01807 590364	Self Catering	★★★		
	Folds Cottage		01340 881616	Self Catering	★★★★		Ⓟ
	Glen Avon Hotel	AB37 9ET	01807 580218	Inn	★★		
	Grant Cottage		01807 590266	Self Catering	★★★		
	Livet Cottage Holidays		01807 580727	Self Catering	★★★		
	Lochranza		01606 75208	Self Catering	★★★★		
	McLeods Cottage		01807 580366	Self Catering	★★★		
	The Croft Inn	AB37 9DP	01807 590361	Awaiting Grading			
	The Croft Inn (Caravan Holiday Homes)	AB37 9DP	01807 590361	Awaiting Grading			
	The Den		01807 590241	Self Catering	★★★	♣	ⓅⓅⓅ
	The Old Kennels		07771 534704	Self Catering	★★★		
	The Old School		01807 590276	Self Catering	★★★★		
	Tomintoul Youth Hostel	AB37 9EX	0870 0041152	Hostel	★★★★		ⓅⓅ
	Woodville	AB37 9AD	01807 500396	Bed & Breakfast	★★★★		
Banchory	Banchory Lodge Country House Hotel	AB31 5HS	01330 822625	Country House Hotel	★★★		
	Birch & Willow Lodges		01330 822622	Self Catering	★★★★	♣	
	Birchlea Cottage	AB31 6NL	01330 824132	Bed & Breakfast	★★★★		
	Bridge of Bennie Cottage		01330 824288	Self Catering	★★★★	♣	
	Burnett Arms Hotel	AB31 5TD	01330 824944	Small Hotel	★★★		
	Burnhead Small Holding	AB31 4RN	01339 883687	Bed & Breakfast	★★★		
	Cairnton Bothy		01339 883536	Self Catering	★★★★		
	Cluny Cottage		01330 825555	Self Catering	★★★		
	Crossroads Hotel	AB31 4RH	01339 883275	Inn	★★		
	Davont	AB31 5JE	01330 844600	Bed & Breakfast	★★★		
	Drumhead Cottage		01330 850771	Self Catering	★★★★		
	East Lodge		0131 2439331	Self Catering	★★★		
	Feughside Caravan Park	AB31 6NT	01330 850669	Holiday Park	★★★★		
	Greenlands		01339 886497	Self Catering	★★★★		

Advertisers' locations have been sorted by postcode. In Scotland, postcodes can cover fairly large geographical areas.
Please check distance of property from specified location with the individual provider. VisitScotland cannot take any responsibility for this.

Location	Property Name	Postcode	Telephone	Classification	Star Rating
Banchory	Inchmarlo Golf Club		01330 826424	Self Catering	★★★★
	Learney Arms Hotel	AB31 4JP	01339 882202	Small Hotel	★★
	Lochton	AB31 6DB	01330 844543	Bed & Breakfast	★★★
	Manse Croft		07702 269609	Self Catering	★★★★
	Mapleview	AB31 4RH	01339 883481	Bed & Breakfast	★★★
	No. 40 Scolty Place		01330 823143	Self Catering	★★★★
	Potarch Hotel	AB31 4BD	01339 884339	Inn	★★★
	Raemoir House Hotel	AB31 4ED	01330 824884	Country House Hotel	★★★
	The Bothy @ Collonach		01330 811116	Self Catering	★★★★
	The Cottage		01330 822919	Self Catering	★★★★
	The Flat		01339 883557	Self Catering	★★★
	The Pine Lodge		01330 825544	Self Catering	★★★★
	Toll Bridge Lodge		01330 822686	Self Catering	★★★★
	Tor-Na-Coille Hotel	AB31 5UB	01330 822242	Awaiting Grading	
	Wester Durris Cottage	AB31 3BQ	01330 844638	Bed & Breakfast	★★
	Woodend Chalet Holidays – Mount Keen		01339 882562	Self Catering	★★★ to ★★★★ 🦽
Banff	1 & 2 Dallochy Cottages		01261 861206	Self Catering	★★★
	1 North High Street		01261 843680	Self Catering	★★★★
	13 Crovie		01563 535790	Self Catering	★★★
	13 Crovie		01563 535790	Self Catering	★★★
	6 Turnkeys		01888 568804	Self Catering	★★★
	6 Turnkeys		01888 568804	Self Catering	★★★
	Academy House	AB45 2SJ	01261 842743	Bed & Breakfast	★★★★★
	Antiquity Cottage		01466 751278	Self Catering	★★★★ 🚶
	Banff Links Caravan Park	AB45 2JJ	01261 812228	Holiday Park	★★★★
	Bankfoot Croft		01261 843003	Self Catering	★★★
	Barton of Muiryhill		01903 767273	Self Catering	★★★★
	Belvedere		01888 544359	Self Catering	★★★
	Bryden	AB45 2LD	01261 861742	Bed & Breakfast	★★★★
	Carmelite House Hotel	AB45 1AY	01261 812152	Guest House	★★★
	Cowfords Cottage		01261 843227	Self Catering	★
	Crovie Cottage (No. 7)		0131 2439335	Self Catering	★★★★
	Eva's Cottage		01382 779818	Self Catering	★★★
	Fife Lodge Hotel	AB45 1BE	01261 812436	Small Hotel	★★★
	Gardenia House	AB45 1DH	01261 812675	Guest House	★★★
	Granny Curly's		01771 637367	Self Catering	★★★★
	Herons		01261 851339	Self Catering	★★★
	Mill of Alvah		01261 818557	Self Catering	★★
	Mitchell's Cottage		07803 503052	Self Catering	★★★★
	Myrus Holiday Park	AB45 3QP	01261 812845	Holiday Park	★★★★★
	No 1 St Brandon House Cottages		01261 843234	Self Catering	★★★★
	No. 131 Harbour Road		07879 604980	Self Catering	★★★
	Old Merchant House	AB45 2PB	01261 843424	Awaiting Grading	
	Palace Farm	AB45 3HS	01261 851261	Farm House	★★★★
	Portsoy Caravan Park	AB45 2RQ	01261 842695	Holiday Park	★★★★
	Sandend Caravan Park	AB4 2UA	01261 842660	Holiday Park	★★★★
	Seilie Cottage		01261 842468	Self Catering	★★★★

♿ Unassisted wheelchair access   🦽 Assisted wheelchair access   🚶 Access for visitors with mobility difficulties
ⓟ Bronze Green Tourism Award   ⓟⓟ Silver Green Tourism Award   ⓟⓟⓟ Gold Green Tourism Award
For further information on our Green Tourism Business Scheme please see page 7.

362   To find out more go to visitscotland.com

Location	Property Name	Postcode	Telephone	Classification	Star Rating		
Banff	Stable Cottage		01261 843434	Self Catering	★★★		
	Station Hotel	AB45 2QT	01261 842327	Inn	★★★		
	The Boyne Hotel	AB45 2PA	01261 842242	Awaiting Grading			
	The Lodge		01261 812436	Self Catering	★★★		
	The Trinity and Alvah Manse	AB45 1DH	01261 812244	Guest House	★★★		
	Tigh-na-Drochaid		01732 456442	Self Catering	★★★		
	Tigh-na-Drochaid		01732 456442	Self Catering	★★★		
	Two Bears Cottage		01772 863214	Self Catering	★★★★		
	Wester Bonnyton Farm Caravan Site	AB45 3EP	01261 832470	Holiday Park	★★★		
Bathgate	Best Western Hilcroft Hotel	EH47 0JU	01501 740818	Hotel	★★★	🦽	🅟
	Bracklin B&B	EH48 1EQ	01506 424487	Awaiting Grading			
	Braeside Cottage B&B	EH47 9DW	01501 772418	Bed & Breakfast	★★		
	Cruachan Guest House	EH47 7QS	01506 655221	Bed & Breakfast	★★★		
	East Badallan Farm	EH47 9AG	01501 770251	Farm House	★★★★		
	Hillview	EH48 4DA	01506 654830	Bed & Breakfast	★★		
	Premier Inn Livingston (Bathgate)	EH48 1LQ	01506 650650	Awaiting Grading			
	Silver Mines		01506 630836	Self Catering	★★★		
	Tarrareoch Farm	EH48 3BJ	01501 730404	Bed & Breakfast	★★★		
	The Cottage Self Catering		01501 752301	Self Catering	★★★		
Beauly	Aigas Holiday Cottages		01463 782423	Self Catering	★★★		
	Broomhill	IV4 7JH	01463 741447	Bed & Breakfast	★★★		
	Cannich Caravan & Camping Park	IV4 7LN	01456 415364	Holiday Park	★★★★		🅟🅟
	Cherry Trees	IV4 7JQ	01463 741368	Farm House	★★★★		
	Cnoc End	IV4 7DJ	01463 782230	Bed & Breakfast	★★★★		
	Cnoc Hotel	IV4 7JU	01463 761264	Small Hotel	★★★		
	Cruachan	IV4 7BQ	01463 782679	Bed & Breakfast	★★★		
	Culligran Cottages		01463 761285	Self Catering	★★ to ★★★		
	Dallas Lodge		01756 720409	Self Catering	★★★	🚶	
	Dunedin		01456 415238	Self Catering	★★★	🚶	
	Dunedin	IV4 7LS	01456 415238	Holiday Caravan			
	Dunsmore Lodges		01463 782424	Self Catering	★★★★	🚶	
	Glen Affric Chalet Park		01456 415369	Self Catering	★★		
	Glen Affric Youth Hostel	IV4 7NO	0870 1553255	Hostel	★		🅟🅟
	Invercannich Farm		01456 415216	Self Catering	★★★		
	Kiltarlity Lodges		01463 741481	Self Catering	★★★		
	Priory Hotel	IV4 7BX	01463 782309	Hotel	★★★		
	Rheindown Farm	IV4 7AB	01463 782461	Holiday Caravan			
	Rheindown Farm Chalets		01463 782461	Self Catering	★		
	Shepherds Cottage		01798 344500	Self Catering	★★		
	Tomich Chalets		01456 415332	Self Catering	★★★ to ★★★★		🅟🅟
	Tomich Hotel	IV4 7LY	01456 415399	Small Hotel	★★★		
	Westward	IV4 7LT	01456 415708	Bed & Breakfast	★★★		
	Willowburn Cottage		01586 830323	Self Catering	★★★★		
Beith	Shotts Farm	KA15 1LB	01505 502273	Farm House	★★★		
	Glasgow Bellsill Premier Inn	ML4 3HH	08701 977106	Budget Hotel			
Bellshill	Hilton Strathclyde	ML4 3JQ	01698 395500	Hotel	★★★★	🚶	

🦽 Unassisted wheelchair access   🦽 Assisted wheelchair access   🚶 Access for visitors with mobility difficulties

🅟 Bronze Green Tourism Award   🅟🅟 Silver Green Tourism Award   🅟🅟🅟 Gold Green Tourism Award

For further information on our Green Tourism Business Scheme please see page 7.

Advertisers' locations have been sorted by postcode. In Scotland, postcodes can cover fairly large geographical areas.
Please check distance of property from specified location with the individual provider. VisitScotland cannot take any responsibility for this.

363

Location	Property Name	Postcode	Telephone	Classification	Star Rating	
Berwick-upon-Tweed	Banrach	TD15 1XQ	01289 386851	Bed & Breakfast	★★★★	
	Bunnahabhain Strathisla and Tomatin		01289 386279	Self Catering	★★★★★	♿
	Foulden Hill Farm		01890 781207	Self Catering	★★★	
	Rose Cottage		01661 820635	Self Catering	★★★	
	The Lodge		01289 386834	Self Catering	★★★★	
	The Lodge		01289 386139	Self Catering	★★★ to ★★★★	
	The Paddock		01289 386339	Self Catering	★★★★	♿ 🅿
	Travelodge Berwick Upon Tweed	TD15 1UP	08719 846279	Budget Hotel		
	Tweed Cottage	TD15 1TE	01890 817186	Awaiting Grading		
Biggar	2 Mitchell Place		01352 714992	Self Catering	★★★	
	Abington Hotel	ML12 6SD	01864 502467	Hotel	★★★	
	Allershaw House	ML12 6TJ	01864 505050	Farm House	★★★★	
	Butlers		01899 308336	Self Catering	★★ to ★★★★	
	Cormiston Farm	ML12 6NS	01899 221507	Bed & Breakfast	★★★★	
	Cornhill House	ML12 6QE	01899 220001	Country House Hotel	★★★	
	Cuil Darach	ML12 6UF	01899 221259	Bed & Breakfast	★★★★	
	Elphinstone Hotel	ML12 6DL	01899 220044	Inn	★★	
	High Meadows B&B	ML12 6NF	01899 308872	Bed & Breakfast	★★★	
	Holmlands Country House	ML12 6TW	01864 502753	Bed & Breakfast	★★	
	Merlindale Holiday Apartment		01899 830221	Self Catering	★★★★★	
	Mount View Caravan Park	ML12 6RW	01864 502808	Holiday Park	★★★★	
	Shieldhill Castle	ML12 6NA	01899 220035	Country House Hotel	★★★★	
	Skirling House	ML12 6HD	01899 860274	Guest House	★★★★★	
	Stonehill Cottage		01864 504217	Self Catering	★★★	🅿🅿
	The New Farmhouse		01899 860245	Self Catering	★★★	
	Victoria Lodge	ML12 6QP	01899 880293	Bed & Breakfast	★★★★★	
Bishopton	Mar Hall	PA7 5NW	0141 8129999	Hotel	★★★★★	
	The Millers House	PA7 5NX	01505 862417	Bed & Breakfast	★★★★	
Blairgowrie	Altamount Country House Hotel	PH10 6JN	01250 873512	Country House Hotel	★★★	
	Alyth Hotel	PH11 8AT	01828 632447	Inn	★★	
	Angus Hotel	PH10 6NQ	01250 872455	Hotel	★★★	
	Ardormie Farm Cottage		01828 633047	Self Catering	★★★★	🅿🅿
	Auchavan Stables		01738 710440	Self Catering	★★★★ to ★★★★★	
	Bankhead	PH10 6SG	01250 884281	Farm House	★★★	
	Blackwater Outdoor Centre	PH10 7HJ	01738 477878	Group Accommodation	★★★	
	Blair Bratach		01142 663188	Self Catering	★★★★	
	Blairgowrie Holiday Park	PH10 7AL	01250 876666	Holiday Park	★★★★★	
	Braveheart Cottage		01828 640445	Self Catering	★★★	
	Bridge of Cally Hotel	PH10 7JJ	01250 886231	Small Hotel	★★★	🚶
	Brown's B&B	PH12 8SD	01828 640020	Bed & Breakfast	★★★★	
	Burrelton Park Inn	PH13 9NX	01828 670206	Inn	★	
	Cairnleith Cottage		01259 218408	Self Catering	★★★	
	Clunskea Farm		01250 881358	Self Catering	★★★	
	Cnoc Liath		01764 683222	Self Catering	★★ to ★★★	
	Corriefodly Holiday Park	PH10 7JG	01250 876666	Holiday Park	★★★★★	
	Cromald Cottages		01250 886391	Self Catering	★★★★	

Directory of all VisitScotland Assured Serviced Establishments, ordered by location.
Establishments highlighted have an advertisement in this guide.

Location	Property Name	Postcode	Telephone	Classification	Star Rating
Blairgowrie	Dalhenzean Lodge	PH10 7QD	01250 885217	Bed & Breakfast	★★★★
	Dalmunzie Castle Hotel	PH10 7QE	01250 885224	Country House Hotel	★★★
	Dalmunzie Highland Cottages – Sauchmore		01250 885226	Self Catering	★★ to ★★★
	Eildon Bank	PH10 6ED	01250 573648	Bed & Breakfast	★★★
	Ericht Holiday Lodges		01250 874686	Self Catering	★★★
	Five Roads Caravan Park	PH11 8NB	01828 632255	Holiday Park	★★★★
	Forter Castle		01575 582305	Self Catering	★★★★
	Garfield House	PH10 6ED	01250 872999	Bed & Breakfast	★★★
	Gilmore House	PH10 6EJ	01250 872791	Bed & Breakfast	★★★★
	Glen prosen, Glen Clova and Glen Isla		01575 530474	Self Catering	★★★★ to ★★★★★
	Glenbeag Mountain Lodges		01250 885204	Self Catering	★★★ to ★★★★ ♈
	Glenisla Hotel	PH11 8PH	01575 582223	Inn	★★
	Glenkilrie Bed and Breakfast	PH10 7LR	01250 882241	Farm House	★★★
	Glensheiling House	PH10 7HZ	01250 874605	Guest House	★★★★
	Glenshieling Lodge		01250 874605	Self Catering	★★★
	Gulabin Lodge	PH10 7QE	01250 885255	Activity Accommodation	★★★
	Heathpark House	PH10 6JT	01250 870700	Bed & Breakfast	★★★★
	Heathpark House Apartment		01250 870700	Self Catering	★★★★
	Heathpark Lodge	PH10 6JT	01250 874929	Bed & Breakfast	★★★★
	Holmrigg	PH10 6RD	01250 884309	Bed & Breakfast	★★★ ♈
	Ivybank Guest House	PH10 7BH	01250 873056	Guest House	★★★★
	Kinloch House Hotel	PH10 6SG	01250 884237	Country House Hotel	★★★★
	Lands of Loyal Hotel	PH11 8JQ	01828 633151	Country House Hotel	★★★★
	Larch Cottage		01575 530258	Self Catering	★★★
	Little Doocot 1 & 2		01250 886349	Self Catering	★★★★
	Lunanbrae	PH10 6RA	01250 884224	Bed & Breakfast	★★★★
	Miramichi		01250 873310	Self Catering	★★★
	Neids		01575 560731	Self Catering	★★★
	Nether Craig Holiday Park	PH11 8HN	01575 560204	Holiday Park	★★★★★
	New Steading Cottage/ Old Steading Cottage		01250 882200	Self Catering	★★★★ ♈
	No 38 Riverside Park		0779 5112201	Self Catering	★★★
	Old Stables	PH11 8BT	01828 632547	Bed & Breakfast	★★★★
	Parkhead Cottage		01575 560374	Self Catering	★★★★
	Pine Lodges Blairgowrie Holiday Park		01250 876666	Self Catering	★★★★
	Pondfauld Holidays Ltd – Marigold Cottage		01250 873284	Self Catering	★★ to ★★★
	Ralston Bothy		01828 650500	Self Catering	★★★★ to ★★★★★ ♈
	Rannagulzion Apt.		01250 886359	Self Catering	★★★
	Red House Hotel	PH13 9AL	01828 628500	Inn	★★★ ♈
	Ridgeway	PH10 6RA	01250 884734	Bed & Breakfast	★★★
	River Cottage		01250 881377	Self Catering	★★★
	Riverview		01250 881416	Self Catering	★★★★
	Rocksite		01383 729618	Self Catering	★★★ ♈
	Rosebank House	PH10 7AF	01250 872912	Guest House	★★★
	The Bothy		01250 884263	Self Catering	★★★★
	The Bothy		01250 870611	Self Catering	★★★ to ★★★★

ᕲ Unassisted wheelchair access ᕳ Assisted wheelchair access ♈ Access for visitors with mobility difficulties
🅟 Bronze Green Tourism Award 🅟🅟 Silver Green Tourism Award 🅟🅟🅟 Gold Green Tourism Award
For further information on our Green Tourism Business Scheme please see page 7.

Advertisers' locations have been sorted by postcode. In Scotland, postcodes can cover fairly large geographical areas.
Please check distance of property from specified location with the individual provider. VisitScotland cannot take any responsibility for this.

Location	Property Name	Postcode	Telephone	Classification	Star Rating	
Blairgowrie	The Coach House	PH10 7QD	01250 885209	Awaiting Grading		
	The Holly Tree Lodge	PH10 7LJ	01250 876566	Awaiting Grading		
	The Laurels Guest House	PH10 6LH	01250 874920	Guest House	★★★	
	The Old Byre		01250 884756	Self Catering	★★★★	
	The Reed & The Toftin		01828 632547	Self Catering	★★★	🕇
	The Whitehouse			Self Catering	★★★	
	Tigh Na Leigh	PH11 8AD	01828 632372	Guest House	★★★★★	
	West Freuchies	PH11 8PG	01575 582716	Bed & Breakfast	★★★★	
Boat of Garten	3 High Terrace		01479 831262	Self Catering	★★	
	Chalet Morlich		01479 831646	Self Catering	★★	
	Cherry Cottage		01875 853491	Self Catering	★★	
	Corronich		01479 831357	Self Catering	★★★★	
	Corrour		07092 397813	Self Catering	★★★	
	Flat 3 Craigview		01698 852901	Self Catering	★★	
	Fraoch Lodge	PH24 3BN	01479 831331	Hostel	★★★★	🍃🍃🍃
	Heath Cottage		01479 831720	Self Catering	★★★	
	Loch Garten Caravan Park	PH24 3BY	01479 831769	Holiday Park	★★★★	
	Meikle House		01479 810694	Self Catering	★★★★	🍃🍃
	Moorfield House	PH24 3BN	01479 831646	Guest House	★★★★	🍃🍃
	Mountain Lodges		01479 831551	Self Catering	★★★	
	The Boat Hotel	PH24 3BH	01479 831258	Hotel	★★★★	
	The Boat House	PH24 3BN	01479 831484	Guest House	★★★	
	Tyndrum		01479 831242	Self Catering	★★★	
Bo'ness	Carriden House	EH51 9SN	01506 829811	Guest House	★★★	
Bonnybridge	Glen Skirlie House & Castle	FK4 1UF	01324 840201	Small Hotel	★★★★	
	Antonine Wall Cottages		01324 811875	Self Catering	★★★★	🕇
	Lawford Lodge		01324 813090	Self Catering	★★★★	🕇
Bonnyrigg	Dalhousie Castle & Spa	EH19 3JB	01875 825716	Hotel	★★★★	
	The Retreat Castle	EH19 3HS	0131 6603200	Small Hotel	★★★	♿
Brechin	Alexandra Lodge	DD9 7TN	01356 648266	Bed & Breakfast	★★★★	
	Blibberhill Farm	DD9 6TH	01307 830323	Farm House	★★★	
	Brathinch Farm	DD9 7QZ	01356 648292	Bed & Breakfast	★★★	
	Cottage at Mill of Lethnot		01224 646239	Self Catering	★★★	🍃🍃
	Doune Guest House	DD9 7TA	01356 648201	Bed & Breakfast	★★★	
	Glenesk Caravan Park	DD9 7YP	01356 648565	Holiday Park	★★★	
	Glenesk Hotel	DD9 7TF	01356 648565	Hotel	★★★	
	Gramarcy House	DD9 6JP	01356 622240	Bed & Breakfast	★★★★	
	Hillview House	DD9 6SY	01356 629061	Bed & Breakfast	★★★	
	Kinnaber	DD9 7TT	01356 648 051	Bed & Breakfast	★★★★	
	Liscara	DD9 6JW	01356 625584	Bed & Breakfast	★★★★	
	Mill of Blackhall		01356 660211	Self Catering	★★★★	
	Negara Bed & Breakfast	DD9 7TA	01356 647463	Bed & Breakfast	★★★	
	Netherton		01356 648426	Self Catering	★★★	
	Newtonmill House	DD9 7PZ	01356 622533	Bed & Breakfast	★★★★	
	No2 Dunlappie Garden Cottage	DD9 7UD	01561 340662	Awaiting Grading		
	North Esk Lodge	DD9 7TA	01356 647409	Bed & Breakfast	★★★	

♿ Unassisted wheelchair access   ♿ Assisted wheelchair access   🕇 Access for visitors with mobility difficulties
🍃 Bronze Green Tourism Award   🍃🍃 Silver Green Tourism Award   🍃🍃🍃 Gold Green Tourism Award
For further information on our Green Tourism Business Scheme please see page 7.

366   To find out more go to visitscotland.com

Location	Property Name	Postcode	Telephone	Classification	Star Rating	
Brechin	Northern Hotel	DD9 6AE	01356 625400	Small Hotel	★★★	♿
	Oakbank		01356 648615	Self Catering	★★★★	
	Panmure Arms Hotel	DD9 7TA	01356 648950	Inn	★★★	
	Parker's Retreat		01356 625354	Self Catering	★★★★★	
	Rose Cottage		01356 647409	Self Catering	★★★	
	The Hayloft	DD9 7PZ	01356 624479	Awaiting Grading		
Bridge of Orchy	Bridge of Orchy Hotel	PA36 4AD	01838 400208	Inn	★★★★	
	The Anchorage		01475 522536	Self Catering	★★★	
Bridge of Weir	The Sycamores	PA11 3PU	01505 613137	Bed & Breakfast	★★★★	
	Maple Cottage – Apartment 1		01505 616044	Self Catering	★★★★	
	Cloverleigh & Oakleigh	KW9 6NG	07900 288884	Awaiting Grading		
Brora	Dalchalm Caravan Club Site	KW9 6LP	01342 336842	Touring Park	★★★★★	
	Inverbrora Farmhouse	KW9 6NJ	01408 621208	Bed & Breakfast	★★★★	
	Royal Marine Hotel	KW9 6GS	01408 621252	Hotel	★★★★	
	The Links Apartments – 5,7,14,15,16		01408 621252	Self Catering	★★★ to ★★★★	
Broxburn	Bankhead Farm	EH52 6NB	01506 811209	Guest House	★★★★	
	Houstoun House Hotel	EH52 6JS	01506 853831	Country House Hotel	★★★	
	Oatridge Hotel	EH52 5DA	01506 856465	Inn	★★	
	The Byre		01506 811209	Self Catering	★★★★★	
Buckie	10 Great Eastern Road		01542 831277	Self Catering	★★★	🚶
	125 Seatown		01779 838040	Self Catering	★★★★	
	16 Albert Terrace		01975 562214	Self Catering	★★★	
	78 Seatown		01464 841696	Self Catering	★★★	
	88 Seatown		01738 812862	Self Catering	★★★	
	Aurora	AB56 4SD	01542 840252	Awaiting Grading		
	Ben Lawers		01542 734999	Self Catering	★★ to ★★★	
	Boat House	AB56 4PX	01224 859810	Awaiting Grading		
	Crannoch Hotel	AB56 4RQ	01542 840210	Inn	★★★	
	Cullen Bay Holiday Park	AB56 4TW	01542 840766	Holiday Park	★★★★	
	Cullen Harbour Hostel	AB56 4AG	01542 841997	Hostel	★★★★	
	Kintrae	AB56 1ES	01542 839755	Bed & Breakfast	★★★★	
	Lismore		01697 20481	Self Catering	★★★	
	No1 Cliff Terrace		01224 323218	Self Catering	★★★	🚶
	Norwood House	AB56 4TE	01542 840314	Guest House	★★★	
	Rosemount	AB56 1ER	01542 833434	Bed & Breakfast	★★★★	
	Seafield Arms Hotel	AB56 4SG	01542 840791	Hotel	★★★	
	Strathlene Caravan Park	AB56 4DJ	01542 834851	Holiday Park	★★★★	
	Taigh Na Mara		01542 841145	Self Catering	★★★	
	The Old Drapery		01343 820304	Self Catering	★★★★	
	Aberdour Hotel	KY3 0SW	01383 860325	Small Hotel	★★★	🚶
	Bankhead Farm		01383 860912	Self Catering	★★★	
	Bay Hotel	KY3 9YE	01592 892215	Hotel	★★★	♿
	Cullaloe Lodge		01383 860575	Self Catering	★★★★	
Burntisland	Gruinard	KY3 9JU	01592 873 877	Bed & Breakfast	★★★★	
	Hideaway Beach House		01592 892535	Self Catering	★★★★	
	Kingswood Hotel	KY3 9LL	01592 872329	Small Hotel	★★★	♿

♿ Unassisted wheelchair access   🦽 Assisted wheelchair access   🚶 Access for visitors with mobility difficulties
🄟 Bronze Green Tourism Award   🄟🄟 Silver Green Tourism Award   🄟🄟🄟 Gold Green Tourism Award
For further information on our Green Tourism Business Scheme please see page 7.

Advertisers' locations have been sorted by postcode. In Scotland, postcodes can cover fairly large geographical areas.
Please check distance of property from specified location with the individual provider. VisitScotland cannot take any responsibility for this.

367

Location	Property Name	Postcode	Telephone	Classification	Star Rating
Burntisland	Kirkton View	KY3 0EW	01592 870481	Awaiting Grading	
	Martins Lodge	KY3 0EN	01592 870481	Bed & Breakfast	★★★
	No 69 Cromwell Road	KY3 9EL	01592 874969	Bed & Breakfast	★★★★
	Riverview		01383 860340	Self Catering	★★★
	Salmon Cottage		0161 4561147	Self Catering	★★★★
	The Chaumer		01383 823872	Self Catering	★★★
	The Wee House		01592 890320	Self Catering	★★★
	The Woodside Hotel	KY3 0SW	01383 860328	Small Hotel	★★★
	Willow Tree Cottage		01383 860 661	Self Catering	★★★ to ★★★★
Cairndow	Achadunan Estate – Inverfyne		01499 600238	Self Catering	★★★
	Cairndow Cottage		01245 231657	Self Catering	★★★★
	Cairndow Stagecoach Inn	PA26 8BN	01499 600286	Inn	★★
	Darroch Mhor Chalets		01301 703249	Self Catering	★★
	Drimsynie & Kingfisher Holiday Village	PA24 8AD	01301 703247	Holiday Park	★★★★★
	Drimsynie House Hotel	PA24 8AD	01301 703247	Small Hotel	★★★
	Halftown Cottages – Loudon & McHugh		01369 860750	Self Catering	★★★★
	Lochgoilhead Hotel	PA24 8AA	01301 703247	Inn	★★
	Lochside Bed and Breakfast	PA24 8AF	01301 703261	Bed & Breakfast	★★★
	The Creggans Inn	PA27 8BX	01369 860279	Small Hotel	★★★
	The Lodge	PA24 8AE	01301 703193	Exclusive Use Venue	★★★★★
	The Shore House Inn	PA24 8AA	01301 703340	Inn	★★★
	Thistle House	PA25 8AZ	01499 302209	Guest House	★★★★
	Tigh An Uillt		0141 3347222	Self Catering	★★★★
	Upper Croitachonie		01436 840040	Self Catering	★★★
Callander	Abbotsford Lodge Guest House	FK17 8DA	01877 330066	Guest House	★★★★
	Annfield Cottage		01877 330234	Self Catering	★★★
	Annfield House	FK17 8EG	01877 330204	Guest House	★★★★
	Ardoch House – Hillside & Woodside		01877 384666	Self Catering	★★★ to ★★★★ _PP_
	Auchenlaich Farmhouse Guest House	FK17 8LQ	01877 331683	Guest House	★★★★
	Braeview		07714 037111	Self Catering	★★★★
	Brook Linn Cottage		01877 330103	Self Catering	★★★★
	Brook Linn Country House	FK17 8AU	01877 330103	Guest House	★★★★
	Burnt Inn House	FK17 8HT	01877 376212	Bed & Breakfast	★★★
	Corriemar	FK17 8LE	01877 330827	Bed & Breakfast	★★★
	Craignethan Cottage		01877 330720	Self Catering	★
	Creagan House	FK18 8ND	01877 384638	Restaurant With Rooms	★★★★★
	Dalgair House Hotel	FK17 8BQ	01877 330283	Small Hotel	★★
	Dreadnought Hotel	FK17 8AN		Awaiting Grading	
	Dunmor House	FK17 8AL	01877 330756	Guest House	★★★★
	Frennich House		01877 376274	Self Catering	★★★★
	Gart Caravan Park	FK17 8LE	01877 330002	Holiday Park	★★★★★
	Highland View			Self Catering	★★
	Immervoulin Caravan & Camping Park	FK18 8NJ	01877 384285	Touring Park	★★★
	Keltie Bridge Caravan Park	FK17 8LQ	01877 330075	Touring Park	★★★★
	Kilravock		01877 330076	Self Catering	★★★★
	Leighton House	FK17 8BG	01877 330291	Bed & Breakfast	★★★
	Lime Tree Cottage		07891 677736	Self Catering	★★★★

  ♿ Unassisted wheelchair access   ♿ Assisted wheelchair access   ♿ Access for visitors with mobility difficulties
  _P_ Bronze Green Tourism Award   _PP_ Silver Green Tourism Award   _PPP_ Gold Green Tourism Award
For further information on our Green Tourism Business Scheme please see page 7.

Location	Property Name	Postcode	Telephone	Classification	Star Rating		
Callander	Loch Achray Hotel	FK17 8HZ	01877 376229	Hotel	★★★		
	Lubnaig House	FK17 8AS	01877 330376	Guest House	★★★★		
	Mid Torrie Farm Cottage		01877 330203	Self Catering	★★★★		
	North Wing	FK17 8HA	01877 331078	Awaiting Grading			
	Poppies Hotel and Restaurant	FK17 8AL	01877 330329	Small Hotel	★★★		
	Riverview House	FK17 8AL	01877 330635	Guest House	★★★		
	Roman Camp Hotel	FK17 8BG	01877 330003	Country House Hotel	★★★★		♠
	Roslin Cottage	FK17 8LE	01877 339787	Bed & Breakfast	★★★		
	Sir Andrew Murray House	FK18 8NQ	01324 562452	Group Accommodation	★★★		♠
	Southfork Villa	FK17 8EA	01877 330831	Guest House	★★★★		
	Straid House B&B	FK17 8LJ	01877 339077	Bed & Breakfast	★★★		
	The Auld Toll Cottage		01877 330635	Self Catering	★★★ to ★★★★		
	The Crags Hotel	FK17 8BQ	01877 330257	Inn	★★★		♠
	The Knowe	FK17 8EL	01877 330076	Guest House	★★★★		
	The Lodge		01877 330568	Self Catering	★★★★		
	The Old Rectory Guest House	FK17 8AL	01877 339215	Inn	★★★		♠
	Trossachs Backpackers	FK17 8HW	01877 331200	Hostel	★★★★		
	Westcot Guest House	FK17 8AL	01877 339812	Awaiting Grading			
	Westerton	FK17 8AJ	01877 330147	Bed & Breakfast	★★★★		
Campbeltown	9 Castleacres		0141 3399353	Self Catering	★★★		
	Allt Mor		01586 830665	Self Catering	★★★		
	Ardshiel Hotel	PA28 6JL	01586 552133	Small Hotel	★★★		
	Avalon	PA28 6JP	01586 552002	Awaiting Grading			
	Ballynacuaig		01583 431234	Self Catering	★★★★		
	Bayview Holiday Cottage	PA28 6UG	01586 554401	Awaiting Grading			
	Bayvoyach		01848 200364	Self Catering	★★		
	Carradale Bay Caravan Park	PA28 6QG	01583 431665	Holiday Park	★★★★		
	Carradale Hotel	PA28 6RY	01583 431223	Small Hotel	★★★		
	Carraig		07778 036137	Self Catering	★★★★		
	Cliff Cottage		01583 431399	Self Catering	★★★★		
	Craigard House	PA28 6EP	01586 554242	Small Hotel	★★★		
	Dalnaspidal Guest House	PA28 6QD	01586 820466	Guest House	★★★★★	♿	
	Daluaine		01738 552553	Self Catering	★★★		
	Dellwood Hotel	PA28 6HD	01586 552465	Small Hotel	★★		
	Dunvalanree	PA28 6SE	01583 431226	Restaurant With Rooms	★★★★	♿	🅟🅟
	Island View		01586 820012	Self Catering	★★★		
	Kiloran Guest House	PA28 6QG	01583 431795	Guest House	★★★		
	Lochain		01583 431612	Self Catering	★★		
	Machrihanish Caravan & Camping Park	PA28 6PT	01586 810366	Touring Park	★★★★		
	Mingulay		01586 553108	Self Catering	★★★		
	Oatfield House	PA28 6PH	01586 551551	Bed & Breakfast	★★★★		
	Ormsary Farm	PA28 6RN	01586 830665	Bed & Breakfast	★★★		
	Peninver Sands Holiday Park	PA28 6QP	01586 552262	Holiday Park	★★★★		
	Peniver Beach	PA28 6PW	01586 810210	Holiday Caravan			
	Pennyseorach Farm	PA28 6RF	01586 830217	Bed & Breakfast	★★★		
	Port Right Cottage		01583 431226	Self Catering	★★★		
	Redknowe	PA28 6PD	01586 550374	Bed & Breakfast	★★★		

♿ Unassisted wheelchair access   🦽 Assisted wheelchair access   ♠ Access for visitors with mobility difficulties
🅟 Bronze Green Tourism Award   🅟🅟 Silver Green Tourism Award   🅟🅟🅟 Gold Green Tourism Award
For further information on our Green Tourism Business Scheme please see page 7.

Advertisers' locations have been sorted by postcode. In Scotland, postcodes can cover fairly large geographical areas.
Please check distance of property from specified location with the individual provider. VisitScotland cannot take any responsibility for this.

369

Location	Property Name	Postcode	Telephone	Classification	Star Rating		
Campbeltown	Rosemount	PA28 6EN	01586 553552	Bed & Breakfast	★★★		
	Seaviews at Pennyseorach Farm	PA28 6RF	01586 830217	Holiday Caravan			
	Shore Cottage West		01474 707616	Self Catering	★★★		
	The Dairy Rhoin Farm		01586 820220	Self Catering	★★★★	氏	丹丹
	Torrisdale Estate Crossaig Kilean and Tangy Apart.		01583 431233	Self Catering	★★ to ★★★		丹
	Westbank Guest House	PA28 6JG	01586 553660	Guest House	★★★		
Canonbie	Blinkbonny	DG14 0RW	01387 371575	Bed & Breakfast	★★★		朮
	Byreburnfoot Country House B&B	DG14 0RA	01387 371209	Bed & Breakfast	★★★★		
	Cross Keys Hotel	DG14 0SY	01387 371205	Inn	★★★		
	Four Oaks	DG14 0TF	01387 371329	Bed & Breakfast	★★★		
	Burnhead Farm	ML8 4QN	01555 771360	Bed & Breakfast	★★★		
	Douglashall Bed & Breakfast	ML8 4PG	01555 750690	Bed & Breakfast	★★★		
Carluke	Wallace Hotel	ML8 4QG	01555 773000	Restaurant With Rooms	★★		
Carnoustie	10 Bruce Court		01241 856133	Self Catering	★★★★		
	74 Dalhousie Court		01592 206087	Self Catering	★★★★		
	Aboukir Hotel	DD7 6AT	01241 852149	Small Hotel	★★		
	Carnoustie Coach House B&B	DD7 6LD	01241 857319	Bed & Breakfast	★★★		朮
	Carnoustie Golf Hotel	DD7 7JE	01241 411999	Awaiting Grading			
	Cottage 1		01241 856465	Self Catering	★★★		
	Morven House	DD7 7SN	01241 852385	Bed & Breakfast	★★★★		
	Park House	DD7 7JA	01241 852101	Bed & Breakfast	★★★★★		
	Seaview Guest House	DD7 6AS	01241 851092	Guest House	★★★★		
	Semi Detached Villa			Self Catering	★★★★		
	The Old Manor	DD7 6JP	01241 854804	Bed & Breakfast	★★★★		
	The Old Manor Cottage		01241 854804	Self Catering	★★★★		
	Twiga Cottage		01241 855203	Self Catering	★★		
	Woodlands Caravan Park	DD7 7SR	01241 851870	Touring Park	★★★★		
Carrbridge	2 Carr Cottage		01463 831479	Self Catering	★★★		
	Carrbridge Hotel	PH23 3AS	01479 841202	Hotel	★★★		
	Carrmoor Guest House	PH23 3AD	01479 841244	Guest House	★★★		
	Craigellachie House	PH23 3AS	01479 841641	Guest House	★★★★		
	Dalrachney Lodge Hotel	PH23 3AT	01479 841252	Country House Hotel	★★★		
	Fairwinds Hotel	PH23 3AA	01479 841240	Small Hotel	★★★		
	Lochanhully Woodland Club		01479 811810	Self Catering	★★★		
	Slochd Mhor Lodge	PH23 3AY	01479 841666	Hostel	★★★★	氏	丹丹
	The Cairn Hotel	PH23 3AS	01479 841212	Inn	★★★		丹
	Tormore		01436 672335	Self Catering	★★★★		
Castle Douglas	1 Tannery Brae		01556 660312	Self Catering	★★★		
	1 Tannery Wynd		01968 674129	Self Catering	★★★		
	45 Academy Street		0131 3364779	Self Catering	★★		
	5 Tannery Wynd		02476 347919	Self Catering	★★★		
	7 (&8) Tannery Brae		01422 843762	Self Catering	★★★		
	Airds Farmhouse	DG7 3BG	01556 670418	Farm House	★★★		
	Airdside		01556 670418	Self Catering	★★★ to ★★★★	氏	
	Albion House	DG7 1LD	01556 502360	Bed & Breakfast	★★★★		

&. Unassisted wheelchair access &. Assisted wheelchair access 朮 Access for visitors with mobility difficulties
丹 Bronze Green Tourism Award 丹丹 Silver Green Tourism Award 丹丹丹 Gold Green Tourism Award
For further information on our Green Tourism Business Scheme please see page 7.

370   To find out more go to visitscotland.com

Location	Property Name	Postcode	Telephone	Classification	Star Rating	
Castle Douglas	Anwoth Holiday Park	DG7 2JU	01557 814333	Holiday Park	★★★★★	
	Auchenlarie Holiday Park	DG7 2EX	01557 840251	Holiday Park	★★★★★	
	Balcary Bay Hotel	DG7 1QZ	01556 640217	Country House Hotel	★★★	♿
	Balcary Mews	DG7 1QZ	01556 640276	Bed & Breakfast	★★★★	
	Balcary Mews		01556 640276	Self Catering	★★★★	
	Ballantines		01556 504954	Self Catering	★★★	
	Barlochan Caravan Park	DG7 1PF	01557 870267	Holiday Park	★★★★	
	Barncrosh Farm – Calf House		01556 680216	Self Catering	★★ to ★★★	
	Bluehill Farm	DG7 1QW	01556 640228	Farm House	★★★★	
	Cally Palace Hotel	DG7 2DL	01557 814341	Hotel	★★★★	
	Carrick Holiday Cottages		01557 814130	Self Catering	★★★	
	Chapelerne Farmhouse		01556 650270	Self Catering	★★★★	♿
	Chipperkyle Bed and Breakfast	DG7 3EY	01556 650223	Bed & Breakfast	★★★★	
	Clachan Cottage		01557 814444	Self Catering	★★★★	
	Clachanside		01683 220870	Self Catering	★★★★	
	Craigadam	DG7 3HU	01556 650233	Farm House	★★★★	
	Craigadam Lodge		01556 650233	Self Catering	★★★★	♿
	Craiglure		07968 873485	Self Catering	★★★	
	Craigrobin		01644 420249	Self Catering	★★★★	
	Craigshall Cottage		01556 640028	Self Catering	★★★	
	Croys	DG7 3EX	01556 650237	Bed & Breakfast	★★★★	
	Croys Lodge		01556 650237	Self Catering	★★★	
	Deeside	DG7 3AU	01556 670239	Bed & Breakfast	★★★	
	Dildawn Courtyard Cottage		01556 680377	Self Catering	★★ to ★★★	
	Douglas Arms Hotel	DG7 1DB	01556 502231	Hotel	★★★	
	Douglas House B&B	DG7 1HS	01556 503262	Bed & Breakfast	★★★★	♿
	Driftwood		01697 473578	Self Catering	★★★★	
	Dukieston Cottage		01644 430230	Self Catering	★★★	
	Ferryboat Cottage		07765 252631	Self Catering	★★★★	
	Galloway Activity Centre	DG7 ENQ	01644 420626	Activity Accommodation	★★★	
	Galloway Cottage		0845 6446547	Self Catering	★★★★	
	Galloway Hideaways – Culreoch		01557 814672	Self Catering	★★ to ★★★	
	Garden Cottage		01557 814215	Self Catering	★★★	♁
	Garden Cottage		02866 385854	Self Catering	★★★	
	Gate Lodge		0131 2439335	Self Catering	★★★	
	Glenfinart Cottage		01387 710409	Self Catering	★★★	
	Glenlee Holiday Houses		01644 430212	Self Catering	★★★	
	Granary Cottage		0131 2439335	Self Catering	★★	
	Hazel Cottage		01556 640210	Self Catering	★★★★	
	Hillowton House	DG7 3EL	01556 502512	Bed & Breakfast	★★★	
	Imperial Hotel	DG7 1AA	01556 502086	Inn	★★★	
	Ironcannie Mill Cottage		01644 420889	Self Catering	★★★	
	Kendoon Youth Hostel	DG7 3UD	0870 1553255	Hostel	★	🄿
	Kings Arms Hotel	DG7 1EL	01556 502626	Inn	★★★	
	Leath		01623 847019	Self Catering	★★★★	
	Livingstone House		01556 504030	Self Catering	★ to ★★	
	Loch Ken Holiday Park	DG7 3NE	01644 470282	Holiday Park	★★★★	

♿ Unassisted wheelchair access   ♿ Assisted wheelchair access   ♁ Access for visitors with mobility difficulties
🄿 Bronze Green Tourism Award   🄿🄿 Silver Green Tourism Award   🄿🄿🄿 Gold Green Tourism Award
For further information on our Green Tourism Business Scheme please see page 7.

Advertisers' locations have been sorted by postcode. In Scotland, postcodes can cover fairly large geographical areas.
Please check distance of property from specified location with the individual provider. VisitScotland cannot take any responsibility for this.

371

Location	Property Name	Postcode	Telephone	Classification	Star Rating		
Castle Douglas	Lochhill Cottages		01557 820225	Self Catering	★★★		
	Lochside Caravan & Camping Site	DG7 1EZ	01556 503806	Touring Park	★★★		
	Market Inn Hotel	DG7 1HX	01556 505070	Inn	★★★		
	Millwheel		0131 2439335	Self Catering	★★		
	Mossyard Caravan Park	DG7 2ET	01557 840226	Holiday Park	★★★★		
	Murray Arms Hotel	DG7 2HY	01557 814207	Small Hotel	★★★		
	Netheryett Caravan	DG7 3JZ	01556 660213	Holiday Caravan			
	Netheryett Cottage		01556 660213	Self Catering	★★★		
	Queenshill Country Cottages – The Lodges		01557 820227	Self Catering	★★★		
	Rangemhor	DG7 3LP	01556 650296	Bed & Breakfast	★★★		
	Redcastle Cottages – Steading Flat 1		01556 660475	Self Catering	★★★	⚡	
	Rusko Holidays – Upper Rusko Farmhouse		01557 814215	Self Catering	★★ to ★★★★	⚡	𝒫𝒫
	Screel Mill/Doach Cottage		01556 502853	Self Catering	★★★★		
	Shilfa		01557 870356	Self Catering	★★★		
	Smithy House	DG7 1TH	01556 503841	Bed & Breakfast	★★★★		
	Studio Cottage		01556 503932	Self Catering	★★		
	The Bank of Fleet Hotel	DG7 2HR	01557 814302	Small Hotel	★★★		
	The Bobbin Guest House	DG7 2HP	01557 814229	Guest House	★★★		
	The Craig	DG7 1BA	01556 504840	Bed & Breakfast	★★★		
	The Old Sunday School		01556 610811	Self Catering	★★★★		
	The Rache		01556 660202	Self Catering	★★★★		
	The Sheilin		01556 660212	Self Catering	★★★		
	The Ship Inn	DG7 2JT	01557 814217	Inn	★★★★		
	The Urr Valley Hotel	DG7 3JG	01556 502188	Country House Hotel	★★		
	TheBreakPad Benmore	DG7 1LB	01556 502693	Bed & Breakfast	★★★		
	Urr Lodge at Herriesdale	DG7 3JZ	01556 660490	Hostel	★★★★	⚡	
	Vital Spark		01557 331303	Self Catering	★★★		
	West Holmhead Cottage		01644 420636	Self Catering	★★★		
Clydebank	The Beardmore Hotel & Conference Centre	G81 4SA	0141 9516000	Hotel	★★★★	♿	𝒫𝒫
	West Park Hotel	G81 6DB	01389 872333	Hotel	★★	⚡	
Cockburnspath	Cloverknowe Cottages		01368 830318	Self Catering	★★★ to ★★★★		𝒫𝒫
	Cockburns Path House	TD13 5YG	01368 862292	Awaiting Grading			
	Neuk Farm Holiday Cottages		01368 830459	Self Catering	★★★★		
	Oldhamstocks Cottage		01368 830233	Self Catering	★★★		
	Pease Bay Caravan Park	TD13 5YP	01368 830206	Holiday Park	★★★★★	♿	
	Red Gauntlet		0778 9791667	Self Catering	★★★★		
	The Sheiling Cottage		07747 174388	Self Catering	★★★		
Coldstream/ Cornhill-on-Tweed/ Mindrum	Abbey House		01890 820359	Self Catering	★★★		
	Babingtons Cottage	TD12 4HA	07831 28652	Awaiting Grading			
	Cotoneaster		01890 882173	Self Catering	★★★	♿	
	Fernyrig Farm	TD12 4NB	01890 830251	Bed & Breakfast	★★★		
	Haymount Guest House	TD12 4DP	01890 883619	Bed & Breakfast	★★★★		
	Meg's Cottage		01890 882124	Self Catering	★★★		

♿ Unassisted wheelchair access   ♿ Assisted wheelchair access   ⚡ Access for visitors with mobility difficulties
𝒫 Bronze Green Tourism Award   𝒫𝒫 Silver Green Tourism Award   𝒫𝒫𝒫 Gold Green Tourism Award
For further information on our Green Tourism Business Scheme please see page 7.

Location	Property Name	Postcode	Telephone	Classification	Star Rating
Coldstream/ Cornhill-on-Tweed/ Mindrum	Nisbet House	TD12 4JL	01890 840279	Bed & Breakfast	★★★★
	Old School House	TD12 4NF	01890 830612	Bed & Breakfast	★★★
	Rowan Tree Cottage		07967 137757	Self Catering	★★★★
	Saint Foin	TD12 4NH	01890 830209	Bed & Breakfast	★★★★
	Ardachearnbeg Farmhouse Cottages- Hayloft & Stable		01369 820272	Self Catering	★★★ to ★★★★
Colintraive	Colintraive Hotel	PA22 3AS	01700 841207	Inn	★★★
	Glendaruel Caravan Park	PA22 3AB	01369 820267	Holiday Park	★★★★
	Home Farm Cottages – Byre Cottage		01463 238238	Self Catering	★★★★
	The Watermill	PA22 3AB	01369 820203	Bed & Breakfast	★★★★
	The Watermill		01369 820203	Self Catering	★★★★
	Waulkmill Cottage		01369 820292	Self Catering	★★
Corrour	Loch Ossian Youth Hostel	PH30 4AA	0870 1553255	Hostel	★★★ 🍃🍃🍃
Crianlarich	4 Clifton		0113 2329360	Self Catering	★★
	Ben Doran Hotel	FK20 8RY	01838 400373	Hotel	★★★
	Burnbrae Cottage		01838 400331	Self Catering	★★★
	By The Way Hostel	FK20 8RY	01838 400333	Hostel	★★★★
	Crianlarich Youth Hostel	FK20 8QN	0870 0041112	Hostel	★★★ 🚶 🍃🍃
	Dalkell Cottages	FK20 8RY	01838 400285	Guest House	★★★
	Ewich House	FK20 8RU	01838 300300	Guest House	★★★★
	Glenardran	FK20 8QS	01838 300236	Guest House	★★★
	Glendochart Caravan Park	FK20 8QT	01567 820637	Touring Park	★★★★
	Glengarry House	FK20 8RY	01838 400224	Guest House	★★★
	Glengarry Lodge		01838 400224	Self Catering	★★★
	Inverardran House	FK20 8QS	01838 300240	Guest House	★★★
	Pine Trees Leisure Park	FK20 8RY	01546 602389	Touring Park	★★★★
	Portnellan – Raven, Ghillies, Pinemartin		01838 300284	Self Catering	★★★★ to ★★★★★
	Riverside Guest House	FK20 8RU	01838 300235	Guest House	★★
	Royal Hotel	FK20 8RZ	01838 400272	Hotel	★★★
	Strathfillan House	FK20 8RU	01838 400228	Bed & Breakfast	★★★
	Strathfillan Wigwams	FK20 8RU	01838 400251	Camping Park	★★★★
	Suie Lodge Hotel	FK20 8QT	01567 820417	Small Hotel	★★
	The Crianlarich Hotel	FK20 8RW	07983 640486	Hotel	★★★
	The Old Church	FK20 8RX	01838 400286	Bed & Breakfast	★★★
	Tyndrum Lodge	FK20 8RY	01838 400219	Inn	★
	West Highland Lodge	FK20 8RU	01838 300283	Guest House	★★★
Crieff	2 Arnottsfield		01764 679657	Self Catering	★★★★
	64 Commissioner Street		01506 671549	Self Catering	★★★
	80 Queens Road		01764 670119	Self Catering	★★★★
	Aberturret Cottage		01764 650064	Self Catering	★★★★
	Arduthie House	PH7 3EQ	01764 653113	Guest House	★★★★
	Avonlea		0141 6203734	Self Catering	★★★★
	Barley Bree Restaurant with Rooms	PH5 2AB	01764 681451	Restaurant With Rooms	★★★★
	Blairmore West Cottage		01764 633625	Self Catering	★★★★

♿ Unassisted wheelchair access   ♿ Assisted wheelchair access   🚶 Access for visitors with mobility difficulties
🍃 Bronze Green Tourism Award   🍃🍃 Silver Green Tourism Award   🍃🍃🍃 Gold Green Tourism Award
For further information on our Green Tourism Business Scheme please see page 7.

Advertisers' locations have been sorted by postcode. In Scotland, postcodes can cover fairly large geographical areas.
Please check distance of property from specified location with the individual provider. VisitScotland cannot take any responsibility for this.

373

Location	Property Name	Postcode	Telephone	Classification	Star Rating
Crieff	Bobbin Mill		01764 679830	Self Catering	★★★★
	Boltachan		0131 4413133	Self Catering	★★★★
	Braehead		01877 384271	Self Catering	★★★
	Braidhaugh Park	PH7 4HP	01764 652951	Holiday Park	★★★
	Comely Bank Guest House	PH7 4DT	01764 653409	Guest House	★★★ ∱
	Comrie Cottage		01764 679633	Self Catering	★★★
	Comrie Croft	PH7 4JZ	01764 670140	Hostel	★★★ to ★★★★
	Comrie Croft	PH7 4JZ	01764 670140	Camping Park	★★★
	Crieff Hydro Hotel	PH7 3LQ	01764 651684	Hotel	★★★★ ∱ *PP*
	Cultoquhey House	PH7 3NE	01764 653253	Guest House	★
	Currochs Holiday Cottages		01764 652159	Self Catering	★★★★
	Drumearn Cottage	PH6 2JU	01764 670030	Bed & Breakfast	★★★★ ∱
	Fendoch Guest House	PH7 3LW	01764 653446	Guest House	★★★ ∱
	Foulford Inn	PH7 3LN	01764 652407	Inn	★★
	Galvelbeg House	PH7 3EQ	01764 655061	Guest House	★★★
	Galvelmore House	PH7 4BY	01764 655721	Bed & Breakfast	★★★ *PP*
	Glen Cottage		01764 671003	Self Catering	★★★
	Glenae Bed & Breakfast	PH7 3DA	01764 652780	Awaiting Grading	
	Glenbuckie Cottage		01764 679413	Self Catering	★★
	Glenbuckie House		01764 670050	Self Catering	★★★★
	Glencairn B&B	PH7 3BD	01764 655700	Bed & Breakfast	★★★
	Hawkshaw House		02072 219017	Self Catering	★★★★
	Highland Heather Lodges		01764 670440	Self Catering	★★★★ ຣ
	Knock Castle Hotel and Spa	PH7 4AN	01764 650088	Small Hotel	★★★
	Ladeside		01764 670640	Self Catering	★★★★
	Leven House Hotel	PH7 4BA	01764 652529	Small Hotel	★★
	Melville House		01764 679200	Self Catering	★★★★
	Merlindale	PH7 3EQ	01764 655205	Bed & Breakfast	★★★★ ∱
	Millhouse Garden Apartment		01764 650443	Self Catering	★★★★ ຣ
	Murraypark Hotel	PH7 3DJ	01764 651670	Hotel	★★★ ຣ
	Old St Michaels		01764 654059	Self Catering	★★★★
	Phase 1 & Phase 2 Lodges		01764 655555	Self Catering	★★★ to ★★★★★ ♿ *P*
	Raith Farmhouse		01764 683468	Self Catering	★★★★
	Riverside Log Cabins		08456 444830	Self Catering	★★★
	Royal Hotel	PH6 2DN	01764 679200	Small Hotel	★★★
	St Margaret's	PH6 2HP	01764 670413	Bed & Breakfast	★★★
	St Ninian's Tower Apartment		07981 623552	Self Catering	★★★★★
	The Bothy		01764 670349	Self Catering	★★★
	The Four Seasons Hotel	PH6 2NF	01764 685333	Small Hotel	★★★
	The Lodge		01764 652586	Self Catering	★★★★ *PPP*
	The Old Bakery		01764 684633	Self Catering	★★★
	The Old Church		07876 654333	Self Catering	★★★★
	The Rowans	PH7 3NH	01764 683720	Bed & Breakfast	★★★★
	The Strathearn		01764 655799	Self Catering	★★★★★ *PP*
	The Uppercrust Apartment		01764 650135	Self Catering	★★★
	The Wee House At The Loaning		01764 681383	Self Catering	★★★★
	The Willows	PH7 3NH	01764 683202	Bed & Breakfast	★★★★
	Towyn House		01453 762169	Self Catering	★★★★

♿ Unassisted wheelchair access   ຣ Assisted wheelchair access   ∱ Access for visitors with mobility difficulties
P Bronze Green Tourism Award   *PP* Silver Green Tourism Award   *PPP* Gold Green Tourism Award
For further information on our Green Tourism Business Scheme please see page 7.

Location	Property Name	Postcode	Telephone	Classification	Star Rating	
Crieff	Tuarach		01835 863485	Self Catering	★★★	
	Viewfield Self Catering Holidays		0141 6162373	Self Catering	★★★★	
	Wallace Lodge		01764 670677	Self Catering	★★★	
	West Lodge Caravan Park	PH6 2LS	01764 670354	Holiday Park	★★★★	
	Westlodge		01764 683365	Self Catering	★★★★	
	Yann's At Glenearn House	PH7 3EQ	01764 650111	Restaurant With Rooms	★★★★	
			01764 650135	Self Catering	★★★	
Cromarty	Lydia Cottage		0131 2439331	Self Catering	★★★	
	Russell House		0131 2439335	Self Catering	★★★	
	Sydney House	IV11 8UZ	01381 600451	Awaiting Grading		
Cumnock	Ashmark Farm Cottage		01290 338830	Self Catering	★★★★	🜊
	Laigh Tarbeg Farm	KA18 2RL	01290 700242	Farm House	★★★★	
	Lochside House Hotel	KA18 4PN	01290 333000	Hotel	★★★★	🜊
	Overcairn Farm Cottage		01290 338273	Self Catering	★★★	
	Royal Hotel	KA18 1BP	01290 420822	Small Hotel	★★★	
	The Beach House		01290 421412	Self Catering	★★★★	♿
Cupar	4 School View		01382 457869	Self Catering	★★★ to ★★★★	
	Abbotshill		01337 840175	Self Catering	★★★★	🄿
	Anvil Cottage B&B	KY15 5LN	01334 840824	Bed & Breakfast	★★★★	
	Athan Cottage		01334 828 361	Self Catering	★★★	
	Bag End		01334 829019	Self Catering	★★★★	
	Baincraig Lodge		01337 828386	Self Catering	★★★★	🄿
	Braehead		01224 638738	Self Catering	★★★★	
	Braemount	KY15 5LS	01334 828169	Bed & Breakfast	★★★★	
	Craigsanquhar Country House Hotel	KY15 4PZ	01334 653426	Country House Hotel	★★★★	
	Dale Cottage		01337 860535	Self Catering	★★★★	
	Eden Cottage		01382 778874	Self Catering	★★★	
	Edenshead Cottage		01337 868500	Self Catering	★★★★	🜊
	Edenshead Stables	KY14 7ST	01337 868500	Bed & Breakfast	★★★★★	
	Fairway	KY15 5UF	01334 850371	Bed & Breakfast	★★★★	
	Garden Cottage		01334 654169	Self Catering	★★★★	
	Gorno Grove House	KY14 7SE	01337 860483	Bed & Breakfast	★★★★	
	Greenmyre Lodges		01337 828883	Self Catering	★★★★	
	Keystone Cottage		01334 656691	Self Catering	★★★	
	Kilninian House	KY15 5TS	01334 654916	Awaiting Grading		
	Ladeddie Barns B&B	KY15 5TX	01334 828357	Bed & Breakfast	★★	
	Ladywell House	KY15 7DE	01337 858414	Bed & Breakfast	★★★★	
	Lindifferon Court Cottages		01337 810752	Self Catering	★★★★	
	Lomond Hills Hotel and Leisure Centre	KY15 7EY	01337 857329	Hotel	★★★	
	Mansfield	KY15 5JF	01334 655120	Bed & Breakfast	★★★★	
	Meadowside Bed & Breakfast	KY15 5DD	01334 650936	Awaiting Grading		
	Meldrums Hotel	KY15 5NA	01334 828286	Inn	★★	
	Middle Cottage		0131 2439335	Self Catering	★★	
	Myres Castle	KY14 7EW	01337 828350	Exclusive Use Venue	★★★★★	
	Ochil Cottage		01786 469172	Self Catering	★★★★	
	Osnaburgh	KY15 4SS	01334 870603	Bed & Breakfast	★★★	
	Robins Nest	KY15 4SR	01334 871466	Bed & Breakfast	★★★★	

♿ Unassisted wheelchair access   ♿ Assisted wheelchair access   🜊 Access for visitors with mobility difficulties
🄿 Bronze Green Tourism Award   🄿🄿 Silver Green Tourism Award   🄿🄿🄿 Gold Green Tourism Award
For further information on our Green Tourism Business Scheme please see page 7.

Advertisers' locations have been sorted by postcode. In Scotland, postcodes can cover fairly large geographical areas.
Please check distance of property from specified location with the individual provider. VisitScotland cannot take any responsibility for this.

375

Location	Property Name	Postcode	Telephone	Classification	Star Rating	
Cupar	Sable		01337 827418	Self Catering	★★★★	🅿🅿
	St Andrews Country Cottages – Gillespie House		01382 330318	Self Catering	★★★ to ★★★★	🕴
	St Andrew's House		0131 2439352	Self Catering	★★★	
	The Bruce	KY15 7BZ	01337 857226	Inn		
	The Cottage	KY14 6DW	01337 840264	Awaiting Grading		
	The Peat Inn	KY15 5LH	01334 840206	Restaurant With Rooms	★★★★★	
	The Strath Tavern	KY14 7PT	01337 860229	Awaiting Grading		
	The Thatched Cottage		01337 842760	Self Catering	★★★	🅿
	Upper West Wing Flat		0131 2439335	Self Catering	★★★	
	West Cottage		0131 2439335	Self Catering	★★★	
Currie	Leonard Horner Hall	EH14 4AS	0131 4513110	Campus	★★	
	Robert Bryson Hall	EH14 4AS	0131 4513110	Campus	★★	🅿🅿
Dalbeattie	Allonby Cottage		01985 850134	Self Catering	★★★	
	Auchenhill Farm Lodges		01556 620268	Self Catering	★★	
	Badgers Cottage		01670 860882	Self Catering	★★★	
	Barn Cottage		01556 610364	Self Catering	★★★★	🅿🅿
	Birchlea Lodge		01556 620125	Self Catering	★★★★	
	Bracken Cottage		01387 780221	Self Catering	★★★★	
	Castle Point Caravan Park	DG5 4QL	01556 630248	Holiday Park	★★★★	
	Clonyard House Hotel	DG5 4QW	01556 630372	Country House Hotel	★★★	🕴
	Corner Cottage		01792 405466	Self Catering	★★★	
	Craigbittern Cottage		01387 780247	Self Catering	★★★	
	Drumbeg		01132 528234	Self Catering	★★★	
	Drumbrae Studio		01556 630217	Self Catering	★★★	
	Elm Cottage		01387 730210	Self Catering	★★★	
	Ercall		01556 620636	Self Catering	★★★ to ★★★★	🕴
	Fonthill		0113 2893460	Self Catering	★★★	
	Glenearly Caravan Park	DG5 4NE	01556 611393	Holiday Park	★★★★	
	Glenstocken Farming Co - Rush Croft		01556 630224	Self Catering	★★★ to ★★★★	
	Heritage Guest House	DG5 4DW	01556 610817	Bed & Breakfast	★★★★	
	Kerr Cottage	DG5 4AZ	01556 612245	Bed & Breakfast	★★★★	♿
	Kippford Holiday Lodges		01475 787251	Self Catering	★★★★	
	Kippford Holiday Park	DG5 4LF	01556 620636	Holiday Park	★★★★★	
	Lochanview		01387 710126	Self Catering	★★★★	
	Millbrae House	DG5 4QG	01556 630217	Bed & Breakfast	★★★★	
	No. 26 Barend Holiday Village		01387 780632	Self Catering	★★	
	Number 9		01697 476254	Self Catering	★★★	
	Pittullie, Barcloy Mill		01458 250868	Self Catering	★★★★	
	Port Donnel Cottage		0131 2439331	Self Catering	★★★	
	Rockyknowe		01556 611549	Self Catering	★★	
	Rosemount	DG5 4LN	01556 620214	Guest House	★★★★	
	Sandyhills Bay Leisure Park	DG5 4NY	01557 870267	Holiday Park	★★★★	
	Thistle Dubh (56 Barend)		01557 820250	Self Catering	★★★ to ★★★★	
	Trewan	DG5 4EE	01556 612337	Bed & Breakfast	★★★	
	Watersedge		01556 630382	Self Catering	★★★	
	Wood End		01885 490286	Self Catering	★★★	

♿ Unassisted wheelchair access   🦽 Assisted wheelchair access   🕴 Access for visitors with mobility difficulties
🅿 Bronze Green Tourism Award   🅿🅿 Silver Green Tourism Award   🅿🅿🅿 Gold Green Tourism Award
For further information on our Green Tourism Business Scheme please see page 7.

376   To find out more go to visitscotland.com

Location	Property Name	Postcode	Telephone	Classification	Star Rating
Dalkeith	AEM Edinburgh Apartments		0131 6633291	Self Catering	★★★★
	Lothian Bridge Caravan Park	EH22 4TP	0131 6636120	Touring Park	★★★★
	Newbattle Abbey College	EH22 3LL	0131 6631921	Campus	★★
	Strathcairn	EH22 1JW	0131 6631208	Bed & Breakfast	★★★
	The County Hotel	EH22 1AY	0131 6633495	Hotel	★★★
	The Guest House @ Eskbank	EH22 3BH	0131 6633291	Guest House	★★★★
	The Sun Inn	EH22 4TR	0131 6632456	Awaiting Grading	
	Wester Cowden Farmhouse	EH22 2QA		Bed & Breakfast	★★★★
Dalmally	Ardbrecknish House – The Old West Wing		01866 833223	Self Catering	★★
	Blarghour Farm		01866 833246	Self Catering	★★★★ ⓟ
	Celtic Cottages/Craig Lora		01245 231657	Self Catering	★★★★
	Craig Villa Guest House	PA33 1AX	01838 200255	Guest House	★★★
	Craigroyston	PA33 1AA	01838 200234	Bed & Breakfast	★★★ ⓟⓟⓟ
	Creagan		01866 822334	Self Catering	★★★
	Dalmally Hotel	PA33 1AY	01838 200444	Hotel	★★★
	Glenorchy Lodge Hotel	PA33 1AA	01838 200312	Small Hotel	★★★ 🚶
	Loch Awe Hotel	PA33 1AQ	01838 200261	Hotel	★★★
	Lochside Apartments – Insh, Rassay & Lunga		01866 833224	Self Catering	★★ to ★★★
	Portsonachan Hotel	PA33 1BJ	01866 833224	Small Hotel	★★★
	Strathorchy	PA33 1AE	01838 200373	Bed & Breakfast	★★★
	The Old House		01838 200399	Self Catering	★★★★
	Troutbeck	PA33 1AW	01838 200476	Awaiting Grading	
Dalry	Baidland Mill		01795 843126	Self Catering	★★★
	Blair House	KA24 4ER	01294 833100	Exclusive Use Venue	★★★★★
	Blair The Stable Flat		01294 833100	Self Catering	★★★★
Dalwhinnie	Balsporran Cottages	PH19 1AF	01528 522389	Bed & Breakfast	★★★
Darvel	Gowanbank House	KA17 0LL	01560 322538	Bed & Breakfast	★★★
Denny	Lochend Farm	FK6 5JJ	01324 822778	Bed & Breakfast	★★★
	Peat Hill and Myot Cottage		01324 812839	Self Catering	★★★★
	The Lodge Home Farm	FK6 5LH	01324 819891	Bed & Breakfast	★★
	Westfield Farm Holiday Lodges		01324 822800	Self Catering	★★★★
	Woodcockfaulds Farm	FK6 6RH	01786 811985	Farm House	★★★
Dingwall	Assynt House	IV16 9XW	01349 832923	Exclusive Use Venue	★★★★★
	Autumn Gold Bed & Breakfast	IV7 8LR	01381 610725	Bed & Breakfast	★★★★
	Balachladdich		001 902 753 3315	Self Catering	★★★★
	Balinoe		01730 267448	Self Catering	★★★★
	Ballyskelly Lodge		01381 610253	Self Catering	★★★
	Ben Wyvis Views	IV7 8JH	01349 877430	Bed & Breakfast	★★★★
	Black Rock Caravan Park	IV16 9UN	01349 830632	Holiday Park	★★★★★
	Cam-mont House	IV7 8HU	01349 877061	Bed & Breakfast	★★★★
	Dingwall Camping & Caravanning Club Site	IV15 9QZ	02476 475318	Touring Park	★★★★
	Dunglass Cottage		01349 861150	Self Catering	★★ to ★★★★
	Dunvournie Farm Cottage		01349 877246	Self Catering	★★

♿ Unassisted wheelchair access   ♿ Assisted wheelchair access   🚶 Access for visitors with mobility difficulties
ⓟ Bronze Green Tourism Award   ⓟⓟ Silver Green Tourism Award   ⓟⓟⓟ Gold Green Tourism Award
For further information on our Green Tourism Business Scheme please see page 7.

Advertisers' locations have been sorted by postcode. In Scotland, postcodes can cover fairly large geographical areas.
Please check distance of property from specified location with the individual provider. VisitScotland cannot take any responsibility for this.

377

Location	Property Name	Postcode	Telephone	Classification	Star Rating	
Dingwall	Kinkell Country House	IV7 8HY	01349 861270	Small Hotel	★★★	🚶
	Lodge Barn		01997 421393	Self Catering	★★★ to ★★★★	
	Magnelia House		01349 877430	Self Catering	★★★★	
	Moydene	IV15 9LE	01349 864965	Bed & Breakfast	★★★	
	Rose Cottage		01997 421436	Self Catering	★★★	
	Solus Or	IV7 8JH	01349 877828	Bed & Breakfast	★★★★	
	Wester Brae Highland Lodges		01349 877609	Self Catering	★★★★	🚶
Dollar	Blashie Cottage		01259 743525	Self Catering	★★★★	Assisted wheelchair access
	Campbell Cottage		01259 743765	Self Catering	★★★★	
	Castle Campbell	FK14 7DE	01259 742519	Small Hotel	★★★	
	Coroghton Guest House	FK14 7JW	01259 781511	Bed & Breakfast	★★★	
	Glendevon Park		01259 781569	Self Catering	★★★	
	Hillfoots Cottage		01786 469172	Self Catering	★★★	
	Kennels Cottage	FK14 7PA	01259 742186	Bed & Breakfast	★★★★	
	Leys Farm	FK14 7JL	01259 781313	Bed & Breakfast	★★★	
	Rosslyn Cottage		01259 781360	Self Catering	★★★	
	The Inn Cottage & The Bothy		01259 781324	Self Catering	★★★★	
	Tigh-Na-Mairi		01259 781270	Self Catering	★★★★	
Dornoch	213 Birichen	IV25 3NE	07789 33202	Awaiting Grading		
	5 Dornoch Square East		01628 486801	Self Catering	★★★★	
	Auchlea	IV25 3HY	07714 981771	Bed & Breakfast	★★★★	🚶
	Collies Lodge		01862 810245	Self Catering	★★★★	🚶
	Corven	IV25 3PT	01862 810128	Bed & Breakfast	★★	
	Dornoch Caravan & Camping Park	IV25 3LX	01862 810423	Holiday Park	★★★★	
	Dornoch Castle Hotel	IV25 3SD	01862 810216	Hotel	★★★	🚶 Bronze Green Tourism Award
	Dornoch Hotel	IV25 3LD	01862 810351	Awaiting Grading		
	Dornoch Links Caravan Park	IV25 3LQ	01862 810366	Holiday Caravan		
	East Dune		01727 840805	Self Catering	★★★★	
	Fairways		01419 550644	Self Catering	★★★	
	Grannies Heilan Hame Holiday Park	IV25 3QD	01862 810383	Holiday Park	★★★★	
	Highfield Guest House	IV25 3H	01862 810909	Bed & Breakfast	★★★★	
	Hillview	IV25 3RD	01862 810151	Bed & Breakfast	★★★★	
	Hilton Lodge	IV25 3PW	01862 811339	Awaiting Grading		
	Kyleview House B&B	IV25 3HR	01862 810999	Bed & Breakfast	★★★★	
	Links Cottage		01408 621252	Self Catering	★★★	
	Oatfield		01235 529940	Self Catering	★★★	
	Seaview Farm Caravan Park	IV25 3PW	01862 810294	Touring Park	★★	
	Strathview B&B	IV25 3JD	01408 633002	Bed & Breakfast		
	Tullochard Bed & Breakfast	IV25 3NN	01862 811122	Bed & Breakfast	★★★★	
Doune	Gled Cottage		01786 850213	Self Catering	★★★★	
	Glenardoch House	FK16 6EA	01786 841489	Bed & Breakfast	★★★★	
Dumbarton	Albion House		01438 869554	Self Catering	★★★	
	Barnhill House		01389 761318	Self Catering	★★★	
	Ben Rhydding	G82 5LL	01389 841659	Bed & Breakfast	★★★★	
	Glenmar Guest House	G82 2HB	01389 731842	Bed & Breakfast	★★★★	
	Kilmalid House	G82 2QL	01389 732030	Bed & Breakfast	★★★	

♿ Unassisted wheelchair access   Assisted wheelchair access   🚶 Access for visitors with mobility difficulties
Bronze Green Tourism Award   Silver Green Tourism Award   Gold Green Tourism Award
For further information on our Green Tourism Business Scheme please see page 7.

Location	Property Name	Postcode	Telephone	Classification	Star Rating	
Dumbarton	Milton Inn	G82 2DT	01389 761401	Inn	★★★	🚶
	Positano	G82 1RE	01389 731943	Bed & Breakfast	★★★	
	The Abbotsford Hotel	G82 2PJ	01389 733304	Hotel	★★★	
	The Cat's Whiskers		01389 762710	Self Catering	★★★★	
	Travelodge Dumbarton	G82 2TY	01389 765202	Budget Hotel		
Dumfries	Abbey Arms Hotel	DG2 8BX	01387 850489	Inn	★★	
	Aberdour Hotel	DG1 1LW	01387 252060	Small Hotel	★★	
	Alder		01387 870608	Self Catering	★★★★	
	Alva House	DG2 8AG	01387 780563	Bed & Breakfast	★★★	
	Arden Holiday Cottages		01387 730309	Self Catering	★★★★	
	Armandii Cottage		01387 820203	Self Catering	★★★	
	Ashwood Lodge		01387 780206	Self Catering	★★★★	🚶
	Aston Hotel	DG1 4ZZ	01387 272410	Hotel	★★★	♿
	Auchenfad Cottage		01387 850267	Self Catering	★★★	
	Averon House	DG1 1QR	01387 711875	Bed & Breakfast	★★★★	
	Barnsoul Farm	DG2 9SQ	01387 730249	Holiday Park	★★★	
	Beechfoot Cottage		01387 830636	Self Catering	★★	
	Beeswing Caravan Park	DG2 8JL	01387 760242	Holiday Park	★★★★	
	Boreland Farm	DG2 0XA	01387 820287	Farm House	★★★	
	Burnbrae Mill		01556 690505	Self Catering	★★★★	
	Burnett House	DG1 1LP	01387 263164	Bed & Breakfast	★★★	
	Cairndale Hotel & Leisure Club	DG1 2DF	01387 254111	Hotel	★★★	
	Cavens	DG2 8AA	01387 880234	Country House Hotel	★★★★	
	Craig Na Mara Cottage		01560 480372	Self Catering	★★	
	Craignair	DG1 1LN	01387 251796	Bed & Breakfast	★★★	
	Dalston House Hotel	DG2 7AH	01387 254422	Small Hotel	★★★	
	Dumfries Premier Inn	DG1 3JX	0870 1977078	Budget Hotel		
	Dumfries Villa	DG1 1LR	01387 248609	Bed & Breakfast	★★★	
	Dun Beag & Dun Mohr		01387 740388	Self Catering	★★★	
	East Brae Cottage	DG2 8QE	01556 690296	Bed & Breakfast	★★	
	Edenbank Hotel	DG2 7AH	01387 252759	Small Hotel	★★★	
	Farmers Inn	DG1 4NF	01387 870675	Inn	★★	
	Friars Carse Hotel	DG2 0SA	01387 740388	Country House Hotel	★★★	
	Glenure Bed and Breakfast	DG1 1NN	01387 252373	Bed & Breakfast	★★★	
	Greenhead Lodge		01387 820396	Self Catering	★★★	
	Gubhill Farm – Shepherd's Flat		01387 860648	Self Catering	★★ to ★★★	♿ 🌿🌿🌿
	Hamilton House	DG1 1NJ	01387 266606	Guest House	★★★★	
	Huntingdon House	DG1 1LZ	01387 254893	Guest House	★★★★	
	Inverallochy	DG1 3AP	01387 267298	Bed & Breakfast	★★★	
	Lighthouse Leisure	DG2 8AZ	01387 880277	Holiday Park	★★★★	
	Little Solway		01387 780262	Self Catering	★★★	
	Lochenlee Guest House	DG1 3AQ	01387 265153	Guest House	★★★	
	Lochview Motel & Restaurant	DG2 8RF	01556 690281	Lodge	★★	
	Low Kirkbride Farmhouse B&B	DG2 0SP	01387 820258	Farm House	★★★	🌿🌿
	Mabie House Hotel	DG2 8HB	01387 263188	Country House Hotel	★★★	
	Marthrown of Mabie	DG2 8HB	01387 247900	Hostel	★★★	
	Merlin	DG2 7QX	01387 261002	Bed & Breakfast	★★★	
	Mews Flat		01387 740548	Self Catering	★★★★	

♿ Unassisted wheelchair access   ♿ Assisted wheelchair access   🚶 Access for visitors with mobility difficulties
🌿 Bronze Green Tourism Award   🌿🌿 Silver Green Tourism Award   🌿🌿🌿 Gold Green Tourism Award
For further information on our Green Tourism Business Scheme please see page 7.

Advertisers' locations have been sorted by postcode. In Scotland, postcodes can cover fairly large geographical areas.
Please check distance of property from specified location with the individual provider. VisitScotland cannot take any responsibility for this.

379

Location	Property Name	Postcode	Telephone	Classification	Star Rating	
Dumfries	Millhill Farm	DG2 8PX	01387 730472	Farm House	★★★★	
	Moreig Hotel	DG1 3EG	01387 255524	Small Hotel	★★★	
	Mossband Caravan Park	DG2 8JP	01387 760505	Touring Park	★★★	
	Nith Hotel	DG1 4RE	01387 770213	Small Hotel	★★	
	North Corner		01768 898214	Self Catering	★★★	
	Park of Brandedleys		01539 563198	Self Catering	★★	
	Park of Brandedleys	DG2 8RG	0845 4561760	Holiday Park	★★★★	
	Pleasance Holiday Letting		01387 253908	Self Catering	★★★	
	Queensberry Hotel	DG1 2BT	01387 739913	Small Hotel	★★	
	Radcliffe Cottage		01387 870213	Self Catering	★★★	
	Rivendell	DG1 1JX	01387 252251	Guest House	★★★★	
	Southerness Holiday Village	DG2 8AZ	01387 880256	Holiday Park	★★★★	᠖
	Southpark Country House	DG1 1QG	01387 711188	Bed & Breakfast	★★★★	
	Station Hotel	DG1 1LT	01387 254316	Hotel	★★★	∱
	Steamboat Inn	DG2 8DS	01387 880631	Inn	★★★	
	The Byre		01387 820258	Self Catering	★★★★	♿
	The Lodge		01387 770205	Self Catering	★★★ to ★★★★	᠖
	The Old Mission Hall		01228 576649	Self Catering	★★★★	∱
	The Old School House		01387 720124	Self Catering	★★★★	
	The Old Shop	DG2 8DS	01387 880799	Bed & Breakfast	★★★	
	The Tower House		01355 303078	Self Catering	★★★	
	Torbay Lodge	DG1 1LR	01387 253922	Guest House	★★★★	∱
	Travelodge Dumfries	DG1 3SE	01387 750658	Budget Hotel		
	Wallamhill House	DG1 1SL	01387 248249	Bed & Breakfast	★★★★	∱
	West Mains Bungalow		01782 680968	Self Catering	★★★	
Dunbar	10B Beachmont Place		0208 3666165	Self Catering	★★★	
	Belhaven Bay Caravan Park	EH42 1TU	01368 865956	Holiday Park	★★★★	᠖
	Belhaven Gardens		07789 693381	Self Catering	★★★	
	Brunt House		01368 862100	Self Catering	★★★★	
	Dunbar Camping & Caravanning Club Site	EH42 1WG	02476 475318	Touring Park	★★★★★	
	Goldenoak Chalet		01368 840669	Self Catering	★★★	
	Haywood Cottage		01368 862018	Self Catering	★★★	
	Nirvana Cottage		01223 356038	Self Catering	★★★	
	Springfield Guest House	EH42 1NH	01368 862502	Guest House	★★★	
	Surfsplash		07970 867089	Self Catering	★★★★	
	The Harbour House		01368 862427	Self Catering	★★★★	
	The Rossborough Hotel	EH42 1LG	01368 862356	Small Hotel	★★★	
	Thurston Manor Holiday Home Park	EH42 1SA	01368 840643	Holiday Park	★★★★★	᠖
Dunbeath	Inver Caravan Park	KW6 6EH	01593 731441	Touring Park	★★★	
	Tormore Farm	KW6 6EH	01593 731240	Farm House	★★	
Dunblane	Cambushinnie Croft		01786 880631	Self Catering	★★★★	᠖
	Ciar Mhor	FK15 9JS	01786 823371	Bed & Breakfast	★★★	
	Craighead Farm		01786 880321	Self Catering	★★★★★	
	Cromlix House	FK15 9JT	01786 822125	Country House Hotel	★★★★	
	Doubletree by Hilton Dunblane Hotel	FK15 0HG	01786 836607	Hotel	★★★★	
	Knockhill Guest House	FK9 4ND	01786 833123	Guest House	★★★★	∱
	Stable Cottage		01786 841200	Self Catering	★★★	∱

♿ Unassisted wheelchair access   ᠖ Assisted wheelchair access   ∱ Access for visitors with mobility difficulties
ⓟ Bronze Green Tourism Award   ⓟⓟ Silver Green Tourism Award   ⓟⓟⓟ Gold Green Tourism Award
For further information on our Green Tourism Business Scheme please see page 7.

Directory of all VisitScotland Assured Serviced Establishments, ordered by location.
Establishments highlighted have an advertisement in this guide.

Location	Property Name	Postcode	Telephone	Classification	Star Rating		
Dundee	8 Bath Street		01382 776676	Self Catering	★★★		
	Aberlaw Guest House	DD4 7JP	01382 456929	Guest House	★★★		
	Abertay Guest House	DD5 2RW	01382 730381	Guest House	★★★		
	Alcorn Guest House	DD2 1HQ	01382 668433	Guest House	★★★		
	Anderson's Guest House	DD2 1JS	01382 668585	Guest House	★★★		
	Apex City Quay Hotel & Spa	DD1 3JP	0845 3650000	Hotel	★★★★		_PPP_
	Ashlea Manor Guest House	DD5 4HP	01382 530015	Bed & Breakfast	★★★★		
	Ashvilla	DD4 7RZ	01382 450831	Bed & Breakfast	★★★		
	Balgowan House B&B	DD2 1LW	01382 200262	Bed & Breakfast	★★★★		
	Balmuirfield House	DD3 0NU	01382 818444	Bed & Breakfast	★★★★		
	Balmuirfield House		01382 818444	Self Catering	★★★★		
	Cullaig Guest House	DD3 6JQ	01382 322154	Guest House	★★★		
	Denhead Cottage		01382 580273	Self Catering	★★★		
	Dundee Backpackers	DD1 1SD	0131 2202200	Hostel	★★★★		
	Dundee Carlton Hotel	DD4 7JR	01382 462056	Small Hotel	★★★		
	Dundee East Premier Inn	DD5 3UP	0870 1977081	Budget Hotel			
	Dundee North Premier Inn	DD2 3SQ	0870 9906420	Budget Hotel			
	Dundee West Premier Inn	DD2 5JU	0870 1977081	Budget Hotel			
	Dunlaw House Hotel	DD3 6JD	01382 221703	Small Hotel	★★		
	East Mains House		01382 320206	Self Catering	★★★		
	Errolbank Guest House	DD4 7JN	01382 462118	Guest House	★★★		
	Forbes of Kingennie – Glen Esk		01382 350777	Self Catering	★★★★	♿	
	Grosvenor Guest House	DD2 1LF	01382 642991	Awaiting Grading			
	Hilton Dundee	DD1 4DE	01382 315515	Hotel	★★★★	♁	_PP_
	Hotel Broughty Ferry	DD5 1AR	01382 480027	Small Hotel	★★★★		
	Invercarse Hotel	DD2 1PG	01382 669231	Hotel	★★★		
	Invergarth	DD5 2NA	01382 736278	Bed & Breakfast	★★★		
	Main Wing	DD4 0PJ	01382 350239	Bed & Breakfast	★★★★	♁	_PP_
	Marlee Guest House	DD5 2SD	01382 779435	Awaiting Grading			
	Milton Hotel	DD5 4LU	01382 539016	Small Hotel	★★★		
	Monument Cottage		01382 370633	Self Catering	★★★★		
	Park House Hotel	DD2 3HY	01382 611151	Small Hotel	★★★		
	Premier Inn Dundee Centre	DD1 4XA	0870 1977079	Budget Hotel			
	Premier Inn Dundee Monifieth	DD5 4HB	0870 977080	Budget Hotel			
	Queens Hotel	DD1 4DU	01382 322515	Hotel	★★★		
	Rainbow 8		01382 581374	Self Catering	★★★★		
	Redmyre Farmhouse		01821 640234	Self Catering	★★★★		
	Redwood Guest House	DD5 2SB	01382 736550	Guest House	★★★★		
	Riverview Caravan Park	DD5 4NN	01382 535471	Holiday Park	★★★★★		
	Seabraes Self Catering Flats		01382 383111	Self Catering	★★	♁	
	Seaton Estate Holiday Park	DD1 5SE	01241 874762	Holiday Park	★★★★		
	Shaftesbury Hotel	DD2 1HQ	01382 669216	Small Hotel	★★★		
	St Leonard B&B	DD3 6HR	01382 227146	Guest House	★		
	Strathdon Guest House	DD2 1JS	01382 665648	Guest House	★★★		
	Taychreggan Hotel	DD5 1JG	01382 778626	Small Hotel	★★★		
	The Craigtay Hotel	DD4 6JE	01382 451142	Small Hotel	★★		
	The Fisherman's Tavern Hotel	DD5 2AD	01382 775941	Small Hotel	★★	♿	
	The Fort Hotel	DD5 2AB	01382 737999	Small Hotel	★★		

♿ Unassisted wheelchair access   ♿ Assisted wheelchair access   ♁ Access for visitors with mobility difficulties
_P_ Bronze Green Tourism Award   _PP_ Silver Green Tourism Award   _PPP_ Gold Green Tourism Award
For further information on our Green Tourism Business Scheme please see page 7.

Advertisers' locations have been sorted by postcode. In Scotland, postcodes can cover fairly large geographical areas.
Please check distance of property from specified location with the individual provider. VisitScotland cannot take any responsibility for this.

381

Location	Property Name	Postcode	Telephone	Classification	Star Rating		
Dundee	The Grampian	DD2 1JS	01382 667785	Guest House	★★★		
	The Hideaway		07939 948796	Self Catering	★★★★		
	The Landmark Hotel	DD2 5JT	01382 641122	Hotel	★★★★	♿	
	The Penthouse	DD1 3BN	01382 200135	Bed & Breakfast	★★★		
	Travelodge Dundee	DD2 4TD	01382 610488	Budget Hotel			
	Travelodge Dundee Central	DD1 1NJ	08719 846134	Budget Hotel			
	West Adamston Farmhouse	DD2 5QX	01382 580215	Farm House	★★★★		
	West Park Centre	DD2 1NN	01382 647171	Campus	★★★	♿	
	Woodlands Hotel	DD5 2QL	01382 823220	Hotel	★★★		
Dunfermline	11 The Beeches	KY11 9SN	01383 822167	Bed & Breakfast	★★★★		
	Auld Mill House Hotel	KY11 4LF	01383 732152	Awaiting Grading			
	Backmarch House	KY11 2RJ	01383 412997	Bed & Breakfast	★★★★		
	Balnacraig B&B	KY12 9TL	01383 852568	Bed & Breakfast	★★★★		
	Bell House	KY12 8AE	01383 723701	Bed & Breakfast	★★★		
	Best Western Keavil House Hotel	KY12 8QW	01383 736258	Country House Hotel	★★★	♿	⑭⑭
	Bowleys Farm Self Catering		01383 721056	Self Catering	★★★		
	Bramble Brae	KY12 8EL	01383 850206	Awaiting Grading			
	Bunree Bed & Breakfast	KY12 9JB	01383 738827	Bed & Breakfast	★★★★		
	Carneil Farm	KY12 9JJ	01383 580285	Farm House	★★★★		
	Clarke Cottage Guest House	KY11 4LA	01383 735935	Guest House	★★★	🚶	
	Cochranes Hotel	KY11 2BA	01383 420101	Lodge	★★	🚶	
	Davaar House Hotel	KY12 8DW	01383 721886	Small Hotel	★★★		
	Express By Holiday Inn Dunfermline	KY11 8DY	0138 748220	Metro Hotel	★★★	♿	
	Garvock House Hotel	KY12 7TU	01383 621067	Hotel	★★★★	♿	
	Grange Farmhouse	KY11 3DG	01383 733125	Bed & Breakfast	★★★★		
	Hillview House	KY11 4PB	01383 726278	Bed & Breakfast	★★★★		
	King Malcolm Hotel	KY11 8DS	01383 722611	Hotel	★★★		
	Kirklands House	KY12 9TS	01383 852737	Bed & Breakfast	★★★★		⑭⑭
	North Dhuloch Cottage		01383 419163	Self Catering	★★★★		
	Pitbauchlie House Hotel	KY11 4PB	01383 722282	Hotel	★★★	🚶	⑭⑭
	Pitreavie Guest House	KY11 4PB	01383 724244	Guest House	★★★		
	Premier Inn Dunfermline	KY11 8EX	0870 6001486	Budget Hotel			
	Rooms at 29 Bruce Street	KY12 7AG	01383 840041	Small Hotel	★★★		
	Roscobie Farmhouse	KY12 0SG	01383 731571	Farm House	★★★★		
	Seaview Apartment		01383 620942	Self Catering	★★★★		
	The Bothy		01383 852286	Self Catering	★★★		
	The Coach House	KY11 9TB	01383 823584	Bed & Breakfast	★★★★		
	The Courtyard		01383 413242	Self Catering	★★★★		
	The Garden Town House		01383 739539	Self Catering	★★★		
	Travelodge Dunfermline	KY11 8PG	08719 846287	Budget Hotel			
Dunkeld	68 Cathedral Street		01350 723200	Self Catering	★★★★		
	Atholl Arms Hotel	PH8 0AQ	0771 3943426	Small Hotel	★★★		
	Byways	PH8 0DH	01350 727542	Bed & Breakfast	★★★		
	Byways Apartment		01350 727542	Self Catering	★★★★		
	City Hall Apartments		01350 727 681	Self Catering	★★★★		
	Erigmore Cottage		01350 727236	Self Catering	★★★	🚶	⑭⑭
	Erigmore House Holiday Park	PH8 0BJ	01350 727236	Holiday Park	★★★★		

♿ Unassisted wheelchair access   ♿ Assisted wheelchair access   🚶 Access for visitors with mobility difficulties
Ⓟ Bronze Green Tourism Award   ⑭⑭ Silver Green Tourism Award   ⑭⑭⑭ Gold Green Tourism Award
For further information on our Green Tourism Business Scheme please see page 7.

382   To find out more go to visitscotland.com

Location	Property Name	Postcode	Telephone	Classification	Star Rating		
Dunkeld	Flat 1		01350 727005	Self Catering	★★★		
	Golden Pond		01350 727137	Self Catering	★★★★		
	Hatton Grange	PH8 0ET	01350 727137	Bed & Breakfast	★★★		
	Hilton Dunkeld	PH8 0HX	01350 727771	Hotel	★★★★	♦	⁄⁄⁄
	Inch Cottage		0131 2255235	Self Catering	★★★		
	Invermill Farm Caravan Park	PH8 0JR	01350 727477	Touring Park	★★★★		
	Kinnaird Estate – Jock Scott		01796 482440	Self Catering	★★★ to ★★★★★		
	Ladyhill Coach House		01592 264369	Self Catering	★★★★		
	Letter Farm	PH8 0HH	01350 724254	Farm House	★★★★		⁄⁄
	Little Puddockwells		01738 710536	Self Catering	★★★		
	Lochview Apartment		01350 724241	Self Catering	★★★ to ★★★★		
	Log Cabin		01324 625019	Self Catering	★★		
	Royal Dunkeld Hotel	PH8 0AR	01350 727322	Hotel	★★★		
	Tayburn House	PH8 0BQ	01350 728822	Bed & Breakfast	★★★		
	The Birnam Guest House	PH8 0BG	01350 727201	Guest House	★★★		
	The Bridge Bed & Breakfast	PH8 0AH	01350 727068	Bed & Breakfast	★★★★		
	The Ell House		0131 2439352	Self Catering	★★		
	The Mill		01350 725213	Self Catering	★★★★		
	Tomnagairn Cottage		01350 723228	Self Catering	★★★		
	Upper Hatton	PH8 0ER	07762 276693	Bed & Breakfast	★★★		
Dunoon	15 Lamont Lodges	PA23 8QT	01369 706591	Awaiting Grading			
	2 Lamont Lodges		01368 863920	Self Catering	★		
	4 Deercroft Hafton		01369 703586	Self Catering	★★★		
	Abbot's Brae Hotel	PA23 7QJ	01369 705021	Small Hotel	★★★★		
	Ardtully Guest House	PA23 3HN	01369 702478	Guest House	★★★		
	Argyll Hotel	PA23 7NE	01369 702059	Hotel	★★★		
	Argyll Lodge		01369 703022	Self Catering	★★★		
	Balmoral		01664 501744	Self Catering	★★★★		
	Bay House	PA23 7HU	01369 704832	Guest House	★★★		⁄
	Bernice Cottage	PA23 8QX	01369 706337	Group Accommodation	★★ to ★★★★		
	Burngill Cottage	PA23 8SB	01369 840625	Awaiting Grading			
	Chase The Wild Goose		01369 840672	Self Catering	★★★		
	Clyde Cottage		01546 510316	Self Catering	★★★★		
	Coylet Inn	PA23 8SG	01369 840426	Inn	★★★		
	Craigen	PA23 7DH	01369 702307	Guest House	★★		
	Craigieburn Guest House	PA23 8AN	01369 702048	Guest House	★★		
	Culzean House		01369 810331	Self Catering	★★★★		
	Dalcamond House		01369 830309	Self Catering	★★★★		
	Dhailling Lodge	PA23 8AW	01369 701253	Guest House	★★★★		
	Duncreggan House	PA23 9TG	01369 840738	Bed & Breakfast	★★★		
	Egmont		0141 6393129	Self Catering	★★★★	♦	
	Eilan Donan		0141 5896811	Self Catering	★★★		
	Eileagan	PA23 7LN	01369 707047	Bed & Breakfast	★★★★		
	Esplanade Hotel	PA23 7HU	01369 704070	Hotel	★★★		
	Fasgadh		01369 701146	Self Catering	★★★		
	Fintry		0141 7763158	Self Catering	★★★		
	Firthview House		01369 702041	Self Catering	★★★		
	Foxbank	PA23 8HJ	01369 703858	Bed & Breakfast	★★		

♿ Unassisted wheelchair access ♿ Assisted wheelchair access ♦ Access for visitors with mobility difficulties
⁄ Bronze Green Tourism Award ⁄⁄ Silver Green Tourism Award ⁄⁄⁄ Gold Green Tourism Award
For further information on our Green Tourism Business Scheme please see page 7.

Advertisers' locations have been sorted by postcode. In Scotland, postcodes can cover fairly large geographical areas.
Please check distance of property from specified location with the individual provider. VisitScotland cannot take any responsibility for this.

383

Location	Property Name	Postcode	Telephone	Classification	Star Rating
Dunoon	Fyne Cottages – Fern Cottage		01369 840206	Self Catering	★★★
	Glenstriven Estate – Highfield		01369 870007	Self Catering	★★★ to ★★★★
	Holly Cottage		0792 1061103	Self Catering	★★★
	Hunters Quay Holiday Village	PA23 8HP	01301 703247	Holiday Park	★★★★★
	Hunters Quay Holiday Village		01301 703247	Self Catering	★★★
	Mayfair Hotel	PA23 8DX	01369 703803	Guest House	★★★
	Merridale		01369 704081	Self Catering	★★★
	Milton Tower Guest House	PA23 7LD	01369 705785	Guest House	★★★
	North Lodge		01592 202564	Self Catering	★★
	Old Kilmun House		01505 843678	Self Catering	★★★★
	Park Hotel	PA23 7LG	01369 702383	Hotel	★★★
	Puck's Lodge	PA23 8QT	07977 079139	Awaiting Grading	
	Royal Marine Hotel	PA23 8HJ	01369 705810	Hotel	★★★
	Sebright	PA23 8AF	01369 702099	Guest House	★★
	Sebright		01369 707408	Self Catering	★★★
	Serendipity		01467 626071	Self Catering	★★★
	St Ives Hotel	PA23 7HU	01369 704825	Small Hotel	★★★
	St Munns Old Manse	PA23 8SD	01369 840311	Bed & Breakfast	★★★
	Stewart's Lodge		01475 638080	Self Catering	★★★
	Strathspey		01480 880395	Self Catering	★★★★
	Stronchullin Holiday Cottages		01369 810246	Self Catering	★★★ 🏃
	The Cedars	PA23 8AF	01369 702425	Guest House	★★★★
	The Old Ticket Office		07799 228435	Self Catering	★★★★
	The Western Hotel	PA23 7HU	01369 704468	Awaiting Grading	
	Undercliff Bed and Breakfast	PA23 8HN	01369 704688	Bed & Breakfast	★★★
	Vaila	PA23 7QY	01369 707540	Bed & Breakfast	★★
	West End Hotel	PA23 7HU	01369 702907	Small Hotel	★★
			07799 228435	Self Catering	★★★★
Duns	2 Kimmerghame Mains Cottages		01325 358725	Self Catering	★★★
	Allanton Inn	TD11 3JZ	01890 818260	Inn	★★★
	Black Bull Hotel	TD11 3AR	01361 883379	Restaurant With Rooms	★★★
	Borthwick Gate B&B	TD11 3NH	01361 883778	Awaiting Grading	
	Chirnside Hall Hotel	TD11 3LD	01890 818219	Country House Hotel	★★★★
	Claymore House	TD11 3AE	01361 883880	Bed & Breakfast	★★
	Courtyard Cottage		01890 840259	Self Catering	★★★★
	Crosshall Farm	TD10 6UL	01890 840220	Farm House	★★★★
	Duns Castle	TD11 3NW	01361 883211	Exclusive Use Venue	★★★★
	Edington Fox Covert		01890 818345	Self Catering	★★★
	Maines North Lodge	TD11 3LD	01890 819171	Bed & Breakfast	★★★★
	Ravelaw Farmhouse	TD11 3NQ	01890 870207	Farm House	★★★★
	The Moorhouse Cottage		01361 840622	Self Catering	★★★
	The Wheatsheaf at Swinton	TD11 3JJ	01890 860257	Restaurant With Rooms	★★★★ ♿
Earlston	Broomfield House	TD4 6DR	01896 848084	Guest House	★★★
	Sorrowlessfield Cottage		01896 849906	Self Catering	★★★

♿ Unassisted wheelchair access 🦽 Assisted wheelchair access 🏃 Access for visitors with mobility difficulties
🏵 Bronze Green Tourism Award   🏵🏵 Silver Green Tourism Award   🏵🏵🏵 Gold Green Tourism Award
For further information on our Green Tourism Business Scheme please see page 7.

Location	Property Name	Postcode	Telephone	Classification	Star Rating
East Linton	Crauchie Farmhouse	EH40 3EB	01620 860124	Bed & Breakfast	★★★★
	Greive's Cottage		01620 870606	Self Catering	★★★ to ★★★★
	Newbyth Garden Cottage		01620 870646	Self Catering	★★★★★
	The Stable		01620 861041	Self Catering	★★★
Edinburgh	21212	EH7 5AB	0131 5231030	Awaiting Grading	
	1 Cranston Street	EH8 8BE	07895 643814	Awaiting Grading	
	1/6 St Leonards Crag		01450 374150	Self Catering	★★★
	10 Glenfinlas Street	EH3 6AQ	0131 2258695	Serviced Apartments	★★★★★
	11 Kings Stables Lane		0131 5552596	Self Catering	★★★
	11 Morrison Circus		01540 673447	Self Catering	★★★★
	11/15 Huntingdon Place		01592 840729	Self Catering	★★★★
	126 High Street	EH4 8EZ	0131 4679060	Serviced Apartments	★★★ to ★★★★
	13 Frederick Street		0175 32 233	Self Catering	★★★★
	13 Stanley Street		0131 6691998	Self Catering	★★★
	16 Waterloo Place (2 bedroom 'minus' & Studios)	EH1 3EG	0131 5581600	Awaiting Grading	
	17/47 The Bond	EH6 7EN	07774 771753	Awaiting Grading	
	2 Rossie Place		0131 6611934	Self Catering	★★★
	2 Seton Place	EH9 2JT	0131 6676430	Bed & Breakfast	★★★★
	21 Mayfield Road	EH9 2NQ	0131 6678435	Bed & Breakfast	★★★
	21 West Mayfield	EH9 1TQ	0131 6682148	Bed & Breakfast	★★★★
	21/2 21/3 Hanover Street		020 72244677	Self Catering	★★★★★
	24 Warrender Park Crescent		0131 6512184	Self Catering	★
	25 Saxe – Coburg Place		01738 812764	Self Catering	★★★★★
	27 Braid Crescent	EH10 6AX	0131 4475830	Bed & Breakfast	★★★
	28 Earl Grey Street	EH3 9DN	01506 859130	Awaiting Grading	
	29b Springfield	EH6 5DU	07788 670520	Awaiting Grading	
	30/3 Abbey Lane		01560 480824	Self Catering	★★★★
	32 Terrars Croft		0131 6657140	Self Catering	★★★
	33 Drummond House		0131 5583479	Self Catering	★★★
	37 Howe Street	EH3 6TF	0131 5573487	Bed & Breakfast	★★
	38 Dublin Street	EH3 6NN	0131 5571789	Bed & Breakfast	★★★★
	3A Clarence Street	EH3 5AE	0131 5579368	Bed & Breakfast	★★
	3D Apartments – Edinburgh Royal Mile		01708 442764	Self Catering	★★★
	4 Hill Street	EH2 3JZ	01312 258884	Guest House	★★★★
	45 Cumberland Street		01387 760230	Self Catering	★★★★★
	45A Dalrymple Loan		0131 6658050	Self Catering	★★★
	46A Drumbrae South	EH12 8SZ	0131 5390909	Bed & Breakfast	★★
	48/1 Candlemaker Row		0131 5380352	Self Catering	★★★★ 𝒫𝒫
	49A North Castle Street		0131 4433182	Self Catering	★★★★
	4A Regent Terrace		0131 5589536	Self Catering	★★★★
	5/2 Ramsay Garden		07904 562723	Self Catering	★★★ to ★★★★
	5/4 Tower House		01875 852881	Self Catering	★★★★
	54/8 St Mary's Street		0131 5581108	Self Catering	★★★
	6 St Giles Street		01835 823248	Self Catering	★★★★
	7 Cambridge Gardens	EH6 5DH	0131 5546196	Bed & Breakfast	★★
	7/6 Chessels Court	EH8 8AD	07786 923386	Awaiting Grading	
	8/6 Powderhall Brae	EH7 4GE	07990 516341	Awaiting Grading	

  ♿ Unassisted wheelchair access   ♿ Assisted wheelchair access   ♈ Access for visitors with mobility difficulties
  𝒫 Bronze Green Tourism Award   𝒫𝒫 Silver Green Tourism Award   𝒫𝒫𝒫 Gold Green Tourism Award
For further information on our Green Tourism Business Scheme please see page 7.

Advertisers' locations have been sorted by postcode. In Scotland, postcodes can cover fairly large geographical areas.
Please check distance of property from specified location with the individual provider. VisitScotland cannot take any responsibility for this.

385

Location	Property Name	Postcode	Telephone	Classification	Star Rating	
Edinburgh	9 Hart Street		0131 5588381	Self Catering	★★★★	
	94/1 Inchview Terrace		0141 6472362	Self Catering	★★★★	
	94DR	EH16 5AF	0131 6629265	Guest House	★★★★★	
	9a Learmonth Terrace	EH4 1PG	01914 167335	Awaiting Grading		
	A Haven Townhouse	EH6 4NS	0131 5546559	Metro Hotel	★★★	
	A Room in Town	EH7 5HB	0131 5578702	Bed & Breakfast	★★★	
	A'Abide'an'Abode	EH14 1PP	0131 4435668	Bed & Breakfast	★★★	
	Aaran Lodge Guest House	EH15 2NW	0131 6575615	Guest House	★★★★	
	Aaron Lodge	EH16 4SD	0131 6642755	Guest House	★★★★	
	Abbey Hotel	EH7 5AH	0131 5570121	Metro Hotel	★★★	
	Abbey Lodge Hotel	EH17 8RJ	0131 6649548	Small Hotel	★★	⋔
	Abbotsford Guest House	EH6 5AL	0131 5542706	Guest House	★★★	
	Abbotshead House	EH9 2BR	0131 6681658	Guest House	★★	
	Abcorn Guest House	EH9 2BU	01316 676548	Guest House	★★★	
	Abercorn Guest House	EH15 2DD	0131 6696139	Guest House	★★★★	
	Acer Lodge Guest House	EH4 7NB	0131 3362554	Guest House	★★★★	
	Adam Drysdale House	EH3 9NQ	0131 2288952	Bed & Breakfast	★★	
	Adria House	EH7 5AB	0131 5567875	Guest House	★★★	
	Afton Guest House	EH10 4LD	0131 2291019	Guest House	★★★	
	Ailsa Craig Hotel	EH7 5AH	0131 5566055	Metro Hotel	★★★	
	Airdenair Guest House	EH16 5DB	0131 6682336	Guest House	★★★	
	Airlie Guest House	EH9 1SB	0131 6673562	Guest House	★★★	
	Alba Executive	EH9 2LX	0131 4462388	Serviced Apartments	★★★★★	
	Albern Morningside Apartment		07914 639962	Self Catering	★★★★	
	Albyn Town House	EH10 4LD	0131 2296459	Guest House	★★★	
	Allison House	EH9 2AX	0131 6678049	Guest House	★★★★	
	Alloway Guest House	EH6 5AY	0131 5541786	Guest House	★★★	
	Almond House	EH12 8HN	0131 4674588	Bed & Breakfast	★★★	
	Amaragua Guest House	EH16 5DR	0131 6676775	Guest House	★★★★	𝓟𝓟
	Annandale Street Apartments		0131 5574676	Self Catering	★★★★	
	Aonach Mor Guesthouse	EH16 5DR	0131 6209999	Guest House	★★★	
	Apartment 39 – Lothian House		0780 1064820	Self Catering	★★★★	
	Apartment By Castle		0131 6205511	Self Catering	★★★★	
	Apartment by Royal Mile		01721 729992	Self Catering	★★★★	𝓟𝓟
	Apex City	EH1 2JF	0845 3650000	Hotel	★★★★	𝓟𝓟𝓟
	Apex European Hotel	EH12 5LQ	0845 3650000	Hotel	★★★	𝓟𝓟𝓟
	Apex International Hotel	EH1 2HY	0845 3650000	Hotel	★★★★	𝓟𝓟𝓟
	Apex Waterloo Place Hotel	EH1 3BH	0131 6665100	Awaiting Grading		
	Appin House	EH9 2AZ	0131 6682947	Guest House	★★★	
	Ardbrae House	EH12 8TD	0131 4675787	Bed & Breakfast	★★★	
	Arden Guest House	EH16 4SD	0131 6643983	Awaiting Grading		
	Ardenlee Guest House	EH3 5ES	0131 5562838	Guest House	★★★	
	Ardgarth Guest House	EH15 2QF	0131 6693021	Guest House	★★★	♿
	Ardleigh Guest House	EH5 3AN	0131 5521833	Guest House	★★★	
	Ardmillan Hotel	EH11 2JW	0131 3379588	Small Hotel	★★	
	Ardmor House	EH6 5AS	0131 5544944	Guest House	★★★★	
	Ard-Na-Said	EH16 5HH	0131 6678754	Guest House	★★★★	
	Argyle Backpackers Hotel	EH9 1JL	0131 6699991	Backpacker	★★★	

♿ Unassisted wheelchair access   ♿ Assisted wheelchair access   ⋔ Access for visitors with mobility difficulties
ℙ Bronze Green Tourism Award   𝓟𝓟 Silver Green Tourism Award   𝓟𝓟𝓟 Gold Green Tourism Award
For further information on our Green Tourism Business Scheme please see page 7.

To find out more go to visitscotland.com

Location	Property Name	Postcode	Telephone	Classification	Star Rating	
Edinburgh	Argyle Suite, McKenzie Suite, Double E/S No 1&2		0131 6691044	Self Catering	★★★	
	Aros House	EH9 1SL	0131 6671585	Bed & Breakfast	★★★	
	Arrandale Guest House	EH9 2BZ	0131 6222232	Guest House	★★★	
	Ascot Garden	EH12 8LS	0131 3392092	Bed & Breakfast	★★★	
	Ascot Guest House	EH16 5AF	0131 6671500	Guest House	★	
	Ashdene House	EH9 2LN	0131 6676026	Guest House	★★★★	🍃🍃🍃
	Ashgrove House	EH12 5HG	0131 3375014	Guest House	★★★	
	Ashlyn Guest House	EH3 5PY	0131 5522954	Guest House	★★★	
	Atholl Brae – The Harland		01721 730679	Self Catering	★★★★	♿
	Auld Alliance Bed & Breakfast	EH4 2AX	0131 3326309	Bed & Breakfast	★★★	
	Auld Reekie Guest House	EH9 2BZ	0131 6676177	Guest House	★★★	
	Aurora Bed & Breakfast	EH12 8JY	07742 661545	Bed & Breakfast	★★	
	Aurora Flat		01382 810526	Self Catering	★★★	
	Averon Guest House	EH3 9NQ	0131 2299932	Guest House	★★	
	Ayden Guest House	EH6 5AS	0131 5542187	Guest House	★★★★	
	Aynetree Guest House	EH15 3AS	0131 2582821	Guest House	★★★	
	B&B Harrison	EH10 6RQ	0131 4481430	Bed & Breakfast	★★★	
	Badjao B&B	EH14 1PP	0131 4433170	Bed & Breakfast	★★	
	Baird, Lee, Ewing and Turner House	EH16 5AY	0131 6512011	Campus	★★	
	Ballantrae Albany Hotel	EH1 3QY	0131 5560397	Awaiting Grading		
	Ballantrae Apartments	EH1 3EP	0131 4784748	Serviced Apartments	★★★★	
	Ballantrae Hotel	EH1 3EP	0131 4784748	Hotel	★★★	
	Ballantrae Hotel At The West End	EH12 5EP	0131 2257033	Awaiting Grading		
	Balmore House	EH3 9NQ	0131 2211331	Guest House	★★★★	
	Barcelo Carlton Hotel	EH1 1SD	0131 4723119	Hotel	★★★★	
	Barony House	EH9 2BZ	0131 6677184	Guest House	★★★	
	Barrosa Guest House	EH6 5AN	0131 5543700	Guest House	★★	
	Belford Hostel	EH4 3DA	0131 2202200	Hostel	★★★	
	Ben Craig House	EH16 5PG	0131 6672593	Guest House	★★★	🚶
	Ben Cruachan	EH7 4LX	0131 5563709	Guest House	★★★★	
	Ben Doran	EH9 2AX	0131 6678488	Guest House	★★★★	
	Best Western Edinburgh City Hotel	EH3 9HZ	0131 6227979	Hotel	★★★	
	Bield B&B	EH4 2EW	0131 3325119	Bed & Breakfast	★★★★	
	Birch Tree House	EH4 7NB	0131 3364790	Bed & Breakfast	★★	
	Blinkbonny House	EH4 3HG	0131 4671232	Bed & Breakfast	★★★	
	Bonnington Guest House	EH6 4NW	0131 5547610	Guest House	★★★★	
	Botanic Garden Apartment		07770 732576	Self Catering	★★★	
	Brae Guest House	EH8 7HN	0131 6610170	Guest House	★★★	
	Brae Lodge Guest House	EH16 6AF	0131 6722876	Guest House	★★★	🚶
	Braid Hills Hotel	EH10 6JD	0131 4478888	Hotel	★★★	
	Brig O'Doon Guest House	EH5 3AN	0131 5523953	Guest House	★★★	
	Brodies 1	EH1 1TB	0131 5566770	Hostel	★★	
	Brodies 2	EH1 1SG	0131 5566697	Hostel	★★★	
	Brothaig House	EH16 5PS	0131 6672202	Guest House	★★★	
	Broughton Apartments		07764 951095	Self Catering	★★★★★	
	Bruntsfield Hotel	EH10 4HH	0131 2291393	Hotel	★★★★	🍃🍃
	Buchan & Haymarket Hotel	EH12 5LG	0131 3371775	Metro Hotel	★★★	

Advertisers' locations have been sorted by postcode. In Scotland, postcodes can cover fairly large geographical areas.
Please check distance of property from specified location with the individual provider. VisitScotland cannot take any responsibility for this.

Location	Property Name	Postcode	Telephone	Classification	Star Rating	
Edinburgh	Budget Backpackers	EH1 1JR	0131 2266351	Backpacker	★★★★	♿
	Budget Backpackers	EH1 1JY	0131 2266351	Backpacker	★★★	
	Burnets Apartment	EH1 1QU	0131 5501150	Awaiting Grading		
	Burns Guest House	EH3 9NU	0131 2291669	Guest House	★★★	
	Caledonian Hilton Hotel	EH1 2AB	0131 2228888	Hotel	★★★★★	♿
	Calton Apartments		0131 5563221	Self Catering	★★★★	
	Canon Court Block A	EH3 5LH	0131 4747000	Serviced Apartments	★★★★	♿ 🄿
	Capital Guest House	EH9 2NG	0131 4660717	Guest House	★★★	
	Caravel Guest House	EH3 6NA	0131 5564444	Guest House	★★	
	Carduus Morrison		01620 826133	Self Catering	★★★	
	Carmichael Cottages		01899 308336	Self Catering	★★★★	
	Carrington	EH6 5AN	0131 5544769	Guest House	★★★	
	Casa Buzzo Guest House	EH16 5DA	0131 6678998	Guest House	★★★	
	Castle Park Guest House	EH3 9NU	0131 2291215	Guest House	★★	
	Castle Rock Hostel	EH1 2PW	0131 2259666	Backpacker	★★	
	Castle View	EH2 3HT	0131 2265784	Guest House	★★★	
	Castle View		01620 829487	Self Catering	★★★★	
	Castle View Apartment		0131 5526300	Self Catering	★★★	
	Channings	EH4 1EZ	0131 2266050	Hotel	★★★★	🄿🄿
	Charleston House Guest House	EH9 2BS	0131 6676589	Guest House	★★★	
	Christopher North House Hotel	EH3 6EF	0131 2252720	Town House Hotel	★★★★	
	Clan Walker Guest House	EH16 5AF	0131 6671244	Guest House	★★★★	
	Claremont Hotel	EH7 4HX	0131 5561487	Metro Hotel	★	
	Classic Guest House	EH9 2NH	0131 6675847	Guest House	★★★	
	Cloughley B&B	EH9 1SW	0131 6673565	Bed & Breakfast	★★★	
	Cluaran House	EH10 4JS	0131 2210047	Guest House	★★★★	
	Cordiner's Land Holiday Apartment	07947 481485	Self Catering	★★★		
	Craigellachie	EH12 6AU	0131 3374076	Guest House	★★★★	
	Craigmore Bed & Breakfast	EH12 8EL	0131 3394225	Bed & Breakfast	★★★★	🄿🄿
	Craigmoss Guest House	EH6 4HS	0131 5543885	Guest House	★★★★	
	Craigwell Cottage		0131 4764011	Self Catering	★★★★	
	Crioch Guest House	EH6 8AD	0131 5545494	Guest House	★★★	
	Cruachan Guest House	EH3 9NT	0131 2296219	Guest House	★★★	
	Cumberland Hotel	EH12 5JQ	0131 4673572	Guest House	★★★	
	Dalry Church Flat		07980 213446	Self Catering	★★★★	
	Davenport House	EH3 6QY	0131 5588495	Guest House	★★★★	
	Dene Guest House	EH3 5ES	0131 5562700	Guest House	★★★	
	Doocote House	EH14 1PE	0131 4435455	Bed & Breakfast	★★★	
	Dorstan House	EH16 5HJ	0131 6676721	Guest House	★★★	
	Dovecot House	EH12 7LE	0131 4677467	Bed & Breakfast	★★★★	
	Drumfin	EH4 3JA	0131 3328209	Bed & Breakfast	★★★	
	Dunedin Guest House	EH16 5HH	0131 6681949	Guest House	★★★★	
	Dunstane City Hotel	EH12 5JD	0131 3376169	Town House Hotel	★★★★	🄿🄿
	Dunstane House Hotel	EH12 5JQ	0131 3376169	Small Hotel	★★★★	
	Duthus Lodge	EH12 5JG	0131 3376876	Guest House	★★★	
	Earl Grey Court	EH3 9BH	0131 6672270	Serviced Apartments	★★★★	
	Ecosse International	EH7 4LX	0131 5564967	Guest House	★★★	
	Edinburgh Agenda Hotel	EH12 8AT	0131 3164466	Hotel	★★	

♿ Unassisted wheelchair access   ♿ Assisted wheelchair access   ♿ Access for visitors with mobility difficulties
🄿 Bronze Green Tourism Award   🄿🄿 Silver Green Tourism Award   🄿🄿🄿 Gold Green Tourism Award
For further information on our Green Tourism Business Scheme please see page 7.

388   To find out more go to visitscotland.com

Location	Property Name	Postcode	Telephone	Classification	Star Rating	
Edinburgh	Edinburgh Apartments City Central (Eyre Crescent)		01727 832820	Self Catering	★★★	🚶
	Edinburgh Backpackers	EH1 1BU	0131 2202200	Hostel	★★★	
	Edinburgh Blair street		0131 6698535	Self Catering	★★★★	
	Edinburgh Brunswick	EH7 5JB	0131 5561238	Guest House	★	
	Edinburgh Capital Hotel	EH12 6UG	0131 5359988	Hotel	★★★	🍃🍃
	Edinburgh Caravan Club Site	EH4 5EN	01342 336842	Touring Park	★★★★★	
	Edinburgh Castle Wynd		01786 822214	Self Catering	★★★	
	Edinburgh Central (Lauriston) Premier Inn	EH3 9HZ	0131 2217130	Budget Hotel		
	Edinburgh Central Youth Hostel	EH7 4AL	0131 5242090	Hostel	★★★★★	
	Edinburgh City Centre Apartments		01463 790483	Self Catering	★★★★	
	Edinburgh City Centre(Morrison St) Premier Inn	EH3 8DN	0870 2383319	Budget Hotel		♿
	Edinburgh East Premier Inn	EH8 7NG	0870 1977091	Budget Hotel		
	Edinburgh First	EH16 5AY	0131 6512189	Campus	★★★	♿
	Edinburgh House	EH7 4LX	0131 5563434	Guest House	★★★	
	Edinburgh Marriott	EH12 8NF	0131 3349191	Hotel	★★★★	♿ 🄿
	Edinburgh Minto Hotel	EH9 9RQ	0131 6681234	Hotel	★★★	
	Edinburgh New Town Apartment		07989 982032	Self Catering	★★★★	
	Edinburgh Self-Catering: Square One Apartment		0131 5536641	Self Catering	★★★ to ★★★★	
	Edinburgh Self-Catering: The Arc Apartment		0131 5536641	Self Catering	★★★ to ★★★★	
	EdinburghFlats – Flat 1, 77 Hanover Street		07973 345559	Self Catering	★★★ to ★★★★★	
	Elas Guest House	EH7 4HX	0131 5561929	Guest House	★	
	Elder York Guest House	EH1 3DX	0131 5561926	Awaiting Grading		
	Ellersly House Hotel	EH12 6HZ	0131 3376888	Awaiting Grading		
	Ellesmere Guest House	EH3 9LN	0131 2294823	Awaiting Grading		
	Emerald House	EH17 8GG	0131 6645918	Guest House	★★★	
	Euro Hostels Limited	EH1 1JT		Hostel	★★★	
	Express By Holiday Inn	EH1 3JT	0131 5582300	Metro Hotel	★★★	♿
	Express By Holiday Inn	EH6 6LA	0131 5554422	Metro Hotel	★★★	♿
	Express by Holiday Inn (Edinburgh Royal Mile)	EH1 1NA	0131 5248400	Metro Hotel	★★★	
	Fairmont		0131 6241258	Self Catering	★★★	
	Fairnington Apartments – 13/4 St Leonards Lane		0131 6677042	Self Catering	★★★ to ★★★★	
	Falcon Crest Guest House	EH5 3NX	0131 5525294	Guest House	★	
	Flat 1, 5 Borthwick's Place		01312 400080	Self Catering	★★★★	
	Flat 11		01224 321681	Self Catering	★★★★	
	Flat 12	EH3 9GG	0131 3432239	Serviced Apartments	★★★★	
	Flat 2		01289 386565	Self Catering	★★★★	
	Flat 2 215 Causewayside		07590 543177	Self Catering	★★★★	
	Flat 2F1 Baillie Fyfes Close		07973 459128	Self Catering	★★★★	
	Flat 2F3		0131 5523084	Self Catering	★★★★	
	Flat 3		0774 7763032	Self Catering	★★★★	
	Flat 4 (Castle View) 1 Upper Bow		0117 9681962	Self Catering	★★★	
	Flat 5		01471 822716	Self Catering	★★	

♿ Unassisted wheelchair access ♿ Assisted wheelchair access 🚶 Access for visitors with mobility difficulties
🄿 Bronze Green Tourism Award 🍃🍃 Silver Green Tourism Award 🍃🍃🍃 Gold Green Tourism Award
For further information on our Green Tourism Business Scheme please see page 7.

Advertisers' locations have been sorted by postcode. In Scotland, postcodes can cover fairly large geographical areas. Please check distance of property from specified location with the individual provider. VisitScotland cannot take any responsibility for this.

389

Location	Property Name	Postcode	Telephone	Classification	Star Rating	
Edinburgh	Flat 6/14 Bethlehem Way		07956 475136	Self Catering	★★★	
	Fountain Court Edinburgh Quay Serviced Apartments	EH3 9QP	0131 6226677	Serviced Apartments	★★★★★	𝑃𝑃
	Fountain Court Grove Apartments	EH3 8AA	0131 6226677	Serviced Apartments	★★★★	
	Fraser Suites Edinburgh	EH1 1PT	0141 5534288	Awaiting Grading		
	Frasers B&B	EH7 4BS	0131 5565123	Bed & Breakfast	★★★	
	Frederick House	EH2 1EX	0131 2261999	Guest Accommodation	★★★★	
	Garden Serviced Apartment		0131 3373454	Self Catering	★ to ★★★	
	Garlands Guest House	EH6 5AL	0131 5544205	Guest House	★★★	
	George Hotel	EH2 2PB	0131 2251251	Hotel	★★★★	𝑃𝑃
	Gifford House	EH16 5AJ	0131 6674688	Guest House	★★★★	
	Gil-Dun Guest House	EH16 5AG	0131 6671368	Guest House	★★★★	
	Gillis Centre	EH9 1BB	0131 6238933	Guest House	★★★	♿
	Gladstone Guest House	EH16 5AF	0131 6674708	Guest House	★★★	
	Glenalmond Guest House	EH9 2BX	0131 6682392	Guest House	★★★★	
	Glendevon	EH12 8HN	0131 5390491	Bed & Breakfast	★★★	
	Granville Guest House	EH10 4PQ	0131 2291676	Guest House	★★	
	Grosvenor Gardens	EH12 5JU	0131 3133415	Guest House	★★★	
	Halcyon House	EH7 5AB	0131 5561032	Guest House	★★	
	Hampton Hotel	EH12 6HN	0131 3371130	Inn	★★★	
	Harvest Guest House	EH15 2BA	0131 6573160	Guest House	★★	
	Herald House Hotel	EH3 8AP	0131 2282323	Metro Hotel	★★	
	Heriott Park Guest House	EH5 3AN	0131 5523456	Guest House	★★★	
	High Street Hostel	EH1 1NE	0131 5573984	Backpacker	★★	
	Highfield Guest House	EH9 3AE	0131 6678717	Guest House	★★★★	
	Hilton Edinburgh Grosvenor	EH12 5EF	0131 2266001	Hotel	★★★	♿
	Holiday Inn Edinburgh	EH12 6UA	0131 3147036	Hotel	★★★★	♿
	Holiday Inn Edinburgh-North	EH4 3HL	0870 4009025	Hotel	★★★	♿
	Holland House	EH16 5AY	0131 6512076	Campus	★★	♀
	Holyrood Aparthotel	EH8 8PE	0131 5243200	Serviced Apartments	★★★★	♀
	Holyrood Hotel	EH8 6AE	0870 1942106	Hotel	★★★★	♀ 𝑃𝑃
	Hotel Ceilidh-Donia	EH16 5HL	0131 6672743	Small Hotel	★★★	
	Hotel Du Vin	EH1 1EZ	0131 2474900	Awaiting Grading		
	Hotel Ibis Edinburgh	EH1 1QW	0131 2407000	Budget Hotel		
	Hotel Missoni	EH1 1AD	0131 2206666	Hotel	★★★★★	
	Hudson Hotel	EH2 4EL	0131 2477000	Metro Hotel	★★★★	
	Inercitylets.com – 4 Fleshmarket Close		07795 634341	Self Catering	★★★	
	Ingleneuk	EH4 8AT	0131 3171743	Bed & Breakfast	★★★	
	Irvine Apartments		0131 3126843	Self Catering	★★★★	
	James Square		0131 2257808	Self Catering	★★★★	
	Joppa Turrets Guest House	EH15 2ER	0131 6695806	Guest House	★★★	
	Judy Guest House	EH12 7AZ	0131 3346159	Guest House	★★	
	Jurys Inn Edinburgh	EH1 1DH	0131 2003300	Hotel	★★★	♿ 𝑃𝑃𝑃
	Kabayan	EH12 8HA	07907 326879	Bed & Breakfast	★★★	
	Kaimes Guest House	EH10 4PQ	0131 2293401	Guest House	★★	
	Kariba Guest House	EH10 4PQ	0131 2293773	Guest House	★★★	
	Kelly's Guest House	EH4 3QP	0131 3323894	Guest House	★★★	♀
	Kenneth MacKenzie Suite	EH8 9ST	0131 6512007	Awaiting Grading		

♿ Unassisted wheelchair access   ♿ Assisted wheelchair access   ♀ Access for visitors with mobility difficulties
🅟 Bronze Green Tourism Award   𝑃𝑃 Silver Green Tourism Award   𝑃𝑃𝑃 Gold Green Tourism Award
For further information on our Green Tourism Business Scheme please see page 7.

Location	Property Name	Postcode	Telephone	Classification	Star Rating		
Edinburgh	Kenvie Guest House	EH16 5DA	0131 6681964	Guest House	★★★		
	Kildonan Lodge Hotel	EH16 5PE	0131 6672793	Small Hotel	★★★★		
	Kilmaurs House	EH16 5DA	0131 6678315	Guest House	★★★		
	Kings Manor Hotel	EH15 2NP	0131 4688003	Hotel	★★★	𝚮	𝒫𝒫𝒫
	Kingsburgh House	EH12 6HN	0131 3131679	Guest House	★★★★★		
	Kingsley Guest House	EH16 5PS	0131 6673177	Guest House	★★★		
	Kingsway Guest House	EH9 1SD	0131 6675029	Guest House	★★★		
	Kirklea Guest House	EH11 1EG	0131 3371129	Guest House	★★★		
	Lauderville House	EH9 2NH	0131 6677788	Guest House	★★★★		
	Le Monde Hotel	EH3 6EE	0131 2703900	Hotel	★★★★		
	Lindsay Guest House	EH11 1NN	0131 3371580	Guest House	★★★	𝚮	
	Links Hotel and Bar	EH9 1DU	0131 5164745	Inn	★★		
	MacIntosh Guest House	EH12 7AU	0131 3343108	Guest House	★★		
	Mackenzie Guest House	EH6 8AA	0131 5543763	Guest House	★★★★		
	Malmaison Hotel et Brasserie	EH6 7DB	0131 4685000	Hotel	★★★★		
	Marchmont Victorian Apartment		07763 342759	Self Catering	★★★★		
	Martin's Guest House	EH10 4PQ	01312 292085	Awaiting Grading			
	Masson House	EH16 5AY	0131 6512076	Campus	★★	𝚮	
	Mayfield Lodge	EH9 3AA	0131 6628899	Guest House	★★★		
	McCrae's	EH7 4JR	0131 5562610	Bed & Breakfast	★★★		
	Melvin House Hotel	EH3 7RY	0131 2255084	Metro Hotel	★★★		
	Menzies Guest House	EH10 4PX	0131 2294629	Guest House	★★		
	Merchiston Apartment		0131 3371066	Self Catering	★★		
	Mercure Point	EH3 9AF	0131 2215555	Hotel	★★★		
	Mews Apartment		0131 4677467	Self Catering	★★★★		
	Mingalar	EH7 4JP	0131 5567000	Guest House	★★★		
	Morita	EH9 2AX	0131 6671337	Bed & Breakfast	★★		
	Mortonhall Caravan Park	EH16 6TJ	0131 6641533	Holiday Park	★★★★	♿	
	Mrs Linda J Allan, 10 Baberton Mains Rise	EH14 3HG	0131 4423619	Bed & Breakfast	★★		
	Murrayfield Hotel	EH12 6HN	0131 6226800	Hotel	★★★		
	MW Town House	EH16 5AG	0131 6551530	Guest House	★★★★		
	Napier Guest House	EH10 4PQ	0131 3373454	Awaiting Grading			
	Napier University Morrison Circus		0131 4553738	Self Catering	★★	♿	
	Napier University Wrights Houses		0131 4553738	Self Catering	★★	♿	
	Nevis		01738 828297	Self Catering	★★★★		
	Newington Lodge	EH16 5DT	01316 670910	Bed & Breakfast	★★		
	Nicolson Apartments		0131 4773680	Self Catering	★★★★		
	No 10 The Arc		0781 1127920	Self Catering	★★★★		
	No 15 & 15a Dundas Street	EH3 6RS	01764 650303	Awaiting Grading			
	No 15 Merchiston Gardens	EH10 5DD	0131 2296565	Awaiting Grading			
	No 22 Dalry Road		0131 3135313	Self Catering	★★★		
	No 3 B&B	EH4 3NH	0131 5380468	Bed & Breakfast	★★★★		
	No 3 Raeburn Mews		01620 894374	Self Catering	★★★		
	No 4		01563 544034	Self Catering	★★★★		
	No 45	EH16 5NS	0131 6673536	Bed & Breakfast	★★★★		
	No 457/4 Lawnmarket		07932 716988	Self Catering	★★★★		
	No 5/3 Hopetoun Crescent		0131 6615665	Self Catering	★★★★		

♿ Unassisted wheelchair access   ♿ Assisted wheelchair access   𝚮 Access for visitors with mobility difficulties
𝒫 Bronze Green Tourism Award   𝒫𝒫 Silver Green Tourism Award   𝒫𝒫𝒫 Gold Green Tourism Award
For further information on our Green Tourism Business Scheme please see page 7.

Advertisers' locations have been sorted by postcode. In Scotland, postcodes can cover fairly large geographical areas.
Please check distance of property from specified location with the individual provider. VisitScotland cannot take any responsibility for this.

391

Location	Property Name	Postcode	Telephone	Classification	Star Rating	
Edinburgh	No 56/15 Belford Road		0131 5588812	Self Catering	★★★★	
	No 7 The Royal Mile Apartment		0131 6673843	Self Catering	★★★	
	No. 23 Mayfield	EH9 2BX	0131 6675806	Guest House	★★★★	
	No. 322 Leith Walk	EH6 5BU	07747 643215	Awaiting Grading		
	No. 85 Lothian House		0131 2258695	Self Catering	★★★★	
	No.4 (2F1)		0782 8122904	Self Catering	★★	
	Nos 1 to 11 Featherhall Garden Court		0845 4301430	Self Catering	★★★	⚡
	Novotel Edinburgh Centre	EH3 9DE	0131 6563500	Hotel	★★★★	♿
	Novotel Edinburgh Park	EH12 9DJ	0131 4465600	Hotel	★★★★	
	Number Ten	EH3 6DF	0131 2252720	Serviced Apartments	★★★★★	
	Ocean Apartments	EH6 6PN	0131 5537394	Serviced Apartments	★★★	
	One O'clock Gunn – 4 York Place		0131 4412373	Self Catering	★★★ to ★★★★	
	One O'clock Gunn – 5 Coates Place		0131 4412373	Self Catering	★★★ to ★★★★	
	One O'clock Gunn – 8 Woodhall Road		0131 4412373	Self Catering	★★★ to ★★★★	
	Osbourne Hotel	EH1 3JD	0131 5565577	Guest Accommodation	★	
	Panda Villa	EH16 5DA	0131 6675057	Bed & Breakfast	★★★	
	Paradise Penthouse		01913 843904	Self Catering	★★★★★	
	Patio Serviced Apartment	EH10 4PQ	0870 7668232	Awaiting Grading		
	Penthouse Flat		01890 771266	Self Catering	★★★★	
	Pilrig House Apartments – Garden Apartment		0131 5544794	Self Catering	★★★★	
	Premier Inn Edinburgh Leith	EH6 4LX	0870 1977093	Budget Hotel		
	Preston Apartment 1	EH8 9QQ	07932 082715	Awaiting Grading		
	Prestonfield	EH16 5UT	0131 2257800	Hotel	★★★★★	
	Priestville Guest House	EH16 5HJ	0131 6672435	Guest House	★★★	
	Quaich Guest House	EH12 6NN	0131 3344440	Bed & Breakfast	★★★	
	Quartermile		0131 4477573	Self Catering	★★★★	
	Quartermile Flat 2	EH3 9BS	01704 539771	Awaiting Grading		
	Queens Guest House	EH2 3NH	0131 2262000	Awaiting Grading		
	Radisson SAS Hotel	EH1 1TH	0131 5579797	Hotel	★★★★	🌿🌿🌿
	Ramada Mount Royal Hotel	EH2 2DG	08448 159017	Hotel	★★★	♿ 🌿
	Ravensdown Guest House	EH5 3AN	0131 5525438	Guest House	★★★	
	Regent House Hotel	EH1 3JX	0131 5561616	Guest House	★★	
	Relax Guest House	EH3 5ES	0131 5561433	Awaiting Grading		
	Rick's	EH2 1LH	0131 2204347	Restaurant With Rooms	★★★★	
	Robertson Guest House	EH10 4LD	0131 2292652	Guest House	★★★	
	Rosehall Hotel	EH16 5AJ	0131 6679372	Metro Hotel	★★★	
	Rosevale House	EH16 5DA	0131 6674781	Guest House	★★	
	Rowan Guest House	EH9 2DQ	0131 6672463	Guest House	★★★	
	Roxburghe Hotel	EH2 4HG	0870 1942108	Hotel	★★★★	⚡ 🌿🌿
	Royal British Hotel	EH2 2AS	0131 5564901	Hotel	★★★	
	Royal Ettrick Hotel	EH10 5BJ	0131 6226800	Small Hotel	★	
	Royal Mile Apartment – Dunbars Close		0131 315 217	Self Catering	★★★★	
	Royal Mile Backpackers	EH1 1SG	0131 5576120	Backpacker	★★	
	Royal Mile Residence	EH1 1PE	0131 2265155	Serviced Apartments	★★★★★	
	Royal Terrace Hotel	EH7 5AQ	0131 5245107	Hotel	★★★★	
	Rutland Hotel	EH1 2AE	0131 2284981	Town House Hotel	★★★★	

♿ Unassisted wheelchair access ♿ Assisted wheelchair access ⚡ Access for visitors with mobility difficulties
🌿 Bronze Green Tourism Award 🌿🌿 Silver Green Tourism Award 🌿🌿🌿 Gold Green Tourism Award
For further information on our Green Tourism Business Scheme please see page 7.

Location	Property Name	Postcode	Telephone	Classification	Star Rating	
Edinburgh	Sakura House	EH8 9PU	0131 6681204	Guest House	★	
	Salisbury Green Hotel Conference Centre	EH16 5AY	01316 622000	Metro Hotel	★★★	ⓘ
	San Marco	EH9 2BZ	0131 6678982	Guest House	★★★★	
	Sandaig Guest House	EH6 8AA	0131 5547357	Guest House	★★★★	
	Sandeman House	EH10 5DR	0131 4478080	Bed & Breakfast	★★★★	
	Sandilands House	EH4 3HB	0131 3322057	Guest House	★★★	
	Shalimar Guest House	EH9 1QS	0131 6672827	Guest House	★★	
	Sheraton Grand Hotel & Spa Edinburgh	EH3 9SR	0131 2299131	Hotel	★★★★★	
	Sheridan Guest House	EH6 4BP	0131 5544107	Guest House	★★★	
	Sherwood Guest House	EH9 2BR	0131 6671200	Guest House	★★★★	
	Silvermills		01224 722243	Self Catering	★★★★	🅿🅿
	Six Brunton Place	EH7 5EG	01316 220042	Guest House	★★★★★	
	Six Marys Place Guest House	EH4 1JH	0131 3328965	Guest House	★★★	🅿🅿
	Smart City Hostel	EH1 1NE	0131 5241989	Hostel	★★★★★	🅿🅿
	Sonas Guest House	EH9 1SD	0131 6672781	Guest House	★★★	
	South Lodge	EH12 7LG	0131 3344651	Bed & Breakfast	★★	
	Southside	EH9 1QS	0131 6684422	Guest House	★★★★	
	Southside Apartments		0131 5240193	Self Catering	★★★★	
	Spring Gardens		01292 264383	Self Catering	★★★★	
	Spylaw Bank House	EH13 0LR	01314 415022	Bed & Breakfast	★★★★	
	St Christophers Inn	EH1 1DE	0131 2261446	Backpacker	★★★	🚶
	St Conan's Guest House	EH9 1SB	0131 6678393	Guest House	★★★	
	St Margaret's	EH12 7SU	0131 3347317	Bed & Breakfast	★★★★	
	St Stephen Street Flat		0131 3313912	Self Catering	★★★	
	St Valery Guest House	EH12 5LE	0131 3371893	Guest House	★★★	
	Star Villa	EH3 9NQ	0131 2294991	Guest House	★★★	
	Stewart's Bed & Breakfast	EH4 2AF	0131 5397033	Bed & Breakfast	★★★	
	Stockbridge Apartment	EH4 1NH	07734 973320	Awaiting Grading		
	Strathallan Guest House	EH9 2BR	0131 6676678	Guest House	★★★	
	Straven Guest House	EH15 2DL	0131 6695580	Guest House	★★★★	🅿🅿🅿
	Swanston Farm Cottages		0131 4455744	Self Catering	★★★★	
	Tailors Hall Hotel	EH1 1JS	0131 6226801	Inn	★★	
	Tania Guest House	EH9 1RQ	0131 6674144	Guest House	★★	
	Tantallon Bed & Breakfast	EH9 1NZ	0131 6671708	Bed & Breakfast	★★★★	
	Ten Hill Place Hotel	EH8 9DS	0131 6689243	Metro Hotel	★★★	🅿🅿🅿
	Teviotdale House	EH9 2ER	0131 6674376	Guest House	★★★★	
	The Alexander Guest House	EH9 2BX	0131 2584028	Guest House	★★★	
	The Apartment		07739 638713	Self Catering	★★★★	
	The Arc	EH8 8JH	07810 560835	Awaiting Grading		
	The Artist's Studio		0131 5588807	Self Catering	★★★	
	The Balmoral Hotel	EH2 2EQ	0131 5562414	Hotel	★★★★★	🅿
	The Bank Hotel	EH1 1LL	0131 5164745	Inn	★★★	
	The Beverley	EH12 6AY	0131 3371128	Guest House	★★★★	
	The Boisdale	EH12 5LG	0131 3371134	Guest House	★★★	
	The Bonham	EH3 7RN	0131 2266050	Hotel	★★★★	🅿🅿🅿
	The Broughton	EH1 3RR	0131 5589792	Guest House	★★★	
	The Cameron Bed & Breakfast	EH16 5LD	0131 6203126	Bed & Breakfast	★★★	

Advertisers' locations have been sorted by postcode. In Scotland, postcodes can cover fairly large geographical areas.
Please check distance of property from specified location with the individual provider. VisitScotland cannot take any responsibility for this.

393

Location	Property Name	Postcode	Telephone	Classification	Star Rating	
Edinburgh	The Chester Residence	EH3 7RF	0131 2262075	Serviced Apartments	★★★★★	
	The Conifers	EH6 5AS	01315 545162	Bed & Breakfast	★★★★	
	The Corstorphine Lodge	EH12 8SG	0131 5394237	Guest House	★★★	
	The Edinburgh Residence	EH3 7RY	0131 2266050	Town House Hotel	★★★★★	🍂🍂
	The Georgian Retreat		0131 6695394	Self Catering	★★★	
	The Gladstone Flat		0131 2265856	Self Catering	★★★	
	The Glasshouse	EH1 3AA	01315 258200	Metro Hotel	★★★★★	
	The Glenora Guest House	EH12 5JY	0131 3371186	Guest House	★★★★	🍂
	The Globetrotter Inn Edinburgh Limited	EH4 5EP	0131 3361030	Hostel	★★★★	
	The Harrison Flat		0131 2439335	Self Catering	★★★	
	The Hedges	EH7 5EB	0131 4789555	Bed & Breakfast	★★★★	
	The Howard	EH3 6QH	0131 2266050	Town House Hotel	★★★★★	🍂🍂🍂
	The Inverleith Hotel	EH3 5NS	0131 5562745	Metro Hotel	★★★	
	The Knight Residence	EH3 9DJ	0131 6228120	Serviced Apartments	★★★★★	
	The Lairg	EH12 5LG	0131 3371050	Guest House	★★★	
	The Laurels	EH17 7PR	0131 6662229	Guest House	★★★	🚶
	The Lodge	EH12 5JD	0131 3373682	Guest House	★★★★	
	The McDonald Guest House	EH7 4LX	0131 5575935	Guest House	★★★	
	The Moorings		01573 224171	Self Catering	★★★★	
	The Parkgate Apartment		07900 447713	Self Catering	★★★★	
	The Parliament House Hotel	EH1 3BJ	0131 4784000	Hotel	★★★	
	The Penthouse		01224 869459	Self Catering	★★★★★	
	The Royal Over-Seas League	EH2 3AB	0131 2251501	Small Hotel	★★★	
	The Royal Scots Club	EH3 6QE	0131 5564270	Hotel	★★★	
	The Salisbury	EH16 5AA	0131 6671264	Small Hotel	★★★★	
	The Scotsman Hotel	EH1 1YT	0207 6578164	Town House Hotel	★★★★★	
	The Town House	EH3 9NU	0131 2291985	Guest House	★★★★	
	The Upper Villa		01314 779645	Self Catering	★★★★	
	The Victorian Townhouse	EH12 5DD	0131 3377088	Bed & Breakfast	★★★★	
	The Walton	EH3 6SD	0131 5561137	Guest House	★★★★	
	The West End Rothesay Apartment		0773 9099257	Self Catering	★★★	
	The Witchery by The Castle	EH1 2NF	0131 2250976	Restaurant With Rooms	★★★★★	
	The Wright Place		0131 467 844	Self Catering	★★★★	
	Thistle Dhu	EH12 8LP	0131 3392862	Bed & Breakfast	★★★	
	Thistle Edinburgh	EH1 3SW	0131 2007758	Hotel	★★★★	♿
	Thistle Hotel	EH3 7EG	0131 2256144	Metro Hotel	★★	
	Thrums	EH9 1RQ	0131 6675545	Guest House	★★★	
	Tigerlily	EH7 4GG	0131 226 1370 ext 26	Hotel	★★★★	
	Toby Carvery & Innkeepers Lodge Edin/West	EH12 8AX	0131 3348235	Lodge	★★★	♿
	Tolbooth Royal Mile		07713 258587	Self Catering	★★★ to ★★★★	
	Travelodge Edinburgh Central	EH1 1TA	0207 8032360	Budget Hotel		
	Travelodge Edinburgh Dreghorn	EH13 9QR	0131 4414296	Budget Hotel		
	Travelodge Edinburgh Haymarket	EH12 5BY	0207 8032277	Budget Hotel		
	Travelodge Edinburgh Shandwick Place	EH2 4RG	0871 9848484	Awaiting Grading		
	Travelodge Edinburgh West End	EH4 3DG	08719 846418	Budget Hotel		
	Travelodge Learmonth Edinburgh	EH4 1PW	08719 846415	Awaiting Grading		

♿ Unassisted wheelchair access   ♿ Assisted wheelchair access   🚶 Access for visitors with mobility difficulties
🍂 Bronze Green Tourism Award   🍂🍂 Silver Green Tourism Award   🍂🍂🍂 Gold Green Tourism Award
For further information on our Green Tourism Business Scheme please see page 7.

Location	Property Name	Postcode	Telephone	Classification	Star Rating
Edinburgh	Two Hillside Crescent	EH7 5DY	0131 5564871	Guest House	★★★★★
	Victoria Park Hotel	EH6 4NN	0131 4777033	Small Hotel	★★★
	Westend Hostel	EH12 5DR	0131 3131031	Hostel	★★★
	Western Manor House	EH12 6JG	0131 5387490	Guest House	★★★
Elgin	Ardent House	IV30 5SY	01343 830694	Bed & Breakfast	★★★★
	Ardvorlich	IV30 1JB	01343 556064	Bed & Breakfast	★★★
	Auchmillan	IV30 1QG	01343 549077	Guest House	★★★
	Cart House		01343 850222	Self Catering	★★★ to ★★★★ ⅙ 🄿
	Curlew Cottage		01343 831114	Self Catering	★★★★ ⋏
	Eight Acres Hotel & Leisure Club	IV30 6UL	01343 543077	Hotel	★★★
	Elgin Premier Inn	IV30 1HY	0870 1977095	Budget Hotel	
	Gamekeepers Cottage		01343 830253	Self Catering	★★★
	Hogarth Whisky Cottage		01343 842460	Self Catering	★★★★
	Laichmoray Hotel	IV30 1QR	01343 540045	Hotel	★★★
	Mayne House		01343 541388	Self Catering	★★★
	Moray Bank Bed and Breakfast	IV30 1QT	01343 547618	Bed & Breakfast	★★★★
	Moraydale	IV30 1AG	01343 546381	Guest House	★★★★
	Old Duffus Farmhouse		01343 830270	Self Catering	★★★
	Old Mills Gardens	IV30 1QE	01343 550944	Awaiting Grading	
	Parkneuk		01343 890233	Self Catering	★★★
	Parrandier The Old Church of Urquhart	IV30 8NH	01343 843063	Bed & Breakfast	★★★★
	Pier Brae		01738 624234	Self Catering	★★★★
	Richmond B&B	IV30 1LT	01343 542561	Bed & Breakfast	★★★★
	Royal Hotel	IV30 1QW	01343 542320	Small Hotel	★★★
	Southbank Guest House	IV30 1LP	01343 547132	Guest House	★★★
	Springburn Log Cabins – Osprey		01343 541939	Self Catering	★★★ to ★★★★
	Station Caravan Park	IV30 5RU	01343 830880	Holiday Park	★★★★
	Sunninghill Hotel	IV30 1NH	01343 547799	Small Hotel	★★★
	The Court Yard	IV30 1NY	01343 547457	Awaiting Grading	
	The Croft	IV30 1QX	01343 546004	Bed & Breakfast	★★★★
	The Lodge	IV30 1QS	01343 549981	Guest House	★★★★
	The Mansefield Hotel	IV30 1NY	01343 540883	Hotel	★★★★
	The Mansion House Hotel	IV30 1AW	01343 548811	Country House Hotel	★★★
	The Pines Guest House	IV30 1XG	01343 552495	Awaiting Grading	
	West End Guest House	IV30 1AQ	01343 549629	Guest House	★★★
	Westmuir		01463 233082	Self Catering	★★★
Ellon	Beechgrove Cottage		0131 2439331	Self Catering	★★★
	Stables Flat		01651 851440	Self Catering	★★★
	Stevenson B&B	AB41 6BH	01358 789017	Bed & Breakfast	★★
Erskine	Erskine Bridge Hotel	PA8 6AN	0141 8120123	Hotel	★★★ ⋏ 🄿🄿🄿
Eyemouth	37 Albert Road		01890 750476	Self Catering	★★
	51 High Street		01961 622030	Self Catering	★★★
	Castle Cottage		01890 771310	Self Catering	★★★★ 🄿🄿🄿
	Courtburn House	TD14 5NS	01890 771266	Bed & Breakfast	★★★
	Crosslaw Caravan Park	TD14 5NS	01890 771316	Holiday Park	★★★★★ ⅙
	Crosslaw Farmhouse		01890 771319	Self Catering	★★★

Advertisers' locations have been sorted by postcode. In Scotland, postcodes can cover fairly large geographical areas.
Please check distance of property from specified location with the individual provider. VisitScotland cannot take any responsibility for this.

Location	Property Name	Postcode	Telephone	Classification	Star Rating	
Eyemouth	Dunlaverock	TD14 5PA	01890 771450	Guest House	★★★★	🚶
	Eye Sleep Inn	TD14 5GN	01890 750913	Guest Accommodation	★★	♿
	Eyemouth Holiday Park	TD14 5BE	01890 751050	Holiday Park	★★★★	
	Glendale Barn Apartment		01361 850207	Self Catering	★★★	
	Gunsgreen House Apartment		01890 752062	Self Catering	★★★	🚶
	Mrs McQueen's B&B	TD14 5TG	01890 750742	Bed & Breakfast	★★★	
	Nisbet's Tower		01890 752062	Self Catering	★★★	
	Priory View	TD14 5NH	01890 771525	Guest House	★★★	
	Redhall Cottage	TD14 5SG	01890 781488	Bed & Breakfast	★★★★	
	Scoutscroft Holiday Centre	TD14 5NB	01890 771338	Holiday Park	★★★★★	
	Seagull Cottage		01289 388938	Self Catering	★★★	
	Seal Cottage		01665 830783	Self Catering	★★	
	Springbank Cottage	TD14 5PW	01890 771477	Bed & Breakfast	★★★	
	St Abbs Haven		01912 614276	Self Catering	★★★★	
	The Anchorage	TD14 5BU	01890 750307	Bed & Breakfast	★★★	
	The Craw Inn	TD14 5LS	01890 61253	Inn	★★★	
	The Stables		01890 771270	Self Catering	★★ to ★★★	
Falkirk	48 Cromwell Road	FK1 1SF	01324 638227	Bed & Breakfast	★★★	
	Airth Castle Hotel & Spa Resort	FK2 8JF	01324 831411	Country House Hotel	★★★★	
	Ashbank	FK2 9UQ	01324 716649	Guest House	★★★★	
	Avon Glen Lodges		01324 861166	Self Catering	★★★	♿
	Best Western Park Hotel	FK1 5RY	01324 628331	Hotel	★★★	
	Bridgend Farm Country B&B	FK2 8RT	01324 832060	Bed & Breakfast	★★★	
	Cladhan Hotel	FK1 1UF	01324 877690	Hotel	★★★	
	Falkirk East Premier Inn	FK2 0YS	08701 977098	Budget Hotel		
	Falkirk North Premier Inn	FK2 8PJ	08701 977099	Budget Hotel		
	Inchyra Grange Hotel	FK2 0YB	01324 711911	Hotel	★★★★	♿
	Lismore House	FK2 0BX	01324 720929	Farm House	★★★★	
	Lower Doune		01324 715597	Self Catering	★★★	
	Oaklands	FK2 9QT	01324 610671	Bed & Breakfast	★★★★	
	Travelodge Falkirk	FK2 0XS	08719 846359	Budget Hotel		
Fochabers	Bayview	IV32 7NP	01343 870210	Bed & Breakfast	★★★	
	Castlehill Cottage	IV32 7LJ	01343 820761	Bed & Breakfast	★★★	
	Darnethills		01343 880240	Self Catering	★★ to ★★★	
	Garmouth Hotel	IV32 7LU	01343 870226	Inn	★★	
	Trochelhill Country House Bed & Breakfast	IV32 7LN	01343 821267	Bed & Breakfast	★★★★	
Forfar	Atholl Cottage	DD8 3JN	01307 465755	Bed & Breakfast	★★★	
	Broom Cottage		01307 850267	Self Catering	★★★	
	Castleton House Hotel	DD8 1SJ	01307 840340	Country House Hotel	★★★	
	Chapelpark House		01307 463972	Self Catering	★★★★	
	Cookston Stables		01307 840332	Self Catering	★★★★	
	Drumshademuir Caravan Park	DD8 1QT	01575 573284	Holiday Park	★★★★★	
	Foresterseat Caravan Park	DD8 2RY	01307 818880	Touring Park	★★★★	
	Holy and Ivy		01307 860305	Self Catering	★★★	
	Kalulu House	DD8 3SF	01307 860205	Bed & Breakfast	★★★★	
	Leckaway Caravan	DD8 1XF	01307 463324	Holiday Caravan		

To find out more go to visitscotland.com

Location	Property Name	Postcode	Telephone	Classification	Star Rating
Forfar	Lochlands Caravan Park	DD8 1XF	01307 463621	Touring Park	★★★★
	Lochside Caravan Park	DD8 1BT	01307 468917	Touring Park	★★★★
	Newton Farm Cottage		01307 820229	Self Catering	★★★
	Newton Farmhouse Bed & Breakfast	DD8 2JU	01307 820229	Bed & Breakfast	★★★
	No 2 Cottage		01307 830208	Self Catering	★★
	The Gida at Arniefoul	DD8 1UD	01307 840208	Awaiting Grading	
	The Granny Flat		01307 860205	Self Catering	★★★ to ★★★★
	Thrums Cottage		01575 572227	Self Catering	★★★
	West Mains of Turin Farmhouse Bed & Breakfast	DD8 2TE	01307 830229	Bed & Breakfast	★★★
	Woodville	DD8 2PS	01307 818090	Bed & Breakfast	★★★
Forres	America Cottage		01343 890454	Self Catering	★★★★
	April Rise	IV36 0HP	01309 674066	Bed & Breakfast	★★★
	Caranrahd	IV36 0DG	01309 672581	Bed & Breakfast	★★★
	Cluny Bank Hotel	IV36 1DW	01309 674304	Small Hotel	★★★★
	Cormack's Lodge		0131 2439331	Self Catering	★★★
	Cottage No1		01309 641205	Self Catering	★
	Daltullich Cottage		0131 3152775	Self Catering	★★★★
	Ferness & Huntly, Eilean & Gamrie		01309 673311	Self Catering	★★★ to ★★★★ ⅙
	Findhorn Bay Holiday Park	IV36 3TY	01309 690203	Holiday Park	★★★
	Findhorn Sands Caravan Park	IV36 0YZ	01309 690324	Holiday Park	★★★★★
	Fisherman's Bothies		01309 611263	Self Catering	★★★
	Heath House	IV36 3WN	01309 691082	Bed & Breakfast	★★★★
	Invercairn House	IV36 2TD	01309 641261	Bed & Breakfast	★★★
	Knockomie Hotel	IV36 0SG	01309 673146	Small Hotel	★★★★ 🄿🄿
	Manse Cottage		01343 890421	Self Catering	★★★
	Mayfield	IV36 3BN	01309 671541	Bed & Breakfast	★★★★
	Millburn Cottage		01977 612525	Self Catering	★★★★
	Milton of Grange Farm	IV36 2TR	01309 676360	Farm House	★★★★
	Morven	IV36 0AN	01309 673788	Bed & Breakfast	★★★
	Ramnee Hotel	IV36 3BN	01309 672410	Hotel	★★★★
	Sherston	IV36 2QT	01309 671087	Bed & Breakfast	★★★★
	South Lodge		0131 2439335	Self Catering	★★★
	Springfield	IV36 3JS	01309 676965	Bed & Breakfast	★★★★
	The Laird's Apartment		0131 2439335	Self Catering	★★★★
	The Old Kirk	IV36 2TL	01309 641414	Bed & Breakfast	★★★★
	Thornhall Chalet		01309 641283	Self Catering	★★★★
	Uralla	IV36 0DG	01309 672082	Bed & Breakfast	★★★★
Forsinard	Corn Mill Bunkhouse	KW13 6YT	01641 571219	Hostel	★★★★
Fort Augustus	7 Monastery		01506 842841	Self Catering	★★★★
	Auchterawe Country House	PH32 4BT	01320 366228	Bed & Breakfast	★★★
	Bon Accord/Caledonian Cottages		01925 740061	Self Catering	★★★
	Caledonian Hotel	PH32 4BQ	01320 366256	Small Hotel	★★★
	Carn A' Chuilinn	PH32 4BY	01320 366387	Bed & Breakfast	★★★★
	Cartref	PH32 4BH	01320 366255	Bed & Breakfast	★★★
	Flat 17 The Raven Wing		01320 340371	Self Catering	★★★★
	Fort Augustus Caravan Park	PH32 4DS	01320 366618	Touring Park	★★★★
	Hillside	PH32 4BT	01320 366253	Bed & Breakfast	★★★

🄳 Unassisted wheelchair access   🄵 Assisted wheelchair access   🅰 Access for visitors with mobility difficulties
🄿 Bronze Green Tourism Award   🄿🄿 Silver Green Tourism Award   🄿🄿🄿 Gold Green Tourism Award
For further information on our Green Tourism Business Scheme please see page 7.

Advertisers' locations have been sorted by postcode. In Scotland, postcodes can cover fairly large geographical areas.
Please check distance of property from specified location with the individual provider. VisitScotland cannot take any responsibility for this.

397

Location	Property Name	Postcode	Telephone	Classification	Star Rating	
Fort Augustus	Inchnacardoch Lodge Hotel LLP	PH32 4BL	01456 450900	Awaiting Grading		
	Livingstone	PH32 3BN	0800 7316651	Awaiting Grading		
	Lorien House	PH32 4AY	01320 366736	Awaiting Grading		
	Mavisburn	PH32 4BT	01320 366417	Bed & Breakfast	★★★	
	Morags Lodge	PH32 4DG	0131 5582342	Hostel	★★★★	🍃🍃
	Mount Pleasant		01809 501289	Self Catering	★★	
	Old School 11 (Eleven)		01456 486631	Self Catering	★★★★	
	Sonas	PH32 4BA	01320 366291	Bed & Breakfast	★★★★	
	St Josephs Bed & Breakfast	PH32 4DW	01320 366771	Bed & Breakfast	★★★	
	Stravaigers Lodge	PH32 4BZ	01320 366257	Hostel	★★★★	
	The Holt	PH32 4BA	01320 366202	Awaiting Grading		
	The Lovat	PH32 4DU	0845 4501100	Hotel	★★★	🍃🍃
	Thistle Dubh	PH32 4BN	01320 366380	Bed & Breakfast	★★★	
	Tigh Na Mairi	PH32 4BA	01320 366766	Awaiting Grading		
Fort William	11 Castle Drive	PH33 7NR	01397 702659	Bed & Breakfast	★★★	
	16 Melantee	PH33 6PZ	01397 703870	Bed & Breakfast	★★	
	24 Henderson Row	PH33 6HT	01397 702711	Bed & Breakfast	★★	
	6 Caberfeidh	PH33 6BE	01397 703756	Bed & Breakfast	★★★	
	Achintee Cottage		01397 702240	Self Catering	★★★	
	Achintee Farm Guest House	PH33 6TE	01397 702240	Bed & Breakfast	★★★	
	Achintee Farm Hostel	PH33 6TE	01397 702240	Hostel	★★	
	Alexandra Hotel	PH33 6AZ	01397 702241	Hotel	★★★	
	Alltshellach	PH33 6SA	01855 821357	Awaiting Grading		
	Alt-An Lodge	PH33 6RN	01397 704546	Bed & Breakfast	★★★	
	Altdarroch Farm		01687 460014	Self Catering	★★★ to ★★★★	
	Alyth 34 Lochaber Road		01687 462210	Self Catering	★★★	
	Aonach Mor House	PH33 6SW	01397 704525	Bed & Breakfast	★★★★	
	Ardblair	PH33 6LJ	01397 705832	Bed & Breakfast	★★★★	
	Ardmory	PH33 6BH	01397 705943	Bed & Breakfast	★★★	
	Ardvullin		0131 3365554	Self Catering	★	
	Argyll House	PH33 6RS	01397 700004	Bed & Breakfast	★★★★	
	Aros Ard	PH33 6RJ	01397 704142	Bed & Breakfast	★★★★	
	Balcarres	PH33 6RJ	01397 704444	Bed & Breakfast	★★★★	
	Bank Cottage		0141 6378591	Self Catering	★★	
	Bank Street Lodge	PH33 6AY	01397 700070	Hostel	★★★	
	Ben Nevis Guest House	PH33 6PF	01397 708817	Guest House	★★★	
	Ben Nevis Hotel & Leisure Club	PH33 6TG	01397 702331	Hotel	★★	
	Ben Nevis Inn	PH33 6TE	01397 701227	Bunkhouse		
	Ben Nevis View	PH33	01397 772131	Bed & Breakfast	★★★	
	Ben View Guest House	PH33 6ER	01397 702966	Guest House	★★★	
	Ben-View Lodges		01397 704124	Self Catering	★★★★	
	Berkeley House	PH33 6BT	01397 701185	Guest House	★★★	
	Berkeley House		01397 701185	Self Catering	★★★	
	Birchbrae		01855 821261	Self Catering	★★★★	
	Blythedale	PH33 6RJ	01397 705523	Bed & Breakfast	★★★★	
	Brae Mhor Cottage		01397 700415	Self Catering	★★★★	🍃
	Braeburn	PH33 7LX	01397 772047	Guest House	★★★★	
	Braeside House	PH33 6LF	01397 705466	Bed & Breakfast	★★★	

To find out more go to visitscotland.com

Location	Property Name	Postcode	Telephone	Classification	Star Rating	
Fort William	Bunree Caravan Club Site	PH33 6SE	01342 336842	Touring Park	★★★★★	
	Bunree Holiday Cottages – Glengower & Glenrigh		01855 821359	Self Catering	★★★	
	Caledonian Hotel	PH33 6RW	01397 703117	Hotel	★★	
	Calluna	PH33 6RE	01397 700451	Bunkhouse		
	Camus House	PH33 6RY	01855 821200	Guest House	★★★	
	Canalside Apartments		07770 533817	Self Catering	★★★★★	
	Carinbrook	PH33 7LX	01397 772318	Guest House	★★★★	
	Carna B&B	PH33 6RQ	01397 708995	Bed & Breakfast	★★★★	
	Cedar Breaks		01397 705897	Self Catering	★★★	
	Chase the Wild Goose Hostel	PH33 7LY	01397 772531	Hostel	★★★	
	Clan MacDuff Hotel	PH33 6RW	01397 702341	Hotel	★★★	₺
	Coorie Doon	PH33 7LX	01397 710439	Hostel	★★★★★	
	Corran Bunkhouse	PH33 6SE	01855 821000	Hostel	★★★★	₺
	Corrieview	PH33 7NX	01397 703608	Bed & Breakfast	★★★	
	Craig Nevis West	PH33 6BU	01397 702023	Guest House	★★	♀
	Creag Mhor Lodge	PH33 6RY	01855 821379	Guest House	★★★★	
	Crolinnhe	PH33 6JF	01397 702709	Bed & Breakfast	★★★★★	
	Cruachan Caravans	PH33 7JG	01397 772573	Holiday Caravan		
	Cruachan Hotel	PH33 6RQ	01397 702022	Hotel	★★★	
	Cuilcheanna House	PH33 6SD	01855 821226	Guest House	★★★★	
	Dailanna Guest House	PH33 7NP	01397 722253	Bed & Breakfast	★★★★	
	Dalaraban		01397 712773	Self Catering	★★★	
	Distillery Guest House	PH33 6LH	01397 700103	Guest House	★★★★	
	Ealasaid		01397 704005	Self Catering	★★★	
	Farr Cottage Lodge	PH33 7LR	01397 772315	Hostel	★★★★	⌑
	Ferndale	PH33 6SP	01397 703593	Bed & Breakfast	★★★	
	Fordon		01397 772737	Self Catering	★★★	
	Fort William Backpackers	PH33 6HB	01397 700711	Backpacker	★★	
	Fort William Premier Inn	PH33 6AN	08701 977104	Budget Hotel		
	Gara-Ni	PH33 6BD	01397 701724	Bed & Breakfast	★★★	
	Glen Loy Lodge	PH33 7PD	01397 712700	Guest House	★★★	⌑⌑
	Glen Nevis Caravan and Camping Park	PH33 6SX	01397 702191	Holiday Park	★★★★★	
	Glen Nevis Lodges		01397 702191	Self Catering	★★★ to ★★★★	
	Glen Nevis Youth Hostel	PH33 6ST	01397 702336	Hostel	★★★	⌑⌑
	Glenaladale House	PH33 6RQ	01397 708609	Bed & Breakfast	★★★★	
	Glengyle	PH33 6PF	01397 708622	Bed & Breakfast	★★★★	
	Glengyle Holiday Home		01397 708622	Self Catering	★★★★	
	Glenlochy Guest House	PH33 6LP	01397 702909	Guest House	★★★	
	Glenshian	PH33 7LY	01397 772174	Bed & Breakfast	★★★★	
	Glentower Lower Observatory	PH33 6PQ	01397 704007	Guest House	★★★★	
	Gowan Brae	PH33 6RB	01397 704399	Bed & Breakfast	★★★	
	Great Glen Holiday Lets	PH33 7PB	01397 701633	Awaiting Grading		
	Guisachan Guest House	PH33 6HA	01397 703797	Guest House	★★★	
	Hawthorn		01343 811303	Self Catering	★★★	
	Highland Croft	PH33 6SD	01855 821557	Awaiting Grading		
	Highland Hotel	PH33 6QY	01397 707500	Hotel	★★★	
	Highland View Bed & Breakfast	PH33 6RY	01855 821555	Bed & Breakfast	★★★★	

♿ Unassisted wheelchair access   ♿ Assisted wheelchair access   ♀ Access for visitors with mobility difficulties
⌑ Bronze Green Tourism Award   ⌑⌑ Silver Green Tourism Award   ⌑⌑⌑ Gold Green Tourism Award
For further information on our Green Tourism Business Scheme please see page 7.

Advertisers' locations have been sorted by postcode. In Scotland, postcodes can cover fairly large geographical areas.
Please check distance of property from specified location with the individual provider. VisitScotland cannot take any responsibility for this.

399

Directory of all VisitScotland Assured Serviced Establishments, ordered by location.
Establishments highlighted have an advertisement in this guide.

Location	Property Name	Postcode	Telephone	Classification	Star Rating	
Fort William	Huntingtower Lodge	PH33 6RP	01397 700079	Bed & Breakfast	★★★★	𝒫𝒫
	Innishfree	PH33 7NX	01397 705471	Bed & Breakfast	★★★★	
	Inverlochy Castle Hotel	PH33 6SN	01397 702177	Country House Hotel	★★★★★	
	Keirlee	PH33 6JF	01397 702803	Bed & Breakfast	★★	
	Kerrera, Lismore & Shuna		07515 580442	Self Catering	★★★ to ★★★★	
	Kildonan	PH33 7JH	01397 772872	Bed & Breakfast	★★★	
	Kilmallie Chalet		01397 772459	Self Catering	★★★	
	Kingairloch House		01967 411242	Self Catering	★★★ to ★★★★★	
	Kintail	PH33 6RJ	01397 701025	Bed & Breakfast	★★★★	
	Langall Cottage		01855 821534	Self Catering	★★★★	𝒫𝒫𝒫
	Lawriestone Guest House	PH33 6RQ	01397 700777	Bed & Breakfast	★★★★	
	Leasona B & B	PH33 6SW	01397 704661	Bed & Breakfast	★★★★	
	Lime Tree An Ealdhain	PH33 6RQ	01397 701806	Small Hotel	★★★	
	Linnhe Lochside Holidays	PH33 7NL	01397 772376	Holiday Park	★★★★★	
	Linnhe Lochside Holidays – Locheil Chalets		01397 772376	Self Catering	★★★ to ★★★★	𝒫𝒫
	Loch Leven Chalets		01855 821272	Self Catering	★★★	
	Loch View		01397 772808	Self Catering	★★★★	
	Lochaber Lodges – Islay, Iona & Tiree		07599 288248	Self Catering	★★★★	
	Lochan Cottage Guest House	PH33 7NX	01397 702695	Guest House	★★★★	⅋
	Lochview		01397 703149	Self Catering	★★★	
	Lochview House	PH33 6RE	01397 703149	Guest House	★★★	
	Lochy Caravan Park	PH33 7NF	01397 703446	Holiday Park	★★★★	
	Lonavla		01397 702600	Self Catering	★★★★	
	Maclean House & Campbell House		01397 713815	Self Catering	★★★★	
	Mansefield Guest House	PH33 7LT	01397 772262	Guest House	★★★★	
	Mayfield	PH33 6SN	01397 703320	Bed & Breakfast	★★★★	
	Melantee	PH33 6RW	01397 705329	Bed & Breakfast	★★	
	Mount Alexander		01397 704466	Self Catering	★★★	
	Number 81	PH33 6HF	01397 703759	Bed & Breakfast	★★	
	Old Blar Cottages		01397 708998	Self Catering	★★★★	
	Quaich Cottage	PH33 7PB	01397 772799	Bed & Breakfast	★★★★	
	Rhiw Goch	PH33 7LY	01397 772373	Bed & Breakfast	★★★	
	Ronaval	PH33 7LX	01397 772206	Bed & Breakfast	★★★	
	Rustic View	PH33 7NX	01397 704709	Bed & Breakfast	★★★★	
	Seafield House	PH33 6RJ	01379 700045	Awaiting Grading		
	Seangan Self Catering		0141 5890014	Self Catering	★★★	
	Smirisary		01397 702918	Self Catering	★	
	Snowgoose Holidays		01397 772467	Self Catering	★★★	
	South Ferry View		01324 554455	Self Catering	★★★★	
	St Anthonys	PH33 6LF	01397 708496	Bed & Breakfast	★★★	
	Stobahn	PH33 6BD	01397 702790	Guest House	★★★	
	Strathavon	PH33 6JF	01397 705033	Bed & Breakfast	★★★	
	Stronchreggan View Guest House	PH33 6RW	01397 704644	Guest House	★★★	
	Taigh Nan Chleirich		01397 702444	Self Catering	★★★	
	Taormina	PH33 7LY	01397 772217	Bed & Breakfast	★	
	Taransay	PH33 6RJ	01397 703964	Bed & Breakfast	★★★★	
	The Barn		01397 772227	Self Catering	★★★ to ★★★★	
	The Gantocks	PH33 6RN	01397 702050	Bed & Breakfast	★★★★★	

 ♿ Unassisted wheelchair access   Assisted wheelchair access   ♱ Access for visitors with mobility difficulties
𝒫 Bronze Green Tourism Award   𝒫𝒫 Silver Green Tourism Award   𝒫𝒫𝒫 Gold Green Tourism Award
For further information on our Green Tourism Business Scheme please see page 7.

Location	Property Name	Postcode	Telephone	Classification	Star Rating
Fort William	The Grange	PH33 6JF	01397 705516	Bed & Breakfast	★★★★★
	The Imperial Hotel	PH33 6DW	01397 702040	Hotel	★★★
	The Inn at Ardgour	PH33 7AA	01855 841225	Inn	★★★
	The Loch Keepers Cottage		0113 2781638	Self Catering	★★★
	The Lodge on the Loch Hotel	PH33 6RY	01855 821237	Small Hotel	★★★
	The Logs		01397 702532	Self Catering	★★★★
	The Moorings Hotel	PH33 7LY	01397 772797	Hotel	★★★
	The Neuk	PH33 7LR	01397 772244	Bed & Breakfast	★★★
	The Old Post House	PH33 7PZ	01397 773752	Awaiting Grading	
	The Old Schoolhouse		01397 703690	Self Catering	★★★
	The Smiddy Bunkhouse and Blacksmiths Backpackers L	PH33 7JH	01397 772467	Bunkhouse	
	The Snuggle Bug		01397 704813	Self Catering	★★★ to ★★★★
	The Steadings B & B	PH33 7AE	01967 411242	Awaiting Grading	
	The White House		01397 705310	Self Catering	★★★
	The Woolly Rock Bed & Breakfast	PH33 6SA	01855 821338	Bed & Breakfast	★★★
	Thistle Cottage	PH33 6SN	01397 702428	Bed & Breakfast	★★★
	Tigh Na Faigh	PH33 6RN	01397 702079	Bed & Breakfast	★★★★
	Tigh-A-Phuirt Holiday Cottages		01397 704610	Self Catering	★★★★
	Tom-na-Creige	PH33 6RY	01855 821547	Bed & Breakfast	★★★
	Torlinnhe Guest House	PH33 6RN	01397 702583	Guest House	★★★
	Torosay		01217 105832	Self Catering	★★★
	Treetops	PH33 7LX	01397 772496	Bed & Breakfast	★★★★
	Viewfield	PH33 6HD	01397 704763	Guest House	★★
	Voringfoss	PH33 6UW	01397 704062	Bed & Breakfast	★★★★
	West End Hotel	PH33 6ED	01397 702614	Hotel	★★
	Whinbrae Cottage		01397 703743	Self Catering	★★★
	Woodside	PH33 6SP	01397 705897	Bed & Breakfast	★★★
Fortrose	17 Marine Terrace	IV10 8UL	01381 620884	Awaiting Grading	
	East Cottage/West Cottage		01381 620946	Self Catering	★★★ to ★★★★
	Fuchsia Cottage		0121 3537750	Self Catering	★★★
	Flowerburn House Holiday Homes		01381 621069	Self Catering	★★★
	Hillhaven	IV10 8RA	01381 620826	Bed & Breakfast	★★★★
	Juniper and Rowan		01381 621184	Self Catering	★★★ to ★★★★
	Rosemarkie Camping & Caravanning Club Site	IV10 8SE	02476 475318	Touring Park	★★★★
	The Byre		01381 620367	Self Catering	★★★
	Waters Edge	IV10 8TT	01381 621202	Bed & Breakfast	★★★★★
			01381 621069	Self Catering	★★★
Fraserburgh	B&B at the Shoppe	AB43 6LD	01346 561214	Awaiting Grading	
	Cairness House	AB43 8XP	01346 582078	Awaiting Grading	
	Cortes House		0207 7948114	Self Catering	★★★★
	Esplanade Caravan Park	AB43 5EU	01346 510041	Holiday Park	★★★
	Fisherman's Cottage		07855 802164	Self Catering	★★★★
	Lonmay Old Manse	AB43 8UJ	01346 532227	Bed & Breakfast	★★★★★
	Newseat		01346 541231	Self Catering	★ to ★★★
	Rosehearty Caravan Park	AB43 7JQ	01467 627622	Touring Park	★★
	The Tufted Duck Hotel	AB43 8ZS	01346 582481	Small Hotel	★★★

Advertisers' locations have been sorted by postcode. In Scotland, postcodes can cover fairly large geographical areas.
Please check distance of property from specified location with the individual provider. VisitScotland cannot take any responsibility for this.

401

Location	Property Name	Postcode	Telephone	Classification	Star Rating	
Gairloch	30 Strath		01289 303197	Self Catering	★★★	
	Apronhill House		01445 741317	Self Catering	★★ *P350*	
	Ard Sheen		01445 741711	Self Catering	★★	
	Ardgrianach		01445 712417	Self Catering	★★	
	Ben Alligin		01445 741755	Self Catering	★★★	
	Cairns Cottage		07762 102760	Self Catering	★★★	
	Carn Dearg Youth Hostel	IV21 2DJ	0870 1553255	Hostel	★★★	𝓟𝓟
	Creag Mhor Chalets		01445 712388	Self Catering	★★★	
	Douglas Cottage		01463 871661	Self Catering	★★★	
	Freyja		01445 771225	Self Catering	★★★	
	Gairloch Caravan & Camping Park	IV21 2BX	01445 712373	Touring Park	★★★★	
	Gairloch Hotel	IV21 2BL	01942 823526	Hotel	★★★	
	Gairloch View B&B	IV21 2BN	01445 712666	Bed & Breakfast	★★★★	
	Heather Croft		01445 712084	Self Catering	★★★	
	Heatherdale	IV21 2AH	01445 712388	Bed & Breakfast	★★★★	
	Kerrysdale House	IV21 2AL	01445 712292	Bed & Breakfast	★★★★	𝓟𝓟
	Iochside		01445 712770	Self Catering	★★★★	
	Lochview	IV21 2DB	01445 712676	Bed & Breakfast	★★★	
	Millcroft Hotel	IV21 2BT	01445 712376	Small Hotel	★★	
	Millcroft Hotel Apartments		01445 712376	Self Catering	★★	
	Rona & Raasay		01445 771225	Self Catering	★★★★	
	Rua Reidh Lighthouse	IV21 2EA	01445 771263	Hostel	★★★★	𝓟𝓟𝓟
	Sands Caravan and Camping	IV21 2DL	01445 712152	Touring Park	★★★★	
	Sands Holiday House		01445 712152	Self Catering	★★★★	
	Shieldaig Lodge Hotel	IV21 2AW	01445 741250	Country House Hotel	★★★	
	Strathlene	IV21 2DB	01445 712170	Bed & Breakfast	★★★	
	The Croft		01903 767803	Self Catering	★★★	
	The Old Inn & The Highland Lodge	IV21 2BD	01445 712006	Small Hotel	★★★	
	Tigh Gael		01252 325119	Self Catering	★★★ to ★★★★	
	Tigh-na-Mhuillean		01505 614343	Self Catering	★★★	
	Tregurnow	IV21 2DB	01445 712116	Bed & Breakfast	★★★★	
	Willow Croft		01445 712448	Self Catering	★★★	℔
Galashiels	Craigielea	TD1 3JQ	01896 753838	Bed & Breakfast	★★★	
	Ettrickvale	TD1 3HW	01896 755224	Bed & Breakfast	★★★	♠
	Monorene	TD1 1BY	01896 753073	Guest House	★★★	
	No 9 Galabank Cottages		01578 730289	Self Catering	★★★★	
	Sunnybrae B&B	TD1 2HZ	01896 758042	Bed & Breakfast	★★★	
	The Coach House		01896 753426	Self Catering	★★★★★	
	Watson Lodge Guest House	TD1 1SW	01896 751630	Guest House	★★★	
Galston	4 Sornhill Cottages		07841 214164	Self Catering	★★★	
Garve	Aultguish Inn	IV23 2PQ	01997 455254	Awaiting Grading		
	Aultguish Inn Bunk House	IV23 2PQ	01997 455254	Awaiting Grading		
	Badrallach Bothy	IV23 2QP	01854 633281	Bothy		𝓟
	Badrallach Bothy & Camp Site	IV23 2QP	01854 633281	Touring Park	★★★★	𝓟
	Badrallach DB&B, Bothy, Cottage & Camping Site		01854 633281	Self Catering	★★★★	𝓟𝓟
	Birch Cottage	IV23 2PS	01997 414237	Bed & Breakfast	★★★	

♿ Unassisted wheelchair access   ℔ Assisted wheelchair access   ♠ Access for visitors with mobility difficulties
𝓟 Bronze Green Tourism Award   𝓟𝓟 Silver Green Tourism Award   𝓟𝓟𝓟 Gold Green Tourism Award
For further information on our Green Tourism Business Scheme please see page 7.

Directory of all VisitScotland Assured Serviced Establishments, ordered by location.

Establishments highlighted have an advertisement in this guide.

Location	Property Name	Postcode	Telephone	Classification	Star Rating	
Garve	Braemore Square Country House		01854 655357	Self Catering	★★★★	🍃🍃
	Broomview		01854 633269	Self Catering	★★★★	
	Clachan Garden Lodge		01854 655201	Self Catering	★★★★	🍃
	Drovers Rest		01977 414384	Self Catering	★★★★	
	Heathmount		01522 539354	Self Catering	★★★★	
	Inchbae Lodge	IV23 2PH	01997 455269	Guest House	★★	
	Inverbroom Estate/Lodge		02075 927660	Self Catering	★★★	
	Leckmelm House		01854 612471	Self Catering	★★★	🍃🍃🍃
	Rhiroy Holiday Bungalow		01854 655229	Self Catering	★★★★	
	Sail Mhor Croft Hostel	IV23 2QT	01854 633224	Hostel	★★★	
	Sail Mhor View		01789 204355	Self Catering	★★★	
	Taigh a'Braoin		01560 484003	Self Catering	★★★★	🚶
	The Peatcutter's Croft	IV23 2QP	01854 633797	Bed & Breakfast	★★★	
	Tigh-na-Mara & Ceol-na-Mara		01854 633237	Self Catering	★★★	
Girvan	7D Wilson Street		01848 500268	Self Catering	★★★	
	Ailsa View		01416 461551	Self Catering	★★★★	
	Ardwell Farm	KA26 0HP	01465 713389	Farm House	★★	
	Auchenflower Cottage		01465 831077	Self Catering	★★★	
	Ballantrae Holiday Park	KA26 0LL	01581 500227	Awaiting Grading		
	Balnowlart Lodge		01465 831343	Self Catering	★★★	
	Bank Cottage		07901 551887	Self Catering	★★	
	Barrhill Holiday Park	KA26 0PZ	01465 821355	Holiday Park	★★★★	
	Bennane Shore Holiday Park	KA26 0JG	01465 891233	Holiday Park	★★★★★	
	Carlenrig Cottage		01465 881265	Self Catering	★★★ to ★★★★	
	Cosses Country House	KA26 0LR	01465 831363	Bed & Breakfast	★★★★★	
	Dalreoch Cottage		01256 882694	Self Catering	★★★	
	Downanhill Cottage		01465 831368	Self Catering	★★★	🚶
	Gladneuk Cottage		01465 861271	Self Catering	★★★	
	Glenapp Castle	KA26 0NZ	01465 831212	Hotel	★★★★★	♿
	Glengennet Cottage		01465 861220	Self Catering	★★ to ★★★★	
	Kilpatrick Farm Cottage	KA26 0TW	01465 841209	Awaiting Grading		
	Kings Arms Hotel	KA26 0NB	01465 831202	Inn	★★	
	Kirkholm		01316 676323	Self Catering	★★★	
	Links Lodge	KA26 9LS	01655 331546	Bed & Breakfast	★★★★	
	Malin Court Hotel & Restaurant	KA26 9PB	01655 331457	Hotel	★★★	🍃
	Milton Wynd Flat 1B & 1C	KA26 9LG	0141 6385760	Awaiting Grading		
	Pinclanty Mill	01465 841219		Self Catering	★★★★	
	Queensland Holiday Park	KA26 0PZ	01465 821364	Holiday Park	★★★★	
	Southfield Hotel	KA26 9DS	01465 714222	Small Hotel	★★	
	The Haven	KA26 0NA	01465 831306	Bed & Breakfast	★★★	
	The Westin Turnberry Resort	KA26 9LT	01655 331000	Hotel	★★★★★	♿
	Turnberry Holiday Park	KA26 9JW	01655 331288	Holiday Park	★★★	
	Woodland Bay Hotel	KA26 0HP	01465 710700	Small Hotel	★★★	
			01465 841219	Self Catering	★★★★	
Glasgow	1 Gartcarron		01943 601729	Self Catering	★★★	
	4 Mount Pleasant Drive		01389 876903	Self Catering	★★	
	8 Sydenham Road		0141 3390008	Self Catering	★★★	

♿ Unassisted wheelchair access   ♿ Assisted wheelchair access   🚶 Access for visitors with mobility difficulties
🍃 Bronze Green Tourism Award   🍃🍃 Silver Green Tourism Award   🍃🍃🍃 Gold Green Tourism Award
For further information on our Green Tourism Business Scheme please see page 7.

Advertisers' locations have been sorted by postcode. In Scotland, postcodes can cover fairly large geographical areas.
Please check distance of property from specified location with the individual provider. VisitScotland cannot take any responsibility for this.

403

Location	Property Name	Postcode	Telephone	Classification	Star Rating	
Glasgow	964 Sauchiehall St			Self Catering	★★★★	
	ABode Glasgow Ltd	G2 2SZ	0141 2216789	Hotel	★★★	
	Acorn Hotel	G3 7AW	0141 3326556	Metro Hotel	★★★★	
	Adelaide's Guest House	G2 4HZ	01412 484970	Guest House	★★	
	Albion Hotel	G20 6NN	0141 3398620	Metro Hotel	★★★	
	Alison Guest House	G31 2JH	0141 5561431	Guest House	★★	
	Allanfauld Farm	G65 9DF	01236 822155	Farm House	★★★	
	Amadeus Guest House	G20 6NN	0141 3398257	Guest House	★★	
	Ambassador Hotel	G20 8QG	0141 9461018	Metro Hotel	★★★	
	Anchorage Cottage	G63 0AW	01360 870394	Bed & Breakfast	★★★★	
	Argyll Guest House	G3 7TH	0141 3575155	Lodge	★★★	
	Argyll Hotel	G3 7TQ	0141 3373313	Hotel	★★★	
	Artto Hotel	G2 6AE	0141 2482480	Awaiting Grading		
	Auchenhowe Cottage B&B	G62 6EL	0141 9564003	Bed & Breakfast	★★★	
	Auchenlea	G69 7RT	0141 7716870	Guest House	★★★	
	Ballat Smithy Cottage		01360 440269	Self Catering	★★★★	PP
	Ballochruin Farm	G63 0LE	01360 440496	Bed & Breakfast	★★★★	
	Balmaha Bunk House	G63 0JQ	01360 870218	Awaiting Grading		
	Bankell Farm Cottage		0141 9564643	Self Catering	★★★	
	Belgrave Guest House	G12 8JD	0141 3371850	Guest House	★★★	
	Benview Holiday Lodges		01360 850001	Self Catering	★★★	
	Best Foot Forward @ West View	G62 6HS	0141 9563046	Bed & Breakfast	★★★	
	Blythswood Square	G2 4AD	0141 2488888	Awaiting Grading		
	Boswell Apartment		0141 5854310	Self Catering	★★★★	
	Botanic Hotel	G12 8RF	0141 3398620	Guest House	★★★	
	Bothwell Bridge Hotel	G71 8EU	01698 852246	Hotel	★★★	
	Braeside	G63 0BP	01360 660989	Awaiting Grading		
	Bridgend Farm	G66 1RT	0141 7761607	Farm House	★★★	
	Bunkum Backpackers	G12 8PY	0141 5814481	Hostel	★★	
	Burnside Hotel	G73 5EA	0141 6341276	Small Hotel	★★	
	Busby Hotel	G76 8RX	0141 6442661	Hotel	★★	
	Cairncross House	G3 8NH	0141 3305385	Hostel	★★★	ⓖ PP
	Caledonian Court	G4 0JF	0141 3313979	Campus	★	
	Campanile Glasgow	G3 8HL	0141 2877700	Hotel	★★★	ⓖ
	Campsie View		01360 660008	Self Catering	★★★	
	Carlton George Hotel	G2 1DH	0141 3536373	Hotel	★★★★	♿
	Cashel Caravan & Campsite	G63 0AW	01283 228607	Touring Park	★★★★	
	Castlecary House Hotel	G68 0HD	01324 840233	Hotel	★★★	♄
	City Apartments		0141 7795868	Self Catering	★★★★	
	City Inn Glasgow	G3 8HN	0141 2401002	Hotel	★★★	P
	City Slicker Apartment		0141 5792360	Self Catering	★★★★	
	Claremont House	G31 2JE	0141 5547312	Bed & Breakfast	★★★	
	Clifton Hotel	G12 8ED	0141 3348080	Guest House	★★	
	Cottage A – East Rogerton		01355 263176	Self Catering	★★★ to ★★★★	
	Craigendmuir Park	G33 6AF	0141 7792973	Holiday Park	★★★	
	Craigielea House	G31 2HY	0141 5543446	Bed & Breakfast	★★	
	Craigpark Guest House	G31 2JG	0141 5544160	Guest House	★★	
	Croftburn Bed & Breakfast	G63 0HA	01360 660796	Bed & Breakfast	★★★	PP

♿ Unassisted wheelchair access ⓖ Assisted wheelchair access ♄ Access for visitors with mobility difficulties
P Bronze Green Tourism Award PP Silver Green Tourism Award PPP Gold Green Tourism Award
For further information on our Green Tourism Business Scheme please see page 7.

404 To find out more go to visitscotland.com

Location	Property Name	Postcode	Telephone	Classification	Star Rating		
Glasgow	Crowne Plaza Hotel	G3 8QT	0870 4431691	Hotel	★★★★	♿	ⓟ
	Crowwood House Hotel	G69 9BJ	0141 7793861	Hotel	★★★		
	Crutherland House Hotel	G75 0QJ	01355 577000	Hotel	★★★★		
	Dalmeny Park Country House Hotel and Gardens	G78 1LG	0141 8819214	Country House Hotel	★★★★		
	Devoncove Hotel	G3 7TQ	0141 3344000	Hotel	★★		
	Drymen Holiday Apartment		01360 660105	Self Catering	★★★★		
	Dubh Loch Cottage		01506 845353	Self Catering	★★★★		
	Dunard Guest House	G72 8PW	0141 6416577	Guest House	★★		
	East Rogerton Lodge	G74 4NZ	01355 263176	Bed & Breakfast	★★		
	Elmbank	G63 0BN	01360 661016	Bed & Breakfast	★★		
	Elmbank		01360 661016	Self Catering	★★★		
	Euro Hostels	G1 4NR	0141 2222828	Hostel	★★★		
	Express by Holiday Inn	G1 2RL	0141 3316800	Metro Hotel	★★★	♿	ⓟ
	Express by Holiday Inn Glasgow	G1 4LT	01415 485000	Metro Hotel	★★★		
	Firfield		01360 550508	Self Catering	★★★		
	Flat 2		07724 428810	Self Catering	★★★★		
	Flat 3		01436 676016	Self Catering	★★★		
	Flat On The Green		07703 314428	Self Catering	★★★		
	Forbes Hall		0141 5534148	Self Catering	★		
	Foxglove Cottages		01360 661128	Self Catering	★★★★★	♿	ⓟⓟⓟ
	Fraser Suites Glasgow	G1 1LH	0141 5534288	Serviced Apartments	★★★★	♿	
	Garfield House Hotel	G33 6HW	01417 792111	Hotel	★★★		
	Glades	G42 8UF	0141 6392601	Hostel	★★★★		
	Glasgow Bearsden Premier Inn	G61 3TA	08709 906532	Budget Hotel			
	Glasgow Cambuslang Premier Inn	G32 8EY	08701 977306	Budget Hotel			
	Glasgow City Centre George Square Premier Inn	G1 1YU	0141 5547312	Budget Hotel			
	Glasgow City Centre Premier Inn (Argyle Street)	G2 4PP	08709 906312	Budget Hotel			ⓟ
	Glasgow City Centre(Charing Cross) Premier Inn	G2 4PP	08708 506358	Budget Hotel			
	Glasgow Cumbernauld Premier Inn	G67 1AX	08701 977108	Budget Hotel			
	Glasgow East Kilbride Central Premier Inn	G75 0JY	08701 977110	Budget Hotel			
	Glasgow East Kilbride Premier Inn (Nerston Toll)	G74 3AW	08708 506324	Budget Hotel			
	Glasgow East Kilbride Premier Inn (Peel Park)	G75 8LW	08709 906542	Budget Hotel			
	Glasgow East Premier Inn	G75 0JY	08701 977109	Budget Hotel			
	Glasgow Hilton	G3 8HT	0141 2045555	Hotel	★★★★★	♿	
	Glasgow Marriott	G3 8RR	0141 2265577	Hotel	★★★★	♿	
	Glasgow Milngavie Premier Inn	G62 6JJ	08701 977112	Budget Hotel			
	Glasgow North East Stepps Premier Inn	G33 6HN	08701 977111	Budget Hotel			
	Glasgow Pond Hotel	G12 0XP	08701 977111	Hotel	★★★		ⓟ
	Glasgow Riverside Apartments		0141 4154546	Self Catering	★★★★		
	Glasgow Youth Hostel	G3 6BY	0141 3323004	Hostel	★★★★		ⓟⓟ
	Glenalva	G63 0AA	01360 660491	Awaiting Grading			
	Green Shadows	G63 0HX	01360 660289	Bed & Breakfast	★★★★		

♿ Unassisted wheelchair access ♿ Assisted wheelchair access ♿ Access for visitors with mobility difficulties
ⓟ Bronze Green Tourism Award ⓟⓟ Silver Green Tourism Award ⓟⓟⓟ Gold Green Tourism Award
For further information on our Green Tourism Business Scheme please see page 7.

Advertisers' locations have been sorted by postcode. In Scotland, postcodes can cover fairly large geographical areas. Please check distance of property from specified location with the individual provider. VisitScotland cannot take any responsibility for this.

Location	Property Name	Postcode	Telephone	Classification	Star Rating		
Glasgow	Green Shadows	G63 0HX	01360 660289	Bed & Breakfast	★★★★		
	Hamilton Drive		0141 6418046	Self Catering	★★★		
	Hampton Court	G3 6TX	0141 3326623	Guest House	★★		
	High Craigton Farm	G62 7HA	01419 561384	Farm House	★★		
	Hillview	G63 0BL	01360 661000	Bed & Breakfast	★★★		
	Hilton Glasgow Grosvenor	G12 0TA	0141 3398811	Hotel	★★★★		
	Holiday Inn	G1 2RL	0141 3528300	Hotel	★★★★	♿	
	Holly House	G51 2TB	0141 275609	Bed & Breakfast	★★		
	Hotel Du Vin at One Devonshire Gardens	G12 0UX	0141 3392001	Town House Hotel	★★★★★		
	Ibis Hotel Glasgow	G2 4DQ	0141 2256000	Budget Hotel		♿	
	Inches		01360 771648	Self Catering	★★★★		
	Ivory Hotel	G41 3AY	0141 6360223	Small Hotel	★★		
	Jurys Inn Glasgow	G1 4QE	0141 3144800	Hotel	★★★	♿	🍃🍃🍃
	Kelvin Apartment		0141 3397143	Self Catering	★★★★		
	Kincaid House Hotel	G66 8BZ	0141 7762226	Small Hotel	★★★		
	Kings Park Hotel	G73 2LX	0141 6475491	Hotel	★★★		
	Laurel Bank 96 Strathblane Road	G62 8HD	0141 5849400	Bed & Breakfast	★★★		
	Loaninghead Farm	G63 0SE	01360 440432	Bed & Breakfast	★★★★		🍃🍃
	Loaninghead Farm Bothy		01360 440432	Self Catering	★★★★		🍃🍃
	Loch Lomond Chalet		01506 203433	Self Catering	★★★★		
	Loch Lomond Lodge		07974 427380	Self Catering	★★★★		
	Loch Lomond Waterfront		01360 870144	Self Catering	★★★★★		🍃
	Lodges 25 & 26		01360 660265	Self Catering	★★★★		
	Lomond Hotel	G12 8EB	01413 392339	Guest House	★★		
	Lomond Lodge	G63 0AR	01236 754075	Awaiting Grading			
	Lomond Luxury Lodges – Inchmurrin		01360 660054	Self Catering	★★★★ to ★★★★★		🍃🍃
	Lomond Mews 7		0141 3411155	Self Catering	★★ to ★★★		
	Manor Park Hotel	G11 7DD	0141 3392143	Guest House	★★★		
	Maple Cottage		01355 500214	Self Catering	★★★		
	Mar Achlais	G63 0JE	01360 870300	Bed & Breakfast	★★★		
	Margaret Macdonald House	G3 6QT	0141 3534507	Hostel	★★		🍃🍃
	Marks Hotel	G2 2EN	0141 3530800	Hotel	★★★	♿	
	McLays Guest House	G3 6TT	0141 3324796	Guest House	★		
	Melville Lodge		01236 722702	Self Catering	★★★★		
	Menteith/Blaine		01360 440496	Self Catering	★★★★		
	Menzies Glasgow	G3 8AZ	0141 2222929	Hotel	★★★★	♿	
	Milarrochy Bay Camping & Caravanning Club Site	G63 0AL	02476 475318	Touring Park	★★★★		
	Murano Street Student Village	G20 7SB	0141 9431424	Hostel	★★★		🍃🍃
	Murray Hall	G4 0NG	0141 5534148	Campus	★		
	Newton House Hotel	G2 4JW	0141 3321666	Guest House	★★★		
	No 38 Bath Street 5/4	G2 1HG	0113 2221234	Serviced Apartments	★★★★ to ★★★★★		
	Northwood Cottage	G63 0AW	01360 870351	Bed & Breakfast	★★		
	Novotel Glasgow Centre	G2 4DT	01412 222775	Hotel	★★★	♿	
	Oak Tree Inn	G63 0JQ	01360 870357	Inn	★★★		
	Oakbank B&B	G63 0EU	07747 181494	Bed & Breakfast	★★★★		
	Oldhall Cottages		01360 440136	Self Catering	★★★		
	Onslow Guest House	G31 2LX	0141 5546797	Guest House	★★★		

  ♿ Unassisted wheelchair access   ♿ Assisted wheelchair access   🚶 Access for visitors with mobility difficulties
🍃 Bronze Green Tourism Award   🍃🍃 Silver Green Tourism Award   🍃🍃🍃 Gold Green Tourism Award
For further information on our Green Tourism Business Scheme please see page 7.

406   To find out more go to visitscotland.com

Location	Property Name	Postcode	Telephone	Classification	Star Rating	
Glasgow	Overmains	G63 0HY	01360 660374	Bed & Breakfast	★★★★	
	Park Inn Glasgow City Centre	G2 3LB	0141 3335712	Hotel	★★★★	
	Premier Inn Glasgow City Centre South	G5 0TW	0870 4236452	Hotel	★★★	Unassisted wheelchair access
	Queen Margaret Hall	G12 0SQ	0141 3342192	Campus	★★	Assisted wheelchair access; Silver Green Tourism Award
	Queens Gate Apartment		0141 3391615	Self Catering	★★★ to ★★★★	
	Rab Ha's	G1 1SH	0141 7792973	Inn	★★	
	Radisson SAS Hotel Glasgow	G2 8DL	01412 043333	Hotel	★★★★★	Gold Green Tourism Award
	Redstones Bar Grill and Rooms	G71 7AS	01698 813774	Restaurant With Rooms	★★★★	
	Rowardennan Lodges		0191 4229581	Self Catering	★★★	
	Rowardennan Youth Hostel	G63 0AR	0870 0041148	Hostel	★★★	Assisted wheelchair access; Silver Green Tourism Award
	Saco House	G1 1HL	0845 1220405	Serviced Apartments	★★★★	
	Sandwood Lodge		0131 4469181	Self Catering	★★★★	
	Seton Guest House	G31 2HU	0141 5567654	Guest House	★★★	
	Sherbrooke Apartments		0141 5854310	Self Catering	★★★ to ★★★★	
	Sherbrooke Castle Hotel	G41 4PG	0141 4274227	Hotel	★★★★	
	Smiths Hotel	G66 1DD	01417750398	Hotel	★★★	
	Strathendrick House		0141 4046493	Self Catering	★★★★	
	Stronend Cottage		01786 870756	Self Catering	★★★★	
	Tambowie Farm	G62 7HD	0141 9561583	Bed & Breakfast	★★★	
	The Alamo Guest House Ltd	G3 7SE	0141 3392395	Guest House	★★★	
	The Balmaha		01389 850245	Self Catering	★★★	
	The Belhaven	G12 0TG	0141 3393222	Guest House	★★★	
	The Claremont Apartment	G3 7XR	0141 3331751	Awaiting Grading		
	The Coach House		0131 2439335	Self Catering	★★★	
	The Fullarton Park Hotel	G32 8HH	0141 7631027	Restaurant With Rooms	★★	
	The Guest Rooms at Matherton	G77 5EY	01416 398931	Bed & Breakfast	★★★	
	The Heritage	G12 8RF	0141 3313979	Guest House	★★★	
	The Kelvin	**G12 8EB**	**0141 3397143**	**Guest House**	**★★**	
	The Kelvingrove	G3 7TH	0141 3395011	Guest House	★★★	
	The Kirklee	G12 9LG	0141 3345555	Guest House	★★★	
	The Knowes		0141 7705213	Self Catering	★★★	Access for visitors with mobility difficulties
	The Lodge		01236 823249	Self Catering	★★★ to ★★★★	
	The Malmaison	G2 4LL	0141 5721000	Hotel	★★★★	
	The Merchant Lodge	G1 1TY	0141 5522424	Guest House	★★★	
	The Millennium Glasgow Hotel	G2 1DS	0141 3326711	Hotel	★★★★	
	The Old Schoolhouse		0141 4237353	Self Catering	★★★★★	
	The Piping Centre	G4 0HW	0141 3535551	Restaurant With Rooms	★★★	
	The Ramada Glasgow City	G1 1DQ	0141 2484401	Hotel	★★★	Access for visitors with mobility difficulties; Bronze Green Tourism Award
	The Sandyford	G3 7TF	0141 3340000	Lodge	★★★	
	The Stables & The Ploughmans Cottage		01360 440325	Self Catering	★★★★	Access for visitors with mobility difficulties
	The Townhouse Hotel	G3 7SL	0141 332 9009	Lodge	★★	
	The Willow	G3 6TX	0141 3322332	Guest House	★★	
	Thistle Glasgow	G2 3HN	0141 3323311	Hotel	★★★★	
	Torrance Hotel	G74 4LN	01355 225241	Small Hotel	★★	
	Townhouse Restaurants	G65 9SG	01236 829201	Restaurant With Rooms	★★★★	Assisted wheelchair access

Unassisted wheelchair access · Assisted wheelchair access · Access for visitors with mobility difficulties
Bronze Green Tourism Award · Silver Green Tourism Award · Gold Green Tourism Award
For further information on our Green Tourism Business Scheme please see page 7.

Directory of all VisitScotland Assured Serviced Establishments, ordered by location.
Establishments highlighted have an advertisement in this guide.

Location	Property Name	Postcode	Telephone	Classification	Star Rating		
Glasgow	Travelodge Glasgow/Paisley Road	G5 8RA	0141 4203882	Budget Hotel			
	Travelodge Glasgow Central	G3 6RP	0141 3331515	Budget Hotel			
	Tullycross Cottage		01360 661124	Self Catering	★★★		
	Twechar Farm B&B	G65 9LH	01236 823216	Farm House	★★★		
	University of Strathclyde	G4 0NG	0141 5534148	Campus	★		
	Uplawmoor Hotel	G78 4AF	01505 850565	Small Hotel	★★★		𝒫𝒫
	Upper flat		0141 6372415	Self Catering	★★★★		
	Westerwood Hotel	G68 0EW	01236 457171	Hotel	★★★★		𝒫𝒫
	White House Apartments – Apartment 18		01417 792111	Self Catering	★★★ to ★★★★		
	Winnock Hotel	G63 0BL	01360 660245	Hotel	★★★	♿	𝒫𝒫
	Wolfson Hall	G20 0TH	0141 3303773	Campus	★	♿	𝒫𝒫
Glenfinnan	Glenfinnan Cottages		01397 722234	Self Catering	★★		
	Glenfinnan Sleeping Car	PH37 4LT	01397 722295	Bunkhouse			
	The Prince's House Hotel	PH37 4LT	01397 722246	Small Hotel	★★★		𝒫𝒫
Glenrothes	Priory Star B&B	KY7 6LQ	01592 754566	Bed & Breakfast	★★★★		
	Balbirnie House Hotel	KY7 6NE	01592 610066	Country House Hotel	★★★★	♿	
	Balbirnie Park Caravan Club Site	KY7 6NR	01342 336842	Touring Park	★★★★		
	Balgeddie House Hotel	KY6 3ET	01592 742511	Hotel	★★★		
	Creg-Ny-Baa		0131 3314753	Self Catering	★★★		
	Cruach Bed & Breakfast	KY7 6ED	01592 751093	Bed & Breakfast	★★★		
	Express by Holiday Inn	KY7 6XX	01592 745509	Metro Hotel	★★★		
	Glenrothes Premier Inn	KY7 4UJ	08701 977114	Budget Hotel			
	Greenhead of Arnot	KY6 3JQ	01592 840459	Bed & Breakfast	★★★★		
	Kingdom Caravan Park	KY6 2NG	01592 772226	Holiday Park	★★★★★		
	Laurel Bank Hotel	KY7 6DB	01592 611205	Inn	★★★		
	Shythrum Farm	KY7 6HB	01592 758372	Bed & Breakfast	★★★		
	The Gilvenbank Hotel	KY7 6RA	01592 742077	Hotel	★★★		
	Town House Hotel	KY7 6DQ	01592 758459	Restaurant With Rooms	★★★★		
	Travelodge Glenrothes	KY7 6GH	08719 846278	Budget Hotel			
	Big Barns Cottage		01406 633332	Self Catering	★★★★		
Golspie	The Golf Links Hotel	KW10 6TT	01408 633408	Small Hotel	★★		
	The Log Cabin		01557 814058	Self Catering	★★		
Gorebridge	Ivory House	EH23 4HH	01875 820755	Guest House	★★★★	♿	
Gourock	Bed & Breakfast Castle Levan	PA19 1AH	01475 659154	Bed & Breakfast	★★★		
	Berghaus	PA19 1JA	01475 634550	Bed & Breakfast	★★★		
	Spinnaker Hotel	PA19 1BU	01475 633107	Inn	★★		🧍
Grangemouth	Grangeburn House	FK3 9BJ	01324 471301	Guest House	★★★★		
	Leapark Hotel	FK3 9BX	01324 486733	Hotel	★★★	♿	
	The Grange Manor	FK3 8XJ	01324 474836	Hotel	★★★★		
Grantown-on-Spey	11 The Square		07973 326505	Self Catering	★★★		
	6 Wood Park		07834 355491	Self Catering	★★★		
	An Cala Guest House	PH26 3JU	01479 873293	Guest House	★★★★★		𝒫𝒫
	Ardenbeg Outdoor Centre	PH26 3LD	01479 872824	Hostel	★★★		
	Auchnagonalin House		01381 610496	Self Catering	★★★		

♿ Unassisted wheelchair access   ♿ Assisted wheelchair access   🧍 Access for visitors with mobility difficulties
🄿 Bronze Green Tourism Award   𝒫𝒫 Silver Green Tourism Award   𝒫𝒫𝒫 Gold Green Tourism Award
For further information on our Green Tourism Business Scheme please see page 7.

To find out more go to visitscotland.com

Location	Property Name	Postcode	Telephone	Classification	Star Rating	
Grantown-on-Spey	Balliefurth Farm	PH26 3NH	01479 821636	Farm House	★★★	🍃🍃🍃
	Bellbec	PH26 3NP	01479 873810	Bed & Breakfast	★★★★	
	Ben Mhor Hotel	PH26 3EG	01479 872056	Hotel	★★★	
	Birchbank		01479 872093	Self Catering	★★★ to ★★★★	
	Brooklynn	PH26 3LA	01479 873113	Guest House	★★★★	
	Cedar Cottage		01475 632830	Self Catering	★★★	
	Craggan Bunkhouse and Bothy	PH26 3NT	01479 873283	Activity Accommodation	★★	
	Craiglynne Hotel	PH26 3JX	01479 872597	Hotel	★★★	🚶
	Craignay		01339 742278	Self Catering	★★★	
	Culdearn House	PH26 3JU	01479 872106	Small Hotel	★★★★	
	Dulnain House		01479 851359	Self Catering	★★★★	
	Dunallan House	PH26 3JN	01479 872140	Guest House	★★★★	
	Easter Duiar Cottage		01620 829488	Self Catering	★★★★	
	Eden House	PH26 3LW	01479 872112	Bed & Breakfast	★★★★	
	Failte		0131 66 6447	Self Catering	★★ to ★★★	
	Fiathail House		01738 624788	Self Catering	★★★★	
	Garth Hotel	PH26 3HN	01479 872836	Small Hotel	★★★	
	Grianan		01479 821636	Self Catering	★★★	🍃🍃
	Kinross Guest House	PH26 3JR	01479 872042	Guest House	★★★★	
	Lanson		01479 851314	Self Catering	★★★	
	Lower Lynemore Croft		01479 872898	Self Catering	★★★	
	Muckrach Castle		01738 477504	Self Catering	★★★★	
	Netherfield B&B	PH26 3PA	01479 851258	Bed & Breakfast	★★★★	
	Old Rectory Cottage		0191 2345222	Self Catering	★★★★	
	Parkburn Guest House	PH26 3EN	01479 873116	Guest House	★★★	
	Ravenscourt House Hotel	PH26 3JG	01479 872286	Small Hotel	★★★★	
	Rosegrove Guest House	PH26 3PA	01479 851335	Guest House	★★★	
	Rossmor Guest House	PH26 3JU	01479 872201	Guest House	★★★★	
	Seafield Lodge Hotel	PH26 3JN	01479 872152	Small Hotel	★★★	
	The Cabrach		01479 851229	Self Catering	★★★★	
	The Dulaig	PH26 3JF	01479 872065	Bed & Breakfast	★★★★★	
	The Pines	PH26 3JR	01479 872092	Guest Accommodation	★★★★★	
	The Strathspey Lodge	PH26 3JA	01382 360648	Awaiting Grading		
	Top Cottage		01334 850 781	Self Catering	★★★	
	West Gorton		01479 872120	Self Catering	★★★	
	Westhaven	PH26 3HZ	01479 872471	Bed & Breakfast	★★★★	
	Willowbank	PH26 3EN	01479 872089	Guest House	★★★	🚶
Greenock	Denholm B&B	PA16 8RJ	01475 781319	Bed & Breakfast	★★	
	Express by Holiday Inn	PA15 4RT	01475 786666	Metro Hotel	★★★	♿
	Glen Brae House		01475 529713	Self Catering	★★★	
	Greenock Premier Inn	PA15 2AJ	01475 730911	Budget Hotel		
	Heather Bed and Breakfast	PA16 8RJ	01475 724002	Bed & Breakfast	★★	
	Inverkip Hotel	PA16 0AS	01475 521478	Inn	★★★	🍃🍃
	James Watt College	PA15 1EN	01475 731360	Campus	★★	♿
	James Watt College			Self Catering	★★	
	Tontine Hotel	PA16 8NG	01475 723316	Hotel	★★★	🚶

Advertisers' locations have been sorted by postcode. In Scotland, postcodes can cover fairly large geographical areas.
Please check distance of property from specified location with the individual provider. VisitScotland cannot take any responsibility for this.

409

Location	Property Name	Postcode	Telephone	Classification	Star Rating		
Gretna	9 Lammerview Terrace		01620 843288	Self Catering	★★		
	Alexander House	DG16 5DU	01461 337056	Guest House	★★★		
	Angus House	DG16 5AF	01461 337533	Bed & Breakfast	★★★		
	Anvil View Guest House	DG16 5EA	01461 338183	Bed & Breakfast	★★		
	Ardurned Guest House	DG16 5EH	01461 338077	Bed & Breakfast	★★★		
	Barrasgate House	DG16 5HU	01461 337577	Bed & Breakfast	★★★		
	Bojangles Guest House	DG16 5DN	01461 338291	Guest House	★★★★		
	Braids Caravan Park	DG16 5DG	01461 337409	Touring Park	★★★★		
	Golf Cottage		01620 842809	Self Catering	★★★★		
	Hunters Lodge Hotel	DG16 5DL	01461 338214	Small Hotel	★★★		♿
	Jadini Garden	EH31 2BA	01620 843343	Bed & Breakfast	★★★		
	Kellagher B&B	EH31 2DT	01620 843348	Bed & Breakfast	★★★★		
	Kilmory	EH31 2AZ	01620 842332	Bed & Breakfast	★★★		
	Kirkcroft	DG16 5DU	01461 337403	Bed & Breakfast	★★★		
	Mallard Hotel	EH31 2AF	01620 843288	Small Hotel	★★		
	Marie Cottage		0131 5515846	Self Catering	★★★		
	Rhone Villa	DG16 5DY	01461 338889	Bed & Breakfast	★★★		♦
	Smiths @ Gretna Green	DG16 5EA	0845 3676768	Hotel	★★★★	♿	🟩🟩
	Solway Lodge Hotel	DG16	01461 338266	Small Hotel	★★★		
	Tern Cottage		01620 893204	Self Catering	★★★★		
	The Bield		01620 861803	Self Catering	★★★ to ★★★★		
	The Garden House Hotel	DG16 5EP	01461 337621	Hotel	★★★	♿	
	The Willows	DG16 5ES	01461 337996	Bed & Breakfast	★★★		♿
Haddington	Carfrae	EH41 4LP	01620 830242	Bed & Breakfast	★★★★		
	Eaglescairnie Mains	EH41 4HN	01620 810491	Farm House	★★★★		🟩🟩
	Greeenfield Bed and Breakfast	EH41 4NW	01620 822458	Bed & Breakfast	★★★		
	Lennoxlove House	EH41 4NZ	01620 828619	Exclusive Use Venue	★★★★★		
	Letham House	EH41 3SS	01620 820055	Guest House	★★★★★		
	Maitlandfield House Hotel	EH41 4BZ	01620 826513	Hotel	★★★	♿	
	No 1 Goodalls Place		07817 435022	Self Catering	★★★★		
	Old Farmhouse B&B	EH41 4JN	01620 810406	Farm House	★★★★		
	Orchard House	EH41 4HB	01620 824898	Bed & Breakfast	★★★		
	The Arches		01620 810476	Self Catering	★★★★		
	The Avenue Restaurant	EH41 3JD	01620 823332	Awaiting Grading			
	The Cottage		01620 810406	Self Catering	★★★		
	The Farmhouse	EH41 4HW	01620 810676	Farm House	★★		
	The Old Bakehouse		01620 830683	Self Catering	★★★		
	The Woodturner's Cottage		01620 810131	Self Catering	★★★★		
	Tyrone Cottage		01620 810378	Self Catering	★★★		
Halkirk	Ulbster Arms Hotel	KW12 6XY	01847 831641	Small Hotel	★★★		
	Upper Clayock Cottage		0208 27666163	Self Catering	★★★		
Hamilton	Avonbridge Hotel	ML3 7DG	01698 420525	Hotel	★★★		
	Avonclyde	ML3 7UL	01698 422917	Bed & Breakfast	★★★		
	Flat – 60 Miller Street		01698 825169	Self Catering	★★★ to ★★★★		
	Glasgow Hamilton Premier Inn	ML3 6JW	08701 977124	Budget Hotel			
	The Villa Hotel	ML3 9AQ	01698 891777	Small Hotel	★★★		

♿ Unassisted wheelchair access   ♿ Assisted wheelchair access   ♦ Access for visitors with mobility difficulties
🟩 Bronze Green Tourism Award   🟩🟩 Silver Green Tourism Award   🟩🟩🟩 Gold Green Tourism Award
For further information on our Green Tourism Business Scheme please see page 7.

Location	Property Name	Postcode	Telephone	Classification	Star Rating	
Hawick	Auld Cross Keys Inn	TD9 8NU	01450 870305	Awaiting Grading		
	Billerwell Farm	TD9 8JF	01450 860656	Farm House	★★★★	🍏🍏
	Dunrovin		01450 870466	Self Catering	★★★	🚶
	Gardeners Cottage		08445 616887	Self Catering	★★★ to ★★★★	
	Granary & Stable		01450 870422	Self Catering	★★★★	
	Hopehill House	TD9 7EH	01450 375042	Bed & Breakfast	★★★	
	Hoscote House		08445 616887	Self Catering	★★★★★	
	Jo's Cottage		01450 860656	Self Catering	★★★★	🚶 🍏
	Kirkton Farmhouse	TD9 8QJ	01450 363464	Bed & Breakfast	★★★★	
	Lux B&B	TD9 9QR	01450 363393	Awaiting Grading		
	Mansfield House Hotel	TD9 8LB	01450 360400	Awaiting Grading		
	Rosemount	TD9 9PQ	01450 375405	Bed & Breakfast	★★★	
	The Laurels	TD9 7AY	01450 370002	Bed & Breakfast	★★★	
	The Old Tearoom	TD9 8TH	01450 860275	Awaiting Grading		
	The Steadings	TD9 8TH	01450 860730	Bed & Breakfast	★★★	
	Whitchester Guest House	TD9 7LN	01450 377477	Guest House	★★★	♿ 🍏🍏
	Willowbank		01450 377754	Self Catering	★★	
	Willowherb Cottage		01450 372414	Self Catering	★	
	Wiltonburn Farm	TD9 7LL	01450 372414	Farm House	★★★	
Hawick/ Newcastleton	10 Mansfield Mills House		01450 373237	Self Catering	★★★★	🚶
	Hizzy's Guest House	TD9 9DB	01450 372101	Guest House	★★★	
	Liddesdale Hotel	TD9 0QD	01387 375255	Inn	★★★	
	Lynnwood Cottage B&B	TD9 0ES	01450 372461	Bed & Breakfast	★★★★	
	Oakwood House	TD9 0EH	01450 372814	Bed & Breakfast	★★★	
	Sorbietrees B&B	TD9 0TL	01387 375215	Bed & Breakfast	★★★	
	Yethouse		01387 375642	Self Catering	★★★★	
Helensburgh	152 East Clyde Street		01436 679095	Self Catering	★★★	
	4 Redclyffe Gardens	G84 9JJ	01436 677688	Bed & Breakfast	★★★	
	An Caladh		01436 831312	Self Catering	★★★★	
	Balmillig	G84 9JP	01436 674922	Bed & Breakfast	★★★★	🍏🍏🍏
	Bellfield	G84 7AJ	01436 673361	Bed & Breakfast	★★★★	
	Craigallion Cottage	G84 0NN	0141 4244587	Awaiting Grading		
	Eastbank	G84 7AW	01436 673665	Bed & Breakfast	★★★	🍏
	Easter Garth	G84 0RF	01436 831007	Guest House	★★★	
	Flat 1 Sinclair House		01436 676301	Self Catering	★★★★	
	Floral Cottage Guest House	G84 8RW	01436 820687	Bed & Breakfast	★★★	
	Garden Cottage		01436 675372	Self Catering	★★★	
	Garemount Lodge		01436 820780	Self Catering	★★★★	
	Gareside Lodge		01436 820745	Self Catering	★★★★	
	Killin Cottage B&B	G84 7PN	01436 670923	Bed & Breakfast	★★★	
	Knockderry Hotel	G84 0NX	01436 842283	Country House Hotel	★★★★	
	Larch View	G84 8QG	01436 674078	Bed & Breakfast	★★★	
	Lethamhill	G84 9AW	01436 676016	Bed & Breakfast	★★★★★	
	Mambeg Country Guest House	G84 0EN	01436 810136	Bed & Breakfast	★★★	
	Maybank	G84 7AG	01436 672865	Bed & Breakfast	★★★	
	Pier View		01436 673713	Self Catering	★★★	

♿ Unassisted wheelchair access   ♿ Assisted wheelchair access   🚶 Access for visitors with mobility difficulties
🍏 Bronze Green Tourism Award   🍏🍏 Silver Green Tourism Award   🍏🍏🍏 Gold Green Tourism Award
For further information on our Green Tourism Business Scheme please see page 7.

Advertisers' locations have been sorted by postcode. In Scotland, postcodes can cover fairly large geographical areas. Please check distance of property from specified location with the individual provider. VisitScotland cannot take any responsibility for this.

411

Location	Property Name	Postcode	Telephone	Classification	Star Rating	
Helensburgh	Ravenswood	G84 9PA	01436 672112	Bed & Breakfast	★★★★	
	Rosneath Castle Caravan Park Ltd	G84 0QS	01436 831208	Holiday Park	★★★★★	
	RSR Braeholm	G84 7HR	01436 671880	Guest House	★★	⚹
	Shandonbank Cottage		01436 820314	Self Catering	★★★★	
	Shiloh Bed & Breakfast	G84 7AJ	01436 671005	Bed & Breakfast	★★★★	
	Sinclair House	G84 8TR	01436 676301	Guest House	★★★★	⟨P⟩
	The Coach House		01436 672865	Self Catering	★★★★	
	The Flat Rhu Lodge		01436 821315	Self Catering	★★★★	
	Timber Cottage	G84 8LH	01436 820611	Bed & Breakfast	★★★★	
	Tolsta		01436 678538	Self Catering	★★★	
Helmsdale	Balvallioch		01234 782578	Self Catering	★★★	
	Broomhill House	KW8 6JS	01431 821259	Bed & Breakfast	★★★	
	Culgower House	KW8 6HP	01431 821268	Bed & Breakfast	★★★★	
	Helmsdale Hostel	KW8 6JR	01431 821636	Hostel	★★★★	
	Kindale House	KW8 6JF	01431 821415	Guest House	★★★★	
Huntly	Bandora	AB54 6BR	01466 730375	Bed & Breakfast	★★★	
	Beggshill Bothy		01466 740325	Self Catering	★★★	
	Castle Hotel	AB54 4SH	01466 792696	Country House Hotel	★★★★	
	Coynachie Guest House	AB54 4SD	01466 720383	Guest House	★★★★	
	Drumdelgie House	AB5 4TH	01466 760346	Bed & Breakfast	★★★★	
	Drumdelgie house – Deveron		01466 760346	Self Catering	★★	♿
	Dunedin Guest House	AB54 8DX	01466 794162	Guest House	★★★	
	Easterton		01888 568327	Self Catering	★★★	
	Gordon Arms Hotel	AB54 8AF	01466 792288	Small Hotel	★★	
	Greenmount Guest House	AB54 8EQ	01466 792482	Guest House	★★★	
	Hillview	AB54 5BB	01466 794870	Bed & Breakfast	★★★	
	Huntly Castle Caravan Park	AB54 4UJ	01466 794999	Holiday Park	★★★★★	
	Huntly Hotel	AB54 8BR	01466 792703	Small Hotel	★★	
	New Marnoch	AB54 8HP	01466 792018	Bed & Breakfast	★★★★	
	Strathlene	AB54 8EW	01466 792664	Bed & Breakfast	★★★★	
	The Cottage		01466 780180	Self Catering	★★★ to ★★★★	
	The Factors House		01466 760219	Self Catering	★★★★	
	West Lodge		0131 2439335	Self Catering	★★	
	Wester Park		01466 700262	Self Catering	★★★ to ★★★★	
Innerleithen	Caddon View	EH44 6HH	01896 830208	Guest House	★★★★	
	Glede Knowe	EH44 6RB	01896 831295	Guest House	★★★★	
	Spinners & Weavers		01896 830874	Self Catering	★★★★	
	The Bothy at Orchard Walls		01896 831227	Self Catering	★★★★★	
	The Old School House	EH44 6PP	01896 830425	Bed & Breakfast	★★	
	Traquair House	EH44 6PW	01896 830323	Bed & Breakfast	★★★★	
	Tweedside Caravan Park	EH44 6JS	01896 831271	Holiday Park	★★★	
Insch	Foggieburn	AB52 6XU	01464 831117	Bed & Breakfast	★★★	
	Green Slate Cottage		07786 999752	Self Catering	★★★★	
	Snipie's Bothy		01464 841394	Self Catering	★★★★	⟨PPP⟩
	The 'Wee' Barn		07707 389504	Self Catering	★★★★	⚹

♿ Unassisted wheelchair access   ♿ Assisted wheelchair access   ⚹ Access for visitors with mobility difficulties
⟨P⟩ Bronze Green Tourism Award   ⟨PP⟩ Silver Green Tourism Award   ⟨PPP⟩ Gold Green Tourism Award
For further information on our Green Tourism Business Scheme please see page 7.

412   To find out more go to visitscotland.com

Location	Property Name	Postcode	Telephone	Classification	Star Rating
Inveraray	Argyll Caravan Park	PA32 8XT	01499 302285	Holiday Park	★★★★★
	Argyll Court Bed and Breakfast	PA32 8UT	01499 302273	Bed & Breakfast	★★★
	Arkland B&B	PA32 8UD	01499 302361	Bed & Breakfast	★★
	Braleckan House – Burnside & Leckan		01499 500662	Self Catering	★★★
	Breagha Lodge	PA32 8YX	01499 302061	Bed & Breakfast	★★★
	Brondeg Lodge, Mr C R Elkin		01546 886655	Self Catering	★★★
	Creag Dhubh	PA32 8XT	01499 302430	Guest House	★★★★
	Inveraray Youth Hostel	PA32 8XD	0870 1553255	Hostel	★★★	🅿🅿
	Killean Farm House	PA32 8XT	01499 302474	Guest House	★★★
	Linwood Cottage		0131 243 9335	Self Catering	★★★
	Loch Fyne Hotel	PA32 8XT	0131 5541713	Hotel	★★★	🅰 🅿
	Maggie's B&B	PA32 8XX	01499 500229	Bed & Breakfast	★★★
	Minard Castle	PA32 8YB	01546 886272	Bed & Breakfast	★★★★	🅰
	No. 15 Upper Flat		01499 302361	Self Catering	★★
	Rudha-Na-Craige	PA32 8YX	01499 302668	Guest House	★★★★
	The Argyll Hotel	PA32 8XB		Awaiting Grading	
	The Paymaster's House		01499 302003	Self Catering	★★★★
Invergarry	Ardgarry Farm	PH35 4HG	01809 501226	Bed & Breakfast	★★★
	Craigard Guest House	PH35 4HG	01809 501258	Guest House	★★★
	Drynachan B&B	PH35 4NL	01809 501353	Bed & Breakfast	★★★★
	Faichemard Farm Camping Site	PH35 4HG	01809 501314	Touring Park	★★★★
	Glengarry Castle Country House Hotel	PH35 4HW	01809 501254	Country House Hotel	★★★
	Highgarry Lodges		01809 501226	Self Catering	★★★ to ★★★★
	Invergarry Hotel	PH35 4HJ	01809 501206	Inn	★★★★
	Invergarry Lodge	PH35 4HP	01809 501412	Hostel	★★★★
	Netherwood B&B	PH35 4HN	01320 366550	Awaiting Grading	
	Tangusdale		01809 501 281	Self Catering	★★★★
	The Shepherds		01809 511292	Self Catering	★★★
Invergordon	Balintraid House Backpackers & Highland Retreat	IV18 0LY	01349 854446	Hostel	★★★
	Balnagowan Estate – Marybank		01862 843601	Self Catering	★★★★★
	Kincraig House Hotel	IV18 0LF	01349 852587	Country House Hotel	★★★★
	The Steading		01667 461007	Self Catering	★★★★
Inverkeithing	Battery House	KY11 1JX	01383 410163	Bed & Breakfast	★★★
	Flat 2		01383 510666	Self Catering	★★ to ★★★
	Inglewood Bed and Breakfast	KY11 1DA	01383 410899	Bed & Breakfast	★★★
	MacKenzies Roost		01383 860271	Self Catering	★★★
	Northcraig Cottage	KY11 1JZ	01383 412299	Bed & Breakfast	★★★
	Queensferry Hotel	KY11 1HP	01383 419708	Hotel	★★★
	Shoreland Studio		01383 413126	Self Catering	★★★
	The Roods	KY11 1NG	01383 415049	Bed & Breakfast	★★★
Inverness	10 Connel Court		01349 877762	Self Catering	★★★★
	14 Glenburn Drive	IV2 4ND	01463 238832	Bed & Breakfast	★★
	16 Wellingtonia Court		02891 816744	Self Catering	★★★★
	21 Crown Drive	IV2 3QF	01463 232614	Bed & Breakfast	★★★
	31 Old Edinburgh Court		01463 236060	Self Catering	★★★ to ★★★★
	38 Glenburn Drive		01463 234817	Self Catering	★★★

& Unassisted wheelchair access   🅰 Assisted wheelchair access   🚶 Access for visitors with mobility difficulties
🅿 Bronze Green Tourism Award   🅿🅿 Silver Green Tourism Award   🅿🅿🅿 Gold Green Tourism Award
For further information on our Green Tourism Business Scheme please see page 7.

Advertisers' locations have been sorted by postcode. In Scotland, postcodes can cover fairly large geographical areas.
Please check distance of property from specified location with the individual provider. VisitScotland cannot take any responsibility for this.

413

Directory of all VisitScotland Assured Serviced Establishments, ordered by location.
Establishments highlighted have an advertisement in this guide.

Location	Property Name	Postcode	Telephone	Classification	Star Rating	
Inverness	4 Elm Park	IV2 4WN	01463 237498	Awaiting Grading		
	6 Connel Court		01463 237086	Self Catering	★★★★	
	Aberfeldy Lodge Guest House	IV2 3BG	01463 231120	Guest House	★★★	
	Abermar Guest House	IV3 5QD	01463 239019	Guest House	★★★	
	Achmony Holidays		01456 450357	Self Catering	★★★★	
	Acorn House	IV3 5ED	01463 717021	Guest House	★★★	
	Advie Lodge	IV2 3QQ	01463 237247	Bed & Breakfast	★★★★	
	Aldourie Castle	IV2 6EL	01463 751309	Hotel	★★★★★	
	Amulree	IV3 5QD	01463 224822	Bed & Breakfast	★★★	
	An Grianan	IV2 3NW	01463 250530	Bed & Breakfast	★★★★	
	Ancarraig Lodges		01456 450377	Self Catering	★★★	
	Anderson Farmhouse	IV63 6XT	01456 450114	Bed & Breakfast	★★★★	
	Ardconnel House	IV2 3EU	01463 240455	Guest House	★★★★	
	Armadale Guest House	IV3 5PX	01463 238970	Bed & Breakfast	★★★	
	Aros	IV2 3NW	01463 235674	Bed & Breakfast	★★★	
	Aslaich	IV63 6UJ	01456 459466	Bed & Breakfast	★★★	⌐⌐⌐
	Aspenwood Cottage		01456 486415	Self Catering	★★★★	
	Atherstone	IV3 5QD	01463 240240	Bed & Breakfast	★★★	
	Atholdene Guest House	IV2 3BG	01463 233565	Guest House	★★★	
	Auchnahillin Caravan & Camping Park	IV2 5XQ	01463 772286	Holiday Park	★★★★	
	Auldness House		01463 792780	Self Catering	★★★	
	Avalon Guest House	IV3 5PB	01463 239075	Guest House	★★★★	♁
	Balblair		01667 493407	Self Catering	★★★	♁ ⌐
	Balcroydon	IV2 3LA	01463 221506	Bed & Breakfast	★★★	
	Balnalurigin		01821 642412	Self Catering	★★★★	
	Bannerman Bed And Breakfast	IV3 5NZ	01463 259199	Bed & Breakfast	★★★	
	Bayview	IV1 2BP	01463 790386	Bed & Breakfast	★★★	
	Bazpackers Hostel	IV2 4AB	01463 772704	Backpacker	★★★	
	Bearnock Cottages		01463 230218	Self Catering	★★★★★	
	Beaufort Hotel	IV2 4AG	01463 222897	Hotel	★★★	
	Beaufort Lodge	IV2 3HR	01463 242123	Awaiting Grading		
	Benleva Hotel	IV63 6UH	01456 450080	Inn	★★	
	Binnilidh Mhor		01320 340258	Self Catering	★★★★★	♁
	Birch Cottage		01667 462213	Self Catering	★★★ to ★★★★	
	Blairbeg Caravan	IV63 6UG	01456 459350	Holiday Caravan		
	Bluebell House	IV3 5DH	01463 238201	Bed & Breakfast	★★★★	
	Bradys	IV63 6TS	01456 450071	Bed & Breakfast	★★★	
	Brae Head	IV2 3NH	01463 224222	Bed & Breakfast	★★★	
	Brambles Cottage		01189 712374	Self Catering	★★★	
	Bridgend House	IV63 6TX	01456 450865	Bed & Breakfast	★★★★	
	Bught Caravan Park	IV3 5SR	01463 236920	Touring Park	★★★	
	Bunchrew House Hotel	IV3 6TA	01463 234917	Country House Hotel	★★★★	
	Buntait Farm Cottage		01456 476256	Self Catering	★★★★	⌐
	Cambeth Lodge	IV3 5QP	01463 231764	Bed & Breakfast	★★★	
	Castleview Guest House	IV3 5NE	01463 241443	Guest House	★★★	
	Cavell House	IV2 4SX	01463 232850	Bed & Breakfast	★★★★	
	Cluanie Inn	IV63 7YW	01320 340238	Small Hotel	★★★	
	Courtyard Cottages		01349 862004	Self Catering	★★★★	
	Craig Villa	IV3 5DH	01463 237568	Bed & Breakfast	★★★★	

♧ Unassisted wheelchair access   ♧ Assisted wheelchair access   ♁ Access for visitors with mobility difficulties
⌐ Bronze Green Tourism Award   ⌐⌐ Silver Green Tourism Award   ⌐⌐⌐ Gold Green Tourism Award
For further information on our Green Tourism Business Scheme please see page 7.

414   To find out more go to visitscotland.com

Location	Property Name	Postcode	Telephone	Classification	Star Rating		
Inverness	Craigdarroch House	IV2 6XU	01456 486400	Restaurant With Rooms	★★★★		
	Craigmonie Hotel	IV2 3HX	01463 231649	Hotel	★★★		
	Craigside Lodge	IV2 3HD	01463 231576	Guest House	★★★		
	Craigview		0777 6027306	Self Catering	★★★ to ★★★★		
	Crathie	IV2 3PG	01463 238259	Bed & Breakfast	★★★		
	Creag Mhor	IV63 6TJ	01456 476329	Bed & Breakfast	★★★★		
	Cruachan	IV63 6UA	01456 450574	Bed & Breakfast	★★★		
	Culbin	IV1 3XF	01463 731455	Bed & Breakfast	★★		
	Culloden House Hotel	IV1 2NZ	01463 790461	Country House Hotel	★★★★		
	Culloden Moor Caravan Club Site	IV2 5EF	01342 336842	Touring Park	★★★★★		
	Culloden Stables		01463 709816	Self Catering	★★★		
	Daisy Cottage	IV3 5PE	01463 234273	Bed & Breakfast	★★★★		
	Dalmore Guest House	IV3 5QQ	01463 237224	Guest House	★★★		
	Dionard	IV2 3HJ	01463 233557	Bed & Breakfast	★★★★		
	Dochgarroch Cottage		0131 2439335	Self Catering	★★★		
	Dolphin Bay Suites		01667 404604	Self Catering	★★★		
	Drumbuie Farm	IV63 6XP	01456 450634	Farm House	★★★★		
	Drumnadrochit Hotel	IV63 6TU	01456 450218	Hotel	★★★		
	Drumnadrocit Lodges		01456 450467	Self Catering	★★★ to ★★★★		
	Dunain Park	IV3 8JN	01463 230512	Country House Hotel	★★★★		
	Dunhallin House	IV2 4BH	01463 220824	Guest House	★★★		
	Dunlichity House	IV2 6XF	01808 521442	Bed & Breakfast	★★★★		
	Easdale		01463 790446	Self Catering	★★★		
	Eastgate Hostel	IV2 3NA	01463 718756	Awaiting Grading			
	Eden House	IV3 5PJ	01463 230278	Guest House	★★★★		
	Eiland View Bed & Breakfast	IV2 5BP	01463 798900	Bed & Breakfast	★★★★		
	Eildon Guest House	IV2 3HJ	01463 231969	Guest House	★★★		
	Eilidh	IV3 5NZ	01463 716106	Bed & Breakfast	★★★		
	Evergreen	IV2 6XR	01456 486717	Bed & Breakfast	★★★★		🍃🍃🍃
	Express by Holiday Inn	IV2 7PA	01463 732700	Metro Hotel	★★★	🚶	
	Fairfield Villa	IV3 5QD	01463 242243	Bed & Breakfast	★★★		
	Fenton House	IV2 3NQ	01463 223604	Bed & Breakfast	★★★		
	Firthview House		01463 790620	Self Catering	★★★★	♿	🍃🍃🍃
	Flat No.9	IV2 3EU	01456 486642	Awaiting Grading			
	Fraser House	IV3 5HS	01463 716488	Guest House	★★★		
	Furan Guest House	IV2 3HT	01463 712094	Guest House	★★★		
	Gate Lodge			Self Catering	★★★★		
	Glen Mhor Hotel	IV2 4SG	01463 234308	Hotel	★★★		
	Glen Rowan House	IV63 6UW	01456 450235	Bed & Breakfast	★★★		
	Glen View Apartment	IV2 3DN	01463 236060	Serviced Apartments	★★★		
	Glencairn and Ardross House	IV3 5NS	01463 232965	Guest House	★★★	♿	
	Glencoe	IV3 5QP	01463 220345	Bed & Breakfast	★★★★		
	Glendale	IV2 3LJ	01463 230204	Awaiting Grading			
	Glendoune B&B	IV3 5QE	01463 231493	Bed & Breakfast	★★★		🍃🍃
	Glenkirk	IV63 6TZ	01454 450802	Bed & Breakfast	★★★★		
	Glenmoriston Town House	IV2 4SF	01463 223777	Hotel	★★★★		
	Glenurquhart House	IV63 6TJ	01456 476234	Restaurant With Rooms	★★★★		
	Glenurquhart Lodges – Cedar & Birch		01456 476234	Self Catering	★★ to ★★★		

♿ Unassisted wheelchair access   ♿ Assisted wheelchair access   🚶 Access for visitors with mobility difficulties
🍃 Bronze Green Tourism Award   🍃🍃 Silver Green Tourism Award   🍃🍃🍃 Gold Green Tourism Award
For further information on our Green Tourism Business Scheme please see page 7.

Advertisers' locations have been sorted by postcode. In Scotland, postcodes can cover fairly large geographical areas.
Please check distance of property from specified location with the individual provider. VisitScotland cannot take any responsibility for this.

415

Location	Property Name	Postcode	Telephone	Classification	Star Rating	
Inverness	Greenlea Bed & Breakfast	IV63 6TX	01456 450546	Bed & Breakfast	★★★	
	Greylag, Rowan, Osprey & Wintergreen		01456 486371	Self Catering	★★★★	
	Grouse & Trout at The Steadings	IV2 6XD	01808 521314	Small Hotel	★★★	
	Hazelgrove		01456 486717	Self Catering	★★★★	ꆆꆆꆆ
	Heathcote B&B	IV3 5PB	01463 236596	Bed & Breakfast	★★★★	
	Heathmount Hotel	IV2 3JU	01463 235877	Small Hotel	★★★	
	Herdsman Cottage		01463 731869	Self Catering	★★★★★	ꆆ
	Heronwood	IV2 4QS	01463 243275	Bed & Breakfast	★★★	
	Highfield House	IV2 3PG	01463 238892	Bed & Breakfast	★★★★	
	Highland Apartments Ltd – Hill Street		01463 717568	Self Catering	★★★★	
	Highland Holidays	IV3 8PN	07791 035574	Awaiting Grading		
	Highlander Hostel	IV1 1HY	01463 221225	Hostel	★★★	
	Hornbeam	IV2 3NT	01463 225655	Bed & Breakfast	★★★	
	Inverglen	IV2 3NW	01463 236281	Guest House	★★★	
	Invermoriston Holidays – Moriston Chalets		01320 351254	Self Catering	★★★ to ★★★★	ᕕ ꆆꆆ
	Inverness Centre Premier Inn	IV2 3QX	08701 977141	Budget Hotel		
	Inverness East Premier Inn	IV2 3BW	08701 977142	Budget Hotel		
	Inverness Millburn Youth Hostel	IV2 3QB	0870 1553255	Hostel	★★★★	ᕕ ꆆꆆ
	Inverness Riverside Apartment		01463 237477	Self Catering	★★★	
	Inverness Student Hotel	IV2 4AB	01463 236556	Backpacker	★★	
	Ivanhoe Guest House	IV3 8HW	01463 223020	Guest House	★★★	
	Ivy Cottage		07525 965874	Self Catering	★★★★	
	Kilmore Farmhouse	IV63 6UF	01456 450524	Bed & Breakfast	★★★★	
	Kiloran Guest House	IV3 3DW	01463 230276	Bed & Breakfast	★★★★	
	Kinbrylie	IV2 6UN	01456 486658	Bed & Breakfast	★★★★	⚲
	Kindeace	IV2 3NT	01463 241041	Bed & Breakfast	★★★	
	Kingsmills Hotel Inverness Ltd	IV2 3LP	01463 237166	Hotel	★★★★	♿
	Knowle B&B	IV63 6UP	01456 450646	Bed & Breakfast	★★★	
	Lakefield	IV2 3JB	01463 238352	Bed & Breakfast	★★★★	
	Lann Dearg Studio Apartments		01456 459083	Self Catering	★★★★	
	Lann Dearg Studios	IV63 7YG	01456 459083	Bed & Breakfast	★★★★	
	Larch Cottage		01456 450358	Self Catering	★★★ to ★★★★	
	Larchview		01463 236763	Self Catering	★★★	
	Leanach Farm	IV1 2EJ	01463 791027	Farm House	★★★★	
	Loch Letter Lodges	IV63 6TJ	07788 855237	Awaiting Grading		
	Loch Ness Backpackers Lodge	IV63 6UJ	01456 450807	Hostel	★★★	
	Loch Ness Caravan Park	IV63 7YE	01320 351207	Touring Park	★★★★★	
	Loch Ness Clansman Hotel	IV3 6LA	01456 450326	Hotel	★★★	
	Loch Ness Cottages		01456 459469	Self Catering	★★★★★	
	Loch Ness Inn	IV63 6UW	07899 496092	Inn	★★★	
	Loch Ness Lodge	IV3 8LA	01456 459469	Exclusive Use Venue	★★★★★	
	Loch Ness Lodge Hotel	IV63 6TU	01456 450342	Hotel	★★★	
	Loch Ness Log Cabins		01463 751251	Self Catering	★★	
	Loch Ness Youth Hostel	IV63 7XD	0870 1553255	Hostel	★★	ꆆꆆ
	Lochardil House Hotel	IV2 4LF	01463 235995	Hotel	★★★★	
	Lodges 1, 2, 3 & 5		01456 476350	Self Catering	★★★ to ★★★★	ꆆꆆ
	Log Cabin		01463 790228	Self Catering	★★ to ★★★	

♿ Unassisted wheelchair access   ᕕ Assisted wheelchair access   ⚲ Access for visitors with mobility difficulties
ꆆ Bronze Green Tourism Award   ꆆꆆ Silver Green Tourism Award   ꆆꆆꆆ Gold Green Tourism Award
For further information on our Green Tourism Business Scheme please see page 7.

416   To find out more go to visitscotland.com

Location	Property Name	Postcode	Telephone	Classification	Star Rating		
Inverness	Lorne House	IV2 3QG	01463 236271	Bed & Breakfast	★★★★		
	Lyndon	IV3 5LE	01463 232551	Bed & Breakfast	★★★★		
	Lynver	IV2 3BG	01463 242906	Bed & Breakfast	★★★★		
	Lynwilg	IV2 4EX	01463 232733	Bed & Breakfast	★		
	MacDonald House	IV3 5NQ	01463 232878	Guest House	★★★		
	MacDougall Clansman Hotel	IV1 1ES	01463 713702	Metro Hotel	★★		
	Malvern	IV3 5PZ	01463 242251	Guest House	★★★		
	Maple Court Hotel	IV3 5SQ	01463 230330	Small Hotel	★★★		
	Melness	IV2 3HF	01463 220963	Bed & Breakfast	★★★★		
	Millness Croft Luxury Cottages		01456 476761	Self Catering	★★★★★	🚶	🌿🌿
	Moalnaceap		0208 8665026	Self Catering	★		
	Moray Park Guest House	IV2 4SX	01463 233528	Guest House	★★★		
	Mount Pleasant	IV1 3XS	01463 731474	Bed & Breakfast	★★★		
	Ness Bank Guest House	IV2 4SF	01463 232939	Guest House	★★★		🌿🌿
	Ness Cottage		01463 232976	Self Catering	★★★★		🌿
	Ness Cottage		01463 751298	Self Catering	★★★		
	Ness-side Cottage		01463 871166	Self Catering	★★★★		
	New Drumossie Hotel	IV1 2BE	01463 236451	Hotel	★★★★	♿	
	No 5 – Cub		01456 476799	Self Catering	★★ to ★★★		
	North Kessock Hotel	IV1 1XN	01463 731208	Small Hotel	★★★		
	Old Drynie House	IV1 3XG	01463 731820	Awaiting Grading			
	Old Stables		01456 476367	Self Catering	★★★★	🚶	🌿
	Palace Hotel	IV3 5NG	01463 223243	Hotel	★★★		
	Park Hill Guest House	IV2 3EU	01463 223300	Guest House	★★★		
	Pine Chalets		01764 654537	Self Catering	★★★		
	Plover Cottage		0151 4252129	Self Catering	★★★		
	Pottery House	IV2 6TR	01463 751267	Bed & Breakfast	★★★★		🌿🌿🌿
	Ramada Jarvis Inverness	IV1 1DX	01463 235181	Hotel	★★★	♿	🌿🌿
	Redcliffe Hotel	IV2 3HD	01463 232767	Small Hotel	★★★		
	Rillan		01923 674525	Self Catering	★★★		
	River Lodge		01463 238238	Self Catering	★★★★ to ★★★★★		
	Riverbank Lodge	IV63 7YA	01320 351287	Bed & Breakfast	★★★★		
	Riverside City Apartment		01466 792696	Self Catering	★★★		
	Riverview Guest House	IV2 4SX	01463 235557	Guest House	★★★★		
	Rocpool Reserve Hotel	IV2 4AG	01463 240089	Small Hotel	★★★★★		
	Rookery Nook		01463 237085	Self Catering	★★★	♿	
	Roseneath Guest House	IV3 5PX	01463 220201	Guest House	★★★		
	Rossmount B&B	IV2 3BB	01463 229749	Bed & Breakfast	★★★		
	Rowan Cottage B&B	IV63 6UW	01456 450944	Bed & Breakfast	★★★★		
	Rowan, Woodpecker, Mountain View		01808 521467	Self Catering	★★★★	♿	🌿🌿
	Royston Guest House	IV2 3PS	01463 231243	Guest House	★★★		
	Stanford House		01667 451762	Self Catering	★★★		
	Stonea	IV1 2NH	01463 791714	Bed & Breakfast	★★★		
	Strathmhor Guest House	IV3 5QQ	01463 235397	Guest House	★★★		
	Strathness House	IV3 5NQ	01463 232765	Guest House	★★★		
	Sunnyholm	IV2 4AE	01463 231336	Bed & Breakfast	★★★		
	Talisker House	IV2 4SF	01463 236221	Guest House	★★★		
	Tamarue	IV3 5PF	01463 239724	Bed & Breakfast	★★★		

♿ Unassisted wheelchair access ♿ Assisted wheelchair access 🚶 Access for visitors with mobility difficulties
🌿 Bronze Green Tourism Award 🌿🌿 Silver Green Tourism Award 🌿🌿🌿 Gold Green Tourism Award
For further information on our Green Tourism Business Scheme please see page 7.

Advertisers' locations have been sorted by postcode. In Scotland, postcodes can cover fairly large geographical areas.
Please check distance of property from specified location with the individual provider. VisitScotland cannot take any responsibility for this.

417

Location	Property Name	Postcode	Telephone	Classification	Star Rating	
Inverness	Tealaggan	IV5 7PX	01463 831621	Awaiting Grading		
	Tenaya		01667 493770	Self Catering	★★★★	
	The Alexander	IV2 4SF	01463 231151	Guest House	★★★★	
	The Chieftain Hotel	IV2 3PS	01463 232241	Awaiting Grading		
	The Croft	IV3 8PN	01463 230225	Holiday Caravan		
	The Dairy at Daviot		01463 772975	Self Catering	★★★★	
	The Garden Flat		01463 222615	Self Catering	★★★★	
	The Gatehouse	IV2 3PG	01463 234590	Bed & Breakfast	★★★★	
	The Ghillies Lodge	IV2 4QS	01463 232137	Bed & Breakfast	★★★★	
	The Glen Urquhart Hostel	IV63 6TN	01463 230218	Hostel	★★★★★	
	The Kemps	IV3 5LE	01463 235780	Bed & Breakfast	★★★	
	The Lodge at Daviot Mains	IV2 5ER	01463 772215	Bed & Breakfast	★★★★★	&
	Thistle Inverness	IV2 3TR	01463 239666	Hotel	★★★	Ⓟ
	Tigh Na Bruach	IV63 7YE	01320 351349	Bed & Breakfast	★★★★★	
	Tigh na Bruaich B&B	IV63 6TH	01456 459341	Bed & Breakfast	★★★★	
	Tordarroch Wing	IV2 6XF	01808 521442	Awaiting Grading		
	Travelodge Inverness	IV2 7PA	08719 846148	Budget Hotel		
	Travelodge Inverness Fairways	IV2 7PA	08719 846285	Budget Hotel		
	Waterside Hotel	IV2 4SF	01463 233065	Hotel	★★★	
	Westerlea	IV2 5BW	01463 792890	Bed & Breakfast	★★★	
	Westhill House	IV2 5BP	01463 793225	Bed & Breakfast	★★	
	Westview House	IV2 5BX	01463 791950	Awaiting Grading		
	Westview House	IV2 5BX	01463 791950	Awaiting Grading		
	Whinpark Guest House	IV3 5NS	01463 232549	Guest House	★★★	
	Whitebridge Hotel	IV2 6UN	01456 486226	Small Hotel	★★	Ⓟ
	Wilderness Cottages – Guisaichan		01456 486358	Self Catering	★★★★	ⓅⓅⓅ
	Wimberley House	IV2 3XJ	01463 224430	Bed & Breakfast	★★★★	
	Winston Guest House	IV3 5NQ	01463 232549	Guest House	★★★	
	Woodlands	IV63 6UJ	01456 450356	Guest House	★★★★	ⓐ
	Wychway	IV2 4SD	01463 239399	Bed & Breakfast	★★★	
Inverurie	5 Kirkton Park	AB51 5HF	01467 681281	Bed & Breakfast	★★★	
	Aquhorthies Cottage		01467 642321	Self Catering	★★★★	♦
	Ashdon Guest House	AB51 5XJ	01467 620980	Awaiting Grading		
	Breaslann Guest House	AB51 4QN	01467 621608	Guest House	★★★	
	Broadsea	AB51 5LB	01467 681386	Farm House	★★★	
	Cairngorm Lodges		01651 882773	Self Catering	★★★	
	Cromlet Hill Guest House	AB51 0DW	01651 872315	Bed & Breakfast	★★★★	
	Grant Arms Hotel	AB51 7HJ	01467 651226	Inn	★★★	ⓐ
	Hillhead Caravan Park	AB51 0YX	01467 632809	Holiday Park	★★★★	
	Inverurie Apartments	AB51 4TW	0800 9178845	Awaiting Grading		
	Iona Bed & Breakfast	AB51 3TT	01467 621917	Bed & Breakfast	★★★★	
	Kingsgait	AB51 3XT	01467 620431	Bed & Breakfast	★★★	
	Meldrum House Hotel Golf Country Estate	AB51 0AE	01651 872294	Country House Hotel	★★★	
	Millbank Cottage		01330 833379	Self Catering	★★★	
	Muirtown Cottage		01467 681321	Self Catering	★★★	
	Pittodrie House Hotel	AB51 5HS	08448 799066	Country House Hotel	★★★	
	Rothie Inn	AB51 8UD	01651 821206	Inn	★★★	

& Unassisted wheelchair access ⓐ Assisted wheelchair access ♦ Access for visitors with mobility difficulties
Ⓟ Bronze Green Tourism Award ⓅⓅ Silver Green Tourism Award ⓅⓅⓅ Gold Green Tourism Award
For further information on our Green Tourism Business Scheme please see page 7.

Location	Property Name	Postcode	Telephone	Classification	Star Rating		
Inverurie	St Andrews Cottage		01467 628950	Self Catering	★★★		
	Strathburn Hotel	AB51 4GY	01467 624422	Hotel	★★★		☂
	Thainstone House Hotel	AB51 5NT	01467 621643	Hotel	★★★		
	The John Bell Flat		0844 4932108	Self Catering	★★★		
	The Redgarth	AB51 0DJ	01651 872353	Inn	★★★★		
	Torryburn Hotel	AB51 0XP	01467 632269	Small Hotel	★★		
	West Wing		01330 833647	Self Catering	★★★★		
	William Lippe Properties		01467 622785	Self Catering	★★★★		
Irvine	Donegal Self Catering		01294 211676	Self Catering	★★★		☂
	Gailes Hotel and Restaurant	KA11 5AE	01294 204040	Hotel	★★★		♿
	Menzies Irvine	KA11 4LD	01294 274272	Hotel	★★★		♿
	Riverview		01332 873522	Self Catering	★★★★		
Isle of Arran	10A Murray Place		01294 471901	Self Catering	★★★		
	23 Hamilton Terrace		01900 825627	Self Catering	★★★		
	5 Alma Park		0161 4450067	Self Catering	★		
	Achagorm		01770 860203	Self Catering	★★★		
	Alltan	KA27 8BY	01770 302937	Bed & Breakfast	★★★★		🗭🗭
	Altachorrie	KA27 8LQ	01770 600468	Awaiting Grading			
	An Caladh		01369 870388	Self Catering	★★★★		
	Apartment on the Bay		01770 303111	Self Catering	★★★		
	Apple Lodge	KA27 8HJ	01770 830229	Guest House	★★★★		
	Ardbeag		01505 850666	Self Catering	★★★		
	Aros Beag		01770 860780	Self Catering	★★★		
	Arran Swiss Cottage		01698 813815	Self Catering	★★★		
	Auchrannie Country House Hotel	KA27 8BZ	01770 302234	Hotel	★★★★	♿	🗭🗭
	Auchrannie Luxury Lodges		01770 302020	Self Catering	★★★★★		🗭
	Auchrannie Spa Resort	KA27 8BZ	01770 302234	Hotel	★★★★	♿	🗭🗭
	Bay View	KA27 8JU	01770 302178	Bed & Breakfast	★★		
	Bayview Cottage		0141 6399175	Self Catering	★★ to ★★★		
	Bellevue Farm Cottage		01770 860251	Self Catering	★★★		
	Belvedere		01770 302397	Self Catering	★★★		☂
	Belvedere Guest House	KA27 8AZ	01770 302397	Guest House	★★★		☂
	Benview Cottage	KA27 8QT	01770 700275	Awaiting Grading			
	Bluebell Cottage		01225 465974	Self Catering	★★		
	Bracklinn		01770 302303	Self Catering	★★★		
	Brae Cottage Bed & Breakfast	KA27 8EP	01770 860780	Awaiting Grading			
	Braehead Cottage		0131 3348693	Self Catering	★★★★		
	Bramble Cottage		0141 8877699	Self Catering	★★★		
	Brandon Lodge		01770 302251	Self Catering	★★★★		
	Brodick Castle		01770 600307	Self Catering	★★★		
	Burnside House		0141 4237939	Self Catering	★★★		
	Butt Lodge Country House		01770 830699	Self Catering	★★★★		
	Carraig Dhubh-No 1		01770 700563	Self Catering	★★★		
	Carrick Lodge	KA27 8BH	01770 302556	Guest House	★★★		
	Clauchlands View Holiday Cottage		01770 600317	Self Catering	★★★★		☂
	Clisham Bed and Breakfast	KA27 8HP	01770 850294	Bed & Breakfast	★★★		
	Cloy Lodge		01294 472772	Self Catering	★★★★		

♿ Unassisted wheelchair access   ♿ Assisted wheelchair access   ☂ Access for visitors with mobility difficulties
🗭 Bronze Green Tourism Award   🗭🗭 Silver Green Tourism Award   🗭🗭🗭 Gold Green Tourism Award
For further information on our Green Tourism Business Scheme please see page 7.

Advertisers' locations have been sorted by postcode. In Scotland, postcodes can cover fairly large geographical areas.
Please check distance of property from specified location with the individual provider. VisitScotland cannot take any responsibility for this.

419

Location	Property Name	Postcode	Telephone	Classification	Star Rating	
Isle of Arran	Craig Dhu Cottage		01770 600276	Self Catering	★★★	
	Craigdhu Farm Cottages – Bushmill		01770 820225	Self Catering	★★★ to ★★★★	
	Craigend		07748 787069	Self Catering	★★★	
	Creagenroin		01770 870263	Self Catering	★★★	
	Croftlea	KA27 8EW	01770 860259	Bed & Breakfast	★★	
	Croftside Cottage		01387 720161	Self Catering	★★★	
	Crovie	KA27 8BL	01770 302193	Bed & Breakfast	★★★	
	Douglas Villa Cottage		0131 4455586	Self Catering	★★★★	
	Drive Houses No. 1		01770 600795	Self Catering	★★★	
	Druid Farmhouse		01292 443769	Self Catering	★★★	
	Drumla Farm – The Whins		01770 820256	Self Catering	★★★ to ★★★★	
	Dunvegan House	KA27 8AJ	01770 302811	Guest House	★★★★	
	Dyemill House	KA27 8NT	01770 600419	Holiday Caravan		
	Dyemill Lodges		01770 600419	Self Catering	★★★	
	Eden Lodge	KA27 8QH	01770 700357	Inn	★★	
	Ellangowan	KA27 8QH	01770 700784	Bed & Breakfast	★★★	
	Evergreen		01786 841966	Self Catering	★★★	
	Ghillie's & Drover's		01770 600291	Self Catering	★★★★	
	Glenartney	KA27 8BX	01770 302220	Guest House	★★★	🍃🍃🍃
	Glencloy Farm Guest House	KA27 8DA	01770 302351	Guest House	★★★	
	Glendale		01560 484898	Self Catering	★★★★	
	Glenisle Hotel	KA27 8LY	01770 600559	Small Hotel	★★★	
	Glenn House	KA27 8DW	01770 302092	Bed & Breakfast	★★★	
	Grans Cottage		01770 302380	Self Catering	★★★★★	
	Greenways Cottage		0141 9428017	Self Catering	★★★	
	Grianan House		01770 820236	Self Catering	★★★★	🚶
	Hayshed & Ploughman's Bothy		01770 870295	Self Catering	★★★	
	Hazelbank		01208 873420	Self Catering	★★★	
	Heathfield House			Self Catering	★★★★	
	Hope Cottage		01770 860377	Self Catering	★★★	
	Invercloy	KA27 8AJ	01770 302225	Guest House	★★★	
	Invermay	KA27 8PZ	01770 700431	Guest House	★★	
	Kennels Lodge		01770 302203	Self Catering	★★★ to ★★★★★	
	Kilbride Farmhouse		01770 302203	Self Catering	★★★★	
	Kildonan Hotel	KA27 8SE	01770 820207	Small Hotel	★★★	♿
	Kildonan School & Schoolhouse		01436 820956	Self Catering	★★★	♿
	Kilmichael Country House Hotel	KA27 8BY	01770 302219	Country House Hotel	★★★★	
	Kilmory Lodge Bunkhouse	KA27 8PQ	01770 870345	Group Accommodation	★★★	
	Kinloch Hotel	KA27 8ET	01770 860444	Hotel	★★★	🍃
	Kirk Kildonan		01770 820682	Self Catering	★★★★	
	Lagg Hotel	KA27 8PQ	01770 870255	Small Hotel	★★★	
	Lamlash Bay Hotel	KA27 8LU	01770 600844	Awaiting Grading		
	Lilybank	KA27 8LS	01770 600230	Guest House	★★★★	🚶
	Liosmor		01770 600752	Self Catering	★★★★	
	Lochranza Hotel	KA27 8HL	01770 830223	Inn	★★	
	Lochranza Youth Hostel	KA27 8HL	0870 1553255	Hostel	★★★	🍃🍃
	Machrie House		01770 840223	Self Catering	★★★	
	Mare	KA27 8AS	01770 820375	Bed & Breakfast	★★★★	

♿ Unassisted wheelchair access ♿ Assisted wheelchair access 🚶 Access for visitors with mobility difficulties
🍃 Bronze Green Tourism Award 🍃🍃 Silver Green Tourism Award 🍃🍃🍃 Gold Green Tourism Award
For further information on our Green Tourism Business Scheme please see page 7.

420   To find out more go to visitscotland.com

Location	Property Name	Postcode	Telephone	Classification	Star Rating	
Isle of Arran	Mill Cottage		01770 860308	Self Catering	★★★	
	Mingulay	KA27 8QH	01770 700346	Bed & Breakfast	★★★	
	Miodar Mor Cottage		01770 820624	Self Catering	★★★★	🏃
	Morvern	KA27 8EU	01770 860254	Bed & Breakfast	★★	
	Moss Cottage		01770 302659	Self Catering	★★★★	
	No 2 Alma Terrace		0141 5614155	Self Catering	★★★	
	Oakwood Cottage		01770 600790	Self Catering	★★★★	
	Old Smiddy Cottage		01770 860261	Self Catering	★★★	
	Ormidale Hotel	KA27 8BY	01770 302293	Small Hotel	★★	
	Ornsay Cottage		01770 830304	Self Catering	★★★	
	Otterburn		01770 302334	Self Catering	★★★★	
	Peacock Cottage		01770 302219	Self Catering	★★★★★	🏃
	Rosaburn Lodge	KA27 8DP	01770 302383	Bed & Breakfast	★★★	
	Rowanbank		01403 822364	Self Catering	★★★ to ★★★★	
	Runrig		0141 9548068	Self Catering	★★★	
	Sandbraes Lodge		01770 700235	Self Catering	★★★	🏃
	Sandmartin Cottage		01770 840227	Self Catering	★★★★	
	Sannaig		01770 860376	Self Catering	★★★	
	Seacliffe Cottages		01770 820323	Self Catering	★★★	
	Seacrest		01899 221678	Self Catering	★★★	
	Sealladh Breagh		01770 860530	Self Catering	★★★★	
	Sealladh Na Mara		07941 325792	Self Catering	★★★	
	Sealshore Camp Site	KA27 8SL	01770 820320	Holiday Park	★★★★	
	Seaview Croft		01770 700680	Self Catering	★★★★	
	Seawinds		01770 810248	Self Catering	★★★★	
	Shannocie Cottages – Eryb		01770 820291	Self Catering	★★★ to ★★★★	
	Spion Kop Cottage		01770 600474	Self Catering	★★★	
	Springbank Farmhouse Apartment		01786 474386	Self Catering	★★★	
	St Columbas		0208 3406069	Self Catering	★★★	
	Strathconon		01586 830323	Self Catering	★★★★	🏃
	Summer House		01770 302121	Self Catering	★★ to ★★★	
	Sunnybank		0114 2680019	Self Catering	★★★	
	The Anchorage		0131 4777033	Self Catering	★★★	
	The Barn	KA27 3DA	01770 303615	Bed & Breakfast	★★★★	
	The Burlington	KA27 8PZ	01770 700255	Guest House	★★★	
	The Flat at Invercloy		01563 571788	Self Catering	★★★	
	The Garden House		01299 269489	Self Catering	★★★	
	The Millhouse		0131 6672267	Self Catering	★★★	
	The Old Farmhouse		0131 4663124	Self Catering	★★★★	
	The Shore		01770 303111	Self Catering	★★★	
	The Shore House		01770 302377	Self Catering	★★	
	The Smiddy		01770 700536	Self Catering	★★★★	
	The Steading		01770 810668	Self Catering	★★ to ★★★	
	The Summer House		01770 700649	Self Catering	★★★	℗℗
	The Wee Rig		01770 850228	Self Catering	★★★	
	The Willows		01292 441161	Self Catering	★★★	
	Trafalgar Cottage		01416 332322	Self Catering	★★★	
	Tulloch-Ard		01786 463414	Self Catering	★★★	

♿ Unassisted wheelchair access   ♿ Assisted wheelchair access   🏃 Access for visitors with mobility difficulties
℗ Bronze Green Tourism Award   ℗℗ Silver Green Tourism Award   ℗℗℗ Gold Green Tourism Award
For further information on our Green Tourism Business Scheme please see page 7.

Advertisers' locations have been sorted by postcode. In Scotland, postcodes can cover fairly large geographical areas.
Please check distance of property from specified location with the individual provider. VisitScotland cannot take any responsibility for this.

421

Location	Property Name	Postcode	Telephone	Classification	Star Rating
Isle of Arran	Viewbank House	KA27 8QT	01770 700326	Guest House	★★★
	Waterfront Apartment		01770 303111	Self Catering	★★★
	Wee Meadow Cottage		01770 850236	Self Catering	★★★★
	Wellingtonia Cottage		0131 4435572	Self Catering	★★
	Whin Cottage		01434 604673	Self Catering	★★★
	Willow Cottage		0141 6372945	Self Catering	★★★
	Woodlands	KA27 8AJ	01770 302564	Awaiting Grading	
	Woodside Cottage		0131 468615	Self Catering	★★★
Isle of Barra	Airds Guest House	HS9 5UY	01871 890720	Bed & Breakfast	★★★ ⟨mobility⟩
	Aros Cottage	HS9 5UT	01871 890355	Bed & Breakfast	★★★
	Bayview	HS9 5XN	01871 810511	Bed & Breakfast	★★★
	Castlebay Hotel	HS9 5XD	01871 810223	Small Hotel	★★★
	Ceum A Bhealaich		01871 810644	Self Catering	★★★
	Craigard Hotel	HS9 5XD	01871 810200	Small Hotel	★★★
	Dunard Hostel	HS9 5XA	01841 810442	Hostel	★★★
	Gearadhmor	HS9 5XS	01871 810688	Bed & Breakfast	★★
	Harbour Cottage		01357 528810	Self Catering	★
	Heathbank Hotel	HS9 5YQ	01871 890266	Inn	★★★
	Isle of Barra Hotel	HS9 5XW	01871 810383	Awaiting Grading	
	Ocean View	HS9 5XR	01871 810590	Bed & Breakfast	★★★
	Orosay	HS9 5UR	01871 810564	Bed & Breakfast	★★★
	Taigh A Bhealaich	HS9 5UH	0141 4273709	Awaiting Grading	
Isle of Benbecula	1 Grimsay Island		01870 602591	Self Catering	★★★
	3 Grimsay	HS7 5PS	01870 602473	Awaiting Grading	
	9 Torlum		01870 603296	Self Catering	★★★
	Am Bothan & Smiddy Steadings		01870 602176	Self Catering	★★★
	Bainbhidh	HS7 5PY	01870 602532	Bed & Breakfast	★★
	Bayview	HS7 5LY	01688 302252	Awaiting Grading	
	Borve Guest House	HS7 5PP	01870 602685	Guest House	★★★★
	Ceann na Pairc Guest House	HS7 5LU	01870 602017	Awaiting Grading	
	Creag Liath	HS7 5QA	01870 602992	Bed & Breakfast	★★★★
	Dark Island Hotel	HS7 5PJ	01870 603030	Hotel	★★
	Ford House		01870 602268	Self Catering	★★★
	Kyles Flodda Bed and Breakfast	HS7 5QR	01870 603145	Bed & Breakfast	★★★★
	Lionacleit Guest House	HS7 5PY	01870 602176	Guest House	★★★
	Moor Cottage	HS7 5LA	01335 342293	Awaiting Grading	
	Shellbay Caravan & Camping Park	HS7 5PJ	01870 602447	Touring Park	★★★
	The Isle of Benbecula House Hotel	HS7 5PG	01870 602024	Hotel	★★★
	The Restful Nest		07801 490274	Self Catering	★★★
	Tigh Curstaig		01870 602536	Self Catering	★★★★
Isle of Bute	Ambrisbeg Cottage		01700 831204	Self Catering	★★★
	Ardencraig House		01700 505077	Self Catering	★★★★
	Argyle House	PA20 0AZ	01700 502424	Guest House	★★
	Arranview @ Stewart Hall		01700 500006	Self Catering	★★★★★
	Balmoral		01700 503371	Self Catering	★★
	Balmory Hall	PA20 9LL	01700 500669	Bed & Breakfast	★★★★★
	Bayview Hotel	PA20 9EB	01700 505411	Guest House	★★★★

& Unassisted wheelchair access   && Assisted wheelchair access   ⟨⟩ Access for visitors with mobility difficulties
⟨P⟩ Bronze Green Tourism Award   ⟨PP⟩ Silver Green Tourism Award   ⟨PPP⟩ Gold Green Tourism Award
For further information on our Green Tourism Business Scheme please see page 7.

422   To find out more go to visitscotland.com

Location	Property Name	Postcode	Telephone	Classification	Star Rating
Isle of Bute	Bute Backpacker		01700 501876	Backpacker	★★★★
	Bute House	PA20 9AF	01700 502481	Guest House	★★★
	Daisy Bank Flats	PA20 9NL	07974 732348	Awaiting Grading	
	Dykenamar		01483 772506	Self Catering	★★★★
	[Flat 9 & Flat 13] Grand Marine Court		01236 755051	Self Catering	★★★
	Glenburn Hotel	PA20 9JB	01700 502500	Hotel	★★★
	Glendale Guest House	PA20 9DU	01700 502329	Guest House	★★★★
	Grand Marine		01323 873688	Self Catering	★★★
	Morningside – Argyle		01700 504237	Self Catering	★★★
	North Lodge		01700 503877	Self Catering	★★★★
	Prospect House		01700 503526	Self Catering	★★★
	Roseland Caravan Park	PA20 9EH	01700 504529	Holiday Park	★★★★
	St Blane's Hotel	PA20 9NW	01700 831224	Small Hotel	★★
	The Ardyne	PA20 9EB	01700 502052	Small Hotel	★★★
	The Commodore	PA20 9DP	01700 502178	Guest House	★★★
	The Moorings	PA20 9DY	01700 502277	Bed & Breakfast	★★★
	West St. Colmac Farm – kames		01700 502144	Self Catering	★★★
	West Wing		01700 500669	Self Catering	★★★★
	Westview		0141 5779091	Self Catering	★★★★
			01700 501876	Backpacker	★★★★
Isle of Canna	The Bothy		0131 2439335	Self Catering	★★
	Lag nam Boitean		0131 2439335	Self Catering	★★
Isle of Coll	Isle of Coll Hotel	PA78 6SZ	01879 230334	Inn	★★★
Isle of Colonsay	Colnatarun Cottage		01951 200355	Self Catering	★★★
	Colonsay Estate Cottages – Drumclach		01951 200312	Self Catering	★★ to ★★★
	Colonsay Keepers Backpackers' Lodge	PA61 7YU	01951 200312	Hostel	★★
	Creag Mhor		01951 200131	Self Catering	★★★★
	Geaspar Lodge		01343 890752	Self Catering	★ to ★★★
	Maghnus Island Lodge		01259 722335	Self Catering	★
	Phoebe		01951 200320	Self Catering	★★★ to ★★★★
	The Colonsay	PA61 7YP	01951 200316	Small Hotel	★★
Isle of Cumbrae	Cumbrae Holiday Apartments – Jura		01475 530041	Self Catering	★★
	Guildford Street – Top Flats Left and Right		01324 554430	Self Catering	★★ to ★★★★
	Lochknowe		01475 530630	Self Catering	★
	The Cathedral of the Isles	KA28 0HE	01475 530353	Guest House	★★★ ♿
	Westbourne	KA28 0HA	01475 530000	Bed & Breakfast	★★★
Isle of Eigg	Glebe Barn	PH42 4RL	01687 482417	Hostel	★★★★ 🌱🌱
	Lageorna Guest House	PH42 4RL	01687 482405	Restaurant With Rooms	★★★★ 🌱🌱
Isle of Gigha	Croft 1		01583 505254	Self Catering	★ to★★★ 🌱
	Gigha Hotel	PA41 7AA	01583 505254	Small Hotel	★★★ 🌱
	The Stable	PA41 7AD	01583 505254	Awaiting Grading	
Isle of Harris	1 Rhenigdale Seaforth Cottage		01859 502447	Self Catering	★★
	5 Caw		01463 223621	Self Catering	★★★
	5 Grosebay	HS3 3EF	01859 511246	Holiday Caravan	
	5 Urgha		01859 502114	Self Catering	★★★

♿ Unassisted wheelchair access   ♿ Assisted wheelchair access   ♿ Access for visitors with mobility difficulties
🌱 Bronze Green Tourism Award   🌱🌱 Silver Green Tourism Award   🌱🌱🌱 Gold Green Tourism Award
For further information on our Green Tourism Business Scheme please see page 7.

Advertisers' locations have been sorted by postcode. In Scotland, postcodes can cover fairly large geographical areas.
Please check distance of property from specified location with the individual provider. VisitScotland cannot take any responsibility for this.

423

Location	Property Name	Postcode	Telephone	Classification	Star Rating	
Isle of Harris	Aisling Cottage		01859 502487	Self Catering	★★★★	
	Am Bothan Leverburgh Bunkhouse	HS5 3UA	01851 520251	Hostel	★★★★★	ฅ
	Ardhasaig House	HS3 3AJ	01859 502500	Restaurant With Rooms	★★★★	๋
	Ashville	HS3 3DJ	07712 886535	Awaiting Grading		
	Atlantic Cottage		01859 550219	Self Catering	★★★★ to ★★★★★	
	Avalon	HS3 3BG	01859 502334	Bed & Breakfast	★★★★	
	Barabhas	HS3 3HL	01859 550400	Awaiting Grading		
	Bayhead		0185 870810	Self Catering	★★★	
	Beachview Cottages	HS3 3JA	01859 520315	Awaiting Grading		
	Beul-na-Mara Bed and Breakfast	HS3 3HP	01859 550205	Bed & Breakfast	★★★★	
	Blacksheep House		01859 560221	Self Catering	★★★★★	
	Buel Na Mara Cottage 1		01859 550205	Self Catering	★★★★	
	Caberfeidh		01422 378983	Self Catering	★★★★★	
	Carminish House	HS5 3UB	01859 520400	Bed & Breakfast	★★★★	๋
	Ceol Na Mara Guest House	HS3 3DP	01859 502464	Guest House	★★★★	℗
	Clisham Cottage		01859 502066	Self Catering	★★★★	
	Cnoc A'Chlachain		01349 877065	Self Catering	★★★★	
	Cnoc Na Ba		01859 530232	Self Catering	★★★★	℗
	Collam Villa	HS3 3DL	0141 5629425	Awaiting Grading		
	Creagan		0113 2756190	Self Catering	★★★	
	Croft Cottage		01859 502338	Self Catering	★★★★★	ฅ ℗℗
	Crook Cottage Holidays		01296 658681	Self Catering	★★★	
	Crowlin		01224 867392	Self Catering	★★★★	
	Dail na Mara	HS3 4XW	01859 540206	Bed & Breakfast	★★★	๋
	Dalhanna		07973 569728	Self Catering	★★★★	
	Drinishader Hostel	HS3 3DX	01859 511255	Hostel	★★	
	Fasgadh Studio		01859 502060	Self Catering	★★★★	
	Fraser Cottage		01859 530251	Self Catering	★★★ to ★★★★	℗
	Gasker House		01859 520265	Self Catering	★★★★	
	Grimisdale	HS5 3TS	01859 520460	Guest House	★★★★	
	Harris Hotel	HS3 3DL	01859 502154	Hotel	★★	
	Harris White Cottage		07787 851155	Self Catering	★★★★	
	Hillcrest		01859 502119	Self Catering	★★★	
	Kinnoull		01573 224751	Self Catering	★★★	
	Kirklea Cottages		01859 502364	Self Catering	★★★	
	Langracleit	HS3 3HQ	01859 502413	Bed & Breakfast	★★★	
	MacLeod Motel	HS3 3DJ	01859 502364	Awaiting Grading		
	Minch View Campsite	HS3 3DX	01859 511207	Touring Park	★★	
	Rhenigidale Hostel	HS3 3BD	01379 890270	Hostel	★	
	Riverside		01859 502156	Self Catering	★★★★	
	Rockview Bunkhouse	HS3 3DJ	01859 502081	Hostel	★★	
	Rodean	HS3 3HQ	01859 502079	Bed & Breakfast	★★★	
	Rodel Valley Log Cabins		01859 520465	Self Catering	★★★★	๋
	Rowan Cottage		01859 502204	Self Catering	★★★★	
	Scaradale Centre	HS3 3AB	01859 502502	Activity Accommodation	★★★★	๋
	Scarista House	HS3 3HX	01859 550238	Guest House	★★★	℗

♿ Unassisted wheelchair access   ฅ Assisted wheelchair access   ๋ Access for visitors with mobility difficulties
℗ Bronze Green Tourism Award   ℗℗ Silver Green Tourism Award   ℗℗℗ Gold Green Tourism Award
For further information on our Green Tourism Business Scheme please see page 7.

424   To find out more go to visitscotland.com

Location	Property Name	Postcode	Telephone	Classification	Star Rating		
Isle of Harris	Seaforth Cottage		01859 502473	Self Catering	★★★★		
	Seaside Cottage		01859 502157	Self Catering	★★★★★		
	Seaside House		01865 858383	Self Catering	★		
	Seaview		01859 502845	Self Catering	★★★		
	Shalom Self Catering		01859 520259	Self Catering	★★★★★		₽₽
	Sorrel Cottage	HS5 3TY	01859 520319	Bed & Breakfast	★★★		
	St Clement's Croft		01463 240788	Self Catering	★★★★		
	Taigh Sheumais		01859 550370	Self Catering	★★★★★		₽₽₽
	Tamh		01416 333744	Self Catering	★★★★		
	Taransay		01540 673531	Self Catering	★★		
	Tetherstone	HS3 3JA	01859 520378	Bed & Breakfast	★★★★		
	The School House		01859 502177	Self Catering	★★★		
	Tigh an Eilein	HS3 3HA	01859 530270	Awaiting Grading			
	Tigh Iomhair		01859 502225	Self Catering	★★★		
	Tigh Na Mara		0141 5863524	Self Catering	★★★		
	Tigh na Seileach		0774 574517	Self Catering	★★		
	Ullabhal & Cleiseabhal		01859 502063	Self Catering	★★★★		
Isle of Iona	Argyll Hotel	PA76 6SJ	01681 700334	Restaurant With Rooms	★★★		
	Iona Hostel	PA76 6SW	01681 700781	Hostel	★★★★	⫯	₽₽₽
	St Columba Hotel	PA76 6SL	01681 700304	Hotel	★★★		₽₽
Isle of Islay	2 Bola na Traigh		01496 850256	Self Catering	★★★		
	2 Mulindry Cottages	PA44 7PZ	01496 810397	Bed & Breakfast	★★★★		
	40 Pier Road	PA42 7DJ	01496 300502	Bed & Breakfast	★★★★		
	9 Shore Street		0141 9565743	Self Catering	★★★★		
	An Cala House		01496 810307	Self Catering	★★★		
	An Cuan B&B	PA43 7HL	01496 810307	Bed & Breakfast	★★★★		
	An Sabhal Cottages		01463 860293	Self Catering	★★★★		
	An Taigh Osda	PA49 7UN	01496 850587	Restaurant With Rooms	★★★★		
	Anchorage	PA49 7UN	01496 850540	Bed & Breakfast	★★		
	Ardatalla Farmhouse		01496 302430	Self Catering	★★ to ★★★★★		
	Ballivicar Farm – Chougherie, Hayloft and Bothy		01496 302251	Self Catering	★★		
	Blackpark Croft		01496 810376	Self Catering	★★★	⌖	
	Bridgend Hotel	PA44 7PJ	01496 810212	Small Hotel	★★★		
	Byre Cottage		01496 850503	Self Catering	★★★★		
	Caberfeidh Cottage		01496 850343	Self Catering	★★★		
	Cala Seimh		01496 850289	Self Catering	★★★		
	Cala Sith		01496 850434	Self Catering	★★★		
	Caladh Sona	PA42 7BD	01496 302694	Bed & Breakfast	★★★		
	Carnain Cottage		0131 3478853	Self Catering	★★★★		
	Clachan Cottage		01496 810440	Self Catering	★★		
	Cladville Dairy		01496 860243	Self Catering	★★★★		
	Claggan Farmhouse		01295 670371	Self Catering	★★		
	Cnoc Ard		01496 810547	Self Catering	★★★★		
	Coillabus Cottage		0131 5531911	Self Catering	★★★		₽
	Coull Farm Holiday Flat		01496 850317	Self Catering	★★★	⫯	

♿ Unassisted wheelchair access   ♿ Assisted wheelchair access   ⫯ Access for visitors with mobility difficulties
₽ Bronze Green Tourism Award   ₽₽ Silver Green Tourism Award   ₽₽₽ Gold Green Tourism Award
For further information on our Green Tourism Business Scheme please see page 7.

Advertisers' locations have been sorted by postcode. In Scotland, postcodes can cover fairly large geographical areas.
Please check distance of property from specified location with the individual provider. VisitScotland cannot take any responsibility for this.

425

Location	Property Name	Postcode	Telephone	Classification	Star Rating
Isle of Islay	Coullabus Keepers Cottage		01496 810293	Self Catering	★★★
	Craigard Holiday Accommodation – Air A Bhuth		01496 810728	Self Catering	★★★ to ★★★★★ ♂ 🐾🐾
	Curlew Cottage		07976 296796	Self Catering	★★★
	Easter Ellister		01555 892785	Self Catering	★★★★
	Glenegedale House	PA42 7AS	01496 300400	Guest House	★★★★★
	High Street		01496 810488	Self Catering	★★
	High View B&B	PA42 7DD	01496 300158	Bed & Breakfast	★★★★
	Islay Holidays	PA42 7AR	01496 300400	Awaiting Grading	
	Klilchiaran Cottage		01496 850248	Self Catering	★★★ to ★★★★
	Kilmeny	PA45 7QW	01496 840668	Guest House	★★★★★
	Kintra Beach Cottages		01496 302051	Self Catering	★★★★
	Lambeth Guest House	PA43 7HL	01496 810597	Awaiting Grading	
	Lambeth Lodge		01496 810792	Self Catering	★★★
	Loch Gorm Cottages		01496 850259	Self Catering	★★★
	Loch Gorm House	PA49 7UN	07775 666850	Bed & Breakfast	★★★★★
	Lorgba Holiday Cottages – Carraig North & South		01496 850208	Self Catering	★★★★
	Lyndon Cottage		01417 776675	Self Catering	★★★
	Lyrabus Moor Croft		01496 850438	Self Catering	★★★
	Machrie Hotel	PA42 7AN	01496 302310	Small Hotel	★★★
	Machrie Hotel Standard Lodges		01496 302310	Self Catering	★ to★★
	Middle Cragabus Cottage		01496 302640	Self Catering	★
	Neriby Cottage		01496 810274	Self Catering	★★★★
	Octomore Cottage		01496 850235	Self Catering	★★★ to ★★★★ 🄿
	Octovullin Farmhouse		01496 810221	Self Catering	★★ to ★★★
	Port Charlotte Youth Hostel	PA48 7TX	0870 1553255	Hostel	★★★ 🐾🐾
	Red Lodge		01496 810235	Self Catering	★★ to ★★★
	Saddlers Brae		0141 9431858	Self Catering	★★★★
	Saligo, Kilchoman and Arndave		0141 9432529	Self Catering	★★★★
	Samhchair	PA42 7AX	01496 302596	Bed & Breakfast	★★★★
	Sgioba Cottage		01496 850334	Self Catering	★★★
	Smiddy Cottage		01496 850420	Self Catering	★★★★
	Stable Cottage		01496 850259	Self Catering	★★★★
	The Cottage		01496 810488	Self Catering	★★
	The Harbour Inn and Restaurant	PA43 7JR	01496 810532	Restaurant With Rooms	★★★★
	The Inns Over-by	PA43 7JR	01496 810330	Awaiting Grading	
	The Meadows	PA44 7PZ	01496 810567	Bed & Breakfast	★★★★
	The Monachs	PA48 7WE	01496 850049	Bed & Breakfast	★★★★★
	The Old Bakery		01496 810671	Self Catering	★★★★
	The Old Schoolroom		01496 810242	Self Catering	★★★★
	The Old Stables		01496 810414	Self Catering	★★★ ♂
	The Trout Fly Bed & Breakfast	PA42 7DF	01496 302204	Bed & Breakfast	★★★
	Tigh Beag		01746 716350	Self Catering	★★★
Isle of Jura	Braeside		0141 9464361	Self Catering	★★
	Heather Cottage		01786 850274	Self Catering	★
	Jura Hotel	PA60 7UX	01496 820243	Small Hotel	★★
	Stalkers Cottage		01584 841234	Self Catering	★

& Unassisted wheelchair access   ♿ Assisted wheelchair access   ♂ Access for visitors with mobility difficulties
🄿 Bronze Green Tourism Award   🐾🐾 Silver Green Tourism Award   🐾🐾🐾 Gold Green Tourism Award
For further information on our Green Tourism Business Scheme please see page 7.

426   To find out more go to visitscotland.com

Location	Property Name	Postcode	Telephone	Classification	Star Rating
Isle of Lewis	10 Glen Gravir		01851 703575	Self Catering	★★★
	10 Tolsta Chaolais		01851 621722	Self Catering	★★★
	11B Riof		02072 634174	Self Catering	★★★
	12 Gravir		01859 520217	Self Catering	★★★
	13 Glen Gravir		0131 5574938	Self Catering	★★★★
	14 Tobson		01851 870706	Self Catering	★★★
	23 Valtos		01749 880380	Self Catering	★★
	25 South Shawbost		01851 710461	Self Catering	★★★★
	25 Valasay		01851 612288	Self Catering	★★★★
	27 Garenin	HS2 9AL	01259 702115	Awaiting Grading	
	33 North Shawbost		01851 710591	Self Catering	★★★
	3A Reef		01463 221558	Self Catering	★★★
	5 Hacklete		01851 612269	Self Catering	★
	6 Tolsta Chaolais		01851 621260	Self Catering	★★★
	8B Calbost		01851 820969	Self Catering	★★★
	Achmore Self Catering		01851 700310	Self Catering	★★★★
	Aultbeithe		01422 378983	Self Catering	★★★★★
	Callan Maran		01851 621706	Self Catering	★★★
	Callanish Farmhouse		01851 621422	Self Catering	★★★★
	Callanish Guest House	HS2 9DY	01851 621279	Awaiting Grading	
	Clearview	HS2 9PT	01851 830472	Bed & Breakfast	★★★
	Creagan		01851 621200	Self Catering	★★★
	Eilean Fraoich Camp Site	HS2 9BQ	01851 710504	Touring Park	★★★
	Eshcol Guest House	HS2 9DY	01851 621357	Guest House	★★★★
	Gallan Head Restaurant and Hotel	HS2 9JA	01851 672474	Restaurant With Rooms	★★★
	Garenin Hostel	HS2 9AL	01379 890270	Hostel	★
	Gearrannan Blackhouse Village – 4A & 4B		01851 643416	Self Catering	★★★ to ★★★★
	Gledfield	HS2 9PN	01851 830233	Bed & Breakfast	★★★
	Glen Eden Cottage	HS2 9LZ	01851 612291	Awaiting Grading	
	Glen House	HS2 9NU	01851 860241	Bed & Breakfast	★★★
	Gravir		01851 704297	Self Catering	★★★
	Hawthorn Cottage		01851 621419	Self Catering	★★★★
	Hollyburn		01851 870483	Self Catering	★★★
	Kingfisher Cottage	HS2 9LS	01851 700119	Awaiting Grading	
	Lag Na Mara	HS2 9HP	01651 851156	Awaiting Grading	
	Leumadair Guest House	HS2 9DY	01851 621706	Guest House	★★★★
	Loch Breacleit View		01259 210599	Self Catering	★★★
	Loch Roag Guest House	HS2 9EF	01851 621357	Guest House	★★★★
	Lochanview Cottage		07768 923740	Self Catering	★★★★
	Lochs House B&B	HS2 9NW	01851 860514	Awaiting Grading	
	Monadh & Eala Lodges		01851 621357	Self Catering	★★★★★
	No 3 Gearrannan	HS2 9AL	01851 643416	Group Accommodation	★★
	Ocean View		01851 704751	Self Catering	★★★★
	Penuel	HS2 9NP	01851 860340	Bed & Breakfast	★★★
	Planasker Old School	HS2 9QP	01851 880476	Bed & Breakfast	★★★★
	Riof Ocean Cottage		01851 672354	Self Catering	★★★★ ⓕ

♿ Unassisted wheelchair access   ♿ Assisted wheelchair access   ⚠ Access for visitors with mobility difficulties
ⓟ Bronze Green Tourism Award   ⓟⓟ Silver Green Tourism Award   ⓟⓟⓟ Gold Green Tourism Award
For further information on our Green Tourism Business Scheme please see page 7.

Advertisers' locations have been sorted by postcode. In Scotland, postcodes can cover fairly large geographical areas. Please check distance of property from specified location with the individual provider. VisitScotland cannot take any responsibility for this.

427

Location	Property Name	Postcode	Telephone	Classification	Star Rating
Isle of Lewis	Scaliscro Lodge		01851 672325	Self Catering	★
	Seaview Cottage	HS2 9NP	01851 860522	Awaiting Grading	
	Shiantview		01851 705283	Self Catering	★★★★
	Suainaval	HS2 9JF	01851 672386	Bed & Breakfast	★★★★
	Ten Tolsta Chaolais	HS2 9DW	01851 621722	Bed & Breakfast	★★★★
	The Cottage		01851 830334	Self Catering	★★★★
	The Loch Erisort Inn	HS2 9RA	01851 830473	Inn	★★★
	The Mollans		01851 705338	Self Catering	★★★★
	Tigh A Bheannaich		01851 672360	Self Catering	★★★
	Tigh Bhisa Blackhouse		01381 610496	Self Catering	★★★★
	Tigh Na Mara		01851 830479	Self Catering	★★★
	Tighnabruaich	HS2 9PN	01851 830742	Bed & Breakfast	★★★
	Tigh-nan-Eilean		01851 672377	Self Catering	★★★ to ★★★★ ♿ 🄿
	Westside		01851 621311	Self Catering	★★★
Isle of Lewis/ Stornoway	22 Braighe Road		01851 706877	Self Catering	★★★
	24 Lower Shader		01494 763074	Self Catering	★★
	6 Laxdale Lane		01851 706966	Self Catering	★★★★
	6 Upper Garrabost	HS2 0PN	01851 870906	Awaiting Grading	
	7a Eader Dha Fhadhail		01296 668118	Self Catering	★★★★
	Baile-Na-Cille	HS2 9SD	01851 672242	Guest House	★★
	Bayview House		01491 612559	Self Catering	★★★
	Beechland Self Catering Annexe		01851 701533	Self Catering	★★★
	Benside Cottage		01851 700369	Self Catering	★★★★
	Borve House Hotel	HS2 0RX	01851 850 223	Awaiting Grading	
	Brackenbury		01851 870576	Self Catering	★★★★
	Braighe House	HS2 0BQ	01851 705287	Guest House	★★★★★
	Braighe Lodge		01851 706073	Self Catering	★★★★
	Broad Bay House	HS2 0LQ	0785 0787094	Guest House	★★★★★ ♿
	Carnan Beag	HS2 0AE	01851 704726	Bed & Breakfast	★★★★
	Ceol-Na-Mara		01851 810429	Self Catering	★★★★
	Ceol-Na-Mara	HS2 0PB	01851 870339	Bed & Breakfast	★★★
	Chalet Cottages		01851 705771	Self Catering	★★
	Comraich		07812 010693	Self Catering	★★★
	Fasgadh	HS2 0HT	01851 705788	Awaiting Grading	
	Galson Farm	HS2 0SH	01851 850492	Hostel	★★★★
	Galson Farm Guest House	HS2 0SH	01851 850492	Guest House	★★★★
	Gladstone House		01851 810269	Self Catering	★★★★
	Harsgeir View Cottage		01851 703612	Self Catering	★★★★
	Kearnaval	HS2 0HS	01851 702853	Bed & Breakfast	★★
	Kirklea Chalet		01851 820379	Self Catering	★★★
	Lasgair	HS2 0QY	01851 840409	Holiday Caravan	
	Lathamor	HS2 0EA	01851 706093	Bed & Breakfast	★★★
	Laxdale Bunkhouse	HS2 0DP	01851 706966	Hostel	★★★★ 🚶
	Laxdale Holiday Park	HS2 0DR	01851 706966	Holiday Park	★★★★
	Moorpark Cottages	HS2 0QZ	01851 840225	Awaiting Grading	
	Newvalley Cottage		01471 822750	Self Catering	★★★★
	Ocean View		01613 8322244	Self Catering	★★★★

♿ Unassisted wheelchair access   ♿ Assisted wheelchair access   🚶 Access for visitors with mobility difficulties
🄿 Bronze Green Tourism Award   🄿🄿 Silver Green Tourism Award   🄿🄿🄿 Gold Green Tourism Award
For further information on our Green Tourism Business Scheme please see page 7.

428   To find out more go to visitscotland.com

Location	Property Name	Postcode	Telephone	Classification	Star Rating
Isle of Lewis Stornoway	Onadune		001 781 383 2842	Self Catering	★★★★
	Park House		01851 703376	Self Catering	★★★★
	Ravenstar	HS2 0JS	01851 820517	Bed & Breakfast	★★★
	Reidhbhat		01851 705008	Self Catering	★★★
	Rockvilla	HS2 0QY	01851 840286	Bed & Breakfast	★★★
	Seaglen Cottage		01772 816105	Self Catering	★★★★
	Seaside Villa	HS2 0LQ	01851 820208	Bed & Breakfast	★★★★
	Sonas		01851 850489	Self Catering	★★
	The Cross Inn	HS2 0SN	01851 810378	Inn	★★★
	The Flat		01851 870258	Self Catering	★★
	The Log Cabin	HS2 0TH	07841 800288	Awaiting Grading	
	The Sheiling		01851 810131	Self Catering	★★★
Isle of Mull	Abbey View	PA66 6BL	01681 700723	Bed & Breakfast	★★★
	Ach Na Brae Cottages		01681 700260	Self Catering	★★★★
	Achaban House	PA66 6BL	01681 700205	Guest House	★★★
	Achadh A'Mhullaich		01244 373862	Self Catering	★★★
	Achnacraig		01688 400309	Self Catering	★★★★
	Achnadrish House	PA75 6QF	01688 400388	Bed & Breakfast	★★★★
	Achnadrish House		01688 400388	Self Catering	★★★
	An Caladh Bed and Breakfast	PA67 6DH	01681 700115	Bed & Breakfast	★★★★
	Ard Mhor House	PA72 6JL	01680 300255	Guest House	★★★
	Ard Shellach		01283 702982	Self Catering	★★★
	Ardachy House Apartment		01681 700505	Self Catering	★★★
	Ardachy House Hotel	PA67 6DS	01681 700505	Small Hotel	★★★
	Ardbeg House	PA75 6QJ	01688 400254	Bed & Breakfast	★★★
	Ardfenaig Coach House		01681 700210	Self Catering	★★★★
	Ardfenaig Farmhouses		01681 700260	Self Catering	★★★★
	Ardness House	PA67 6DU	01681 700260	Bed & Breakfast	★★★
	Ardtun House	PA67 6DG	01681 700264	Bed & Breakfast	★★★
	Ardtun House & Cottage – The Stables		01681 700264	Self Catering	★★ to ★★★
	Arle Lodge	PA72 6JS	01680 300299	Hostel	★★★
	Aros View	PA72 6JB	01680 300372	Bed & Breakfast	★★★
	Assynt		01282 692816	Self Catering	★★★★
	Baliscate Guest House	PA75 6QA	01688 302048	Guest House	★★★
	Balmeanach Park	PA65 6BA	01680 300342	Touring Park	★★★★
	Barn Cottage and Stables	PA71 6HR	01680 300451	Bed & Breakfast	★★★
	Barrachandroman Farmhouse		01680 814220	Self Catering	★★★★
	Beach	PA70 6HE	0131 6693082	Awaiting Grading	
	Bealach an Dreathan- Donn Cottage		01688 302517	Self Catering	★★★★
	Beech & Willow Cill-Mhoire		01688 400445	Self Catering	★★★
	Bellachroy Hotel	PA75 6QW	01688 400314	Inn	★★★
	Benmore Estate – Drive Cottage		01680 300543	Self Catering	★★ to ★★★★
	Birchgrove	PA64 4AP	01680 812364	Bed & Breakfast	★★★★
	Braeside House		01623 477670	Self Catering	★★★★
	Brockville	PA75 6RS	01688 302741	Bed & Breakfast	★★★★
	Bruach Roineach		01688 400213	Self Catering	★★★★
	Buel-na-Atha	PA75 6QZ	01688 302560	Bed & Breakfast	★★★

♿ Unassisted wheelchair access   ♿ Assisted wheelchair access   ⚊ Access for visitors with mobility difficulties
🄿 Bronze Green Tourism Award   🄿🄿 Silver Green Tourism Award   🄿🄿🄿 Gold Green Tourism Award
For further information on our Green Tourism Business Scheme please see page 7.

Advertisers' locations have been sorted by postcode. In Scotland, postcodes can cover fairly large geographical areas.
Please check distance of property from specified location with the individual provider. VisitScotland cannot take any responsibility for this.

429

Location	Property Name	Postcode	Telephone	Classification	Star Rating
Isle of Mull	Burnside		0208 9473181	Self Catering	★★
	Burnside Blacksmiths & Gamekeepers Cottages		01688 302251	Self Catering	★★★★
	Calgary Hotel	PA75 6QW	01688 400256	Restaurant With Rooms	★★★
	Calve and Aros		01688 302193	Self Catering	★★★
	Caol-Ithe	PA66 6BL	01681 700375	Bed & Breakfast	★★★★
	Caol-Ithe Self Catering		01681 700375	Self Catering	★★★
	Caorann	PA72 6JS	01680 300355	Bed & Breakfast	★★★
	Carnaburg	PA75 6NT	01688 302409	Guest House	★★
	Clachan Cottage		01688 400303	Self Catering	★★★
	Coille Grianach		01438 798700	Self Catering	★★★
	Copeland House	PA75 6PZ	01688 302049	Bed & Breakfast	★★★
	Corrieyairack & Fas Na Cloich		01899 220473	Self Catering	★★★★ ♠
	Courtyard Cottage		01680 300581	Self Catering	★★★★
	Craig Rowan	PA70 6HB	01681 704230	Bed & Breakfast	★★★★
	Craignure Bay House		01539 620343	Self Catering	★★★★
	Crannich Holiday Caravans	PA72 6JP	01680 300495	Holiday Caravan	
	Crosslake		0141 9444473	Self Catering	★★★
	Cuidhe Leathain	PA75 6PD	01688 302504	Bed & Breakfast	★★★
	Cuin Lodge	PA75 6QL	01688 400346	Bed & Breakfast	★★★★
	Dee-Emm Bed & Breakfast	PA65 6AY	01680 812440	Bed & Breakfast	★★★
	Dervaig Bunkrooms	PA75 6JN	01688 400249	Bunkhouse	
	Druimgigha Farm		01688 400228	Self Catering	★★★★
	Druimnacroish	PA75 6QW	01688 400274	Guest House	★★★
	Druimnacroish		01688 400274	Self Catering	★★★
	Dunan	PA67 6DH	01681 700665	Bed & Breakfast	★★
	Dunara Cottage		01688 302321	Self Catering	★★★ to ★★★★★
	Failte Guest House	PA75 6NU	01688 302495	Guest House	★★★
	Faoileann Ghlas		01271 370582	Self Catering	★★★★
	Fascadail	PA72 6JB	01680 300444	Bed & Breakfast	★★★
	Fisherman's Cottage		01688 302251	Self Catering	★★★
	Frachadil Farm Steadings		01688 400265	Self Catering	★★★
	Fuaran	PA75 6PY	01688 302888	Bed & Breakfast	★★★
	Garden Cottage		01688 302075	Self Catering	★★★ to ★★★★ 🄿🄿🄿
	Glen Cottage		01688 400518	Self Catering	★★★
	Glenaros Farm Cottage – Tigh Beag		01631 770369	Self Catering	★★
	Glenaros Lodge	PA72 6JP	01680 300301	Hostel	★★
	Glengorm Castle	PA75 6QE	01688 302321	Bed & Breakfast	★★★★
	Glenview	PA75 6QJ	01688 400239	Bed & Breakfast	★★★★
	Glenview		01688 400239	Self Catering	★★★
	Half-Moon House		01260 298512	Self Catering	★★★★
	Harvey's House		0131 2439335	Self Catering	★★★
	Heatherbank		01680 300342	Self Catering	★★★
	Hector's House		0131 2439335	Self Catering	★★★
	Hideaway Lodges – Staffa, Ulva and Eorsa		01680 300567	Self Catering	★★★★
	Highland Cottage	PA75 6PD	01688 302030	Small Hotel	★★★★ ♠
	Inverlussa	PA65 6BD	01680 812436	Holiday Caravan	

♿ Unassisted wheelchair access   ♿ Assisted wheelchair access   ♠ Access for visitors with mobility difficulties
🄿 Bronze Green Tourism Award   🄿🄿 Silver Green Tourism Award   🄿🄿🄿 Gold Green Tourism Award
For further information on our Green Tourism Business Scheme please see page 7.

Location	Property Name	Postcode	Telephone	Classification	Star Rating	
Isle of Mull	Iona Cottage		01315 568794	Self Catering	★★	
	Isle of Mull Hotel	PA65 6BB	01680 812351	Hotel	★★★	
	Kathleen & Mabel Cottages		01680 814214	Self Catering	★★	
	Keills Cottage		01786 860739	Self Catering	★★★	
	Killoran House	PA75 6QR	01688 400362	Guest House	★★★★	
	Kilninian Schoolhouse		01721 724428	Self Catering	★★★	
	Knockan		01786 825510	Self Catering	★★★	
	Lochnameal	PA75 6QB	01688 302364	Holiday Caravan		
	Lonan	PA75 6RA	01688 302082	Bed & Breakfast	★★★	
	Maolbhuidhe B&B	PA66 6BP	01681 700718	Bed & Breakfast	★★★	
	Maple Cottage		01416 477288	Self Catering	★★★	
	McLean Cottage		01680 300332	Self Catering	★★★	
	Morvern and Sunart		01688 302629	Self Catering	★★★	
	Na Croitean		01681 700471	Self Catering	★★★★	🕈
	Newcrofts	PA67 6DS	01681 700471	Farm House	★★★	
	Newcrofts	PA67 6PS	01681 700471	Holiday Caravan		
	No 2 Royal Buildings		01330 850663	Self Catering	★★	
	No 6		01355 236317	Self Catering	★★	
	No.5 Eas Brae Apartments		01688 302821	Self Catering	★★★	
	Oakfield Cottage		0131 4411259	Self Catering	★★★	
	Oaklee	PA75 6PS	01688 302520	Bed & Breakfast	★★★★	
	Old Mill Cottage	PA64 6AP	01680 812442	Bed & Breakfast	★★★★	
	Oran-Na-Mara	PA67 6DG	01681 700087	Bed & Breakfast	★★★★	
	Oxlip Cottage		01688 302534	Self Catering	★★★	
	Park Lodge Hotel	PA75 6PR	01688 302430	Small Hotel	★★	
	Penmore Beg		01604 770868	Self Catering	★★★	
	Pennygate Lodge	PA65 6AY	01680 812333	Guest House	★★★	
	Pennyghael Hotel	PA70 6HB	01681 704288	Small Hotel	★★★	🕈
	Pennygown Farm	PA72 6JN	01680 300335	Holiday Caravan		
	Puffer		01680 300389	Self Catering	★★★★	
	Raraig House		01688 302390	Self Catering	★★★	
	Raraig House West Wing Suite	PA75 6PU	01688 302390	Bed & Breakfast	★★★	
	Roan Cottage		07746 437600	Self Catering	★★★	
	Salachran		01786 472900	Self Catering	★★★	🕈
	Sands Cottage		0208 4882543	Self Catering	★★★	
	Saorphin Cottages – Tigh Beag & Tigh Mor		01256 381275	Self Catering	★★	
	Seaview	PA66 6BL	01681 700235	Bed & Breakfast	★★★★	🌿🌿🌿
	Seaview Cottage		01355 227194	Self Catering	★★★★	
	Shieling Holidays	PA65 6AY	01680 812496	Camping Park	★★★★★	
	Shieling Holidays Cottage		01680 812496	Self Catering	★★★	
	Shore Cottage		01680 812421	Self Catering	★★★	
	Shuna		01688 302044	Self Catering	★★★★ to ★★★★★	
	Spey Cottage		01506 811488	Self Catering	★★★	
	Staffa Cottages Bed & Breakfast	PA75 6PL	01688 302464	Bed & Breakfast	★★	
	Staffa House	PA66 6BL	01681 700677	Bed & Breakfast	★★★	
	Strongarbh House	PA75 6PR	01688 302319	Bed & Breakfast	★★★★	
	Sunart View	PA75 6QA	01688 302439	Bed & Breakfast	★★★	

Advertisers' locations have been sorted by postcode. In Scotland, postcodes can cover fairly large geographical areas. Please check distance of property from specified location with the individual provider. VisitScotland cannot take any responsibility for this.

Location	Property Name	Postcode	Telephone	Classification	Star Rating	
Isle of Mull	Taigh Foise		01681 700509	Self Catering	★★★★	♁
	The Barn	PA62 6AA	01680 814220	Bed & Breakfast	★★★★	
	The Bothy		01688 400229	Self Catering	★★★	
	The Long House		01228 710661	Self Catering	★	
	The Old Mill		01688 400242	Self Catering	★★★★	𝑃𝑃
	The Old School House		01962 771557	Self Catering	★★ to ★★★	
	The Sheiling		01688 400249	Self Catering	★★★ to ★★★★	ᵹ 𝑃𝑃𝑃
	The Smithy		01491 639299	Self Catering	★★★	
	The Stables		01680 300371	Self Catering	★★★	
	The Steading		01681 705217	Self Catering	★★★★	
	Tigh An Solas	PA72 6JN	01680 300506	Bed & Breakfast	★★★	
	Tigh Bhan		01680 300424	Self Catering	★★★	
	Tigh Na Acha		01372 728525	Self Catering	★★★	
	Tigh Na Caora		01206 263800	Self Catering	★★	
	Tiroran House	PA69 6ES	01681 705232	Small Hotel	★★★★	
	Tobermory Campsite	PA75 6QF	01688 302624	Touring Park	★★★	
	Tobermory Youth Hostel	PA75 6NU	0870 0041151	Hostel	★★★	𝑃𝑃𝑃
	Torness		01688 302496	Self Catering	★★★★	
	Torr a'Clachan		01688 400251	Self Catering	★★★	
	Torr Buan House	PA73 6LY	01688 500121	Bed & Breakfast	★★★★	𝑃𝑃𝑃
	Torr Gorm	PA72 6JB	01680 300250	Awaiting Grading		
	Tostarie House		0131 4772130	Self Catering	★★★	
	Tostary Cottage		01223 352860	Self Catering	★★★	
	Tralee		01922 624091	Self Catering	★★★★	
	Twelve Oaks		01680 812187	Self Catering	★★★	
	Upstairs Apartment		01688 300307	Self Catering	★★★ to ★★★★	
	Victoria Cottage		01270 528045	Self Catering	★★★	
	Western Isles Hotel	PA75 6 P	01688 302012	Awaiting Grading		
	Wild Cottage	PA64 6AP	01680 812105	Bed & Breakfast	★★★	
Isle of North Uist	12 Balemore		01876 510342	Self Catering	★★	
	17 Kersavagh		01372 469340	Self Catering	★★★	
	18 Illeray		01876 580672	Self Catering	★★★	
	Airigh An Obain		01876 580229	Self Catering	★★★★	
	An T-Seann Dachaidh		01343 550805	Self Catering	★★★	
	Ardnastruban	HS6 5HT	01870 602452	Bed & Breakfast	★★★★	
	Bonnie View	HS6 5EJ	01876 580211	Bed & Breakfast	★★★★	
	Clachan		01876 580644	Self Catering	★★	
	Coille Gorm	HS6 5EB	07909 993863	Awaiting Grading		
	Glendale		01870 602029	Self Catering	★★★	
	Heisker		01434 603401	Self Catering	★★★★	
	John MacIsaac		01224 825509	Self Catering	★★★★★	
	Kintail Cottage		01876 500899	Self Catering	★★★★	
	Knockintorran		01876 510379	Self Catering	★★★	
	Langass Lodge	HS6 5EX	01876 580285	Small Hotel	★★★	𝑃𝑃
	Larkfield House		01876 560238	Self Catering	★★★	
	Loch Portain House		0131 4479911	Self Catering	★★★	
	Lochmaddy Hotel	HS6 5AA	01876 500331	Small Hotel	★★	
	No. 19 Knockline	HS6 5DT	01876 510390	Bed & Breakfast	★★★★	

ᵹ Unassisted wheelchair access   ᵹ Assisted wheelchair access   ♁ Access for visitors with mobility difficulties
𝑃 Bronze Green Tourism Award   𝑃𝑃 Silver Green Tourism Award   𝑃𝑃𝑃 Gold Green Tourism Award
For further information on our Green Tourism Business Scheme please see page 7.

Location	Property Name	Postcode	Telephone	Classification	Star Rating
Isle of North Uist	Old Shop House	HS6 5DS	01876 510395	Bed & Breakfast	★★★
	Redburn House	HS6 5AA	01876 500301	Bed & Breakfast	★★★ ⋏
	Rona View		01606 44422	Self Catering	★★★
	Rushlee House	HS6 5AE	01876 500274	Bed & Breakfast	★★★★
	Sgeir Ruadh	HS6 5DL	01876 510312	Bed & Breakfast	★★★
	Shivinish	HS6 5JA	01870 602481	Bed & Breakfast	★★★★
	Taigh Mairi		0131 4660781	Self Catering	★★★★
	The Boathouse		01671 402554	Self Catering	★★★★
	The Moorings		01505 614660	Self Catering	★★★
	The Smiddy	HS6 5BJ	01876 540235	Awaiting Grading	
	Tigh Alasdair		0141 5853155	Self Catering	★★★
	Tigh Dearg Hotel	HS6 5AE	01876 500700	Small Hotel	★★★★ 🦽
	Tigh Geal	HS6 5BS	0131 3461458	Awaiting Grading	
	Tigh Na Boireach & Boreray		01876 560403	Self Catering	★★★★★
	Tigh-na-Mara		07930 164013	Self Catering	★★★★★
	Torran Gorm		01876 500391	Self Catering	★★★★
	Uist Outdoor Centre	HS6 5AE	01876 500480	Group Accommodation	★★
Isle of Scalpay	Hamarsay		01463 236049	Self Catering	★★★★
	Highcroft	HS4 3YB	01859 540305	Bed & Breakfast	★★★★
	Hirta House	HS4 3XZ	01859 540394	Bed & Breakfast	★★★★
	New Haven	HS4 3XZ	01859 540325	Bed & Breakfast	★★★★
	Stac Pollaidh		01859 540394	Self Catering	★★★★
Isle of Skye	1 Eynort		01851 701790	Self Catering	★★★
	1/2 of 2		0777 5954481	Self Catering	★★★★
	11 Hallin Park		0208 8763054	Self Catering	★★★
	17 Kyleside	IV41 8PW	01599 534197	Bed & Breakfast	★★★
	21 Fiscavaig		01478 640365	Self Catering	★★
	7 Geary		01470 592276	Self Catering	★
	Achalochan House	IV56 8FJ	01470 572323	Bed & Breakfast	★★★★
	Ardmore		01471 822372	Self Catering	★★★★★
	Ardmore Holiday Cottage		01470 592305	Self Catering	★★★ to ★★★★★ 🦽
	Ardmorn	IV55 8ZD	01470 521354	Bed & Breakfast	★★★★
	Ardtreck Cottage	IV47 8SN	01478 640744	Bed & Breakfast	★★★★
	Ardvasar Hotel	IV45 8RS	01471 844223	Small Hotel	★★★
	Ashaig Campsite	IV42 8PZ	07846 485310	Awaiting Grading	
	Auld Orwell Cottage		01470 592363	Self Catering	★★★★ 🦽
	Balmeanach House	IV56 8FH	01470 572320	Bed & Breakfast	★★★★
	Beinn an Fhraoich		0161 9413440	Self Catering	★★★
	Berabhaigh Bed & Breakfast	IV49 9AE	01471 822372	Bed & Breakfast	★★★★
	Bla Bheinn	IV47 8SP	01478 640269	Bed & Breakfast	★★★★
	Blairdhu House	IV41 8PQ	01599 534760	Guest House	★★★★
	Boat Lodge	IV47 8SR	01478 640396	Awaiting Grading	
	Bracadale Holiday Cottages		01470 572231	Self Catering	★★★
	Braigh A' Roid	IV49 9AQ	01471 820221	Bed & Breakfast	★★★★
	Broadford Hotel	IV49 9AB	01471 822414	Hotel	★★★★
	Broadford Youth Hostel	IV49 9AA	0870 1553255	Hostel	★★★ 𝄞𝄞
	Bruaich Mhor	IV42 8QB	01471 820304	Awaiting Grading	

🦽 Unassisted wheelchair access   🦽 Assisted wheelchair access   ⋏ Access for visitors with mobility difficulties
𝄞 Bronze Green Tourism Award   𝄞𝄞 Silver Green Tourism Award   𝄞𝄞𝄞 Gold Green Tourism Award
For further information on our Green Tourism Business Scheme please see page 7.

Advertisers' locations have been sorted by postcode. In Scotland, postcodes can cover fairly large geographical areas.
Please check distance of property from specified location with the individual provider. VisitScotland cannot take any responsibility for this.

433

Location	Property Name	Postcode	Telephone	Classification	Star Rating	
Isle of Skye	But n Ben	IV42 8SL	01478 640254	Hostel	★★★★	
	Carter's Rest	IV55 8WY	01470 511272	Guest House	★★★★	
	Clach Ghlas	IV55 8NR	01470 511205	Bed & Breakfast	★★★★★	
	Clisham	IV49 9AQ	01471 822320	Awaiting Grading		
	Clover Hill Holiday Cottage		01471 822763	Self Catering	★★★★	
	Coille Challtainn	IV43 8QU	01471 833711	Bed & Breakfast	★★★	
	Corran Guest House	IV41 8PL	01599 534859	Guest House	★★★★	
	Corriegorm Beag		01471 822515	Self Catering	★★★	⚹
	Croft Bunkhouse	IV42 8SL	01478 640254	Hostel	★★★	
	Crofter's Cottage		01470 572374	Self Catering	★★★★★	
	Crossal House	IV47 8SP	01478 640745	Bed & Breakfast	★★★	
	Denekin		07957 752001	Self Catering	★★	
	Duisdale Hotel	IV43 8QW	01471 833202	Country House Hotel	★★★★	
	Dun Caan Hostel	IV41 8PL	01599 534087	Hostel	★★★★	
	Dunmara B&B	IV49 9AJ	01471 820319	Bed & Breakfast	★★★	
	Dunollie Hotel	IV49 9AE		Hotel	★★	
	Dunorin House Hotel	IV55 8GZ	01470 521488	Small Hotel	★★★	
	Fernlea	IV42 8PY	01471 822107	Bed & Breakfast	★★★	
	Fineviews	IV47 8SL	07810 710485	Bed & Breakfast	★★★	
	Flora MacDonald Hostel	IV44 8RG	01471 844272	Hostel	★★★	
	Flora MacDonald's Apartment		01471 844305	Self Catering	★★★ to ★★★★	
	Gesto Cottage		01470 592281	Self Catering	★★★	
	Glenarroch	IV41 8PH	01599 534845	Guest House	★★★	
	Glenbrittle Youth Hostel	IV47 8TA	0870 1553255	Hostel	★★★	🏅
	Glendrynoch Cottages – The Old School House		01478 640218	Self Catering	★★ to ★★★	
	Grianan	IV56 8FH	01470 572374	Bed & Breakfast	★★★	
	Henderson House		01470 592235	Self Catering	★★★★	
	Hillview	IV49 9AE	01471 822083	Bed & Breakfast	★★★★	
	Homeleigh	IV45 8RU	01471 844752	Bed & Breakfast	★★★	
	Hotel Eilean Iarmain	IV43 8QR	01471 833332	Small Hotel	★★★	
	Inver Rose		0191 3840151	Self Catering	★★★★	
	Kings Arms Hotel	IV41 8PH		Hotel	★★	
	Kinloch Campsite	IV55 8WQ	01470 521210	Touring Park	★★★	
	Kinloch Lodge	IV43 8QY	01471 833214	Country House Hotel	★★★★	
	La Bergerie		01470 592282	Self Catering	★★★★	♿
	Loch Aluinn B&B	IV48 8TD	01478 650288	Bed & Breakfast	★★★★	
	Loch Aluinn S/C	IV48 8TD	01478 650288	Awaiting Grading		
	Loch View		01463 235793	Self Catering	★★	
	Lochbay Boathouse		01470 592354	Self Catering	★★★★	
	Luib House	IV49 9AN	01471 820334	Bed & Breakfast	★★★	
	Maltby B&B	IV42 8PY	01471 822642	Bed & Breakfast	★★★★	
	Mavis Bank		01471 833455	Self Catering	★★★★	
	Meadale Cottage		01470 572216	Self Catering	★★★	
	Mo-Dhachaidh	IV41 8PR	01599 534724	Bed & Breakfast	★★★★	
	No. 8 crossal		01786 471455	Self Catering	★★★★	
	Number Ten		01470 511795	Self Catering	★★★★★	
	Oak Tree Cottage		0113 2781638	Self Catering	★★★	

♿ Unassisted wheelchair access   ♿ Assisted wheelchair access   ⚹ Access for visitors with mobility difficulties
🏅 Bronze Green Tourism Award   🏅 Silver Green Tourism Award   🏅 Gold Green Tourism Award
For further information on our Green Tourism Business Scheme please see page 7.

434   To find out more go to visitscotland.com

Location	Property Name	Postcode	Telephone	Classification	Star Rating	
Isle of Skye	Ord House	IV44 8RN	01471 855212	Bed & Breakfast	★★★★★	
	Osdale Farmhouse		01349 877039	Self Catering	★★★★	
	Osedale House	IV56 8FJ	01470 572317	Bed & Breakfast	★★★	
	Phoenix House Bed & Breakfast	IV47 8SR	01478 640775	Bed & Breakfast	★★★★	
	Puffin Cottage		01761 239008	Self Catering	★★★★	
	Roskhill Barn		07899 660200	Self Catering	★★★	
	Roskhill Barn Bed & Breakfast	IV55 8ZD	01470 521755	Bed & Breakfast	★★★	
	Roskhill House	IV55 8ZD	01483 740910	Guest House	★★★★	
	Rowan Cottage		01470 521755	Self Catering	★★★	
	Ruisgarry	IV42 8PY	01471 822850	Bed & Breakfast	★★★★	
	Salento B&B	IV41 8PR	01599 534771	Bed & Breakfast	★★★	
	Saucy Mary's Lodge	IV41 8PL	01599 534845	Hostel	★★★	
	Scalpay View	IV49 9AJ	01471 820229	Bed & Breakfast	★★★	
	Sea Drift		01471 822531	Self Catering	★★★	⋀
	Seagull's Nest		01470 511272	Self Catering	★★★★	
	Seaview	IV49 9AB	01471 820308	Guest House	★★★	⋀
	Shira	IV49 9AE	01471 822848	Awaiting Grading		
	Silverdale	IV55 8ZS	01470 521251	Bed & Breakfast	★★★★	
	Skye Backpackers	IV41 8PH	01599 534510	Backpacker	★★	
	Skyewalker Hostel	IV47 8SL	01478 640250	Hostel	★★★★	
	Slapin View	IV49 9BA	01471 822672	Farm House	★★	
	Sligachan Bunkhouse	IV47 8SW	01478 650204	Hostel	★★★	
	Stein Inn	IV55 8GA	01470 592362	Inn	★★★	℗℗℗
	Stein Inn Apartment		01470 592362	Self Catering	★★★	
	Strathgorm	IV42 8PY	01471 822508	Bed & Breakfast	★★★★	
	Tarnershiel		01494 758348	Self Catering	★★	
	The Cedars			Self Catering	★★	
	The Old Byre	IV56 8FJ	01470 572774	Bed & Breakfast	★★★	
	The Old Church		01270 759635	Self Catering	★★★	
	The Old Church	IV49 9BA	01422 884276	Awaiting Grading		
	The Old Mission Hall		0141 5853155	Self Catering	★★★	
	The Rowans	IV47 8SL	01478 640478	Bed & Breakfast	★★★★	
	The Schoolhouse		+0033 1473 40358	Self Catering	★★	
	The Skye Picture House	IV49 9AJ	01471 822531	Guest House	★★★	
	The Waterfront Bunkhouse	IV47 8SR	01478 640205	Hostel	★★★	
	Three Chimneys	IV55 8ZT	01470 511258	Restaurant With Rooms	★★★★★	
	Tigh an Dochais	IV49 9AQ	01471 820022	Bed & Breakfast	★★★★★	
	Tigh Na Cairigh		07860 219861	Self Catering	★★★★	
	Tigh Na Mara		01463 715939	Self Catering	★★★	
	Tigh Seonag, Tigh Phadruig & Tigh Mairi		01471 866275	Self Catering	★★★★	
	Tighban		01202 460241	Self Catering	★★★★	
	Tir Alainn	IV42 8PY	01471 822366	Bed & Breakfast	★★★★	
	Toravaig House Hotel	IV44 8RE	01471 833231	Small Hotel	★★★★	
	Torgorm Cottage		01626 852266	Self Catering	★★★	
	Trien Cottage		01478 640463	Self Catering	★★	
	Uiginish Farmhouse	IV55 8ZR	01470 521431	Farm House	★★★	

♿ Unassisted wheelchair access   ♿ Assisted wheelchair access   ⋀ Access for visitors with mobility difficulties
℗ Bronze Green Tourism Award   ℗℗ Silver Green Tourism Award   ℗℗℗ Gold Green Tourism Award
For further information on our Green Tourism Business Scheme please see page 7.

Advertisers' locations have been sorted by postcode. In Scotland, postcodes can cover fairly large geographical areas. Please check distance of property from specified location with the individual provider. VisitScotland cannot take any responsibility for this.

435

Location	Property Name	Postcode	Telephone	Classification	Star Rating
Isle of Skye	Ullinish Country Lodge	IV56 8FD	01470 572214	Restaurant With Rooms	★★★★★
	Woodburn Cottage		01470 592708	Self Catering	★★★
Isle of South Uist	2 Sandwick		01189 782587	Self Catering	★★★
	298 Kilpheader		01878 700204	Self Catering	★★★
	363 Leth Meadhanach	HS8 5TE	01878 700586	Bed & Breakfast	★★★
	6 Milton	HS8 5RY	01878 710214	Holiday Caravan	
	6 North Locheynort	HS8 5SN	01878 710363	Holiday Caravan	
	An Seann Tigh		01870 620322	Self Catering	★★★
	Anglers Retreat	HS8 5QY	01870 610325	Guest House	★★★
	Anglers Retreat	HS8 5QY	01870 610325	Holiday Caravan	
	Ard Na Mara	HS8 5TB	01878 700452	Bed & Breakfast	★★★
	Benview		0208 71382399	Self Catering	★★★
	Borrodale Hotel	HS8 5SS	01878 700444	Small Hotel	★★★
	Brae Lea House	HS8 5TH	01878 700497	Guest House	★★★
	Caloraidh	HS8 5RY	01878 710365	Bed & Breakfast	★★★ ♀
	Chalet	HS8 5PE	01870 610274	Awaiting Grading	
	Clanranald Self Catering	HS8 5SS	01878 700266	Awaiting Grading	
	Corncrake Cottage		01878 700371	Self Catering	★★★★
	Croft House B&B	HS8 5RY	01878 710224	Bed & Breakfast	★★★
	Crossroads	HS8 5SD	01870 620321	Bed & Breakfast	★★★ ♿
	Crossroads	HS8 5SD	01870 620321	Holiday Caravan	
	Eriskay Self-Catering		0141 3399143	Self Catering	★★★★ ♀
	Kiaora	HS8 5TU	01878 700382	Bed & Breakfast	★★★
	Kilchoan	HS8 5TN	01878 700517	Bed & Breakfast	★★★
	Kilvale	HS8 5SX	01878 700394	Bed & Breakfast	★★★
	Kinloch	HS8 5RR	01870 620316	Bed & Breakfast	★★★
	Lasgair House		01851 840409	Self Catering	★★★
	Lochboisdale Hotel	HS8 5TH	01878 700332	Small Hotel	★★
	Lochside Cottage	HS8 5TN	01878 700472	Holiday Caravan	
	Ocean View		01878 700383	Self Catering	★★★★ to ★★★★★
	Ocean View	HS8 5TU	01878 700383	Holiday Caravan	
	Oir Na Mara	HS8 5JL	01878 720216	Awaiting Grading	
	Orasay Inn	HS8 5PD	01870 610298	Small Hotel	★★★ ♿
	Polochar Inn	HS8 5TT	01878 700215	Inn	★★★★
	The Old School House		01878 700295	Self Catering	★★★★
Isle of Tiree	Cottage at Port A Mhuillin		01879 220538	Self Catering	★★★
	Kenoreef		01879 220321	Self Catering	★★★★
	Millhouse Hostel	PA77 6XA	01879 220435	Hostel	★★★★
	Tiree Lodge Hotel	PA77 6TW	01879 220368	Awaiting Grading	
	Tiree Scarinish Hotel	PA77 6UH	01879 220308	Inn	★★
Jedburgh	14 Tweed Cottages		07929 736374	Self Catering	★★★★
	3 Under Nags Head Close		0207 5895231	Self Catering	★★★★
	Airenlea	TD8 6EX	07817 141705	Bed & Breakfast	★★★★
	Allerton House	TD8 6QQ	01835 869633	Guest House	★★★★ ♀
	Ancrum Craig	TD8 6UN	01835 830280	Bed & Breakfast	★★★★
	Edgerston Mill	TD8 6NF	01835 840343	Bed & Breakfast	★★★

♿ Unassisted wheelchair access ♿ Assisted wheelchair access ♀ Access for visitors with mobility difficulties
ⓟ Bronze Green Tourism Award ⓟⓟ Silver Green Tourism Award ⓟⓟⓟ Gold Green Tourism Award
For further information on our Green Tourism Business Scheme please see page 7.

To find out more go to visitscotland.com

Location	Property Name	Postcode	Telephone	Classification	Star Rating
Jedburgh	Fernlea	TD8 6LG	01835 862318	Bed & Breakfast	★★★★
	Glenacre Bed & Breakfast	TD8 6PJ	01835 840671	Bed & Breakfast	★★★★
	Glenbank House Hotel	TD8 6BD	01835 862258	Small Hotel	★
	Jedburgh Camping & Caravanning Club Site	TD8 6EF	02476 475318	Touring Park	★★★★
	Jedwater Caravan Park	TD8 6PJ	01835 840219	Holiday Park	★★★★
	Log Lodge		01835 862201	Self Catering	★★★
	Meadhon House	TD8 6BB	01835 862504	Guest House	★★★★
	Nisbet Old Schoolhouse		01835 862201	Self Catering	★★★
	Overwells Country Cottages		01835 863020	Self Catering	★★★★
	Spinney Self Catering		01835 863525	Self Catering	★★★★
	The School House	TD8 6PW	01835 840627	Bed & Breakfast	★★★★★
	The Spinney	TD8 6PB	01835 863525	Bed & Breakfast	★★★★
	Wild Rose Cottage		01835 840389	Self Catering	★★★
	Willow Court	TD8 6BN	01835 863702	Bed & Breakfast	★★★★★
	Woodend Mill		01835 830591	Self Catering	★★★★
Johnstone	Barnbrock Campsite	PA10 2PZ	01505 614791	Camping Park	★★★
	Bowfield Hotel & Country Club	PA9 1DB	01505 705225	Hotel	★★★
	Heather Cottage		01505 690628	Self Catering	★★★
Keith	Anvil Cottage		01343 820304	Self Catering	★★★★
	Braehead Villa	AB55 4AN	01340 820461	Bed & Breakfast	★★★ ♿
	Chapelhill Croft	AB55 6LQ	01542 870302	Farm House	★★★
	Craighurst Guest House	AB55 5BS	01542 880345	Bed & Breakfast	★★★★
	Davaar	AB55 4AR	01340 820464	Bed & Breakfast	★★★
	Earlsmount Fine Accommodation	AB55 5DW	01542 888397	Bed & Breakfast	★★★★
	Farm Steading		01542 882218	Self Catering	★★★★
	Fernbank House	AB55 4DL	01340 820136	Bed & Breakfast	★★★★
	Meikle Cantlay	AB55 6LJ	01542 870634	Awaiting Grading	
	Moray Cottages		01340 820007	Self Catering	★★★★
	Nashville	AB55 4AB	01340 820553	Bed & Breakfast	★★★
	Tannochbrae Guest House & Scotts Restaurant	AB55 4AL	01340 820541	Guest House	★★★★
Kelso	3 Lambing Field Cottage		01573 420241	Self Catering	★★
	Benfield	TD5 8QG	01890 817186	Awaiting Grading	
	Branston Bothy		01423 321480	Self Catering	★★★
	Burnbrae Holidays		01573 225570	Self Catering	★★★★ 🚶 PPP
	Chelsea Cottage		01337 831477	Self Catering	★★★★
	Courtyard House		01573 430241	Self Catering	★★★★
	Craggs Cottage		01573 460318	Self Catering	★★★★
	Cross Keys Hotel	TD5 7HL	01573 223303	Hotel	★★★ 🚶
	East Cottage		01573 223495	Self Catering	★★★★ PP
	Eckford Hall Steading	TD5 8LQ	01835 850715	Bed & Breakfast	★★★★★
	Edenbank House	TD5 7SX	01573 226734	Bed & Breakfast	★★★★
	Edenmouth Farm	TD5 7QB	01890 830391	Bed & Breakfast	★★★ 🚶
	Edenmouth Lodge		01890 830391	Self Catering	★★★ to ★★★★ 🚶
	Ednam House Hotel	TD5 7HT	01573 224168	Hotel	★★★
	Glebe House		07971 522040	Self Catering	★★★

♿ Unassisted wheelchair access   ♿ Assisted wheelchair access   🚶 Access for visitors with mobility difficulties
P Bronze Green Tourism Award   PP Silver Green Tourism Award   PPP Gold Green Tourism Award
For further information on our Green Tourism Business Scheme please see page 7.

Advertisers' locations have been sorted by postcode. In Scotland, postcodes can cover fairly large geographical areas.
Please check distance of property from specified location with the individual provider. VisitScotland cannot take any responsibility for this.

437

Location	Property Name	Postcode	Telephone	Classification	Star Rating	
Kelso	Inglestone House	TD5 7HQ	01573 225800	Guest House	★★★	𝕝ᵣ
	Kirk Yetholm Youth Hostel	TD5 8PG	0870 1553255	Hostel	★★	𝒫𝒫
	Marmion	TD5 7SP	01279 320411	Awaiting Grading		
	Mill House B&B	TD5 8PE	01573 420604	Bed & Breakfast	★★★★	
	Plough Hotel	TD5 8RF	01573 420215	Inn	★★	
	Plum Tree Cottage		01573 225028	Self Catering	★★★ to ★★★★	♠
	Roxburgh Barns Cottages – Keepers Cottage		01573 450257	Self Catering	★★★★	𝒫𝒫
	Roxburghe Hotel and Golf Course	TD5 8JZ	01573 223333	Country House Hotel	★★★	
	Roxburghe Hotel and Golf Course	TD5 8JZ	01573 223333	Country House Hotel	★★★	
	Stables Cottage		07789 938600	Self Catering	★★★★	
	Swallow Cottage		01573 450250	Self Catering	★★★★	♠
	The Bield	TD5 7TS	01573 470349	Bed & Breakfast	★★★	
	The Border Hotel	TD5 8PQ	01573 420237	Inn	★★★★	
	The Hermitage B&B	TD5 7AN	01573 229090	Bed & Breakfast	★★★★	
Kelty	The Watermill	KY4 0HS	01383 624321	Awaiting Grading		
	Yellowscott Country Park	KY4 0UN	07867 975561	Awaiting Grading		
Kilbirnie	Moorpark House Hotel	KA25 7LD	01505 683503	Country House Hotel	★★★★	
Killin	Am Bathach – 'The Barn'	FK21 8UT	01567 820286	Bed & Breakfast	★★★	𝒫𝒫
	Ardlochay Lodge	FK21 8TN	01567 820962	Bed & Breakfast	★★★	
	Ballinloan		01567 820562	Self Catering	★★★	
	Braveheart Backpackers	FK21 8TP	01567 829089	Bunkhouse		
	Breadalbane House	FK21 8UT	01567 820134	Guest House	★★★	
	Bridge of Lochay Hotel	FK21 8TS	01567 820272	Inn	★★★	
	Bridge Park Cottage		01225 837545	Self Catering	★★	
	Byre Cottage		01567 820270	Self Catering	★★★	
	Craigbuie Guest House	FK21 8UH	01567 820439	Guest House	★★★	
	Cruachan Farm Caravan & Camping Park	FK21 8TY	01567 820302	Holiday Park	★★★	
	Dall Lodge Country House	FK21 8TN	01567 820217	Guest House	★★★★	
	Drumfinn Country Guest House	FK21 8UY	01567 820900	Guest House	★★★	
	Fairview House	FK21 8UT	01567 820667	Guest House	★★★	
	Fiddlers Bay Lodge		01835 863250	Self Catering	★★★★	
	Gracedieu		01567 820396	Self Catering	★★★	
	Greenbank		01567 820462	Self Catering	★★	
	Kettle Rock		01567 820323	Self Catering	★★★ to ★★★★	
	Killin Highland Lodges – Lodges 10/11		08456 444866	Self Catering	★★★ to ★★★★	♠
	Kinnell Farm Cottage		01567 820814	Self Catering	★★	
	Major's Rock		01642 784757	Self Catering	★★★	
	Maragowan Caravan Club Site	FK21 8TN	01342 336842	Touring Park	★★★★★	
	Morenish Mews		01567 820527	Self Catering	★★★★	𝒫𝒫
	Succoth Farm	FK21 8SY	01567 820005	Bed & Breakfast	★★★★	
	Tarmachan		01567 820646	Self Catering	★★★	
	The Ardeonaig Hotel	FK21 8SU	01567 820400	Small Hotel	★★★★	
	The Coach House Hotel	FK21 8TN	01567 820349	Inn	★★	
	The Falls of Dochart Inn	FK21 8SL	07810 555520	Inn	★★★	
	Tigh Na Eilean		01567 820961	Self Catering	★★★★	♠

& Unassisted wheelchair access   𝕝ᵣ Assisted wheelchair access   ♠ Access for visitors with mobility difficulties
𝒫 Bronze Green Tourism Award   𝒫𝒫 Silver Green Tourism Award   𝒫𝒫𝒫 Gold Green Tourism Award
For further information on our Green Tourism Business Scheme please see page 7.

438   To find out more go to visitscotland.com

Location	Property Name	Postcode	Telephone	Classification	Star Rating	
Kilmacolm	Hillside Cottage		01505 872077	Self Catering	★★★	
Kilmarnock	Aulton Farm	KA3 2PQ	01563 538208	Farm House	★★★	
	Beggar Ha		01563 525269	Self Catering	★★★	
	Best Western Fenwick Hotel	KA3 6AU	01560 600478	Hotel	★★★	
	Dean Park Guest House	KA3 1DZ	01563 572794	Guest House	★★★	
	Heughmill	KA1 5NQ	01563 860389	Bed & Breakfast	★★★★	
	Kilmarnock (Cotton Mills) Premier Inn	KA1 2RS	08701 977148	Budget Hotel		
	Lily Cottage	KA1 5RA	01563 830921	Awaiting Grading		
	Moorfield Cottage		07909 841361	Self Catering	★★★	
	No 2 Old Rome Mews		01563 850265	Self Catering	★★★★	
	Park Hotel	KA1 1UR	01563 545999	Hotel	★★★★	♿
	Tamarind	KA3 1TP	01563 571788	Bed & Breakfast	★★★	
	Travelodge Kilmarnock	KA1 5LQ	01563 573810	Budget Hotel		
	Underwood House	KA1 5NG	01563 830887	Bed & Breakfast	★★★	
Kilwinning	Ailsa Craig View		01294 552361	Self Catering	★★★★	♿
	Blairholme	KA13 6JU	01294 552023	Bed & Breakfast	★★	
	High Smithstone Farmhouse	KA13 6PG	01294 552361	Farm House	★★★★	
	Montgrennan House	KA13 7QZ	01294 850005	Awaiting Grading		
Kinbrace	Maggie's Croft		01343 544799	Self Catering	★★★	
Kingussie	Allt Gynack Guest House	PH21 1HS	01540 661081	Guest House	★★★	
	Alvie Holiday Cottages – Park Cottage		01540 651255	Self Catering	★★★	
	Aonach		01540 661636	Self Catering	★★★	
	Arden House	PH21 1HE	01540 661369	Guest House	★★★★	
	Ardselma	PH21 1JZ	07786 696384	Bed & Breakfast	★★★	
	Aspen		0131 6542192	Self Catering	★★★★	
	Balbeag		01963 220250	Self Catering	★★★	
	Benula		01865 890750	Self Catering	★★★★	
	Braeriach Guest House	PH21 1QA	01540 651369	Guest House	★★★★	
	Calum's Cottage		01540 661442	Self Catering	★★★★	
	Carrick House		01540 661305	Self Catering	★★★	
	Columba House Hotel & Garden Restaurant	PH21 1JF	01540 661402	Small Hotel	★★★	♿
	Duke of Gordon Hotel	PH21 1HE	0845 6441781	Hotel	★★★	
	Feshieway Cottage		01462 423198	Self Catering	★★	
	Fraser & Telford Cottages		01540 651377	Self Catering	★★★	🍃🍃
	Glen Feshie Hostel	PH21 1NH	01540 651323	Bunkhouse		
	Glenfeshie House		0131 4411431	Self Catering	★★★★	
	Glengarry	PH21 1JS	01540 661386	Bed & Breakfast	★★★★	
	Grant Arms Hotel	PH21 3HF	01479 872526	Hotel	★★★	
	Greenfield Croft	PH21 1NT	01540 661010	Bed & Breakfast	★★★	
	Homewood Lodge	PH21 1HD	01540 661507	Bed & Breakfast	★★★★	🍃🍃
	Insh Hall Lodge	PH21 1NU	01540 651272	Hostel	★★★	
	Insh House Guest House	PH21 1NU	01540 651377	Guest House	★★★	🍃🍃
	Kate's Cabins – Little Birch Cabin		01540 661829	Self Catering	★★★	
	Kullbery		01540 661560	Self Catering	★★★	
	Loch Insh Chalets		01540 651272	Self Catering	★★ to ★★★	
	Netherwood		0131 4736151	Self Catering	★★★★	

Advertisers' locations have been sorted by postcode. In Scotland, postcodes can cover fairly large geographical areas.
Please check distance of property from specified location with the individual provider. VisitScotland cannot take any responsibility for this.

Location	Property Name	Postcode	Telephone	Classification	Star Rating		
Kingussie	Ptarmigan	PH21 1NG	01540 651265	Activity Accommodation	★★★		
	Ruthven House	PH21 1NR	01540 661226	Bed & Breakfast	★★★★		
	Ruthven Steadings	PH21 1NR	01540 662328	Bed & Breakfast	★★★★		
	Slemish B&B	PH21 1JN	01540 662360	Bed & Breakfast	★★★★		🄿🄿
	Sonas		01236 730615	Self Catering	★★★		
	Spindrift Cottage		01540 662328	Self Catering	★★★★		🄿
	St Helens	PH21 1JX	01540 661430	Bed & Breakfast	★★★★		
	Suie Guest House	PH21 1NA	01540 651344	Guest House	★★★		
	The Cross at Kingussie	PH21 1LB	01540 661166	Restaurant With Rooms	★★★★		🄿🄿
	The Hermitage Guest House	PH21 1HN	01540 662137	Guest House	★★★★	🕴	🄿🄿
	The Lairds Bothy	PH21 1HZ	01540 661334	Hostel	★★		
	The Scot House Hotel	PH21 1HE	01540 661351	Small Hotel	★★★		
	West Wing of Clifton	PH21 1EY	01540 661248	Bed & Breakfast	★★★★		
			01540 661226	Self Catering	★★		
Kinlochleven	Blackwater Hostel	PH50 4SG	01855 831253	Hostel	★★★★	♿	
	Caolasnacon Caravan and Camping Park	PH50 4RJ	01855 831279	Holiday Park	★★★		
	Edencoille	PH50 4SE	01855 831358	Guest House	★★★★		
	Highland Getaway	PH50 4RP	01855 831506	Restaurant With Rooms	★★★		
	MacDonald Hotel	PH50 4QR	01855 831539	Small Hotel	★★★		
	Tailrace Inn	PH50 4QH	01855 831777	Inn	★★★		
	Tigh-Na-Cheo	PH50 4SE	01855 831434	Guest House	★★★★	♿	
Kinross	Arisaig	KY13 9HP	01592 840063	Bed & Breakfast	★★★★		
	Burnbank	KY13 8AZ	01764 670055	Bed & Breakfast	★★★★		🄿🄿
	Dalqueich Farmhouse	KY13 0RG	01577 862599	Bed & Breakfast	★★★★		
	Gallowhill Farm Camping & Caravan Park	KY13 0RD	01577 862364	Touring Park	★★★		
	Gateside Farm Cottage		01577 840223	Self Catering	★★		
	Kirklands Hotel and Restaurant	KY13 8AN	01577 863313	Small Hotel	★★★		
	Mawcarse House	KY13 9SJ	01577 862220	Farm House	★★★★		
	Park House	KY13 9HN	01592 840237	Bed & Breakfast	★★★★		
	The Green Hotel	KY13 8AS	01577 863467	Hotel	★★★★		🄿
	The Grouse and Claret	KY13 0NQ	01577 864212	Restaurant With Rooms	★★★		
	The Lodge		01592 840403	Self Catering	★★★		
	Travelodge Kinross M90	KY13 7NQ	08700 850950	Budget Hotel			
	Tullibole Castle Long House	KY13 0QN	01577 840236	Awaiting Grading			
	Windlestrae Hotel	KY13 8AS	01577 863217	Awaiting Grading			
Kirkcaldy	54 Haig Avenue		02476 491448	Self Catering	★★★	♿	
	Ahaven	KY1 1LB	01592 267779	Bed & Breakfast	★★★★		
	Annies'Lan	KY2 5RB	01592 262231	Bed & Breakfast	★★★		
	Ashgrove B&B	KY1 1PF	01592 561354	Bed & Breakfast	★★★		
	Dean Park Hotel	KY2 6QW	01592 261635	Hotel	★★★		
	Dorothy Cottage		01132 590815	Self Catering	★★★★		
	East Wing Lawers		01592 781656	Self Catering	★★★ to ★★★★		

♿ Unassisted wheelchair access ♿ Assisted wheelchair access 🕴 Access for visitors with mobility difficulties
🄿 Bronze Green Tourism Award 🄿🄿 Silver Green Tourism Award 🄿🄿🄿 Gold Green Tourism Award
For further information on our Green Tourism Business Scheme please see page 7.

440   To find out more go to visitscotland.com

Location	Property Name	Postcode	Telephone	Classification	Star Rating	
Kirkcaldy	Invertiel B&B	KY2 5QJ	01592 264849	Bed & Breakfast	★★★★	
	Kilrie Granary		01592 269035	Self Catering	★★★★	
	North Hall	KY1 1DQ	01592 268864	Bed & Breakfast	★★★★	
	The Elbow Room	KY1 3HT	01592 654826	Inn	★★★	
	The Kyle atop Ravenscraig		01592 642221	Self Catering	★★★★	
	The Strathearn Hotel	KY1 2AS	01592 652210	Small Hotel	★★	
Kirkcudbright	1 Gordon Place	DG6 4LA	01557 330472	Bed & Breakfast	★★★	
	1 High Kirkland		01557 330684	Self Catering	★★★	
	13A High Street		01422 843762	Self Catering	★★★	
	Anchorlee	DG6 4EL	01557 330197	Bed & Breakfast	★★★★	
	Arnot's Cottage		01455 212955	Self Catering	★★★	
	Baytree House	DG6 4JQ	01557 330824	Bed & Breakfast	★★★★	
	Benutium	DG6 4BS	01557 330788	Bed & Breakfast	★★★★	
	Blackcroft Cottage		01557 331931	Self Catering	★★★★	
	Blaven	DG6 4HN	01557 331415	Bed & Breakfast	★★★	
	Blue Door		0131 2439335	Self Catering	★★★★	
	Brighouse Bay Holiday Park	DG6 4TS	01557 870267	Holiday Park	★★★★★	🌿🌿🌿
	Brighouse Bay Lodges		01557 870409	Self Catering	★★ to ★★★	
	Brookland		01677 470396	Self Catering	★★	
	Cannee Cottages		01557 330245	Self Catering	★★★★	
	Cormorant Cottage		01557 870606	Self Catering	★★★★	
	Craig Cottage		01557 870217	Self Catering	★★★	
	Dee Cottage	DG6 4LT	01557 330338	Bed & Breakfast	★★★★	
	Doon Cottage		0141 4239024	Self Catering	★★★★	
	Fludha Guest House	DG6 4UU	01557 331443	Guest House	★★★★★	♿
	Gladstone House	DG6 4JX	01557 331734	Guest House	★★★★	
	Glenauld Cottage		01557 330656	Self Catering	★★★	
	Gordon House Hotel	DG6 4JQ	01557 330670	Small Hotel	★★★	
	Grooms Cottage		01995 671909	Self Catering	★★★★	
	Haven Cottage		01557 331960	Self Catering	★★★	
	Kilkerran	DG6 4NY	01557 860057	Bed & Breakfast	★★★	
	Kirkland Mill		01671 820354	Self Catering	★★★★	
	Linthorpe	DG6 4PB	01557 860662	Bed & Breakfast	★★★	
	Low Newton		0796 8558920	Self Catering	★★★	
	Marks	DG6 4XR	01557 330854	Farm House	★★★	
	Mews Lane Cottage		01557 331673	Self Catering	★★★	
	Milk House and Honey House		01557 500588	Self Catering	★★★★	
	Millstones		01506 847535	Self Catering	★★★	
	Nathaniels Cottage		01254 581273	Self Catering	★★★★	
	Number One Bed & Breakfast	DG6 4JE	01557 330540	Bed & Breakfast	★★★★	
	Orroland Holiday Cottages		01557 500697	Self Catering	★★★ to ★★★★	
	Rivergarth	DG6 4UT	01557 332054	Bed & Breakfast	★★★★	🚶
	Sassoon House	DG6 4JZ	01557 330390	Bed & Breakfast	★★★★	
	Seaward Caravan Park	DG6 4TJ	01557 870267	Holiday Park	★★★★	
	Selkirk Arms Hotel	DG6 4JG	01557 330402	Small Hotel	★★★	
	Senwick Glebe		01557 870137	Self Catering	★★★	
	Silvercraigs Caravan & Camping Site	DG6 4BT	01556 503806	Touring Park	★★★★	
	Solway View Caravan & Camping Site	DG6 4TR	01557 870206	Touring Park	★★★	

Advertisers' locations have been sorted by postcode. In Scotland, postcodes can cover fairly large geographical areas.
Please check distance of property from specified location with the individual provider. VisitScotland cannot take any responsibility for this.

441

Location	Property Name	Postcode	Telephone	Classification	Star Rating
Kirkcudbright	The Dhoon		01744 889855	Self Catering	★★★
	The Haven		01557 332363	Self Catering	★★★
	The Shieling		01557 860349	Self Catering	★★★★
	The Star Hotel	DG6 4NT	01557 860279	Inn	★★
Kirkliston	Almondhill Guest House	EH29 9EQ	0131 3331570	Bed & Breakfast	★★★★
Kirknewton	A Room in the Country	EH27 8LR	01506 884850	Awaiting Grading	
	The Marriott Dalmahoy Hotel	EH27 8EP	0131 3331845	Hotel	★★★★
Kirkwall	1 Papdale Close	KW15 1QP	01856 874201	Bed & Breakfast	★★★
	10 & 12 Clay Loan	KW15 1QP	01856 875556	Self Catering	★★★
	14 Buttquoy Park		01856 861267	Self Catering	★★★
	2 + 2A Wellington Street		01856 875265	Self Catering	★★ to ★★★
	2 Willow Road	KW15 1PH	01856 879784	Awaiting Grading	
	8 West Tankerness Lane		01856 878594	Self Catering	★★★★
	Albert Hotel	KW15 1JZ	01856 876000	Small Hotel	★★★
	Apartment B		01856 874404	Self Catering	★★★★
	Ardconnel	KW15 1TB	01856 873885	Bed & Breakfast	★★★
	Auld Smokehoose		01856 861385	Self Catering	★★★★
	Avalon House	KW15 1UE	01856 876665	Guest House	★★★★
	Ayre Hotel	KW15 1QX	01856 873001	Hotel	★★★
	Bellavista	KW15 1UE	01856 872306	Guest House	★★★
	Benbradagh Flat	KW15 1SP	01856 874332	Awaiting Grading	
	Berstane House	KW15 1SZ	01856 876277	Bed & Breakfast	★★★
	Blinkbonny Holiday Homes – Units 1 & 2		01856 870208	Self Catering	★★★ to ★★★★
	Bon Accord	KW15 1BT	01856 873034	Bed & Breakfast	★★★
	Broad Street Gardens Apartments		07702 366933	Self Catering	★★★★
	Broadsands Self-Catering		01856 876038	Self Catering	★★★★
	Courtyard Apartment		01856 878477	Self Catering	★★★★
	Crossford	KW15 1SY	01856 876142	Bed & Breakfast	★★★
	Eastbank Cottages – Cottage 5		01856 873561	Self Catering	★★★
	Fairhaven	KW15 1PX	01856 872944	Bed & Breakfast	★★★
	Foveran Hotel	KW15 1SF	01856 872389	Small Hotel	★★★
	Grimbister Farm Cottage		01856 761318	Self Catering	★★★
	High Park Lodges		01856 873541	Self Catering	★★★★
	Hildeval Bed and Breakfast	KW15 1LY	01856 872989	Bed & Breakfast	★★★★
	Hoy Centre	KW15 3NJ	01856 873535	Hostel	★★★★
	Inganess Lodge		01856 870646	Self Catering	★★★★
	Innisgarth		01856 873256	Self Catering	★★★★
	John Brightman		01856 872899	Self Catering	★★★ to ★★★★
	Kingston Self Catering		0790 4521351	Self Catering	★★★★
	Kirkwall Hotel	KW15 1LF	01856 872232	Hotel	★★★
	Kirkwall Youth Hostel	KW15 1BB	0870 1553255	Hostel	★★ 🚶 ⓟ
	Kjarstad		0141 2222098	Self Catering	★★★★
	Laingbrae Cottage		01856 877573	Self Catering	★★★★ ♿
	Laurel House	KW15 1LB	01856 870285	Awaiting Grading	
	Lav'rockha Guest House	KW15 1SP	01856 876107	Guest House	★★★★ ♿
	Lerona	KW15 1LW	01856 874538	Bed & Breakfast	★★★

♿ Unassisted wheelchair access ♿ Assisted wheelchair access 🚶 Access for visitors with mobility difficulties
ⓟ Bronze Green Tourism Award ⓟⓟ Silver Green Tourism Award ⓟⓟⓟ Gold Green Tourism Award
For further information on our Green Tourism Business Scheme please see page 7.

442   To find out more go to visitscotland.com

Location	Property Name	Postcode	Telephone	Classification	Star Rating	
Kirkwall	Lynn View Self Catering		0779 6498068	Self Catering	★★★★★	
	Lynnfield Hotel	KW15 1SU	01856 872505	Small Hotel	★★★★	
	Nabban House		01856 873404	Self Catering	★★★★	
	Narvik	KW15 1LS	01856 879049	Bed & Breakfast	★★★★	
	No 5 Ingale	KW15 1UY	01856 875721	Awaiting Grading		
	No. 5 Highbury Villas		01857 677394	Self Catering	★★★	
	Orcades Hostel	KW15 1JQ	01856 873745	Hostel	★★★★	
	Orkney Hotel	KW15	01856 873477	Hotel	★★★	⌂⌂
	Overscapa Cottage		01856 874100	Self Catering	★★★★	♿
	Peedie Hostel	KW15 1QX	01856 875477	Hostel	★★★	
	Peter McKinlay B&B	KW15 1PA	01856 872249	Bed & Breakfast	★★★	
	Polrudden Guest House	KW15 1UH	01856 874761	Guest House	★★★	
	Royal Oak Guest House	KW15 1PY	01856 877177	Guest House	★★★	
	Sanderlay Guest House	KW15 1RB	01856 875587	Guest House	★★★	
	Scapa House	KW15 1SE		Awaiting Grading		
	Soulisquoy Barn		01856 874425	Self Catering	★★★★	
	St Ola Guest House	KW15 1LE	01856 875090	Guest House	★★★	
	Sunrise Apartment		01856 872174	Self Catering	★★★	
	The Brig Apartments		01856 872239	Self Catering	★★★	
	The Cottage		01856 873235	Self Catering	★★★ to ★★★★	
	The Pickaquoy Centre Caravan Park	KW15 1JG	01856 879900	Touring Park	★★★★	
	The Shore Rooms Restaurant Bar	KW15 1LG	01856 872200	Inn	★★★	
	West End Hotel	KW15 1BU	01856 872368	Small Hotel	★★★	
	West Greenigoe	KW15 1SG	01856 871618	Bed & Breakfast	★★★★	
Kirriemuir	Brankam		01575 560364	Self Catering	★★★ to ★★★★	♸
	Crepto	DD8 4JW	01575 572746	Bed & Breakfast	★★	
	Falls of Holm	DD8 5HY	01575 575867	Bed & Breakfast	★★★★	
	Glen Clova Hotel	DD8 4QS	01575 550350	Small Hotel	★★★	
	Glen Prosen Hostel	DD8 4SA	01575 540302	Hostel	★★★★	♸
	Glenprosen Cottages – Tinkerbell		01575 540302	Self Catering	★ to ★★★	⌂
	Kenny Farm Cottages – Charlies Cottage		01575 560292	Self Catering	★★★	
	Littleton of Airlie Farm Cottages – No's 1 & 2		01575 530422	Self Catering	★★★	⌂⌂
	Lochside Lodge & Roundhouse Restaurant	DD8 5JJ	01575 560340	Restaurant With Rooms	★★★★	♿
	Muirhouses Farm	DD8 4QG	01575 573128	Farm House	★★★★	⌂⌂
	Pearsie Lodge		01575 540234	Self Catering	★★★★	♿
	Purgavie Farm	DD8 5HZ	01575 560213	Farm House	★★★★	
	The Bothy	DD8 4QU	01575 540330	Awaiting Grading		
	The Crowe's Nest		01575 573604	Self Catering	★★	
	The Steading Bunkhouse	DD8 4QS	01575 550350	Hostel	★★★	♿
	Thrums Hotel	DD8 4BE	01575 572758	Inn	★★★	
	Weaver's Cottage		01575 572085	Self Catering	★★★	
	Winters Cottage		01608 682570	Self Catering	★★★	
Kyle	A'Chomraich	IV40 8DA	01599 534210	Bed & Breakfast	★★	
	Balmacara Lodge B & B	IV40 8DP	01599 566282	Bed & Breakfast	★★★	
	Balmacara Mains Guest House	IV40 8DN	01599 566240	Guest House	★★★★	
	Birchwood Holiday Cottage		01599 534823	Self Catering	★★★★	

Advertisers' locations have been sorted by postcode. In Scotland, postcodes can cover fairly large geographical areas.
Please check distance of property from specified location with the individual provider. VisitScotland cannot take any responsibility for this.

443

Directory of all VisitScotland Assured Serviced Establishments, ordered by location.
Establishments highlighted have an advertisement in this guide.

Location	Property Name	Postcode	Telephone	Classification	Star Rating
Kyle	Borodale House	IV40 8PB	01478 660222	Small Hotel	★★★ 𝙭
	Brook Cottage		01599 555201	Self Catering	★★★
	Caberfeidh Guest House	IV40 8DY	01599 555293	Guest House	★★★
	Ceol-Na-Mara	IV40 8DH	01599 566208	Bed & Breakfast	★★★★
	Conchra Farm Cottages – Gardeners Cottage		01599 555752	Self Catering	★★ to ★★★
	Conchra House	IV40 8DZ	01599 555233	Guest House	★★★
	Craggan Cottage		0131 2439331	Self Catering	★★★
	Craig Cottage		01382 477462	Self Catering	★★★
	Dornie Hotel	IV40 8DT	01599 555205	Small Hotel	★★
	Duirinish Lodge East Wing		0131 5560101	Self Catering	★★★★★
	Eilean A Cheo	IV40 8DY	01599 555485	Guest House	★★★
	Ferry Cottage		0131 2439335	Self Catering	★★★
	Glomach House	IV40 8HN	01599 511222	Bed & Breakfast	★★★★
	Granny's Croft House		01599 544204	Self Catering	★★★★ 𝙭
	Holly Cottage		01202 298775	Self Catering	★★★★
	John Fishers Cottage		01626 889098	Self Catering	★★★ 🄿
	Kilimanjaro		01224 865763	Self Catering	★★★★
	Kintail		01539 560242	Self Catering	★★★★
	Kintail Lodge Hotel	IV40 8HL	01599 511275	Small Hotel	★★★
	Kyle Hotel	IV40 8AB		Awaiting Grading	
	Lamont Bungalow		01599 522231	Self Catering	★★★
	Mo-dhachaidh	IV40 8HB	01599 511351	Bed & Breakfast	★★★
	Morvich Caravan Club Site	IV40 8HQ	01342 336842	Touring Park	★★★★★
	Raasay House	IV40 8PB	01478 660266	Awaiting Grading	
	Raasay Youth Hostel	IV40 8NT	0870 1553255	Hostel	★★★
	Ratagan Youth Hostel	IV40 8HP	08701 553255	Hostel	★★★★ 🄿🄿
	Red House Dornie		01274 832001	Self Catering	★★★★
	Reraig Caravan Site	IV40 8DH	01599 566215	Touring Park	★★★★
	Rosdail		01599 511351	Self Catering	★★★
	Seadrift	IV40 8EQ	01599 555415	Bed & Breakfast	★★★
	Seadrift chalet		01599 555415	Self Catering	★★★
	Sealladh Mara	IV40 8EY	01599 555296	Bed & Breakfast	★★★
	Sealoch Cottages		01463 790253	Self Catering	★★★★ to ★★★★★
	Seaview		01224 899421	Self Catering	★★★
	Shoreside		01599 511227	Self Catering	★★★★
	The Lodge – Tigh Na Creag		01599 522226	Self Catering	★★★★
	Tighe Mo Cridhe		01506 872063	Self Catering	★★★★
	Tingle Creek Hotel	IV40 8BB	01599 534430	Small Hotel	★★★
	Tir Nan Og	IV40 8DY	01599 555231	Holiday Caravan	
Lairg	142 Oldshoremore	IV27	01971 521335	Awaiting Grading	
	252 Culkein		01463 230985	Self Catering	★★
	Achmelvich Youth Hostel	IV27 4JB	08701 553255	Hostel	★ 🄿🄿
	Achnacairn Chalets		01571 855240	Self Catering	★★
	Ambleside	IV27 4EG	01549 402130	Bed & Breakfast	★★★
	An Caladh		01971 502400	Self Catering	★★★★
	An Tigh Earna		01382 580358	Self Catering	★★★★
	Ardsaile	IV27 4SB	01571 844363	Bed & Breakfast	★★★★

♿ Unassisted wheelchair access ♿ Assisted wheelchair access 𝙭 Access for visitors with mobility difficulties
🄿 Bronze Green Tourism Award 🄿🄿 Silver Green Tourism Award 🄿🄿🄿 Gold Green Tourism Award
For further information on our Green Tourism Business Scheme please see page 7.

Location	Property Name	Postcode	Telephone	Classification	Star Rating
Lairg	Ardvar Cottage		01571 844756	Self Catering	★★★★
	Arkle		01580 892750	Self Catering	★★★
	Badnabay and Kinnoch Cottage		01971 500221	Self Catering	★★★
	Ben Loyal Hotel	IV27 4XE	01847 611216	Small Hotel	★★★
	Benmore Cottage	IV27 4DB	01253 393576	Awaiting Grading	
	Blar na Leisg at Drunbeg House	IV27 4NW	01571 833325	Restaurant With Rooms	★★★★★
	Brown Villa		01779 473116	Self Catering	★★★
	Buailard House		001 289 252 0581	Self Catering	★★★
	Burnside House		01628 628474	Self Catering	★★ to ★★★
	Cathair Dhubh Estate		01571 855277	Self Catering	★★★★ 🕅
	Ceannebeinne		01732 882320	Self Catering	★★★
	Clachtoll Cottage		01358 720163	Self Catering	★★★★
	Clashmore Holiday Cottages		01571 855226	Self Catering	★★★
	Cloisters	IV27 4YP	01847 601286	Bed & Breakfast	★★★★ ♿
	Cnoclochan		01483 274846	Self Catering	★★
	Creigard		01571 844448	Self Catering	★★★★
	Cruachan Lodge Guest House	IV27 4JE	01571 855303	Guest House	★★★★
	Davar	IV27 4LJ	01571 844501	Bed & Breakfast	★★★★
	Duchally Lodge		01862 843601	Self Catering	★★★★
	Dunroamin Caravan Park	IV27 4AR	01549 402447	Holiday Park	★★★★
	Durness Youth Hostel	IV27 4QA	01971 511244	Bunkhouse	ⴹ
	Eddrachilles Hotel	IV27 4TH	01971 502080	Small Hotel	★★★
	Fasgadh	IV27 4TG	01971 502402	Bed & Breakfast	★★★
	Glenaladale Bed And Breakfast	IV27 4UN	01971 511329	Bed & Breakfast	★★★
	Glencorse		01857 600459	Self Catering	★★★★
	Glendarroch House		01431 821207	Self Catering	★★★★ 🕅
	Glengolly	IV27 4PN	01971 511255	Bed & Breakfast	★★★
	Gull Cottage (The Barn)		01971 521717	Self Catering	★★★
	Heather Cottage		01571 844383	Self Catering	★★★★
	Highland House	IV27 4DH	01549 402414	Bed & Breakfast	★★★★
	Hill Cottage		01786 880631	Self Catering	★★★
	Horseshoe Cottage		01971 521729	Self Catering	★★★ to ★★★★ 🕅
	Inchnadamph Lodge Hostel	IV27 4HL	01571 822218	Hostel	★★★
	Inver Lodge Hotel	IV27 4LU	01571 844496	Hotel	★★★★
	Invercassley Cottage		01264 773319	Self Catering	★★★
	Invermudale Annexe		01549 411250	Self Catering	★★★★ 🕅
	Kinlochbervie Hotel	IV27 4RP	01971 521275	Hotel	★★
	Kirkaig Hill Caravan	IV27 4LR	01571 844115	Holiday Caravan	
	Lagbuie		01549 402223	Self Catering	★★★
	Lairg Highland Hotel	IV27 4DB	01549 402243	Small Hotel	★★★
	Lazy Crofter	IV27 4PN	01971 511202	Hostel	★★★
	Lochinver Holiday Cottages		01571 844318	Self Catering	★★★★
	Lochview	IV27 4EH	01549 402578	Bed & Breakfast	★★★★
	Milnclarin Holiday Homes		01408 634300	Self Catering	★★★★
	Milton Cottage		01862 843601	Self Catering	★★★★ to ★★★★★
	Morven	IV27 4QB	01971 511252	Bed & Breakfast	★★★

♿ Unassisted wheelchair access   ♿ Assisted wheelchair access   🕅 Access for visitors with mobility difficulties
ⴹ Bronze Green Tourism Award   Silver Green Tourism Award   Gold Green Tourism Award
For further information on our Green Tourism Business Scheme please see page 7.

Advertisers' locations have been sorted by postcode. In Scotland, postcodes can cover fairly large geographical areas.
Please check distance of property from specified location with the individual provider. VisitScotland cannot take any responsibility for this.

Location	Property Name	Postcode	Telephone	Classification	Star Rating	
Lairg	Mountview Self-catering		01571 844648	Self Catering	★★★★	𝒾ఉ
	Mullach		01356 626011	Self Catering	★★★★	
	no. 143 Skinnet		+0039 3351 733682	Self Catering	★★★	
	Old Post Office		0141 9563753	Self Catering	★★★	
	Old School Restaurant & Rooms	IV27 4RH	01971 521383	Restaurant With Rooms	★★★	
	Park House	IV27 4AU	01549 402208	Guest House	★★★★	
	Polcraig Guest House	IV27 4LD	01571 844429	Guest House	★★★★	
	Post Office Flat		01847 601250	Self Catering	★★	𝙠
	Reid's Cottage		01403 891989	Self Catering	★★★★	
	Rhian Cottage	IV27 4FX	01847 611257	Guest House	★★★	𝒫𝒫
	Rhiconich Hotel	IV27 4RN	01971 521224	Small Hotel	★★	
	Ruddyglow Park Country House	IV27 4HB	01571 822216	Bed & Breakfast	★★★★★	𝙠
	Scourie Guest House	IV27 4TE	01971 502001	Guest House	★★★	
	Scourie Hotel	IV27 4SX	01971 502396	Small Hotel	★★★	
	Scourie Lodge	IV27 4SX	01971 502248	Bed & Breakfast	★★★★	
	Seafield House		01223 500910	Self Catering	★★	
	Sealladh Na Mara		01287 660076	Self Catering	★★★★	
	Stac Fada B&B	IV27 4JE	01571 855366	Bed & Breakfast	★★★	
	Strathan Midtown and Assynt		01571 844457	Self Catering	★★★★	
	The Albannach	IV27 4LP	015718 44407	Restaurant With Rooms	★★★★	
	The Old Library		0131 5552565	Self Catering	★★★	
	The Overscaig House Hotel	IV27 4NY	01549 431203	Small Hotel	★★★	
	The Sheiling		01862 842665	Self Catering	★★	
	Tigh Beag		01571 844414	Self Catering	★★★	
	Tigh Na Craig		01337 840178	Self Catering	★★★★	
	Tigh na Mara		01571 844377	Self Catering	★★★	
	Tigh Nan Shian		01571 855363	Self Catering	★★★	
	Tongue Hotel	IV27 4XD	01847 611206	Small Hotel	★★★★	𝒫
	Tongue Youth Hostel	IV27 4XH	08701 553255	Hostel	★★★	𝒫𝒫
	Tuinne-Na-Mara		01463 234420	Self Catering	★★★	
	Unapool House Cottages – Quaing Cottage		01971 502344	Self Catering	★★★ to ★★★★	
	Unst		01673 857516	Self Catering	★★★	
	Veyatie	IV27 4LP	01571 844424	Bed & Breakfast	★★★★	𝒫𝒫
	Wild Orchid Guest House	IV27 4PN	01971 511280	Guest House	★★★	
			01971 500221	Self Catering	★★★	
Lanark	6 Carstairs Road	ML11 8QD	01555 871513	Awaiting Grading		
	Bankhead Accommodation – Corner House		01555 666560	Self Catering	★★★★	
	Carnwath Vineyard B&B	ML11 8HR	01555 840156	Bed & Breakfast	★★★★	
	Cartland Bridge Country House Hotel	ML11 9UE	01555 664426	Country House Hotel	★★★	
	Clarkston Farm	ML11 9UN	01555 663388	Farm House	★★★	
	Cleugh Farm		01555 811932	Self Catering	★★★★	
	Corehouse Farm	ML11 9TQ	01555 661377	Farm House	★★★	𝒫𝒫
	Duneaton	ML11 9BG	01555 665487	Bed & Breakfast	★★★	
	Dunsyre Mains Farm	ML11 8NQ	01899 810251	Farm House	★★★	
	Dykecroft Farm	ML11 0JQ	01555 892226	Farm House	★★	

♧ Unassisted wheelchair access   Assisted wheelchair access   Access for visitors with mobility difficulties
𝒫 Bronze Green Tourism Award   𝒫𝒫 Silver Green Tourism Award   𝒫𝒫𝒫 Gold Green Tourism Award
For further information on our Green Tourism Business Scheme please see page 7.

Location	Property Name	Postcode	Telephone	Classification	Star Rating		
Lanark	Fearn		01555 661739	Self Catering	★		
	Muirhall Holiday Cottages		01501 785240	Self Catering	★★★★★		
	New Lanark Mill Hotel	ML11 9DB	01555 661345	Hotel	★★★	♿	🍃🍃🍃
	New Lanark Youth Hostel	ML11 9DJ	0870 1553255	Hostel	★★★		🍃🍃
	Oak Lodge Beech Lodge	ML11 9UH	01555 662192	Awaiting Grading			
	Scottish Equi B&B	ML11 9TA	01555 661853	Bed & Breakfast	★★★		
	Shodshill Mill Farm		01555 870725	Self Catering	★★★★		
	St Catherines B&B	ML11 7BL	01555 662295	Bed & Breakfast	★★★		
	Summerlea	ML11 9AE	01555 664889	Bed & Breakfast	★★★		
	The Annexe		01555 870906	Self Catering	★★★★		
	The Robertson Arms Hotel	ML11 8JZ	01555 840060	Small Hotel	★★★		
	The Water Houses		01555 667200	Self Catering	★★★★		🍃🍃🍃
	Town House		01555 665283	Self Catering	★★★		
	Unit 3 Corehouse Farm Self Catering		01555 661377	Self Catering	★★★		
	Wester Walston Lodge		01889 810335	Self Catering	★★★★		
Langholm	Border House	DG13 0JH	01387 380376	Bed & Breakfast	★★★		
	Bush of Ewes Farmhouse	DG13 0HN	01387 381241	Farm House	★★★		
	Carnlea	DG13 0EE	01387 380284	Bed & Breakfast	★★★		
	Ewes Water Caravan & Camping Park	DG13 0DH	01387 380386	Touring Park	★★★		
	Georgefield Cottage		01387 370227	Self Catering	★★★		
	Jamestown Cottage		01387 371420	Self Catering	★★★★		
	Wauchope Cottage	DG13 0AY	01387 380429	Bed & Breakfast	★★★		
	Whitshiels Caravan Park	DG13 0HG	01387 380494	Holiday Park	★★★★		
Larbert	Carronvale House/The Boys' Brigade	FK5 3LH	01324 562800	Group Accommodation	★★★		
	Falkirk (Larbert/M876) Premier Inn	FK5 4EG	08709 906550	Budget Hotel			
	3c Kirklands		01475 673873	Self Catering	★★★		
	62 Irvine road	KA30 8HP	01475 686268	Bed & Breakfast	★★★★		
	Bayview		0141 5701258	Self Catering	★★★		
	Brisbane House Hotel	KA30 8NE	01475 687200	Awaiting Grading			
	Broom Lodge	KA30 8DR	01475 674290	Bed & Breakfast	★★★★		
Largs	Douglas House		01475 673992	Self Catering	★★★★		
	East Wing		01475 673757	Self Catering	★★★ to ★★★★		
	Fencefoot Farm		01475 568918	Self Catering	★★★		
	Ferry Row B&B	KA29 0AJ	01475 568687	Bed & Breakfast	★★★		🍃🍃
	Flat 1A		01475 673387	Self Catering	★		
	Glendarroch	KA30 8HW	01475 676305	Bed & Breakfast	★★★		
	Harbour View		01475 521916	Self Catering	★★★		
	Seger Property Mgnt		01475 686369	Self Catering	★★★★	🚶	
	South Whittlieburn Farm	KA30 8SN	01475 675881	Bed & Breakfast	★★★★		
	St Leonard's Guest House	KA30 8JP	01475 673318	Bed & Breakfast	★★★		
	The Old Rectory	KA30 8PR	01475 674405	Bed & Breakfast	★★★★		
	Tigh An Struan	KA30 8BU	01475 670668	Guest House	★★★		
	Tigh-Na-Ligh	KA30 8NN	01475 673975	Guest House	★★★		
	Whin-Park Guest House	KA30 8PS	01475 673437	Guest House	★★★★		
	Willowbank Hotel	KA30 8PG	01475 672311	Hotel	★★★		
	Zion House		01475 673162	Self Catering	★★★		

Advertisers' locations have been sorted by postcode. In Scotland, postcodes can cover fairly large geographical areas.
Please check distance of property from specified location with the individual provider. VisitScotland cannot take any responsibility for this.

447

Location	Property Name	Postcode	Telephone	Classification	Star Rating
Larkhall	Bramble Cottage		01698 889021	Self Catering	★★★ to ★★★★
	Shawlands Hotel	ML9 2TZ	01698 791111	Hotel	★★★ 🕴
	The Studio		01698 884060	Self Catering	★★★
Lasswade	Droman House	EH18 1HA	0131 6639239	Bed & Breakfast	★★
	Gorton House East		0131 4404332	Self Catering	★★ to ★★★
	Pine Cottage		0131 6633456	Self Catering	★★★★
	The Laird & Dog Inn	EH18 1NA	0131 6639219	Awaiting Grading	
Latheron	Craiglea		0208 7317771	Self Catering	★★★★
	Studio Apartment		01593 741740	Self Catering	★★★
Lauder	Black Bull Hotel	TD2 6SR	01578 722208	Inn	★★★
	Lamont		01578 750642	Self Catering	★★★★ to ★★★★★ 🦽 𝄞𝄞
	Lauder Camping & Caravanning Club Site	TD2 6RA	02476 475318	Touring Park	★★★★
	Lornebank Homestay	TD2 6SU	01578 722317	Bed & Breakfast	★★★★
	No 16 Market Place	TD2 6SR	01578 718776	Bed & Breakfast	★★★
	The Lodge at Carfraemill	TD2 6RA	01578 750750	Restaurant With Rooms	★★★★
	Thirlestane Castle Caravan Park	TD2 6RU	01578 718884	Touring Park	★★★★
	Thirlestane Castle Trust	TD2 6RU	01578 722430	Serviced Apartments	★★★★★
	Thirlestane Farm Cottages		01578 722216	Self Catering	★★★
	Timber Chalets	TD2 6RA	0845 130 7631	Awaiting Grading	
Laurencekirk	Arbuthnott Holiday Lets – Grey Granite		01561 320417	Self Catering	★★★
	Brownmuir Caravan Park	AB30 1SJ	01561 320786	Holiday Park	★★★
	Dovecot Caravan Park	AB30 1QL	01674 840630	Holiday Park	★★★★
	Drumtochty Stables		01561 360387	Self Catering	★★★★
	East Wing		01561 320230	Self Catering	★★★ to ★★★★
	The Cottage		01561 3203400	Self Catering	★★
	The Redhall Arms Hotel	AB30 1NN	01561 320526	Bed & Breakfast	★★
Leven	1 School Wynd		07915 075754	Self Catering	★★★★
	60 Main Street		01788 890942	Self Catering	★★
	Afton Cottage	KY8 6DF	01333 320915	Awaiting Grading	
	Balhousie Farm	KY8 5QN	01333 360680	Bed & Breakfast	★★★
	Bayview	KY8 6JD	01333 360454	Bed & Breakfast	★★★★ 🕴
	Caledonian Hotel	KY8 4NG	01333 424101	Hotel	★★★
	Crusoe Hotel	KY8 6BT	01333 320759	Small Hotel	★★★
	Dunclutha	KY8 4EX	01333 425515	Guest House	★★★★
	Elie Letting		01333 330219	Self Catering	★★★★ 🕴
	Fantasia B&B	KY8 4GD	01333 421247	Bed & Breakfast	★★★
	Fluthers Wood	KY8 5NN	01333 351167	Bed & Breakfast	★★★
	Holly Tree Cottage		01333 360297	Self Catering	★★★★
	Kerrera Cottage		001 613 830 3840	Self Catering	★★★
	Letham Feus Caravan Park	KY8 4HR	01333 351900	Holiday Park	★★★★★
	Lorne House	KY8 4TB	01333 423255	Bed & Breakfast	★★★★
	Lundin Links Hotel	KY8 6AP	01333 320207	Awaiting Grading	
	Monturpie Caravan Park	KY8 5QS	01333 360254	Touring Park	★★★
	Monturpie Guest House	KY8 5QS	01333 360254	Guest House	★★★
	No 18 Links Road	KY8 6AU	01333 320497	Bed & Breakfast	★★★

♿ Unassisted wheelchair access   🦽 Assisted wheelchair access   🕴 Access for visitors with mobility difficulties
𝄞 Bronze Green Tourism Award   𝄞𝄞 Silver Green Tourism Award   𝄞𝄞𝄞 Gold Green Tourism Award
For further information on our Green Tourism Business Scheme please see page 7.

448   To find out more go to visitscotland.com

Location	Property Name	Postcode	Telephone	Classification	Star Rating
Leven	No 18 Links Road		01333 320497	Self Catering	★★★
	Northfield		01333 340214	Self Catering	★★★★ ⋔
	Old Manor Hotel	KY8 6AJ	01333 320368	Hotel	★★★
	Rockpool Cottage		01333 320844	Self Catering	★★★★
	Sandilands B&B	KY8 6AH	01333 329881	Bed & Breakfast	★★★★
	Seascape	KY9	01334 479542	Awaiting Grading	
	Shell Bay Caravan	KY9 1HB	0131 6051888	Holiday Caravan	
	Shell Bay Caravan Park	KY9 1HB	01334 474250	Holiday Park	★★★
	South Cassingray Cottage		01334 840254	Self Catering	★★★
	St. Anne's		0131 3321357	Self Catering	★★★
	Stenton Cottage		01738 442953	Self Catering	★★★
	Sunnybraes		01333 320019	Self Catering	★★★★
	Sunnyside	KY9 1DN	01334 208171	Awaiting Grading	
	The Granary		07946 535314	Self Catering	★★★★
	The Inn At Lathones	KY9 1JE	01334 840494	Inn	★★★★
	Thistle Cottage		01333 360259	Self Catering	★★★★ ⋔
	Tweedbank		01333 300058	Self Catering	★★★
	Units 26		01333 340501	Self Catering	★★★★ to ★★★★★
	Viewforth Cottage		01224 209151	Self Catering	★★★
	West Lingo Farm Cottage		01334 828873	Self Catering	★★★
	Woodland Gardens Caravan & Camping Park	KY8 5QG	01333 360319	Holiday Park	★★★★
Linlithgow	26 Cameron Knowe	EH49 6RL	01506 834284	Bed & Breakfast	★★★
	Aran House	EH49 6QE	01506 842088	Bed & Breakfast	★★
	Arden House	EH49 6QE	01506 670172	Bed & Breakfast	★★★★★
	Beecraigs Caravan and Camping Site	EH49 6PL	01506 844516	Touring Park	★★★★
	Belsyde Farm	EH49 6QE	01506 842098	Bed & Breakfast	★★★★ Ⓟ
	Bomains Farm	EH49 7RQ	01506 822188	Bed & Breakfast	★★★★
	Craigs Lodges – Tunuri		01506 845025	Self Catering	★★★
	Linlithgow Cottages		01506 840793	Self Catering	★★★★
	Lumsdaine	EH49 6QE	01506 845001	Bed & Breakfast	★★★
	Strawberry Bank House	EH49 6BL	01506 848372	Bed & Breakfast	★★★★
	The Bonsyde House Hotel	EH49 7NU	01506 842229	Small Hotel	★★★
	The Star & Garter Hotel	EH49 7AB	01506 846362	Inn	★★★
	West Port Hotel	EH49 7AZ	01506 847456	Small Hotel	★
	Linwater Caravan Park	EH53 0HT	0131 3333326	Touring Park	★★★★
	Livingston (M8/J3) Premier Inn	EH54 8AD	08701 977161	Budget Hotel	
Livingston	Overshiel Farm	EH53 0HT	01506 880469	Bed & Breakfast	★★★
	Ramada Livingston	EH54 6QB	01506 431222	Hotel	★★★ ⋔ Ⓟ
	Redcraig Bed and Breakfast	EH53 0JT	01506 884249	Bed & Breakfast	★★★★
	Travelodge Livingston	EH54 6QX	08719 846151	Budget Hotel	
	Whitecroft	EH53 0ET	01506 882494	Bed & Breakfast	★★★
Loanhead	Aaron Glen Guest House	EH20 9AU	0131 4401293	Guest House	★★★ ⋔
Lochailort	Glenuig Inn	PH38 4NG	01687 470219	Inn	★★
Lochearnhead	Ballimore Farm Cottage		01877 384287	Self Catering	★★★★
	Bute, Cumbrae and Arran		01567 830238	Self Catering	★★★ ⋔

Location	Property Name	Postcode	Telephone	Classification	Star Rating	
Lochearnhead	Cnoc Fuar		07946 740404	Self Catering	★★★	🅟
	Gartnafuaran Farm Holiday Cottage		01877 384221	Self Catering	★★★★	
	Kings House Cottages		01877 384646	Self Catering	★★★	
	King's House Hotel	FK19 8NY	01877 384646	Small Hotel	★★	
	Lochearn House	FK19 8NR	01567 830380	Guest House	★★★★	
	Lochearnhead Lochside Chalets		01567 830268	Self Catering	★★★	
	Lochside Cottages		01877 384219	Self Catering	★★★★	♿
	Mansewood Country House	FK19 8NS	01567 830213	Guest House	★★★★	
	Monachyle Mhor	FK19 8PQ	01877 384622	Small Hotel	★★★★	
	No's 1, 2 & 3		01567 830293	Self Catering	★★★ to ★★★★	
Lochgelly	Balbedie Farm Cottage		01592 882242	Self Catering	★★	
Lochgilphead	Aird House		01852 500224	Self Catering	★★★★ to ★★★★★	
	Allt-Na-Craig House	PA30 8EP	01546 603245	Guest House	★★★★	
	Auchenbeag	PA31 8PW	01546 870241	Bed & Breakfast	★★★	
	Brenfield Shores – Cottage 1		01546 603284	Self Catering	★★★★	
	Cairnbaan Hotel	PA31 8SJ	01546 603668	Small Hotel	★★★	
	Clachandubh		01546 810215	Self Catering	★★★	
	Crinan Hotel	PA31 8SR	01546 830261	Small Hotel	★★★★	
	Crinan House		07747 409648	Self Catering	★★★★	
	Drumalban		01852 500207	Self Catering	★★★★	
	Ellary Estate – The Bungalow		01880 770209	Self Catering	★★ to ★★★★	
	Empire Travel Lodge	PA31 8JS	01546 602381	Lodge	★★★	♿
	Ford House	PA31 8RH	01546 810273	Guest House	★★★	
	Gallanach cottage		01738 626644	Self Catering	★★	
	Greenacre	PA31 1PJ	01631 710756	Guest House	★★★	
	Islay		0131 6612783	Self Catering	★★★★	
	Kilmahumaig Barn Flats		01546 830238	Self Catering	★★	
	Lochnell Arms Hotel	PA31 1RP	01631 710408	Awaiting Grading		
	Ormsary Estate – Barnlongart House		01880 770700	Self Catering	★ to ★★★	🚶
	The Bothy		01546 510283	Self Catering	★★★	
	The Bullock Shed		01546 510316	Self Catering	★★★★	
	The Corran	PA31 8LR	01546 603866	Bed & Breakfast	★★★★	
	The Deckhouse		07808 781464	Self Catering	★★★★	
	The Stables B&B	PA31 8PX	01546 850276	Bed & Breakfast	★★★★	
	The Steading No 3		01546 870294	Self Catering	★★★★	
	Tigha Charnain		01546 810286	Self Catering	★★★	
Lochwinnoch	East Kerse Farm	PA12 4DU	01505 502400	Farm House	★★★	
	East Lochhead Cottages – Loch View		01505 842610	Self Catering	★★★★	♿ 🅟🅟🅟
	The Hungry Monk	PA12 4JF	01505 843848	Inn	★★★★	
Lockerbie	Bonshawbrae		01505 690202	Self Catering	★★★	
	Bruce Suite		01461 800285	Self Catering	★★★★	
	Carlyle House	DG11 3DG	01576 300322	Bed & Breakfast	★★★	
	Cressfield Caravan Park	DG11 3DR	01576 300702	Holiday Park	★★★★	
	Cressfield Country House Hotel	DG11 3DR	01576 300281	Small Hotel	★★★	
	Dalton Pottery		01387 840236	Self Catering	★★★ to ★★★★	
	Dryfesdale Country House Hotel	DG11 2SF	01576 202427	Hotel	★★★★	♿
	Halleaths Caravan & Camping Park	DG11 1NA	01387 810630	Holiday Park	★★★★	

♿ Unassisted wheelchair access   ♿ Assisted wheelchair access   🚶 Access for visitors with mobility difficulties
🅟 Bronze Green Tourism Award   🅟🅟 Silver Green Tourism Award   🅟🅟🅟 Gold Green Tourism Award
For further information on our Green Tourism Business Scheme please see page 7.

450   To find out more go to visitscotland.com

Location	Property Name	Postcode	Telephone	Classification	Star Rating
Lockerbie	Hoddom Castle Caravan Park	DG11 1AS	01576 300244	Holiday Park	★★★★★
	King Robert the Bruce's Cave	DG11 3AT	01461 800285	Holiday Park	★★★★
	Kings Arms Hotel	DG11 2JL	01576 202410	Small Hotel	★★★
	Kirkconnell Hall Hotel	DG11 3JH	01576 300277	Awaiting Grading	
	Kirkloch Caravan & Camping Site	DG11 1PZ	01556 503806	Touring Park	★★★
	Kirkwood Cottages – Roe Deer		01576 510200	Self Catering	★★ to ★★★
	Lockerbie Premier Inn (Annandale Water)	DG11 1HD	08701 977163	Budget Hotel	
	Nether Boreland	DG11 2LL	01576 610248	Bed & Breakfast	★★★
	Queens Hotel	DG11 2RB	01576 202415	Hotel	★★★
	Ravenshill House Hotel	DG11 2EF	01576 202882	Small Hotel	★★
	Smithy Cottage		01387 840270	Self Catering	★★★★
	Somerton House Hotel	DG11 2DR	01576 202384	Small Hotel	★★★
	Torbeckhill Bungalow	DG11 3EX	01461 600683	Bed & Breakfast	★★★★
	Williamwood	DG11 3LN	01461 500213	Awaiting Grading	
Longniddry/ Prestonpans	1 A Wemyss Place		01875 815737	Self Catering	★★★
	Aberlady Station Caravan Park	EH32 0PZ	01875 870666	Touring Park	★★★
	Green Craigs	EH32 0PY	01875 870301	Small Hotel	★★★★★
	Kilspindie House Hotel	EH32 0RE	01875 870682	Restaurant With Rooms	★★★
	Seton Sands Holiday Village	EH32 0QF	0131 3328851	Holiday Caravan	
	Seton Sands Holiday Village	EH32 0QF	01442 230300	Holiday Park	★★★★
	Upper Flat Sunset View		01875 870405	Self Catering	★★★
Lossiemouth	Ardivot House B&B	IV31 6RY	01343 811076	Farm House	★★★
	Beachview Apartment		01343 813815	Self Catering	★★★
	Beachview Holiday Flat		0141 9424135	Self Catering	★★★★
	Ceilidh B&B	IV31 6DP	01343 815848	Bed & Breakfast	★★★ ♿
	Covesea Skerry		0131 2439335	Self Catering	★★★
	Golf View Apartment		01343 813430	Self Catering	★★★★★
	Halliman		0131 2439335	Self Catering	★★★
	Links Lodge	IV31 6QS	01343 813815	Guest House	★★★★ �
	Lossiemouth House	IV31 6DP	01343 813397	Bed & Breakfast	★★★
	No. 1 Pitgaveny Court		01343 813495	Self Catering	★★★
	Norland	IV31 6QP	01343 813570	Guest House	★★★★
	Silver Sands Leisure Park	IV31 6SP	01343 813262	Holiday Park	★★★★
	Stotfield Hotel	IV31 6QS		Awaiting Grading	
	The Skerry Brae Hotel	IV31 6QS	01343 812040	Inn	★★★
Lybster	Canisp House	KW3 6BD	01593 721758	Bed & Breakfast	★★★
	Taigh an Clachair		01398 341692	Self Catering	★★★
	The Croft House	KW3 6BT	01593 721342	Bed & Breakfast	★★★
Macduff	Knowes Hotel	AB44 1LL	01261 832152	Small Hotel	★★
	Mariner's Cottage		01261 832414	Self Catering	★★★★
	Monica & Martin's B&B	AB44 1TN	01261 832336	Bed & Breakfast	★★★★
Mallaig	Ceithir Raithean		0161 4066010	Self Catering	★★★★
	Creag-Eiridh		01747 852289	Self Catering	★★★

♿ Unassisted wheelchair access   ♿ Assisted wheelchair access   � Access for visitors with mobility difficulties
⌖ Bronze Green Tourism Award   ⌖⌖ Silver Green Tourism Award   ⌖⌖⌖ Gold Green Tourism Award
For further information on our Green Tourism Business Scheme please see page 7.

Advertisers' locations have been sorted by postcode. In Scotland, postcodes can cover fairly large geographical areas.
Please check distance of property from specified location with the individual provider. VisitScotland cannot take any responsibility for this.

451

Location	Property Name	Postcode	Telephone	Classification	Star Rating
Mallaig	Doune Stone Lodges	PH41 4PU	01687 462667	Restaurant With Rooms	★★★
	Essan Cottage		01687 460014	Self Catering	★★★
	Fois A Chridhe		0131 3333677	Self Catering	★★★
	Garramore House	PH40 4PD	01687 450268	Guest House	★★
	Kilchoan Farmhouse		01687 462133	Self Catering	★★★ to ★★★★
	Morar Hotel	PH40 4PA	01687 462346	Hotel	★★★
	Sandholm Cottages		01687 462592	Self Catering	★★★
	Seaview	PH41 4QS	01687 462059	Guest House	★★★
	Sheenas Backpackers Lodge	PH41 4PU	01687 462764	Hostel	★★★
	The Gathering	PH41 4PL	01687 460051	Bed & Breakfast	★★★★
	The Moorings	PH41 4PQ	01687 462225	Guest House	★★★
	The Old Byre	PH41 4PL	01687 462639	Group Accommodation	★★★★
	West Highland Hotel	PH41 4QZ	01687 462210	Hotel	★★★
	Western Isles Guest House	PH41 4QG	01687 462320	Guest House	★★★
Mauchline	Ardwell	KA5 5BH	01290 552987	Bed & Breakfast	★★★
	Darnhay Cottage Holidays		01290 559428	Self Catering	★★★★
	Dykefield Farm	KA5 6EY	01290 553170	Farm House	★★
	Middlemuir Park	KA5 5NR	01292 541647	Holiday Park	★★★★
	Overtoun Farm Cottage		01290 550337	Self Catering	★★★
Maybole	12 Carrick Drive	KA19 7RH	01292 443830	Awaiting Grading	
	Blairquhan Castle Holiday Cottages – Kennedy Cottage		01655 770239	Self Catering	★★ to ★★★
	Brewhouse Flat		01655 884455	Self Catering	★★★
	Croyburnfoot Holiday Park	KA19 8JS	01292 500239	Holiday Park	★★★★
	Culzean Bay Holiday Park	KA19 8JS	01292 500444	Holiday Park	★★★★
	Culzean Castle Camping & Caravanning Club Site	KA19 8JX	02476 475318	Touring Park	★★★★
	Doonan's Cottage		01655 770665	Self Catering	★★★ to ★★★★
	Dove and Rainbow Cottages		01292 560426	Self Catering	★★★★★
	Kileekie Cottage		01655 740236	Self Catering	★★★
	Loch Ayim Cottage		01292 264022	Self Catering	★★★
	North Segganwell		0131 2439335	Self Catering	★★
	Old Mill Holiday Park – Maidens	KA19 8JZ	01581 500227	Awaiting Grading	
	Royal Artillery Cottage		0131 2439335	Self Catering	★★★
	South Segganwell		0131 2439335	Self Catering	★★
	The Ranch	KA19 8DU	01655 882446	Holiday Park	★★★★
	Walled Garden Camping & Caravan Park	KA19 7SL	01655 740323	Touring Park	★★★★
Melrose	12 Glentress		0148 3534877	Self Catering	★★★
	Barnhill		01573 450250	Self Catering	★★★★
	Braidwood	TD6 9LD	01896 822488	Guest House	★★★★
	Buccleuch Arms Hotel	TD6 0EW	01835 822243	Small Hotel	★★★
	Burts Hotel	TD6 9PL	01896 822285	Small Hotel	★★★
	Clint Lodge Cottage		01835 822027	Self Catering	★★★★
	Clint Lodge Country House	TD6 0DZ	01835 822027	Guest House	★★★★
	Courtyard Cottage		01896 822183	Self Catering	★★★
	Dimpleknowe Mill		01835 870333	Self Catering	★★★ to ★★★★

♿ Unassisted wheelchair access ♿ Assisted wheelchair access 🚶 Access for visitors with mobility difficulties
🄿 Bronze Green Tourism Award 🄿🄿 Silver Green Tourism Award 🄿🄿🄿 Gold Green Tourism Award
For further information on our Green Tourism Business Scheme please see page 7.

452   To find out more go to visitscotland.com

Location	Property Name	Postcode	Telephone	Classification	Star Rating	
Melrose	Drumblair		01896 823648	Self Catering	★★★★	
	Dryburgh Abbey Hotel	TD6 0RQ	01835 822261	Country House Hotel	★★★★	
	Dunfermline House	TD6 9LB	01896 822411	Guest House	★★★	
	Easter Cottage	TD6 9JD	01835 870281	Bed & Breakfast	★★★★	🚶
	Eildon Holiday Cottages – The Granary		01896 823258	Self Catering	★★★ to ★★★★	♿
	Fauhope House	TD6 9LU	01896 823184	Bed & Breakfast	★★★★★	
	Fiorlin	TD6 9PX	01896 822984	Bed & Breakfast	★★★	
	Fishermans		01835 822356	Self Catering	★★★	
	Four Market Square		01896 820224	Self Catering	★★★★	
	George & Abbotsford Hotel	TD6 9PD	01896 822308	Hotel	★★	
	Gibson Park Caravan Club Site	TD6 9RY	01342 336842	Touring Park	★★★★★	
	Glendevon		0131 4660760	Self Catering	★★★	
	Harmony Cottage		0131 2439335	Self Catering	★★	
	Harmony House	TD6 9LJ	0131 2439335	Awaiting Grading		
	Mainhill	TD6 0HG	01835 823788	Bed & Breakfast	★★★	
	Melrose Youth Hostel	TD6 9EF	01786 891300	Hostel	★★★	🍃
	Newstead Mill		01896 820388	Self Catering	★★★★	
	No. 9 Townhead Way	TD6 9BU	01896 820435	Bed & Breakfast	★★★★	
	Old Abbey School	TD6 9SH	01896 823432	Bed & Breakfast	★★★	
	Old Bank House	TD6 9LB	01896 823712	Bed & Breakfast	★★★★	
	Pavilion Cottage		01896 820388	Self Catering	★★★★	
	Pear Cottage		0131 2439335	Self Catering	★★★	
	Priory Cottage	TD6 9LU	01896 820333	Awaiting Grading		
	Stables Cottage		01896 822300	Self Catering	★★★★	
	Swallow Cottage		01896 822608	Self Catering	★★	
	Swallow Cottage		01896 820388	Self Catering	★★★★	
	The Cloister House		0845 0900194	Self Catering	★★★★	
	The Lodge		01835 824400	Self Catering	★★★★	
	The Old Dairy		01507 606757	Self Catering	★★★★	
	The Town House Hotel	TD6 9PQ	01896 822645	Town House Hotel	★★★	
	Waverley Castle Hotel	TD6 9AA	01896 822244	Hotel	★★★	
	Whitehouse	TD6 0ED	01573 460343	Bed & Breakfast	★★★★★	
Menstrie	Broomhall Castle	FK11 7EA	01259 763360	Guest Accommodation	★★★	
	Menstrie Castle		01259 212478	Self Catering	★★★	
Moffat	1, Macadam House		01683 221676	Self Catering	★★★★ to ★★★★★	
	Annandale Arms Hotel	DG10 9HF	01683 220013	Small Hotel	★★★	
	Auchen Castle Hotel	DG10 9SH	01683 300407	Country House Hotel	★★★	
	Balmoral Hotel	DG10 9DL	01683 220288	Inn	★★★	
	Blairdrummond House	DG10 9AX	01683 221240	Bed & Breakfast	★★★★	
	Bridge House	DG10 9JT	01683 220558	Guest House	★★★★	
	Buccleuch Arms Hotel	DG10 9ET	01683 220003	Small Hotel	★★★	🍃🍃🍃
	Buchan Guest House	DG10 9RS	01683 220378	Guest House	★★★	
	Dell-Mar	DG10 9RS	01683 220260	Bed & Breakfast	★★★	
	Dye Mill Cottage		01683 220681	Self Catering	★★	
	Flat 4 St Mary's Church	DG10 9LW	0207 2432455	Awaiting Grading		
	Hartfell House & The Limetree Restaurant	DG10 9AL	01683 220153	Guest House	★★★★	

♿ Unassisted wheelchair access   🖐♿ Assisted wheelchair access   🚶 Access for visitors with mobility difficulties
🍃 Bronze Green Tourism Award   🍃🍃 Silver Green Tourism Award   🍃🍃🍃 Gold Green Tourism Award
For further information on our Green Tourism Business Scheme please see page 7.

Advertisers' locations have been sorted by postcode. In Scotland, postcodes can cover fairly large geographical areas.
Please check distance of property from specified location with the individual provider. VisitScotland cannot take any responsibility for this.

453

Directory of all VisitScotland Assured Serviced Establishments, ordered by location.
Establishments highlighted have an advertisement in this guide.

Location	Property Name	Postcode	Telephone	Classification	Star Rating	
Moffat	Hillview		01683 221021	Self Catering	★★	
	Holmedale		0191 2901461	Self Catering	★★★	
	Kirsty Cottage		01527 585585	Self Catering	★★★	
	Limetree House	DG10 9AE	01683 220001	Guest House	★★★★	⚹
	Lochhouse Farm Retreat Centre	DG10 9SG	01683 300451	Bed & Breakfast	★★★	♿
	Lochhouse Farm Retreat Centre		01683 300451	Self Catering	★★★	♿
	Moffat Camping & Caravanning Club Site	DG10 9QL	02476 475318	Touring Park	★★★★	
	Morlich House	DG10 9JU	01683 220589	Bed & Breakfast	★★★★	
	Queensberry House	DG10 9RS	01683 220538	Bed & Breakfast	★★★★	
	Riverdale		0791 77533302	Self Catering	★★★	
	Rockhill Guest House	DG10 9RS	01683 220283	Guest House	★★★	
	Rosebery House	DG10 9QJ	01683 221976	Bed & Breakfast	★★★	
	Seamore House	DG10 9HW	01683 220404	Guest House	★★★	
	Seven Oaks at 2 St. Mary's Church	DG10 9HP	01683 220584	Bed & Breakfast	★★★★	
	Stag Hotel	DG10 9HL	01683 220343	Inn	★★	
	Star Hotel	DG10 9EF	01683 220156	Small Hotel	★★	
	The Bonnington Hotel	DG10 9DL	01683 221888	Awaiting Grading		
	Well View	DG10 9JU	01683 220184	Restaurant With Rooms	★★★★	
	Woodhead Farm	DG10 9LU	01683 220225	Bed & Breakfast	★★★★	
Montrose	21 King Street		0141 5695275	Self Catering	★★★	
	36 The Mall	DD10 8SS	01674 673646	Bed & Breakfast	★★★★	
	Anniston Farm Cottages		01561 361402	Self Catering	★★★★	♿
	Auld Smiddy		01561 362841	Self Catering	★★★	
	Best Western Links Hotel	DD10 8RL	01674 671000	Hotel	★★★★	⚹
	East Bowstrips Caravan Park	DD10 0DE	01674 850328	Holiday Park	★★★★★	
	Ellington	DD10 0JD	01561 362756	Bed & Breakfast	★★★★	
	Eskview Farm	DD10 0AQ	01674 830890	Bed & Breakfast	★★★★	
	Inverbervie Caravan Park	DD10 0SP	07791 678997	Holiday Park	★★★	
	Lilybank Cottage		01975 651474	Self Catering	★★★	
	Monaidh Rois	DD10 8RS	01224 747894	Awaiting Grading		
	North Flat		01674 810264	Self Catering	★★★	
	Oaklands	DD10 9NN	01674 672018	Guest House	★★★	
	Park Hotel	DD10	01674 673415	Hotel	★★★	
	South Flat		0131 2439335	Self Catering	★★★	
	South Links Caravan Park	DD10 8AJ	01674 672105	Touring Park	★★★	
	St Cyrus Park	DD10 0DJ	01674 850316	Holiday Park	★★★	
	Stable Cottage & Dairy Cottage		01561 362453	Self Catering	★★★★	⚹
	The Green House		01224 864458	Self Catering	★★★	
	Wairds Park Caravan Park	DD10 0HD	01561 362395	Holiday Park	★★★★	
	Westerton of Rosie Cottage	DD10 9TN	01674 675837	Awaiting Grading		
	Woodland Glade	DD10 0PX	01561 361567	Bed & Breakfast	★★★	
	Woodston Bothy	DD10 0DG	01639 883800	Awaiting Grading		
Motherwell	Dakota Hotel	ML1 4UD	01698 835444	Hotel	★★★	
	Express By Holiday Inn	ML1 3RB	0169 8858585	Metro Hotel	★★★	♿
	Glasgow Motherwell Premier Inn	ML1 5SY	08701 977164	Budget Hotel		
	Moorings Hotel	ML1 3DG	01698 258131	Hotel	★★★	♿

♿ Unassisted wheelchair access ♿ Assisted wheelchair access ⚹ Access for visitors with mobility difficulties
🄿 Bronze Green Tourism Award 🄿🄿 Silver Green Tourism Award 🄿🄿🄿 Gold Green Tourism Award
For further information on our Green Tourism Business Scheme please see page 7.

To find out more go to visitscotland.com

Location	Property Name	Postcode	Telephone	Classification	Star Rating	
Motherwell	Motherwell College	ML1	01698 232323	Campus	★★★	♿
	Strathclyde Country Park	ML1 3ED	01698 402084	Touring Park	★★★	
	The Alona Hotel	ML1 3RT	01698 333888	Hotel	★★★★	♿
Muir Of Ord	Balvraid Cottage		01463 870326	Self Catering	★★★	✦
	Benview		0770 6134891	Self Catering	★★★★	
	Caberfeidh		01997 477252	Self Catering	★★★	
	Dungrianach	IV6 7TN	01463 870316	Bed & Breakfast	★★★	
	Hillview Park	IV6 7TU	01463 870787	Bed & Breakfast	★★★★	✦
	Home Farm Bed and Breakfast	IV6 7XN	01463 871779	Bed & Breakfast	★★★★	
	Honeysuckle Cottage		01997 871060	Self Catering	★★★	
	Kilcoy Chalets		01463 741797	Self Catering	★★★	
	Ord House Hotel	IV6 7UH	01463 870492	Country House Hotel	★★	
	Wester Muckernich	IV6 7SA	01349 861222	Bed & Breakfast	★★★★	
Munlochy	Kinneskie House	IV8 8PF	01463 811779	Bed & Breakfast	★★★★	
Musselburgh	18 Woodside Gardens	EH21 7LJ	0131 6653170	Bed & Breakfast	★★	
	19 Bridge Street	EH21 6AA	0131 6656560	Bed & Breakfast	★★	
	Arden House	EH21 7LL	0131 6650663	Guest House	★★★★	
	Carberry Tower	EH21 8PY	0131 6653135	Guest Accommodation	★★★	
	Edinburgh (Newcraighall) Premier Inn	EH21 8RX	0870 9906336	Budget Hotel		
	Edinburgh Inveresk Premier Inn	EH21 8PT	0870 1977092	Budget Hotel		
	Eildon	EH21 7AS	0131 6653981	Bed & Breakfast	★★★	🌿🌿🌿
	QMU Capital Campus	EH21 6UD	0131 4740000	Awaiting Grading		♿
	Travelodge Edinburgh Musselburgh	EH21 8RE	08719 846138	Budget Hotel		
Nairn	6 The Moorings		01309 691266	Self Catering	★★★	
	Altonburn Cottage		01667 493305	Self Catering	★★★★	
	Aurora Hotel	IV12 4RJ	01667 453 551	Small Hotel	★★	
	Banchor Cottage		01667 404401	Self Catering	★★★★	
	Boath House	IV12 5TE	01667 454896	Country House Hotel	★★★★	
	Boath Stables – North & South		01667 451300	Self Catering	★★★★	🌿🌿
	Braeval Hotel	IV12 4NB	01667 452341	Small Hotel	★★★	
	Cawdor Cottages – Fishermans Cottage		01667 402402	Self Catering	★★★★	
	Cawdor House	IV12 4QD	01667 455855	Guest House	★★★★	
	Ceolmara Garden Flat		01667 452495	Self Catering	★★★★	
	Claymore House Hotel	IV12 4EY	01667 452341	Small Hotel	★★★★	
	Cottar House		01667 455137	Self Catering	★★★★	
	Covenanters' Inn	IV12 5TG	01667 452456	Inn	★★★	♿
	Dunbar View		01667 456995	Self Catering	★★★★	
	Easter Arr Bed & Breakfast	IV12 5HZ	01667 451051	Awaiting Grading		
	Firth View Cottage		01309 641505	Self Catering	★★★★	
	Flora's Cottage		0207 3591507	Self Catering	★★★	
	Glebe End	IV12 4ED	01667 451659	Bed & Breakfast	★★★★	
	Golf View Hotel	IV12 4HD	01667 452301	Hotel	★★★★	✦
	Greenlawns	IV12 4HG	01667 452738	Guest House	★★★★	
	Hadden		01259 742341	Self Catering	★★★	
	Hidden Glen Holidays – Rowantree		01667 454630	Self Catering	★★ to ★★★★	♿
	Inveran	IV12 4HG	01667 455666	Bed & Breakfast	★★★★	

♿ Unassisted wheelchair access ♿ Assisted wheelchair access ✦ Access for visitors with mobility difficulties
🌿 Bronze Green Tourism Award 🌿🌿 Silver Green Tourism Award 🌿🌿🌿 Gold Green Tourism Award
For further information on our Green Tourism Business Scheme please see page 7.

Advertisers' locations have been sorted by postcode. In Scotland, postcodes can cover fairly large geographical areas.
Please check distance of property from specified location with the individual provider. VisitScotland cannot take any responsibility for this.

455

Location	Property Name	Postcode	Telephone	Classification	Star Rating		
Nairn	Invernairne Guest House	IV12 4EZ	01667 452039	Guest House	★★★		
	Inverwick Cottage		01667 455050	Self Catering	★★★★		
	Laikenbuie	IV12 5QN	01667 454630	Holiday Caravan			
	Marina View		01667 454464	Self Catering	★★★		
	Mill Lodge		01667 454635	Self Catering	★★★★	⅃	
	Nairn Camping & Caravanning Club Site	IV12 5NX	02476 475318	Touring Park	★★★★		
	Nairn Lochloy Holiday Park	IV12 4DE	01667 453764	Holiday Park	★★★★		
	Number 5		01667 493815	Self Catering	★★★★		
	Redburn	IV12 4AA	01667 452238	Bed & Breakfast	★★★		
	Redburn House	IV12 5JE	01309 651323	Awaiting Grading			
	Sunny Brae Hotel	IV12 4AE	01667 452309	Small Hotel	★★★★		℗℗℗
	The Cottage		01667 453261	Self Catering	★★★		
	The Pine Tree House		01667 456930	Self Catering	★		
	The Sheiling			Self Catering	★★★		
	Torrich House Apartment		01667 404679	Self Catering	★★★		
	Windsor Hotel	IV12 4HP	01667 453108	Hotel	★★★	♿	
Nethy Bridge	Abernethy Bunkhouses	PH25 3DN	01479 821370	Awaiting Grading			
	Abernethy Bunkhouses (Nethy Station)	PH25 3DN	01479 821370	Group Accommodation	★★		℗
	Badanfhuarain Forest Cottages		01479 821642	Self Catering	★★★★	⅃	℗℗
	Balnagowan Mill		01786 824957	Self Catering	★★★★		
	Birch Beag		01479 821613	Self Catering	★★★ to ★★★★		℗℗
	Cluny-Mhore		01479 872675	Self Catering	★★★★	⅃	℗
	Coire Choille B&B	PH25 3DY	01479 821716	Bed & Breakfast	★★★		
	Corner Cottage		0131 558 9391	Self Catering	★★★★		
	Dell of Abernethy Cottages – East Dell (Building 1)		0845 0179636	Self Catering	★★ to ★★★	♁	℗
	Derraid		01479 821803	Self Catering	★★★		
	Fern Cottage		0776 7846474	Self Catering	★★★		
	Gowanlea		01315 315078	Self Catering	★★★		
	Innis Bhroc		01479 831711	Self Catering	★★★★		
	Lazy Duck Hostel	PH25 3ED	01479 821642	Hostel	★★★★	⅃	℗℗
	Lorien		0141 5637830	Self Catering	★★★		
	Mountain Bear Lodge		01479 812266	Self Catering	★★★★★		
	Mountview Hotel	PH25 3EB	01479 821248	Small Hotel	★★★		℗℗
	Nethybridge Hotel	PH25 3DP	01479 821203	Hotel	★★★	⅃	
	No. 6 Lynstock Park		01312 209212	Self Catering	★★★		
	Osprey House		01330 844344	Self Catering	★★★★★	♁	
	Ryvoan Lodge			Self Catering	★★★★		℗℗
	The Lodge		01479 831384	Self Catering	★★★★		
	The Lodge		01479 821473	Self Catering	★★★★ to ★★★★★		
	Tigh Na Fraoch	PH25 3DA	01479 821400	Bed & Breakfast	★★★★		℗℗
	Woodbridge		01479 821226	Self Catering	★★★		
Newbridge	Hilton Edinburgh Airport	EH28 8LL	01315 194400	Hotel	★★★★	⅃	
	Norton House Hotel	EH28 8LX	0131 3331275	Country House Hotel	★★★★		
	The Quality Hotel Edinburgh Airport	EH28 8AU	0131 3334331	Hotel	★★★		

♿ Unassisted wheelchair access ⅃ Assisted wheelchair access ♁ Access for visitors with mobility difficulties
℗ Bronze Green Tourism Award ℗℗ Silver Green Tourism Award ℗℗℗ Gold Green Tourism Award
For further information on our Green Tourism Business Scheme please see page 7.

456   To find out more go to visitscotland.com

Location	Property Name	Postcode	Telephone	Classification	Star Rating
Newport-on-Tay	Braemore	DD6 8AR	01382 542516	Bed & Breakfast	★★★★
	Fernbrae House Apartment		01382 542088	Self Catering	★★★★
	The Ice Barn		01264 850344	Self Catering	★★★★
	Thorndene		01382 542274	Self Catering	★★★
Newton Stewart	15 Cowgate		0141 3574551	Self Catering	★★★★
	2 Laigh Isle	DG8 8LS	01229 468946	Awaiting Grading	
	41 Main Street		02085 606820	Self Catering	★
	42 Laigh Isle		023 92593468	Self Catering	★★
	5 Laigh Isle		02870 868396	Self Catering	★★
	Amisfield		01988 700284	Self Catering	★★★★
	Anne's Lodge		01671 840252	Self Catering	★★★ to ★★★★
	Ash Tree Cottage		01671 830287	Self Catering	★★ to ★★★
	Barholm Croft		01671 820440	Self Catering	★★
	Bladnoch Inn	DG8 9AB	01671 402727	Inn	★★
	Bridge Croft & Heron Crofts		01224 633872	Self Catering	★★★★
	Brigton Farm		01671 840278	Self Catering	★★★
	Cairnhouse Farm		01988 403217	Self Catering	★★★★
	Castle Cary Holiday Park	DG8 7DQ	01671 820264	Holiday Park	★★★★
	Castlewigg Holiday Park	DG8 9DL	01988 500616	Holiday Park	★★★
	Chapel Outon Farmhouse	DG8 8DH	01988 500136	Bed & Breakfast	★★★
	Cherrytrees	DG8 7JB	01671 820229	Bed & Breakfast	★★★
	Craiglemine Cottage B&B	DG8 8NE	01988 500594	Bed & Breakfast	★★
	Craiglemine Tigh	DG8 8NE	01988 500490	Bed & Breakfast	★★★
	Craw's Nest Bungalow		01213 781844	Self Catering	★★★
	Cree Cottage		01671 403341	Self Catering	★★★★
	Creebridge Caravan Park	DG8 6AJ	01671 402324	Holiday Park	★★★
	Creebridge House Hotel	DG8 6NP	01671 402121	Small Hotel	★★★
	Creetown Caravan Park	DG8 7HU	01581 500227	Holiday Park	★★★★
	Dirnow Schoolhouse		01671 830297	Self Catering	★★★★
	Drumroamin Farm Camping & Caravan Site	DG8 9DB	01988 840613	Holiday Park	★★★★
	East Culkae Farm House	DG8 8AS	01988 850214	Farm House	★★★
	East Culkae Farmhouse	DG8 8AS	01988 850214	Holiday Caravan	
	Galloway Arms Hotel	DG8 6DB	01671 402653	Inn	★★★
	Garheugh Croft		01892 655045	Self Catering	★★★
	Glenalmar		01988 500203	Self Catering	★★★
	Glencaird Farmhouse		0208 4557124	Self Catering	★★★★
	Glenluce Caravan & Camping Park	DG8 0QR	01581 300412	Holiday Park	★★★★
	Glentrool Holiday Park	DG8 6RN	01671 840280	Holiday Park	★★★★
	Granary & Stables		01988 402266	Self Catering	★★★
	High Killantrae Cottage		07968 032741	Self Catering	★★★
	Hillcrest House	DG8 9EU	01988 402018	Guest House	★★★
	Hilltop		01776 810486	Self Catering	★★★
	Holmpark Cottages		01671 402499	Self Catering	★★★★
	Kilwarlin	DG8 6LN	01671 403047	Bed & Breakfast	★★★
	Kirroughtree House	DG8 6AN	01671 402141	Country House Hotel	★★★
	Low Cordorcan Cottage		01671 840311	Self Catering	★★★★

  Unassisted wheelchair access   Assisted wheelchair access   Access for visitors with mobility difficulties
Ⓟ Bronze Green Tourism Award   ⒫⒫ Silver Green Tourism Award   ⒫⒫⒫ Gold Green Tourism Award
For further information on our Green Tourism Business Scheme please see page 7.

Advertisers' locations have been sorted by postcode. In Scotland, postcodes can cover fairly large geographical areas.
Please check distance of property from specified location with the individual provider. VisitScotland cannot take any responsibility for this.

457

Location	Property Name	Postcode	Telephone	Classification	Star Rating		
Newton Stewart	Luce Bay Holiday Park & Lodges	DG8 0JT	01581 500227	Holiday Park	★★★★		
	Maidland Lodge		01988 403270	Self Catering	★★★		
	Mid Bishopton Bungalow		01988 500754	Self Catering	★★★		
	Minnigaff Youth Hostel	DG8 6PL	0870 1553255	Hostel	★★		🄿
	Muirfad Farmhouse B&B	DG8 7BA	0791 5059103	Bed & Breakfast	★★★		
	Pend House		01988 500469	Self Catering	★★★★		
	Ravenstone House	DG8 8DU	01988 700756	Bed & Breakfast	★★★★		
	Ravenstone Mains Cottage		01988 850377	Self Catering	★★★ to ★★★★		
	Rowallan	DG8 6JB	01671 402520	Guest House	★★★		
	Seabank		01581 600228	Self Catering	★★★		
	Spittal Cottages		01671 820224	Self Catering	★★★		
	Stables Guest House	DG8 6JB	01671 402157	Guest House	★★★		
	Tha Butchach	DG8 0AW	01581 600217	Bed & Breakfast	★★		
	The Barn At Glenturk No 1		01988 402281	Self Catering	★★★★		
	The Bruce Hotel	DG8 6JL	01671 402294	Hotel	★★★		
	The Chalet	DG8 8AD	01988 600248	Awaiting Grading			
	The Crown Hotel	DG8 6JW	01671 402727	Small Hotel	★★★		
	The Nether Barr Steading		01671 404326	Self Catering	★★★		
	The Steam Packet Inn	DG8 8LL	01988 500334	Inn	★★		
	The Wigtown Ploughman Hotel	DG8 9HG	01988 402852	Inn	★★★		
	Three Lochs Holiday Park	DG8 0EP	01671 830304	Holiday Park	★★★★		
	West Barr Cottage		01988 700367	Self Catering	★★★		
	Whitecairn Farm Caravan Park	DG8 0NZ	01581 300267	Holiday Park	★★★★★		
Newtonmore	Alvey House	PH20 1AT	01540 673260	Guest House	★★★		
	Ard-Na-Coille	PH20 1AY	01540 673214	Guest House	★★★★★		
	Ardverikie Estate Houses – Gate Lodge		01528 544300	Self Catering	★★ to ★★★		
	Bail nan Cnoc		01528 544336	Self Catering	★★★ to ★★★★	🏃	🄿🄿
	Balgowan House		01528 544368	Self Catering	★★★★		
	Biallid House		07974 226862	Self Catering	★★★		
	Clune House	PH20 1DR	01540 673359	Bed & Breakfast	★★★		🄿🄿
	Cluny Mains		01462 673410	Self Catering	★★★★		
	Coig Na Shee	PH20 1DG	01540 670109	Guest House	★★★★		
	Craigower Lodge	PH20 1AT	01540 673319	Activity Accommodation	★★★	♿	
	Creag Meagaidh Bed & Breakfast	PH20 1DP	01540 673798	Bed & Breakfast	★★★★		
	Crubenbeg Holiday Cottages		01540 673566	Self Catering	★★★★		🄿🄿🄿
	Crubenbeg House	PH20 1BE	01540 673300	Guest House	★★★★	♿	
	Glenavon House	PH20 1DR	01540 673701	Bed & Breakfast	★★★★		
	Greenways	PH20 1AT	01540 670136	Bed & Breakfast	★★★★		
	Highlander Hotel	PH20 1AY		Hotel	★★		
	Invernahavon Caravan Site	PH20 1BE	01540 673534	Touring Park	★★★★		
	Larick House B&B	PH20 1AT	01540 673762	Bed & Breakfast	★★★		
	Monadhliath Hotel	PH20 1BT	01528 544276	Small Hotel	★★★		
	Newtonmore Hostel	PH20 1DA	01540 673360	Hostel	★★★		
	Pottery Bunkhouse	PH20 1BT	01528 544231	Group Accommodation	★★★★		
	Stable Cottage and The Loft		07921 729249	Self Catering	★★ to ★★★	♿	
	Steading 5 Balvatin Cottages		01355 260498	Self Catering	★★★		

♿ Unassisted wheelchair access   ♿ Assisted wheelchair access   🏃 Access for visitors with mobility difficulties
🄿 Bronze Green Tourism Award   🄿🄿 Silver Green Tourism Award   🄿🄿🄿 Gold Green Tourism Award
For further information on our Green Tourism Business Scheme please see page 7.

To find out more go to visitscotland.com

Location	Property Name	Postcode	Telephone	Classification	Star Rating	
Newtonmore	Strathspey Mountain Hostel	PH20 1DR	01540 673694	Hostel	★★★	ⓕ
	The Rumblie	PH20 1AH	01528 544766	Guest House	★★★★	🅟🅟🅟
	Tigh an Each B&B	PH20 1BS	01528 544709	Awaiting Grading		
	Treetops		0114 2668626	Self Catering	★★★	
	Woodlands		0131 4452070	Self Catering	★★★	
			07921 729249	Self Catering	★★	ⓕ
North Berwick	1 Church Road		01620 893204	Self Catering	★★	
	11 Lorne Lane		01620 890555	Self Catering	★★★	
	12 Quality Street	EH39 4HP	01620 892529	Restaurant With Rooms	★★★	
	14 Cromwell Road		01620 893204	Self Catering	★★★★	
	15C Balfour Street		01855 850355	Self Catering	★★★	
	2 Milsey Court		01620 893334	Self Catering	★★★	
	25G Melbourne Place		01620 893204	Self Catering	★★	
	30 Royal Apartments		01620 893204	Self Catering	★★★★	
	31 Westgate		01620 890204	Self Catering	★★★★	
	4 Milsey Court		01620 892638	Self Catering	★★★	
	45 Westgate		0191 3781097	Self Catering	★★★	
	5 Lorne Lane		01620 893435	Self Catering	★★★	
	5 Viewforth		07815 060445	Self Catering	★★★★	
	90A High Street		01223 690 157	Self Catering	Awaiting Grading	
	90 High Street		01620 893204	Self Catering	★★★	
	Aaran Apartment		0131 6654608	Self Catering	★★★★★	
	Aviemore		01620 893204	Self Catering	★★★	
	Beach Haven		01620 893204	Self Catering	★★★	
	By The Sea		01620 893204	Self Catering	★★★	
	Cairnsmore – Top Flat		01620 894554	Self Catering	★★★	
	Chelmsford		0141 5849608	Self Catering	★★★	
	Cottage Garden		01777 719107	Self Catering	★★★★	
	Denis Duncan House		01787 372343	Self Catering	★★★★	♿
	Drem Farmhouse	EH39 5AP	01620 850563	Bed & Breakfast	★★★★	
	Fenton Tower	EH39 5JH	01620 890089	Exclusive Use Venue	★★★★★	
	Fishermens Hall		0131 3313878	Self Catering	★★★★	
	Flat 3		01620 893204	Self Catering	★★★	
	Flat 6 Hyndford House		01620 893204	Self Catering	★★★	
	Gilsland Caravan Park	EH39 53A	01620 892205	Holiday Park	★★★	
	Glenconner Cottage		01642 700431	Self Catering	★★★	
	Glentruim	EH39 4BL	01620 890064	Bed & Breakfast	★★★★	
	Glentruim Self-Catering Cottage		01620 890064	Self Catering	★★★★	
	Ithaca House		0131 3373617	Self Catering	★★★	
	Kirkpatrick Self Catering		0131 3345951	Self Catering	★	
	Kirkview		01620 893204	Self Catering	★★★	
	MacDonald Marine Hotel & Spa	EH39 4LZ	01620 894301	Hotel	★★★★	
	Mews Cottage		01620 892030	Self Catering	★★★★★	
	Nether Abbey Hotel	EH39 4BQ	01620 892802	Small Hotel	★★★	
	Newmains Farm Steading		07967 689831	Self Catering	★★★★	
	Nia Roo		0131 3324320	Self Catering	★★★	
	No 8 & 9 Scoughall Farm Cottages		01620 870210	Self Catering	★★	

Advertisers' locations have been sorted by postcode. In Scotland, postcodes can cover fairly large geographical areas.
Please check distance of property from specified location with the individual provider. VisitScotland cannot take any responsibility for this.

459

Location	Property Name	Postcode	Telephone	Classification	Star Rating	
North Berwick	No 8 Marine Parade		01620 893204	Self Catering	★★★★	
	No 8 Melbourne Place		01620 893204	Self Catering	★★	
	North Berwick Golf Lodge		01620 892457	Self Catering	★★★★★	
	Open Arms Hotel	EH39 5EG	01620 850241	Small Hotel	★★★	
	Seafield		01620 893204	Self Catering	★★	
	Seaholm	EH39 4LB	01620 895150	Bed & Breakfast	★★★★	
	Stewart Lodge		01620 893204	Self Catering	★★★	
	Tantallon Caravan Park	EH39 5NJ	01620 893348	Holiday Park	★★★★	ঌ
	The Garden Flat B&B	EH39 4LX	07734 033058	Awaiting Grading		
	The Glebe House	EH39 4PL	01620 892608	Bed & Breakfast	★★★★	
	The Hideaway		01620 893204	Self Catering	★★	
	The House at the Beach		01382 778928	Self Catering	★★★	
	The Neuk		01620 671966	Self Catering	★★★	
	The Retreat Cottage		01620 892429	Self Catering	★★★	
	The Wing	EH39 4LD	01620 893162	Bed & Breakfast	★★★	
	Troon	EH39 5DF	01620 893555	Bed & Breakfast	★★★	
	Vale End		0131 3321544	Self Catering	★★★★	
	West Fenton Court Cottages		01620 842154	Self Catering	★★★★	
	Winterfield Lodge	EH39 4LY	01620 892962	Bed & Breakfast	★★	
	Yellowcraig Caravan Club Site	EH39 5DS	01342 336842	Touring Park	★★★★★	
Oban	12 High Street		01631 565368	Self Catering	★★	
	15 Albany Apartments		01631 563987	Self Catering	★★★★	
	19 Albany Apts		0141 8806707	Self Catering	★★★	
	23 Albany Apartments		01631 710569	Self Catering	★★★★	
	29 Albany Apartments		01631 562089	Self Catering	★★★★	
	3 Oban Times Buildings		01631 562815	Self Catering	★★★	
	9 Knipoch Place		01631 564833	Self Catering	★★★★	
	Achnacroish Cottage		02086 611834	Self Catering	★★★	
	Achnamara	PA37 1DT	01631 710705	Bed & Breakfast	★★★★	
	Achranich	PA34 5UZ	01967 421288	Awaiting Grading		
	Albany Apartments 3		01631 566909	Self Catering	★★★★	
	Alexandra Hotel	PA34 5AA		Hotel	★★★	
	Alltavona	PA34 5AQ	01631 565067	Guest House	★★★★	
	An Acail		02392 553433	Self Catering	★★★	
	An Cladach – West Wing		01347 878418	Self Catering	★★★	
	An Rubha		07831 838717	Self Catering	★★	
	An Struan	PA37 1ST	01631 720301	Bed & Breakfast	★★★★	
	An Tobar	PA34 4SE	01631 565081	Holiday Caravan		
	Annabells		01631 710737	Self Catering	★★★★	
	Anvil Edgemont Annexe		01631 569499	Self Catering	★★★	
	Ard Struan	PA34 5JN	01631 563689	Bed & Breakfast	★★★	
	Ardara		01852 300379	Self Catering	★★	
	Ardchoille	PA37 1ST	01631 720432	Bed & Breakfast	★★★	
	Ardenstur Cottages – Croft		01429 267266	Self Catering	★★ to ★★★★	
	Ardlynn		01786 842889	Self Catering	★★★★	
	Ardmaddy Castle Holiday Cottages – The Lodge		01852 300353	Self Catering	★★★★	♿
	Ardoran Marine Chalet		01631 566123	Self Catering	★★★	

♿ Unassisted wheelchair access   ঌ Assisted wheelchair access   ♿ Access for visitors with mobility difficulties
P Bronze Green Tourism Award   *PP* Silver Green Tourism Award   *PPP* Gold Green Tourism Award
For further information on our Green Tourism Business Scheme please see page 7.

460   To find out more go to visitscotland.com

Location	Property Name	Postcode	Telephone	Classification	Star Rating	
Oban	Ards House	PA37 1PT	01631 710255	Guest House	★★★★	
	Ardshellach		01494 891614	Self Catering	★★★★	
	Arduaine Cottage	PA34 4XQ	01852 200216	Awaiting Grading		
	Ardura	PA34 5DU	01631 562380	Bed & Breakfast	★★★	
	Ardura Flat		01631 562380	Self Catering	★★★	
	Aros Ard	PA34 5JN	01631 565500	Bed & Breakfast	★★★★	
	Ayres Guest House	PA34 5JL	01631 562260	Guest House	★★	
	Baravullin Cottage		01631 710569	Self Catering	★★★	
	Barcaldine House Cottages	PA37 1SL	01631 720219	Awaiting Grading		
	Barcaldine House Hotel	PA37 1SG	01670 789048	Small Hotel		
	Bay View		01631 570552	Self Catering	★★★	
	Bayview Caravans	PA37 1QS	01631 720397	Awaiting Grading		
	Beech Grove Guest House	PA34 5JL	01631 566111	Guest House	★★★★	
	Blair Villa South	PA34 5DQ	01631 564813	Bed & Breakfast	★★★	
	Blaran		0191 2811695	Self Catering	★★★★	
	Blarcreen House	PA37 1RG	01631 750272	Bed & Breakfast	★★★★	
	Bracken Cottage		01631 770283	Self Catering	★★★★	
	Braeside Guest House	PA34 4QR	01631 770243	Guest House	★★★★	
	Briarbank	PA34 4DN	01631 566549	Bed & Breakfast	★★★★	
	Broomhill	PA34 5DY	01631 566182	Bed & Breakfast	★★★★	
	Cawdor Terrace Apartment		01505 874180	Self Catering	★★★★	
	Ceo Na Mara		07789 150826	Self Catering	★★★	
	Cherry Tree Cottage	PA34 4QA	01631 565421	Awaiting Grading		
	Clan Cottages		01631 770372	Self Catering	★★★★	🍃🍃
	Clohass	PA34 5TX	01631 563647	Bed & Breakfast	★★★	
	Cluaran House	PA37 1RN	01631 710051	Awaiting Grading		
	Corran House Hostel	PA34 5PN	01631 563344	Hostel	★★★★	
	Corriemar	PA34 5AQ	01631 562476	Guest House	★★★★	
	Creagard Country House		0141 6394592	Self Catering	★★★★	
	Creran Chalets		01631 720253	Self Catering	★★★	
	Croft Cottage		01852 300457	Self Catering	★★★★	🚶
	Cuilfail Hotel	PA34 4XA	01852 200274	Small Hotel	★★	
	Dalachullish	PA37 1SQ	01631 730452	Bed & Breakfast	★★★	
	Don-Muir	PA34 4LX	01631 564536	Bed & Breakfast	★★★★	
	Dungallan Country House	PA34 4PD	01631 563799	Guest House	★★★★★	
	Dunheanish Guest House	PA34 5DW	01631 566556	Guest House	★★★★	
	East Kames		01943 601729	Self Catering	★★★★	
	Elderberry – Self Catering	PA37 1QS	01631 720322	Holiday Caravan		
	Eredine	PA34 5DW	01631 563917	Bed & Breakfast	★★★	
	Esplanade Court Apart. – Apart. 401 Lismore – Type A		01631 562067	Self Catering	★★★ to ★★★★	
	Failte Bed and Breakfast	PA34 5DQ	01631 570219	Bed & Breakfast	★★★	
	Falls of Lora Hotel	PA37 1PB	01631 710483	Hotel	★★★	
	Fearnach Bay House		01852 200263	Self Catering	★★★★★	
	Garragh Mhor	PA34 4RF	01852 300513	Bed & Breakfast	★★★	
	Glen Cottage	PA34 5JU	01631 563420	Bed & Breakfast	★★★	
	Glen Cottage			Self Catering	★★★	
	Glenara Guest House	PA34 5DQ	01631 563172	Bed & Breakfast	★★★★	

♿ Unassisted wheelchair access ♿ Assisted wheelchair access 🚶 Access for visitors with mobility difficulties
🍃 Bronze Green Tourism Award 🍃🍃 Silver Green Tourism Award 🍃🍃🍃 Gold Green Tourism Award
For further information on our Green Tourism Business Scheme please see page 7.

Advertisers' locations have been sorted by postcode. In Scotland, postcodes can cover fairly large geographical areas.
Please check distance of property from specified location with the individual provider. VisitScotland cannot take any responsibility for this.

461

Location	Property Name	Postcode	Telephone	Classification	Star Rating
Oban	Glenbervie Guest House	PA34	01631 564770	Guest House	★★★★
	Glenburnie	PA34 5AQ	01631 562089	Guest House	★★★★
	Glengorm	PA34 5PH	01631 564386	Guest House	★★★
	Glenrigh Guest House	PA34 5AQ	01631 562991	Guest House	★★★★
	Glenroy Guest House	PA34 5DQ	01631 562585	Guest House	★★★
	Gramarvin Guest House	PA34 5PE	01631 564622	Guest House	★★★
	Great Western Hotel	PA34 5PP	01631 563101	Hotel	★★★
	Greencourt Guest House	PA34 5EF	01631 563987	Guest House	★★★★
	Grove House	PA37 1PA	01631 710599	Guest House	★★★★
	Hawthorn	PA37 1QS	01631 720452	Bed & Breakfast	★★★★
	Hawthornbank Guest House	PA34 5JE	01631 562041	Guest House	★★★★
	Heatherfield House	PA34 5EY	01631 562806	Guest House	★★★★
	High Cliff	PA34 4EW	01631 564134	Guest House	★★★★
	Individually names Lodges		01631 720255	Self Catering	★★★ to ★★★★
	Innis Chonain	PA37 1RT	01631 720550	Bed & Breakfast	★★★
	Insh Cottage		01852 300573	Self Catering	★★★★
	Inverasdale	PA34 4SA	01631 571031	Bed & Breakfast	★★★★
	Isle of Eriska Hotel	PA37 1SD	01631 720371	Country House Hotel	★★★★★	ⓚ
	Jeremy Inglis Hostel	PA34 55J	01631 565065	Hostel	★
	Kathmore Guest House	PA34 4JF	01631 562104	Guest House	★★★
	Katie's Flat		01631 562272	Self Catering	★★★
	Kelvin Hotel	PA34 4LQ	01631 562150	Guest House	★
	Kilchrenan House	PA34 5AQ	01631 562663	Guest House	★★★★
	Killbride Cottage		01852 300475	Self Catering	★★★
	Knipoch Hotel	PA34 4QT	01852 316251	Small Hotel	★★★★
	Lagganbeg Guest House	PA34 5PH	01631 563151	Guest House	★★★
	Lagganbuie	PA34 4QT	01631 770218	Bed & Breakfast	★★★★
	Lagnakeil Lodge – Millstone		01631 562746	Self Catering	★★★ to ★★★★
	Latheron	PA34 5JU	01631 564974	Bed & Breakfast	★★★
	Loch Melfort Hotel	PA34 4XG	01852 200233	Hotel	★★★
	Lochnagar & Ben Nevis		01631 564653	Self Catering	★★★
	Lochside Lodges		01631 720265	Self Catering	★★★
	Lochvoil House	PA34 4NE	01631 562645	Bed & Breakfast	★★★★
	Lochvoil House Bothy		01631 562645	Self Catering	★★★
	Lorne View	PA34 5DW	01631 566841	Bed & Breakfast	★★★
	Mactalla	PA37 1PJ	01631 710465	Guest House	★★★
	Maridon House	PA34 4NE	01631 562670	Guest House	★★★
	Melfort Village – Walled Garden Cottages 2 3 5 & 8		01852 200257	Self Catering	★★★★	🍃🍃🍃
	No 1 & 2 Tramway Cottages		01852 300112	Self Catering	★★★★
	No 7 Tramway		07810 710494	Self Catering	★★★★
	No. 6 Feochan Cottages		01852 200346	Self Catering	★★★
	North Ledaig Co Ltd	PA37 1RT	01631 710291	Touring Park	★★★★★
	Oban Backpackers	PA34 5NZ	01631 562107	Backpacker	★★★
	Oban Bay Hotel	PA34 5AE	01631 562051	Hotel	★★★	🍃
	Oban Camping & Caravanning Club Site	PA37 1SG	02476 475318	Touring Park	★★★★
	Oban Caravan & Camping Park	PA34 4QH	01631 562425	Touring Park	★★★
	Oban Holiday Home	PA34 5JH	01631 562536	Awaiting Grading	

& Unassisted wheelchair access ⓚ Assisted wheelchair access 🕴 Access for visitors with mobility difficulties
🍃 Bronze Green Tourism Award 🍃🍃 Silver Green Tourism Award 🍃🍃🍃 Gold Green Tourism Award
For further information on our Green Tourism Business Scheme please see page 7.

462 To find out more go to visitscotland.com

Location	Property Name	Postcode	Telephone	Classification	Star Rating	
Oban	Oban Seil Farm – Steading Cottages		01852 300245	Self Catering	★★★★	
	Oban Youth Hostel	PA34 5AF	0870 0041144	Hostel	★★★ to ★★★★	⅍
	Oiseanbeag	PA37 1RX	01871 810916	Awaiting Grading		
	Regent Hotel	PA34 5PZ	01631 562341	Hotel	★★	
	Rhonelin		01631 710288	Self Catering	★★★ to ★★★★	⋏
	Rockmount Cottage		01631 564647	Self Catering	★★	
	Ronebhal Guest House	PA37 1PJ	01631 710310	Guest House	★★★★	
	Rose View Caravan Park	PA34 4QJ	01631 562755	Touring Park	★★★★	
	Rosebank	PA37 1PA	01631 710316	Bed & Breakfast	★	
	Roseneath Guest House	PA34 5EQ	01631 562929	Guest House	★★★	
	Rowantree Cottage B & B	PA37 1QP	01631 720433	Bed & Breakfast	★★★	
	Rowantree Hotel	PA34 5NX	01631 562954	Hotel	★★	
	Royal Hotel	PA34 4BE	01631 563021	Hotel	★★★	
	Sabden Brook	PA34 5DY	01631 562649	Bed & Breakfast	★★★	
	Scotholm	PA37 1PG	01631 710549	Bed & Breakfast	★★★★	
	Seabank		01631 720602	Self Catering	★★★★	
	Seil Chalet Balvicar Chalets		01324 812927	Self Catering	★★★	
	Sgeir Mhaol	PA34 4JF	01631 562650	Awaiting Grading		
	Shenavallie	PA37 1QU	01631 720240	Bed & Breakfast	★★★★	
	Shian Bed & Breakfast	PA34 4LE	01631 564763	Bed & Breakfast	★★★★	
	St Anne's Guest House & Arbour Guest House	PA34 5PH	01631 562743	Guest House	★★	
	Staffa Annexe		01631 710681	Self Catering	★★★	
	Strathnaver Guest House	PA34 5JQ	01631 563305	Guest House	★★★	
	Strumhor	PA37 1PJ	01631 710167	Bed & Breakfast	★★★	
	Sunnybrae	PA34 4TU	01852 314274	Holiday Park	★★★★	🅟🅟
	Sutherland Guest House	PA34 5PN	01631 562539	Guest House	★★	
	Teanga-Bhuidhe	PA34 4QA	01631 564719	Holiday Caravan		
	The Barn at Scammadale Farm		01852 316282	Self Catering	★★★★	⋏ 🅟
	The Barriemore	PA34 5AQ	01631 566356	Guest House	★★★★	
	The Bolt-hole		01904 492111	Self Catering	★★★★	
	The Bothy Self Catering Cottage	PA34 4TX	01852 314388	Awaiting Grading		
	The Caledonian Hotel	PA34 5RT	01631 563133	Hotel	★★★	⋏
	The Cottage		01631 562878	Self Catering	★★	
	The Gallery Flat	PA34 4AY	01768 778518	Awaiting Grading		
	The Granary		07768 038247	Self Catering	★★★★	
	The Haven		01786 825582	Self Catering	★★★★	
	The Kimberley House	PA34 5EQ	01631 571115	Guest House	★★★★	
	The Manor House	PA34 4LS	01631 562087	Restaurant With Rooms	★★★★	
	The Old Manse	PA34 5JE	01631 564886	Guest House	★★★★	
	The Oyster Inn	PA37 1PJ	01631 710666	Inn	★★★★	
	The Queens Hotel	PA34 5AG	01631 562505	Awaiting Grading		
	Thornloe Guest House	PA34 5EJ	01631 562879	Guest House	★★★★	🅟🅟
	Torlin Guest House	PA34 4EP	01631 570642	Bed & Breakfast	★★★	
	Tralee Bay Purple Thistle Holidays	PA37 1QR	01631 720255	Holiday Park	★★★★★	
	Tralee Beach House		01631 710568	Self Catering	★★★★	
	Ulva Cottage		01631 563042	Self Catering	★★★	
	Ulva Villa	PA34 4JF	01631 563042	Guest House	★★★	

      ዽ Unassisted wheelchair access   ዽ Assisted wheelchair access   ⋏ Access for visitors with mobility difficulties
      🅟 Bronze Green Tourism Award   🅟🅟 Silver Green Tourism Award   🅟🅟🅟 Gold Green Tourism Award
For further information on our Green Tourism Business Scheme please see page 7.

Advertisers' locations have been sorted by postcode. In Scotland, postcodes can cover fairly large geographical areas.
Please check distance of property from specified location with the individual provider. VisitScotland cannot take any responsibility for this.

463

Location	Property Name	Postcode	Telephone	Classification	Star Rating	
Oban	Units 5 to 18 & Paddoch Lodge		01631 564501	Self Catering	★★★ to ★★★★	🏃‍♿
	Wellpark House	PA34 5AQ	01631 562948	Guest House	★★★★	
	Wide Mouthed Frog	PA37 1PX	01631 567005	Restaurant With Rooms	★★★	♿
	Willowdene	PA34 4EW	01631 563412	Bed & Breakfast	★★★	
Orkney	Ashleigh	KW17 2JA	01856 771378	Bed & Breakfast	★★★★	🧍
	Atlantis Lodges		01856 761581	Self Catering	★★★★	
	Auldkirk Apartments		01856 875488	Self Catering	★★★★	
	Ayres Rock Hostel	KW17 2AY	01857 600410	Hostel	★★★★	
	Backaskaill B&B	KW17 2BA	01857 600298	Bed & Breakfast	★★★	
	Bayview		01856 761543	Self Catering	★★★	
	Belmont Swanway	KW17 2NR	01856 721281	Holiday Caravan		
	Bethany Cottage		01856 871169	Self Catering	★★★	
	Birsay Outdoor Centre	KW17 2LY	01856 873535	Hostel	★★★	
	Braemill		01856 741240	Self Catering	★★★	
	Breckan		01856 771442	Self Catering	★★★	
	Brekkan		01856 721407	Self Catering	★★★	
	Bryameadow Farm	KW17 2JH	01856 841803	Holiday Caravan		
	Buan House		01856 761442	Self Catering	★★★★	
	Buxa Farm Chalets		01856 811360	Self Catering	★★★★	🧍
	Byre at Heddle		01856 761437	Self Catering	★★★★ to ★★★★★	🍂🍂
	Castlehill	KW17 2PJ	01856 751228	Bed & Breakfast	★★★★	
	Cauldhame		01856 831266	Self Catering	★★★★	🍂🍂
	Choin	KW17 2ND	01856 721488	Bed & Breakfast	★★★★	
	Cleaton House	KW17 2DB	01857 677508	Small Hotel	★★★★	
	Clouston Lodges		01856 811268	Self Catering	★★★★	
	Commodore Chalets		01856 781319	Self Catering	★★★	
	Commodore Chalets	KW17 2RU	01856 781319	Guest House	★★★	
	Corkaquina		01856 874100	Self Catering	★★★★	
	Corks		0131 5567051	Self Catering	★★★★	
	Craebreck House		01856 781231	Self Catering	★★★	
	Craigview		0115 9825014	Self Catering	★★★	
	Crearhowe		01334 850310	Self Catering	★★★★	
	Creel Cottage		01856 811739	Self Catering	★★★	
	Cullya-Quoy		01856 872265	Self Catering	★★★★	🧍
	Daisy Cottage		01857 677398	Self Catering	★★★	
	Daybreak		01856 876579	Self Catering	★★★	
	Deersound Cottage		01856 741331	Self Catering	★★★★	🏃‍♿
	Dennishill		01856 874486	Self Catering	★★★	
	Easterbister Cottage	KW17 2RY	01856 781387	Awaiting Grading		
	Findlays Cottage		01588 640941	Self Catering	★★★	
	Forst		01856 721323	Self Catering	★★	
	Furso		01856 875135	Self Catering	★★★	
	Garleton		01493 488609	Self Catering	★★★	
	Gorse Cottage		01856 751400	Self Catering	★★★	
	Gray's Inn		01856 811393	Self Catering	★★	
	Greenvale Self Catering	KW17 2SX	01856 731338	Awaiting Grading		
	Hilton Farmhouse	KW17 2EA	01856 711239	Farm House	★★★★	

♿ Unassisted wheelchair access   🏃‍♿ Assisted wheelchair access   🧍 Access for visitors with mobility difficulties
🍂 Bronze Green Tourism Award   🍂🍂 Silver Green Tourism Award   🍂🍂🍂 Gold Green Tourism Award
For further information on our Green Tourism Business Scheme please see page 7.

464   To find out more go to visitscotland.com

Location	Property Name	Postcode	Telephone	Classification	Star Rating		
Orkney	Holland House	KW17 2LQ	01856 771400	Bed & Breakfast	★★★★★		
	Holm View		01857 644211	Self Catering	★★★★	♿	
	House		01857 677374	Self Catering	★★★		
	Houton Bay Lodge	KW17 2RD	01856 811320	Inn	★★★★	♣	
	Howe Cottage		01856 831234	Self Catering	★★★		
	Iona Cottage	KW17 2EA	01224 867184	Awaiting Grading			
	Kenila	KW17 2LE	01856 771431	Bed & Breakfast	★★★		
	Lash		01856 811318	Self Catering	★★		
	Links House	KW17 2LX	01856 721221	Bed & Breakfast	★★★★		
	Linnadale	KW17 2EG	01856 761300	Bed & Breakfast	★★★★		
	Little Bu		01604 843275	Self Catering	★★★		
	Lochland Chalets		01856 771340	Self Catering	★★★ to ★★★★	♣	🅿
	Loons Cottage		01856 721386	Self Catering	★★★		
	Mallard Cottage		01785 812290	Self Catering	★★★★		
	Merkister Hotel	KW17 2LF	01856 771366	Country House Hotel	★★★		🅿
	Mid-Comloquoy Cottage		01856 721218	Self Catering	★★		
	Midhouse – Burness		01856 781327	Self Catering	★★★		
	Mill O' Cara		01856 781376	Self Catering	★★★★		
	Murray Arms Hotel	KW17 2SP	01856 831205	Awaiting Grading			
	Netherbutton 1		01856 781312	Self Catering	★★★★		
	New Breckan Flat		01856 771233	Self Catering	★★★		
	New Lighthouse		01856 741326	Self Catering	★★★★		
	No1 Broughton	KW17 2DA	01857 677726	Bed & Breakfast	★★★★		
	North Wald Cottage		01856 821398	Self Catering	★★★		
	Northfield	KW17 2QL	01856 741353	Bed & Breakfast	★★★★		
	Norton Cottage		01856 771284	Self Catering	★★★★		
	Nurses Cottage		01856 771865	Self Catering	★★★		
	Observatory Guest House	KW17 2BE	01857 633200	Guest House	★★★	♿	
	Orcadee		01952 727814	Self Catering	★★★		
	Orkney Self Catering – The Boat House		01856 761581	Self Catering	★★★★		
	Orkney Shore Cottage		01856 811772	Self Catering	★★★		
	Owlswood Lodge		01856 873596	Self Catering	★★★★	♿	🅿🅿
	Palace Cottage		01856 721418	Self Catering	★★★		
	Park Cottage		01856 731246	Self Catering	★★★		
	Pierowall Hotel	KW17 2BZ	01857 677472	Inn	★★★		
	Poppy's Place		01856 731349	Self Catering	★★★		
	Primrose Cottage	KW17 2NB	01856 721384	Bed & Breakfast	★★★		
	Rickla		01856 761575	Self Catering	★★★★★		
	Roadside	KW17 2AA	01857 622303	Bed & Breakfast	★★★		
	Roadside, Burnside, The Kiln and Bayview		01856 877782	Self Catering	★★★★	♣	
	Rousay Hostel	KW17 2PU	01856 821252	Hostel	★★★		
	Rowan Cottage		01856 761551	Self Catering	★★★★		
	Sands Hotel	KW17 2SS	01856 731298	Small Hotel	★★★★		
	Scorralee	KW17 2RF	01856 811268	Bed & Breakfast	★★★		🅿🅿
	Seaquoys		01856 871169	Self Catering	★★★★		
	Seaview and Seal Cottage		01856 831605	Self Catering	★★★ to ★★★★		
	Seaview Ground Floor		01856 876277	Self Catering	★★★		

Advertisers' locations have been sorted by postcode. In Scotland, postcodes can cover fairly large geographical areas.
Please check distance of property from specified location with the individual provider. VisitScotland cannot take any responsibility for this.

Location	Property Name	Postcode	Telephone	Classification	Star Rating		
Orkney	Shoreside		01856 831560	Self Catering	★★★★		
	Skesquoy		01856 761581	Self Catering	★★★		
	Smithfield Hotel	KW17 2HT	01856 771215	Inn	★★		
	Springwell	KW17 2BA	01856 873235	Awaiting Grading			
	St Margarets Hope Backpackers	KW17 2SR	01856 831225	Backpacker	★★★		
	St. Margarets Cottage Bed & Breakfast	KW17 2SR	01856 831637	Bed & Breakfast	★★★		
	Stable		01856 751254	Self Catering	★★★		
	Sties		02089 415291	Self Catering	★★★		
	Sties		02089 415291	Self Catering	★★★		
	Stoo Bed & Breakfast	KW17 2NN	01856 751761	Bed & Breakfast	★★★		
	The Barn	KW17 2BZ	01857 677214	Hostel	★★★★		
	The Bothy		01856 811212	Self Catering	★★★		
	The Creel Restaurant & Rooms	KW17 2SL	01856 831311	Restaurant With Rooms	★★★★		
	The Inn B&B	KW17 2RU	01856 781786	Guest House	★★★		
	The Noust		01856 811348	Self Catering	★★★★		
	The Noust	KW17 2RB	01856 811348	Bed & Breakfast	★★★★		
	The Observatory Hostel	KW17 2BE	01857 633200	Hostel	★★★★		
	The Old St Nicholas Manse		01856 781758	Self Catering	★★		
	The Peedie Hoose		01856 841724	Self Catering	★★★★		
	The Peedie House		01856 831240	Self Catering	★★★★		⌂⌂
	The Quoy of Houton	KW17 2RD	01856 811237	Bed & Breakfast	★★★★		
	The Taversoe	KW17 2PT	01856 821325	Inn	★★★		
	Upper Barswick	KW17 2AY	0773 4810577	Awaiting Grading			
	Upper Quoys		01856 751298	Self Catering	★★★		
	Walkerhouse Mill	KW17 2PQ	01856 874150	Awaiting Grading			
	Wattle House		01856 721206	Self Catering	★★★★		
	West Shaird House		01856 831265	Self Catering	★★★		
	Westend B&B	KW17 2SL	01856 831877	Bed & Breakfast	★★★		
	Widefirth Cottages		01856 761028	Self Catering	★★★★	♿	⌂⌂⌂
	Woodwick House	KW17 2PQ	01856 751330	Guest House	★★★		
	Yeldavale		01856 771303	Self Catering	★★		
Paisley	Ardgowan Town House Hotel	PA3 4BJ	0141 8894763	Guest House	★★★	♠	
	Ashtree House	PA1 2DL	01418 486411	Guest House	★★★★		
	Dryesdale	PA3 2PR	01418 897178	Guest House	★★		
	Duncreggan House		01369 840738	Self Catering	★★★		
	Express by Holiday Inn Glasgow Airport	PA3 2TJ	0141 8421100	Metro Hotel	★★★	♿	
	Flat 4 Brough Hall		01583 431226	Self Catering	★★★		
	Glasgow Airport Premier Inn	PA3 2TH	08702 383321	Budget Hotel			
	Glasgow Paisley Premier Inn	PA1 2BH	08701 977113	Budget Hotel			
	Holiday Inn Glasgow Airport	PA3 2TR	01418 478209	Hotel	★★★	♿	⌂⌂
	Ivybank Villa	PA2 0HX	01700 505064	Bed & Breakfast	★★★★		
	Muirholm Bed & Breakfast	PA2 6DO	0141 8893854	Bed & Breakfast	★★★★★		
	Ramada Glasgow Airport	PA3 2SJ	0141 8402200	Hotel	★★★	♿	⌂
	Scotscraig House	PA2 6JW	0141 8842082	Bed & Breakfast	★★★★★		
	Travelodge Glasgow Airport	PA3 2SJ		Budget Hotel			

♿ Unassisted wheelchair access   ♿ Assisted wheelchair access   ♠ Access for visitors with mobility difficulties
⌂ Bronze Green Tourism Award   ⌂⌂ Silver Green Tourism Award   ⌂⌂⌂ Gold Green Tourism Award
For further information on our Green Tourism Business Scheme please see page 7.

466   To find out more go to visitscotland.com

Location	Property Name	Postcode	Telephone	Classification	Star Rating
Peebles	6 Northgate Vennel		01434 682220	Self Catering	★★★★
	Cardrona Breaks – 12 Mains Farm Steading		01896 830371	Self Catering	★★★ to ★★★★
	Castle Venlaw Hotel	EH45 8QG	01721 720384	Country House Hotel	★★★★
	Castlehill		01721 740630	Self Catering	★★★
	Castlehill Knowe	EH45 9JN	01721 740218	Bed & Breakfast	★★★★
	Cherryville & Belmore Cottages		01721 720188	Self Catering	★★ to ★★★
	Coachman's Cottage		01721 720007	Self Catering	★★
	Courtyard Cottages		01721 721264	Self Catering	★★★★ ⟨🚶⟩
	Craiguart Bed & Breakfast	EH45 8LZ	01721 720219	Bed & Breakfast	★★★
	Cringletie House Hotel	EH45 8PL	01721 725750	Country House Hotel	★★★★ ⟨♿⟩
	Cristine Napier, 7 Rosetta Road		01603 301702	Self Catering	★★★
	Crossburn Caravan Park	EH45 8ED	01721 720501	Holiday Park	★★★★★
	Hillview		01721 740221	Self Catering	★★★ to ★★★★
	Kerfield Coach House		01721 720264	Self Catering	★★★★
	Lindores	EH45 8JE	01721 722072	Guest House	★★★
	Lyne Farmhouse	EH45 8NR	01721 740255	Farm House	★★★
	Macdonald Cardrona Hotel & Golf Course	EH45 8NE	01896 833600	Hotel	★★★★ ⟨♿⟩
	Mains Farm Steading		01896 830436	Self Catering	★★★
	Peebles Hotel Hydro	EH45 8LX	01721 720602	Hotel	★★★★
	Rowanbrae	EH45 8BU	01721 721630	Bed & Breakfast	★★★★
	The Horseshoe Inn	EH45 8QP	01721 730225	Restaurant With Rooms	★★★★
	The Park Hotel	EH45 8BA	01721 720451	Hotel	★★★
	Tontine Hotel	EH45 8AJ	01721 720892	Hotel	★★★
	Torhill B&B	EH45 8NQ	01721 729882	Bed & Breakfast	★★★★
	Tweed View Bed and Breakfast	EH45 9HL	01896 831771	Bed & Breakfast	★★★★
	Venlaw Farm	EH45 8QG	01721 722040	Bed & Breakfast	★★★★
	Venlaw View		01721 722073	Self Catering	★★★
	Whitestone House	EH45 8B	01721 720337	Bed & Breakfast	★★★
	Whitie's	EH45 8AN	01721 721605	Bed & Breakfast	★★★
	Winkston Farmhouse	EH45 8PH	01721 721264	Farm House	★★★★
Penicuik	Allan Ramsay Hotel	EH26 9NF	01968 660258	Awaiting Grading	
	Braidwood Farm	EH26 9LP	01968 679959	Bed & Breakfast	★★★
	Eastside Farm Holiday Cottages – The Stables		01968 677842	Self Catering	★★★★
	Flotterstone Cottage		01968 673717	Self Catering	★★★
	Glenferndale	EH26 9AD	01968 676972	Bed & Breakfast	★★★
	Patieshill Farm + B6091	EH26 9ND	01968 660551	Farm House	★★★
	Peggyslea Farm	EH26 9LX	01968 660930	Guest House	★★★★
Perth	12 Affric Avenue		01796 472214	Self Catering	★★★★
	21 Vasart Court		07766 024999	Self Catering	★★★★
	2B South Inch Court		01577 863367	Self Catering	★★★★
	Aaron	PH2 0PQ	01738 446112	Guest House	★★★
	Acer Guest House	PH2 8AX	01738 444966	Bed & Breakfast	★★★
	Achnacarry Guest House	PH2 7HT	01738 621421	Guest House	★★★★
	Ackinnoull Guest House	PH2 7HT	01738 634165	Guest House	★★★★

Advertisers' locations have been sorted by postcode. In Scotland, postcodes can cover fairly large geographical areas.
Please check distance of property from specified location with the individual provider. VisitScotland cannot take any responsibility for this.

467

Location	Property Name	Postcode	Telephone	Classification	Star Rating		
Perth	Adam Guest House	PH2 7HT	01738 627179	Guest House	★★★		
	Albert Villa Guest House	PH1 5RP	01738 622730	Guest House	★★★		
	Alexander Residence – Barossa Apt		01738 450455	Self Catering	★★★★★		
	Almond Villa Guest House	PH1 5RP	01738 629356	Guest House	★★★★		
	Ardfern Guest House	PH2 7HT	01738 637031	Guest House	★★★★		
	Arisaig Guest House	PH2 7HT	01738 628240	Guest House	★★★★	⚥	🍃🍃🍃
	Ballathie House Hotel	PH1 4QN	01250 883268	Country House Hotel	★★★★	⚥	
	Ballathie House Sportsman's Lodge	PH1 4QN	01250 883268	Lodge	★★★		
	Battledown Bed & Breakfast	PH2 9EL	01738 812471	Bed & Breakfast	★★★★	♿	
	Beech Hedge Caravan Park	PH2 6DU	01250 883249	Holiday Park	★★★		
	Beech Hedge Chalets		01250 883249	Self Catering	★★★ to ★★★★		
	Beeches	PH2 7HU	01738 624486	Bed & Breakfast	★★★		
	Bijou		01337 827789	Self Catering	★★★★		
	Bronton Cottage B&B	PH2 9PP	01738 815997	Bed & Breakfast	★★★		
	Buchanan's Bothy		01738 860765	Self Catering	★★★★		
	Cherrybank Guest House	PH2 0NB	01738 451982	Guest House	★★★★		
	Cherrybank Inn	PH2 0NA	01738 624 349	Inn	★★★	⚥	
	Clifton House	PH2 0PB	01738 621997	Guest House	★★★★		
	Cloag Farm Cottages		01738 840239	Self Catering	★★★		🍃
	Clock Tower & Coach House 3		01738 446577	Self Catering	★★★★	⚥	
	Clunie Guest House	PH2 7HT	01738 623625	Guest House	★★★★		
	Comely Bank Cottage	PH2 7HT	01738 631118	Bed & Breakfast	★★★		
	Dalvey	PH1 5RP	01738 621714	Bed & Breakfast	★★★★		
	Dunallan Guest House	PH2 7TH	01738 622551	Guest House	★★★★		
	Duncrub Holidays – The Tower House		01764 684100	Self Catering	★★★★ to ★★★★★	⚥	🍃🍃
	Earnview Glenfoot	PH2 9LS	01738 850353	Bed & Breakfast	★★★		
	Easter Deuglie		01241 879111	Self Catering	★★★		
	Eppies & Flisk		01828 686231	Self Catering	★★★★		
	Express by Holiday Inn	PH1 3AQ	01738 636666	Metro Hotel	★★★		
	Fingask		01241 430730	Self Catering	★★★★ to ★★★★★		🍃🍃🍃
	Fingask Cottages – Sycamore, Rowan		01821 670777	Self Catering	★★★		
	Finlaggan House	PH1 3TH	01738 880234	Bed & Breakfast	★★★★		
	Fiscal's Flat		01738 587899	Self Catering	★★★★		
	Forest Lodge	PH1 4BN	01738 787150	Bed & Breakfast	★★★		
	Four Seasons		01299 403421	Self Catering	★★★★	⚥	
	Garden Flat		01738 583882	Self Catering	★★★★		
	Grampian Hotel	PH2 8EH	01738 621057	Small Hotel	★★★		
	Greenacres	PH1 3TQ	01738 880302	Bed & Breakfast	★★★		🍃🍃🍃
	Halton House B&B	PH1 1BA	01738 643446	Bed & Breakfast	★★★★		
	Hazeldene Guest House	PH2 7HP	01738 623550	Guest House	★★★★		
	Heidl Guest House	PH2 8EH	01738 635031	Guest House	★★★		
	Hilltop View	PH1 5QZ	01738 445776	Awaiting Grading			
	Huntingtower Hotel	PH1 3JT	01738 583771	Hotel	★★★	♿	
	Huntingtower Lodges		01738 582444	Self Catering	★★★		
	Inchtuthill Coachhouse		01738 710332	Self Catering	★★★★		
	Little Pines	PH2 7BN	01738 636140	Awaiting Grading			
	Lovat Hotel	PH2 0LT	01738 636555	Hotel	★★★		🍃
	Marshall House	PH2 8AH	01738 442886	Bed & Breakfast	★★★		

♿ Unassisted wheelchair access   ♿ Assisted wheelchair access   ⚥ Access for visitors with mobility difficulties
🍃 Bronze Green Tourism Award   🍃🍃 Silver Green Tourism Award   🍃🍃🍃 Gold Green Tourism Award
For further information on our Green Tourism Business Scheme please see page 7.

468   To find out more go to visitscotland.com

Location	Property Name	Postcode	Telephone	Classification	Star Rating	
Perth	Meikleour Hotel	PH2 6EB	01250 883206	Inn	★★★★	
	Moulinalmond Cottage		01738 583206	Self Catering	★★★	𝒫𝒫
	Murrayshall Hotel	PH2 7PH	01738 551171	Country House Hotel	★★★★	
	New County Hotel	PH2 8EE	01738 623355	Hotel	★★★	
	Newhill Granary		01577 830616	Self Catering	★★★★★	
	Newmill Farm	PH1 4PS	01738 828281	Farm House	★★★	
	No 9 & No 13 Beaumont House Apartments		01738 447933	Self Catering	★★★ to ★★★★	
	Noahs Arc Caravan Park		01738 440456	Awaiting Grading		
	Northlees Farm	PH2 7LJ	01738 860852	Farm House	★★	
	Oakwood House	PH2 6DW	01821 650800	Bed & Breakfast	★★★★	
	Old Cottage		01577 830434	Self Catering	★★★★	
	Old Smiddy Cottage		01250 883236	Self Catering	★★★	
	Orchard Cottage		01738 620783	Self Catering	★★★★	🯅
	Ordie View	PH1 4PR	01738 827191	Bed & Breakfast	★★★	
	Parklands Hotel	PH2 8EB	01738 622451	Small Hotel	★★★★	𝒫
	Pear Tree		01738 621342	Self Catering	★★★	
	Perth Airport Skylodge	PH2 6PL	01738 550009	Lodge	★★★	🯅
	Petra's B&B	PH1 2BD	01738 563050	Bed & Breakfast	★★★	🯅
	Pitcullen Guest House	PH2 7HT	01738 626506	Guest House	★★★	
	Quality Hotel Perth	PH2 8HE	01738 624141	Hotel	★	
	Queens Hotel	PH2 8HB	01738 442222	Hotel	★★★	𝒫
	Ramada Hotel	PH1 5QP	01738 628281	Hotel	★★★	𝒫
	River Edge Lodges – Lodge 15		01738 812370	Self Catering	★★★	🯅
	Riverside Apartment		01738 449381	Self Catering	★★★★	
	Rowanlea	PH2 0PQ	01738 621922	Guest House	★★★★	
	Salutation Hotel	PH2 8PH	01738 630066	Hotel	★★	𝒫𝒫
	Scone Camping & Caravanning Club Site	PH2 6BB	02476 475318	Touring Park	★★★★	
	Shenval Farm Steading		01738 787867	Self Catering	★★★★	
	Strathearn Holidays Ltd		01738 840263	Self Catering	★★★★	
	Strathmore View Cottage		01738 828463	Self Catering	★★★ to ★★★★	
	Summerfield View		01821 640760	Self Catering	★★★★	🯅
	Sunbank House	PH2 7BA	01738 624882	Metro Hotel	★★★★	🯅
	Tayside Hotel	PH1 4NL	01738 828249	Small Hotel	★★★	
	Taythorpe House	PH2 7HQ	01738 447994	Bed & Breakfast	★★★★	
	The Coach House		01764 684250	Self Catering	★★★★	
	The Courtyard	PH2 7RS	01821 670435	Bed & Breakfast	★★★★	
	The Doocot		01764 684358	Self Catering	★★★★	
	The Famous Bein Inn	PH2 9PY	01577 830216	Inn	★★★	
	The Gables Guest House	PH1 5RW	01738 624717	Guest House	★★★	
	The Last Cast	PH2 9PL	01738 812578	Guest House	★★★	
	The Millers Cottage		01577 830445	Self Catering	★★★★	
	The Royal George	PH1 5LD	01738 624455	Hotel	★★★	
	The Townhouse	PH2 8AG	01738 446179	Guest House	★★★	
	Tower View		01738 813045	Self Catering	★★★★	
	Travelodge Perth Broxden Junction	PH2 0PL	07879 662014	Budget Hotel		
	Wayside Cottage		01738 583237	Self Catering	★★★★	

♿ Unassisted wheelchair access   ♿ Assisted wheelchair access   🯅 Access for visitors with mobility difficulties
𝒫 Bronze Green Tourism Award   𝒫𝒫 Silver Green Tourism Award   𝒫𝒫𝒫 Gold Green Tourism Award
For further information on our Green Tourism Business Scheme please see page 7.

Advertisers' locations have been sorted by postcode. In Scotland, postcodes can cover fairly large geographical areas.
Please check distance of property from specified location with the individual provider. VisitScotland cannot take any responsibility for this.

469

Location	Property Name	Postcode	Telephone	Classification	Star Rating	
Perth	Wester Caputh Lodge	PH1 4JH	01738 710449	Hostel	★★★★	👨‍🦽
	Westview	PH1 5RP	01738 627787	Bed & Breakfast	★★★★	
	WMB Properties Ltd	PH2 7JZ	07967 135204	Awaiting Grading		
	WoodLea Hotel	PH2 8EP	01738 621744	Small Hotel	★★★	
Peterculter	Furain Guest House	AB14 0QN	01224 732189	Guest House	★★★	
	Gordon House Self Catering Apartment		01224 732284	Self Catering	★★★★	
Peterhead	Aden Caravan Park	AB42 8FQ	01467 627622	Holiday Park	★★★★★	
	Aden House	AB42 5LN	01771 622573	Guest House	★★★	
	Bank House	AB42 5LN	01771 623463	Bed & Breakfast	★★★★	
	Berryhill Cottage		01779 472225	Self Catering	★★★	
	Buchan Braes Hotel	AB42 3AR	01779 871471	Hotel	★★★★	
	Carrick Guest House	AB42 1DU	01779 470610	Guest House	★★	
	Craighead Caravan Park	AB42 0PL	01779 812251	Holiday Park	★★★	
	Durie House	AB42 5BE	01771 622823	Bed & Breakfast	★★★	
	Greenbrae Farmhouse	AB42 4JX	01779 821051	Bed & Breakfast	★★★	🧍 🍂🍂🍂
	Palace Hotel	AB42 6PL	01779 474821	Hotel	★★★	
	Peterhead Lido Caravan Park	AB42 2YP	01467 627622	Holiday Park	★★★★	
	Pond View	AB42 4QN	01771 613675	Bed & Breakfast	★★★★	
	Rattray Head Hostel	AB42 3HA	01346 532236	Hostel	★★★	
	Rose Lodge	AB42 4HX	01346 531148	Bed & Breakfast	★★★★	
	Saplinbrae House Hotel	AB42 4LP	01771 623515	Small Hotel	★★	
	Skerry Cottage		01779 470476	Self Catering	★★★★	
	The Kilmarnock Arms Hotel	AB42 0HD	01779 812213	Small Hotel	★★★	
Pitlochry	127 Atholl Road	PH16 5AG	01796 470446	Awaiting Grading		
	1A Robertson Crescent		01796 473353	Self Catering	★★★★	
	3B Robertson Crescent		01796 472157	Self Catering	★★★	
	4 Viewbank Gardens		04961 0343252	Self Catering	★★★	
	Acarsaid Hotel and Lodge	PH16 5BX	01796 472389	Hotel	★★★	
	Almond Lee	PH16 5HU	01796 474048	Guest House	★★★	
	An Treasaite		01796 472170	Self Catering	★★★	
	Annslea Guest House	PH16 5AR	01796 472430	Guest House	★★★	
	Ardenlea		01796 472758	Self Catering	★★★ to ★★★★	
	Ardvane	PH16 5DS	01796 472683	Bed & Breakfast	★★★★	
	Ardvane		01796 472683	Self Catering	★★★★	
	Ashbank House	PH16 5JA	01796 472711	Bed & Breakfast	★★★	
	Atholl Arms Hotel	PH18 5SG	01796 481205	Hotel	★★★	
	Atholl Baptist Centre	PH16 5BX	01796 473044	Awaiting Grading		
	Atholl Villa		01796 473820	Self Catering	★★★	
	Atholl Villa Guest House	PH16 5BX	01796 473820	Guest House	★★★	
	Atom Crow Cottage		01796 473444	Self Catering	★★★	🧍
	Balbeagan	PH9 0PY	01796 482627	Bed & Breakfast	★★★★	
	Beinn Bhracaigh	PH16 5HT	01796 470355	Guest House	★★★★	
	Bendarroch House	PH9 0PG	01887 840420	Guest House	★★★	
	Blair Castle Caravan Park	PH18 5SR	01796 481355	Holiday Park	★★★★★	🍂🍂
	Blithe Nook		01382 826680	Self Catering	★★★★	
	Bridge House	PH16 5BL	01796 474062	Bed & Breakfast	★★★	
	Bridge of Gaur Guest House	PH17 2QD	01882 633356	Awaiting Grading		

♿ Unassisted wheelchair access   👨‍🦽 Assisted wheelchair access   🧍 Access for visitors with mobility difficulties
🍂 Bronze Green Tourism Award   🍂🍂 Silver Green Tourism Award   🍂🍂🍂 Gold Green Tourism Award
For further information on our Green Tourism Business Scheme please see page 7.

Location	Property Name	Postcode	Telephone	Classification	Star Rating	
Pitlochry	Bridge of Tilt Hotel	PH18 5SU	01796 481333	Hotel	★★	
	Bruach Cottage		01506 429162	Self Catering	★★★★	
	Buttonboss Lodge	PH16 5BX	01796 472065	Guest House	★★★	
	Caberfeidh		01882 632303	Self Catering	★★★	
	Caravan Holiday Home	PH18 5TE	01307 819043	Holiday Caravan		
	Carie Estate – Factors House		07980 634784	Self Catering	★★★★★	
	Carra Beag Guest House	PH16 5HG	01796 472835	Guest House	★★★	
	Cherry Cottage		01796 482409	Self Catering	★★★★	
	Cnoc Aluinn		01506 848104	Self Catering	★★★	
	Cnoc Eoghainn		0779 9232700	Self Catering	★★★	🅿🅿
	Convalloch Lodge		01796 481355	Self Catering	★★★	
	Corrie Beag Self Catering		01796 473003	Self Catering	★★★	
	Courtyard Cottage		01796 474433	Self Catering	★★★★	
	Craigard – Chalet		01796 473695	Self Catering	★★ to ★★★	
	Craigatin House & Courtyard	PH16 5QL	01796 472478	Guest House	★★★★	🚶
	Craiglynn		01796 472065	Self Catering	★★★★	
	Craigmhor Lodge	PH16 5EF	01796 472123	Guest House	★★★★	
	Craigroyston Guest House	PH16 5HQ	01796 472053	Guest House	★★★★	
	Craigroyston Lodge		01796 472053	Self Catering	★★★	
	Craigvar		01882 632353	Self Catering	★★★	
	Craigvrack Hotel	PH16 5EQ	01796 472399	Small Hotel	★★★	🚶
	Croiscrag		01883 714039	Self Catering	★★	
	Dail Na Coille Garden Cottage		01796 473449	Self Catering	★★★	
	Dalgreine Guest House	PH16 5SX	01796 481276	Guest House	★★★★	
	Dall Mill		0131 3375780	Self Catering	★★★	
	Dalshian Chalets		01796 473080	Self Catering	★★★★	♿
	Dalshian House	PH16 5TD	01796 472173	Guest House	★★★	
	Dawn Cottage		01292 443979	Self Catering	★★★★	
	Derrybeg Guest House	PH16 5DS	01796 472070	Guest House	★★★★	
	Dunalastair Holiday Houses – Bridge Cottage		01882 632314	Self Catering	★★★ to ★★★★	♿ 🅿
	Dunalastair Hotel	PH16 5PW	01882 632323	Hotel	★★★	♿
	Dundarach Hotel	PH16 5DJ	01796 472862	Hotel	★★★	
	Dunmurray Lodge Guest House	PH16 5ED	01796 473624	Guest House	★★★★	
	East Haugh House Country Hotel & Res	PH16 5TE	01796 473121	Small Hotel	★★★★	🚶
	East Haugh Lodge		01796 473121	Self Catering	★★★★	
	Easter Croftinloan Farmhouse	PH16 5TA	01796 473454	Guest House	★★★★	
	Easter Dunfallandy Country House B&B	PH16 5NA	01796 474128	Bed & Breakfast	★★★★★	
	Ellangowan	PH16 5DS	01796 473704	Bed & Breakfast	★★★	
	Elmwood Apartments		01796 474355	Self Catering	★★★	
	Elnagar Cottage		01796 472871	Self Catering	★★★	
	Esk Cottage		01796 472322	Self Catering	★★★	
	Farragon	PH16 5HH	01796 470051	Bed & Breakfast	★★★★	
	Fasganeoin Country House	PH16 5DJ	01796 472387	Guest House	★★★	
	Faskally Caravan Park	PH16 5LA	01796 472007	Holiday Park	★★★★	
	Ferrymans Cottage	PH16 5ND	01796 473681	Bed & Breakfast	★★★★	
	Garrybank		01592 564435	Self Catering	★★★	
	Glen Bruar Lodge		01796 481355	Self Catering	★★★	

Advertisers' locations have been sorted by postcode. In Scotland, postcodes can cover fairly large geographical areas.
Please check distance of property from specified location with the individual provider. VisitScotland cannot take any responsibility for this.

471

Directory of all VisitScotland Assured Serviced Establishments, ordered by location.
Establishments highlighted have an advertisement in this guide.

Location	Property Name	Postcode	Telephone	Classification	Star Rating		
Pitlochry	Glen Garry	PH16 5AP	0179 6474465	Bed & Breakfast	★★★		
	Glengoulandie Country Park	PH16 5NL	01887 830495	Holiday Park	★★★		
	Green Park Hotel	PH16 5JY	01796 473248	Country House Hotel	★★★★	🚶	🅿
	Gushat Cottage		01481 263991	Self Catering	★★★★		
	Holiday Lodges @ Old Faskally		01796 473436	Self Catering	★★★		
	Ivy Cottage		01314 477494	Self Catering	★★★★		
	Kindrochet Lodge		01796 481355	Self Catering	★★★★		
	Kinloch Rannoch Centre	PH16 5PQ	01738 477878	Awaiting Grading			
	Kinnaird Woodland Lodges		01796 472843	Self Catering	★★★★		
	Knockendarroch	PH16 5HT	01796 473473	Small Hotel	★★★★		
	Kynachan Loch Tummel Hotel	PH16 5SB	01389 713713	Hotel	★★★	♿	
	Lassintullich Lodge		01882 632330	Self Catering	★★★★		
	Lavalette	PH16 5EP	01796 472364	Bed & Breakfast	★★★		
	Loch Rannoch Hotel	PH16 5PS	0844 8799059	Hotel	★★★		
	Lodges – Kinnaird, Moulin, Garry, Tay & Tummel		01796 472400	Self Catering	★★★ to ★★★★		
	Logierait Pine lodges		01796 482253	Self Catering	★★★		
	Macdonalds Restaurant & Guest House	PH16 5AG	01796 472170	Guest House	★★★		
	Markova		01796 472364	Self Catering	★★★		
	Milton of Fonab Caravan Park	PH16 5NA	01796 472882	Holiday Park	★★★★		
	Moulin Hotel	PH16 5EW	01796 472196	Hotel	★★★		
	Moulin Mill		01383 839393	Self Catering	★★★★★		
	Moville	PH16 5JL	01796 470100	Bed & Breakfast	★★★★		
	No. 7 Dean Court		01796 482278	Self Catering	★★★		
	Oak Cottage		01796 472046	Self Catering	★★★★		
	Old Blair Lodge		01796 481355	Self Catering	★★★		
	Old Mill Inn	PH16 5BH	01796 474020	Inn	★★★★		
	Old Post Office Cottage		01577 863245	Self Catering	★★★		
	Orchard Cottage	PH18 5SY	01796 481676	Awaiting Grading			
	Pine Trees Country House Hotel	PH16 5QR	01796 472121	Country House Hotel	★★★★		
	Pitcastle Estate	PH9 0PJ	01887 840412	Exclusive Use Venue	★★★★★		
	Pitlochry Backpackers	PH16 5AB	01796 470044	Hostel	★★★		
	Pitlochry Hydro Hotel	PH16 5JH	01796 472666	Hotel	★★★		
	Pitlochry Youth Hostel	PH16 5HJ	0870 0041145	Hostel	★★★		🅿🅿
	Ptarmigan House	PH18 5SZ	01796 481269	Guest House	★★★		
	Rannoch Lodge Estate – Ghillie's Cottage		01882 633204	Self Catering	★★★		
	Roseburn B&B	PH16 5EA	01796 470002	Bed & Breakfast	★★★★		
	Rosehill	PH16 5BX	01796 472958	Guest House	★★★		
	Rosemount Hotel	PH16 5HT	01796 472302	Small Hotel	★★★		
	Scotlands Hotel	PH16 5BT	0870 9506276	Hotel	★★★		
	Strathgarry Hotel	PH16 5AG	01796 473826	Restaurant With Rooms	★★★		
	Strathmhor Cottages	PH9 0PB	01887 840323	Awaiting Grading			
	Talladh-a-Bheithe Lodge	PH17 2QW	01882 633203	Guest House	★★★		
	The Atholl Palace	PH16 5LY	01796 472400	Hotel	★★★★	🚶	🅿
	The Claymore	PH16 5AR	01796 472888	Guest House	★★★		
	The Dell B & B	PH16 5QX	01796 470306	Bed & Breakfast	★★★		
	The Firs	PH18 5TA	01796 481256	Guest House	★★★		🅿🅿

♿ Unassisted wheelchair access   ♿ Assisted wheelchair access   🚶 Access for visitors with mobility difficulties
🅿 Bronze Green Tourism Award   🅿🅿 Silver Green Tourism Award   🅿🅿🅿 Gold Green Tourism Award
For further information on our Green Tourism Business Scheme please see page 7.

To find out more go to visitscotland.com

Location	Property Name	Postcode	Telephone	Classification	Star Rating	
Pitlochry	The Firs Lodge		01796 481256	Self Catering	★★★	
	The Gardens	PH16 5PB	01882 632434	Bed & Breakfast	★★★	
	The Inn on the Tay	PH9 0PL	01887 840760	Inn	★★★	
	The Old Coach House		07738 801210	Self Catering	★★★	
	The Old Mill		01738 730336	Self Catering	★★★★	
	The Poplars	PH16 5DS	01796 472129	Guest House	★★★★	ⵏ
	The River Tilt Park	PH18 5TE	01796 481467	Holiday Park	★★★★★	
	The Rowans Bed and Breakfast	PH16 5DD	01796 474469	Bed & Breakfast	★★★★	
	The Well House	PH16 5HG	01796 472239	Guest House	★★★★	ⵏ
	The White House		01453 823992	Self Catering	★★	
	Tigh Na Cloich Hotel	PH16 5AS	01796 472216	Small Hotel	★★★	🅿🅿
	Tir Aluinn	PH16 5HT	01796 473811	Guest House	★★★	
	Torrdarach House	PH16 5AU	01796 472136	Guest House	★★★★	
	Tummel Valley Holiday Park		01882 634221	Self Catering	★★★★	
	Tummel Valley Holiday Park	PH16 5SA	01882 634221	Holiday Park	★★★★	
	Wellwood House	PH16 5EA	01796 474288	Guest House	★★★★	
	Wester Knockfarrie	PH16 5DN	01796 472020	Bed & Breakfast	★★★★	
	Westlands Hotel	PH16 5AR	01796 472266	Small Hotel	★★★	
	Windsor Gardens	PH16 5BE	01796 474351	Bed & Breakfast	★★★	
	Woodburn House	PH16 5DD	01796 473818	Bed & Breakfast	★★★	
	Woodshiel	PH16 5EA	01796 470358	Bed & Breakfast	★★★	
	Woodside		01382 541024	Self Catering	★★★★	
Plockton	30a Harbour Street		01851 702085	Self Catering	★★	
	7 Harbour Street		01387 269762	Self Catering	★★ to ★★★★	
	Creag Liath	IV52 8TY	01599 544341	Bed & Breakfast	★★★★	
	Hillview B&B	IV52 8TQ	01599 544226	Bed & Breakfast	★★★	
	Plockton Cottages		01599 544255	Self Catering	★★★	
	Plockton Inn	IV52 8TW	01599 544222	Inn	★★★	
	Plockton Station	IV52 8TF	01599 544235	Bunkhouse		
	The Haven Hotel	IV52 8TW	01599 544223	Small Hotel	★★	
	Tomac's	IV52 8TQ	01599 544321	Bed & Breakfast	★★★	
Port Glasgow	Gleddoch House Hotel	PA14 6YE		Awaiting Grading		
Portree	1 Grealin		01449 760428	Self Catering	★★★★	
	11 Earlish	IV51 9XL	01470 542319	Bed & Breakfast	★★★	
	25 Urquhart Place	IV51 9HJ	01478 612374	Bed & Breakfast	★★★	
	52 Aird	IV51 9NU	01470 532471	Bed & Breakfast	★★★	
	6 Knott		01865 514204	Self Catering	★★★	
	9 Stormyhill Road	IV51 9DY	01478 613332	Bed & Breakfast	★★★	
	Aird View		01470 521755	Self Catering	★★★	
	Aite Sithiel Self Catering		01470 532745	Self Catering	★★★★	
	Almondbank	IV51 9EU	01478 612696	Guest House	★★★★	
	An Acarsaid	IV51 9ES	01478 612252	Bed & Breakfast	★★★	
	An Airidh	IV51 9EU	01478 612250	Guest House	★★★	
	Apartment 1	IV51 9HX	01478 612851	Serviced Apartments	★★★★	
	Ard Dearg		01478 612749	Self Catering	★★★	
	Ashaig B&B	IV51 9PU	01470 582336	Bed & Breakfast	★★★★	
	Auchendinny	IV51 9NX	01470 532470	Guest House	★★★	ⵏ

Advertisers' locations have been sorted by postcode. In Scotland, postcodes can cover fairly large geographical areas.
Please check distance of property from specified location with the individual provider. VisitScotland cannot take any responsibility for this.

473

Location	Property Name	Postcode	Telephone	Classification	Star Rating	
Portree	Balloch	IV51 9ES	01478 612093	Guest House	★★★★	
	Barnellan		01729 824624	Self Catering	★★★★	
	Bayfield Backpackers	IV51 9EW	01478 612231	Hostel	★★★★	
	Bayview Croft		01667 452547	Self Catering	★★★★	
	Beatons Cottage		0131 2439331	Self Catering	★★★	
	Brescalan Cottage		01470 532425	Self Catering	★★★	&#x267F;
	Brook Cottage		01478 612980	Self Catering	★★★★	
	Buaile Nan Carn		01470 552279	Self Catering	★★★	
	Carnbeag	IV51 9XL	01470 542398	Bed & Breakfast	★★★	
	Cliff Cottage		01478 612555	Self Catering	★★★	
	Cnoc Preasach	IV51 9UY	01470 542406	Bed & Breakfast	★★★	
	Colgrain		01270 759635	Self Catering	★★★★	
	Coolin Lodge		01478 613240	Self Catering	★★★★★	
	Coolin View Guest House	IV51 9DG	01478 611280	Guest House	★★★	
	Corran Guest House	IV51 9XE	01470 532311	Guest House	★★★★	
	Corran Holiday Home		01470 532311	Self Catering	★★★★	
	Creagalain Cottage		01470 532391	Self Catering	★★★	
	Crepigill Lodge		01470 532785	Self Catering	★★★★★	
	Crepigilll Cottage		01478 613104	Self Catering	★★★ to ★★★★★	
	Croit Anna	IV51 9NS	01470 532760	Bed & Breakfast	★★	
	Cruinn Bheinn	IV51 9XB	01470 532459	Bed & Breakfast	★★★★	
	Cuil Lodge	IV51 9YB	01470 542216	Bed & Breakfast	★★★★	
	Cuillin Hills Hotel	IV51 9QU	01478 612003	Country House Hotel	★★★★	&#x267F;
	Cul Na Creagan	IV51 9LN	01478 611356	Bed & Breakfast	★★★	
	Dalriada	IV51 9HT	01478 612397	Guest House	★★★	
	Dalrigh		0141 9565056	Self Catering	★★★★	
	Drumorell	IV51 9DS	01478 613058	Bed & Breakfast	★★★★	
	Dry Harbour Cottages – Skeyscape		07775 593055	Self Catering	★★★ to ★★★★	
	Dun Eighre Bed & Breakfast	IV51 9XE	01470 532439	Bed & Breakfast	★★★★	
	Dun Flashader		0131 2439335	Self Catering	★★★	
	Dun Flodigarry Hostel	IV51 9HZ	01470 552212	Hostel	★★★	
	Easdale	IV51 9ER	01478 613244	Bed & Breakfast	★★★	
	Edinbane Holiday Homes		01470 582270	Self Catering	★★★	
	Edinbane Self Catering		01470 582221	Self Catering	★★★	🧍 🄿🄿
	Feochan	IV51 9EU	01478 613508	Guest House	★★★	
	Ferry Inn Hotel	IV51 9XP	01478 611216	Inn	★★★	
	Fisherfield Self Catering		01478 612696	Self Catering	★★★★★	
	Flat 1 Bayfield House		0141 9426531	Self Catering	★★★★	
	Flodigarry Country House Hotel	IV51 9HZ	01470 552203	Country House Hotel	★★★	
	Foreland	IV51 9DT	01478 612752	Bed & Breakfast	★★★	
	Gairloch View	IV51 9LA	01470 562718	Bed & Breakfast	★★★	
	Garybuie B&B	IV51 9UX	01470 542310	Bed & Breakfast	★★★	
	Givendale Guest House	IV51 9GU	01478 612183	Guest House	★★	
	Gleann an Ronnaich	IV51 9HS	01478 611529	Bed & Breakfast	★★★	
	Gleniffer House		01609 772433	Self Catering	★★★★	
	Glenview	IV51 9JH	01470 562248	Restaurant With Rooms	★★★	
	Greshornish House Hotel	IV51 9PN	01470 582266	Country House Hotel	★★★★	

♿ Unassisted wheelchair access   ♿ Assisted wheelchair access   🧍 Access for visitors with mobility difficulties
🄿 Bronze Green Tourism Award   🄿🄿 Silver Green Tourism Award   🄿🄿🄿 Gold Green Tourism Award
For further information on our Green Tourism Business Scheme please see page 7.

474   To find out more go to visitscotland.com

Location	Property Name	Postcode	Telephone	Classification	Star Rating	
Portree	Hallaig Bed And Breakfast	IV51 9JG	01470 562250	Guest House	★★★★	
	Harbour View		01471 855253	Self Catering	★★★	
	Heronfield	IV51 9GU	01478 613050	Bed & Breakfast	★★★	
	Highfield	IV51 9ES	01478 612781	Bed & Breakfast	★★★	
	Hillcroft	IV51 9NX	01470 582304	Bed & Breakfast	★★★★	
	Kerrysdale	IV51 9EU	01478 613170	Bed & Breakfast	★★★	
	Kingsburgh Boathouse Skye	IV51 9UT	01470 532350	Awaiting Grading		
	Kirsty's Cottage		01478 650349	Self Catering	★★★	
	Lawries Thatched Cottage		01470 542409	Self Catering	★★★	⌂⌂
	Lochview	IV51 9NT	0532 736	Bed & Breakfast	★★★★	
	MacLeod Estates – Laundry		01470 521206	Self Catering	★★ to ★★★	
	Marmalade	IV51 9LX	01478 611711	Small Hotel	★★★	
	Meadowbank House	IV51 9ES	01478 612059	Guest House	★★★	
	Medina	IV51 9NB	01478 612 821	Bed & Breakfast	★★★★	
	Number 6		01478 613167	Self Catering	★★★	♿
	Orasay	IV51 9XU	01470 542316	Bed & Breakfast	★★★	
	Otterburn	IV51 9LU	01478 613588	Bed & Breakfast	★★★★	
	Park Cottage		01463 221526	Self Catering	★★★	
	Peinmore House	IV51 9LG	01478 612574	Guest House	★★★★	
	Portree Bay Cottage		07917 628982	Self Catering	★★★	
	Portree Garden Cottages		01478 613713	Self Catering	★★★	
	Portree Independent Hostel	IV51 9BT	01478 613737	Hostel	★★★	
	Quiraing Guest House	IV51 9ES	01478 612870	Guest House	★★★★	
	Resolis		01470 562328	Self Catering	★★★★	
	Rona Bunk House	IV51 9RA	07831 293963	Awaiting Grading		
	Rosebank House	IV51 9QX	01478 612282	Guest House	★★★	
	Rosedale Hotel	IV51 9DF	01478 613131	Hotel	★★★	
	Royal Hotel	IV51 9BU	01478 612525	Hotel	★★★	
	Sandgrounder Bed and Breakfast	IV51 9JA	01478 612321	Bed & Breakfast	★★★	
	Seacroft Cottage		01202 708847	Self Catering	★★★★	
	Sgiathan Mara	IV51 9HS	01478 612927	Bed & Breakfast	★★★	
	Skeabost Country House Hotel	IV51 9NP		Hotel	★★★	
	Skye Camping & Caravanning Club Site	IV51 9PS	01470 582230	Touring Park	★★★★	
	Steading Cottage		01667 451578	Self Catering	★★★★	
	Storr Lochs Lodge		0208 8765777	Self Catering	★★★	
	Taigh Na H-Aibhne		0131 3326622	Self Catering	★★★★	
	Tarven Cottage		01478 612679	Self Catering	★★★★	
	Teeny's Cottage		01470 582777	Self Catering	★★★★	
	The Bosville Hotel	IV51 9DG	01478 612846	Hotel	★★★★	
	The Bothy		01470 562204	Self Catering	★★★★	⌂
	The Cedar		0113 2781638	Self Catering	★★★★	
	The Cottage		01470 532382	Self Catering	★★★	
	The Cottage		01478 612217	Self Catering	★★★	
	The Cottage		01470 562235	Self Catering	★★★	
	The Orde of Greshornish	IV51 9PN	0207 2310953	Awaiting Grading		
	The Spoons	IV51 9NU	01470 532217	Bed & Breakfast	★★★★★	
	Tigh Cilmartin		01372 363998	Self Catering	★★★★	
	Tigh Nighean Bhan		01470 552353	Self Catering	★★★★	

Location	Property Name	Postcode	Telephone	Classification	Star Rating	
Portree	Tir Alainn – Kildonan	IV51 9PU	01470 582335	Bed & Breakfast	★★★★	
	Torvaig Caravan & Camping Park	IV51 9HU	01478 611849	Touring Park	★★★	
	Torwood	IV51 9LW	01470 532479	Bed & Breakfast	★★★	
	Uig Hotel	IV51 9YE	01470 542205	Small Hotel	★★★	
	Uig Youth Hostel	IV51 9YD	01470 542211	Hostel	★★★	⏀⏀
	Viewfield House Hotel	IV51 9EU	01478 612217	Guest Accommodation	★★★★	♿
	Witch Hazel House	IV51 9HT	01478 612327	Bed & Breakfast	★★★	
	Woodlands	IV51 9EU	01478 612980	Bed & Breakfast	★★★★	
Prestonpans	Drummohr Caravan Park	EH21 8JS	0131 6656867	Touring Park	★★★★★	
Prestwick	Appletree B&B	KA9 1SY	01292 478680	Bed & Breakfast	★★★	
	Ayr Premier Inn	KA9 2RJ	0870 1977020	Budget Hotel		
	Fernbank Guest House	KA9 1LH	01292 475027	Guest House	★★★	⏀
	Fionn Fraoch	KA9 1RR	0787 9695187	Bed & Breakfast	★★★	
	Firhill	KA9 1QS	01292 478225	Bed & Breakfast	★★★	
	Golf View	KA9 1QG	01292 671234	Guest House	★★★★	
	Keeru's B&B	KA9 1LA	01292 475833	Awaiting Grading		
	Kincraig House	KA9 1SY	01292 479480	Guest House	★★★	
	Knox	KA9 1TN	01292 478808	Bed & Breakfast	★★★	
	No 6 The Crescent	KA9 1BQ	01292 471234	Bed & Breakfast	★★★	
	North Beach Hotel	KA9 1QG	01292 479069	Small Hotel	★★	
	Parkstone Hotel	KA9 1QN	01292 477286	Hotel	★★★	♿
	The Barrels	KA9 2QL	01292 671391	Bed & Breakfast	★★★	
	The Dormie House	KA9 2DL	01292 477292	Bed & Breakfast	★★★★	
	Western House Hotel	KA9 0JE	0870 8505666	Hotel	★★★★	♿
Renfrew	Glynhill Hotel	PA4 8XB	0141 8865555	Hotel	★★★★	
	The Normandy Hotel	PA4 5EJ	0141 8864100	Hotel	★★★	⏀⏀
	Travelodge Glasgow Braehead	PA4 8ZL	08719 846372	Budget Hotel		
Rogart	Aultibea		01408 633512	Self Catering	★★★	
	Elcaila		01408 641361	Self Catering	★★★	
	Glebe House		01408 641363	Self Catering	★★★	
	Sleeperzzz.com	IV28 3XA	01408 641343	Hostel	★★★	
Rosewell	Carrick Cottage		0131 4480888	Self Catering	★★★	♿
	Park Neuk		01506 653095	Self Catering	★★★	🚶
	Hillwood	EH24 9AU	01314 482844	Bed & Breakfast	★★	
Roslin	Original Rosslyn Inn	EH25 9LE	0131 4402384	Inn	★★	
	Rosslyn Cottage		0131 4402196	Self Catering	★★★	
	The Steading	EH25 9PU	0131 4401608	Bed & Breakfast	★★★★	
Roy Bridge	Bunroy Camping & Caravan Site	PH31 4AG	01397 712332	Touring Park	★★★★	
	Bunroy Holiday Lodges		01397 712332	Self Catering	★★★	
	Dunhafen B&B	PH31 4AS	01397 712830	Bed & Breakfast	★★★	
	Fersit Log Cottage		01397 732323	Self Catering	★★★★	⏀
	Grey Corrie Lodge	PH31 4AN	01397 712236	Bunkhouse		
	Homagen	PH31 4AN	01397 712411	Bed & Breakfast	★★★	
	Roy Bridge Hotel	PH31 4AN	01397 712236	Inn	★★	
	The Stronlossit Inn	PH31 4AG	01397 712253	Small Hotel	★★★	♿
	Torr An Daimh	PH31 4AR	0131 4783551	Awaiting Grading		

♿ Unassisted wheelchair access   ♿ Assisted wheelchair access   🚶 Access for visitors with mobility difficulties
⏀ Bronze Green Tourism Award   ⏀⏀ Silver Green Tourism Award   ⏀⏀⏀ Gold Green Tourism Award
For further information on our Green Tourism Business Scheme please see page 7.

476   To find out more go to visitscotland.com

Directory of all VisitScotland Assured Serviced Establishments, ordered by location.
Establishments highlighted have an advertisement in this guide.

Location	Property Name	Postcode	Telephone	Classification	Star Rating		
Saltcoats		KA21 5JN	0870 4429312	Holiday Park	★★★		
Sanquhar	Blackaddie House Hotel	DG4 6JJ	01659 50270	Country House Hotel	★★★		
	Newark	DG4 6HN	01659 50263	Farm House	★★★	ዼ	
	Nith Riverside Lodges		01659 50270	Self Catering	★★★	ዼ	
	No 3 Mountain Lodge		0791 7753302	Self Catering	★★★		
Selkirk	Abbey Court/Kelso/Melrose/Dryburgh		01750 20118	Self Catering	★★★ to ★★★★		
	Broadmeadows House		01750 725014	Self Catering	★★★★		
	Broadmeadows Youth Hostel	TD7 5LZ	0870 1553255	Hostel	★★		℗
	Buxton House B&B	TD7 4PU	01750 21431	Bed & Breakfast	★★★★★		
	Elspinhope		01750 62259	Self Catering	★★★★	ዼ	℗℗℗
	Headshaw Farm Holiday Cottages – Skye		01750 32233	Self Catering	★★★★		
	Heatherlie House Hotel	TD7 5AL	01750 721200	Small Hotel	★★★		
	Ivy Bank	TD7 4LT	01750 21270	Bed & Breakfast	★★		
	Nether Whitlaw Farm Cottage		01750 21217	Self Catering	★★★★		
	New Woll Estate		01750 32711	Self Catering	★★★★		
	St Mary's House	TD7 5NE	01750 82287	Bed & Breakfast	★★★		
	Sunnybrae House	TD7 4LS	01750 21156	Bed & Breakfast	★★★		
	Synton Mains Farm		01750 32388	Self Catering	★★★★	ዼ	
	The County Hotel	TD7 4BZ	01750 721233	Small Hotel	★★★		
	The Firs	TD7 5LS	01750 20409	Bed & Breakfast	★★★★		
	The Glen Hotel	TD7 5AS	01750 20259	Small Hotel	★★★		
	The Mill @ Lewinshope		07732 653861	Self Catering	★★★★★	🕴	
	The Philipburn Country House Hotel	TD7 5LS	01750 720747	Country House Hotel	★★★★		
	Tower Street Guest House	TD7 4LR	01750 23222	Guest House	★★★		
	Tushielaw Inn	TD7 5HT	01750 62205	Inn	★★		
	Victoria Caravan Park	TD7 5DN	01750 20897	Touring Park	★★★		
	West Deloraine	TD7 5HR	01750 62207	Holiday Caravan			
Shetland	11A King Herald Apartments		01595 694014	Self Catering	★★★		
	16 Monthooly Street		01950 477350	Self Catering	★★★		
	2 Bothies	ZE2 9AQ	01806 566429	Awaiting Grading			
	25 Westerloch Drive		01595 695649	Self Catering	★★★★		
	4 Greenfield Square		01595 696056	Self Catering	★★★		
	4-6 Burns Lane		01595 695922	Self Catering	★★★★		
	59A King Harald Street		01595 693054	Self Catering	★★★		
	6 Water Lane		01595 760248	Self Catering	★★★		
	64B Burgh Road		01595 696381	Self Catering	★★★		
	8 Thorfinn Street		01595 692317	Self Catering	★★★		
	9 Hillside Brae		01595 694418	Self Catering	★★★★		
	9 Navy Lane		01595 694152	Self Catering	★★		
	Abateg Apartment		01595 840458	Self Catering	★★★		
	Aesthus		01806 577274	Self Catering	★★★★		
	Aithbank Camping Bod	ZE2 9DJ	01595 694688	Bod			
	Alderlodge Guest House	ZE1 0BR	01595 695705	Guest House	★★★		
	Almara	ZE2 9RH	01806 503261	Bed & Breakfast	★★★★		℗℗℗
	Almara Chalet		01806 503261	Self Catering	★★★★		
	Anderlea		01595 840484	Self Catering	★★		

Advertisers' locations have been sorted by postcode. In Scotland, postcodes can cover fairly large geographical areas.
Please check distance of property from specified location with the individual provider. VisitScotland cannot take any responsibility for this.

Directory of all VisitScotland Assured Serviced Establishments, ordered by location. Establishments highlighted have an advertisement in this guide.

Location	Property Name	Postcode	Telephone	Classification	Star Rating
Shetland	Apartment @ Ovrevagen		01950 477633	Self Catering	★★★
	Betty Mouat's	ZE3 9JW	01595 694688	Bod	
	Blydest Self Catering		01950 431496	Self Catering	★★★
	Boatsroom B&B	ZE2 9QF	01806 577328	Bed & Breakfast	★★
	Bod of Nesbister	ZE2 9LJ	01595 694688	Bod	
	Braewick		01806 577269	Self Catering	★★★
	Braewick Cafe & Caravan Park	ZE2 9RS	01806 503345	Touring Park	★★★★
	Breiview	ZE1 0RJ	01595 695956	Guest House	★★★
	Brekka Lodge		01950 477687	Self Catering	★★★★
	Brentham House	ZE1 0LR	01950 460201	Guest Accommodation	★★★★
	Burnside Cottage		01595 809366	Self Catering	★★
	Burrastow House	ZE2 9PD	01595 809307	Guest House	★★★★ ⎣
	Busta House Hotel	ZE2 9QN	01806 522506	Country House Hotel	★★★
	Cee Aa	ZE1 0PR	01595 693362	Bed & Breakfast	★★★
	Chalet 1		01595 810222	Self Catering	★★
	Clickimin Caravan & Camping Site	ZE1 0PJ	01595 741000	Touring Park	★★★★★
	Coel Na Mara		01957 702102	Self Catering	★★★
	Crawton		01950 460409	Self Catering	★★★
	Croft Cottage		01806 577224	Self Catering	★★★
	Culswick Crofthouse Apartments		01595 810222	Self Catering	★★★★
	Cymrund		01595 840673	Self Catering	★★★
	Da Barn		01957 755255	Self Catering	★★
	Dale Cottage		01957 711315	Self Catering	★★★★
	Delting Boat Club Caravan Park	ZE2 9QJ	01806 522524	Awaiting Grading	
	East Cottage and West Cottage		01595 694688	Self Catering	★★★
	Easterhoull Chalets 4&5		07818 845385	Self Catering	★★ to ★★★
	Eddlewood Guest House	ZE1 0BR	01595 692772	Guest House	★★★
	Eshaness Lighthouse		01595 694 688	Self Catering	★★
	Fair Isle Bird Observatory Lodge	ZE2 9JU	01595 760258	Awaiting Grading	
	Fairview		07770 955830	Self Catering	★★★★
	Fishers Croft Hamnavoe		01223 208437	Self Catering	★★★★
	Fjael	ZE2 9JX	01595 697488	Bed & Breakfast	★★★
	Flat 55 King Harald Street		01595 695758	Self Catering	★★★
	Fort Charlotte Guest House	ZE1 0JL	01595 692140	Guest House	★★★
	Gardiesfauld Youth Hostel	ZE2 9DW	01957 755279	Hostel	★★★ ⎣
	Gaza		01806 522239	Self Catering	★★★
	Gerratoun	ZE2 9EF	01957 711323	Bed & Breakfast	★★
	Glen Orchy Guest House	ZE1 0AX	01595 692031	Guest House	★★★ 🕇 🄟
	Gord Bed and Breakfast	ZE2 9DJ	01957 733227	Bed & Breakfast	★★★
	Gord Holiday Cottages		01950 477384	Self Catering	★★★
	Grand Hotel	ZE1 0HX	01595 692826	Hotel	★★★
	Gremister		01856 850651	Self Catering	★★★★
	Grieve House		01595 694688	Bod	Pass Pass
	Hannigarth		01452 831881	Self Catering	★★★
	Harbour Penthouse	ZE1 0LR	01595 696901	Awaiting Grading	
	Heart Stanes		01595 741471	Self Catering	★★
	Herrislea House	ZE2 9SB	01595 840208	Restaurant With Rooms	★★★★ 🄟🄟

⎣ Unassisted wheelchair access   ⎣ Assisted wheelchair access   🕇 Access for visitors with mobility difficulties
🄟 Bronze Green Tourism Award   🄟🄟 Silver Green Tourism Award   🄟🄟🄟 Gold Green Tourism Award
For further information on our Green Tourism Business Scheme please see page 7.

To find out more go to visitscotland.com

Location	Property Name	Postcode	Telephone	Classification	Star Rating
Shetland	Highmount		01595 880647	Self Catering	★★★
	Hurdiback Packpackers Hostel	ZE2 9PW	01595 873227	Awaiting Grading	
	Irvine		01595 810325	Self Catering	★★★★
	Islehavn Chalet		01595 890342	Self Catering	★★★
	Johnnie Notions	ZE2	01595 693434	Bod	
	Kinlea		01595 880961	Self Catering	★★★★
	Kveldsro House Hotel	ZE1 0AN	01595 692195	Small Hotel	★★★
	Lerwick Hotel	ZE1 0RB	01595 692166	Hotel	★★★
	Lerwick Youth Hostel	ZE1 0EQ	01595 692114	Hostel	★★★★★
	Linga		01950 477596	Self Catering	★★★★
	Longwell Cottage		01595 744432	Self Catering	★★★
	Lower Cottage		01595 810439	Self Catering	★★
	Lunna House	ZE2 9QF	0845 6448609	Bed & Breakfast	★★★
	Lurnea		01595 859413	Self Catering	★★★
	Marshvale		01595 810378	Self Catering	★★★
	Maryfield House Hotel	ZE2 9EL	01595 820207	Restaurant With Rooms	★
	Melstadr		01950 422368	Self Catering	★★★
	Midfield Cottage		01806 544277	Self Catering	★★★ to ★★★★
	Muckle Hus	ZE2 9HX	01950 422370	Bed & Breakfast	★★★★
	Nilmurhaa		01595 860240	Self Catering	★★★★
	No 5 Queens Place		01806 566577	Self Catering	★★
	No 7A Hillhead		01595 696774	Self Catering	★★★
	Nordagerdi		01950 461929	Self Catering	★★
	North Booth		01343 860227	Self Catering	★★
	North Dale		01957 711579	Self Catering	★★ to ★★★
	Northern Lights Holistic Spa	ZE2 9ES	01595 820733	Guest House	★★★★
	Office Lodge	ZE1 0JL		Serviced Apartments	★★★
	Orca Country Inn	ZE2 9HL	01950 431226	Guest House	★★★
	Overby		01325 710143	Self Catering	★★★
	Pomona	ZE2 9NR	01595 810438	Bed & Breakfast	★★
	Prestegaard	ZE2 9DL	01957 755234	Bed & Breakfast	★★★
	Queans		01595 810231	Self Catering	★★★★
	Queen's Hotel	ZE1 0AB	01595 692826	Hotel	★★★
	Roadside Cottage		01950 477350	Self Catering	★★★
	Sail Loft	ZE2	01595 694688	Bod	
	Sandibanks		01595 692701	Self Catering	★★★★
	Saxa Vord		01957 881273	Self Catering	★★★
	Saxa Vord Ltd	ZE2 9TJ	01479 870022	Hostel	★★★
	Scalloway Hotel	ZE1 0RT	01595 880444	Small Hotel	★★
	Scarvataing		01595 810421	Self Catering	★★★★
	Scraefield		013527 13094	Self Catering	★
	Seafield Farm	ZE1 0RN	01595 693853	Bed & Breakfast	★★★
	Setterbrae	ZE2 9JE	01950 460468	Bed & Breakfast	★★★★
	Shalders	ZE2 9HX	01950 422229	Bed & Breakfast	★★★★
	Shetland Hotel	ZE1 0PW	01595 695515	Hotel	★★★ ᕫ
	Shorehaven	ZE2 9TJ	01806 522447	Awaiting Grading	
	Skeld Camping Bod	ZE2 9NL	01595 694688	Bod	

ᕫ Unassisted wheelchair access   ᕫ Assisted wheelchair access   ♁ Access for visitors with mobility difficulties
Ⓟ Bronze Green Tourism Award   ⒫⒫ Silver Green Tourism Award   ⒫⒫⒫ Gold Green Tourism Award
For further information on our Green Tourism Business Scheme please see page 7.

Advertisers' locations have been sorted by postcode. In Scotland, postcodes can cover fairly large geographical areas.
Please check distance of property from specified location with the individual provider. VisitScotland cannot take any responsibility for this.

479

Location	Property Name	Postcode	Telephone	Classification	Star Rating	
Shetland	Skeld Caravan & Camping Site	ZE2 9NL	01595 860287	Touring Park	★★★	
	Skeoverick	ZE2 9PJ	01595 809349	Bed & Breakfast	★★★	
	Smola	ZE2 0HX	07880 950222	Awaiting Grading		
	Solbrekke	ZE2 9HP	01950 431410	Bed & Breakfast	★★	
	Solheim Guest House	ZE1 0EQ	01595 695275	Guest House	★★★	
	Spiggie Hotel	ZE2 9JE	01950 460409	Small Hotel	★★★	
	Spiggie House		01950 460152	Self Catering	★★★	
	St Magnus Bay Hotel	ZE2 9RW	01806 503372	Awaiting Grading		
	Sumburgh Hotel	ZE3 9JN	01950 460201	Hotel	★★★	
	Sumburgh Lighthouse		01595 694688	Self Catering	★★	
	Sumburgh Lodge	ZE3 9JN	01950 460201	Awaiting Grading		
	Swarthoull		01806 503397	Self Catering	★★★	
	Tenko		01595 695727	Self Catering	★★★	
	The Booth		01224 791327	Self Catering	★★★	
	The Cottage		01595 693782	Self Catering	★★	
	The Cottage		01806 522589	Self Catering	★★★	
	The Croft House		01595 820332	Self Catering	★★★	
	The Flats		01595 692793	Self Catering	★★★	ふ
	The Lodge		01595 810280	Self Catering	★★★	
	Thorfinn Apartment		01595 693034	Self Catering	★★★	
	Top Floor Flat		01595 697137	Self Catering	★★	
	Tresta		01957 733231	Self Catering	★★★★	
	Trondheim	ZE7 0XL	01595 830220	Awaiting Grading		
	Upper Garden		01806 577215	Self Catering	★★★★	
	Valeind		01595 830219	Self Catering	★★★	
	Valley B&B	ZE2 9SE	01595 840403	Bed & Breakfast	★★★	
	Virdafjell	ZE2 9TX	01595 694336	Bed & Breakfast	★★★★	𝗂
	Voe House	ZE2 9PB	01595 694688	Bod		
	Voeview Cottage		01957 702307	Self Catering	★★	
	Westayre B&B	ZE2 9QW	01806 522368	Bed & Breakfast	★★★★	
	Westhall	ZE1 0RN	01595 694247	Bed & Breakfast	★★★★	
	Westhall Cottage	ZE1 0RN	01595 694247	Awaiting Grading		
	Wildrig		01950 460373	Self Catering	★★★★	
	Windhouse Croft	ZE2 9TA	01950 422459	Awaiting Grading		
	Windhouse Lodge		01595 694688	Bod	Pass	Pass	
	Windrush	ZE2 9HE	07894 644681	Bed & Breakfast	★★★	
	Windward	ZE1 0UN	01595 880769	Bed & Breakfast	★★★	
	Woosung	ZE1 0EN	01595 693687	Bed & Breakfast	★★	
Shotts	Blairmains	ML7 5TJ	01501 751278	Guest House	★★	
Skelmorlie	Mallowdale Cottage		01475 529166	Self Catering	★★★★	
	Dakota Forth Bridge	EH30 9QZ	0870 4234293	Hotel	★★★★	
South Queensferry	Dundas Castle	EH30 9SP	0131 3192039	Exclusive Use Venue	★★★★★	
	Edinburgh South Queensferry Premier Inn	EH30 9YJ	0870 1977094	Budget Hotel		
	Forth Reflections Self Catering		0131 3191118	Self Catering	★★★	
	Priory Lodge	EH30 9NS	0131 3314345	Guest House	★★★★	𝗂
	The Boat House		0131 3192039	Self Catering	★★★★	

Location	Property Name	Postcode	Telephone	Classification	Star Rating
Spean Bridge	2 Balmaglaster	PH34 4EB	01809 501289	Holiday Caravan	
	Achaneich Chalet		01397 712715	Self Catering	★★★★
	Achnabobane Farmhouse	PH34 4EX	01397 712919	Farm House	★★★
	Apartment At No.3	PH34 4EU	01397 712690	Awaiting Grading	
	Burnbank Lodges		01397 712520	Self Catering	★★★ ⟨PP⟩
	But N Ben No.1		0151 9315382	Self Catering	★★★
	Coinachan	PH34 4EG	01397 712417	Bed & Breakfast	★★★★
	Coire Glas Guest House	PH34 4EU	01397 712272	Guest House	★★★
	Corriegour Lodge Hotel	PH34 4EA	01397 712685	Small Hotel	★★★★
	Corrieview Lodges		01397 712395	Self Catering	★★★★
	Distant Hills Guest House	PH34 4EU	01397 712452	Guest House	★★★★
	Dreamweavers	PH34 4EQ	01397 712548	Bed & Breakfast	★★★★ ♀
	Faegour House	PH34 4EU	01397 712903	Bed & Breakfast	★★★★
	Forest Lodge	PH34 4EA	01809 501219	Guest House	★★★
	Gairlochy Holiday Park		01397 712711	Self Catering	★★★★
	Great Glen Hostel	PH34 4EA	01809 501451	Hostel	★★★★
	Highland Lodges		01809 501225	Self Catering	★★★
	Inverour Guest House	PH34 4EU	01397 712218	Guest House	★★★
	Mehalah Riverside House	PH34 4EU	01397 712893	Bed & Breakfast	★★★★
	Oak Lodge Larch Cottage & Gorries Lair		01397 712398	Self Catering	★★★★
	Old Pines Hotel and Restaurant	PH34 4EG	01397 712324	Small Hotel	★★★ ♿
	Old Smiddy Restaurant with Rooms	PH34 4EU	01397 712335	Restaurant With Rooms	★★★★
	Riverside Lodge Gardens B&B	PH34 4EN	01397 712702	Bed & Breakfast	★★★★
	Riverside Lodges	PH34 4DY	01397 712684	Bed & Breakfast	★★★★
	Riverside Lodges		01397 712684	Self Catering	★★★★
	Spean Bridge Hotel	PH34 4ES	01397 712250	Hotel	★★
	Spean Cottage		01397 712004	Self Catering	★★★ to ★★★★
	Spean Lodge	PH34 4EP	01397 712004	Bed & Breakfast	★★★★
	Springburn	PH34 4DX	01397 712707	Bed & Breakfast	★★★★
	Springburn Self Catering		01397 712707	Self Catering	★★★★
	The Braes Guest House	PH34 4EU	01397 712437	Guest House	★★★
	The Heathers	PH34 4DY	01397 712077	Guest House	★★★★ ♀
	The Heathers (Fraoch Cottage)		01397 712077	Self Catering	★★★★
	The Old Smiddy		01397 712335	Self Catering	★★★★
	The Wee Floating Bunkhouse	PH34 4EA	07789 858567	Awaiting Grading	
	Tirindrish Steading		01603 788448	Self Catering	★★★★
St. Andrews	1 Greenside Court		01419 562532	Self Catering	★★★
	11 Queens Gardens	KY16 9TA	01334 478751	Guest House	★★★★
	12 Golf Place		01333 330241	Self Catering	★★★★
	12 Grange Road	KY16 8LF	01334 471949	Bed & Breakfast	★★★★
	140 North Street		07841 506683	Self Catering	★★★★
	143 Market Street		0207 9176233	Self Catering	★★★
	150A North Street		01333 313659	Self Catering	★★★★
	16 Kilrymont Road		0141 5480614	Self Catering	★★★
	17 Queens Gardens		01483 424743	Self Catering	★★★
	18 Queens Terrace	KY16 9QF	01334 478849	Bed & Breakfast	★★★★
	18 The Scores		01248 6442577	Self Catering	★★★★

& Unassisted wheelchair access   Assisted wheelchair access   ♀ Access for visitors with mobility difficulties
⟨P⟩ Bronze Green Tourism Award   ⟨PP⟩ Silver Green Tourism Award   ⟨PPP⟩ Gold Green Tourism Award
For further information on our Green Tourism Business Scheme please see page 7.

Advertisers' locations have been sorted by postcode. In Scotland, postcodes can cover fairly large geographical areas.
Please check distance of property from specified location with the individual provider. VisitScotland cannot take any responsibility for this.

481

Location	Property Name	Postcode	Telephone	Classification	Star Rating	
St. Andrews	185 South Street		07798 806801	Self Catering	★★★	
	2 Chamberlain Street		01625 611975	Self Catering	★★	
	20 College Street		01620 895520	Self Catering	★★★	
	247 Lamond Drive		0151 5262116	Self Catering	★★★	
	25 City Road		07909 521082	Self Catering	★★★★	
	25 Sloan Street		01224 722243	Self Catering	★★★	⌂
	29 North Street		0131 3329499	Self Catering	★★★★	
	30 Drumcarrow Road	KY16 8SE	01334 472036	Bed & Breakfast	★★★	
	3C Gillespie Terrace		01327 704797	Self Catering	★★★	
	4 & 5 Abbotsford Place		01382 330318	Self Catering	★★★★	
	4 Mount Melville		01505 335246	Self Catering	★★★	
	41 Auldburn Park		0141 8896327	Self Catering	★★	
	6 Livingstone Place		01464 820871	Self Catering	★★★	
	6 Queens Gardens		01345 9452385	Self Catering	★★★★	
	8 Dempster Terrace	KY16 9QQ	01389 874509	Awaiting Grading		
	Abbey Cottage	KY16 9LB	01334 473727	Bed & Breakfast	★★	
	Acorn B & B	KY16 8DJ	01334 476009	Bed & Breakfast	★★★★	
	Albany Apartments		0131 3468662	Self Catering	★★★★★	
	Albany Hotel	KY16 9AH	01334 477737	Metro Hotel	★★★	
	Amberside	KY16 9AW	01334 474644	Guest House	★★★	
	Anderson House	KY16 8DA	01334 477286	Bed & Breakfast	★★★	
	Annandale Guest House	KY16 9AW	01334 475310	Guest House	★★★★	
	Ardgowan Hotel	KY16 9HX	01334 472970	Small Hotel	★★★	
	Arran House	KY16 9AW	01334 474724	Guest House	★★★	
	Aslar House	KY16 9AF	01334 473460	Guest House	★★★★	
	Balmashie Holiday Cottages		01334 880666	Self Catering	★★★★	♿
	Balrymonth B&B	KY16 8XT	01334 470855	Bed & Breakfast	★★★	
	Barnhay	KY16 8NA	01334 477791	Bed & Breakfast	★★★★	
	Bell Craig	KY16 9AW	01334 472962	Guest House	★★★	
	Beveridge House	KY16 9PW	01334 477453	Bed & Breakfast	★★★	
	Braeside House	KY16 8AJ	01334 473375	Bed & Breakfast	★★★★	
	Braid		0141 6163491	Self Catering	★★★ to ★★★★	
	Bramley House	KY16 9RP	01334 850955	Awaiting Grading		
	Brooksby House	KY16 9ER	01334 470723	Guest House	★★★★★	
	Brownlees	KY16 9AP	01334 473868	Guest House	★★★★	
	Burness House	KY16 9AW	01334 474314	Guest House	★★★★	
	Burnside		01334 473180	Self Catering	★★★	
	Cairnsmill Caravan Park	KY16 8NN	01334 475058	Holiday Park	★★★★	
	Cambo House	KY16 8QD	01333 450313	Bed & Breakfast	★★★★	⌂⌂
	Cameron House	KY16 9AW	01334 472306	Guest House	★★★★	
	Canongate		07881 775967	Self Catering	★★★	
	Caravan C4	KY16 8PX	01698 816839	Holiday Caravan		
	Castlemount	KY16 9AR	01334 475579	Bed & Breakfast	★★★★	
	Charlesworth House	KY16 9AP	01334 476528	Guest House	★★★★	
	Clayton Caravan Park	KY16 9YB	01334 870242	Holiday Park	★★★★★	
	Cleveden Guest House	KY16 9AP	01334 474212	Guest House	★★★★	
	Cobwebs		01764 685482	Self Catering	★★★★	♁
	Craigmore Guest House	KY16 9AW	01334 472142	Guest House	★★★★	

♿ Unassisted wheelchair access   ♿ Assisted wheelchair access   ♁ Access for visitors with mobility difficulties
⌂ Bronze Green Tourism Award   ⌂⌂ Silver Green Tourism Award   ⌂⌂⌂ Gold Green Tourism Award
For further information on our Green Tourism Business Scheme please see page 7.

To find out more go to visitscotland.com

Location	Property Name	Postcode	Telephone	Classification	Star Rating	
St. Andrews	Craigtoun Meadows Holiday Park	KY16 8PQ	01334 475959	Holiday Park	★★★★★	
	Daisybank & The Smithy		0141 9511331	Self Catering	★★★★	
	David Russell Hall		01334 462000	Self Catering	★★★	🍃🍃🍃
	Deveron House	KY16 9AH	01334 473513	Guest House	★★★	
	Doune House	KY16 9AP	01334 475195	Guest House	★★★★	
	Drumoig Hotel & Golf Resort	KY16 0BE	07880 551372	Awaiting Grading		
	Drumtilly House	KY16 8SE	01334 470954	Bed & Breakfast	★★★	
	Ducks Crossing	KY16 9QQ	01334 477010	Bed & Breakfast	★★★	
	Dunvegan Hotel	KY16 9HZ	01334 473105	Small Hotel	★★★	
	East & Mid Cottage		01333 450313	Self Catering	★★★ to ★★★★	🍃🍃
	Edenside House	KY16 9QS	01334 838108	Guest House	★★★	
	Fairmont St Andrews	KY16 8PN	01334 468005	Hotel	★★★★★	🍃🍃
	Fairnie House	KY16 9LA	01334 474094	Bed & Breakfast	★★★	
	Five Pilmour Place	KY16 9HZ	01334 478665	Guest House	★★★★	
	Flat B Hepburn Gardens		01334 473989	Self Catering	★★★ to ★★★★	
	Flat No 1		01333 312613	Self Catering	★★★	
	Flowers of May Cottage		01334 880616	Self Catering	★★★★	
	Garden Flat & 1st Floor Flat		01343 812212	Self Catering	★★	
	Glenderran Guest House	KY16 9AW	01334 477951	Guest House	★★★★	
	Greyfriars Hotel	KY16 9AG	01334 474906	Small Hotel	★★★	
	Hawthorne House	KY16 9RY	01334 580855	Bed & Breakfast	★★★★	
	Hayston Farm	KY16 0AJ	01334 870210	Bed & Breakfast	★★★	
	Hazelbank Hotel	KY16 9AS	01334 472466	Metro Hotel	★★★	
	Hilltop Bed and Breakfast	KY16 9RX	01334 850667	Bed & Breakfast	★★★	
	Hillwood House	KY16 8PD	01334 840396	Bed & Breakfast	★★★	
	Inchdairnie – 5 West Grange		01334 477011	Self Catering	★★★ to ★★★★	
	Ivybank		01344 626431	Self Catering	★★★	
	Jules House B&B	KY16 8XD	01334 472735	Bed & Breakfast	★★★	
	Kildonan House		01334 473446	Self Catering	★★★	
	Kinburn Guest House	KY16 9DT	01334 474711	Guest House	★★★★	
	Kingask Country Cottages – Kirkmay Cottage 1 and 2		01334 472011	Self Catering	★★★	
	Kinkell Braes Caravan Park	KY16 8PX	01259 751270	Holiday Caravan		
	Kinkell Braes Caravan Park	KY16 8PX	01383 851851	Holiday Park	★★★	
	Ladybrand		0121 4727404	Self Catering	★★★	
	Larch & Ash		01334 850217	Self Catering	★★★ to ★★★★	
	Linskill House		01334 473040	Self Catering	★★★	
	Little Balone		01334 470051	Self Catering	★★★★	
	Little Carron Cottage	KY16 8QN	01334 474039	Bed & Breakfast	★★★★	
	Lone Star	KY16 8NA	01334 476837	Bed & Breakfast	★★★★★	
	Lorimer House	KY16 9AW	01334 476599	Guest House	★★★★	
	Macdonald Rusacks Hotel	KY16 9JQ	01334 474 321	Hotel	★★★★	
	Mansedale House	KY16 9RY	01334 850850	Bed & Breakfast	★★★★	
	McIntosh Hall	KY16 9HT	01334 467000	Campus	★★	
	Millhouse	KY16 9TY	01334 850557	Bed & Breakfast	★★★★	
	Milton Lea B&B	KY16 0AB	05602 988677	Bed & Breakfast	★★★★	
	Monksholm House	KY16 9SJ	01334 850023	Bed & Breakfast	★★★	
	Montague House	KY16 9AW	01334 479287	Guest House	★★★	

♿ Unassisted wheelchair access ♿ Assisted wheelchair access 🚶 Access for visitors with mobility difficulties
🍃 Bronze Green Tourism Award   🍃🍃 Silver Green Tourism Award   🍃🍃🍃 Gold Green Tourism Award
For further information on our Green Tourism Business Scheme please see page 7.

Advertisers' locations have been sorted by postcode. In Scotland, postcodes can cover fairly large geographical areas.
Please check distance of property from specified location with the individual provider. VisitScotland cannot take any responsibility for this.

483

Location	Property Name	Postcode	Telephone	Classification	Star Rating	
St. Andrews	Morton of Pitmilly		01334 880466	Self Catering	★★★★	🍃🍃🍃
	Nethan House	KY16 9AW	01334 472104	Guest House	★★★★	🍃🍃
	New Hall University of St Andrews	KY16 9XW	01334 462496	Hotel	★★★	🍃🍃🍃
	No 24 Chamberlain Street		01383 723069	Self Catering	★★★	
	No 6		01727 832065	Self Catering	★★★★	
	Ogstons on North Street	KY16 9AG	01334 473387	Inn	★★★	
	Ogston's on Pilmour	KY16 9HZ	01334 473252	Inn	★★	
	Old Course Hotel Golf Resort & Spa	KY16 9SP	01334 474371	Hotel	★★★★★	
	Old Fishergate House	KY16 9BG	01334 470874	Bed & Breakfast	★★★★	
	Park Mill Cottage		01334 880254	Self Catering	★★	
	Pinewood Country House	KY16 0DU	01334 839860	Guest House	★★★★	
	Pitmilly West Lodge	KY16 8QA	01334 880581	Bed & Breakfast	★★★★	🚶
	Rigg's End		01334 473310	Self Catering	★★★★★	
	Riverview Guest House	KY16 9SQ	01334 838009	Guest House	★★★	
	Royal George		01334 473365	Self Catering	★★★★	
	Rufflets Country House Hotel	KY16 9TX	01334 472594	Country House Hotel	★★★★	♿ 🍃🍃🍃
	Sandmill House		01333 450549	Self Catering	★★★★	
	Scores Hotel	KY16 9BB	01334 472451	Hotel	★★★	
	Scotscraig	KY16 9SA	01334 850748	Awaiting Grading		
	Shandon House	KY16 9AP	01334 472412	Guest House	★★★	
	Six Murray Park	KY16 9AW	01334 473319	Guest House	★★★★	
	Spinkstown Farmhouse	KY16 8PN	01334 473475	Bed & Breakfast	★★★★	
	St Andrews Golf Hotel	KY16 9AS	01334 472611	Hotel	★★★★	
	St Marys		0141 639 3860	Self Catering	★★★	
	St Michaels Inn	KY16 0DU	01334 839220	Inn	★★★	
	St Nicholas	KY16 8LD	01334 473090	Bed & Breakfast	★★★	
	St. Andrews Coach Houses		01334 477593	Self Catering	★★★★	
	Strathkinness House		01334 850506	Self Catering	★★★★	
	Stravithie Castle	KY16 8LT	01334 880251	Bed & Breakfast	★★★	
	Swilken View		01828 686261	Self Catering	★★★★	
	The Auld Hoose		07748 700458	Self Catering	★★★★	
	The Barns at Kingsbarns	KY16 8TA	01334 460820	Awaiting Grading		
	The Bothy		01334 479127	Self Catering	★★★★	
	The Coach House		01334 475844	Self Catering	★★ to ★★★	
	The Dunes		07789 722488	Self Catering	★★★★	
	The Hirsel Cottage		01334 472578	Self Catering	★★★	
	The Humble Rowan B&B	KY16 8LG	01334 475322	Awaiting Grading		
	The Larches	KY16 0XA	01334 838008	Bed & Breakfast	★★★	
	The New Inn	KY16 8AZ	01334 461333	Inn	★★★	
	The Old Station Country Guest House	KY16 8LR	01334 880505	Guest House	★★★★	♿
	The Paddock	KY16 9XP	01334 850888	Bed & Breakfast	★★★★	🍃🍃
	The Russell Hotel	KY16 9AS	01334 473447	Small Hotel	★★★	
	The Spindle	KY16 9QQ	01334 477185	Awaiting Grading		
	The Vintage	KY16 9AU	+0041 (7920) 11074	Awaiting Grading		
	The West Port	KY16 9EG	01334 473186	Inn	★★★	
	The Whins 1 Chambers Place		07796 440954	Self Catering	★★★★	
	The White House	KY16 0EY	01334 838227	Bed & Breakfast	★★★★	
	The Yards B&B	KY16 8ST	01334 880317	Awaiting Grading		

Location	Property Name	Postcode	Telephone	Classification	Star Rating	
St. Andrews	Vardon House	KY16 9AW	01334 475787	Bed & Breakfast	★★★	
	Vardon House		01334 475787	Self Catering	★★★	
	Vicarsford Lodge	KY16 0DT	01334 834356	Bed & Breakfast	★★★★	
	Vicarsford Lodge	KY16 0DT	01334 834356	Awaiting Grading		
	West and East Cottages		0131 2401114	Self Catering	★★★★	
	Yorkston House	KY16 9BU	01334 472019	Guest House	★★★	
Stevenston	Ardeer Steading	KA20 3DD	01294 465438	Farm House	★★★★	
Stirling	10 Gladstone Place	FK8 2NN	01786 472681	Bed & Breakfast	★★★★	
	14 Melville Terrace	FK8 2NE	01786 475361	Bed & Breakfast	★★★	
	14a Melville Terrace			Self Catering	★★	
	27 King Street	FK8 1DN	01786 471082	Bed & Breakfast	★★	
	5 Individually named units		01479 811244	Self Catering	★★★★	
	5 Randolph Terrace	FK7 9AA	01786 472454	Bed & Breakfast	★★★	
	8 Staball 'Ard		01786 871197	Self Catering	★★★★	
	9 Glebe Crescent	FK8 2JB	01786 473433	Bed & Breakfast	★★★	
	Abercromby Apartments Flat 2		01738 450445	Self Catering	★★★★	
	Acorn Cottage		01877 382266	Self Catering	★★★★	
	Adamo	FK9 4HP	01786 833268	Small Hotel	★★★★	♿
	Adamo Hotel	FK8 2DT	01786 430891	Restaurant With Rooms	★★★★	
	Ainslie Cottage		07966 414996	Self Catering	★★★	
	Alberts	FK9 5LF	01786 478728	Bed & Breakfast	★	
	Allan Park Hotel	FK8 2QG	01786 473598	Metro Hotel	★	
	Allen Cottage		01360 850233	Self Catering	★★★★	
	Allerton	FK8 2AF	01786 465677	Bed & Breakfast	★★★	
	Arnvicar		01877 385775	Self Catering	★★★	
	Auchenbowie Caravan Site	FK7 8HE	01324 823999	Holiday Park	★★★	
	Barcelo Stirling Highland Hotel	FK8 1DU	01786 272727	Hotel	★★★★	
	Barnsdale House	FK7 0PT	01786 461729	Bed & Breakfast	★★★	
	Bellview		01786 860543	Self Catering	★★★★	♀
	Ben Lomond Lodges		01877 382614	Self Catering	★★★★	
	Bonnie Braes	FK8 3QL	01786 850225	Bed & Breakfast	★★★	
	Brockville B&B	FK8 2PG	01786 475225	Bed & Breakfast	★★★	
	Broom Farm		01786 474329	Self Catering	★★★	♀
	Buchlyvie Bed and Breakfast	FK8 3NA	01360 850580	Bed & Breakfast	★	
	Burns View	FK8 2QL	01786 451002	Guest House	★★★	
	Castle View	FK9 5EG	01786 469922	Awaiting Grading		
	Cobleland Caravan and Campsite	FK8 3RR	01283 228607	Touring Park	★★★	🄿
	Corrie Glen B&B	FK8 3XF	01877 382427	Bed & Breakfast	★★★	
	Cotkerse House		01259 761423	Self Catering	★★★★	
	Craigard	FK9 5EY	01786 460540	Bed & Breakfast	★★★	
	Craigmore Guest House	FK8 3SZ	01877 382436	Guest House	★★★	
	Craigquarter Farm	FK7 9QP	01786 812668	Farm House	★★★★	
	Cressington	FK9 5EU	01786 462435	Bed & Breakfast	★★★	
	Currach	FK8 3RA	01877 385699	Bed & Breakfast	★★★	
	Dunardry		01942 816010	Self Catering	★★★	
	Express by Holiday Inn – Stirling	FK7 7XH	01786 449922	Metro Hotel	★★★	♿

Advertisers' locations have been sorted by postcode. In Scotland, postcodes can cover fairly large geographical areas.
Please check distance of property from specified location with the individual provider. VisitScotland cannot take any responsibility for this.

485

Directory

of all VisitScotland Assured Serviced Establishments, ordered by location. Establishments highlighted have an advertisement in this guide.

Location	Property Name	Postcode	Telephone	Classification	Star Rating	
Stirling	Firgrove	FK8 2AQ	01786 475805	Bed & Breakfast	★★★★	
	Fordhead Cottage		01786 870329	Self Catering	★★★★	
	Forest Hills Hotel	FK8 3TL	08448 799057	Hotel	★★★★	♿
	Forth Guest House	FK8 1UD	01786 471020	Guest House	★★★★	
	Front Apartment	FK8 2RQ	01786 462064	Awaiting Grading		
	Garfield Guest House	FK8 2QZ	01786 473730	Guest House	★★★	
	Gartmore House	FK8 3SZ	07801 767499	Guest Accommodation	★★	
	Gillies Cottage		01786 470616	Self Catering	★★★	
	Glendale Cottage		01786 811162	Self Catering	★★★	
	Glenny Cottages		01877 385229	Self Catering	★★★	
	Hawthorn Cottage		01786 472523	Self Catering	★★★★	♿ ⓟ
	Hillview Holiday Cottage		0141 9428299	Self Catering	★★★	
	Inchie Farm	FK8 3JZ	01877 385233	Bed & Breakfast	★★★	
	Inverard Lodge B&B	FK8 3TD	01877 389113	Bed & Breakfast	★★★	
	Inverard Lodge Cabin		01877 389113	Self Catering	★★	
	Inversnaid Bunkhouse	FK8 3TU	01877 386249	Awaiting Grading		
	Inversnaid Hotel	FK8 3TU	01877 386223	Hotel	★★★	
	King Robert Hotel	FK7 OLJ	01786 811666	Hotel	★★★	
	Lake of Menteith Hotel	FK8 3RA	01877 385258	Small Hotel	★★★	
	Larne Coach House		01786 871197	Self Catering	★★★★	
	Laurinda	FK7 8PJ	01786 815612	Bed & Breakfast	★★★	
	Ledard Farm Bothies	FK8 3TL	01877387219	Bunkhouse		
	Linden Guest House	FK7 7PQ	01786 448850	Guest House	★★★★	
	Loch Dhu Cottage		01877 387712	Self Catering	★★★	
	Lochend Chalets		01877 385268	Self Catering	★★★ to ★★★★	ⓟ
	Logie Barn		01786 833343	Self Catering	★★★	
	Lomond View Cottage		01877 382427	Self Catering	★★★★	
	Lynedoch	FK9 4QU	01786 832178	Bed & Breakfast	★★★	♁
	Munro Guest House	FK8 1HQ	01786 472685	Guest House	★★★	
	Neidpath B&B	FK7 7PQ	01786 469017	Bed & Breakfast	★★★	
	New Holme		01786 442001	Self Catering	★★★★	
	No 31 Kenningknowes Road	FK7 9JF	01786 475511	Bed & Breakfast	★★	
	Norrieston East Wing		01786 850234	Self Catering	★★★	
	Park Lodge Hotel	FK8 2JS	01786 474862	Small Hotel	★★★	
	Pendreich Way Chalets		01786 466188	Self Catering	★★★	
	Plumtree Cottage		01324 832060	Self Catering	★★★★	
	Queen's Guest House	FK8 1HN	01786 471043	Bed & Breakfast	★★	
	Redcarr Lodge		01786 477210	Self Catering	★★★★	
	Redhall Farm	FK8 3AE	01786 860204	Holiday Caravan		
	Rob Roy Hotel	FK8 3UX	01877 382245	Hotel	★★	♁
	Rowan & Oak		01877 382075	Self Catering	★★★★	ⓟⓟ
	Royal Hotel	FK9 4HG	01786 832284	Hotel	★★★	
	Southfield	FK8 2ND	01786 464872	Bed & Breakfast	★★★	
	St Alma	FK9 5EG	01786 465795	Guest House	★★	
	Stillrovin in Scotland	FK7 7BG	01786 818899	Awaiting Grading		
	Stirling Management Centre	FK9 4LA	01786 451666	Hotel	★★★	♿ ⓟⓟ
	Stirling Premier Inn	FK7 8EX	08701 977241	Budget Hotel		
	Stirling Youth Hostel	FK8 1EA	01786 473442	Hostel	★★★★	♿ ⓟⓟ

♿ Unassisted wheelchair access   ♿ Assisted wheelchair access   ♁ Access for visitors with mobility difficulties
ⓟ Bronze Green Tourism Award   ⓟⓟ Silver Green Tourism Award   ⓟⓟⓟ Gold Green Tourism Award
For further information on our Green Tourism Business Scheme please see page 7.

To find out more go to visitscotland.com

Location	Property Name	Postcode	Telephone	Classification	Star Rating	
Stirling	StoneyPark	FK8 3SZ	01877 382208	Bed & Breakfast	★★★	
	Stoneypark Cottage		01877 382208	Self Catering	★★★	
	Strathard		01877 387366	Self Catering	★★★	
	Stronachlachar Lodge		0141 9550772	Self Catering	★★★	
	The Bield	FK8 3SX	01877 382351	Bed & Breakfast	★★★★	
	The Cottage	FK7 9JR	01786 478246	Bed & Breakfast	★★★	
	The Courtyard		01786 469433	Self Catering	★★★★	
	The Forth Inn	FK8 3UQ	01877 382372	Inn	★★★	
	The Golden Lion Hotel	FK8 1BD	01786 475351	Hotel	★★★	
	The Haven	FK9 5EU	01786 464060	Bed & Breakfast	★★★	
	The Hayloft Forth House		01877 382696	Self Catering	★★★	
	The Old Manse	FK7 9AJ	01786 463264	Bed & Breakfast	★★★	
	The Old Tram House	FK9 5EY	01786 449774	Bed & Breakfast	★★★★	
	The Pine	FK9 5NP	07843 339538	Awaiting Grading		
	The Portcullis	FK8 1AG	01786 472290	Inn	★★★	
	The Whitehouse	FK7 0PA	01786 462636	Guest House	★★★	
	Thorntree Barn		01786 870710	Self Catering	★★★	🄿
	Travelodge Stirling	FK7 8EU	08700 850950	Budget Hotel		
	Trossachs Holiday Park	FK8 3SA	01877 382614	Holiday Park	★★★★★	🄿🄿🄿
	Watergate		01259 761667	Self Catering	★★★	
	Wattie Cottage		0141 3394400	Self Catering	★★★	
	West Drip Farm	FK9 4UJ	01786 472523	Holiday Caravan		
	West Plean House	FK7 8HA	01786 812208	Bed & Breakfast	★★★★	
	Willow Cottage		01786 480178	Self Catering	★★★	
	Willy Wallace Hostel	FK8 1AU	01786 446773	Backpacker	★★	
	Witches Craig Caravan Park	FK9 5PX	01786 474947	Touring Park	★★★★★	
Stonehaven	60C High Street		01183 773050	Self Catering	★★	
	Ambleside B&B	AB39 3RB	01569 731105	Bed & Breakfast	★★★	
	Arduthie Garden Flat		01569 766241	Self Catering	★★★	
	Aspen & Hollyburn Lodges		01569 730210	Self Catering	★★★★	
	Bayview B&B	AB39 2BD	01569 766933	Bed & Breakfast	★★★★	
	Beachgate House	AB39 2BD	01569 763155	Bed & Breakfast	★★★★	
	Beachview B&B	AB39 2NZ	01569 765267	Bed & Breakfast	★★★	
	Cardowan B&B	AB39 2DU	01569 762759	Bed & Breakfast	★★★★	
	Cloak Caravan Park	AB39	01569 750232	Holiday Caravan		
	Cowie Mill	AB39 3BH	0141 6499555	Awaiting Grading		
	Dunnottar Mains Farm	AB39 2TL	01569 762621	Farm House	★★★★	
	Ellerslie House		01569 762504	Self Catering	★★★★	
	Gleniffer	AB39 2EH	01569 765272	Bed & Breakfast	★★★★	
	Heugh Hotel	AB39 2EE	01569 762379	Small Hotel	★★★	
	Marine Hotel	AB39 2XJ	01569 762155	Awaiting Grading		
	Pitgaveny	AB39 2SP	01569 764719	Bed & Breakfast	★★★★	
	Queen Elizabeth Caravan Park	AB39 2RP	01467 627622	Holiday Park	★★★	
	Tewel Farmhouse	AB39 3UU	01569 762306	Farm House	★★	
	The Belvedere Hotel	AB39 2ET	01569 762672	Small Hotel	★★	
	The Korner House	AB39 2HG	01569 766164	Bed & Breakfast	★★★	
	The Royal Hotel	AB39 2BU	0156 9762979	Awaiting Grading		
	The Ship Inn	AB39 2JY	01569 762617	Inn	★★	

Advertisers' locations have been sorted by postcode. In Scotland, postcodes can cover fairly large geographical areas.
Please check distance of property from specified location with the individual provider. VisitScotland cannot take any responsibility for this.

487

Location	Property Name	Postcode	Telephone	Classification	Star Rating		
Stonehaven	Upper Crawton	AB39 2TU	01569 750243	Bed & Breakfast	★★★		
	Woodside of Glasslaw	AB39 3XQ	01569 763799	Guest House	★★★★		
Stornoway	26 Newton Street	HS1 2RE	01851 702824	Bed & Breakfast	★★★		
	8 Esplanade Court		01851 871007	Self Catering	★★★★		
	Ardmor	HS1 2TX	01851 702796	Bed & Breakfast	★★★		
	Cabarfeidh Hotel	HS1 2EU	01851 702604	Hotel	★★★		
	Cairn Dhu Apartment	HS1 2LA	01851 612851	Serviced Apartments	★★★★		
	Caladh Inn	HS1 2QN	01851 702740	Hotel	★★		
	Dunard		01851 702458	Self Catering	★★★★		
	Fernlea	HS1 2NQ	01851 702125	Bed & Breakfast	★★★★		
	Hal-O The Wynd	HS1 2RE	01851 706073	Guest House	★★★		
	Heb Hostel	HS1 2DR	01851 709889	Backpacker	★★★★		
	Hebridean Guest House	HS1 2DZ	01851 702268	Guest House	★★★★		
	Iolaire & Metagama		0800 2343271	Self Catering	★★★★★		
	Jannel	HS1 2TU	01851 705324	Bed & Breakfast	★★★★	⸙	𝒫𝒫
	Kitale	HS1 2UE	01851 702568	Awaiting Grading			
	Number Six	HS1 2QR	01851 703014	Guest House	★★★★		
	Park Guest House	HS1 2QN	01851 702485	Guest House	★★★		
	Plasterfield Cottage		01851 701038	Self Catering	★★★★		
	Primrose Villa	HS1 2JL	01851 703 387	Bed & Breakfast	★★		
	Royal Hotel	HS1 2DG	01851 702109	Hotel	★★		
	Seacote		01851 700100	Self Catering	★★★★	♿	𝒫𝒫
	Solas		01851 702970	Self Catering	★★★★		
	Sula Sgeir	HS1 2UE	01851 705893	Bed & Breakfast	★★★		
	The Croft House	HS1 2UG	01851 701889	Bed & Breakfast	★★★		
	Valtos Cottage		01851 703957	Self Catering	★★★★★	⸙	
	Vancouver		01851 612347	Self Catering	★★★		
	Westwinds	HS1 2RW	01851 703408	Bed & Breakfast	★★★		
Stranraer	Aird Donald Caravan Park	DG9 8RN	01776 702025	Touring Park	★★★★		
	Auld Diary Cottage		01776 840242	Self Catering	★★★★	⸙	
	Balyett House B&B	DG9 8QL	01776 703395	Bed & Breakfast	★★★★		
	Barnhills Farm	DG9 0QG	01776 853236	Bed & Breakfast	★★★★		
	Braefield Guest House	DG9 8TA	01776 810255	Guest House	★★★	⸙	
	Braeside Cottage		01776 820684	Self Catering	★★★		
	Cairnryan House	DG9 8QX	01581 200624	Guest House	★★★		
	Clanna Susaidh		01776 810555	Self Catering	★★★★		
	Crosshaven Guest House	DG9 7AL	01776 700598	Bed & Breakfast	★★★		
	Culmore Bridge Cottages		01776 830539	Self Catering	★★★★	♿	
	Dairy Cottage East Challoch Farmhouse		01581 400391	Self Catering	★★★		
	Drumlochart Caravan Park	DG9 0RN	01776 870232	Holiday Park	★★★★★		
	Dundrum Cottage		07769 806259	Self Catering	★★★★★		
	Dunskey Estate Cottages – Blair Cottage		01776 810211	Self Catering	★★		
	Dunskey Guest House	DG9 8TD	01776 810241	Guest House	★★		
	East Challoch Farmhouse	DG9 8PY	01581 400391	Farm House	★★★		
	East Muntloch Croft B&B	DG9 9HN	01776 840264	Bed & Breakfast	★★★★		
	Fernhill Hotel	DG9 8TD	01776 810220	Hotel	★★★	⸙	
	Fernlea	DG9 7AQ	01776 703 037	Bed & Breakfast	★★★★		

♿ Unassisted wheelchair access   ♿ Assisted wheelchair access   ⸙ Access for visitors with mobility difficulties
𝒫 Bronze Green Tourism Award   𝒫𝒫 Silver Green Tourism Award   𝒫𝒫𝒫 Gold Green Tourism Award
For further information on our Green Tourism Business Scheme please see page 7.

488   To find out more go to visitscotland.com

Location	Property Name	Postcode	Telephone	Classification	Star Rating	
Stranraer	Glen Auchie Cottage		01776 840264	Self Catering	★★★	
	Glenlee Cottage		01776 840326	Self Catering	★★★★	
	Glenotter	DG9 0EP	01776 703199	Bed & Breakfast	★★★★	
	Harbour Guest House	DG9 7RF	01776 704626	Guest House	★★★	
	Harbour Lights Guest House	DG9 7JY	01776 706261	Guest House	★★★	
	Harbour Row – Gigha		01776 840631	Self Catering	★★★ to ★★★★	
	Ivy House & Ferry Link	DG9 8ER	01776 704176	Guest House	★★★	
	Keek Afar		01581 600228	Self Catering	★★★	
	Kildonan	DG9 8HP	01776 704186	Bed & Breakfast	★★★★	
	Kittiwake House		0131 2439335	Self Catering	★★★	
	Knockinaam Lodge	DG9 9AD	01776 810471	Small Hotel	★★★★	
	Mid Muntloch Farm		01776 840225	Self Catering	★★★	
	Morroch Cottage		01457 862128	Self Catering	★★★ to ★★★★	
	Mull of Galloway Holiday Park	DG9 9RD	01581 500227	Holiday Park	★★★★	
	New England Bay Caravan Club Site	DG9 9NX	01342 336842	Touring Park	★★★★★	
	No 3D Hill Street		0141 5809113	Self Catering	★★★	
	North West Castle Hotel	DG9 8EH	01776 704413	Hotel	★★★★	
	Old Lighthouse Keepers' Cottage		0131 2439335	Self Catering	★★★	
	Plantings Inn	DG9 8SQ	01581 400633	Inn	★★★	
	Port-O-Spittal Bungalow		01776 810412	Self Catering	★★★★	
	Portpatrick Hotel	DG9 8TQ	01776 810333	Hotel	★★	⚐
	Port-side Cottage		02893 341733	Self Catering	★★	
	Puffin House		0131 2439335	Self Catering	★★★	
	Rhins of Galloway	DG9 8QU	01581 200294	Guest House	★★★	
	Rickwood House Hotel	DG9 8TD	01776 810270	Guest House	★★★	
	Sandeel House		01449 744287	Self Catering	★★★	
	Sands of Luce Holiday Park	DG9 9JN	01776 830456	Holiday Park	★★★★	
	Southpark Bed & Breakfast	DG9 8AD	01776 889706	Bed & Breakfast	★★	
	The Homestead	DG9 8QX	01581 200203	Bed & Breakfast	★★★	
	The Knowe		01655 770343	Self Catering	★★★★	
	The Lodge		01776 703833	Self Catering	★★★	⚐
	The Loft		01776 702994	Self Catering	★★★★	
	The Port House		07786 262082	Self Catering	★★★★	
	The Stable & The Hayloft		01776 704086	Self Catering	★★★	
	The Waterfront Hotel	DG9 8SX	01776 810800	Small Hotel	★★★	
	Tigh-Na-Mara Hotel & Restaurant	DG9 9JF	01776 830210	Restaurant With Rooms	★★★	
	Torrs Warren Country House Hotel	DG9 9DH	01776 830204	Small Hotel	★★★	
	Wig Bay Holiday Park	DG9 0PS	01776 853233	Holiday Park	★★★★	
Strathaven	Drumboy Lodge		01357 440544	Self Catering	★★★★	⚐
	Rissons at Springvale	ML10 6AD	01357 521131	Restaurant With Rooms	★★★	⚐
	Strathaven Hotel	ML10 6SZ	01357 521778	Hotel	★★★	🄿
	The Sheiling	ML10 6DA	01357 520477	Bed & Breakfast	★★	
Strathcarron	Airdaniar Cottage		01520 744320	Self Catering	★★★	
	Applecross Campsite	IV54 8ND	01520 744268	Touring Park	★★★	
	Applecross Inn	IV54 8LR	01520 744262	Inn	★★★	🄿🄿
	Aurora B&B	IV54 8XN	01520 755246	Bed & Breakfast	★★★★	

♿ Unassisted wheelchair access ♿ Assisted wheelchair access ⚐ Access for visitors with mobility difficulties
🄿 Bronze Green Tourism Award 🄿🄿 Silver Green Tourism Award 🄿🄿🄿 Gold Green Tourism Award
For further information on our Green Tourism Business Scheme please see page 7.

Advertisers' locations have been sorted by postcode. In Scotland, postcodes can cover fairly large geographical areas.
Please check distance of property from specified location with the individual provider. VisitScotland cannot take any responsibility for this.

489

Directory of all VisitScotland Assured Serviced Establishments, ordered by location.
Establishments highlighted have an advertisement in this guide.

Location	Property Name	Postcode	Telephone	Classification	Star Rating
Strathcarron	Campbell House		0151 5472356	Self Catering	★★★
	Ceol-Na-Mara		01463 220858	Self Catering	★★★
	Craig Cottage		01520 755367	Self Catering	★★★★
	Fearnmore Church		01520 744263	Self Catering	★★★
	Holly's House		01520 744399	Self Catering	★★★★
	Lochcarron Holiday Properties – Seabank		01520 766288	Self Catering	★★★ to ★★★★
	Lotta Dubh	IV54 8YL	01520 722405	Bed & Breakfast	★★★
	Rockvilla Hotel	IV54 8YB	01520 722379	Inn	★★★
	Rose Cottage		01706 826590	Self Catering	★★★★
	Rowan Cottage		01252 852382	Self Catering	★★★★
	Struan Cottage		01309 690267	Self Catering	★★★
	Tigh Ruaraidh		0116 2605726	Self Catering	★★★★
	Tortola Log Cabin		01520 755248	Self Catering	★★★★
Strathdon	Auld Cummerton	AB36 8UP	01975 651337	Bed & Breakfast	★★★★★
	Buchaam Farm – Gammock & Cairnbeg		01975 651238	Self Catering	★★★
	Craigiedows Cottage		01975 564334	Self Catering	★★★
	Jenny's Bothy Crofthouse	AB36 8YP	01975 651449	Hostel	★★★
	Kildrummy Castle Hotel	AB36 8RA	01975 571288	Country House Hotel	★★★★
	The Colquhonnie House Hotel	AB36 8UN	01975 651210	Inn	★★★
Strathpeffer	8 Kinellan Drive		01997 421506	Self Catering	★★★
	An Darach	IV14 9EL	01997 421408	Bed & Breakfast	★★★★
	Ben Wyvis Hotel	IV14 9DN	0870 9506264	Hotel	★★★
	Ben Wyvis Lodges – Eagle Cottage		01224 318520	Self Catering	★★★
	Birch Cottage		01997 421075	Self Catering	★★★
	Birch Lodge	IV14 9BA	01997 420118	Bed & Breakfast	★★★
	Coul House Hotel	IV14 9ES	01997 421487	Country House Hotel	★★★
	Craigvar	IV14 9DL	01997 421622	Bed & Breakfast	★★★★
	Garden House	IV14 9BJ	01997 421242	Guest House	★★★
	Highland Hotel	IV14 9AS	01997 421457	Hotel	★★
	Kinettas Cottage		01997 421053	Self Catering	★★★
	Nutwood House		01997 421344	Self Catering	★★★★
	Riverside Chalets & Caravan Park	IV14 9ES	07765 633482	Touring Park	★★
	White Lodge	IV14 9AL	01997 421730	Bed & Breakfast	★★★★
Strome Ferry	Portachullin Holidays		01599 577267	Self Catering	★★★★
	Soluis Mu Thuath	IV53 8UP	01599 577219	Guest House	★★★
Stromness	10 Graham Place		01856 850581	Self Catering	★★
	16 Graham Place		01856 850818	Self Catering	★★★
	2 Victoria House	KW16 3AJ	01856 761543	Awaiting Grading	
	30 Hillside Road		01856 850042	Self Catering	★★★
	41 & 43 John Street		01856 850469	Self Catering	★★★
	45 John Street	KW16 3AD	01856 850949	Bed & Breakfast	★★★
	52 Dundas Street		01856 850255	Self Catering	★★★★
	Asgard	KW16 3JS	01856 851699	Bed & Breakfast	★★★★
	Bachylis Self Catering		01856 811363	Self Catering	★★★
	Ben End		01651 862234	Self Catering	★★★★
	Braehead Farm		01856 851313	Self Catering	★★★★
	Brown's Hostel	KW16 3BS	01856 850661	Hostel	★★★

Location	Property Name	Postcode	Telephone	Classification	Star Rating
Stromness	Burnhouse		01856 870058	Self Catering	★★★
	Burnlee		01856 811242	Self Catering	★★★★
	Burnside B&B	KW16 3LJ	01856 850723	Awaiting Grading	
	Camusbeag		01856 851043	Self Catering	★★★
	Cliffgate		01856 771231	Self Catering	★★★★
	Congesquoy No 1		01856 850302	Self Catering	★★★
	Cottage of Oback		01856 751283	Self Catering	★★★
	Ferry Inn	KW16 3AA	01856 850280	Inn	★★
	Ferrybank	KW16 3AG	01856 851250	Bed & Breakfast	★★★★
	Fisherman's Cottage	KW16 3DF	01856 850345	Awaiting Grading	
	Hall of Clestrain		01856 850365	Self Catering	★★★
	Hamnavoe Hostel	KW16 3AG	01856 851202	Hostel	★★★★
	Harbourlee House		01856 850661	Self Catering	★★★
	Harbourside Self Catering		01856 851969	Self Catering	★★★
	Ingasquoy Lets		01357 520813	Self Catering	★★★
	Langaskaill Flat 1		01856 761200	Self Catering	★★★
	Lenahowe Apt. 1 & 2	KW16 3JA	01856 841523	Awaiting Grading	
	Lindisfarne	KW16 3LL	01856 850828	Bed & Breakfast	★★★
	Lindisfarne		01856 850828	Self Catering	★★★
	Lochend		01856 851003	Self Catering	★★★
	Mill of Eyrland	KW16 3HA	01856 850136	Bed & Breakfast	★★★★
	Millers House & Harbourside B&B	KW16 3AD	01856 851969	Guest House	★★★
	Netherstove Cottage		01856 841625	Self Catering	★★
	Newcott		01856 850072	Self Catering	★★★
	Odin		01224 593029	Self Catering	★★★★
	Old Hall	KW16 3PQ	01856 701213	Awaiting Grading	
	Orca Guest House	KW16 3BS	01856 850447	Guest House	★★
	Outbrecks Cottages		01856 851223	Self Catering	★★★
	Overbigging		07802 204141	Self Catering	★★★★
	Peedie Cottage		01856 850438	Self Catering	★★★
	Pier House		01856 850415	Self Catering	★★★★
	Point of Ness Caravan & Camping Site	KW16	01856 873535	Touring Park	★★★
	Pools		01856 701211	Self Catering	★★★★
	Pools		01856 701211	Self Catering	★★★★
	Portsmouth Point		01856 851209	Self Catering	★★★
	Quildon Apartment 1 Quildon Apartment 2		01856 851830	Self Catering	★★★★
	Quoydale	KW16 3NJ	01856 791315	Bed & Breakfast	★★★
	Rackwick Outdoor Centre	KW16 3NJ	01856 873535	Hostel	★★★
	South Heddle		01856 761282	Self Catering	★★★
	Springfield		01856 850776	Self Catering	★★★★
	Standing Stones Hotel	KW16 3JX	01856 850449	Small Hotel	★★★
	Stromabank	KW16 3PA	01856 701494	Small Hotel	★★★
	Stromness Hotel	KW16 3AA	01856 850298	Hotel	★★★
	Summerdale Self Catering		01856 811285	Self Catering	★★★
	The Ben Quoybow		01856 851476	Self Catering	★★★
	The Cottage		01856 851032	Self Catering	★★★
	The Peedie Hoose		01856 876933	Self Catering	★★★★
	Upper Flat		01856 851202	Self Catering	★★★★

 ♿ Unassisted wheelchair access ♿ Assisted wheelchair access ▲ Access for visitors with mobility difficulties
 Ⓩ Bronze Green Tourism Award ℕℕ Silver Green Tourism Award ℕℕℕ Gold Green Tourism Award
For further information on our Green Tourism Business Scheme please see page 7.

Advertisers' locations have been sorted by postcode. In Scotland, postcodes can cover fairly large geographical areas.
Please check distance of property from specified location with the individual provider. VisitScotland cannot take any responsibility for this.

491

Location	Property Name	Postcode	Telephone	Classification	Star Rating
Stromness	Voe Cottages		01856 851077	Self Catering	★★★
	Westslate	KW16 3JN	01856 851234	Awaiting Grading	
	Wild Heather B&B At Millhouse	KW16 3NU	01856 791098	Bed & Breakfast	★★★★
Tain	Achintoul Lets		07944 255097	Self Catering	★★★
	Broomton Farmhouse	IV20 1XN	01862 832831	Awaiting Grading	
	Carringtons	IV19 1PY	01862 892635	Bed & Breakfast	★★★
	Cartomie	IV19 1LB	01862 821599	Bed & Breakfast	★★★
	Dolphin View – The Cottages		01862 871576	Self Catering	★★★★
	Dornoch Firth Caravan Park	IV19 1JX	01862 892292	Holiday Park	★★★★
	Dunbius Guest House	IV19 1HP	01862 894902	Guest House	★★★
	Edderton Inn	IV19 1LB	01862 821588	Inn	★★★ ♿
	Fearn Hotel	IV20 1TJ	01862 832234	Awaiting Grading	Awaiting Grading
	Golf View Guest House	IV19 1BN	01862 892856	Guest House	★★★★
	Hamilton Cottage		07775 826108	Self Catering	★★★
	Mo Dhachaidh		01356 623543	Self Catering	★★★★
	Morangie B&B	IV19 1PY	01862 893855	Bed & Breakfast	★★★
	No 3 Tarrel Farm Cottages		020 84402826	Self Catering	★★★
	Ross Villa	IV19 1BN	01862 894746	Awaiting Grading	
	Royal Hotel	IV19 1AB	01862 892013	Hotel	★★★
	Shepherd's Cottage		01862 832720	Self Catering	★★★★
	Sycamore Country Lettings		07997 458207	Self Catering	★★★★
Tarbert	Afton Lodge		0141 9422792	Self Catering	★★★
	Ardglass	PA29 6TR	01880 820884	Bed & Breakfast	★★★
	Ardyne		07940 564192	Self Catering	★★★★
	Barr Na Criche	PA29 6YA	01880 820833	Bed & Breakfast	★★★
	Barr Na Criche Cottage		01880 820833	Self Catering	★★★
	Crossaig Lodge	PA29 6YQ	01880 760369	Awaiting Grading	
	Crubasdale Lodge Chalet		01583 421358	Self Catering	★★
	Dunivaig B&B	PA29 6UG	01880 820896	Bed & Breakfast	★★★
	Dunmore Court		01880 820833	Self Catering	★★
	Dunultach	PA29 6XW	01880 740650	Bed & Breakfast	★★★★
	Jura		01583 421207	Self Catering	★★★ ♟
	Killean Estate – Killean House		01257 266511	Self Catering	★★★
	Knap Guest House	PA29 6SX	01880 820015	Guest House	★★★★
	Laundry Cottage		01880 770217	Self Catering	★★★
	Marviesta		0141 3577134	Self Catering	★★★
	Petersville		0141 3343935	Self Catering	★★★
	Point Sands	PA29 6XG	01583 441263	Holiday Park	★★★
	Port Ban Holiday Park Ltd	PA29 6YD	01880 770224	Holiday Park	★★★★
	Rhu House	PA29 6YF	01880 820231	Bed & Breakfast	★★★
	Skipness Holiday Cottages – Middle Seaview		01880 760207	Self Catering	★★
	Stables Cottage		01880 740635	Self Catering	★★★
	Stonefield Castle Hotel	PA29 6YJ		Awaiting Grading	
	Struan House B&B	PA29 6UD	01880 820190	Bed & Breakfast	★★★★
	Tigh-Na-Creage		01583 421270	Self Catering	★
	Wee Dunultach		01880 740650	Self Catering	★★★★
	West Loch Hotel	PA29 6YF	01880 820283	Inn	★★

Location	Property Name	Postcode	Telephone	Classification	Star Rating		
Taynuilt	Achadacallan		01866 822775	Self Catering	★★★		
	Airdeny Chalets – Muckairn/Bonawe & Kilchurn		01866 822648	Self Catering	★★★	♿	🌿
	Airds Cottage		01866 822349	Self Catering	★★★		
	Ardabhaigh		01499 302736	Self Catering	★★★★		
	Ardanaiseig Hotel	PA35 1HE	01866 833333	Country House Hotel	★★★★		
	Ballimore House		07775 802050	Self Catering	★★★★		
	Collaig House	PA35 1HG	01866 833202	Bed & Breakfast	★★★★		
	Cruailinn	PA35 1HY	01866 822351	Bed & Breakfast	★★★		
	Cuilreoch	PA35 1HG	01866 833236	Holiday Caravan	Pass	Pass	
	Curacao Holiday Caravan	PA35 1HW	01866 822636	Holiday Caravan			
	Druimdarroch Cottage		01416 479016	Self Catering	★★★		
	Garden Cottage		01866 844212	Self Catering	★★★		
	Holly and Garden and Hydrangea		01866 822309	Self Catering	★★★		🌿
	Kirkton Cottage		01866 822657	Self Catering	★★★		
	Literature		01866 844065	Self Catering	★★		
	Loch Awe Holiday Park	PA35 1HT	01866 822666	Holiday Park	★★★		
	Roineabhal Country House	PA35 1HD	01866 833207	Bed & Breakfast	★★★★	♿	
	Sithean		01866 822110	Self Catering	★★★★	♿	🌿
	Tanglewood Lodge Bed and Breakfast	PA35 1HP	01866 822114	Bed & Breakfast	★★★★		
	Taychreggan Hotel	PA35 1HQ	01866 833211	Country House Hotel	★★★		
	Taynuilt Hotel	PA35 1JN	01866 822437	Inn	★★★		
	Tigh an Daraich – Rowan Tree		01866 822693	Self Catering	★★★★	♿	
Tayport	Forgan B&B	DD6 9AE	01382 552682	Bed & Breakfast	★★★		
	Tayport B&B	DD6 9JZ	01382 552272	Bed & Breakfast	★★★		
Thornhill	Buccleuch & Queensberry Hotel	DG3 5LU	01848 330215	Inn	★★★		
	Causies Cross Guest House	DG3 4HN	01848 200719	Bed & Breakfast	★★★		
	Clonwood		01524 791283	Self Catering	★★★		
	Hillcrest Barn		01848 331557	Self Catering	★★★		
	Hope Cottage		01848 331510	Self Catering	★★★★		
	Millhouse Cotage		07765 252760	Self Catering	★★★		
	Morton Mains Cottage		0770 2880574	Self Catering	★		
	Old Tannery Cottage		01848 330116	Self Catering	★★★★		
	Penpont Caravan Park	DG3 4BQ	07710 267547	Holiday Park	★★★		
	Scaurbank Cottage		01848 330933	Self Catering	★★★★		
	Templand Cottages – Thomas Carlyle		01848 330775	Self Catering	★★★		
	The Bothy at the Garth		01848 200364	Self Catering	★★★		
	The Flying School		01848 332260	Self Catering	★★★★★		
	The Thornhill Inn	DG3 5LU	01848 330326	Inn	★★★		
	Volunteer Arms Hotel	DG3 4BP	01848 330381	Inn	★★★		
Thurso	1 Granville Crescent	KW14 7NP	01847 892993	Bed & Breakfast	★★★★		
	25 Airdneiskich		01847 831544	Self Catering	★★★★		
	9 Couper Street	KW14 8AR	01847 894529	Bed & Breakfast	★★★		
	Armadale Farm Cottage	KW14 7SA	01325 300347	Awaiting Grading			
	Ash Cottage		01847 821633	Self Catering	★★★		
	Bairlinnean		01847 895653	Self Catering	★★★		
	Bighouse Lodge	KW14 7YJ	01641 531207	Awaiting Grading			
	Borgie Lodge Hotel	KW14 7TH	01641 521332	Small Hotel	★★		

♿ Unassisted wheelchair access   ♿ Assisted wheelchair access   🚶 Access for visitors with mobility difficulties
🌿 Bronze Green Tourism Award   🌿 Silver Green Tourism Award   🌿 Gold Green Tourism Award
For further information on our Green Tourism Business Scheme please see page 7.

Advertisers' locations have been sorted by postcode. In Scotland, postcodes can cover fairly large geographical areas.
Please check distance of property from specified location with the individual provider. VisitScotland cannot take any responsibility for this.

493

Location	Property Name	Postcode	Telephone	Classification	Star Rating		
Thurso	Castle Arms Hotel	KW14 8XH	01847 851992	Small Hotel	★★		
	Celtic Firs	KW14 8XW	01847 581851	Holiday Caravan	Pass		
	Creag Na Mara	KW14 8XL	01847 851850	Guest House	★★★	⋏	𝘱𝘱
	Curlew Cottage		01847 895638	Self Catering	★★★★	⋏	
	Dhualton		01159 403352	Self Catering	★★		
	Dunnet Bay Caravan Club Site	KW14 8XD	01342 336842	Touring Park	★★★★★		
	Forss House Hotel	KW14 7XY	01847 861201	Country House Hotel	★★★★	⋏	𝘱
	Halladale Inn Caravan Park	KW14 7YJ	01641 531282	Touring Park	★★★★		
	Halladale Inn Chalet Park		01641 531282	Self Catering	★★		
	Hughag's House		01452 525627	Self Catering	★★★		
	Lau-ren House	KW14 8SY	01847 851717	Bed & Breakfast	★★★		
	Melvich Hotel	KW14 7YJ	01641 531206	Small Hotel	★★★		
	Midskerry Cottage		01307 463324	Self Catering	★★		
	Murray House	KW14 7HD	01847 895759	Bed & Breakfast	★★★		
	Park Hotel	KW14 8RE	01847 893251	Small Hotel	★★★	♿	𝘱𝘱
	Pentland Hotel	KW14 7AA	01847 893202	Hotel	★★★		
	Pentland Lodge House	KW14 7JN	01847 895103	Guest House	★★★★	♿	
	Poulouriscaig	KW14 7SA	01641 541269	Holiday Caravan			
	Rhivale		0121 4442683	Self Catering	★★★		
	Royal Hotel	KW14 8EH		Awaiting Grading			
	Sandra's Hostel	KW14 7BQ	01847 894575	Hostel	★★★★		
	Scrabster Caravan Park	KW14 8BN	01847 893524	Holiday Caravan			
	Sharvedda	KW14 7RY	01641 541311	Bed & Breakfast	★★★★		
	Sheigra	KW14 7EL	01847 892559	Bed & Breakfast	★★★		
	Shormary Cottage		01847 892892	Self Catering	★★★		
	Skara	KW14 8YN	01847 890062	Bed & Breakfast	★★★		
	St Clair Hotel	KW14 7AJ	01847 896481	Hotel	★★★		
	Starbank		01476 561239	Self Catering	★★★		
	Station Hotel	KW14 7DH	01847 892003	Hotel	★★★		
	Strath Halladale Partnership		01641 571271	Self Catering	★★★		
	Straven	KW14 8YN	01847 893850	Bed & Breakfast	★★★		
	The Castletown Hotel	KW14 8TP	01847 821656	Hotel	★★		
	The Croft		01847 851889	Self Catering	★★★★		
	The Ferry Inn	KW14 7UJ	01847 892814	Inn	★★★		
	The Holborn	KW14 7BQ	01847 892771	Inn	★★		
	The Old Inn	KW14 7RE	01847 811554	Bed & Breakfast	★★★		
	The Sheiling	KW14 7YG	01641 531256	Awaiting Grading			
	The Strathy Inn	KW14 7RY	01641 541205	Awaiting Grading			
	Weigh Inn Hotel	KW14 7UG	01847 893722	Hotel	★★★		𝘱
Tighnabruaich	Acharossan House		01369 860377	Self Catering	★★★★★		
	Connas Cottage		01700 811346	Self Catering	★★		
	Glenahuil		01700 811616	Self Catering	★★★		
	Kames Hotel	PA21 2AF	01700 811489	Inn	★★★		
	Kilfinan Hotel	PA21 2EP	01700 821201	Inn	★★★		
	The Annexe		01700 821235	Self Catering	★★		
Tillicoultry	Bramble Cottage	FK13 6BU	01259 751341	Bed & Breakfast	★★★		
	Harviestoun Country Hotel & Restaurant	FK13 6PQ	01259 752522	Small Hotel	★★★		

♿ Unassisted wheelchair access ♿ Assisted wheelchair access ⋏ Access for visitors with mobility difficulties
𝘱 Bronze Green Tourism Award 𝘱𝘱 Silver Green Tourism Award 𝘱𝘱𝘱 Gold Green Tourism Award
For further information on our Green Tourism Business Scheme please see page 7.

Location	Property Name	Postcode	Telephone	Classification	Star Rating		
Tillicoultry	West Wing – Westbourne House		01259 750314	Self Catering	★★★★		
	Westbourne	FK13 6PA	01259 750314	Bed & Breakfast	★★★		
	Wyvis	FK13 6EA	01259 751513	Bed & Breakfast	★★★★		🄿
Tranent	47 Carlaverock Avenue	EH33 2PW	01875 614008	Bed & Breakfast	★★★		
	Adniston Manor	EH33 1EA	01875 611190	Guest House	★★★★	🜊	
	Bramble Cottage		01875 340547	Self Catering	★★★★★		
	Elvingston Apartment		01875 408020	Self Catering	★★★		
	Oor Ecks, 103 Preston Avenue		0131 665 6113	Self Catering	★★★		
	Rosebank Guest House	EH33 1LP	01875 610967	Guest House	★★★		
	Schiehallion	EH33 1BA	01875 611224	Bed & Breakfast	★★★★		
	The Tower	EH33 2LE	0131 6657654	Bed & Breakfast	★★★★		
	Wintonhill Farmhouse		01875 340222	Self Catering	★★★★	🜊	
	Woodside		0131 6657654	Self Catering	★★★★		
Troon	124a Bentinck Drive		0207 6373225	Self Catering	★★★		
	24H Bradan Road		07770 220840	Self Catering	★★★		
	Barcelo Troon Marine Hotel	KA10 6HE	01292 314444	Hotel	★★★	🜊	
	Copper Beech	KA10 6JB	01292 314100	Bed & Breakfast	★★★★		
	Hillcrest		01292 312534	Self Catering	★★★		
	Hillhouse	KA10 7HU	01292 676400	Exclusive Use Venue	★★★★★		
	Lochgreen House	KA10 7EN	01292 313343	Hotel	★★★★★		
	No 2 Troon Road	KA10 7EY	01292 679927	Bed & Breakfast	★★★★		
	Piersland House Hotel	KA10 6HD	01292 314747	Hotel	★★★★	🜊	
	Portland Villa		07773 297674	Self Catering	★★★★		
	Rutland House		0141 6384428	Self Catering	★★★★		
	South Beach Hotel	KA10 6EG	01292 312033	Hotel	★★★	♿	
	Tigh Dearg	KA10 6JF	01292 311552	Bed & Breakfast	★★★		
Turriff	Ardmiddle Mains Self Catering Cottages		01888 562443	Self Catering	★★★★		🄿
	Ashwood		01888 563479	Self Catering	★★★	♿	
	Deveron Lodge B&B Guesthouse	AB53 4ES	01888 563613	Guest House	★★★★	♿	🄿🄿🄿
	Fife Arms Hotel	AB53 4AE	01888 563124	Restaurant With Rooms	★★★		
	Garden Cottage		01888 544230	Self Catering	★★★★	♿	
	Garden Cottage		0131 2439335	Self Catering	★★★★		
	Monydeen Enterprises	AB53 5RA	01888 568937	Bed & Breakfast	★★★★		
	Nettle Cottages		01888 511168	Self Catering	★★★★		
	Penelopefield House		01888 562486	Self Catering	★★		
	Preston Tower Apartment		0131 2439331	Self Catering	★★★		
	Seggat Farm Cottages		01888 511223	Self Catering	★★★★	🜊	
	Stonefolds Farm Cottages		01651 891267	Self Catering	★★★★	🜊	
	Tehillah Farm Cottage (The Bothy)		01651 806376	Self Catering	★★★★		
	The Bothy		01464 871272	Self Catering	★★★★	🜊	
	The Gables	AB53 4ER	01888 568715	Bed & Breakfast	★★★		
	Turriff Caravan Park	AB53 7ER	01888 568867	Holiday Park	★★★★		
			01888 562443	Self Catering	★★★★		🄿
Ullapool	3 Castle Terrace	IV26 2XD	01854 612409	Bed & Breakfast	★★★		
	3 Vyner Place	IV26 2XR	01854 612023	Bed & Breakfast	★★★★		
	Achininver Youth Hostel	IV26 2YL	08701 553255	Hostel	★★		🄿

♿ Unassisted wheelchair access   ♿ Assisted wheelchair access   🜊 Access for visitors with mobility difficulties
🄿 Bronze Green Tourism Award   🄿🄿 Silver Green Tourism Award   🄿🄿🄿 Gold Green Tourism Award
For further information on our Green Tourism Business Scheme please see page 7.

Advertisers' locations have been sorted by postcode. In Scotland, postcodes can cover fairly large geographical areas.
Please check distance of property from specified location with the individual provider. VisitScotland cannot take any responsibility for this.

495

Location	Property Name	Postcode	Telephone	Classification	Star Rating	
Ullapool	Ailleag		0208 4687086	Self Catering	★★★★	
	Ardmair House		0141 6341681	Self Catering	★★★	
	Ardvreck		01294 216991	Self Catering	★★★	
	Ardvreck Guest House	IV26 2TH	01854 612028	Guest House	★★★★	
	Beinn Ghobhlach		01854 666217	Self Catering	★★★	
	Benwell House	IV26 2UB	01971 502039	Awaiting Grading		
	Bothan na Tilleadh		01854 622448	Self Catering	★★	
	Braemore Square	IV23 2RX	01854 655357	Bed & Breakfast	★★★★	𝒫𝒫
	Broombank	IV26 2XD	01854 612247	Bed & Breakfast	★★★	
	Caberfeidh		01339 886232	Self Catering	★★★	
	Caledonian Hotel	IV26 2UG		Hotel	★★	
	Chenoweth Bed and Breakfast	IV26 2TP	01854 666331	Bed & Breakfast	★★★	
	Cottage		018546 22361	Self Catering	★★★	
	Croft House		01854 622340	Self Catering	★★★ to ★★★★	
	Dolphin Flat		01235 763139	Self Catering	★★	
	Dromnan Guest House	IV26 2SX	01854 612333	Guest House	★★★★	⋏
	Eilean Donan Guest House	IV26 2XE	01854 612524	Guest House	★★★	
	Essex Cottage	IV26 2UU	01854 612663	Bed & Breakfast	★★★	
	Farm Cottage		01854 622348	Self Catering	★★★★	
	Hallival		01854 612680	Self Catering	★★★★	
	Highveld		01854 612947	Self Catering	★★★	
	Island View		01463 223225	Self Catering	★★★	⋏
	Kilbrannan		01854 612236	Self Catering	★★★★	
	Newton		01971 502221	Self Catering	★★★★	
	No 3 Broom Cottages		01854 613126	Self Catering	★★★	
	Oakworth	IV26 2TE	01854 612290	Bed & Breakfast	★★★	
	Point Cottage	IV26 2UR	01854 612494	Guest House	★★★★	
	Riverside	IV26 2UE	01854 612239	Guest House	★★★	
	Royal Hotel	IV26 2SY	01854 612181	Hotel	★★★	
	Rubha Mor Self Catering		01854 612323	Self Catering	★★★★	♿
	Seagulls		0208 3360843	Self Catering	★★★★	
	Tamarin	IV26 2SZ	01854 612667	Bed & Breakfast	★★★★	
	The Argyll Hotel	IV26 2UB	01854 612422	Small Hotel	★★	
	The Chalet & The Cottage		01854 612272	Self Catering	★★	
	The Ferry Boat Inn	IV26 2UJ	01854 612366	Inn	★★★	
	The Haven		01463 234826	Self Catering	★★	
	The Old Post Office		01483 421524	Self Catering	★★★	
	The Steading		01854 622416	Self Catering	★★★★	⋏
	Tigh Na Reultan		01854 012775	Self Catering	★★★★	
	Tigh Na Sith		01732 367827	Self Catering	★★★	
	Torran	IV23 2SG	01854 655227	Bed & Breakfast	★★★	
	Ullapool Youth Hostel	IV26 2UJ	08701 553255	Hostel	★★★	𝒫𝒫
	Waterfront Cottage		01854 613454	Self Catering	★★★	
	West House Bed & Breakfast	IV26 2TY	01854 613126	Bed & Breakfast	★★★	
	Westlea Guest House	IV26 2XE	01854 612594	Guest House	★★★★	
			01854 622340	Self Catering	★★★	

♿ Unassisted wheelchair access   ♿ Assisted wheelchair access   ⋏ Access for visitors with mobility difficulties
𝒫 Bronze Green Tourism Award   𝒫𝒫 Silver Green Tourism Award   𝒫𝒫𝒫 Gold Green Tourism Award
For further information on our Green Tourism Business Scheme please see page 7.

496   To find out more go to visitscotland.com

Location	Property Name	Postcode	Telephone	Classification	Star Rating		
Walkerburn	Eliburn Cottage		01896 870218	Self Catering	★★★★		
	The George Hotel	EH43 6AF	01896 870336	Inn	★★		
	Windlestraw Lodge	EH43 6AA	01896 870636	Country House Hotel	★★★★		
Wemyss Bay	Wemyss Bay Holiday Park	PA18 6BA	01475 520812	Holiday Park	★★★★		𝒫𝒫
West Calder	Limefield House	EH55 8QL	01506 871237	Awaiting Grading			
	Orlege		01501 785205	Self Catering	★★★	ⓖ	𝒫𝒫𝒫
West Kilbride	Millstonford House Bed & Breakfast	KA23 9PS	01294 823430	Bed & Breakfast	★★★		
	Portencross Holiday Cottage		01294 829236	Self Catering	★★★		
	Seamill Hydro	KA23 9NB	01294 822217	Hotel	★★★		𝒫𝒫
	The Ploughman's Rest		01294 822281	Self Catering	★★★★		
West Linton	Anne's Cottage		01968 682256	Self Catering	★★★		
	Croft Loft		01968 661333	Self Catering	★★★★		
	Drochil Castle Farm	EH46 7DD	01721 752249	Bed & Breakfast	★★★★	ⓖ	𝒫
	Ingraston Farm B&B	EH46 7AA	01968 682219	Farm House	★★★	𝝜	
	Jerviswood	EH46 7DT	01968 660429	Bed & Breakfast	★★		
	Loch Cottage		01968 660401	Self Catering	★★★		
	Mill Cottage		01968 660887	Self Catering	★★★★	𝝜	
	Millburn House Bed & Breakfast	EH46 7AF	01968 682252	Bed & Breakfast	★★★★		
	The Meadows	EH46 7JD	01968 661798	Bed & Breakfast	★★★		
Westhill	Aberdeen Westhill Premier Inn	AB32 6HF	0870 9906348	Budget Hotel	Pass	Pass	
	Holiday Inn Aberdeen West	AB32 6TT	01224 270300	Hotel	★★★★	♿	
	Kilnhall	AB32 6TB	01224 742440	Guest House	★★★★		
	Pond Cottage		01224 743033	Self Catering	★★★★		
	Struan	AB32 6UL	01330 860799	Bed & Breakfast	★★★★		
Wick	Auld Post Office B&B	KW1 5XR	01847 841391	Bed & Breakfast	★★★★		
	Bank House Bed & Breakfast	KW1 4NG	01955 604001	Guest House	★★★		
	Bayview	KW1 4JJ	01955 604054	Bed & Breakfast	★★★		
	Belhaven	KW1 4JJ	01955 603411	Bed & Breakfast	★★★		
	Bencorragh House	KW1 4YD	01955 611449	Farm House	★★★		
	Bower Old Free Church House	KW1 4YY	01955 661222	Awaiting Grading			
	Corner House		01955 603500	Self Catering	★★★★		
	Gardeners Cottage		01955 621226	Self Catering	★★★★		
	Horseman's Cottage		01955 611239	Self Catering	★★★		
	John O'Groats Caravan Park	KW1 4YR	01955 611329	Touring Park	★★★		
	John O'Groats Youth Hostel	KW1 4YH	08701 553255	Hostel	★★★		𝒫𝒫
	Mackays Hotel	KW1 5ED	07775 671630	Hotel	★★★		
	Mill House	KW1 4YR	01955 611239	Bed & Breakfast	★★★		
	Nethercliffe Hotel	KW1 4NS	01955 602044	Small Hotel	★★★		
	Queens Hotel	KW1 5PZ	01955 602992	Small Hotel	★★		
	Seaview Guest House	KW1 4JH	01955 602735	Bed & Breakfast	★★★		
	Seaview Hotel	KW1 4YR	01955 611220	Small Hotel	★★		𝒫𝒫
	Sinclair Bay Hotel	KW1 4UY	01955 631233	Inn	★★		
	The Clachan	KW1 5NJ	01955 605384	Bed & Breakfast	★★★★		
	Wick Caravan & Camping Park	KW1 4RG	01955 605420	Touring Park	★★★★		
Wishaw	Herdshill Guest House	ML2 8HA	01698 381579	Guest House	★★★		

♿ Unassisted wheelchair access   ⓖ Assisted wheelchair access   𝝜 Access for visitors with mobility difficulties
𝒫 Bronze Green Tourism Award   𝒫𝒫 Silver Green Tourism Award   𝒫𝒫𝒫 Gold Green Tourism Award
For further information on our Green Tourism Business Scheme please see page 7.

Advertisers' locations have been sorted by postcode. In Scotland, postcodes can cover fairly large geographical areas.
Please check distance of property from specified location with the individual provider. VisitScotland cannot take any responsibility for this.

497

To find out more go to visitscotland.com

To find out more go to visitscotland.com